Dawn Terrick

Discovering the Student

INTRODUCTION TO
COLLEGE WRITING

seventh edition

Discovering the Self

Kendall Hunt
publishing company

Cover image © Shutterstock, Inc.

Kendall Hunt
publishing company

www.kendallhunt.com
Send all inquiries to:
4050 Westmark Drive
Dubuque, IA 52004-1840

Contents

Why do I like or dislike reading and writing? What impact do my past literacy experiences have on my present and future literacy experiences? How do I locate my strengths and weaknesses? How do I gain confidence and create a plan to improve my writing? Why is process so important in writing? What are the stages in the writing process and how do I create a process that works for me?

Now that I have an interview subject, what questions do I ask? How do I write and organize my questions? How do I ensure that I will get enough relevant and detailed information from my interview subject?

Now that my interview is complete, what do I do? How do I go from my notes and recording to an academic essay?

What does a "good" student interview paper look like?

Why are collaboration, conferencing and feedback important parts of the writing process? How do I provide helpful feedback and suggestions to my peers? How will helping my peers help my own writing?

What is text-based academic writing? What is critical thinking and reading? Why is it so important?

What are the different ways to respond to a text? How do I know which response is appropriate? How do I strengthen my critical reading skills and develop my responses?

How do I integrate sources? How do I find an effective balance between my own ideas and experiences on the one hand and information from the text on the other? Does academic essay structure change as I integrate sources? How do I distinguish between my ideas and experiences and those of the author?

How do I decide upon an issue and what conversation I want to join? How do I start writing a draft for a text-based essay/paper? How do I structure an argument about an issue or event using textual evidence? What does a "good" student text-based essay/paper look like?

Why are collaboration, conferencing and feedback important parts of the writing process? How do I provide helpful feedback and suggestions to my peers? How will helping my peers help my own writing?

III. Using and Documenting Sources   293

What is plagiarism? What are the different kinds of plagiarism? What are the dangers of plagiarism? How can I avoid all types of plagiarism? What is the difference between a quote and a paraphrase? What is MLA?

How do I format and cite sources within the text?

How do I cite sources at the end of the text? How do I prepare the list of works cited?

This is confusing. How do I remember all of these rules? Can I practice formatting and citing before I write my essay/paper?

IV. End of Semester Reflection   299

What have I really learned this semester? How can I apply what I have learned in other courses?

V. Sentence Construction and Grammar Instruction   301

Why are sentence structure and grammar important? What should I focus on as I edit my draft? What strategies and exercises should I use?

VI. Student Essays   353

Introduction   353

This all seems very difficult—how can I accomplish all of this and write a successful essay/paper? What does a successful student essay/paper look like? What can I learn from reading other student essays/papers?

Appendix: Writer's Workshop

Instructor's Resource Guide: *This electronic supplement will help instructors get the most out of Discovering the Student, Discovering the Self by providing a course syllabus and assignment schedule, detailed assignments, discussions and examples of instructor feedback/evaluation/grading of student papers as well as the theory behind the textbook and its lessons.*

Preface for Instructors

For those of us who teach in the field of developmental or introductory college writing, we are currently faced with myriad changes—changes in what we do, who we serve and how we are viewed by others. Amidst growing enrollments, budget cuts and questions of the validity of developmental writing programs, as Director of Developmental Writing for the past 15 years at a 4-year open admissions university, I have seen vast changes in the last years. As our student population grows and evolves, it is a struggle to maintain retention rates and continue to prove that all of these students deserve a place in the academy. Now, with less funding and more institutional, state and national pressure to increase retention rates, we must restructure our courses and re-envision our students in order to withstand the scrutiny from outside and create a course that will provide students with the critical thinking, reading and writing skills and intellectual curiosity they need to be successful students and citizens. *Discovering the Student, Discovering the Self: Introduction to College Writing* was created from a developmental writing program that was a past recipient of the Conference on Basic Writing's Award for Innovation and provides faculty and students with the tools to successfully navigate the new face of academia.

Discovering the Student, Discovering the Self espouses the idea or theory that teachers have a fundamental belief in their students and in the power of language. This textbook encourages and cultivates meaningful reading and writing. However, before I explain the structure of the textbook, I would like to share with you the impetus behind it. In many ways, it began with Kate Ronald's essay, "Style: The Hidden Agenda in Composition Classes," where, at the end of her essay, she uses Stoppard's play *The Real Thing* to illustrate what she means by style through his metaphor of the cricket bat and ball: " [The cricket bat] is actually several pieces of particular wood cunningly put together . . . If you get it right, the cricket ball will travel two hundred yards in four seconds . . . what we're trying to do is write cricket bats, so when we throw up an idea and give it a little knock, it might . . . travel," Yes, I wanted my students' stories and ideas to travel. Ronald goes on to ask, "But how to transform lumps of wood into cricket bats? It seems to me the key lies in the play's other theme—the real thing, meaning real love and passion." We must provide students with meaningful reading and writing assignments so they will fully invest in their writing, fully invest in the messy and uncomfortable journey to find their identities and voice.

Identity and voice are the two themes I wish to focus upon because they are a focus of the textbook and from where its title, *Discovering the Student, Discovering the Self*, comes. An effective curriculum must speak to students' personal experiences, must validate a positive self and group identity and must be culturally relevant. So the first step in students finding their voice and dissecting, understanding and developing their identities, is for them to read and write about them. This textbook is filled with essays from authors who look like them, who have had similar experiences and who have faced similar obstacles. It is important that students see their lives reflected in the syllabus in a meaningful way, a way that does not always set up an opposition between blue and white collar, working class and middle class, black and white, heterosexual and homosexual but invites thought, analysis and provides students with the means to navigate through these oppositions, finding their place both within and against the mainstream. Students also find connections to and learn from those authors who do not look like them, and this is what creates a sense of community and the courage to write in the classroom. With the help of these reading and writing assignments, students write not only about their own experiences, but write about them in relation to the authors they read. Can authors' works provide context and history for students' identities and struggles? Are these authors still trying to negotiate and create their own identities? What experiences do the authors and students share and not share?

Discovering the Student, Discovering the Self looks back to the history of remedial, basic or developmental writing as well as looks forward to the future of writing and English classes at the university. This textbook, and the theory it espouses, does not cling to the antiquated definitions of remedial writing. Rather, *Discovering the Student, Discovering the Self* sees writing as Mike Rose does when he insists, "Writing assumes a richer epistemology and demands fuller participation. It requires a complete, active struggling engagement, an encounter of the discipline's texts and incorporation of them into one's own work." As a result, this textbook proposes to redefine the place of the developmental writing program as well as the language used to describe it and

- defines writing as a discipline and not a skill
- judges writing not on errors but in a qualitative sense
- has full status and is the heart of the curriculum
- understands students as having knowledge, but that the knowledge is incomplete, fragmented or disorganized
- combines reading and writing
- centers on holistic pedagogies
- focuses on academically oriented assignments
- teaches and discusses writing as discovery and a meaning-making process
- focuses on language as an active force in the way we constitute reality

The reading and writing assignments in this textbook

- are personal *and* academic in nature
- are transformative
- utilize texts
- reflect students' lives and struggles as well as force students to examine their own situations, families, communities, social and political structures, etc.
- are collaborative and social
- are constructed so instruction and evaluation are inherently connected
- reflect the writing process, focusing on revision and reflection
- connect to outside of the classroom as well

Discovering the Student, Discovering the Self is a textbook and writing course that expects much from its students. However, a key difference in this textbook and course is that it breaks down all assignments, tasks and requirements into smaller, more manageable exercises. Instructors of developmental, beginning or introductory writers should never change or lower their expectations but, rather, change how they approach and instruct. If an instructor, with the help of a textbook, can break down every part of the thinking, reading and writing processes for students, students will be able to comprehend each part and, thus, comprehend academic inquiry and writing while building their engagement and confidence.

Features

Discovering the Student, Discovering the Self contains not only readings/professional essays but also critical thinking, reading and writing exercises and assignments that will take instructors and students throughout an entire semester, a Writer's Workshop supplemental instruction model, student essays and instruction in grammar and sentence construction. Furthermore, for instructors, there is a supplemental Instructor's Resource Guide.

Student-Focused Content, Tone and Language: The most important audience for *Discovering the Student, Discovering the Self* is the student so it is written *to* students in order to show respect for and confidence in our students. Assignments are written in a way that offers clear explanations and examples while addressing common student questions and concerns. Students are not expected to just passively read the textbook, but are expected to actively engage in the activities that take them through the writing process. The inclusion of real student writing/essays complements this student focus.

Readings/Professional Essays: These essays are organized by theme and correspond to the four major writing assignments or Task Papers. Themes include identity (in terms of race, class, culture, place, gender and sexual orientation), education, language and literacy and the voices are both mainstream and marginal. Students' intellectual curiosity will be sparked by these authors and essays.

Writing Instruction: This section moves students from personal to academic writing, offering tutorials beginning with detail, description, narration and basic academic essay structure and culminating with activities in critical reading, summary writing and integration of borrowed material resulting in meaningful engagement with texts. Activities and lessons directly correspond to the formal essay/paper (Task Paper) assignments in the Instructor's Resource Guide but can also be used on their own. In addition, you will find a Writer's Workshop supplemental instruction model that can be implemented by the instructor and/or a peer writing tutor.

Grammar Instruction and Sentence Construction: This section covers the key areas in grammar and sentence structure to help students understand the parts of speech and how each part of a sentence truly works. Helpful lists such as "Do's and Don'ts" and exercises allow students to apply what they have read and practiced in class. This section directs students in competent, correct and clear writing.

Student Essays: This section includes real student essays that have not been edited or revised from students in the ENG 100 program from Missouri Western State University. These essays are an effective teaching tool and provide various modeling opportunities for the instructor. In a larger sense, assigning students these essays can provide them with ideas and insights for topics and help them to address questions and concerns such as, "How do I find a topic?" "I do not have anything significant to write about," "What do you want?" and "How should this paper look?" Once students find a focus and topic, these essays provide effective instruction on thesis statements, paragraph construction, use of detail and description, incorporation of text and borrowed material and response to and analysis of others' words and ideas. Model essays also provide students with the confidence they need to find their own voices and commit them to paper.

Instructor's Resource Guide: This supplement helps you get the most out of *Discovering the Student, Discovering the Self* by providing a course syllabus and schedule, detailed assignments, examples and explanations of instructor feedback/evaluation/grading of student papers as well as the theory behind the textbook and its lessons. The formal essay/paper (Task Paper) assignments in the Instructor's Resource Guide connect to the textbook information and activities; therefore, the information and activities in the Writing Instruction sections can be used in tandem with the formal writing assignments or on their own.

Preface for Students

"One thing that is always with the writer —no matter how long he has written or how good he is—is the continuing process of learning how to write."

—Flannery O'Connor

"There is no greater agony than bearing an untold story inside you."

—Maya Angelou

In this course you will discuss writing as a process. And you may ask, what does this statement mean? The truth is, no one just sits down and instantly produces a perfect piece of writing. There are many steps a writer goes through when producing a text, including prewriting (or gathering and organizing ideas and thoughts), writing, revising and editing, and we will discuss these steps in this course. By breaking down these steps, hopefully, the writing process will seem less difficult. In discovering writing as a process, you will discover the reading and writing strategies and processes that work best for you. The emphasis here is on you and your attention to the topics. I know that you will not survive in this course if you come to class unprepared, if you do not revise your writing, if you do not ask questions, if you do not solicit help from your Instructor and peers, if you wait until the last minute to draft an essay or build a portfolio. I also know that you probably will succeed if you become someone who connects reading and writing to your life, to your experiences, and who reflects on the impact of these connections. Becoming a critical and thoughtful writer is essential for success in college and for life after college. This textbook has been designed to help you make this effort.

The primary goals of *Discovering the Student, Discovering the Self* are to help you learn how to

- shape the academic paper with introduction, focused body paragraphs and conclusion
- state a clear, insightful thesis and strong topic sentences
- reflect meaningfully on your own experiences and offer your personal experience as evidence in support of your thesis
- critically read and understand written (and other) texts
- connect your experiences and opinions to others' (written texts, interviews, etc.) and blend/integrate those into your text-based essays/papers
- grapple with and reflect upon the significance of your topic and claim
- gain a greater awareness of the present (current events, social and political issues, etc.) through an understanding and a reading of past events, biographies and historical periods

- develop a unique voice, style and tone
- introduce, explain and cite borrowed information
- control conventions of correctness (punctuation, spelling, sentence construction)

If all of the above seems overwhelming or if you have ever exclaimed, "I don't know what to write!" or asked, "What does a good student paper look like?" then this textbook is for you. One unique feature of *Discovering the Student, Discovering the Self* that guides your writing process is the student essays. These essays were written by students just like you. They provide insight into your assignments, ideas for topics and models for your writing. Furthermore, this is not a textbook you just passively read; it is designed so you can actively engage in reading and writing activities on your own and with your peers.

As you sit in class on the first day or, perhaps, flip through this book even before you get to class and read the list above, you may be thinking, "What does this all *really* mean?" "Why is this all important?" "Why do I need this course?" "Why is this textbook so important?" Well, let's look at the title of this textbook, *Discovering the Student, Discovering the Self*, because it will tell you lots.

This course and textbook will not only help you to become a successful student but also a successful citizen of the larger world. Text-based writing, or academic writing, is at the heart of all college-level work; you will find this type of writing in most of your college courses and across fields and disciplines. As a result, this textbook focuses on the inextricable link between reading and writing. You will respond to your readings in various ways: you will form personal responses, summarize, analyze and evaluate. You will discover that the more you read, the better writer you will become. You will learn to make both personal and public/social connections to what you read in order to better understand yourself and the world around you. Through these reading and writing assignments, you will be introduced to new voices and viewpoints and learn how to integrate them into your own. You will discover the power of language and the impact not only of others' stories but also of your own stories. Writing can be cathartic for you and constructive for your audience. Critical thinking, reading and writing dominate the world outside of college as well. The ever-changing and challenging workplace requires you to effectively solve problems and respond to a multitude of situations and information. The digital world, where you are relentlessly bombarded with information in various modes and media, requires you to analyze and evaluate that information in order to make informed decisions about your life and the lives of those who matter most to you. My hope is that, at the end of this semester, you will not only have grown as a student and be prepared for the challenges in your college courses, but you will also have grown as an individual. The person who you are right now, on the first day of class, will be different from the person who you are on the last day of class. Through critical thinking, discovery, reading, writing and reflection, I hope that you discover the same things that past students have discovered: during your first semesters in college you are discovering yourself, realizing you are part of many communities, including this academic community, and defining yourself as an individual, student, scholar and citizen.

Acknowledgments

I first must thank my family. I am grateful to my husband, Tim, for his unconditional love, support and patience as I continually ask, "Can you read this?" or "Wouldn't this book/article/TV show/movie be great for my class?" and have spent too many dinner and weekend conversations on work. I am also grateful to my sister, Kristi, who has been my cheerleader ever since we were kids. And my eternal gratitude to my grandparents, Rose and Mickey, who although no longer alive, are by my side every day reminding me of my worth and believing in me.

Early on, I benefitted from the guidance of my graduate professors, and I still feel their impact on my work. I offer my thanks to Dr. Lois Green who made me realize that I wanted to teach composition rather than literature and to Dr. Christopher Ferry who challenged, chided yet always encouraged me while he opened up this whole new world of composition theory to me as a brand-new graduate student.

I have also been fortunate to have many colleagues, both within and outside of the English and Modern Languages Department at Missouri Western State University, who have encouraged me, supported my program, attended every English 100 Publication Reception and responded to my incessant requests for recruiting tutors, evaluating placement exams and a hundred other things I do not have room to write in. I want to especially offer my gratitude to my fabulous English 100 Instructors—Dana Andrews, Patricia Brost, Brooksie Kluge, Joe Marmaud, Amy Miller, Leanne Murray, Tom Pankiewicz, Beth Reinert, Kay Siebler and Kristy Weiberg—who amaze me with their passion, purpose and ability to reach and teach so many of our students.. We are truly a family. I offer thanks to my Chairpersons who have supported my program and my crazy ideas. I want to thank Dr. Martin Johnson, former Dean of Liberal Arts and Sciences at Missouri Western State University, who took a huge chance on me, many years ago, when he appointed me the Director of Developmental Writing and Placement.

I have been fortunate to work with the professional and committed team at Kendall Hunt. I distinctly remember the first day that Angela Lampe and Nicole Mathers walked into my office. Within minutes, I knew that my book and I had found a home.

Finally, I want to wholeheartedly thank my students—past, present and future—who motivate and inspire me. *Discovering the Student, Discovering the Self* is for and because of them. I also want to thank the English 100 students and Writer's Workshop Leaders at Missouri Western State University whose work is featured in this book—Debra Anderson, Christopher Bennett, Nora Cogdill, Erica Cook, Stephaney Ferguson, James A. Garrison, Nikki Groom, Tori Kibbe, Prince Chuck Mosley, Laura Sapp, Chayata Faye Thammarat and Au-sha Ramirez-Quevado—and I hope they realize what a privilege it is.

Dawn Terrick

PART I

READINGS

1

Identity

Place

by Dorothy Allison

What do you notice when you first enter a story? Who is talking? Who are they talking to? Where are they standing? What's going on in the background? Is there a background?

There are two primary reasons why people read; boredom, which is my disease, and the need for reliable information, which is my constant motivation. I want to know everything. And I do, indeed, pick up books just to get the information that, in my upbringing, I missed. But I cannot tell you how many stories I pick up, and two people are having a conversation about their sex lives—which is a great place to begin, sex is always a good place to begin—but I don't know who they are, and I don't know where they are. It makes me crazy to step into a story and not know where I am. It makes me crazy when characters are arguing about sex, and I don't know what sex means for them. The story seems to take place in no place.

Most Americans no longer have the history of growing up in a town where their parents grew up and their grandparents grew up and handed down stories about what came before. We no longer necessarily know the story of *nobody goes down that road at night because the colonel killed a bunch of people out there and the ghosts walk the roads*. Used to be that story was told for generations. No more. If you're American, you've probably moved at least three times in the last decade. You probably do not live where you were born. Almost surely, you do not live close to your parents. Almost surely, you have to invent the place that you are writing-about.

And you're jealous of people you think come from a place that is generally recognizable—Southerners, who all have porches and pickup trucks and grandmothers (never mind that bunches of Southerners come from Atlanta); Bostonians, who can remember that last great blizzard that shut down the city; people from the Chicago projects; Jews from Staten Island or Queens or the Lower East Side, who eat pickles and go to the Second Avenue Deli and also have a grandmother. Everybody knows these places and the people in these places are all assumed to share the same food and the same language. Their place is a given.

But if you're from a place that no one knows, you have to invent it on the page.

I grew up among truck drivers and waitresses, and, for me, the place where most stories take place is the place that is no place for most other people. The truck stop: no place. The diner: no place. The grocery store: an empty landscape that you do not ascribe as being a real place. But for me those places are real places, with a population I recognize and can describe, a people I love even if they do not always love me.

I can give you detail. I can describe for you the tile they use in most truck stops because truckers have a horrible tendency to puke after having drunk great quantities of beer on top of chili. I know the colors of those tiles. I know, in fact, why 7-Elevens are designed the way they are. I've worked there. I recognize why diners are they way they are—why, in fact, I'll make more money waiting on a booth than on the counter. Those places are real places for me. You probably read my stories to learn more about diners. And waitresses. And truck drivers. And I read to learn about the Jews in Brooklyn, the fishermen of Maine, and the combine drivers in Iowa. I'm lusting after those people I know little about: Bostonians who run along the Charles River in shorts even on snowy gray mornings, South Americans who live halfway up a hillside and speak Portuguese, Amish who somehow wound up in Hawaii and live out near Hilo and grow mangoes and passion fruit. All of these people are profoundly exotic to me, and I ache to know their secrets—especially their secret places.

Place is often something you don't see because you're so familiar with it that you devalue it or dismiss it or ignore it. But in fact it is the information your reader most wants to know.

When I went to college, I would sneak into other people's dorms and look in their rooms. I wasn't out to rob anyone but to learn about who they were and what they had. That, too, is place. All the stuff you've got that you don't see is place—and me, I am your reader, and I want to know all about it. Your reader comes into your narrative to steal knowledge—who you are and what is all around you, what you use, or don't use, what you need, or fear, or want—all that sweet reverberating detail. It is just like me going into those dorm rooms and taking a good solid look around. Your stuff provides telling details from which I can derive all kinds of information about you. I can imagine your self-consciousness, your prejudices, your need to be in control, and maybe even what you are willing to risk or share or not risk or not share. I am making you up in my mind, deriving you from clues you provide, you and your story.

So let's review what place is.

Place is visual detail: manicured grass or scrubby weeds, broken concrete or pristine tarmac glistening with morning dew. Place is conditions: weather, atmosphere. Are the roads crowded or are they empty? When you step outside your house in the morning and you hit that clean, cool sidewalk, are there people walking around? Are they looking at you or are they looking away? Are you lonely? Are you nervous?

Place requires context. Is it responsive? Does it notice me? Or is it porcelain, pristine, and just ignoring my passage through? Are there people on the street who flinch when I smile at them? Is there a reason they do that? Place is where the "I" goes. Place is what that "I" looks at, what it doesn't look at. Is it happy? Is it sad? Is it afraid? Is it curious?

What I am trying to say is that place is not just landscape—a list of flora and fauna and street names. That's not place, that's not even decent research. Which brings me to my other point.

I cannot abide a story told to me by a numb, empty voice that never responds to anything that's happening, that doesn't express some feelings in response to what it sees. Place is not just what your feet are crossing to get to somewhere. Place is feeling, and feeling is something a character expresses. More, it is something the writer puts on the page—articulates with deliberate purpose. If you keep giving me these eyes that note all the details —if you tell me the lawn is manicured but you don't tell me that it makes your character both deeply happy and slightly anxious—then I'm a little bit frustrated with you. I want a story that'll pull me in. I want a story that makes me drunk. I want a story that feeds me glory. And most of all, I want a story I can trust. I want a story that is happening in a real place, which means a place that has meaning and that evokes emotions in the person who's telling me the story. Place is emotion.

So I'm going to say some unscrupulous, terrible, horrible things that are absolutely true in my mind, if not in yours:

Central Florida is despair.

New York City is sex.

California is smug.

Boston has never gotten over Henry James.

Seattle and Portland lie about their weather.

Iowa City is one hotel room and a chlorine stink away from the suburbs of hell.

I keep a list. I keep track of the places I have been and what I have decided about those places from stories I have experienced or read or heard or dreamed. It's a writer's game, but also a game for anyone who grew up with a sense of not knowing much and trying to figure out what everyone else knows or thinks they know.

Now I'll tell you the place I don't want.

A motel in Iowa City whose windows open onto the swimming pool. Have you been there? Not a Motel 6 or a Days Inn. Probably a Sheraton, maybe the Hyatt, but more likely the Marriott, and definitely not the Four Seasons.

For a year I took a picture of every motel room I stayed in. I lined them up. The only thing different as the year went on was that I was more and more often in rooms with minibars. And you could tell it was a minibar. That was the only difference I could see. The bed is always the bed. There is always a TV; there is always a remote control. Sometimes there are extra pillows. Sometimes there aren't.

It's nowhere. It's no place. And there you are.

If you're lucky, Oprah is on at eleven thirty at night. And you can check out what she's done lately. Try, try, try not to start channel-hopping and watching the ads. You can't afford any of that stuff anyway. It's the middle of the night, three o'clock in the morning, and you're in a room in which the art on the wall is a stylized painting of a flower or an unknown landscape. And I do mean an unknown landscape. Someone is doing these paintings and making money, but it's not an actual artist and that landscape is nowhere you recognize. Also, the mattress is kind of soggy, and you've got one of those covers that you are too hot if you have it on you and too cold if you pull it off. You're awake at three o'clock in the morning and you are nowhere; this is not a place.

Hyatts, Sheratons—that's where all those stories take place in which there is no landscape, in which there is not the mention of a tree or the grass or the weather. There is no weather in a Hyatt. Stories that take place in no place—why would you leave out the thing that will most bring alive what you're trying to do? You think the most important thing is that confident voice of that "I" narrator who, let's be clear, is really you when you were twenty-two, and they didn't treat you right, didn't fuck you right, didn't love you right—Momma, first lover, Daddy, I don't care who it was. But I want the story to burn me. I want the page to crisp my fingers.

You were in that room with him when he said no, he did not want you, and you walked out of the room and it felt as if you were bleeding into your own belly. You went down the stairs, out into the night, and you smelled—what did you smell? Was there the distinct odor of spilled beer on the steps? Were you thinking about how when your daddy left that was all that you could smell on the front steps after he was gone? Is it torn-up weeds that you smell? Somebody was sitting on those steps earlier and she was crying, and she didn't have anything else so she reached down and pulled up the grass and ripped it, and you can smell the tom grass in the air.

Or is it your own skin? You had put on perfume. You had bathed carefully. You had washed your hair. You had used that new soap with lavender scent and flowers. You wanted to be wanted, and no one can ever understand how terrible it felt to be told, no, I don't want you. But you smell your skin, and it stinks of sour disappointment, and you don't want you. You can understand why he didn't want to have sex with you. That's place—the smell in the air, the memory, the association. It's all history. You are somebody real who comes from somewhere, and you have been hurt in specific, deep, terrible ways.

Or, it could be that other story.

You have been cared for and loved and made joyful. You expect good things. You expect love. Take a deep breath and what do you smell? Mmmm. You've opened your suitcase and your mother, or your girlfriend, or—oh, my God—your husband of one year who still gets tears in his eyes when you reach for him has tucked something inside. You open up the suitcase and lying there, wrapped in plastic, carefully prepared, is a sugar cookie with anisette. The smell is enough to make your whole body flush with lust. You open it up and breathe it in; you won't eat it now. You think about it. Your mother or your lover or your husband or your best friend sneaked that in there for you to find. You are a person to whom wonderful things happen. And tonight, tonight, when you come back to the Hyatt, more wonderful things will happen. The manager will have left chocolates and a bottle of some perfect complimentary wine, with a glass sitting by it waiting for you, or maybe there will be strawberries dipped in chocolate. You are a person to whom wonderful things happen.

That's place, a place more of us should get to more often.

Place is people.

Place is people with self-consciousness.

Place is people with desire.

My major reason for reading stories is that I get off on knowing other people's secrets. On every level, I get off—I tremble from the power of the sexual charge of the secret and the electrical excitement of suddenly discovering the connections I never made before. I want to know everything and so I need an actual person walking the landscape, responding to it, telling me, in fact, how he or she wound up there. What was the decision-making process? Who is that person in this place? I need to know the person walking the landscape, seeing the landscape, remembering another landscape, putting that landscape on top of this landscape. Then suddenly I'm not in one place, I'm in two places. And there's a narrator, and the narrator is making

Story is negotiated. Story happens from what we put on the page and what the reader takes off the page. The reader does not always take off the page what we imagine we have put there. Because, as I said, there's a whole bunch of stuff you don't even see anymore. And you don't know who your reader might be. When I read your story, I read it with my imagination and my landscape, my sense of place. I can see the place you tell me only through the filter of the places I can imagine, unless you're really good. And it's not going to be good enough just to tell me that a place is all red brick and that kind of off-white limestone. That's not sufficient. I grew up in Greenville, South Carolina, with clapboard houses. No bricks. What I have is the landscape in which I grew up and the landscapes that I have adapted from every damned book I've ever read, and every damned book I've ever read is in the back of my head while I'm reading yours. Every place every other writer has taken me is in me.

Can you take me somewhere no one else has?

Can you show me a place I don't already have a reference for?

Place is the desire for a door. Place is the desire to get out of where you are. Place is experiencing where you are as a trap. Are you in hell on your way to heaven? Are you momentarily safe in heaven, fearful of falling into hell? Characters that interest me, about whom I am most curious, are always engaged in a journey.

Fear is a wonderful place for writers. A character who is genuinely terrified is in the best place because the reader is going to be terrified as well. The reader is going to be sweaty, anxious, wanting something to happen, turning pages. It's a better place if there are loud noises about which a character is not entirely sure of the cause. Fearful places. The lights have gone out, and the rain's coming down so hard, and loud, she can't hear anything, and it's dark and somebody might be chasing her and she's running and the floor is slippery. The tiles are slippery, they're old and they're worn and she's barefoot and sweaty and sliding, and she thinks she can hear somebody coming behind her. She can hear his boots. She can smell his sweat. He's close enough that she can smell him. He's real. Oh God! He's so damn close! And you know what? You know what?

It's better if the fear is real.

You're sitting at home. You're reading this essay. The lights aren't going to go off; it's not raining. There's nothing to be afraid of. Probably not, anyway. Unless, wait. It's not just anybody running up the hall; it's you—not second-person you, first-person YOU. I'm describing you; I'm in your body. Now, how do I make you know this? How do I make you know you're running up the hall, and you're terrified, and sweat's pouring off you, and you're sliding on the slippery linoleum, and the person behind you with a knife is somebody you have reason to be afraid of?

I'm going to use specific details. I'm going to put you in Portland, Oregon. It's July. It's the last night of a writing conference. Everybody was drinking heavy. The students were all exchanging addresses and phone numbers. And you, you wouldn't give this one guy your phone number. You were feeling really full of yourself because your workshop teacher liked that story you showed her and she said she wanted to read the rest of it and you could send it to her, and you were just feeling so good, and good stuff happens to you, it always does. And you go back to the dorm later than you'd planned, but there's nobody else in the dorm. Listen. It's raining. And the back door slams and there he is. And you didn't give him your phone number, and he's like, "Who the fuck do you think you are?" He's coming up the hall and you're barefoot and you're sweating and you're running and the lights go out and it's raining hard. And just before the lights go out, you see what he has in his hand: he's going to gut you from front to back. Run hard, run fast. It's a specific place. It is your specific tender body that your momma loves so much. That's place.

Dorothy Allison is the bestselling author of several novels including Bastard Out of Carolina, Cavedweller, *and* Two Or Three Things I Know For Sure. *The recipient of numerous awards, she has been the subject of many profiles and a short documentary film of her life,* Two or Three Things but Nothing For Sure. Essay from *The Writer's Notebook: Craft Essays from Tin House.*

Graduation Day

by Maya Angelou

The children in Stamps trembled visibly with anticipation. Some adults were excited too, but to be certain the whole young population had come down with graduation epidemic. Large classes were graduating from both the grammar school and the high school. Even those who were years removed from their own day of glorious release were anxious to help with preparations as a kind of dry run. The junior students who were moving into the vacating classes' chairs were tradition-bound to show their talents for leadership and management. They strutted through the school and around the campus exerting pressure on the lower grades. Their authority was so new that occasionally if they pressed a little too hard it had to be overlooked. After all, next term was coming, and it never hurt a sixth grader to have a play sister in the eighth grade, or a tenth-year student to be able to call a twelfth grader Bubba. So all was endured in a spirit of shared understanding. But the graduating classes themselves were the nobility. Like travelers with exotic destinations on their minds, the graduates were remarkably forgetful. They came to school without their books, or tablets or even pencils. Volunteers fell over themselves to secure replacements for the missing equipment. When accepted, the willing workers might or might not be thanked, and it was of no importance to the pregraduation rites. Even teachers were respectful of the now quiet and aging seniors, and tended to speak to them, if not as equals, as beings only slightly lower than themselves. After tests were returned and grades given, the student body, which acted like an extended family, knew who did well, who excelled, and what piteous ones had failed.

Unlike the white high school, Lafayette County Training School distinguished itself by having neither lawn, nor hedges, nor tennis court, nor climbing ivy. Its two buildings (main classrooms, the grade school and home economics) were set on a dirt hill with no fence to limit either its boundaries or those of bordering farms. There was a large expanse to U1e left of the school which was used alternately as a baseball diamond or basketball court. Rusty hoops on swaying poles represented the permanent recreational equipment, although bats and balls could be borrowed from the P.E. teacher if the borrower was qualified and if the diamond wasn't occupied.

Over this rocky area relieved by a few shady tall persimmon trees the graduating class walked. The girls often held hands and no longer bothered to speak to the lower students. There was a sadness about them, as if this old world was not their home and they were bound for higher ground. The boys, on the other hand, had become more friendly, more outgoing. A decided change from the closed attitude they projected while studying for finals. Now they seemed not ready to give up the old school, the familiar paths and classrooms. Only a small percentage would be continuing on to college-one of the South's A & M (agricultural and mechanical) schools, whim trained Negro youths to be carpenters, farmers, handymen, masons, maids, cooks and baby nurses. Their future rode heavily on their shoulders, and blinded them to the collective joy that had pervaded the lives of the boys and girls in the grammar school graduating class.

Parents who could afford it had ordered new shoes and ready-made clothes for themselves from Sears and Roebuck or Montgomery Ward. They also engaged the best seamstresses to make the floating graduating dresses and to cut down secondhand pants which would be pressed to a military slickness for the important event.

Oh, it was important, all right. Whitefolks would attend the ceremony, and two or three would speak of God and home, and the Southern way of life, and Mrs. Parsons, the principal's wife, would play the graduation march while the lower-grade graduates paraded down the aisles and took their seats below the platform. The high school seniors would wait in empty classrooms to make their dramatic entrance.

In the Store I was the person of the moment. The birthday girl. The center. Bailey had graduated the year before, although to do so he had had to forfeit all pleasures to make up for his time lost in Baton Rouge. My class was wearing butter-yellow piqué dresses, and Momma launched out on mine. She smocked the yoke into tiny crisscrossing puckers, then on mine. She smocked the yoke into tiny crisscrossing puckers, then shirred the rest of the bodice. Her dark fingers ducked in and out of the lemony cloth as she embroidered raised daisies around the hem. Before she considered herself finished she had added a crocheted cuff on the puff sleeves, and a pointy crocheted collar.

I was going to be lovely. A walking model of all the various styles of fine hand sewing and it didn't worry me that I was only twelve years old and merely graduating from the eighth grade. Besides, many teachers in Arkansas Negro schools had only that diploma and were licensed to impart wisdom.

The days had become longer and more noticeable. The faded beige of former times had been replaced with strong and sure colors. I began to see my classmates' clothes, their skin tones, and the dust that waved off pussy willows. Clouds that lazed across the sky were objects of great concern to me. Their shiftier shapes might have held a message that in my new happiness and with a little bit of time I'd soon decipher. During that period I looked at the arch of heaven so religiously my neck kept a steady ache. I had taken to smiling more often, and my jaws hurt from the unaccustomed activity. Between the two physical sore spots, I suppose I could have been uncomfortable, but that was not the case. As a member of the winning team (the graduating class of 1940) l had outdistanced unpleasant sensations by miles. l was headed for the freedom of open fields.

Youth and social approval allied themselves with me and we trammeled memories of slights and insults. The wind of our swift passage remodeled my features. Lost tears were pounded to mud and then to dust. Years of withdrawal were brushed aside and left behind, as hanging ropes of parasitic moss.

My work alone had awarded me a top place and I was going to be one of the first called in the graduating ceremonies. On the classroom blackboard, as well as on the bulletin board in the auditorium, there were blue stars and white stars and red stars. No absences, no tardinesses, and my academic work was among the best of the year. I could say the preamble lo the Constitution even faster than Bailey. We timed ourselves often: "WethepeopleoftheUnitedStatesinordertoformamoreperfectunion . . . " I had memorized the Presidents of the United States from Washington to Roosevelt in chronological as well as alphabetical order.

My hair pleased me too. Gradually the black mass had lengthened and thickened, so that it kept at last to its braided pattern, and I didn't have to yank my scalp off when I tried to comb it.

Louise and I had rehearsed the exercises until we tired out ourselves. Henry Reed was class valedictorian. He was a small, very black boy with hooded eyes, a long, broad nose and an oddly shaped head. I had admired him for years because each term he and I vied for the best grades in our class. Most often he bested me, but instead of being disappointed l was pleased that we shared top places between us. Like many Southern Black children, he lived with his grandmother, who was as strict as Momma and as kind as she knew how to be. He was courteous, respectful and soft-spoken to elders, but on the playground he chose to play the roughest games. I admired him. Anyone, I reckoned, sufficiently afraid or sufficiently dull could be polite. But to be able to operate at a top level with both adults and children was admirable.

His valedictory speech was entitled "To Be or Not to Be." The rigid tenth-grade teacher had helped him write it. He'd been working on the dramatic stresses for months.

The weeks until graduation were filled with heady activities. A group of small children were to be presented in a play about buttercups and daisies and bunny rabbits. They could be heard throughout the building practicing their hops and their little songs that sounded like silver bells. The older girls (nongraduates, of course) were assigned the task of making refreshments for the night's festivities. A tangy scent of ginger, cinnamon, nutmeg and chocolate wafted around the home economics building as the budding cooks made samples for themselves and their learners.

In every corner of the workshop, axes and saws split fresh timber as the woodshop boys made sets and stage scenery. Only the graduates were left out of the general bustle. We were free to sit in the library at the back of the building or look in quite detachedly, naturally, on the measures being taken for our event.

Even the minister preached on graduation the Sunday before. His subject was, "Let your light so shine that men will see your good works and praise your Father, Who is in Heaven." Although the sermon was purported to be addressed to us, he used the occasion to speak to backsliders, gamblers and general ne'er-do-wells. But since he had called our names at the beginning of the service we were mollified.

Among Negroes the tradition was to give presents to children going only from one grade to another. How much more important this was when the person was graduating at the top of the class. Uncle Willie and Momma had sent away for a Mickey Mouse watch like Bailey's. Louise gave me four embroidered handkerchiefs. (I gave her crocheted doilies.) Mrs. Sneed, the minister's wife, made me an undershirt to wear for graduation, and nearly every customer gave me a nickel or maybe even a dime with the instruction "Keep on moving to higher ground," or some such encouragement.

Amazingly the great day finally dawned and I was out of bed before I knew it. I threw open the back door to see it more clearly, but Momma said, "Sister, come away from that door and put your robe on.c

I hoped the memory of that morning would never leave me. Sunlight was itself young, and the day had none of the insistence maturity would bring it in a few hours. In my robe and barefoot in the backyard, under cover of going to see about my new beans, I gave myself up to the gentle warmth and thanked God that no matter what evil I had done in my life He had allowed me to live to see this day. Somewhere in my fatalism I had expected to die, accidentally, and never have the chance to walk up the stairs in the auditorium and gracefully receive my hard-earned diploma. Out of God's merciful bosom I had won reprieve.

Bailey came out in his robe and gave me a box wrapped in Christmas paper. He said he had saved his money for months to pay for it. It felt like a box of chocolates, but I knew Bailey wouldn't save money to buy candy when we had all we could want under our noses.

He was as proud of the gift as I. It was a soft-leather-bound copy of a collection of poems by Edgar Allan Poe, or, as Bailey and l called him, "Eap." l turned to "Annabel Lee" and we walked up and down the garden rows, the cool dirt between our toes, reciting the beautifully sad lines.

Momma made a Sunday breakfast although it was only Friday. After we finished the blessing, l opened my eyes to find the watch on my plate. It was a dream of a day. Everything went smoothly and to my credit. l didn't have to be reminded or scolded for anything. Near evening I was too jittery to attend to chores, so Bailey volunteered to do all before his bath.

Days before, we had made a sign for the Store, and as we turned out the lights Momma hung the cardboard over the doorknob. It read clearly: CLOSED. GRADUATION.

My dress fitted perfectly and everyone said that I looked like a sunbeam in it. On the hill, going toward the school, Bailey walked behind with Uncle Willie, who muttered, "Go on, Ju." He wanted him to walk ahead with us because it embarrassed him to have to walk so slowly. Bailey said he'd let the ladies walk together, and the men would bring up the rear. We all laughed, nicely.

Little children dashed by out of the dark like fireflies. Their crepepaper dresses and butterfly wings were not made for running and we heard more than one rip, dryly, and the regretful "uh uh" that followed.

The school blazed without gaiety. The windows seemed cold and unfriendly from the lower hill. A sense of ill-fated timing crept over me, and if Momma hadn't reached for my hand I would have drifted back to Bailey and Uncle Willie, and possibly beyond. She made a few slow jokes about my feet getting cold, and tugged me along to the now-strange building.

Around the front steps, assurance came back. There were my fellow "greats," the graduating class. Hair brushed back, legs oiled, new dresses and pressed pleats, fresh pocket handkerchiefs and little handbags, all homesewn. Oh, we were up to snuff, all right. I joined my comrades and didn't even see my family go in to find seats in the crowded auditorium.

The school band struck up a march and all classes filed in as had been rehearsed. We stood in front of our seats, as assigned, and on a signal from the choir director, we sat. No sooner had this been accomplished than the band started to play the national anthem. We rose again and sang the song, after which we recited the pledge of allegiance. We remained standing for a brief minute before the choir director and the principal signaled to us, rather desperately I thought, to take our seats. The command was so unusual that our carefully rehearsed and smooth-running machine was thrown off. For a full minute we fumbled for our chairs and bumped into each other awkwardly. Habits change or solidify under pressure, so in our state of nervous tension we had been ready to follow our usual assembly pattern: the American national anthem, then the pledge of allegiance, then the song every Black person I knew called the Negro National Anthem. All done in the same key, with the same passion and most often standing on the same foot.

Finding my seat at last, I was overcome with a presentiment of worse things to come. Something unrehearsed, unplanned, was going to happen, and we were going to be made to look bad. I distinctly remember being explicit in the choice of pronoun. It was "we," the graduating class, the unit, that concerned me then.

The principal welcomed "parents and friends" and asked the Baptist minister to lead us in prayer. His invocation was brief and punchy, and for a second I thought we were getting on the high road to right action. When the principal came back to the dais, however, his voice had changed. Sounds always affected me profoundly and the principal's voice was one of my favorites. During assembly it melted and lowed weakly into the audience. It had not been in my plan to listen to him, but my curiosity was piqued and I straightened up to give him my attention.

He was talking about Booker T. Washington, our "late great leader," who said we can be as close as the fingers on the hand, etc.

. . . Then he said a few vague things about friendship and the friendship of kindly people to those less fortunate than themselves. With that his voice nearly faded, thin, away. Like a river diminishing to a stream and then to a trickle. But he cleared his throat and said, "Our speaker tonight, who is also our friend, came from Texarkana to deliver the commencement address, but due to the irregularity of the train schedule, he's going to, as they say, 'speak and run.'" He said that we understood and wanted the man to know that we were most grateful for the time he was able to give us and then something about how we were willing always to adjust to another's program, and without more ado— "I give you Mr. Edward Donleavy."

Not one but two white men came through the door off-stage. The shorter one walked to the speaker's platform, and the tall one moved to the center seat and sat down. But that was our principal's seat, and already occupied. The dislodged gentleman bounced around for a long breath or two before the Baptist minister gave him his chair, then with more dignity than the situation deserved, the minister walked off the stage.

Donleavy looked at the audience once (on reflection, I'm sure that he wanted only to reassure himself that we were really there), adjusted his glasses and began to read from a sheaf of papers.

He was glad "to be here and to see the work going on just as it was in the other schools."

At the first "Amen" from the audience I willed the offender to immediate death by choking on the word. But Amens and Yes, sir's began to fall around the room like rain through a ragged umbrella.

He told us of the wonderful changes we children in Stamps had in store. The Central School (naturally, the white school was Central) had already been granted improvements that would be in use in the fall. A well-known artist was coming from Little Rock to teach art to them. They were going to have the newest microscopes and chemistry equipment for their laboratory. Mr. Donleavy didn't leave us long in the dark over who made these improvements available to Central High. Nor were we to be ignored in the general betterment scheme he had in mind.

He said that he had pointed out to people at a very high level that one of the first-line football tacklers at Arkansas Agricultural and Mechanical College had graduated from good old Lafayette County Training School. Here fewer Amen's were heard. Those few that did break through lay dully in the air with the heaviness of habit.

He went on to praise us. He went on to say how he had bragged that "one of the best basketball players at Fisk sank his first ball right here at Lafayette County Training School."

The white kids were going to have a chance to become Galileos and Madame Curies and Edisons and Gauguins, and our boys (the girls weren't even in on it) would try to be Jesse Owenses and Joe Louises.

Owens and the Brown Bomber were great heroes in our world, but what school official in the white-goddom of Little Rock had the right to decide that those two men must be our only heroes? Who decided that for Henry Reed to become a scientist he had to work Iike George Washington Carver, as a bootblack, to buy a lousy microscope? Bailey was obviously always going to be too small to be an athlete, so which concrete angel glued to what country seat had decided that if my brother wanted to become a lawyer he had to first pay penance for his skin by picking cotton and hoeing corn and studying correspondence books at night for twenty years?

The man's dead words fell like bricks around the auditorium and too many settled in my belly. Constrained by hard-learned manners I couldn't look behind me, but to my left and right the proud graduating class of 1940 had dropped their heads. Every girl in my row had found something new to do with her handkerchief. Some folded the tiny squares into love knots, some into triangles, but most were wadding them, then pressing them flat on their yellow laps.

On the dais, the ancient tragedy was being replayed. Professor Parsons sat, a sculptor's reject, rigid. His large, heavy body seemed devoid of will or willingness, and his eyes said he was no longer with us. The other teachers examined the flag (which was draped stage right) or their notes, or the windows which opened on our nowfamous playing diamond.

Graduation, the hush-hush magic time of frills and gifts and congratulations and diplomas, was finished for me before my name was called. The accomplishment was nothing. The meticulous maps, drawn in three colors of ink, learning and spelling decasyllabic words, memorizing the whole of *The Rape of Lucrece*—it was for nothing. Donleavy had exposed us.

We were maids and farmers, handymen and washerwomen, and anything higher that we aspired to was farcical and presumptuous.

Then I wished that Gabriel Prosser and Nat Turner had killed all whitefolks in their beds and that Abraham Lincoln had been assassinated before the signing of the Emancipation Proclamation, and that Harriet Tubman had been killed by that blow on her head and Christopher Columbus had drowned in the *Santa Maria*.

It was awful to be a Negro and have no control over my life. It was brutal to be young and already trained to sit quietly and listen to charges brought against my color, with no chance of defense. We should all be dead. I thought I should like to see us all dead, one on top of the other. A pyramid of flesh with the whitefolks on the bottom, as the broad base, then the Indians with their silly tomahawks and teepees and wigwams and treaties, the Negroes with their mops and recipes and cotton sacks and spirituals sticking out of their mouths. The Dutch children should all stumble in their wooden shoes and break their necks. The French should choke to death on the Louisiana Purchase (1803) while silkworms ate all the Chinese with their stupid pigtails. As a species, we were an abomination. All of us.

Donleavy was running for election, and assured our parents that if he won we could count on having the only colored paved playing field in that part of Arkansas. Also—he never looked up to acknowledge the grunts of acceptance—also, we were bound to get some new equipment for the home economics building and the workshop.

He finished, and since there was no need to give any more than the most perfunctory thank-you's, he nodded to the men on the stage, and the tall white man who was never introduced joined him at the door. They left with the attitude that now they were off to something really important. (The graduation ceremonies at Lafayette County Training School had been a mere preliminary.)

The ugliness they left was palpable. An uninvited guest who wouldn't leave. The choir was summoned and sang a modern arrangement of "Onward, Christian Soldiers," with new words pertaining to graduates seeking their place in the world. But it didn't work. Elouise, the daughter of the Baptist minister, recited "Invictus," and I could have cried at the impertinence of "I am the master of my fate, I am the captain of my soul."

My name had lost its ring of familiarity and I had to be nudged to go and receive my diploma. All my preparations had fled. I neither marched up to the stage like a conquering Amazon, nor did I look in the audience for Bailey's nod of approval. Marguerite Johnson, I heard the name again, my honors were read, there were noises in the audience of appreciation, and I took my place on the stage as rehearsed.

I thought about colors I hated: ecru, puce, lavender, beige and black.

There was shuffling and rustling around me, then Henry Reed was giving his valedictory address, "To Be or Not to Be." Hadn't he heard the whitefolks? We couldn't *be*, so the question was a waste of time. Henry's voice came out clear and strong. I feared to look at him. Hadn't he got the message? There was no "nobler in the mind" for Negroes because the world didn't think we had minds, and they let us know it. "Outrageous fortune"? Now, that was a joke. When the ceremony was over I had to tell Henry Reed some things. That is, if I still cared. Not "rub," Henry, "erase." "Ah, there's the erase." Us.

Henry had been a good student in elocution. His voice rose on tides of promise and fell on waves of warnings. The English teacher had helped him to create a sermon winging through Hamlet's soliloquy. To be a man, a doer, a builder, a leader, or to be a tool, an unfunny joke, a crusher of funky toadstools. I marveled that Henry could go through with the speech as if we had a choice.

I had been listening and silently rebutting each sentence with my eyes closed; then there was a hush, which in an audience warns that something unplanned is happening. I looked up and saw

Henry Reed, the conservative, the proper, the A student, turn his back to the audience and turn to us (the proud graduating class of 1940) and sing, nearly speaking,

"Lift ev'ry voice and sing

Till earth and heaven ring

Ring with the harmonies of Liberty . . "

It was the poem written by James Weldon Johnson. It was the music composed by J. Rosamond Johnson. It was the Negro national anthem. Out of habit we were singing it.

Our mothers and fathers stood in the dark hall and joined the hymn of encouragement. A kindergarten teacher led the small children onto the stage and the buttercups and daisies and bunny rabbits marked time and tried to follow:

"Stony the road we trod

Bitter the chastening rod

Felt in the days when hope, unborn, had died. Yet with a steady beat

Have not our weary feet

Come to the place for which our fathers sighed?"

Each child l knew had learned that song with his ABC's and along with "Jesus Loves Me This I Know." But I personally had never heard it before. Never heard the words, despite the thousands of times I had sung them. Never thought they had anything to do with me.

On the other hand, the words of Patrick Henry had made such an impression on me that I had been able to stretch myself tall and trembling and say, "l know not what course others may take, but as for me, give me liberty or give me death."

And now l heard, really for the first time:

"We have come over a way that with tears has been watered,

We have come, treading our path through the blood of the slaughtered."

While echoes of the song shivered in the air, Henry Reed bowed his head, said "Thank you," and returned to his place in the line. The tears that slipped down many faces were not wiped away in shame.

We were on top again. As always, again. We survived. The depths had been icy and dark, but now a bright sun spoke to our souls. I was no longer simply a member of the proud graduating class of 1940; l was a proud member of the wonderful, beautiful Negro race.

Oh, Black known and unknown poets, how often have your auctioned pains sustained us? Who will compute the lonely nights made less lonely by your songs, or the empty pots made less tragic by your tales?

If we were a people much given to revealing secrets, we might raise monuments and sacrifice to the memories of our poets, but slavery cured us of that weakness. It may be enough, however, to have it said that we survive in exact relationship to the dedication of our poets (include preachers, musicians and blues singers).

Sister Flowers

by Maya Angelou

For nearly a year, I sopped around the house, the Store, the school and the church, like an old biscuit, dirty and inedible. Then I met, or rather got to know, the lady who threw me my first life line.

Mrs. Bertha Flowers was the aristocrat of Black Stamps. She had the grace of control to appear warm in the coldest weather, and on the Arkansas summer days it seemed she had a private breeze which swirled around, cooling her. She was thin without the taut look of wiry people, and her printed voile dresses and flowered hats were a right for her a denim overalls for a farmer. She was our side's answer to the richest white woman in town.

Her skin was a rich black that would have peeled like a plum if snagged, but then no one would have thought of getting close enough to Mrs. Flowers to ruffle her dress, let alone snag her skin. She didn't encourage familiarity. She wore gloves too.

I don't think I ever saw Mrs. Flowers laugh, but she smiled often. A slow widening of her thin black lips to show even, small white teeth, then the slow effortless closing. When she chose to smile on me, I always wanted to thank her. The action was so graceful and inclusively benign.

She was one of the few gentlewomen I have ever known, and has remained throughout my life the measure of what a human being can be.

Momma had a strange relationship with her. Most often when she passed on the road in front of the Store, she spoke to Momma in that soft yet carrying voice, "Good day, Mrs. Henderson." Momma responded with "How you, Sister Flowers?"

Mrs. Flowers didn't belong to our church, nor was she Momma's familiar. Why on earth did she insist on calling her Sister Flowers? Shame made me want to hide my face. Mrs. Flowers deserved better than to be called Sister. Then, Momma left out the verb. Why not ask, "How are you, Mrs. Flowers?" With the unbalanced passion of the young, I hated her for showing her ignorance to Mrs. Flowers. It didn't occur to me for many years that they were as alike as sisters, separated only by formal education.

Although I was upset, neither of the women was in the least shaken by what I thought an unceremonious greeting. Mrs. Flowers would continue her easy gait up the hill to her little bungalow, and Momma kept on shelling peas or doing whatever had brought her to the front porch.

Occasionally, though, Mrs. Flowers would drift off the road and down to the Store and Momma would say to me, "Sister, you go on and play." As I left I would hear the beginning of an intimate conversation. Momma persistently using the wrong verb, or none at all.

"Brother and Sister Wilcox is sho'ly the meanest —" "Is," Momma? "Is"? Oh, please, not "is," Momma, for two or more. But they talked, and from the side of the building where I waited for the ground to open up and swallow me, I heard the soft voiced Mrs. Flowers and the textured voice of my grandmother merging and melting. They were interrupted from time to time by giggles that must have come from Mrs. Flowers (Momma never giggled in her life). Then she was gone.

She appealed to me because she was like people I had never met personally. Like women in English novels who walked the moors (whatever they were) with their loyal dogs racing at a respectful distance. Like the women who sat in front of roaring fireplaces, drinking tea incessantly from silver trays full of scones and crumpets. Women who walked over the "health" and read morocco-bound books and had two last names divided by a hyphen. It would be safe to say that she made me proud to be Negro, just by being herself.

She acted just as refined as whitefolks in the movies and books and she was more beautiful, for none of them could have come near that warm color without looking gray by comparison.

I was fortunate that I never saw her in the company of powhitefolks. For since they tend to think of their whiteness as an evenizer, I'm certain that I would have had to hear her spoken to commonly as Bertha, and my image of her would have been shattered like the unmendable Humpty-Dumpty.

One summer afternoon, sweet-milk fresh my memory, she stopped at the Store to buy provisions. Another Negro woman of her health and age would have been expected to carry the paper sacks home in one hand, but Momma said, "Sister Flowers, I'll send Bailey up to your house with these things."

She smiled that show dragging smile, "Thank you, Mrs. Henderson. I'd prefer Marguerite, though." My name was beautiful when she said it. "I've been meaning to talk to her, anyway." They gave each other age-group looks.

Momma said, "Well, that's all right then, Sister, go and change your dress. You going to Sister Flowers's."

The chifforobe was a maze. What on earth did one put on to go to Mrs. Flowers' house? I knew I shouldn't put on a Sunday dress. It might be sacrilegious. Certainly not a house dress, since I was already wearing a fresh one. I chose a school dress, naturally. It was formal without suggesting that going to Mrs. Flowers' house was equivalent to attending church.

I trusted myself back into the Store.

"Now, don't you look nice." I had chosen the right thing, for once. . . .

There was a little path beside the rocky road, and Mrs. Flowers walked in front swinging her arms and picking her way over the stones.

She said, without turning her head, to me, "I hear you're doing very good school work, Marguerite, but that it's all written. The teachers report that they have trouble getting you to talk in class." We passed the triangular farm on our left and the path widened to allow us to walk together. I hung back in the separate unasked and unanswerable questions.

"Come and walk along with me, Marguerite." I couldn't have refused even if I wanted to. She pronounced my name so nicely. Or more correctly, she spoke each word with such clarity that I was certain a foreigner who didn't understand English could have understood her.

"Now no one is going to make you talk—possibly no one can. But bear in mind, language is man's way of communicating with his fellow man and it is language alone which separates him from the lower animals." That was a totally new idea to me, and I would need time to think about it.

"Your grandmother says you read a lot. Every chance you get. That's good, but not good enough. Words mean more than what is set down on paper. It takes the human voice to infuse them with the shades of deeper meaning."

I memorized the part about the human voice infusing words. It seemed so valid and poetic.

She said she was going to give me some books and that I not only must read them, I must read them aloud. She suggested that I try to make a sentence sound in as many different ways as possible.

"I'll accept no excuse if you return a book to me that has been badly handled." My imagination boggled at the punishment I would deserve if in fact I did abuse a book of Mrs. Flowers's. Death would be too kind and brief.

The odors in the house surprised me. Somehow I had never connected Mrs. Flowers with food or eating or any other common experience of common people. There must have been an outhouse, too, but my mind never recorded it.

The sweet scent of vanilla had met us as she opened the door.

"I made tea cookies this morning. You see, I had planned to invite you for cookies and lemonade so we could have this little chat. The lemonade is in the icebox."

It followed that Mrs. Flowers would have ice on an ordinary day, when most families in our town bought ice late on Saturdays only a few times during the summer to be used in the wooden ice-cream freezers.

She took the bags from me and disappeared through the kitchen door. I looked around the room that I had never in my wildest fantasies imagined I would see. Browned photographs leered or threatened from the walls and the white, freshly done curtains pushed against themselves and against the wind. I wanted to gobble up the room entire and take it to Bailey, who would help me analyze and enjoy it.

"Have a seat, Marguerite. Over there by the table." She carried a platter covered with a tea towel. Although she warned that she hadn't tried her hand at baking sweets for some time, I was certain that like everything else about her the cookies would be perfect.

They were flat round wafers, slightly browned on the edges and butter yellow in the center. With the cold lemonade they were sufficient for childhood's lifelong diet. Remembering my manners, I took nice little ladylike bites off the edges. She said she had made them expressly for me and that she had a few in the kitchen that I could take home to my brother. So I jammed one whole cake in my mouth and the rough crumbs scratched the insides of my jaws, and if I hadn't had to swallow, it would have been a dream come true.

As I ate she began the first of what we later called "my lessons in living." She said that I must always be intolerant of ignorance but understanding of illiteracy. That some people, unable to go to school, were more educated and even more intelligent than college professors. She encouraged me to listen carefully to what country people called mother wit. That in those homely sayings was couched the collective wisdom of generations.

When I finished the cookies she brushed off the table and brought a thick, small book from the bookcase. I had read A *Tale of Two Cities* and found it up to my standards as a romantic novel. She opened the first page and I heard poetry for the first time in my life.

"It was the best of times and the worst of times . . ." Her voice slid in and curved down through and over the words. She was nearly singing. I wanted to look at the pages. Were they the same that I had read? Or were there notes, music, lined on the pages, as in a hymn book? Her sounds began cascading gently. I knew from listening to a thousand preachers that she was nearing the end of her reading, and I hadn't really heard, heard to understand, a single word.

"How do you like that?"

It occurred to me that she expected a response. The sweet vanilla flavor was still on my tongue and her reading was a wonder in my ears. I had to speak.

I said, "Yes, ma'am." It was the least I could do, but it was the most also.

"There's one more thing. Take this book of poems and memorize one for me. Next time you pay me a visit, I want you to recite."

I have tried often to search behind the sophistication of years for the enchantment I so easily found in those gifts. The essence escapes but its aura remains. To be allowed, no, invited, into the private lives of strangers, and to share their joys and fears, was a chance to exchange the Southern bitter wormwood for a cup of mead with Beowulf or a hot cup of tea and milk with Oliver Twist. When I said aloud, "It is a far, far better thing that I do, than I have ever done . . ." tears of love filled my eyes at my selflessness.

On that first day, I ran down the hill and into the road (few cars ever came along it) and had the good sense to stop running before I reached the Store.

I was liked, and what a difference it made. I was respected not as Mrs. Henderson's grandchild or Bailey's sister but for just being Marguerite Johnson.

Childhood's logic never asks to be proved (all conclusions are absolute). I didn't question why Mrs. Flowers had singled me out for attention, nor did it occur to me that Momma might have asked her to give me a little talking to. All I cared about was that she had made tea cookies for *me* and read to *me* from her favorite book. It was enough to prove that she liked me.

Notes of a Native Son

by James Baldwin

1

On the twenty-ninth of July, in 1943, my father died. On the same day, a few hours later, his last child was born. Over a month before this, while all our energies were concentrated in waiting for these events, there had been, in Detroit, one of the bloodiest race riots of the century. A few hours after my father's funeral, while he lay in state in the undertaker's chapel, a race riot broke out in Harlem. On the morning of the third of August, we drove my father to the graveyard through a wilderness of smashed plate glass.

The day of my father's funeral had also been my nineteenth birthday. As we drove him to the graveyard, the spoils of injustice, anarchy, discontent, and hatred were all around us. It seemed to me that God himself had devised, to mark my father's end, the most sustained and brutally dissonant of codas. And it seemed to me, too, that the violence which rose all about us as my father left the world had been devised as a corrective for the pride of his eldest son. I had declined to believe in that apocalypse which had been central to my father's vision; very well, life seemed to be saying, here is something that will certainly pass for an apocalypse until the real thing comes along. I had inclined to be contemptuous of my father for the conditions of his life, for the conditions of our lives. When his life had ended I began to wonder about that life and also, in a new way, to be apprehensive about my own.

I had not known my father very well. We had got on badly, partly because we shared, in our different fashions, the vice of stubborn pride. When he was dead I realized that I had hardly ever spoken to him. When he had been dead a long time I began to wish I had. It seems to be typical of life in America, where opportunities, real and fancied, are thicker than anywhere else on the globe, that the second generation has no time to talk to the first. No one, including my father, seems to have known exactly how old he was, but his mother had been born during slavery. He was of the first generation of free men. He, along with thousands of other Negroes, came North after 1919 and I was part of that generation which had never seen the landscape of what Negroes sometimes call the Old Country.

He had been born in New Orleans and had been a quite young man there during the time that Louis Armstrong, a boy, was running errands for the dives and honky-tonks of what was always presented to me as one of the most wicked of cities—to this day, whenever I think of New Orleans, I also helplessly think of Sodom and Gomorrah. My father never mentioned Louis Armstrong, except to forbid us to play his records; but there was a picture of him on our wall for a long time. One of my father's strong-willed female relatives had placed it there and forbade my father to take it down. He never did, but he eventually maneuvered her out of the house and when, some years later, she was in trouble and near death, he refused to do anything to help her.

He was, I think, very handsome. I gather this from photographs and from my own memories of him, dressed in his Sunday best and on his way to preach a sermon somewhere, when I was little. Handsome, proud, and ingrown, "like a toenail," somebody said. But he looked to me, as I grew older, like pictures I had seen of African tribal chieftains: he really should have been naked, with warpaint on and barbaric mementos, standing among spears. He could be chilling in the pulpit and indescribably cruel in his personal life and he was certainly the most bitter man I have ever met; yet it must be said that there was something else in him, buried in him, which lent him his tremendous power and, even, a rather crushing charm. It had something to do with his blackness, I think—he was very black—with his blackness and his beauty, and with the fact that he knew that he was black but did not know that he was beautiful. He claimed to be proud of his blackness but it had also been the cause of much humiliation and it had fixed bleak boundaries to his life. He was not a young man when we were growing up and he had already suffered many kinds of ruin; in his outrageously demanding and protective way he loved his children, who were black like him and menaced, like him; and all these things sometimes showed in his face when he tried, never to my knowledge with any success, to establish contact with any of us. When he took one of his children on his knee to play, the child always became fretful and began to cry; when he tried to help one of us with our homework the absolutely unabating tension which emanated from him caused our minds and our tongues to become paralyzed, so that he, scarcely knowing why, flew into a rage and the child, not knowing why, was punished. If it ever entered his head to bring a surprise home for his children, it was, almost unfailingly, the wrong surprise and even the big watermelons he often brought home on his back in the summertime led to the most appalling scenes. I do not remember, in all those years, that one of his children was ever glad to see him come home. From what I was able to gather of his early life, it seemed that this inability to establish contact with other people had always marked him and had been one of the things which had driven him out of New Orleans. There was something in him, therefore, groping and tentative, which was never expressed and which was buried with him. One saw it most clearly when he was facing new people and hoping to impress them. But he never did, not for long. We went from church to smaller and more improbable church, he found himself in less and less demand as a minister, and by the time he died none of his friends had come to see him for a long time. He had lived and died in an intolerable bitterness of spirit and it frightened me, as we drove him to the graveyard through those unquiet, ruined streets, to see how powerful and overflowing this bitterness could be and to realize that this bitterness now was mine.

When he died I had been away from home for a little over a year. In that year I had had time to become aware of the meaning of all my father's bitter warnings, had discovered the secret of his proudly pursed lips and rigid carriage: I had discovered the weight of white people in the world. I saw that this had been for my ancestors and now would be for me an awful thing to live with and that the bitterness which had helped to kill my father could also kill me.

He had been ill a long time—in the mind, as we now realized, reliving instances of his fantastic intransigence in the new light of his affliction and endeavoring to feel a sorrow for him which never, quite, came true. We had not known that he was being eaten up by paranoia, and the discovery that his cruelty, to our bodies and our minds, had been one of the symptoms of his illness was not, then, enough to enable us to forgive him. The younger children felt, quite simply, relief that he would not be coming home anymore. My mother's observation that it was he, after all, who had kept them alive all these years meant nothing because the problems of keeping children alive are not real for children. The older children felt, with my father gone, that they could invite their friends to the house without fear that their friends would be insulted or, as had sometimes happened with me, being told that their friends were in league with the devil and intended to rob our family of everything we owned. (I didn't fail to wonder, and it made me hate him, what on earth we owned that anybody else would want.)

His illness was beyond all hope of healing before anyone realized that he was ill. He had always been so strange and had lived, like a prophet, in such unimaginably close communion with the Lord that his long silences which were punctuated by moans and hallelujahs and snatches of old songs while he sat at the living-room window never seemed odd to us. It was not until he refused to eat because, he said, his family was trying to poison him that my mother was forced to accept as a fact what had, until then, been only an unwilling suspicion. When he was committed, it was discovered that he had tuberculosis and, as it turned out, the disease of his mind allowed the disease of his body to destroy him. For the doctors could not force him to eat, either, and, though he was fed intravenously, it was clear from the beginning that there was no hope for him.

In my mind's eye I could see him, sitting at the window, locked up in his terrors; hating and fearing every living soul including his children who had betrayed him, too, by reaching toward the world which had despised him. There were nine of us. I began to wonder what it could have felt like for such a man to have had nine children whom he could barely feed. He used to make little jokes about our poverty, which never, of course, seemed very funny to us; they could not have seemed very funny to him, either, or else our all too feeble response to them would never have caused such rages. He spent great energy and achieved, to our chagrin, no small amount of success in keeping us away from the people who surrounded us, people who had all-night rent parties to which we listened when we should have been sleeping, people who cursed and drank and flashed razor blades on Lenox Avenue. He could not understand why, if they had so much energy to spare, they could not use it to make their lives better. He treated almost everybody on our block with a most uncharitable asperity and neither they, nor, of course, their children were slow to reciprocate.

The only white people who came to our house were welfare workers and bill collectors. It was almost always my mother who dealt with them, for my father's temper, which was at the mercy of his pride, was never to be trusted. It was clear that he felt their very presence in his home to be a violation: this was conveyed by his carriage, almost ludicrously stiff, and by his voice, harsh and vindictively polite. When I was around nine or ten I wrote a play which was directed by a young, white schoolteacher, a woman, who then took an interest in me, and gave me books to read and, in order to corroborate my theatrical bent, decided to take me to see what she somewhat tactlessly referred to as "real" plays. Theater-going was forbidden in our house, but, with the really cruel intuitiveness of a child, I suspected that the color of this woman's skin would carry the day for me. When, at school, she suggested taking me to the theater, I did not, as I might have done if she had been a Negro, find a way of discouraging her, but agreed that she should pick me up at my house one evening. I then, very cleverly, left all the rest to my mother, who suggested to my father, as I knew she would, that it would not be very nice to let such a kind woman make the trip for nothing. Also, since it was a schoolteacher, I imagine that my mother countered the idea of sin with the idea of "education," which word, even with my father, carried a kind of bitter weight.

Before the teacher came my father took me aside to ask why she was coming, what interest she could possibly have in our house, in a boy like me. I said I didn't know but I, too, suggested that it had something to do with education. And I understood that my father was waiting for me to say something—I didn't quite know what; perhaps that I wanted his protection against this teacher and her "education." I said none of these things and the teacher came and we went out. It was clear, during the brief interview in our living room, that my father was agreeing very much against his will and that he would have refused permission if he had dared. The fact that he did not dare caused me to despise him: I had no way of knowing that he was facing in that living room a wholly unprecedented and frightening situation.

Later, when my father had been laid off from his job, this woman became very important to us. She was really a very sweet and generous woman and went to a great deal of trouble to be of help to us, particularly during one awful winter. My mother called her by the highest name she knew: she said she was a "christian." My father could scarcely disagree but during the four or five years of our relatively close association he never trusted her and was always trying to surprise in her open, Midwestern face the genuine, cunningly hidden, and hideous motivation. In later years, particularly when it began to be clear that this "education" of mine was going to lead me to perdition, he became more explicit and warned me that my white friends in high school were not really my friends and that I would see, when I was older, how white people would do anything to keep a Negro down. Some of them could be nice, he admitted, but none of them were to be trusted and most of them were not even nice. The best thing was to have as little to do with them as possible. I did not feel this way and I was certain, in my innocence, that I never would.

But the year which preceded my father's death had made a great change in my life. I had been living in New Jersey, working in defense plants, working and living among southerners, white and black. I knew about the South, of course, and about how southerners treated Negroes and how they expected them to behave, but it had never entered my mind that anyone would look at me and expect *me* to behave that way. I learned in New Jersey that to be a Negro meant, precisely, that one was never looked at but was simply at the mercy of the reflexes the color of one's skin caused in other people. I acted in New Jersey as I had always acted, that is as though I thought a great deal of myself—I had to act that way—with results that were, simply, unbelievable. I had scarcely arrived before I had earned the enmity, which was extraordinarily ingenious, of all my superiors and nearly all my co-workers. In the beginning, to make matters worse, I simply did not know what was happening. I did not know what I had done, and I shortly began to wonder what anyone could possibly do, to bring about such unanimous, active, and unbearably vocal hostility. I knew about jim crow but I had never experienced it. I went to the same self-service restaurant three times and stood with all the Princeton boys before the counter, waiting for a hamburger and coffee; it was always an extraordinarily long time before anything was set before me; but it was not until the fourth visit that I learned that, in fact, nothing had ever been set before me: I had simply picked something up. Negroes were not served there, I was told, and they had been waiting for me to realize that I was always the only Negro present. Once I was told this, I determined to go there all the time. But now they were ready for me and, though some dreadful scenes were subsequently enacted in that restaurant, I never ate there again.

It was the same story all over New Jersey, in bars, bowling alleys, diners, places to live. I was always being forced to leave, silently, or with mutual imprecations. I very shortly became notorious and children giggled behind me when I passed and their elders whispered or shouted-they really believed that I was mad. And it did begin to work on my mind, of course; I began to be afraid to go anywhere and to compensate for this I went places to which I really should not have gone and where, God knows, I had no desire to be. My reputation in town naturally enhanced my reputation at work and my working day became one long series of acrobatics designed to keep me out of trouble. I cannot say that these acrobatics succeeded. It began to seem that the machinery of the organization I worked for was turning over, day and night, with but one aim: to eject me. I was fired once, and contrived, with the aid of a friend from New York, to get back on the payroll; was fired again, and bounced back again. It took a while to fire me for the third time, but the third time took. There were no loopholes anywhere. There was not even any way of getting back inside the gates.

That year in New Jersey lives in my mind as though it were the year during which, having an unsuspected predilection for it, I first contracted some dread, chronic disease, the unfailing symptom of which is a kind of blind fever, a pounding in the skull and fire in the bowels. Once this disease is contracted, one can never be really carefree again, for the fever, without an instant's warning, can recur at any moment. It can wreck more important things than race relations. There is not a Negro alive who does not have this rage in his blood—one has the choice, merely, of living with it consciously or surrendering to it. As for me, this fever has recurred in me, and does, and will until the day I die.

My last night in New Jersey, a white friend from New York took me to the nearest big town, Trenton, to go to the movies and have a few drinks. As it turned out, he also saved me from, at the very least, a violent whipping. Almost every detail of that night stands out very clearly in my memory. I even remember the name of the movie we saw because its title impressed me as being so patly ironical. It was a movie about the German occupation of France, starring Maureen O'Hara and Charles Laughton and called *This Land Is Mine*. I remember the name of the diner we walked into when the movie ended: it was the "American Diner." When we walked in the counterman asked what we wanted and I remember answering with the casual sharpness which had become my habit: "We want a hamburger and a cup of coffee, what do you think we want?" I do not know why, after a year of such rebuffs, I so completely failed to anticipate his answer, which was, of course, "we don't serve Negroes here." This reply failed to discompose me, at least for the moment. I made some sardonic comment about the name of the diner and we walked out into the streets.

This was the time of what was called the "brownout," when the lights in all American cities were very dim. When we reentered the streets something happened to me which had the force of an optical illusion, or a nightmare. The streets were very crowded and I was facing north. People were moving in every direction but it seemed to me, in that instant, that all of the people I could see, and many more than that, were moving toward me, against me, and that everyone was white. I remember how their faces gleamed. And I felt, like a physical sensation, a click at the nape of my neck as though some interior string connecting my head to my body had been cut. I began to walk. I heard my friend call after me, but I ignored him. Heaven only knows what was going on in his mind, but he had the good sense not to touch me—I don't know what would have happened if he had—and to keep me in sight. I don't know what was going on in my mind, either; I certainly had no conscious plan. I wanted to do something to crush these white faces, which were crushing me. I walked for perhaps a block or two until I came to an enormous, glittering, and fashionable restaurant in which I knew not even the intercession of the Virgin would cause me to be served. I pushed through the doors and took the first vacant seat I saw, at a table for two, and waited.

I do not know how long I waited and I rather wonder, until today, what I could possibly have looked like. Whatever I looked like, I frightened the waitress who shortly appeared, and the moment she appeared all of my fury flowed toward her. I hated her for her white face, and for her great, astounded, frightened eyes. I felt that if she found a black man so frightening I would make her fright worthwhile.

She did not ask me what I wanted, but repeated, as though she had earned it somewhere, "We don't serve Negroes here." She did not say it with the blunt, derisive hostility to which I had grown so accustomed, but, rather, with a note of apology in her voice, and fear. This made me colder and more murderous than ever. I felt I had to do something with my hands. I wanted her to come close enough for me to get her neck between my hands.

So I pretended not to have understood her, hoping to draw her closer. And she did step a very short step closer, with her pencil poised incongruously over her pad, and repeated the formula: ". . . don't serve Negroes here."

Somehow, with the repetition of that phrase, which was already ringing in my head like a thousand bells of a nightmare, I realized that she would never come any closer and that I would have to strike from a distance. There was nothing on the table but an ordinary watermug half full of water, and I picked this up and hurled it with all my strength at her. She ducked and it missed her and shattered against the mirror behind the bar. And, with that sound, my frozen blood abruptly thawed, I returned from wherever I had been, I saw, for the first time, the restaurant, the people with their mouths open, already, as it seemed to me, rising as one man, and I realized what I had done, and where I was, and I was frightened. I rose and began running for the door. A round, potbellied man grabbed me by the nape of the neck just as I reached the doors and began to beat me about the face. I kicked him and got loose and ran into the streets. My friend whispered, "Run!" and I ran.

My friend stayed outside the restaurant long enough to misdirect my pursuers and the police, who arrived, he told me, at once. I do not know what I said to him when he came to my room that night. I could not have said much. I felt, in the oddest, most awful way, that I had somehow betrayed him. I lived it over and over and over again, the way one relives an automobile accident after it has happened and one finds oneself alone and safe. I could not get over two facts, both equally difficult for the imagination to grasp, and one was that I could have been murdered. But the other was that I had been ready to commit murder. I saw nothing very clearly but I did see this: that my life, my real life, was in danger, and not from anything other people might do but from the hatred I carried in my own heart.

2

I had returned home around the second week in June—in great haste because it seemed that my father's death and my mother's confinement were both but a matter of hours. In the case of my mother, it soon became clear that she had simply made a miscalculation. This had always been her tendency and I don't believe that a single one of us arrived in the world, or has since arrived anywhere else, on time. But none of us dawdled so intolerably about the business of being born as did my baby sister. We sometimes amused ourselves, during those endless, stifling weeks, by picturing the baby sitting within in the safe, warm dark, bitterly regretting the necessity of becoming a part of our chaos and stubbornly putting it off as long as possible. I understood her perfectly and congratulated her on showing such good sense so soon. Death, however, sat as purposefully at my father's bedside as life stirred within my mother's womb and it was harder to understand why he so lingered in that long shadow. It seemed that he had bent, and for a long time, too, all of his energies toward dying. Now death was ready for him but my father held back.

All of Harlem, indeed, seemed to be infected by waiting. I had never before known it to be so violently still. Racial tensions throughout this country were exacerbated during the early years of the war, partly because the labor market brought together hundreds of thousands of ill-prepared people and partly because Negro soldiers, regardless of where they were born, received their military training in the south. What happened in defense plants and army camps had repercussions, naturally, in every Negro ghetto. The situation in Harlem had grown bad enough for clergymen, policemen, educators, politicians, and social workers to assert in one breath that there was no "crime wave" and to offer, in the very next breath, suggestions as to how to combat it. These suggestions always seemed to involve playgrounds, despite the fact that racial skirmishes were occurring in the playgrounds, too. Playground or not, crime wave or not, the Harlem police force had been augmented in March, and the unrest grew—perhaps, in fact, partly as a result of the ghetto's instinctive hatred of policemen. Perhaps the most revealing news item, out of the steady parade of reports of muggings, stabbings, shootings, assaults, gang wars, and accusations of police brutality, is the item concerning six Negro girls who set upon a white girl in the subway because, as they all too accurately put it, she was stepping on their toes. Indeed she was, all over the nation.

I had never before been so aware of policemen, on foot, on horseback, on corners, everywhere, always two by two. Nor had I ever been so aware of small knots of people. They were on stoops and on corners and in doorways, and what was striking about them, I think, was that they did not seem to be talking. Never, when I passed these groups, did the usual sound of a curse or a laugh ring out and neither did there seem to be any hum of gossip. There was certainly, on the other hand, occurring between them communication extraordinarily intense. Another thing that was striking was the unexpected diversity of the people who made up these groups. Usually, for example, one would see a group of sharpies standing on the street corner, jiving the passing chicks; or a group of older men, usually, for some reason, in the vicinity of a barber shop, discussing baseball scores, or the numbers, or making rather chilling observations about women they had known. Women, in a general way, tended to be seen less often together—unless they were church women, or very young girls, or prostitutes met together for an unprofessional instant. But that summer I saw the strangest combinations: large, respectable, churchly matrons standing on the stoops or the corners with their hair tied up, together with a girl in sleazy satin whose face bore the marks of gin and the razor, or heavy-set, abrupt, no-nonsense older men, in company with the most disreputable and fanatical "race" men, or these same "race" men with the sharpies, or these sharpies with the churchly women. Seventh Day Adventists and Methodists and Spiritualists seemed to be hobnobbing with Holyrollers and they were all, alike, entangled with the most flagrant disbelievers; something heavy in their stance seemed to indicate that they had all, incredibly, seen a common vision, and on each face there seemed to be the same strange, bitter shadow.

The churchly women and the matter-of-fact, no-nonsense men had children in the Army. The sleazy girls they talked to had lovers there, the sharpies and the "race" men had friends and brothers there. It would have demanded an unquestioning patriotism, happily as uncommon in this country as it is undesirable, for these people not to have been disturbed by the bitter letters they received, by the newspaper stories they read, not to have been enraged by the posters, then to be found all over New York, which described the Japanese as "yellow-bellied Japs." It was only the "race" men, to be sure, who spoke ceaselessly of being revenged-how this vengeance was to be exacted was not clear-for the indignities and dangers suffered by Negro boys in uniform; but everybody felt a directionless, hopeless bitterness, as well as that panic which can scarcely be suppressed when one knows that a human being one loves is beyond one's reach, and in danger. This helplessness and this gnawing uneasiness does something, at length, to even the toughest mind. Perhaps the best way to sum all this up is to say that the people I knew felt, mainly, a peculiar kind of relief when they knew that their boys were being shipped out of the south, to do battle overseas. It was, perhaps, like feeling that the most dangerous part of a dangerous journey had been passed and that now, even if death should come, it would come with honor and without the complicity of their countrymen. Such a death would be, in short, a fact with which one could hope to live.

It was on the twenty-eighth of July, which I believe was a Wednesday, that I visited my father for the first time during his illness and for the last time in his life. The moment I saw him I knew why I had put off this visit so long. I had told my mother that I did not want to see him because I hated him. But this was not true. It was only that I had hated him and I wanted to hold on to this hatred. I did not want to look on him as a ruin: it was not a ruin I had hated. I imagine that one of the reasons people cling to their hates so stubbornly is because they sense, once hate is gone, that they will be forced to deal with pain.

We traveled out to him, his older sister and myself, to what seemed to be the very end of a very Long Island. It was hot and dusty and we wrangled, my aunt and I, all the way out, over the fact that I had recently begun to smoke and, as she said, to give myself airs. But I knew that she wrangled with me because she could not bear to face the fact of her brother's dying. Neither could I endure the reality of her despair, her unstated bafflement as to what had happened to her brother's life, and her own. So we wrangled and I smoked and from time to time she fell into a heavy reverie. Covertly, I watched her face, which was the face of an old woman; it had fallen in, the eyes were sunken arid lightless; soon she would be dying, too.

In my childhood—it had not been so long ago—I had thought her beautiful. She had been quick-witted and quick-moving and very generous with all the children and each of her visits had been an event. At one time one of my brothers and myself had thought of running away to live with her. Now she could no longer produce out of her handbag some unexpected and yet familiar delight. She made me feel pity and revulsion and fear. It was awful to realize that she no longer caused me to feel affection. The closer we came to the hospital the more querulous she became and at the same time, naturally, grew more dependent on me. Between pity and guilt and fear I began to feel that there was another me trapped in my skull like a jack-in-the-box who might escape my control at any moment and fill the air with screaming.

She began to cry the moment we entered the room and she saw him lying there, all shriveled and still, like a little black monkey. The great, gleaming apparatus which fed him and would have compelled him to be still even if he had been able to move brought to mind, not beneficence, but torture; the tubes entering his arm made me think of pictures I had seen when a child, of Gulliver, tied down by the pygmies on that island. My aunt wept and wept, there was a whistling sound in my father's throat; nothing was said; he could not speak. I wanted to take his hand, to say something. But I do not know what I could have said, even if he could have heard me. He was not really in that room with us, he had at last really embarked on his journey; and though my aunt told me that he said he was going to meet Jesus, I did not hear anything except that whistling in his throat. The doctor came back and we left, into that unbearable train again, and home. In the morning came the telegram saying that he was dead. Then the house was suddenly full of relatives, friends, hysteria, and confusion and I quickly left my mother and the children to the care of those impressive women, who, in Negro communities at least, automatically appear at times of bereavement armed with lotions, proverbs, and patience, and an ability to cook. I went downtown. By the time I returned, later the same day, my mother had been carried to the hospital and the baby had been born.

3

For my father's funeral I had nothing black to wear and this posed a nagging problem all day long. It was one of those problems, simple, or impossible of solution, to which the mind insanely clings in order to avoid the mind's real trouble. I spent most of that day at the downtown apartment of a girl I knew, celebrating my birthday with whisky and wondering what to wear that night. When planning a birthday celebration one naturally does not expect that it will be up against competition from a funeral and this girl had anticipated taking me out that night, for a big dinner and a nightclub afterwards. Sometime during the course of that long day we decided that we would go out anyway, when my father's funeral service was over. I imagine I decided it, since, as the funeral hour approached, it became clearer and dearer to me that I would not know what to do with myself when it was over. The girl, stifling her very lively concern as to the possible effects of the whisky on one of my father's chief mourners, concentrated on being conciliatory and practically helpful. She found a black shirt for me somewhere and ironed it and, dressed in the darkest pants and jacket I owned, and slightly drunk, I made my way to my father's funeral.

The chapel was full, but not packed, and very quiet. There were, mainly, my father's relatives, and his children, and here and there I saw faces I had not seen since childhood, the faces of my father's one-time friends. They were very dark and solemn now, seeming somehow to suggest that they had known all along that something like this would happen. Chief among the mourners was my aunt, who had quarreled with my father all his life; by which I do not mean to suggest that her mourning was insincere or that she had not loved him. I suppose that she was one of the few people in the world who had, and their incessant quarreling proved precisely the strength of the tie that bound them. The only other person in the world, as far as I knew, whose relationship to my father rivaled my aunt's in depth was my mother, who was not there.

It seemed to me, of course, that it was a very long funeral. But it was, if anything, a rather shorter funeral than most, nor, since there were no overwhelming, uncontrollable expressions of grief, could it be called—if I dare to use the word—successful. The minister who preached my father's funeral sermon was one of the few my father had still been seeing as he neared his end. He presented to us in his sermon a man whom none of us had ever seen—a man thoughtful, patient, and forbearing, a Christian inspiration to all who knew him; and a model for his children. And no doubt the children, in their disturbed and guilty state, were almost ready to believe this; he had been remote enough to be anything and, anyway, the shock of the incontrovertible, that it was really our father lying up there in that casket, prepared the mind for anything. His sister moaned and this grief-stricken moaning was taken as corroboration. The other faces held a dark, noncommittal thoughtfulness. This was not the man they had known, but they had scarcely expected to be confronted with him; this was, in a sense deeper than questions of fact, the man they had not known, and the man they had not known may have been the real one. The real man, whoever he had been, had suffered and now he was dead: this was all that was sure and all that mattered now. Every man in the chapel hoped that when his hour came he, too, would be eulogized, which is to say forgiven, and that all of his lapses, greeds, errors, and strayings from the truth would be invested with coherence and looked upon with charity. This was perhaps the last thing human beings could give each other and it was what they demanded, after all, of the Lord. Only the Lord saw the midnight tears, only He was present when one of His children, moaning and wringing hands, paced up and down the room. When one slapped one's child in anger the recoil in the heart reverberated through heaven and became part of the pain of the universe. And when the children were hungry and sullen and distrustful and one watched them, daily, growing wilder, and further away, and running headlong into danger, it was the Lord who knew what the charged heart endured as the strap was laid to the backside; the Lord alone who knew what one would have said if one had had, like the Lord, the gift of the living word. It was the Lord who knew of the impossibility every parent in that room faced: how to prepare the child for the day when the child would be despised and how to create in the child—by what means?—a stronger antidote to this poison than one had found for oneself. The avenues, side streets, bars, billiard halls, hospitals, police stations, and even the playgrounds of Harlem—not to mention the houses of correction, the jails, and the morgue-testified to the potency of the poison while remaining silent as to the efficacy of whatever antidote, irresistibly raising the question of whether or not such an antidote existed; raising, which was worse, the question of whether or not an antidote was desirable; perhaps poison should be fought with poison. With these several schisms in the mind and with more terrors in the heart than could be named, it was better not to judge the man who had gone down under an impossible burden. It was better to remember: *Thou knowest this man's fall; but thou knowest not his wrassling.*

While the preacher talked and I watched the children—years of changing their diapers, scrubbing them, slapping them, taking them to school, and scolding them had had the perhaps inevitable result of making me love them, though I am not sure I knew this then—my mind was busily breaking out with a rash of disconnected impressions. Snatches of popular songs, indecent jokes, bits of books I had read, movie sequences, faces, voices, political issues—I thought I was going mad; all these impressions suspended, as it were, in the solution of the faint nausea produced in me by the heat and liquor. For a moment I had the impression that my alcoholic breath, inefficiently disguised with chewing gum, filled the entire chapel. Then someone began singing one of my father's favorite songs and, abruptly, I was with him, sitting on his knee, in the hot, enormous, crowded church which was the first church we attended. It was the Abyssinian Baptist Church on 138th Street. We had not gone there long. With this image, a host of others came. I had forgotten, in the rage of my growing up, how proud my father had been of me when I was little. Apparently, I had had a voice and my father had liked to show me off before the members of the church. I had forgotten what he had looked like when he was pleased but now I remembered that he had always been grinning with pleasure when my solos ended. I even remembered certain expressions on his face when he teased my mother—had he loved her? I would never know. And when had it all begun to change? For now it seemed that he had not always been cruel. I remembered being taken for a haircut and scraping my knee on the footrest of the barber's chair and I remembered my father's face as he soothed my crying and applied the stinging iodine. Then I remembered our fights, fights which had been of the worst possible kind because my technique had been silence.

I remembered the one time in all our life together when we had really spoken to each other.

It was on a Sunday and it must have been shortly before I left home. We were walking, just the two of us, in our usual silence, to or from church. I was in high school and had been doing a lot of writing and I was, at about this time, the editor of the high school magazine. But I had also been a Young Minister and had been preaching from the pulpit. Lately, I had been taking fewer engagements and preached as rarely as possible. It was said in the church, quite truthfully, that I was "cooling off."

My father asked me abruptly, "You'd rather write than preach, wouldn't you?"

I was astonished at his question—because it was a real question. I answered, "Yes."

That was all we said. It was awful to remember that that was all we had ever said.

The casket now was opened and the mourners were being led up the aisle to look for the last time on the deceased. The assumption was that the family was too overcome with grief to be allowed to make this journey alone and I watched while my aunt was led to the casket and, muffled in black, and shaking, led back to her seat. I disapproved of forcing the children to look on their dead father, considering that the shock of his death, or, more truthfully, the shock of death as a reality, was already a little more than a child could bear, but my judgment in this matter had been overruled and there they were, bewildered and frightened and very small, being led, one by one, to the casket. But there is also something very gallant about children at such moments. It has something to do with their silence and gravity and with the fact that one cannot help them. Their legs, somehow, seem exposed, so that it is at once incredible and terribly clear that their legs are all they have to hold them up.

I had not wanted to go to the casket myself and I certainly had not wished to be led there, but there was no way of avoiding either of these forms. One of the deacons led me up and I looked on my father's face. I cannot say that it looked like him at all. His blackness had been equivocated by powder and there was no suggestion in that casket of what his power had or could have been. He was simply an old man dead, and it was hard to believe that he had ever given anyone either joy or pain. Yet, his life filled that room. Further up the avenue his wife was holding his newborn child. Life and death so close together, and love and hatred, and right and wrong, said something to me which I did not want to hear concerning man, concerning the life of man.

After the funeral, while I was downtown desperately celebrating my birthday, a Negro soldier, in the lobby of the Hotel Braddock, got into a fight with a white policeman over a Negro girl. Negro girls, white policemen, in or out of uniform, and Negro males—in or out of uniform—were part of the furniture of the lobby of the Hotel Braddock and this was certainly not the first time such an incident had occurred. It was destined, however, to receive an unprecedented publicity, for the fight between the policeman and the soldier ended with the shooting of the soldier. Rumor, flowing immediately to the streets outside, stated that the soldier had been shot in the back, an instantaneous and revealing invention, and that the soldier had died protecting a Negro woman. The facts were somewhat different—for example, the soldier had not been shot in the back, and was not dead, and the girl seems to have been as dubious a symbol of womanhood as her white counterpart in Georgia usually is, but no one was interested in the facts. They preferred the invention because this invention expressed and corroborated their hates and fears so perfectly. It is just as well to remember that people are always doing this. Perhaps many of those legends, including Christianity, to which the world clings began their conquest of the world with just some such concerted surrender to distortion. The effect, in Harlem, of this particular legend was like the effect of a lit match in a tin of gasoline. The mob gathered before the doors of the Hotel Braddock simply began to swell and to spread in every direction, and Harlem exploded.

The mob did not cross the ghetto lines. It would have been easy, for example, to have gone over Morningside Park on the west side or to have crossed the Grand Central railroad tracks at 125th Street on the east side, to wreak havoc in white neighborhoods. The mob seems to have been mainly interested in something more potent and real than the white face, that is, in white power, and the principal damage done during the riot of the summer of 1943 was to white business establishments in Harlem. It might have been a far bloodier story, of course, if, at the hour the riot began, these establishments had still been open. From the Hotel Braddock the mob fanned out, east and west along 125th Street, and for the entire length of Lenox, Seventh, and Eighth avenues. Along each of these avenues, and along each major side street—116th, 125th, 135th, and so on-bars, stores, pawnshops, restaurants, even little luncheonettes had been smashed open and entered and looted—looted, it might be added, with more haste than efficiency. The shelves really looked as though a bomb had struck them. Cans of beans and soup and dog food, along with toilet paper, corn flakes, sardines and milk tumbled every which way, and abandoned cash registers and cases of beer leaned crazily out of the splintered windows and were strewn along the avenues. Sheets, blankets, and clothing of every description formed a kind of path, as though people had dropped them while running. I truly had not realized that Harlem had so many stores until I saw them all smashed open; the first time the word wealth ever entered my mind in relation to Harlem was when I saw it scattered in the streets. Bur one's first, incongruous impression of plenty was countered immediately by an impression of waste. None of this was doing anybody any good. It would have been better to have left the plate glass as it had been and the goods lying in the stores.

It would have been better, but it would also have been intolerable, for Harlem had needed something to smash. To smash something is the ghetto's chronic need. Most of the time it is the members of the ghetto who smash each other, and themselves. But as long as the ghetto walls are standing there will always come a moment when these outlets do not work. That summer, for example, it was not enough to get into a fight on Lenox Avenue, or curse out one's cronies in the barber shops. If ever, indeed, the violence which fills Harlem's churches, pool halls, and bars erupts outward in a more direct fashion, Harlem and its citizens are likely to vanish in an apocalyptic flood. That this is not likely to happen is due to a great many reasons, most hidden and powerful among them the Negro's real relation to the white American. This relation prohibits, simply, anything as uncomplicated and satisfactory as pure hatred. In order really to hate white people, one has to blot so much out of the mind—and the heart—that this hatred itself becomes an exhausting and self-destructive pose. But this does not mean, on the other hand, that love comes easily: the white world is too powerful, too complacent, too ready with gratuitous humiliation, and, above all, too ignorant and too innocent for that. One is absolutely forced to make perpetual qualifications and one's own reactions are always canceling each other out. It is this, really, which has driven so many people mad, both white and black. One is always in the position of having to decide between amputation and gangrene. Amputation is swift but time may prove that the amputation was not necessary—or one may delay the amputation too long. Gangrene is slow, but it is impossible to be sure that one is reading one's symptoms right.

The idea of going through life as a cripple is more than one can bear, and equally unbearable is the risk of swelling up slowly, in agony, with poison. And the trouble, finally, is that the risks are real even if the choices do not exist.

"But as for me and my house," my father had said, "we will serve the Lord." I wondered, as we drove him to his resting place, what this line had meant for him. I had heard him preach it many times. I had preached it once myself, proudly giving it an interpretation different from my father's. Now the whole thing came back to me, as though my father and I were on our way to Sunday school and I were memorizing the golden text: *And if it seem evil unto you to serve the Lord, choose you this day whom you will serve; whether the gods which your fathers served that were on the other side of the flood, or the gods of the Amorites, in whose land ye dwell: but as for me and my house, we will serve the Lord.* I suspected in these familiar lines a meaning which had never been there for me before. All of my father's texts and songs, which I had decided were meaningless, were arranged before me at his death like empty bottles, waiting to hold the meaning which life would give them for me. This was his legacy: nothing is ever escaped. That bleakly memorable morning I hated the unbelievable streets and the Negroes and whites who had, equally, made them that way. But I knew that it was folly, as my father would have said, this bitterness was folly. It was necessary to hold on to the things that mattered. The dead man mattered, the new life mattered; blackness and whiteness did not matter; to believe that they did was to acquiesce in one's own destruction. Hatred, which could destroy so much, never failed to destroy the man who hated and this was an immutable law.

It began to seem that one would have to hold in the mind forever two ideas which seemed to be in opposition. The first idea was acceptance, the acceptance, totally without rancor, of life as it is, and men as they are: in the light of this idea, it goes without saying that injustice is a commonplace. But this did not mean that one could be complacent, for the second idea was of equal power: that one must never, in one's own life, accept these injustices as commonplace but must fight them with all one's strength. This fight begins, however, in the heart and it now had been laid to my charge to keep my own heart free of hatred and despair. This intimation made my heart heavy and, now that my father was irrecoverable, I wished that he had been beside me so that I could have searched his face for the answers which only the future would give me now.

Rite of Passage

by Anthony Brandt

Some things that happen to us can't be borne, with the paradoxical result that we carry them on our backs the rest of our lives. I have been half obsessed for almost thirty years with the death of my grandmother. I should say with her dying: with the long and terrible changes that came at the worst time for a boy of twelve and thirteen, going through his own difficult changes. It felt like and perhaps was the equivalent of a puberty rite: dark, frightening, aboriginal, an obscure emotional exchange between old and young. It has become part of my character.

I grew up in New Jersey in a suburban town where my brother still lives and practices law. One might best describe it as quiet, protected, and green; it was no preparation for death. Tall, graceful elm trees lined both sides of the street where we lived. My father's brother-in-law, a contractor, built our house; we moved into it a year after I was born. My grandmother and grandfather (my mother's parents; they were the only grandparents who mattered) lived up the street "on the hill"; it wasn't much of a hill, the terrain in that part of New Jersey being what it is, but we could ride our sleds down the street after it snowed, and that was hilly enough.

Our family lived, or seemed to a young boy to live, in very stable, very ordinary patterns. My father Commuted to New York every day, taking the Jersey Central Railroad, riding in cars that had windows you could open, getting off the train in Jersey City and taking a ferry to Manhattan. He held the same job in the same company for more than thirty years. The Son of Swedish immigrants, he was a funny man who could wiggle his ears without raising his eyebrows and made up the most dreadful puns. When he wasn't being funny he was quiet, the newspaper his shield and companion, or the *Saturday Evening Post*, which he brought home without fail every Wednesday evening, or *Life*, which he brought home Fridays. It was hard to break through the quiet and the humor, and after he died my mother said, as much puzzled as disturbed, that she hardly knew him at all.

She, the backbone of the family, was fierce, stern, the kind of person who can cow you with a glance. My brother and I, and my cousins, were all a little in awe of her. The ruling passion in her life was to protect her family; she lived in a set of concentric circles, nephews, brothers, parents, then more distant relatives, and outside that a few friends, very few. No one and nothing else existed for her; she had no interest in politics, art, history, or even the price of eggs. "Fierce" is the best word for her, or single-minded. In those days (I was born in 1936) polio was every parent's bugbear; she, to keep my brother and me away from places where the disease was supposed to be communicated, particularly swimming pools, took us every summer for the entire summer to the Jersey shore, first to her parents' cottage, later to a little cottage she and my father bought. She did that even though it meant being separated from my father for nearly three months, having no body to talk to, having to handle my brother and me on her own. She hated it, she told us years later, but she did it: fiercely. Or there's the story of one of my cousins who got pregnant when she was sixteen or seventeen; my mother took her into our house, managed somehow to hide her condition from the neighbors, then, after the birth, arranged privately to have the child adopted by a family the doctor recommended, all this being done without consulting the proper authorities, and for the rest of her life never told a single person how she made these arrangements or where she had placed the child. She was a genuine primitive, like some tough old peasant woman. Yet her name was Grace, her nickname Bunny; if you saw through the fierceness, you understood that it was a version of love.

Her mother, my grandmother, seemed anything but fierce. One of our weekly routines was Sunday dinner at their house on the hill, some five or six houses from ours. When I was very young, before World War II, the house had a mansard roof, a barn in the back, lots of yard space, lots of rooms inside, and a cherry tree. I thought it was a palace. Actually it was rather small, and became smaller when my grandmother insisted on tearing down the mansard roof and replacing it with a conventional peaked roof; the house lost three attic rooms in the process. Sunday dinner was invariably roast beef or chicken or leg of lamb with mashed potatoes and vegetables, standard American fare but cooked by my grandparents' Polish maid, Josephine, not by my grandmother. Josephine made wonderful pies in an old cast-iron coal stove and used to let me tie her with string to the kitchen sink. My grandfather was a gentle man who smoked a pipe, had a bristly reddish moustache, and always seemed to wind up paying everybody else's debts in the family; my mother worshipped him. There were usually lots of uncles at these meals, and they were a playful bunch. I have a very early memory of two of them tossing me back and forth between them, and another of the youngest, whose name was Don, carrying me on his shoulders into the surf. I also remember my grandmother presiding at these meals. She was gray-haired and benign.

Later they sold that house. My benign grandmother, I've been told since, was in fact a restless, unsatisfied woman; changing the roof line, moving from house to house, were her ways of expressing that dissatisfaction. In the next house, I think it was, my grandfather died; my grandmother moved again, then again, and then to a house down the street, at the bottom of the hill this time, and there I got to know her better. I was nine or ten years old. She let me throw a tennis ball against the side of the house for hours at a time; the noise must have been terribly aggravating. She cooked lunch for me and used to make pancakes the size of dinner plates, and corn fritters. She also made me a whole set of yarn figures a few inches long, rolling yarn around her hand, taking the roll and tying off arms, legs, and a head, then sewing a face onto the head with black thread. I played with these and an odd assortment of hand-me-down toy soldiers for long afternoons, setting up wars, football games, contests of all kinds, and designating particular yarn figures as customary heroes. Together we played a spelling game: I'd be on the floor playing with the yarn figures, she'd be writing a letter and ask me how to spell "appreciate" (it was always that word), and I'd spell it for her while she pretended to be impressed with my spelling ability and I pretended that she hadn't asked me to spell that same word a dozen times before. I was good, too, at helping her find her glasses.

One scene at this house stands out. My uncle Bob came home from the whole family, his young wife, other uncles, my mother and father and brother and I, gathered at the house to meet him, and he came in wearing his captain's uniform and looking to me, I swear it, like a handsome young god. In fact he was an ordinary man who spent the rest of his life selling insurance. He had been in New Guinea, a ground officer in the Air Corps, and the story I remember is of the native who came into his tent one day and took a great deal of interest in the scissors my uncle was using. The native asked in pidgin English what my uncle would require for the scissors in trade, and he jokingly said, well, how about a tentful of bananas. Sure enough, several days later two or three hundred natives came out of the jungle, huge bunches of bananas of their shoulders, and filled my uncle's tent.

Things went on this way for I don't know how long, maybe two years, maybe three. I don't want to describe it as idyllic. Youth has its problems. But this old woman who could never find her glasses was wonderful to me, a grandmother in the true likeness of one, and I couldn't understand the changes when they came. She moved again, against all advice, this time to a big, bare apartment on the other side of town. She was gradually becoming irritable and difficult, not much fun to be around. There were no more spelling games; she stopped writing letters. Because she moved I saw her less often, and her home could no longer be a haven for me. She neglected it, too; it grew dirtier and dirtier, until my mother eventually had to do her cleaning for her.

Then she began to see things that weren't there. A branch in the back yard became a woman, I remember, who apparently wasn't fully clothed, and a man was doing something to her, something unspeakable. She developed diabetes and my mother learned to give her insulin shots, but she wouldn't stop eating candy, the worst thing for her, and the diabetes got worse. Her face began to change, to slacken, to lose its shape and character. I didn't understand these things; arteriosclerosis, hardening of the arteries, whatever the explanation, it was only words. What I noticed was that her white hair was getting thinner and harder to control, that she herself seemed to be shrinking even as I grew, that when she looked at me I wasn't sure it was me she was seeing anymore.

After a few months of this, we brought her to live with us. My mother was determined to take care of her, and certain family pressures were brought to bear too. That private man my father didn't like the idea at all, but he said nothing, which was his way. And she was put in my brother's bedroom over the garage, my brother moving in with me. It was a small house, six rooms and a basement, much too small for what we had to face.

What we had to face was a rapid deterioration into senile dementia and the rise from beneath the surface of this smiling, kindly, white-haired old lady of something truly ugly. Whenever she was awake she called for attention, calling, calling a hundred times a day. Restless as always, she picked the bedclothes off, tore holes in sheets and pillows, took off her nightclothes and sat naked talking to herself. She hallucinated more and more frequently, addressing her dead husband, a dead brother, scolding, shouting at their apparitions. She became incontinent and smeared feces on herself, the furniture, the walls. And always calling—"Bunny, where are you? Bunny, I want you!"—scolding, demanding; she could seldom remember what she wanted when my mother came. It became an important event when she fell asleep; to make sure she stayed asleep to radio was kept off, the four of us tiptoed around the house, and when I went out to close the garage door, directly under her window (it was an overhead door and had to be pulled down), I did it so slowly and carefully, half an inch at a time, that it sometimes took me a full fifteen minutes to get it down.

That my mother endured this for six months is a testimony to her strength and determination, but it was really beyond her and almost destroyed her health. My grandmother didn't often sleep through the night; she would wake up, yell, cry, a creature of disorder, a living *memento mori*, and my mother would have to tend to her. The house began to smell in spite of all my mother's efforts to keep my grandmother's room clean. My father, his peace gone, brooded in his chair behind his newspaper. My brother and I fought for *Lebensraum*, each of us trying to grow up in his own way. People avoided us. My uncles were living elsewhere—Miami, Cleveland, Delaware. My grandmother's two surviving sisters, who lived about ten blocks away, never came to see her. Everybody seemed to sense that something obscene was happening, and stayed away. Terrified, I stayed away, too. I heard my grandmother constantly, but in the six months she lived with us I think I went into her room only once. That was as my mother wished it. She was a nightmare, naked and filthy without warning.

After six months, at my father's insistence, after a night nurse had been hired and left, after my mother had reached her limits and beyond, my parents started looking for a nursing home, anyplace they could put her. It became a family scandal; the two sisters were outraged that my mother would consider putting her own mother in a home, there were telephone calls back and forth between them and my uncles, but of course the sisters had never come to see her themselves, and my mother never forgave them. One of my uncles finally came from Cleveland, saw what was happening, and that day they put my grandmother in a car and drove her off to the nearest state mental hospital. They brought her back the same day; desperate as they were, they couldn't leave her in hell. At last, when it had come time to go to the shore, they found a nursing home in the middle of the Pine Barrens, miles from anywhere, and kept her there for a while. That, too, proving unsatisfactory, they put her in a small nursing home in western New Jersey, about two hours away by car. We made the drive every Sunday for the next six months, until my grandmother finally died. I always waited in the car while my mother visited her. At the funeral I refused to go into the room for one last look at the body. I was afraid of her still. The whole thing had been a subtle act of violence, a violation of the sensibilities, made all the worse by the fact that I knew it wasn't really her fault, that she was a victim of biology, of life itself. Hard knowledge for a boy just turned fourteen. She became the color of all my expectations.

Life is savage, then, and even character is insecure. Call no man happy until he be dead, said the Greek lawgiver Solon. But what would a wise man say to this? In that same town in New Jersey, that town I have long since abandoned as too flat and too good to be true, my mother, thirty years older now, weighing in at ninety-two pounds, incontinent, her white hair wild about her head, sits strapped into a chair in another nursing home taking incoherently to her fellow patients and working her hands at the figures she thinks she sees moving around on the floor. It's enough to make stones weep to see this fierce, strong woman, who paid her dues, surely, ten times over, reduced to this.

Yet she is *cheerful*. This son comes to see her and she quite literally babbles with delight, introduces him (as her father, her husband—the connections are burnt out) to the aides, tells him endless stories that don't make any sense at all, and *shines*, shines with a clear light that must be her soul. Care and bitterness vanish in her presence. Helpless, the victim of numerous tiny strokes—"shower strokes," the doctors call them—that are gradually destroying her brain, she has somehow achieved a radiant serenity that accepts everything that happens and incorporates and transforms it.

Is there a lesson in this? Is some pattern larger than life working itself out; is this some kind of poetic justice on display, a mother balancing a grandmother, gods demonstrating reasons beyond our comprehension? It was a bitter thing to put her into that place, reeking of disinfectant, full of senile, dying old people, and I used to hate to visit her there, but as she has deteriorated she has also by sheer force of example managed to change my attitude. If she can be reconciled to all this, why can't I? It doesn't last very long, but after I've seen her, talked to her for half an hour, helped feed her, stroked her hair, I walk away amazed, as if I had been witness to a miracle.

Anthony Brandt, journalist, essayist, and author of *Reality Police*, is at work on a book on the American Dream.

Casa: A Partial Remembrance of a Puerto Rican Childhood

by Judith Ortiz Cofer

At three or four o'clock in the afternoon, the hour of *café con leche*, the women of my family gathered in Mamá's living room to speak of important things and retell familiar stories meant to be overheard by us young girls, their daughters. In Mamá's house (everyone called my grandmother Mamá) was a large parlor built by my grandfather to his wife's exact specifications so that it was always cool, facing away from the sun. The doorway was on the side of the house so no one could walk directly into her living room. First they had to take a little stroll through and around her beautiful garden where prize-winning orchids grew in the trunk of an ancient tree she had hollowed out for that purpose. This room was furnished with several mahogany rocking chairs, acquired at the births of her children, and one intricately carved rocker that had passed down to Mamá at the death of her own mother.

It was on these rockers that my mother, her sisters, and my grandmother sat on these afternoons of my childhood to tell their stories, teaching each other, and my cousin and me, what it was like to be a woman, more specifically, a Puerto Rican woman. They talked about life on the island, and life in *Los Nueva Yores*, their way of referring to the United States from New York City to California: the other place, not home, all the same. They told real-life stories though, as I later learned, always embellishing them with a little or a lot of dramatic detail. And they told *cuentos*, the morality and cautionary tales told by the women in our family for generations: stories that became a part of my subconscious as I grew up in two worlds, the tropical island and the cold city, and that would later surface in my dreams and in my poetry.

One of these tales was about the woman who was left at the altar. Mamá liked to tell that one with histrionic intensity. I remember the rise and fall of her voice, the sighs, and her constantly gesturing hands, like two birds swooping through her words. This particular story usually would come up in a conversation as a result of someone mentioning a forthcoming engagement or wedding. The first time I remember hearing it, I was sitting on the floor at Mamá's feet. I pretending to read a comic book. I may have been eleven or twelve years old, at that difficult age when a girl was no longer a child who could be ordered to leave the room if the women wanted freedom to take their talk into forbidden zones, nor really old enough to be considered a part of their conclave. I could only sit quietly, pretending to be in another world, while absorbing it all in a sort of unspoken agreement of my status as silent auditor. On this day, Mamá had taken my long, tangled mane of hair into her ever-busy hands. Without looking down at me and with no interruption of her flow of words, she began braiding my hair, working at it with the quickness and determination that characterized all her actions. My mother was watching us impassively from her rocker across the room. On her lips played a little ironic smile. I would never sit still for her ministrations, but even then, I instinctively knew that she did not possess Mamá's matriarchal power to command and keep everyone's attention. This was never more evident than in the spell she cast when telling a story.

It is not like it used to be when I was a girl," Mamá announced. "Then, a man could leave a girl standing at the church altar with a bouquet of fresh flowers in her hands and disappear off the face of the earth. No way to track him down if he was from another town. He could be a married man, with maybe even two or three families all over the island. There was no way to know. And there were men who did this. Hombres with the devil in their flesh who would come to a pueblo, like this one, take a job at one of the haciendas, never meaning to stay, only to have a good time and to seduce the women."

The whole time she was speaking, Mamá would be weaving my hair into a flat plait that required pulling apart the two sections of hair with little jerks that made my eyes water; but knowing how grandmother detested whining and boba (sissy) tears, as she called them, I just sat up as straight and stiff as I did at La Escuela San Jose, where the nuns enforced good posture with a flexible plastic ruler they bounced off of slumped shoulders and heads. As Mamá's story progressed, I noticed how my young Aunt Laura lowered her eyes, refusing to meet Mamá's meaningful gaze. Laura was seventeen, in her last year of high school, and already engaged to a boy from another town who had staked his claim with a tiny diamond ring, then left for Los Nueva Yores to make his fortune. They were planning to get married in a year. Mamá had expressed serious doubts that the wedding would ever take place. In Mamá's eyes, a man set free without a legal contract was a man lost. She believed that marriage was not something men desired, but simply the price they had to pay for the privilege of children and, of course, for what no decent (synonymous with "smart") woman would give away for free.

"María La Loca was only seventeen when *it* happened to her." I listened closely at the mention of this name. María was a town character, a fat middle-aged woman who lived with her old mother on the outskirts of town. She was to be seen around the pueblo delivering the meat pies the two women made for a living. The most peculiar thing about María, in my eyes, was that she walked and moved like a little girl though she had the thick body and wrinkled face of an old woman. She would swing her hips in an exaggerated, clownish way and sometimes even hop and skip up to someone's house. She spoke to no one. Even if you asked her a question, she would just look at you and smile, showing her yellow teeth. But I had heard that if you got close enough, you could hear her humming a tune without words. The kids yelled out nasty things at her calling her *La Loca*, and the men who hang out at the bodega playing dominoes sometimes whistled mockingly as she passed by with her funny, outlandish walk. But María seemed impervious to it all, carrying her basket of *pasteles* like a grotesque Little Red Riding Hood through the forest.

María La Loca interested me, as did all the eccentrics and crazies of our pueblo. Their weirdness was a measuring stick I used in my serious quest for a definition of normal. As a Navy brat shuttling between New Jersey and the pueblo, I was constantly made to feel like an oddball by my peers, who made fun of my two-way accent: a Spanish accent when I spoke English, and when I spoke Spanish I was told that I sounded like a *Gringa*. Being the outsider had already turned my brother and me into cultural chameleons. We developed early on the ability to blend into a crowd, to sit and read quietly in a fifth story apartment building for days and days when it was too bitterly cold to play outside, or, set free, to run wild in Mamá's realm, where she took charge of our lives, releasing Mother for a while from the intense fear for our safety that our father's absences instilled in her. In order to keep us from harm when Father was away, Mother kept us under strict surveillance. She even walked us to and from Public School No. 11, which we attended during the months we lived in Paterson, New Jersey, our home base in the states. Mamá freed all three of us like pigeons from a cage. I saw her as my liberator and my model. Her stories were parables from which to glean the *Truth*.

"María La Loca was once a beautiful girl. Everyone thought she would marry the Mendez boy." As everyone knew, Rogelio Mendez was the richest man in town. "But," Mamá continued, knitting my hair with the same intensity she was putting into her story, ""this *macho* made a fool out of her and ruined her life." She paused for the effect of her use of the word ""Macho," which at that time had not yet become a popular epithet for an unliberated man. This word had for us the crude and comical connotation of "male of the species," stud: a *macho* was what you put in a pen to increase your stock.

I peeked over my comic book at my mother. She too was under Mamá's spell, smiling conspiratorially at this little swipe at men. She was safe from Mamá's contempt in this area. Married at an early age, an unspotted lamb, she had been accepted by a good family of strict Spaniards whose name was old and respected, though their fortune had been lost long before my birth. In a rocker Papa had painted sky blue sat Mamá's oldest child, Aunt Nena. Mother of three children, stepmother of two more. She was a quiet woman who liked books but had married an ignorant and abusive widower whose main interest in life was accumulating wealth. He too was in the mainland working on his dream of returning home rich and triumphant to buy the *finca* of his dreams. She was waiting for him to send for her. She would leave her children with Mamá for several years while the two of them slaved away in factories. He would one day be a rich man, and she a sadder woman. Even now her life-light was dimming. She spoke little, an aberration in Mamá's house, and she read avidly, as if storing up spiritual food for the long winters that awaited her in Los Nueva Yores without her family. But even Aunt Nena came alive to Mamá's words, rocking gently, her hands over a thick book in her lap.

Her daughter, my cousin Sara, played jacks by herself on the tile porch outside the room where we sat. She was a year older than I. We shared a bed and all our family's secrets. Collaborators in search of answers, Sara and I discussed everything we heard the women say, trying to fit it all together like a puzzle that, once assembled, would reveal life's mysteries to us. Though she and I still enjoyed taking part in boys' games-chase, volleyball, and even *vaqueros*, the island version of cowboys and Indians involving cap-gun battles and violent shoot-outs under the mango tree in Mamá's backyard-we loved best the quiet hours in the afternoon when the men were still at work, and the boys had gone to play serious baseball at the park. Then Mamá's house belonged only to us women. The aroma of coffee perking in the kitchen, the mesmerizing creaks and groans of the rockers, and the women telling their lives in cuentos are forever woven into the fabric of my imagination, braided like my hair that day I felt my grandmother's hands teaching me about strength, her voice convincing me of the power of storytelling.

That day Mamá told how the beautiful María had fallen prey to a man whose name was never the same in subsequent versions of the story; it was Juan one time, Jose, Rafael, Diego, another. We understood that neither the name nor any of the *facts* were important, only that a woman had allowed love to defeat her. Mamá put each of us in María's place by describing her wedding dress in loving detail: how she looked like a princess in her lace as she waited at the altar. Then, as Mamá approached the tragic denouement of her story, I was distracted by the sound of my aunt Laura's violent rocking. She seemed on the verge of tears. She knew the fable was intended for her. That week she was going to have her wedding gown fitted, though no firm date had been set for the marriage. Mamá ignored Laura's obvious discomfort, digging out a ribbon from the sewing basket she kept by her rocker while describing María's long illness, "a fever that would not break for days." She spoke of a mother's despair: ""that woman climbed the church steps on her knees every morning, wore only black as a *promesa* to the Holy Virgin in exchange for her daughter's health." By the time María returned from her honeymoon with death, she was ravished, no longer young or sane. "As you can see, she is almost as old as her mother already," Mamá lamented while tying the ribbon to the ends of my hair, pulling it back with such force that I just knew I would never be able to close my eyes completely again.

"That María's getting crazier every day." Mamá's voice would take a lighter tone now, expressing satisfaction, either for the perfection of my braid, or for a story well told-it was hard to tell. 1."You know that tune María is always humming?" Carried away by her enthusiasm, I tried to nod, but Mamá still had me pinned between her knees.

"Well, that's the wedding march." Surprising us all, Mamá sang out, "Da, da, dara . . . da, da, dara." Then lifting me off the floor by my skinny shoulders, she would lead me around the room in an impromptu waltz-another session ending with the laughter of women, all of us caught up in the infectious joke of our lives.

Being Country

by Bobbie Ann Mason

Food was the center of our lives. Everything we did and thought revolved around it. We planted it, grew it, harvested it, peeled it, cooked it, served it, consumed it—endlessly, day after day, season after season. This was life on a farm—as it had been time out of mind.

The area around Clear Springs, on Panther Creek, was one of the first white settlements in the Jackson Purchase. In the spring of 1820, Peyton Washam, his fifteen-year-old son Peter, and a third man whose name has been forgotten came to Panther Creek from Virginia with a plan to build a cabin and plant some corn. Mrs. Washam and the seven other children, whom they had left in a settlement about a hundred miles away, would come along later. Before the men could begin building, they had to slash a clearing from the wilderness. It was tougher than they expected. They had plenty of water, for the place abounded with springs, but they soon ran out of food and supplies. They sent for more, but before these arrived they were reduced to boiling and eating their small treasure (half a bushel) of seed corn—the dried corn that would have let them get out a crop. Then Peyton Washam came down with a fever. He sent for his wife to come quickly. She arrived late at night and got lost in the canebrake—a thicket of canes growing up to thirty feet high. Frightened in the noisy darkness, she waited, upright and sleepless, beneath an old tree till daylight, according to the accounts. She hurried on then, propelled by worry, but when she reached her husband's camp, she was too late. He had died during the night. Afterwards, she lived out his dream, settling in the vicinity with her children. The area her husband had chosen eventually grew into the community where a dozen branches of my family took root.

This story vexes me. What a bold but pathetic beginning! What careless, untrained pioneers. How could Peyton Washam and his cohorts have run out of food so soon? If they arrived in the spring, they should have planted that seed corn before long (between mid-April and mid-May). Why, in a mild Kentucky spring, did they not get a garden out right away? How could they have run out of supplies before they got their corn in the ground? Of course they had to clear some canebrake, which wasn't easy. But it wasn't as hard as clearing trees. You can even eat cane like a vegetable. In May, there would have been a carpet of wild strawberries. If Peyton Washam was too sick to forage, why didn't the kid and the other guy go pick something? What kind of pioneer eats his seed corn? Why didn't they shoot a squirrel?

Mrs. Washam is the hero of the tale. She survived and her children joined her. She probably could handle a gun. I'm sure she knew how to get out a garden. I picture her coming alone with a basket of cornbread and fried pies, looking for her sick, hungry husband, trying to follow directions scribbled on a piece of paper. Turn left *before* the canebrake. Follow the creek to the large old tree. Or maybe Peyton Washam's handwriting was bad—maybe he meant an *oak* tree.

This was the rough and foolhardy beginning of Clear Springs. The expedition was a man's notion, with a woman coming to the rescue. The men were starving without her. It makes perfect sense to me, in light of everything I know about the rural life that came down to me from that community. When I think of Clear Springs, I think first of the women cooking. Every Christmas we went out to the Mason homeplace for a grand celebration dinner that included at least a dozen cakes. And in the summer we went to big homecoming feasts—called dinner-on-the-ground—at nearby McKendree Methodist Church, which was on Mason land.

One day Mama and Granny were shelling beans and talking about the proper method of drying apples. I was nearly eleven and still entirely absorbed with the March girls in *Little Women*. Drying apples was not in my dreams. Beth's death was weighing darkly on me at that moment, and I threw a little tantrum—what Mama called a hissy fit.

"Can't y'all talk about anything but food?" I screamed.

There was a shocked silence. "Well, what else is there?" Granny asked.

Granny didn't question a woman's duties, but I did. I didn't want to be hulling beans in a hot kitchen when I was fifty years old. I wanted to *be* somebody, maybe an airline stewardess. Also, I had been listening to the radio. I had notions.

Our lives were haunted by the fear of crop failure. We ate as if we didn't know where our next meal might come from. All my life I have had a recurrent food dream: I face a buffet or cafeteria line, laden with beautiful foods. I spend the entire dream choosing the foods I want. My anticipation is deliciously agonizing. I always wake up just as I've made my selections but before I get to eat.

Working with food was fraught with anxiety and desperation. In truth, no one in memory had missed a meal—except Peyton Washam on the banks of Panther Creek wistfully regarding his seed corn. But the rumble of poor Peyton's belly must have survived to trouble our dreams. We were at the mercy of nature, and it wasn't to be trusted. My mother watched the skies at evening for a portent of the morrow. A cloud that went over and then turned around and came back was an especially bad sign. Our livelihood—even our lives—depended on forces outside our control.

I think this dependence on nature was at the core of my rebellion. I hated the constant sense of helplessness before vast forces, the continuous threat of failure. Farmers didn't take initiative, I began to see; they reacted to whatever presented itself. I especially hated women's part in the dependence.

My mother allowed me to get spoiled. She never even tried to teach me to cook. "You didn't want to learn," she says now. "You were a lady of leisure, and you didn't want to help. You had your nose in a book."

I believed progress meant freedom from the field and the range. That meant moving to town, I thought.

Because we lived on the edge of Mayfield, I was acutely conscious of being country. I felt inferior to people in town because we grew our food and made our clothes, while they bought whatever they needed. Although we were self-sufficient and resourceful and held clear title to our land, we lived in a state of psychological poverty. As I grew older, this acute sense of separation from town affected me more deeply. I began to sense that the fine life in town—celebrated in magazines, on radio, in movies—was denied us. Of course we weren't poor at all. Poor people had too many kids, and they weren't landowners; they rented decrepit little houses with plank floors and trash in the yard. "Poor people are wormy and eat wild onions," Mama said. We weren't poor, but we were country.

We had three wardrobes—everyday clothes, school clothes, and Sunday clothes. We didn't wear our school clothes at home, but we could wear them to town. When we got home from church, we had to change back into everyday clothes before we ate Mama's big Sunday dinner.

"Don't eat in your good clothes!" Mama always cried. "You'll spill something on them."

Mama always preferred outdoor life, but she was a natural cook. At harvest time, after she'd come in from the garden and put out a wash, she would whip out a noontime dinner for the men in the field—my father and grandfather and maybe some neighbors and a couple of hired hands: fried chicken with milk gravy, ham, mashed potatoes, lima beans, field peas, corn, slaw, sliced tomatoes, fried apples, biscuits, and peach pie. This was not considered a banquet, only plain hearty food, fuel for work. All the ingredients except the flour, sugar, and salt came from our farm—the chickens, the hogs, the milk and butter, the Irish potatoes, the beans, peas, corn, cabbage, apples, peaches. Nothing was processed, except by Mama. She was always butchering and plucking and planting and hoeing and shredding and slicing and creaming (scraping cobs for the creamed corn) and pressure-cooking and canning and freezing and thawing and mixing and shaping and baking and frying.

We would eat our pie right on the same plate as our turnip greens so as not to mess up another dish. The peach cobbler oozed all over the turnip-green juice and the pork grease. "It all goes to the same place," Mama said. It was boarding-house reach, no "Pass the peas, please." Conversation detracted from the sensuous pleasure of filling yourself. A meal required meat and vegetables and dessert. The beverages were milk and iced tea ("ice-tea"). We never used napkins or ate tossed salad. Our salads were Jell-O and slaw. We ate "poke salet" and wilted lettuce. Mama picked tender, young pokeweed in the woods in the spring, before it turned poison, and cooked it a good long time to get the bitterness out. We liked it with vinegar and minced boiled eggs. Wilted lettuce was tender new lettuce, shredded, with sliced radishes and green onions, and blasted with hot bacon grease to blanch the rawness. "Too many fresh vegetables in summer gives people the scours," Daddy said.

Food was better in town, we thought. It wasn't plain and everyday. The centers of pleasure were there—the hamburger and barbecue places, the movie shows, all the places to buy things. Woolworth's, with the pneumatic tubes overhead rushing money along a metallic mole tunnel up to a balcony; Lochridge & Ridgway, with an engraved sign on the third-story cornice: STOVES, APPLI-ANCES, PLOWS. On the mezz anine at that store, I bought my first phonograph records, brittle 78s of big-band music—Woody Herman and Glenn Miller, and Glen Gray and his Casa Loma Orchestra playing "No Name Jive." A circuit of the courthouse square took you past the grand furniture stores, the two dime stores, the shoe stores, the men's stores, the ladies' stores, the banks, the drugstores. You'd walk past the poolroom and an exhaust fan would blow the intoxicating smell of hamburgers in your face. Before she bought a freezer, Mama stored meat in a rented food locker in town, near the ice company. She stored the butchered calf there, and she fetched hunks of him each week to fry. But hamburgers in town were better. They were greasier, and they came in waxed-paper packages.

At the corner drugstore, on the square, Mama and Janice and I sat at filigreed wrought-iron tables on a black-and-white mosaic tile floor, eating peppermint ice cream. It was very cold in there, under the ceiling fans. The ice cream was served elegantly, in paper cones sunk into black plastic holders. We were uptown.

The A&P grocery, a block away, reeked of the rich aroma of ground coffee. Daddy couldn't stand the smell of coffee, but Mama loved it. Daddy retched and scoffed in his exaggerated fashion. "I can't stand that smell!" Granny perked coffee, and Granddaddy told me it would turn a child black. I hated coffee. I wouldn't touch it till I was thirty. We savored store-bought food—coconuts, pineapples, and Vienna sausages and potted meat in little cans that opened with keys. We rarely went to the uptown A&P. We usually traded at a small mom- and-pop grocery, where the proprietors slapped the hands of black children who touched the candy case. I wondered if they were black from coffee.

In the summer of 1954, when I was about to enter high school, my mother got a chance to run a nearby restaurant on the highway across the train track. My parents knew the owner, and one day he stopped by and asked Mama if she'd like to manage the place. She wasn't working at the Merit at that time, and she jumped at the opportunity.

"Why, anybody could cook hamburgers and French fries for the public," Mama said confidently. "That would be easy."

I went with her to inspect the restaurant—a square cinder-block building with a picture-window view of the highway. There were no trees around, just a graveled parking area. It was an informal sort of place, with a simple kitchen, a deep fryer, a grill, some pots and pans. There were five or six tables and a counter with stools. Mama saw potential.

"Catfish platters," she said. "Fish. Hush puppies. Slaw. French fries."

I was so excited I couldn't sleep. Running our own little restaurant could mean we wouldn't have to work in the garden. I wanted nothing more to do with okra and beans. Besides, the restaurant had an apartment above it. I wanted to live there, on the highway. Marlene was still running her frozen-custard stand nearby, and now I too would get to meet strangers traveling through. Mama and I inspected the apartment: a living room, a kitchen, and two bedrooms. It was all new and fresh. I loved it.

"Oh, please, let's move here," I begged, wishing desperately for novelty, deliverance, and an endless supply of Co'-Colas.

Mama's eyes lit up. "We'll see," she said.

A restaurant would be ideal for her. "It's a chance to make big money," she told me. She told the owner she would try it for a while, to see how she liked it. If she became the manager, then she would rent it for a hundred dollars a month.

"If it works out, maybe I could make a hundred dollars a *week*," she said.

I tagged along with her when she worked at the restaurant. I felt important waiting on customers—strangers driving along the highway and stopping for a bite to eat right where I was. I wanted to meet somebody from New York. When I drew glasses of foamy Coca-Cola from the fountain, the Coke fizzed over crushed ice. I made grilled-cheese sandwiches in the grilled-cheese machine. I experimented with milk shakes. I was flying.

Most of all, I loved the jukebox. The jukebox man came by to change records and insert new red-rimmed paper strips of titles: Doris Day and Johnnie Ray duets, "Teardrops from My Eyes" by Ruth Brown, and "P.S. I Love You" by a Kentucky vocal group called the Hilltoppers. I listened avidly to everything. I was fourteen and deeply concerned about my suntan, and I was saving pocket money to buy records.

The restaurant had a television set, which sat in a corner with something called a television light on top—a prism of soft colors which supposedly kept people from ruining their eyes on TV rays. I had hardly ever watched television, and I was captivated by Sid Caesar's variety show and *I Love Lucy*. When the evening crowd came in, Mama trotted back and forth from the kitchen with her hamburger platters and catfish platters. She would stop and laugh at something Lucy and Ethel were doing on the screen.

Mama had to give up the restaurant even before the trial period ended. She didn't do it voluntarily. Granddaddy stepped in and told her she had to.

"We need you here at home," he said. "Running a eating place out on the highway ain't fitten work."

Daddy didn't stand up for her. "How would you make anything?" he asked her. "By the time you pay out that hundred dollars a month and all the expenses, you won't have nothing left. First thing you know, you'll get behind and then you'll be owing *him*."

Granny said, "And who's going to do your cooking here?"

That was that. Afterwards, Mama cooked her hamburger platters at home, but they weren't the same without the fountain Cokes and the jukebox and the television. I thought I saw a little fire go out of her then. Much later, her fire would almost die. But my own flame was burning brighter. I had had a glimpse of life outside the farm, and I wanted it.

I can still see Mama emerging from that restaurant kitchen, carrying two hamburger platters and gabbing with her customers as if they were old friends who had dropped in to visit and sit a spell. In the glass of the picture window, reflections from the TV set flicker like candles at the church Christmas service.

And then the blackberries were ripe. We spent every July and August in the berry patch. The tame berries had spread along the fencerows and creek banks. When they ripened, Mama would exclaim in wonder, "There are *worlds* of berries down there!" She always "engaged" the berries to customers. By June, she would say, "I've already got forty gallons of berries engaged."

We strode out at dawn, in the dew, and picked until the mid-morning sun bore down on our heads. To protect her hands from the briars, Mama made gloves from old bluejeans. Following the berries down the creek bank, we perched on ledges and tiptoed on unsure footing through thickets. We tunneled. When Mama saw an especially large berry just out of reach, she would manage to get it somehow, even if she had to lean her body against the bush and let it support her while she plucked the prize. We picked in quart baskets, then poured the berries into red-and-white Krey lard buckets. The berries settled quickly, and Mama picked an extra quart to top off the full buckets. By nine o'clock the sun was high, and I struggled to the house with my four gallons, eager to wash the chiggers off and eat some cereal.

From picking blackberries, I learned about money. I wouldn't eat the berries, even on my cereal: I wanted the money. One summer I picked eighty gallons and earned eighty dollars—much more than Mama made in a week when she worked at the Merit. Granny said food was everything, but I was hungry for something else—a kind of food that didn't grow in the ground. Yet I couldn't deny that we were always feasting. We ate sumptuous meals, never missing dessert. Once in a while, Daddy brought home exotic treats—fried oysters in little goldfish cartons or hot tamales wrapped in corn shucks. At Christmas, the dairy he drove for produced jugs of boiled custard, and we slurped gallons of it even though it was not really as good as Granny's, which was naturally yellow from fresh country eggs. Granny complained that store-bought eggs were pale. When the cows needed feed, Daddy took a load of corn from the corncrib to the feed mill and had it ground and mixed with molasses and wheat and oats. He brought it home and filled the feed bin, a big box with a hinged lid, like a giant coffin. I would chew a mouthful now and then for the sweetening.

One spring I rode the corn planter behind Daddy on the tractor. He had plowed and disked and harrowed the ground. Sitting in a concave metal seat with holes in it, I rode the planter, which drilled furrows to receive the seed. At the end of each row I closed the hoppers so they wouldn't release seed while he turned the tractor in a wide loop. When he nosed down the next row, I opened the hoppers at his signal, so that the seed would trickle out again, evenly spaced, behind the drill. The planter covered the seed behind us. We didn't talk much in our awkward caravan. As we rode the long hot rows, rich floods of remembered music accompanied me as vividly as if I had been wearing a Walkman. Top Ten numbers like "Ruby," "The Song from Moulin Rouge," and "Rags to Riches" rolled through my head with the promise that I would not have to plant corn when I grew up.

As I look back, the men recede into the furrows, into the waves of the ocean, and the women stand erect, churning and frying.

Yes, Ma'am

by Deirdre N. McCloskey

It's hard to pass. You just try it, Dee would say. I mean really try to pass as the opposite gender> not just put on a joke dress and a lampshade hat for the Lions picnic. You'll be surprised at how many gender clues there are and how easy it is to get them wrong. Scores of them, natural and unnatural, genetic and socially constructed.

No, hundreds. Women stand and sit at angles. Men offer their hands to shake. Women put their hands to their chests when speaking of themselves. Men barge through. Women look frequently at nonspeaking participants in a conversation. Men don't look at each other when talking. Women carry papers and books clutched to their midriffs, men balance things on their hips. Women smile at other women when entering their space. Men never smile at male strangers. Women put their hands on their hips with fingers pointing backward. Men use wide gestures. Women frequently fold their hands together in their laps. Men walk from their shoulders, women from their hips. And on and on.

Dee watched other women in her culture for characteristic gestures and practiced them on the spot. *The way the hands gesture together, as though in a little dance. The way the fingers lie up the arm when the arms are crossed. Standing with feet in a ballet pose. Pulling your hair from under a coat just put on.* (It was some time before her hair was long enough to make that feminine gesture useful.) Years into her transition she could amuse herself in a dull moment in a mall or airport by breaking down other women's gestures and trying them out. Like square dancing: hundreds of calls.

Rest one elbow on the back of the other hand, laid horizontally across your middle, the free hand stretching vertically to frame your face from the bottom, palm out. In touching your face, which you should do frequently, hold the hand in a graceful pose. For situations such as display at the dinner table, learn the hand pose used in ballet—fingers arched and separated, middle finger almost touching the thumb. Pinky up, but not too much, since it's an obvious parody of the ladylike. Overacting evokes the theatrical tradition of drag. Try to create a somewhat splayed effect with the fingers, angled up, instead of masculine cupping. When shaking hands—don't be the first to offer—use no strong grip, and place your hand sideward into the other person's. Check your hair frequently. Play idly with your jewelry. Check your clothing (a set of gestures that women's clothes require more often than men's, or else you stride out of the ladies' room with the back of your skirt up around your behind). Always stand more on one foot than the other. Stand with your legs crossed (a youngish gesture, this). Never stand manlike with feet parallel and legs spread wide. Angle your feet when you stop at the corner before crossing. Rest with hands together, not sprawled all over like a man's. When sitting cross your legs, either knee over knee angled to one side (never lower leg crossed horizontally over the knee, like the Greek boy in the statue removing a splinter) or to one side beneath the chair ankle over ankle. Never slouch when you sit. Stick your rear end solidly into the back of the chair and never stretch your legs out, crossed at the ankles. Keep your knees together when you sit—"close the gates of hell" used to be the misogynist joke about it-which is easier if your knees are naturally angled inward, as girls' and especially women's are. If your feet are not crossed when sitting, keep your legs together from feet to knees. "Take up less space" is one formula; another is "keep your wrists loose," and still another "keep your elbows close to your body," this one imitating the effect of a female angle in the elbow, a piece of biology. But the formulas are hard to apply, like formal grammatical rules. Imitate, imitate, the way girls learn it. Deirdre was congratulated three years into full time: "Last year your motions were a little abrupt; now they are convincingly feminine." The gesture language is probably imitated with the same ease and at the same age as the spoken language, and like the spoken language it is hard to learn as an adult. Little girls act different from little boys, independent of the slight structural differences in their bodies. By age ten many girls even know the secret smile.

Much of behavior is gendered. A lot of it is culturally specific and variable from person to person. European men cross their legs in a way that in America is coded as feminine. American soldiers in Vietnam would sneer at what they read as femininity in their Vietnamese allies and enemies: "They're all queer, you know." Mediterranean and Middle Eastern women make broader gestures, not the little dance of hands that upper-middle-class women in America use. The gender clues figure in any culture in an abundance that only a gender crosser or Dustin Hoffman preparing for *Tootsie* can grasp.

Of course if you are *aiming* to be funny then you want to be read, even if you are skillful at giving appropriate gender clues. Passing is not at issue. The Australian comedian who has developed the character "Dame Edna" is good at it. Without a leer or a nudge, he simply is the absurd Dame and sometimes spends hours in character, yet of course his audience knows. Miss Piggy of the Muppets is similar. She is gloriously who she is, yet everyone knows it's cross-speaking-her voice is always that of a man using falsetto. Getting read is part of the joke.

If you are not trying to be funny, you do not want to get read. Really, you don't. A sincere but detected attempt to jump the gender border from male to female—and no joking about it—creates anxiety in men, to be released by laughter if they can handle it or by a length of steel pipe if they can't. A 1997 survey claimed that 60 percent of cross-gendered people had been assaulted. Deirdre knew a gender crosser who had been beaten by four young men outside a bar even in peaceful Iowa City. The director of Gender PAC noted that "RuPaul is funny so long as she stays in a television studio. But try walking to the subway and she'll be a grease spot on the sidewalk before she makes it home." (If a female-to-male crosser was read by men maybe he would be regarded as cute, or rational: after all, it's rational to prefer to be a man, isn't it? Like the daily prayer by Orthodox Jewish men thanking God for not making them women. On the other hand, Brandon Teena, a pre-op female-to-male thief outed by the Falls City, Nebraska, police department was raped, complained about it to the police, who did nothing, and the next week in 1993 was murdered. Not by women.)

The anxiety is weirdly strong. A standard routine in the movies is that two men are forced to sleep with each other by circumstances (oh, sure), and then one of them dreams that he's sleeping with a woman. The other man, horrified by the amorous advances, rejects them violently, and the awakened dreamer is ashamed. The routine enacts over and over again the male anxiety about being homosexual, much less being a woman, and the violent reaction the anxiety arouses. With this threat of violence in mind, Donald's sister had given him her own pepper spray. The pepper spray though, wouldn't be much good against a steel pipe.

Women who read a crossdresser are not violent, but frightened and indignant. Who is this guy? What's he up to? Deirdre knew from being a woman on trains late at night in Holland or walking by

Dutch cafés in the summertime or living later in the less demonstrative but more dangerous environment of America that women have daily experiences of men in fact being up to something, often something sexual, often enough something dangerous. At first it was flattering, the knocking on windows of the *eetcafé* as she went by, the propositions to come into the jazz club and have a drink. Then it was tedious or frightening. Women experience dangerous men all day long and are on the alert. The alertness is not male bashing, merely prudence in the company of people with greater upper-body strength and the inclination to use it, intoxicated by lethal fantasies about What She Really Wants. Women who read a gender crosser are putting her in this category of dangerous men. To be read by women is utterly demoralizing. After all, the gender crosser is trying to join the women, to pass as one, and instead they are treating her like a man, maybe nuts, probably dangerous, definitely another one of those bloody *men*.

On all counts it is better for a gender crosser to pass rapidly to the other side, and making the crossing rapid ought to be the purpose of medical intervention, such as facial surgery, and social intervention, such as counseling on gender clues. Women acquainted with a gender crosser sometimes think of her interest in facial surgery as vanity. Natural-born women have no problem passing as women. "You're silly to want operations," says a woman out of a face with pointed chin, no browridges, high cheekbones. Deirdre's mother declared that getting electrolysis, which she regarded as merely temporary, was "vain." But a nose job or a facelift or electrolysis that ·will make a gender crosser passable will also make her less likely to be scorned or raped or killed—at any rate at no more than the shocking rates for genetic women. Deirdre knew a note very passable gender crosser in tolerant Holland who had been raped three times. It is merely prudent to pass.

Some radical feminists object to gender crossing. They complain of the gender crosser that she (when they have the ruth to call her "she") is adopting oppressive stereotypes about women and therefore contributing to society's discrimination. The gender crosser, they claim, is pulling women back to the 1950s, white gloves and pill-box hats, lovely garden parties, and a *Leave It to Beaver* vision of a woman's life.

There is little truth in the stereotype argument. The crossphobe who uses it ordinarily doesn't know any gender crossers. A gender crosser with a job or career outside the home tries to keep it and does not in practice dissolve into a 1950s heaven of full-time cookie baking and teatime gossip. Far from becoming passive and stereotypically feminine, the gender crossers Deirdre knew often retained much of their masculine sides. The crossphobes mix up gender crossers with drag queens or female impersonators, whose shtick is indeed a parody of women—sometimes demeaning and stereotypical, though often enough loving and amusing. In 1958 the sociologist Harold Garfinkel described a gender crosser named Agnes. Latter-day crossphobes attack Agnes as "displaying rigidly traditional ideas of what a woman is" or having "stereotypical views of femininity" or "constructing an extremely narrow and constricted view of womanhood." Agnes was nineteen, a typist, at the height of the feminine mystique. But no allowances: "I don't support you in your effort to have an operation, because you have stereotypical views of what it means to be a woman." Unlike all the other nineteen-year-old typists in 1958. (Agnes had the operation, and was fine, because Garfinkel and a psychiatrist named Stoller did support her.)

A gender crosser trying to be a woman must reproduce enough of the characteristic gestures to escape being read, and often—especially in voice—this is difficult. It becomes second nature, and a comfort to oneself even when alone. But if you fail you are classed with people stereotyping women. Or murdered. The crossphobe radical feminists are allies in hatred with the gay-bashing murderers of Matthew Shephard.

The complaint about stereotyping will be delivered by a genetic woman whose every gesture and syllable is stereotypically feminine. At seminars in which Deirdre was attacked for stereotyping she would reply with the same stereotypically feminine gestures or turns of phrase just used by the crossphobe—who had been practicing them since she was a little girl. This was Garfinkel's point, that gender is something "done," a performance, not an essence springing from genitals or chromosomes. Deirdre would say, "Of course I [putting her hand to her chest in the feminine way of referring to oneself, just used by the crossphobe] would never [doing a deprecating double flap with her hands in the style of American middle-class women] want to damage women by *stereotyping* [raising her voice in the falsetto of emphasis stereotypical of women, for instance, the crossphobe attacking the genuineness of gender crossers]."

The passing worked better, slowly, each month, if she dressed carefully and worked at it. Ech little acceptance delighted her. The signal was being called "mevrouw" in Holland, "ma'am" in America, "madame" in France, "madam" in England. *Yes: call me madam.*

She is getting up to leave a Dutch tram at Oostzeedijk, intent on how to make the transfer of the subway. *Let's see: across there and down. Remember to watch for the bicycles.* The tram has almost stopped and she is pressing the exit button when she hears finally through her English thoughts and the haze of a foreign tongue, *"Mevrouw! Mevrouw!" It's me they're calling,* she thinks. *Oh. I've left a package.* She smiles in thanks and snatches up the package, slipping out the door as it closes, still smiling. They see her as "ma'am."

At the grocery store she is accosted by a woman giving out samples of a Dutch delicacy. It doesn't look very good. The woman babbles at Dee in Dutch, and Dee catches only the blessed "mevrouw." She smiles and shakes her head no thank you and pushes the cart toward the canned goods.

In May in Paris with an economist friend, Nancy, who is visiting there for a year, she walks out of a hat store, wearing the lovely lace floppy number just purchased. An elegant Frenchman goes by and says with a smile, "Un beau chapeau, madame!" Deirdre's French is poor, and she is still wondering if he could have said what she thought he had said when he politely repeats it in English over his shoulder as he walks on, "A beautiful hat, madame!" She would say when telling the story, "I could have kissed him. If he had proposed, I would have married him on the spot. Even though he was shorter."

A month later she wears the hat (which can be worn only in Paris or at special events) to a daylong concert of classical music in the park in Rotterdam. Sitting at luncheon on the grass with some members of her women's group, she feels particularly lovely. A Dutchman passes by and makes in Dutch the same remark the Frenchman had made, "A beautiful hat, mevrouw!"

The women's group meets at a restaurant in Rotterdam. It is a year since she abandoned the male role. The waiter asks the *"dames"* (DAH-mez) what they want, including Deirdre without notice or comment. *One of the dames. Yes.*

For other viewpoints about gender, read and discuss the following:

"Jay-Z, Prince Harry, Brad Pitt, and the New Frontier of Male Vulnerability" by Monica Lewinski from Vanity Fair: http://www.vanityfair.com/style/2017/07/jay-z-prince-harry-brad-pitt-male-vulnerability

"The Picture for Men: Superhero or Slacker" by Sameer Pandya from the Research of Culture blog for Pacific Standard: http://www.sameerpandya.net/portfolio/essays-and-analysis/the-picture-for-men-superhero-or-slacker/

"What About the Boys?" by Michael Kimmel: This is a lengthy and in-depth essay, so it is effective to focus on only one section of the essay: HYPERLINK "https://quod.lib.umich.edu/cgi/t/text/text-idx?cc=mfsfront;c=mfs;c=mfsfront;idno=ark5583.0014.001;g=mfsg;rgn=main;view=text;xc=1" \t "_blank" https://quod.lib.umich.edu/cgi/t/text/text-idx?cc=mfsfront;c=mfs;c=mfsfront;idno=ark5583.0014.001;g=mfsg;rgn=main;vie

"Your Life as a Girl" by Curtis Sittenfeld
http://www.angelfire.com/fl/automaticpansy/asgirl.html

The Things They Carried

by Tim O'Brien

First Lieutenant Jimmy Cross carried letters from a girl named Martha, a junior at Mount Sebastian College in New Jersey. They were not love letters, but Lieutenant Cross was hoping, so he kept them folded in plastic at the bottom of his rucksack. In the late afternoon, after a day's march, he would dig his foxhole, wash his hands under a canteen, unwrap the letters, hold them with the tips of his fingers, and spend the last hour of light pretending. He would imagine romantic camping trips into the White Mountains in New Hampshire. He would sometimes taste the envelope flaps, knowing her tongue had been there. More than anything, he wanted Martha to love him as he loved her, but the letters were mostly chatty, elusive on the matter of love. She was a virgin, he was almost sure. She was an English major at Mount Sebastian, and she wrote beautifully about her professors and roommates and midterm exams, about her respect for Chaucer and her great affection for Virginia Woolf. She often quoted lines of poetry; she never mentioned the war, except to say, Jimmy, take care of yourself. The letters weighed 10 ounces. They were signed Love, Martha, but Lieutenant Cross understood that Love was only a way of signing and did not mean what he sometimes pretended it meant. At dusk, he would carefully return the letters to his rucksack. Slowly, a bit distracted, he would get up and move among his men, checking the perimeter, then at full dark he would return to his hole and watch the night and wonder if Martha was a virgin.

The things they carried were largely determined by necessity. Among the necessities or near-necessities were P-38 can openers, pocket knives, heat tabs, wristwatches, dog tags, mosquito repellent, chewing gum, candy, cigarettes, salt tablets, packets of Kool-Aid, lighters, matches, sewing kits, Military Payment Certificates, C rations, and two or three canteens of water. Together, these items weighed between 15 and 20 pounds, depending upon a man's habits or rate of metabolism. Henry Dobbins, who was a big man, carried extra rations; he was especially fond of canned peaches in heavy syrup over pound cake. Dave Jensen, who practiced field hygiene, carried a toothbrush, dental floss, and several hotel-sized bars of soap he'd stolen on R&R in Sydney, Australia. Ted Lavender, who was scared, carried tranquilizers until he was shot in the head outside the village of Than Khe in mid-April. By necessity, and because it was SOP, they all carried steel helmets that weighed 5 pounds including the liner and camouflage cover. They carried the standard fatigue jackets and trousers. Very few carried underwear. On their feet they carried jungle boots—2.1 pounds—and Dave Jensen carried three pairs of socks and a can of Dr. Scholl's foot powder as a precaution against trench foot. Until he was shot, Ted Lavender carried 6 or 7 ounces of premium dope, which for him was a necessity. Mitchell Sanders, the RTO, carried condoms. Norman Bowker carried a diary. Rat Kiley carried comic books. Kiowa, a devout Baptist, carried an illustrated New Testament that had been presented to him by his father, who taught Sunday school in Oklahoma City, Oklahoma. As a hedge against bad times, however, Kiowa also carried his grandmother's distrust of the white man, his grandfather's old hunting hatchet. Necessity dictated. Because the land was mined and booby-trapped, it was SOP for each man to carry a steel-centered, nylon-covered flak jacket, which weighed 6.7 pounds, but which on hot days seemed much heavier. Because you could die so quickly, each man carried at least one large compress bandage, usually in the helmet band for easy access. Because the nights were cold, and because the monsoons were wet, each carried a green plastic poncho that could be used as a raincoat or groundsheet or makeshift tent. With its quilted liner, the poncho weighed almost 2 pounds, but it was worth every ounce. In April, for instance, when Ted Lavender was shot, they used his poncho to wrap him up, then to carry him across the paddy, then to lift him into the chopper that took him away.

They were called legs or grunts.

To carry something was to hump it, as when Lieutenant Jimmy Cross humped his love for Martha up the hills and through the swamps. In its intransitive form, to hump meant to walk, or to march, but it implied burdens far beyond the intransitive.

Almost everyone humped photographs. In his wallet, Lieutenant Cross carried two photographs of Martha. The first was a Kodacolor snapshot signed Love, though he knew better. She stood against a brick wall. Her eyes were gray and neutral, her lips slightly open as she stared straight- on at the camera. At night, sometimes, Lieutenant Cross wondered who had taken the picture, because he knew she had boyfriends, because he loved her so much, and because he could see the shadow of the picture- taker spreading out against the brick wall. The second photograph had been clipped from the 1968 Mount Sebastian yearbook. It was an action shot—women's volleyball—and Martha was bent horizontal to the floor, reaching, the palms of her hands in sharp focus, the tongue taut, the expression frank and competitive. There was no visible sweat. She wore white gym shorts. Her legs, he thought, were almost certainly the legs of a virgin, dry and without hair, the left knee cocked and carrying her entire weight, which was just over 100 pounds. Lieutenant Cross remembered touching that left knee. A dark theater, he remembered, and the movie was *Bonnie and Clyde*, and Martha wore a tweed skirt, and during the final scene, when he touched her knee, she turned and looked at him in a sad, sober way that made him pull his hand back, but he would always remember the feel of the tweed skirt and the knee beneath it and the sound of the gunfire that killed Bonnie and Clyde, how embarrassing it was, how slow and oppressive. He remembered kissing her good night at the dorm door. Right then, he thought, he should've done something brave. He should've carried her up the stairs to her room and tied her to the bed and touched that left knee all night long. He should've risked it. Whenever he looked at the photographs, he thought of new things he should've done.

What they carried was partly a function of rank, partly of field specialty.

As a first lieutenant and platoon leader, Jimmy Cross carried a compass, maps, code books, binoculars, and a.45-caliber pistol that weighed 2.9 pounds fully loaded. He carried a strobe light and the responsibility for the lives of his men.

As an RTO, Mitchell Sanders carried the PRC-25 radio, a killer, 26 pounds with its battery.

As a medic, Rat Kiley carried a canvas satchel filled with morphine and plasma and malaria tablets and surgical tape and comic books and all the things a medic must carry, including M&M's for especially bad wounds, for a total weight of nearly 20 pounds.

As a big man, therefore a machine gunner, Henry Dobbins carried the M-60, which weighed 23 pounds unloaded, but which was almost always loaded. In addition, Dobbins carried between 10 and 15 pounds of ammunition draped in belts across his chest and shoulders.

As PFCs or Spec 4s, most of them were common grunts and carried the standard M-16 gas-operated assault rifle. The weapon weighed 7.5 pounds unloaded, 8.2 pounds with its full 20-round magazine. Depending on numerous factors, such as topography and psychology, the riflemen carried anywhere from 12 to 20 magazines, usually in cloth bandoliers, adding on another 8.4 pounds at minimum, 14 pounds at maximum. When it was available, they also carried M-16 maintenance gear—rods and steel brushes and swabs and tubes of LSA oil—all of which weighed about a pound. Among the grunts, some carried the M-79 grenade launcher, 5.9 pounds unloaded, a reasonably light weapon except for the ammunition, which was heavy. A single round weighed 10 ounces. The typical load was 25 rounds. But Ted Lavender, who was scared, carried 34 rounds when he was shot and killed outside Than Khe, and he went down under an exceptional burden, more than 20 pounds of ammunition, plus the flak jacket and helmet and rations and water and toilet paper and tranquilizers and all the rest, plus the unweighed fear. He was dead weight. There was no twitching or flopping. Kiowa, who saw it happen, said it was like watching a rock fall, or a big sandbag or something—just boom, then down—not like the movies where the dead guy rolls around and does fancy spins and goes ass over teakettle—not like that, Kiowa said, the poor bastard just flat-fuck fell. Boom. Down. Nothing else. It was a bright morning in mid-April. Lieutenant Cross felt the pain. He blamed himself. They stripped off Lavender's canteens and ammo, all the heavy things, and Rat Kiley said the obvious, the guy's dead, and Mitchell Sanders used his radio to report one U.S. KIA and to request a chopper. Then they wrapped Lavender in his poncho. They carried him out to a dry paddy, established security, and sat smoking the dead man's dope until the chopper came. Lieutenant Cross kept to himself. He pictured Martha's smooth young face, thinking he loved her more than anything, more than his men, and now Ted Lavender was dead because he loved her so much and could not stop thinking about her. When the dustoff arrived, they carried Lavender aboard. Afterward they burned Than Khe. They marched until dusk, then dug their holes, and that night Kiowa kept explaining how you had to be there, how fast it was, how the poor guy just dropped like so much concrete. Boom-down, he said. Like cement.

In addition to the three standard weapons—the M-60, M-16, and M-79—they carried whatever presented itself, or whatever seemed appropriate as a means of killing or staying alive. They carried catch-as-catch-can. At various times, in various situations, they carried M-14s and CAR-15s and Swedish Ks and grease guns and captured AK-47s and Chi-Coms and RPGs and Simonov carbines and black market Uzis and .38-caliber Smith & Wesson handguns and 66 mm LAWs and shotguns and silencers and blackjacks and bayonets and C-4 plastic explosives. Lee Strunk carried a slingshot; a weapon of last resort, he called it. Mitchell Sanders carried brass knuckles. Kiowa carried his grandfather's feathered hatchet. Every third or fourth man carried a Claymore antipersonnel mine—3.5 pounds with its firing device. They all carried fragmentation grenades—14 ounces each. They all carried at least one M-18 colored smoke grenade—24 ounces. Some carried CS or tear gas grenades. Some carried white phosphorus grenades. They carried all they could bear, and then some, including a silent awe for the terrible power of the things they carried.

In the first week of April, before Lavender died, Lieutenant Jimmy Cross received a good-luck charm from Martha. It was a simple pebble, an ounce at most. Smooth to the touch, it was a milky white color with flecks of orange and violet, oval-shaped, like a miniature egg. In the accompanying letter, Martha wrote that she had found the pebble on the Jersey shoreline, precisely where the land touched water at high tide, where things came together but also separated. It was this separate-but-together quality, she wrote, that had inspired her to pick up the pebble and to carry it in her breast pocket for several days, where it seemed weightless, and then to send it through the mail, by air, as a token of her truest feelings for him. Lieutenant Cross found this romantic. But he wondered what her truest feelings were, exactly, and what she meant by separate-but-together. He wondered how the tides and waves had come into play on that afternoon along the Jersey shoreline when Martha saw the pebble and bent down to rescue it from geology. He imagined bare feet. Martha was a poet, with the poet's sensibilities, and her feet would be brown and bare, the toenails unpainted, the eyes chilly and somber like the ocean in March, and though it was painful, he wondered who had been with her that afternoon. He imagined a pair of shadows moving along the strip of sand where things came together but also separated. It was phantom jealousy, he knew, but he couldn't help himself. He loved her so much. On the march, through the hot days of early April, he carried the pebble in his mouth, turning it with his tongue, tasting sea salt and moisture. His mind wandered. He had difficulty keeping his attention on the war. On occasion he would yell at his men to spread out the column, to keep their eyes open, but then he would slip away into daydreams, just pretending, walking barefoot along the Jersey shore, with Martha, carrying nothing. He would feel himself rising. Sun and waves and gentle winds, all love and lightness.

What they carried varied by mission.

When a mission took them to the mountains, they carried mosquito netting, machetes, canvas tarps, and extra bug juice.

If a mission seemed especially hazardous, or if it involved a place they knew to be bad, they carried everything they could. In certain heavily mined AOs, where the land was dense with Toe Poppers and Bouncing Betties, they took turns humping a 28-pound mine detector. With its headphones and big sensing plate, the equipment was a stress on the lower back and shoulders, awkward to handle, often useless because of the shrapnel in the earth, but they carried it anyway, partly for safety, partly for the illusion of safety.

On ambush, or other night missions, they carried peculiar little odds and ends. Kiowa always took along his New Testament and a pair of moccasins for silence. Dave Jensen carried night-sight vitamins high in carotene. Lee Strunk carried his slingshot; ammo, he claimed, would never be a problem. Rat Kiley carried brandy and M&M's candy. Until he was shot, Ted Lavender carried the starlight scope, which weighed 6.3 pounds with its aluminum carrying case. Henry Dobbins carried his girlfriend's pantyhose wrapped around his neck as a comforter. They all carried ghosts. When dark came, they would move out single file across the meadows and paddies to their ambush coordinates, where they would quietly set up the Claymores and lie down and spend the night waiting.

Other missions were more complicated and required special equipment. In mid-April, it was their mission to search out and destroy the elaborate tunnel complexes in the Than Khe area south of Chu Lai. To blow the tunnels, they carried one-pound blocks of pentrite high explosives, four blocks to a man, 68 pounds in all. They carried wiring, detonators, and battery-powered clackers. Dave Jensen carried earplugs. Most often, before blowing the tunnels, they were ordered by higher command to search them, which was considered bad news, but by and large they just shrugged and carried out orders. Because he was a big man, Henry Dobbins was excused from tunnel duty. The others would draw numbers. Before Lavender died there were 17 men in the platoon, and whoever drew the number 17 would strip off his gear and crawl in headfirst with a flashlight and Lieutenant Cross's .45-caliber pistol. The rest of them would fan out as security. They would sit down or kneel, not facing the hole, listening to the ground beneath them, imagining cobwebs and ghosts, whatever was down there—the tunnel walls squeezing in—how the flashlight seemed impossibly heavy in the hand and how it was tunnel vision in the very strictest sense, compression in all ways, even time, and how you had to wiggle in—ass and elbows—a swallowed-up feeling—and how you found yourself worrying about odd things: Will your flashlight go dead? Do rats carry rabies? If you screamed, how far would the sound carry? Would your buddies hear it? Would they have the courage to drag you out? In some respects, though not many, the waiting was worse than the tunnel itself. Imagination was a killer.

On April 16, when Lee Strunk drew the number 17, he laughed and muttered something and went down quickly. The morning was hot and very still. Not good, Kiowa said. He looked at the tunnel opening, then out across a dry paddy toward the village of Than Khe. Nothing moved. No clouds or birds or people. As they waited, the men smoked and drank Kool-Aid, not talking much, feeling sympathy for Lee Strunk but also feeling the luck of the draw. You win some, you lose some, said Mitchell Sanders, and sometimes you settle for a rain check. It was a tired line and no one laughed.

Henry Dobbins ate a tropical chocolate bar. Ted Lavender popped a tranquilizer and went off to pee.

After five minutes, Lieutenant Jimmy Cross moved to the tunnel, leaned down, and examined the darkness. Trouble, he thought—a cave-in maybe. And then suddenly, without willing it, he was thinking about Martha. The stresses and fractures, the quick collapse, the two of them buried alive under all that weight. Dense, crushing love. Kneeling, watching the hole, he tried to concentrate on Lee Strunk and the war, all the dangers, but his love was too much for him, he felt paralyzed, he wanted to sleep inside her lungs and breathe her blood and be smothered. He wanted her to be a virgin and not a virgin, all at once. He wanted to know her. Intimate secrets: Why poetry? Why so sad? Why that grayness in her eyes? Why so alone? Not lonely, just alone—riding her bike across campus or sitting off by herself in the cafeteria—even dancing, she danced alone—and it was the aloneness that filled him with love. He remembered telling her that one evening. How she nodded and looked away. And how, later, when he kissed her, she received the kiss without returning it, her eyes wide open, not afraid, not a virgin's eyes, just flat and uninvolved.

Lieutenant Cross gazed at the tunnel. But he was not there. He was buried with Martha under the white sand at the Jersey shore. They were pressed together, and the pebble in his mouth was her tongue. He was smiling. Vaguely, he was aware of how quiet the day was, the sullen paddies, yet he could not bring himself to worry about matters of security. He was beyond that. He was just a kid at war, in love. He was twenty-four years old. He couldn't help it.

A few moments later Lee Strunk crawled out of the tunnel. He came up grinning, filthy but alive. Lieutenant Cross nodded and closed his eyes while the others clapped Strunk on the back and made jokes about rising from the dead.

Worms, Rat Kiley said. Right out of the grave. Fuckin' zombie. The men laughed. They all felt great relief.

Spook city, said Mitchell Sanders.

Lee Strunk made a funny ghost sound, a kind of moaning, yet very happy, and right then, when Strunk made that high happy moaning sound, when he went Ahhooooo, right then Ted Lavender was shot in the head on his way back from peeing. He lay with his mouth open. The teeth were broken. There was a swollen black bruise under his left eye.

The cheekbone was gone. Oh shit, Rat Kiley said, the guy's dead. The guy's dead, he kept saying, which seemed profound—the guy's dead. I mean really.

The things they carried were determined to some extent by superstition. Lieutenant Cross carried his good-luck pebble. Dave Jensen carried a rabbit's foot. Norman Bowker, otherwise a very gentle person, carried a thumb that had been presented to him as a gift by Mitchell Sanders. The thumb was dark brown, rubbery to the touch, and weighed 4 ounces at most. It had been cut from a VC corpse, a boy of fifteen or sixteen. They'd found him at the bottom of an irrigation ditch, badly burned, flies in his mouth and eyes. The boy wore black shorts and sandals. At the time of his death he had been carrying a pouch of rice, a rifle, and three magazines of ammunition.

You want my opinion, Mitchell Sanders said, there's a definite moral here.

He put his hand on the dead boy's wrist. He was quiet for a time, as if counting a pulse, then he patted the stomach, almost affectionately, and used Kiowa's hunting hatchet to remove the thumb.

Henry Dobbins asked what the moral was. Moral?

You know. *Moral*.

Sanders wrapped the thumb in toilet paper and handed it across to Norman Bowker. There was no blood. Smiling, he kicked the boy's head, watched the flies scatter, and said, It's like with that old TV show— Paladin. Have gun, will travel.

Henry Dobbins thought about it.

Yeah, well, he finally said. I don't see no moral. There it Is, man.

Fuck off.

They carried USO stationery and pencils and pens. They carried Sterno, safety pins, trip flares, signal flares, spools of wire, razor blades, chewing tobacco, liberated joss sticks and statuettes of the smiling Buddha, candles, grease pencils, *The Stars and Stripes*, fingernail clippers, Psy Ops leaflets, bush hats, bolos, and much more. Twice a week, when the resupply choppers came in, they carried hot chow in green mermite cans and large canvas bags filled with iced beer and soda pop. They carried plastic water containers, each with a 2-gallon capacity. Mitchell Sanders carried a set of starched tiger fatigues for special occasions. Henry Dobbins carried Black Flag insecticide. Dave Jensen carried empty sandbags that could be filled at night for added protection. Lee Strunk carried tanning lotion. Some things they carried in common. Taking turns, they carried the big PRC-77 scrambler radio, which weighed 30 pounds with its battery. They shared the weight of memory. They took up what others could no longer bear. Often, they carried each other, the wounded or weak. They carried infections. They carried chess sets, basketballs, Vietnamese-English dictionaries, insignia of rank, Bronze Stars and Purple Hearts, plastic cards imprinted with the Code of Conduct. They carried diseases, among them malaria and dysentery. They carried lice and ringworm and leeches and paddy algae and various rots and molds. They carried the land itself—Vietnam, the place, the soil—a powdery orange-red dust that covered their boots and fatigues and faces. They carried the sky. The whole atmosphere, they carried it, the humidity, the monsoons, the stink of fungus and decay, all of it, they carried gravity. They moved like mules. By daylight they took sniper fire, at night they were mortared, but it was not battle, it was just the endless march, village to village, without purpose, nothing won or lost. They marched for the sake of the march. They plodded along slowly, dumbly, leaning forward against the heat, unthinking, all blood and bone, simple grunts, soldiering with their legs, toiling up the hills and down into the paddies and across the rivers and up again and down, just humping, one step and then the next and then another, but no volition, no will, because it was automatic, it was anatomy, and the war was entirely a matter of posture and carriage, the hump was everything, a kind of inertia, a kind of emptiness, a dullness of desire and intellect and conscience and hope and human sensibility. Their principles were in their feet. Their calculations were biological. They had no sense of strategy or mission. They searched the villages without knowing what to look for, not caring, kicking over jars of rice, frisking children and old men, blowing tunnels, sometimes setting fires and sometimes not, then forming up and moving on to the next village, then other villages, where it would always be the same. They carried their own lives. The pressures were enormous. In the heat of early afternoon, they would remove their helmets and flak jackets, walking bare, which was dangerous but which helped ease the strain. They would often discard things along the route of march. Purely for comfort, they would throw away rations, blow their Claymores and grenades, no matter, because by nightfall the resupply choppers would arrive with more of the same, then a day or two later still more, fresh watermelons and crates of ammunition and sunglasses and woolen sweaters—the resources were stunning—sparklers for the Fourth of July, colored eggs for Easter—it was the great American war chest—the fruits of science, the smokestacks, the canneries, the arsenals at Hartford, the Minnesota forests, the machine shops, the vast fields of corn and wheat— they carried like freight trains; they carried it on their backs and shoulders—and for all the ambiguities of Vietnam, all the mysteries and unknowns, there was at least the single abiding certainty that they would never be at a loss for things to carry.

After the chopper took Lavender away, Lieutenant Jimmy Cross led his men into the village of Than Khe. They burned everything. They shot chickens and dogs, they trashed the village well, they called in artillery and watched the wreckage, then they marched for several hours through the hot afternoon, and then at dusk, while Kiowa explained how Lavender died, Lieutenant Cross found himself trembling.

He tried not to cry. With his entrenching tool, which weighed 5 pounds, he began digging a hole in the earth.

He felt shame. He hated himself. He had loved Martha more than his men, and as a consequence Lavender was now dead, and this was something he would have to carry like a stone in his stomach for the rest of the war.

All he could do was dig. He used his entrenching tool like an ax, slashing, feeling both love and hate, and then later, when it was full dark, he sat at the bottom of his foxhole and wept. It went on for a long while. In part, he was grieving for Ted Lavender, but mostly it was for Martha, and for himself, because she belonged to another world, which was not quite real, and because she was a junior at Mount Sebastian College in New Jersey, a poet and a virgin and uninvolved, and because he realized she did not love him and never would.

Like cement, Kiowa whispered in the dark. I swear to God—boom, down. Not a word.

I've heard this, said Norman Bowker.

A pisser, you know? Still zipping himself up. Zapped while zipping. All right, fine. That's enough.

Yeah, but you had to see it, the guy just—

I heard, man. Cement. So why not shut the fuck up?

Kiowa shook his head sadly and glanced over at the hole where Lieutenant Jimmy Cross sat watching the night. The air was thick and wet. A warm dense fog had settled over the paddies and there was the stillness that precedes rain.

After a time Kiowa sighed.

One thing for sure, he said. The lieutenant's in some deep hurt. I mean that crying jag—the way he was carrying on—it wasn't fake or anything, it was real heavy-duty hurt. The man cares.

Sure, Norman Bowker said.

Say what you want, the man does care. We all got problems.

Not Lavender.

No, I guess not, Bowker said. Do me a favor, though. Shut up?

That's a smart Indian. Shut up.

Shrugging, Kiowa pulled off his boots. He wanted to say more, just to lighten up his sleep, but instead he opened his New Testament and arranged it beneath his head as a pillow. The fog made things seem hollow and unattached. He tried not to think about Ted Lavender, but then he was thinking how fast it was, no drama, down and dead, and how it was hard to feel anything except surprise. It seemed unchristian. He wished he could find some great sadness, or even anger, but the emotion wasn't there and he couldn't make it happen. Mostly he felt pleased to be alive. He liked the smell of the New Testament under his cheek, the leather and ink and paper and glue, whatever the chemicals were. He liked hearing the sounds of night. Even his fatigue, it felt fine, the stiff muscles and the prickly awareness of his own body, a floating feeling. He enjoyed not being dead. Lying there, Kiowa admired Lieutenant Jimmy Cross's capacity for grief. He wanted to share the man's pain, he wanted to care as Jimmy Cross cared. And yet when he closed his eyes, all he could think was Boom-down, and all he could feel was the pleasure of having his boots off and the fog curling in around him and the damp soil and the Bible smells and the plush comfort of night.

After a moment Norman Bowker sat up in the dark.

What the hell, he said. You want to talk, talk. Tell it to me. Forget it.

No, man, go on. One thing I hate, it's a silent Indian.

For the most part they carried themselves with poise, a kind of dignity. Now and then, however, there were times of panic, when they squealed or wanted to squeal but couldn't, when they twitched and made moaning sounds and covered their heads and said Dear Jesus and flopped around on the earth and fired their weapons blindly and cringed and sobbed and begged for the noise to stop and went wild and made stupid promises to themselves and to God and to their mothers and fathers, hoping not to die. In different ways, it happened to all of them. Afterward, when the firing ended, they would blink and peek up. They would touch their bodies, feeling shame, then quickly hiding it. They would force themselves to stand. As if in slow motion, frame by frame, the world would take on the old logic—absolute silence, then the wind, then sunlight, then voices. It was the burden of being alive. Awkwardly, the men would reassemble themselves, first in private, then in groups, becoming soldiers again. They would repair the leaks in their eyes. They would check for casualties, call in dustoffs, light cigarettes, try to smile, clear their throats and spit and begin cleaning their weapons. After a time someone would shake his head and say, No lie, I almost shit my pants, and someone else would laugh, which meant it was bad, yes, but the guy had obviously not shit his pants, it wasn't that bad, and in any case nobody would ever do such a thing and then go ahead and talk about it. They would squint into the dense, oppressive sunlight. For a few moments, perhaps, they would fall silent, lighting a joint and tracking its passage from man to man, inhaling, holding in the humiliation. Scary stuff, one of them might say. But then someone else would grin or flick his eyebrows and say, Roger-dodger, almost cut me a new asshole, *almost*.

There were numerous such poses. Some carried themselves with a sort of wistful resignation, others with pride or stiff soldierly discipline or good humor or macho zeal. They were afraid of dying but they were even more afraid to show it.

They found jokes to tell.

They used a hard vocabulary to contain the terrible softness. *Greased* they'd say. *Offed, lit up, zapped while zipping*. It wasn't cruelty, just stage presence. They were actors. When someone died, it wasn't quite dying, because in a curious way it seemed scripted, and because they had their lines mostly memorized, irony mixed with tragedy, and because they called it by other names, as if to encyst and destroy the reality of death itself. They kicked corpses. They cut off thumbs. They talked grunt lingo. They told stories about Ted Lavender's supply of tranquilizers, how the poor guy didn't feel a thing, how incredibly tranquil he was.

There's a moral here, said Mitchell Sanders.

They were waiting for Lavender's chopper, smoking the dead man's dope.

The moral's pretty obvious, Sanders said, and winked. Stay away from drugs. No joke, they'll ruin your day every time.

Cute, said Henry Dobbins.

Mind blower, get it? Talk about wiggy. Nothing left, just blood and brains.

They made themselves laugh.

There it is, they'd say. Over and over—there it is, my friend, there it is—as if the repetition itself were an act of poise, a balance between crazy and almost crazy, knowing without going, there it is, which meant be cool, let it ride, because Oh yeah, man, you can't change what can't be changed, there it is, there it absolutely and positively and fucking well *is*.

They were tough.

They carried all the emotional baggage of men who might die. Grief, terror, love, longing—these were intangibles, but the intangibles had their own mass and specific gravity, they had tangible weight. They carried shameful memories. They carried the common secret of cowardice barely restrained, the instinct to run or freeze or hide, and in many respects this was the heaviest burden of all, for it could never be put down, it required perfect balance and perfect posture. They carried their reputations. They carried the soldier's greatest fear, which was the fear of blushing. Men killed, and died, because they were embarrassed not to. It was what had brought them to the war in the first place, nothing positive, no dreams of glory or honor, just to avoid the blush of dishonor. They died so as not to die of embarrassment. They crawled into tunnels and walked point and advanced under fire. Each morning, despite the unknowns, they made their legs move. They endured. They kept humping. They did not submit to the obvious alternative, which was simply to close the eyes and fall. So easy, really. Go limp and tumble to the ground and let the muscles unwind and not speak and not budge until your buddies picked you up and lifted you into the chopper that would roar and dip its nose and carry you off to the world. A mere matter of falling, yet no one ever fell. It was not courage, exactly; the object was not valor. Rather, they were too frightened to be cowards.

By and large they carried these things inside, maintaining the masks of composure. They sneered at sick call. They spoke bitterly about guys who had found release by shooting off their own toes or fingers. Pussies, they'd say. Candy-asses. It was fierce, mocking talk, with only a trace of envy or awe, but even so the image played itself out behind their eyes.

They imagined the muzzle against flesh. So easy: squeeze the trigger and blow away a toe. They imagined it. They imagined the quick, sweet pain, then the evacuation to Japan, then a hospital with warm beds and cute geisha nurses.

And they dreamed of freedom birds.

At night, on guard, staring into the dark, they were carried away by jumbo jets. They felt the rush of takeoff. *Gone!* they yelled. And then velocity—wings and engines—a smiling stewardess—but it was more than a plane, it was a real bird, a big sleek silver bird with feathers and talons and high screeching. They were flying. The weights fell off; there was nothing to bear. They laughed and held on tight, feeling the cold slap of wind and altitude, soaring, thinking *It's over, I'm gone!*—they were naked, they were light and free—it was all lightness, bright and fast and buoyant, light as light, a helium buzz in the brain, a giddy bubbling in the lungs as they were taken up over the clouds and the war, beyond duty, beyond gravity and mortification and global entanglements—*Sin loi!* they yelled. *I'm sorry, motherfuckers, but I'm out of it, I'm goofed, I'm on a space cruise, I'm gone!*—and it was a restful, unencumbered sensation, just riding the light waves, sailing that big silver freedom bird over the mountains and oceans, over America, over the farms and great sleeping cities and cemeteries and highways and the golden arches of McDonald's, it was flight, a kind of fleeing, a kind of falling, falling higher and higher, spinning off the edge of the earth and beyond the sun and through the vast, silent vacuum where there were no burdens and where everything weighed exactly nothing—*Gone!* they screamed. *I'm sorry but I'm gone!*—and so at night, not quite dreaming, they gave themselves over to lightness, they were carried, they were purely borne.

On the morning after Ted Lavender died, First Lieutenant Jimmy Cross crouched at the bottom of his foxhole and burned Martha's letters. Then he burned the two photographs. There was a steady rain falling, which made it difficult, but he used heat tabs and Sterno to build a small fire, screening it with his body, holding the photographs over the tight blue flame with the tips of his fingers.

He realized it was only a gesture. Stupid, he thought. Sentimental, too, but mostly just stupid.

Lavender was dead. You couldn't burn the blame.

Besides, the letters were in his head. And even now, without photographs, Lieutenant Cross could see Martha playing volleyball in her white gym shorts and yellow T-shirt. He could see her moving in the rain.

When the fire died out, Lieutenant Cross pulled his poncho over his shoulders and ate breakfast from a can.

There was no great mystery, he decided.

In those burned letters Martha had never mentioned the war, except to say, Jimmy, take care of yourself. She wasn't involved. She signed the letters Love, but it wasn't love, and all the fine lines and technicalities did not matter. Virginity was no longer an issue. He hated her. Yes, he did. He hated her. Love, too, but it was a hard, hating kind of love.

The morning came up wet and blurry. Everything seemed part of everything else, the fog and Martha and the deepening rain.

He was a soldier, after all.

Half smiling, Lieutenant Jimmy Cross took out his maps. He shook his head hard, as if to clear it, then bent forward and began planning the day's march. In ten minutes, or maybe twenty, he would rouse the men and they would pack up and head west, where the maps showed the country to be green and inviting. They would do what they had always done. The rain might add some weight, but otherwise it would be one more day layered upon all the other days.

He was realistic about it. There was that new hardness in his stomach.

He loved her but he hated her.

No more fantasies, he told himself.

Henceforth, when he thought about Martha, it would be only to think that she belonged elsewhere. He would shut down the daydreams. This was not Mount Sebastian, it was another world, where there were no pretty poems or midterm exams, a place where men died because of carelessness and gross stupidity. Kiowa was right. Boom-down, and you were dead, never partly dead.

Briefly, in the rain, Lieutenant Cross saw Martha's gray eyes gazing back at him. He understood.

It was very sad, he thought. The things men carried inside. The things men did or felt they had to do.

He almost nodded at her, but didn't.

Instead he went back to his maps. He was now determined to perform his duties firmly and without negligence. It wouldn't help Lavender, he knew that, but from this point on he would comport himself as an officer. He would dispose of his good-luck pebble. Swallow it, maybe, or use Lee Strunk's slingshot, or just drop it along the trail. On the march he would impose strict field discipline. He would be careful to send out flank security, to prevent straggling or bunching up, to keep his troops moving at the proper pace and at the proper interval. He would insist on clean weapons. He would confiscate the remainder of Lavender's dope. Later in the day, perhaps, he would call the men together and speak to them plainly. He would accept the blame for what had happened to Ted Lavender. He would be a man about it. He would look them in the eyes, keeping his chin level, and he would issue the new SOPs in a calm, impersonal tone of voice, a lieutenant's voice, leaving no room for argument or discussion. Commencing immediately, he'd tell them, they would no longer abandon equipment along the route of march. They would police up their acts. They would get their shit together, and keep it together, and maintain it neatly and in good working order.

He would not tolerate laxity. He would show strength, distancing himself.

Among the men there would be grumbling, of course, and maybe worse, because their days would seem longer and their loads heavier, but Lieutenant Jimmy Cross reminded himself that his obligation was not to be loved but to lead. He would dispense with love; it was not now a factor. And if anyone quarreled or complained, he would simply tighten his lips and arrange his shoulders in the correct command posture. He might give a curt little nod. Or he might not. He might just shrug and say, Carry on, then they would saddle up and form into a column and move out toward the villages west of Than Khe.

Love

Many years after the war Jimmy Cross came to visit me at my home in Massachusetts, and for a full day we drank coffee and smoked cigarettes and talked about everything we had seen and done so long ago, all the things we still carried through our lives. Spread out across the kitchen table were maybe a hundred old photographs. There were pictures of Rat Kiley and Kiowa and Mitchell Sanders, all of us, the faces incredibly soft and young. At one point, I remember, we paused over a snapshot of Ted Lavender, and after a while Jimmy rubbed his eyes and said he'd never forgiven himself for Lavender's death. It was something that would never go away, he said quietly, and I nodded and told him I felt the same about certain things. Then for a long time neither of us could think of much to say. The thing to do, we decided, was to forget the coffee and switch to gin, which improved the mood, and not much later we were laughing about some of the craziness that used to go on. The way Henry Dobbins carried his girlfriend's pantyhose around his neck like a comforter. Kiowa's moccasins and hunting hatchet. Rat Kiley's comic books. By midnight we were both a little high, and I decided there was no harm in asking about Martha. I'm not sure how I phrased it—just a general question—but Jimmy Cross looked up in surprise. "You writer types," he said, "you've got long memories." Then he smiled and excused himself and went up to the guest room and came back with a small framed photograph. It was the volleyball shot: Martha bent horizontal to the floor, reaching, the palms of her hands in sharp focus.

"Remember this?" he said.

I nodded and told him I was surprised. I thought he'd burned it.

Jimmy kept smiling. For a while he stared down at the photograph, his eyes very bright, then he shrugged and said, "Well, I did—I burned it. After Lavender died, I couldn't . . . This is a new one. Martha gave it to me herself."

They'd run into each other, he said, at a college reunion in 1979. Nothing had changed. He still loved her. For eight or nine hours, he said, they spent most of their time together. There was a banquet, and then a dance, and then afterward they took a walk across the campus and talked about their lives. Martha was a Lutheran missionary now. A trained nurse, although nursing wasn't the point, and she had done service in Ethiopia and Guatemala and Mexico. She had never married, she said, and probably never would. She didn't know why. But as she said this, her eyes seemed to slide sideways, and it occurred to him that there were things about her he would never know. Her eyes were gray and neutral. Later, when he took her hand, there was no pressure in return, and later still, when he told her he still loved her, she kept walking and didn't answer and then after several minutes looked at her wristwatch and said it was getting late. He walked her back to the dormitory. For a few moments he considered asking her to his room, but instead he laughed and told her how back in college he'd almost done something very brave. It was after seeing *Bonnie and Clyde*, he said, and on this same spot he'd almost picked her up and carried her to his room and tied her to the bed and put his hand on her knee and just held it there all night long. It came close, he told her—he'd almost done it. Martha shut her eyes. She crossed her arms at her chest, as if suddenly cold, rocking slightly, then after a time she looked at him and said she was glad he hadn't tried it. She didn't understand how men could do those things. What things? he asked, and Martha said, The things men do. Then he nodded. It began to form. Oh, he said, those things. At breakfast the next morning she told him she was sorry. She explained that there was nothing she could do about it, and he said he understood, and then she laughed and gave him the picture and told him not to burn this one up.

Jimmy shook his head. "It doesn't matter," he finally said. "I love her." For the rest of his visit I steered the conversation away from Martha. At the end, though, as we were walking out to his car, I told him that I'd like to write a story about some of this. Jimmy thought it over and then gave me a little smile. "Why not?" he said. "Maybe she'll read it and come begging. There's always hope, right?"

"Right," I said.

He got into his car and rolled down the window. "Make me out to be a good guy, okay? Brave and handsome, all that stuff. Best platoon leader ever." He hesitated for a second. "And do me a favor. Don't mention anything about—"

"No," I said, "I won't."

Spin

The war wasn't all terror and violence.

Sometimes things could almost get sweet. For instance, I remember a little boy with a plastic leg. I remember how he hopped over to Azar and asked for a chocolate bar—"GI number one," the kid said—and Azar laughed and handed over the chocolate. When the boy hopped away, Azar clucked his tongue and said, "War's a bitch." He shook his head sadly. "One leg, for Chrissake. Some poor fucker ran out of ammo."

I remember Mitchell Sanders sitting quietly in the shade of an old banyan tree. He was using a thumbnail to pry off the body lice, working slowly, carefully depositing the lice in a blue USO envelope. His eyes were tired. It had been a long two weeks in the bush. After an hour or so he sealed up the envelope, wrote FREE in the upper right-hand corner, and addressed it to his draft board in Ohio.

On occasions the war was like a Ping-Pong ball. You could put fancy spin on it, you could make it dance.

I remember Norman Bowker and Henry Dobbins playing checkers every evening before dark. It was a ritual for them. They would dig a foxhole and get the board out and play long, silent games as the sky went from pink to purple. The rest of us would sometimes stop by to watch. There was something restful about it, something orderly and reassuring. There were red checkers and black checkers. The playing field was laid out in a strict grid, no tunnels or mountains or jungles. You knew where you stood. You knew the score. The pieces were out on the board, the enemy was visible, you could watch the tactics unfolding into larger strategies. There was a winner and a loser. There were rules.

I'm forty-three years old, and a writer now, and the war has been over for a long while. Much of it is hard to remember. I sit at this typewriter and stare through my words and watch Kiowa sinking into the deep muck of a shit field, or Curt Lemon hanging in pieces from a tree, and as I write about these things, the remembering is turned into a kind of rehappening. Kiowa yells at me. Curt Lemon steps from the shade into bright sunlight, his face brown and shining, and then he soars into a tree. The bad stuff never stops happening: it lives in its own dimension, replaying itself over and over.

But the war wasn't all that way.

Like when Ted Lavender went too heavy on the tranquilizers. "How's the war today?" somebody would say, and Ted Lavender would give a soft, spacey smile and say, "Mellow, man. We got ourselves a nice mellow war today."

And like the time we enlisted an old poppa-san to guide us through the mine fields out on the Batangan Peninsula. The old guy walked with a limp, slow and stooped over, but he knew where the safe spots were and where you had to be careful and where even if you were careful you could end up like popcorn. He had a tightrope walker's feel for the land beneath him—its surface tension, the give and take of things. Each morning we'd form up in a long column, the old poppa-san out front, and for the whole day we'd troop along after him, tracing his footsteps, playing an exact and ruthless game of follow the leader. Rat Kiley made up a rhyme that caught on, and we'd all be chanting it together: *Step out of line, hit a mine; follow the dink, you're in the pink.* All around us, the place was littered with Bouncing Betties and Toe Poppers and booby- trapped artillery rounds, but in those five days on the Batangan Peninsula nobody got hurt. We all learned to love the old man.

It was a sad scene when the choppers came to take us away. Jimmy Cross gave the old poppa-san a hug. Mitchell Sanders and Lee Strunk loaded him up with boxes of C rations.

There were actually tears in the old guy's eyes. "Follow dink," he said to each of us, "you go pink."

If you weren't humping, you were waiting. I remember the monotony. Digging foxholes. Slapping mosquitoes. The sun and the heat and the endless paddies. Even in the deep bush, where you could die in any number of ways, the war was nakedly and aggressively boring. But it was a strange boredom. It was boredom with a twist, the kind of boredom that caused stomach disorders. You'd be sitting at the top of a high hill, the flat paddies stretching out below, and the day would be calm and hot and utterly vacant, and you'd feel the boredom dripping inside you like a leaky faucet, except it wasn't water, it was a sort of acid, and with each little droplet you'd feel the stuff eating away at important organs. You'd try to relax. You'd uncurl your fists and let your thoughts go. Well, you'd think, this isn't so bad. And right then you'd hear gunfire behind you and your nuts would fly up into your throat and you'd be squealing pig squeals. That kind of boredom.

I feel guilty sometimes. Forty-three years old and I'm still writing war stories. My daughter Kathleen tells me it's an obsession, that I should write about a little girl who finds a million dollars and spends it all on a Shetland pony. In a way, I guess, she's right: I should forget it. But the thing about remembering is that you don't forget. You take your material where you find it, which is in your life, at the intersection of past and present. The memory-traffic feeds into a rotary up on your head, where it goes in circles for a while, then pretty soon imagination flows in and the traffic merges and shoots off down a thousand different streets. As a writer, all you can do is pick a street and go for the ride, putting things down as they come at you. That's the real obsession. All those stories.

Not bloody stories, necessarily. Happy stories, too, and even a few peace stories.

Here's a quick peace story:

A guy goes AWOL. Shacks up in Danang with a Red Cross nurse. It's a great time—the nurse loves him to death—the guy gets whatever he wants whenever he wants it. The war's over, he thinks. Just nookie and new angles. But then one day he rejoins his unit in the bush. Can't wait to get back into action. Finally one of his buddies asks what happened with the nurse, why so hot for combat, and the guy says, "All that peace, man, it felt so good it hurt. I want to hurt it *back*."

I remember Mitchell Sanders smiling as he told me that story. Most of it he made up, I'm sure, but even so it gave me a quick truth-goose. Because it's all relative. You're pinned down in some filthy hellhole of a paddy, getting your ass delivered to kingdom come, but then for a few seconds everything goes quiet and you look up and see the sun and a few puffy white clouds, and the immense serenity flashes against your eyeballs—the whole world gets rearranged—and even though you're pinned down by a war you never felt more at peace.

What sticks to memory, often, are those odd little fragments that have no beginning and no end:

Norman Bowker lying on his back one night, watching the stars, then whispering to me, "I'll tell you something, O'Brien. If I could have one wish, anything, I'd wish for my dad to write me a letter and say it's okay if I don't win any medals. That's all my old man talks about, nothing else. How he can't wait to see my goddamn medals."

Or Kiowa teaching a rain dance to Rat Kiley and Dave Jensen, the three of them whooping and leaping around barefoot while a bunch of villagers looked on with a mixture of fascination and giggly horror. Afterward, Rat said, "So where's the rain?" and Kiowa said, "The earth is slow, but the buffalo is patient," and Rat thought about it and said, "Yeah, but where's the *rain*?"

Or Ted Lavender adopting an orphan puppy—feeding it from a plastic spoon and carrying it in his rucksack until the day Azar strapped it to a Claymore antipersonnel mine and squeezed the firing device.

The average age in our platoon, I'd guess, was nineteen or twenty, and as a consequence things often took on a curiously playful atmosphere, like a sporting event at some exotic reform school. The competition could be lethal, yet there was a childlike exuberance to it all, lots of pranks and horseplay. Like when Azar blew away Ted Lavender's puppy. "What's everybody so upset about?" Azar said. "I mean, Christ, I'm just a *boy*."

I remember these things, too.

The damp, fungal scent of an empty body bag.

A quarter moon rising over the nighttime paddies.

Henry Dobbins sitting in the twilight, sewing on his new buck- sergeant stripes, quietly singing, "A tisket, a tasket, a green and yellow basket."

A field of elephant grass weighted with wind, bowing under the stir of a helicopter's blades, the grass dark and servile, bending low, but then rising straight again when the chopper went away.

A red clay trail outside the village of My Khe. A hand grenade.

A slim, dead, dainty young man of about twenty.

Kiowa saying, "No choice, Tim. What else could you do?" Kiowa saying, "Right?"

Kiowa saying, "Talk to me."

Forty-three years old, and the war occurred half a lifetime ago, and yet the remembering makes it now. And sometimes remembering will lead to a story, which makes it forever. That's what stories are for. Stories are for joining the past to the future. Stories are for those late hours in the night when you can't remember how you got from where you were to where you are. Stories are for eternity, when memory is erased, when there is nothing to remember except the story.

On the Rainy River

This is one story I've never told before. Not to anyone. Not to my parents, not to my brother or sister, not even to my wife. To go into it, I've always thought, would only cause embarrassment for all of us, a sudden need to be elsewhere, which is the natural response to a confession. Even now, I'll admit, the story makes me squirm. For more than twenty years I've had to live with it, feeling the shame, trying to push it away, and so by this act of remembrance, by putting the facts down on paper, I'm hoping to relieve at least some of the pressure on my dreams. Still, it's a hard story to tell. All of us, I suppose, like to believe that in a moral emergency we will behave like the heroes of our youth, bravely and forthrightly, without thought of personal loss or discredit. Certainly that was my conviction back in the summer of 1968. Tim O'Brien: a secret hero. The Lone Ranger. If the stakes ever became high enough—if the evil were evil enough, if the good were good enough—I would simply tap a secret reservoir of courage that had been accumulating inside me over the years. Courage, I seemed to think, comes to us in finite quantities, like an inheritance, and by being frugal and stashing it away and letting it earn interest, we steadily increase our moral capital in preparation for that day when the account must be drawn down. It was a comforting theory. It dispensed with all those bothersome little acts of daily courage; it offered hope and grace to the repetitive coward; it justified the past while amortizing the future.

In June of 1968, a month after graduating from Macalester College, I was drafted to fight a war I hated. I was twenty-one years old. Young, yes, and politically naive, but even so the American war in Vietnam seemed to me wrong. Certain blood was being shed for uncertain reasons. I saw no unity of purpose, no consensus on matters of philosophy or history or law. The very facts were shrouded in uncertainty: Was it a civil war? A war of national liberation or simple aggression? Who started it, and when, and why? What really happened to the *USS Maddox* on that dark night in the Gulf of Tonkin? Was Ho Chi Minh a Communist stooge, or a nationalist savior, or both, or neither? What about the Geneva Accords? What about SEATO and the Cold War? What about dominoes? America was divided on these and a thousand other issues, and the debate had spilled out across the floor of the United States Senate and into the streets, and smart men in pinstripes could not agree on even the most fundamental matters of public policy. The only certainty that summer was moral confusion. It was my view then, and still is, that you don't make war without knowing why. Knowledge, of course, is always imperfect, but it seemed to me that when a nation goes to war it must have reasonable confidence in the justice and imperative of its cause. You can't fix your mistakes. Once people are dead, you can't make them undead.

In any case those were my convictions, and back in college I had taken a modest stand against the war. Nothing radical, no hothead stuff, just ringing a few doorbells for Gene McCarthy, composing a few tedious, uninspired editorials for the campus newspaper. Oddly, though, it was almost entirely an intellectual activity. I brought some energy to it, of course, but it was the energy that accompanies almost any abstract endeavor; I felt no personal danger; I felt no sense of an impending crisis in my life. Stupidly, with a kind of smug removal that I can't begin to fathom, I assumed that the problems of killing and dying did not fall within my special province.

The draft notice arrived on June 17, 1968. It was a humid afternoon, I remember, cloudy and very quiet, and I'd just come in from a round of golf. My mother and father were having lunch out in the kitchen. I remember opening up the letter, scanning the first few lines, feeling the blood go thick behind my eyes. I remember a sound in my head. It wasn't thinking, just a silent howl. A million things all at once—I was too *good* for this war. Too smart, too compassionate, too everything. It couldn't happen. I was above it. I had the world dicked—Phi Beta Kappa and summa cum laude and president of the student body and a full-ride scholarship for grad studies at Harvard. A mistake, maybe—a foul-up in the paperwork. I was no soldier. I hated Boy Scouts. I hated camping out. I hated dirt and tents and mosquitoes. The sight of blood made me queasy, and I couldn't tolerate authority, and I didn't know a rifle from a slingshot. I was a *liberal*, for Christ sake: If they needed fresh bodies, why not draft some back-to-the-stone-age hawk? Or some dumb jingo in his hard hat and Bomb Hanoi button, or one of LBJ's pretty daughters, or Westmoreland's whole handsome family—nephews and nieces and baby grandson. There should be a law, I thought. If you support a war, if you think it's worth the price, that's fine, but you have to put your own precious fluids on the line. You have to head for the front and hook up with an infantry unit and help spill the blood. And you have to bring along your wife, or your kids, or your lover. A *law*, I thought.

I remember the rage in my stomach. Later it burned down to a smoldering self-pity, then to numbness. At dinner that night my father asked what my plans were. "Nothing," I said. "Wait."

I spent the summer of 1968 working in an Armour meatpacking plant in my hometown of Worthington, Minnesota. The plant specialized in pork products, and for eight hours a day I stood on a quarter-mile assembly line—more properly, a disassembly line—removing blood clots from the necks of dead pigs. My job title, I believe, was Declotter. After slaughter, the hogs were decapitated, split down the length of the belly, pried open, eviscerated, and strung up by the hind hocks on a high conveyer belt. Then gravity took over. By the time a carcass reached my spot on the line, the fluids had mostly drained out, everything except for thick clots of blood in the neck and upper chest cavity. To remove the stuff, I used a kind of water gun. The machine was heavy, maybe eighty pounds, and was suspended from the ceiling by a heavy rubber cord. There was some bounce to it, an elastic up-and-down give, and the trick was to maneuver the gun with your whole body, not lifting with the arms, just letting the rubber cord do the work for you. At one end was a trigger; at the muzzle end was a small nozzle and a steel roller brush. As a carcass passed by, you'd lean forward and swing the gun up against the clots and squeeze the trigger, all in one motion, and the brush would whirl and water would come shooting out and you'd hear a quick splattering sound as the clots dissolved into a fine red mist. It was not pleasant work. Goggles were a necessity, and a rubber apron, but even so it was like standing for eight hours a day under a lukewarm blood-shower. At night I'd go home smelling of pig. It wouldn't go away. Even after a hot bath, scrubbing hard, the stink was always there—like old bacon, or sausage, a dense greasy pig-stink that soaked deep into my skin and hair. Among other things, I remember, it was tough getting dates that summer. I felt isolated; I spent a lot of time alone. And there was also that draft notice tucked away in my wallet.

In the evenings I'd sometimes borrow my father's car and drive aimlessly around town, feeling sorry for myself, thinking about the war and the pig factory and how my life seemed to be collapsing toward slaughter. I felt paralyzed. All around me the options seemed to be narrowing, as if I were hurtling down a huge black funnel, the whole world squeezing in tight. There was no happy way out. The government had ended most graduate school deferments; the waiting lists for the National Guard and Reserves were impossibly long; my health was solid; I didn't qualify for CO status—no religious grounds, no history as a pacifist. Moreover, I could not claim to be opposed to war as a matter of general principle. There were occasions, I believed, when a nation was justified in using military force to achieve its ends, to stop a Hitler or some comparable evil, and I told myself that in such circumstances I would've willingly marched off to the battle. The problem, though, was that a draft board did not let you choose your war.

Beyond all this, or at the very center, was the raw fact of terror. I did not want to die. Not ever. But certainly not then, not there, not in a wrong war. Driving up Main Street, past the courthouse and the Ben Franklin store, I sometimes felt the fear spreading inside me like weeds. I imagined myself dead. I imagined myself doing things I could not do— charging an enemy position, taking aim at another human being.

At some point in mid-July I began thinking seriously about Canada. The border lay a few hundred miles north, an eight-hour drive. Both my conscience and my instincts were telling me to make a break for it, just take off and run like hell and never stop. In the beginning the idea seemed purely abstract, the word Canada printing itself out in my head; but after a time I could see particular shapes and images, the sorry details of my own future—a hotel room in Winnipeg, a battered old suitcase, my father's eyes as I tried to explain myself over the telephone. I could almost hear his voice, and my mother's. Run, I'd think. Then I'd think, Impossible. Then a second later I'd think, *Run*.

It was a kind of schizophrenia. A moral split. I couldn't make up my mind. I feared the war, yes, but I also feared exile. I was afraid of walking away from my own life, my friends and my family, my whole history, everything that mattered to me. I feared losing the respect of my parents. I feared the law. I feared ridicule and censure. My hometown was a conservative little spot on the prairie, a place where tradition counted, and it was easy to imagine people sitting around a table down at the old Gobbler Cafe on Main Street, coffee cups poised, the conversation slowly zeroing in on the young O'Brien kid, how the damned sissy had taken off for Canada. At night, when I couldn't sleep, I'd sometimes carry on fierce arguments with those people. I'd be screaming at them, telling them how much I detested their blind, thoughtless, automatic acquiescence to it all, their simple-minded patriotism, their prideful ignorance, their love-it- or-leave-it platitudes, how they were sending me off to fight a war they didn't understand and didn't want to understand. I held them responsible. By God, yes, I *did*. All of them—I held them personally and individually responsible—the polyestered Kiwanis boys, the merchants and farmers, the pious churchgoers, the chatty housewives, the PTA and the Lions club and the Veterans of Foreign Wars and the fine upstanding gentry out at the country club.

They didn't know Bao Dai from the man in the moon. They didn't know history. They didn't know the first thing about Diem's tyranny, or the nature of Vietnamese nationalism, or the long colonialism of the French—this was all too damned complicated, it required some reading—but no matter, it was a war to stop the Communists, plain and simple, which was how they liked things, and you were a treasonous pussy if you had second thoughts about killing or dying for plain and simple reasons.

I was bitter, sure. But it was so much more than that.

The emotions went from outrage to terror to bewilderment to guilt to sorrow and then back again to outrage. I felt a sickness inside me. Real disease.

Most of this I've told before, or at least hinted at, but what I have never told is the full truth. How I cracked. How at work one morning, standing on the pig line, I felt something break open in my chest. I don't know what it was. I'll never know. But it was real, I know that much, it was a physical rupture—a cracking-leaking-popping feeling. I remember dropping my water gun. Quickly, almost without thought, I took off my apron and walked out of the plant and drove home. It was midmorning, I remember, and the house was empty. Down in my chest there was still that leaking sensation, something very warm and precious spilling out, and I was covered with blood and hog-stink, and for a long while I just concentrated on holding myself together. I remember taking a hot shower. I remember packing a suitcase and carrying it out to the kitchen, standing very still for a few minutes, looking carefully at the familiar objects all around me. The old chrome toaster, the telephone, the pink and white Formica on the kitchen counters. The room was full of bright sunshine. Everything sparkled. My house, I thought. My life. I'm not sure how long I stood there, but later I scribbled out a short note to my parents.

What it said, exactly, I don't recall now. Something vague. Taking off, will call, love Tim. I drove north.

It's a blur now, as it was then, and all I remember is a sense of high velocity and the feel of the steering wheel in my hands. I was riding on adrenaline. A giddy feeling, in a way, except there was the dreamy edge of impossibility to it—like running a dead-end maze—no way out—it couldn't come to a happy conclusion and yet I was doing it anyway because it was all I could think of to do. It was pure flight, fast and mindless. I had no plan. Just hit the border at high speed and crash through and keep on running. Near dusk I passed through Bemidji, then turned northeast toward International Falls. I spent the night in the car behind a closed-down gas station a half mile from the border. In the morning, after gassing up, I headed straight west along the Rainy River, which separates Minnesota from Canada, and which for me separated one life from another. The land was mostly wilderness. Here and there I passed a motel or bait shop, but otherwise the country unfolded in great sweeps of pine and birch and sumac. Though it was still August, the air already had the smell of October, football season, piles of yellow-red leaves, everything crisp and clean. I remember a huge blue sky. Off to my right was the Rainy River, wide as a lake in places, and beyond the Rainy River was Canada.

For a while I just drove, not aiming at anything, then in the late morning I began looking for a place to lie low for a day or two. I was exhausted, and scared sick, and around noon I pulled into an old fishing resort called the Tip Top Lodge. Actually it was not a lodge at all, just eight or nine tiny yellow cabins clustered on a peninsula that jutted northward into the Rainy River. The place was in sorry shape. There was a dangerous wooden dock, an old minnow tank, a flimsy tar paper boathouse along the shore.

The main building, which stood in a cluster of pines on high ground, seemed to lean heavily to one side, like a cripple, the roof sagging toward Canada. Briefly, I thought about turning around, just giving up, but then I got out of the car and walked up to the front porch.

The man who opened the door that day is the hero of my life. How do I say this without sounding sappy? Blurt it out—the man saved me. He offered exactly what I needed, without questions, without any words at all. He took me in. He was there at the critical time—a silent, watchful presence. Six days later, when it ended, I was unable to find a proper way to thank him, and I never have, and so, if nothing else, this story represents a small gesture of gratitude twenty years overdue.

Even after two decades I can close my eyes and return to that porch at the Tip Top Lodge. I can see the old guy staring at me. Elroy Berdahl: eighty-one years old, skinny and shrunken and mostly bald. He wore a flannel shirt and brown work pants. In one hand, I remember, he carried a green apple, a small paring knife in the other. His eyes had the bluish gray color of a razor blade, the same polished shine, and as he peered up at me I felt a strange sharpness, almost painful, a cutting sensation, as if his gaze were somehow slicing me open. In part, no doubt, it was my own sense of guilt, but even so I'm absolutely certain that the old man took one look and went right to the heart of things—a kid in trouble. When I asked for a room, Elroy made a little clicking sound with his tongue. He nodded, led me out to one of the cabins, and dropped a key in my hand. I remember smiling at him. I also remember wishing I hadn't. The old man shook his head as if to tell me it wasn't worth the bother.

"Dinner at five-thirty," he said. "You eat fish?" "Anything," I said.

Elroy grunted and said, "I'll bet."

We spent six days together at the Tip Top Lodge. Just the two of us. Tourist season was over, and there were no boats on the river, and the wilderness seemed to withdraw into a great permanent stillness. Over those six days Elroy Berdahl and I took most of our meals together. In the mornings we sometimes went out on long hikes into the woods, and at night we played Scrabble or listened to records or sat reading in front of his big stone fireplace. At times I felt the awkwardness of an intruder, but Elroy accepted me into his quiet routine without fuss or ceremony. He took my presence for granted, the same way he might've sheltered a stray cat—no wasted sighs or pity—and there was never any talk about it. Just the opposite. What I remember more than anything is the man's willful, almost ferocious silence. In all that time together, all those hours, he never asked the obvious questions: Why was I there? Why alone? Why so preoccupied? If Elroy was curious about any of this, he was careful never to put it into words.

My hunch, though, is that he already knew. At least the basics. After all, it was 1968, and guys were burning draft cards, and Canada was just a boat ride away. Elroy Berdahl was no hick. His bedroom, I remember, was cluttered with books and newspapers. He killed me at the Scrabble board, barely concentrating, and on those occasions when speech was necessary he had a way of compressing large thoughts into small, cryptic packets of language. One evening, just at sunset, he pointed up at an owl circling over the violet-lighted forest to the west. "Hey, O'Brien," he said. "There's Jesus." The man was sharp—he didn't miss much. Those razor eyes. Now and then he'd catch me staring out at the river, at the far shore, and I could almost hear the tumblers clicking in his head. Maybe I'm wrong, but I doubt it.

One thing for certain, he knew I was in desperate trouble. And he knew I couldn't talk about it. The wrong word—or even the right word— and I would've disappeared. I was wired and jittery. My skin felt too tight. After supper one evening I vomited and went back to my cabin and lay down for a few moments and then vomited again; another time, in the middle of the afternoon, I began sweating and couldn't shut it off. I went through whole days feeling dizzy with sorrow. I couldn't sleep; I couldn't lie still. At night I'd toss around in bed, half awake, half dreaming, imagining how I'd sneak down to the beach and quietly push one of the old man's boats out into the river and start paddling my way toward Canada. There were times when I thought I'd gone off the psychic edge. I couldn't tell up from down, I was just falling, and late in the night I'd lie there watching weird pictures spin through my head. Getting chased by the Border Patrol—helicopters and searchlights and barking dogs—I'd be crashing through the woods, I'd be down on my hands and knees—people shouting out my name—the law closing in on all sides— my hometown draft board and the FBI and the Royal Canadian Mounted Police. It all seemed crazy and impossible. Twenty-one years old, an ordinary kid with all the ordinary dreams and ambitions, and all I wanted was to live the life I was born to—a mainstream life—I loved baseball and hamburgers and cherry Cokes—and now I was off on the margins of exile, leaving my country forever, and it seemed so impossible and terrible and sad.

I'm not sure how I made it through those six days. Most of it I can't remember. On two or three afternoons, to pass some time, I helped Elroy get the place ready for winter, sweeping down the cabins and hauling in the boats, little chores that kept my body moving. The days were cool and bright. The nights were very dark. One morning the old man showed me how to split and stack firewood, and for several hours we just worked in silence out behind his house. At one point, I remember, Elroy put down his maul and looked at me for a long time, his lips drawn as if framing a difficult question, but then he shook his head and went back to work. The man's self-control was amazing. He never pried. He never put me in a position that required lies or denials. To an extent, I suppose, his reticence was typical of that part of Minnesota, where privacy still held value, and even if I'd been walking around with some horrible deformity—four arms and three heads—I'm sure the old man would've talked about everything except those extra arms and heads. Simple politeness was part of it. But even more than that, I think, the man understood that words were insufficient. The problem had gone beyond discussion. During that long summer I'd been over and over the various arguments, all the pros and cons, and it was no longer a question that could be decided by an act of pure reason. Intellect had come up against emotion. My conscience told me to run, but some irrational and powerful force was resisting, like a weight pushing me toward the war. What it came down to, stupidly, was a sense of shame. Hot, stupid shame. I did not want people to think badly of me. Not my parents, not my brother and sister, not even the folks down at the Gobbler Cafe. I was ashamed to be there at the Tip Top Lodge. I was ashamed of my conscience, ashamed to be doing the right thing.

Some of this Elroy must've understood. Not the details, of course, but the plain fact of crisis.

Although the old man never confronted me about it, there was one occasion when he came close to forcing the whole thing out into the open. It was early evening, and we'd just finished supper, and over coffee and dessert I asked him about my bill, how much I owed so far. For a long while the old man squinted down at the tablecloth.

"Well, the basic rate," he said, "is fifty bucks a night. Not counting meals. This makes four nights, right?"

I nodded. I had three hundred and twelve dollars in my wallet.

Elroy kept his eyes on the tablecloth. "Now that's an on-season price. To be fair, I suppose we should knock it down a peg or two." He leaned back in his chair. "What's a reasonable number, you figure?"

"I don't know," I said. "Forty?"

"Forty's good. Forty a night. Then we tack on food—say another hundred? Two hundred sixty total?"

"I guess."

He raised his eyebrows. "Too much?"

"No, that's fair. It's fine. Tomorrow, though . . . I think I'd better take off tomorrow."

Elroy shrugged and began clearing the table. For a time he fussed with the dishes, whistling to himself as if the subject had been settled. After a second he slapped his hands together.

"You know what we forgot?" he said. "We forgot wages. Those odd jobs you done. What we have to do, we have to figure out what your time's worth. Your last job—how much did you pull in an hour?"

"Not enough," I said. "A bad one?"

"Yes. Pretty bad."

Slowly then, without intending any long sermon, I told him about my days at the pig plant. It began as a straight recitation of the facts, but before I could stop myself I was talking about the blood clots and the water gun and how the smell had soaked into my skin and how I couldn't wash it away. I went on for a long time. I told him about wild hogs squealing in my dreams, the sounds of butchery, slaughterhouse sounds, and how I'd sometimes wake up with that greasy pig-stink in my throat.

When I was finished, Elroy nodded at me.

"Well, to be honest," he said, "when you first showed up here, I wondered about all that. The aroma, I mean. Smelled like you was awful damned fond of pork chops." The old man almost smiled. He made a snuffling sound, then sat down with a pencil and a piece of paper. "So what'd this crud job pay? Ten bucks an hour? Fifteen?"

"Less."

Elroy shook his head. "Let's make it fifteen. You put in twenty-five hours here, easy. That's three hundred seventy-five bucks total wages. We subtract the two hundred sixty for food and lodging, I still owe you a hundred and fifteen."

He took four fifties out of his shirt pocket and laid them on the table. "Call it even," he said.

"No."

"Pick it up. Get yourself a haircut."

The money lay on the table for the rest of the evening. It was still there when I went back to my cabin. In the morning, though, I found an envelope tacked to my door. Inside were the four fifties and a two-word note that said

EMERGENCY FUND.

The man knew.

Looking back after twenty years, I sometimes wonder if the events of that summer didn't happen in some other dimension, a place where your life exists before you've lived it, and where it goes afterward. None of it ever seemed real. During my time at the Tip Top Lodge I had the feeling that I'd slipped out of my own skin, hovering a few feet away while some poor yo-yo with my name and face tried to make his way toward a future he didn't understand and didn't want. Even now I can see myself as I was then. It's like watching an old home movie: I'm young and tan and fit. I've got hair—lots of it. I don't smoke or drink. I'm wearing faded blue jeans and a white polo shirt. I can see myself sitting on Elroy Berdahl's dock near dusk one evening, the sky a bright shimmering pink, and I'm finishing up a letter to my parents that tells what I'm about to do and why I'm doing it and how sorry I am that I'd never found the courage to talk to them about it. I ask them not to be angry. I try to explain some of my feelings, but there aren't enough words, and so I just say that it's a thing that has to be done. At the end of the letter I talk about the vacations we used to take up in this north country, at a place called Whitefish Lake, and how the scenery here reminds me of those good times. I tell them I'm fine. I tell them I'll write again from Winnipeg or Montreal or wherever I end up.

On my last full day, the sixth day, the old man took me out fishing on the Rainy River. The afternoon was sunny and cold. A stiff breeze came in from the north, and I remember how the little fourteen-foot boat made sharp rocking motions as we pushed off from the dock. The current was fast. All around us, I remember, there was a vastness to the world, an unpeopled rawness, just the trees and the sky and the water reaching out toward nowhere. The air had the brittle scent of October.

For ten or fifteen minutes Elroy held a course upstream, the river choppy and silver-gray, then he turned straight north and put the engine on full throttle. I felt the bow lift beneath me. I remember the wind in my ears, the sound of the old outboard Evinrude. For a time I didn't pay attention to anything, just feeling the cold spray against my face, but then it occurred to me that at some point we must've passed into Canadian waters, across that dotted line between two different worlds, and

I remember a sudden tightness in my chest as I looked up and watched the far shore come at me. This wasn't a daydream. It was tangible and real. As we came in toward land, Elroy cut the engine, letting the boat fishtail lightly about twenty yards off shore. The old man didn't look at me or speak. Bending down, he opened up his tackle box and busied himself with a bobber and a piece of wire leader, humming to himself, his eyes down.

It struck me then that he must've planned it. I'll never be certain, of course, but I think he meant to bring me up against the realities, to guide me across the river and to take me to the edge and to stand a kind of vigil as I chose a life for myself.

I remember staring at the old man, then at my hands, then at Canada. The shoreline was dense with brush and timber. I could see tiny red berries on the bushes. I could see a squirrel up in one of the birch trees, a big crow looking at me from a boulder along the river. That close— twenty yards—and I could see the delicate latticework of the leaves, the texture of the soil, the browned needles beneath the pines, the configurations of geology and human history. Twenty yards. I could've done it. I could've jumped and started swimming for my life. Inside me, in my chest, I felt a terrible squeezing pressure. Even now, as I write this, I can still feel that tightness. And I want you to feel it—the wind coming off the river, the waves, the silence, the wooded frontier. You're at the bow of a boat on the Rainy River. You're twenty-one years old, you're scared, and there's a hard squeezing pressure in your chest.

What would you do?

Would you jump? Would you feel pity for yourself? Would you think about your family and your childhood and your dreams and all you're leaving behind? Would it hurt? Would it feel like dying? Would you cry, as I did?

I tried to swallow it back. I tried to smile, except I was crying.

Now, perhaps, you can understand why I've never told this story before. It's not just the embarrassment of tears. That's part of it, no doubt, but what embarrasses me much more, and always will, is the paralysis that took my heart. A moral freeze: I couldn't decide, I couldn't act, I couldn't comport myself with even a pretense of modest human dignity.

All I could do was cry. Quietly, not bawling, just the chest-chokes.

At the rear of the boat Elroy Berdahl pretended not to notice. He held a fishing rod in his hands, his head bowed to hide his eyes. He kept humming a soft, monotonous little tune. Everywhere, it seemed, in the trees and water and sky, a great worldwide sadness came pressing down on me, a crushing sorrow, sorrow like I had never known it before. And what was so sad, I realized, was that Canada had become a pitiful fantasy. Silly and hopeless. It was no longer a possibility. Right then, with the shore so close, I understood that I would not do what I should do. I would not swim away from my hometown and my country and my life. I would not be brave. That old image of myself as a hero, as a man of conscience and courage, all that was just a threadbare pipe dream. Bobbing there on the Rainy River, looking back at the Minnesota shore, I felt a sudden swell of helplessness come over me, a drowning sensation, as if I had toppled overboard and was being swept away by the silver waves. Chunks of my own history flashed by. I saw a seven-year-old boy in a white cowboy hat and a Lone Ranger mask and a pair of holstered six-shooters; I saw a twelve-year-old Little League shortstop pivoting to turn a double play; I saw a sixteen-year-old kid decked out for his first prom, looking spiffy in a white tux and a black bow tie, his hair cut short and flat, his shoes freshly polished. My whole life seemed to spill out into the river, swirling away from me, everything I had ever been or ever wanted to be. I couldn't get my breath; I couldn't stay afloat; I couldn't tell which way to swim. A hallucination, I suppose, but it was as real as anything I would ever feel. I saw my parents calling to me from the far shoreline. I saw my brother and sister, all the townsfolk, the mayor and the entire Chamber of Commerce and all my old teachers and girlfriends and high school buddies. Like some weird sporting event: everybody screaming from the sidelines, rooting me on—a loud stadium roar. Hotdogs and popcorn—stadium smells, stadium heat. A squad of cheerleaders did cartwheels along the banks of the Rainy River; they had megaphones and pompoms and smooth brown thighs. The crowd swayed left and right. A marching band played fight songs. All my aunts and uncles were there, and Abraham Lincoln, and Saint George, and a nine-year-old girl named Linda who had died of a brain tumor back in fifth grade, and several members of the United States Senate, and a blind poet scribbling notes, and LBJ, and Huck Finn, and Abbie Hoffman, and all the dead soldiers back from the grave, and the many thousands who were later to die—villagers with terrible burns, little kids without arms or legs—yes, and the Joint Chiefs of Staff were there, and a couple of popes, and a first lieutenant named Jimmy Cross, and the last surviving veteran of the American Civil War, and Jane Fonda dressed up as Barbarella, and an old man sprawled beside a pigpen, and my grandfather, and Gary Cooper, and a kind-faced woman carrying an umbrella and a copy of Plato's *Republic*, and a million ferocious citizens waving flags of all shapes and colors—people in hard hats, people in headbands—they were all whooping and chanting and urging me toward one shore or the other. I saw faces from my distant past and distant future. My wife was there.

My unborn daughter waved at me, and my two sons hopped up and down, and a drill sergeant named Blyton sneered and shot up a finger and shook his head. There was a choir in bright purple robes. There was a cabbie from the Bronx. There was a slim young man I would one day kill with a hand grenade along a red clay trail outside the village of My Khe.

The little aluminum boat rocked softly beneath me. There was the wind and the sky.

I tried to will myself overboard.

I gripped the edge of the boat and leaned forward and thought, *Now*. I did try. It just wasn't possible.

All those eyes on me—the town, the whole universe—and I couldn't risk the embarrassment. It was as if there were an audience to my life, that swirl of faces along the river, and in my head I could hear people screaming at me. Traitor! they yelled. Turncoat! Pussy! I felt myself blush. I couldn't tolerate it. I couldn't endure the mockery, or the disgrace, or the patriotic ridicule. Even in my imagination, the shore just twenty yards away, I couldn't make myself be brave. It had nothing to do with morality. Embarrassment, that's all it was.

And right then I submitted.

I would go to the war—I would kill and maybe die—because I was embarrassed not to.

That was the sad thing. And so I sat in the bow of the boat and cried. It was loud now. Loud, hard crying.

Elroy Berdahl remained quiet. He kept fishing. He worked his line with the tips of his fingers, patiently, squinting out at his red and white bobber on the Rainy River. His eyes were flat and impassive. He didn't speak. He was simply there, like the river and the late-summer sun. And yet by his presence, his mute watchfulness, he made it real. He was the true audience. He was a witness, like God, or like the gods, who look on in absolute silence as we live our lives, as we make our choices or fail to make them.

"Ain't biting," he said.

Then after a time the old man pulled in his line and turned the boat back toward Minnesota.

I don't remember saying goodbye. That last night we had dinner together, and I went to bed early, and in the morning Elroy fixed breakfast for me. When I told him I'd be leaving, the old man nodded as if he already knew. He looked down at the table and smiled.

At some point later in the morning it's possible that we shook hands—I just don't remember—but I do know that by the time I'd finished packing the old man had disappeared. Around noon, when I took my suitcase out to the car, I noticed that his old black pickup truck was no longer parked in front of the house. I went inside and waited for a while, but I felt a bone certainty that he wouldn't be back. In a way, I thought, it was appropriate. I washed up the breakfast dishes, left his two hundred dollars on the kitchen counter, got into the car, and drove south toward home.

The day was cloudy. I passed through towns with familiar names, through the pine forests and down to the prairie, and then to Vietnam, where I was a soldier, and then home again. I survived, but it's not a happy ending. I was a coward. I went to the war.

Enemies

One morning in late July, while we were out on patrol near LZ Gator, Lee Strunk and Dave Jensen got into a fistfight. It was about something stupid—a missing jackknife—but even so the fight was vicious. For a while it went back and forth, but Dave Jensen was much bigger and much stronger, and eventually he wrapped an arm around Strunk's neck and pinned him down and kept hitting him on the nose. He hit him hard. And he didn't stop. Strunk's nose made a sharp snapping sound, like a firecracker, but even then Jensen kept hitting him, over and over, quick stiff punches that did not miss. It took three of us to pull him off. When it was over, Strunk had to be choppered back to the rear, where he had his nose looked after, and two days later he rejoined us wearing a metal splint and lots of gauze.

In any other circumstance it might've ended there. But this was Vietnam, where guys carried guns, and Dave Jensen started to worry. It was mostly in his head. There were no threats, no vows of revenge, just a silent tension between them that made Jensen take special precautions. On patrol he was careful to keep track of Strunk's whereabouts. He dug his foxholes on the far side of the perimeter; he kept his back covered; he avoided situations that might put the two of them alone together. Eventually, after a week of this, the strain began to create problems. Jensen couldn't relax. Like fighting two different wars, he said. No safe ground: enemies everywhere. No front or rear. At night he had trouble sleeping—a skittish feeling—always on guard, hearing strange noises in the dark, imagining a grenade rolling into his foxhole or the tickle of a knife against his ear. The distinction between good guys and bad guys disappeared for him. Even in times of relative safety, while the rest of us took it easy, Jensen would be sitting with his back against a stone wall, weapon across his knees, watching Lee Strunk with quick, nervous eyes. It got to the point finally where he lost control. Something must've snapped. One afternoon he began firing his weapon into the air, yelling Strunk's name, just firing and yelling, and it didn't stop until he'd rattled off an entire magazine of ammunition. We were all flat on the ground. Nobody had the nerve to go near him. Jensen started to reload, but then suddenly he sat down and held his head in his arms and wouldn't move. For two or three hours he simply sat there.

But that wasn't the bizarre part.

Because late that same night he borrowed a pistol, gripped it by the barrel, and used it like a hammer to break his own nose.

Afterward, he crossed the perimeter to Lee Strunk's foxhole. He showed him what he'd done and asked if everything was square between them.

Strunk nodded and said, Sure, things were square.

But in the morning Lee Strunk couldn't stop laughing. "The man's crazy," he said. "I stole his fucking jackknife."

Friends

Dave Jensen and Lee Strunk did not become instant buddies, but they did learn to trust each other. Over the next month they often teamed up on ambushes. They covered each other on patrol, shared a foxhole, took turns pulling guard at night. In late August they made a pact that if one of them should ever get totally rucked up—a wheelchair wound—the other guy would automatically find a way to end it. As far as I could tell they were serious. They drew it up on paper, signing their names and asking a couple of guys to act as witnesses. And then in October Lee Strunk stepped on a rigged mortar round. It took off his right leg at the knee. He managed a funny little half step, like a hop, then he tilted sideways and dropped. "Oh, damn," he said. For a while he kept on saying it, "Damn oh damn," as if he'd stubbed a toe. Then he panicked. He tried to get up and run, but there was nothing left to run on. He fell hard. The stump of his right leg was twitching. There were slivers of bone, and the blood came in quick spurts like water from a pump. He seemed bewildered. He reached down as if to massage his missing leg, then he passed out, and Rat Kiley put on a tourniquet and administered morphine and ran plasma into him.

There was nothing much anybody could do except wait for the dustoff. After we'd secured an LZ, Dave Jensen went over and kneeled at Strunk's side. The stump had stopped twitching now. For a time there was some question as to whether Strunk was still alive, but then he opened his eyes and looked up at Dave Jensen. "Oh, Jesus," he said, and moaned, and tried to slide away and said, "Jesus, man, don't kill me."

"Relax," Jensen said.

Lee Strunk seemed groggy and confused. He lay still for a second and then motioned toward his leg. "Really, it's not so bad, Not terrible. Hey, *really*—they can sew it back on—*really*."

"Right, I'll bet they can." "You think?"

"Sure I do."

Strunk frowned at the sky. He passed out again, then woke up and said, "Don't kill me."

"I won't," Jensen said. "I'm *serious*."

"Sure."

"But you got to promise. Swear it to me—swear you won't kill me." Jensen nodded and said, "I swear," and then a little later we carried

Strunk to the dustoff chopper. Jensen reached out and touched the good

leg. "Go on now," he said. Later we heard that Strunk died somewhere over Chu Lai, which seemed to relieve Dave Jensen of an enormous weight.

How to Tell a True War Story

This is true.

I had a buddy in Vietnam. His name was Bob Kiley, but everybody called him Rat.

A friend of his gets killed, so about a week later Rat sits down and writes a letter to the guy's sister. Rat tells her what a great brother she had, how together the guy was, a number one pal and comrade. A real soldier's soldier, Rat says. Then he tells a few stories to make the point, how her brother would always volunteer for stuff nobody else would volunteer for in a million years, dangerous stuff, like doing recon or going out on these really badass night patrols. Stainless steel balls, Rat tells her. The guy was a little crazy, for sure, but crazy in a good way, a real daredevil, because he liked the challenge of it, he liked testing himself, just man against gook. A great, great guy, Rat says.

Anyway, it's a terrific letter, very personal and touching. Rat almost bawls writing it. He gets all teary telling about the good times they had together, how her brother made the war seem almost fun, always raising hell and lighting up villes and bringing smoke to bear every which way. A great sense of humor, too. Like the time at this river when he went fishing with a whole damn crate of hand grenades. Probably the funniest thing in world history, Rat says, all that gore, about twenty zillion dead gook fish. Her brother, he had the right attitude. He knew how to have a good time. On Halloween, this real hot spooky night, the dude paints up his body all different colors and puts on this weird mask and hikes over to a ville and goes trick-or-treating almost stark naked, just boots and balls and an M-16. A tremendous human being, Rat says. Pretty nutso sometimes, but you could trust him with your life.

And then the letter gets very sad and serious. Rat pours his heart out. He says he loved the guy. He says the guy was his best friend in the world. They were like soul mates, he says, like twins or something, they had a whole lot in common. He tells the guy's sister he'll look her up when the war's over.

So what happens?

Rat mails the letter. He waits two months. The dumb cooze never writes back. A true war story is never moral. It does not instruct, nor encourage virtue, nor suggest models of proper human behavior, nor restrain men from doing the things men have always done. If a story seems moral, do not believe it. If at the end of a war story you feel uplifted, or if you feel that some small bit of rectitude has been salvaged from the larger waste, then you have been made the victim of a very old and terrible lie. There is no rectitude whatsoever. There is no virtue. As a first rule of thumb, therefore, you can tell a true war story by its absolute and uncompromising allegiance to obscenity and evil. Listen to Rat Kiley. Cooze, he says. He does not say bitch. He certainly does not say woman, or girl. He says cooze. Then he spits and stares. He's nineteen years old— it's too much for him—so he looks at you with those big sad gentle killer eyes and says cooze, because his friend is dead, and because it's so incredibly sad and true: she never wrote back.

You can tell a true war story if it embarrasses you. If you don't care for obscenity, you don't care for the truth; if you don't care for the truth, watch how you vote. Send guys to war, they come home talking dirty.

Listen to Rat: "Jesus Christ, man, I write this beautiful fuckin' letter, I slave over it, and what happens? The dumb cooze never writes back."

The dead guy's name was Curt Lemon. What happened was, we crossed a muddy river and marched west into the mountains, and on the third day we took a break along a trail junction in deep jungle. Right away, Lemon and Rat Kiley started goofing. They didn't understand about the spookiness. They were kids; they just didn't know. A nature hike, they thought, not even a war, so they went off into the shade of some giant trees—quadruple canopy, no sunlight at all—and they were giggling and calling each other yellow mother and playing a silly game they'd invented. The game involved smoke grenades, which were harmless unless you did stupid things, and what they did was pull out the pin and stand a few feet apart and play catch under the shade of those huge trees. Whoever chickened out was a yellow mother. And if nobody chickened out, the grenade would make a light popping sound and they'd be covered with smoke and they'd laugh and dance around and then do it again.

It's all exactly true.

It happened, to *me*, nearly twenty years ago, and I still remember that trail junction and those giant trees and a soft dripping sound somewhere beyond the trees. I remember the smell of moss. Up in the canopy there were tiny white blossoms, but no sunlight at all, and I remember the shadows spreading out under the trees where Curt Lemon and Rat Kiley were playing catch with smoke grenades. Mitchell Sanders sat flipping his yo-yo. Norman Bowker and Kiowa and Dave Jensen were dozing, or half dozing, and all around us were those ragged green mountains.

Except for the laughter things were quiet.

At one point, I remember, Mitchell Sanders turned and looked at me, not quite nodding, as if to warn me about something, as if he already *knew*, then after a while he rolled up his yo-yo and moved away.

It's hard to tell you what happened next.

They were just goofing. There was a noise, I suppose, which must've been the detonator, so I glanced behind me and watched Lemon step from the shade into bright sunlight. His face was suddenly brown and shining. A handsome kid, really. Sharp gray eyes, lean and narrow-waisted, and when he died it was almost beautiful, the way the sunlight came around him and lifted him up and sucked him high into a tree full of moss and vines and white blossoms.

In any war story, but especially a true one, it's difficult to separate what happened from what seemed to happen. What seems to happen becomes its own happening and has to be told that way. The angles of vision are skewed. When a booby trap explodes, you close your eyes and duck and float outside yourself. When a guy dies, like Curt Lemon, you look away and then look back for a moment and then look away again. The pictures get jumbled; you tend to miss a lot. And then afterward, when you go to tell about it, there is always that surreal seemingness, which makes the story seem untrue, but which in fact represents the hard and exact truth as it *seemed*.

In many cases a true war story cannot be believed. If you believe it, be skeptical. It's a question of credibility. Often the crazy stuff is true and the normal stuff isn't, because the normal stuff is necessary to make you believe the truly incredible craziness.

In other cases you can't even tell a true war story. Sometimes it's just beyond telling.

I heard this one, for example, from Mitchell Sanders. It was near dusk and we were sitting at my foxhole along a wide muddy river north of Quang Ngai. I remember how peaceful the twilight was. A deep pinkish red spilled out on the river, which moved without sound, and in the morning we would cross the river and march west into the mountains. The occasion was right for a good story.

"God's truth," Mitchell Sanders said. "A six-man patrol goes up into the mountains on a basic listening-post operation. The idea's to spend a week up there, just lie low and listen for enemy movement. They've got a radio along, so if they hear anything suspicious—anything—they're supposed to call in artillery or gunships, whatever it takes. Otherwise they keep strict field discipline. Absolute silence. They just listen."

Sanders glanced at me to make sure I had the scenario. He was playing with his yo-yo, dancing it with short, tight little strokes of the wrist.

His face was blank in the dusk.

"We're talking regulation, by-the-book LP. These six guys, they don't say boo for a solid week. They don't got tongues. *All* ears."

"Right," I said. "Understand me?" "Invisible." Sanders nodded.

"Affirm," he said. "Invisible. So what happens is, these guys get themselves deep in the bush, all camouflaged up, and they lie down and wait and that's all they do, nothing else, they lie there for seven straight days and just listen. And man, I'll tell you—it's spooky. This is mountains. You don't *know* spooky till you been there. Jungle, sort of, except it's way up in the clouds and there's always this fog—like rain, except it's not raining—everything's all wet and swirly and tangled up and you can't see jack, you can't find your own pecker to piss with. Like you don't even have a body. Serious spooky. You just go with the vapors—the fog sort of takes you in . . . And the sounds, man. The sounds carry forever. You hear stuff nobody should overhear."

Sanders was quiet for a second, just working the yo-yo, then he smiled at me.

"So after a couple days the guys start hearing this real soft, kind of wacked-out music. Weird echoes and stuff. Like a radio or something, but it's not a radio, it's this strange gook music that comes right out of the rocks. Faraway, sort of, but right up close, too. They try to ignore it. But it's a listening post, right? So they listen. And every night they keep hearing that crazyass gook concert. All kinds of chimes and xylophones. I mean, this is wilderness—no way, it can't be real—but there it *is*, like the mountains are tuned in to Radio fucking Hanoi. Naturally they get nervous. One guy sticks Juicy Fruit in his ears. Another guy almost flips. Thing is, though, they can't report music. They can't get on the horn and call back to base and say, 'Hey, listen, we need some firepower, we got to blow away this weirdo gook rock band.' They can't do that. It wouldn't go down. So they lie there in the fog and keep their mouths shut. And what makes it extra bad, see, is the poor dudes can't horse around like normal. Can't joke it away. Can't even talk to each other except maybe in whispers, all hush-hush, and that just revs up the willies. All they do is listen."

Again there was some silence as Mitchell Sanders looked out on the river. The dark was coming on hard now, and off to the west I could see the mountains rising in silhouette, all the mysteries and unknowns.

"This next part," Sanders said quietly, "you won't believe." "Probably not," I said.

"You won't. And you know why?" He gave me a long, tired smile. "Because it happened. Because every word is absolutely dead-on true."

Sanders made a sound in his throat, like a sigh, as if to say he didn't care if I believed him or not. But he did care. He wanted me to feel the truth, to believe by the raw force of feeling. He seemed sad, in a way.

"These six guys," he said, "they're pretty fried out by now, and one night they start hearing voices. Like at a cocktail party. That's what it sounds like, this big swank gook cocktail party somewhere out there in the fog. Music and chitchat and stuff. It's crazy, I know, but they hear the champagne corks. They hear the actual martini glasses. Real hoity-toity, all very civilized, except this isn't civilization. This is Nam.

"Anyway, the guys try to be cool. They just lie there and groove, but after a while they start hearing—you won't believe this—they hear chamber music. They hear violins and cellos. They hear this terrific mama-san soprano. Then after a while they hear gook opera and a glee club and the Haiphong Boys Choir and a barbershop quartet and all kinds of weird chanting and Buddha-Buddha stuff. And the whole time, in the background, there's still that cocktail party going on. All these different voices. Not human voices, though. Because it's the mountains. Follow me? The rock—it's *talking*. And the fog, too, and the grass and the goddamn mongooses. Everything talks. The trees talk politics, the monkeys talk religion. The whole country. Vietnam. The place talks. It talks. Understand? Nam—it truly *talks*.

"The guys can't cope. They lose it. They get on the radio and report enemy movement—a whole army, they say—and they order up the firepower. They get arty and gunships. They call in air strikes. And I'll tell you, they fuckin' crash that cocktail party. All night long, they just smoke those mountains. They make jungle juice. They blow away trees and glee clubs and whatever else there is to blow away. Scorch time. They walk napalm up and down the ridges. They bring in the Cobras and F-4s, they use Willie Peter and HE and incendiaries. It's all fire. They make those mountains burn.

"Around dawn things finally get quiet. Like you never even *heard* quiet before. One of those real thick, real misty days—just clouds and fog, they're off in this special zone—and the mountains are absolutely dead- flat silent. Like *Brigadoon*—pure vapor, you know? Everything's all sucked up inside the fog. Not a single sound, except they still *hear* it.

"So they pack up and start humping. They head down the mountain, back to base camp, and when they get there they don't say diddly. They don't talk. Not a word, like they're deaf and dumb. Later on this fat bird colonel comes up and asks what the hell happened out there. What'd they hear? Why all the ordnance? The man's ragged out, he gets down tight on their case. I mean, they spent six trillion dollars on firepower, and this fatass colonel wants answers, he wants to know what the fuckin' story is.

"But the guys don't say zip. They just look at him for a while, sort of funny like, sort of amazed, and the whole war is right there in that stare. It says everything you can't ever say. It says, man, you got wax in your ears. It says, poor bastard, you'll never know—wrong frequency—you don't *even* want to hear this. Then they salute the fucker and walk away, because certain stories you don't ever tell."

You can tell a true war story by the way it never seems to end. Not then, not ever. Not when Mitchell Sanders stood up and moved off into the dark.

It all happened.

Even now, at this instant, I remember that yo-yo. In a way, I suppose, you had to be there, you had to hear it, but I could tell how desperately Sanders wanted me to believe him, his frustration at not quite getting the details right, not quite pinning down the final and definitive truth.

And I remember sitting at my foxhole that night, watching the shadows of Quang Ngai, thinking about the coming day and how we would cross the river and march west into the mountains, all the ways I might die, all the things I did not understand.

Late in the night Mitchell Sanders touched my shoulder. "Just came to me," he whispered. "The moral, I mean. Nobody listens. Nobody hears nothin'. Like that fatass colonel. The politicians, all the civilian types. Your girlfriend. My girlfriend. Everybody's sweet little virgin girlfriend. What they need is to go out on LP. The vapors, man. Trees and rocks— you got to *listen* to your enemy."

And then again, in the morning, Sanders came up to me. The platoon was preparing to move out, checking weapons, going through all the little rituals that preceded a day's march. Already the lead squad had crossed the river and was filing off toward the west.

"I got a confession to make," Sanders said. "Last night, man, I had to make up a few things."

"I know that."

"The glee club. There wasn't any glee club." "Right."

"No opera."

"Forget it, I understand."

"Yeah, but listen, it's still true. Those six guys, they heard wicked sound out there. They heard sound you just plain won't believe."

Sanders pulled on his rucksack, closed his eyes for a moment, then almost smiled at me. I knew what was coming.

"All right," I said, "what's the moral?" "Forget it."

"No, go ahead."

For a long while he was quiet, looking away, and the silence kept stretching out until it was almost embarrassing. Then he shrugged and gave me a stare that lasted all day.

"Hear that quiet, man?" he said. "That quiet—just listen. There's your moral."

In a true war story, if there's a moral at all, it's like the thread that makes the cloth. You can't tease it out. You can't extract the meaning without unraveling the deeper meaning. And in the end, really, there's nothing much to say about a true war story, except maybe "Oh."

True war stories do not generalize. They do not indulge in abstraction or analysis.

For example: War is hell. As a moral declaration the old truism seems perfectly true, and yet because it abstracts, because it generalizes, I can't believe it with my stomach. Nothing turns inside.

It comes down to gut instinct. A true war story, if truly told, makes the stomach believe.

This one does it for me. I've told it before—many times, many versions—but here's what actually happened.

We crossed that river and marched west into the mountains. On the third day, Curt Lemon stepped on a booby-trapped 105 round. He was playing catch with Rat Kiley, laughing, and then he was dead. The trees were thick; it took nearly an hour to cut an LZ for the dustoff.

Later, higher in the mountains, we came across a baby VC water buffalo. What it was doing there I don't know—no farms or paddies—but we chased it down and got a rope around it and led it along to a deserted village where we set up for the night. After supper Rat Kiley went over and stroked its nose.

He opened up a can of C rations, pork and beans, but the baby buffalo wasn't interested.

Rat shrugged.

He stepped back and shot it through the right front knee. The animal did not make a sound. It went down hard, then got up again, and Rat took careful aim and shot off an ear. He shot it in the hindquarters and in the little hump at its back. He shot it twice in the flanks. It wasn't to kill; it was to hurt. He put the rifle muzzle up against the mouth and shot the mouth away. Nobody said much. The whole platoon stood there watching, feeling all kinds of things, but there wasn't a great deal of pity for the baby water buffalo. Curt Lemon was dead. Rat Kiley had lost his best friend in the world. Later in the week he would write a long personal letter to the guy's sister, who would not write back, but for now it was a question of pain. He shot off the tail. He shot away chunks of meat below the ribs. All around us there was the smell of smoke and filth and deep greenery, and the evening was humid and very hot. Rat went to automatic. He shot randomly, almost casually, quick little spurts in the belly and butt. Then he reloaded, squatted down, and shot it in the left front knee. Again the animal fell hard and tried to get up, but this time it couldn't quite make it. It wobbled and went down sideways. Rat shot it in the nose. He bent forward and whispered something, as if talking to a pet, then he shot it in the throat. All the while the baby buffalo was silent, or almost silent, just a light bubbling sound where the nose had been. It lay very still. Nothing moved except the eyes, which were enormous, the pupils shiny black and dumb.

Rat Kiley was crying. He tried to say something, but then cradled his rifle and went off by himself.

The rest of us stood in a ragged circle around the baby buffalo. For a time no one spoke. We had witnessed something essential, something brand-new and profound, a piece of the world so startling there was not yet a name for it.

Somebody kicked the baby buffalo.

It was still alive, though just barely, just in the eyes.

"Amazing," Dave Jensen said. "My whole life, I never seen anything like it."

"Never?"

"Not hardly. Not once."

Kiowa and Mitchell Sanders picked up the baby buffalo. They hauled it across the open square, hoisted it up, and dumped it in the village well.

Afterward, we sat waiting for Rat to get himself together.

"Amazing," Dave Jensen kept saying. "A new wrinkle. I never seen it before."

Mitchell Sanders took out his yo-yo. "Well, that's Nam," he said. "Garden of Evil. Over here, man, every sin's real fresh and original."

How do you generalize?

War is hell, but that's not the half of it, because war is also mystery and terror and adventure and courage and discovery and holiness and pity and despair and longing and love. War is nasty; war is fun. War is thrilling; war is drudgery. War makes you a man; war makes you dead.

The truths are contradictory. It can be argued, for instance, that war is grotesque. But in truth war is also beauty. For all its horror, you can't help but gape at the awful majesty of combat. You stare out at tracer rounds unwinding through the dark like brilliant red ribbons. You crouch in ambush as a cool, impassive moon rises over the nighttime paddies. You admire the fluid symmetries of troops on the move, the harmonies of sound and shape and proportion, the great sheets of metal-fire streaming down from a gunship, the illumination rounds, the white phosphorus, the purply orange glow of napalm, the rocket's red glare. It's not pretty, exactly. It's astonishing. It fills the eye. It commands you. You hate it, yes, but your eyes do not. Like a killer forest fire, like cancer under a microscope, any battle or bombing raid or artillery barrage has the aesthetic purity of absolute moral indifference—a powerful, implacable beauty—and a true war story will tell the truth about this, though the truth is ugly.

To generalize about war is like generalizing about peace. Almost everything is true. Almost nothing is true. At its core, perhaps, war is just another name for death, and yet any soldier will tell you, if he tells the truth, that proximity to death brings with it a corresponding proximity to life. After a firefight, there is always the immense pleasure of aliveness. The trees are alive. The grass, the soil—everything. All around you things are purely living, and you among them, and the aliveness makes you tremble. You feel an intense, out-of-the-skin awareness of your living self—your truest self, the human being you want to be and then become by the force of wanting it. In the midst of evil you want to be a good man. You want decency. You want justice and courtesy and human concord, things you never knew you wanted. There is a kind of largeness to it, a kind of godliness. Though it's odd, you're never more alive than when you're almost dead. You recognize what's valuable. Freshly, as if for the first time, you love what's best in yourself and in the world, all that might be lost. At the hour of dusk you sit at your foxhole and look out on a wide river turning pinkish red, and at the mountains beyond, and although in the morning you must cross the river and go into the mountains and do terrible things and maybe die, even so, you find yourself studying the fine colors on the river, you feel wonder and awe at the setting of the sun, and you are filled with a hard, aching love for how the world could be and always should be, but now is not.

Mitchell Sanders was right. For the common soldier, at least, war has the feel—the spiritual texture—of a great ghostly fog, thick and permanent. There is no clarity. Everything swirls. The old rules are no longer binding, the old truths no longer true. Right spills over into wrong. Order blends into chaos, love into hate, ugliness into beauty, law into anarchy, civility into savagery. The vapors suck you in. You can't tell where you are, or why you're there, and the only certainty is overwhelming ambiguity.

In war you lose your sense of the definite, hence your sense of truth itself, and therefore it's safe to say that in a true war story nothing is ever absolutely true.

Often in a true war story there is not even a point, or else the point doesn't hit you until twenty years later, in your sleep, and you wake up and shake your wife and start telling the story to her, except when you get to the end you've forgotten the point again. And then for a long time you lie there watching the story happen in your head. You listen to your wife's breathing. The war's over. You close your eyes. You smile and think, Christ, what's the *point*?

This one wakes me up.

In the mountains that day, I watched Lemon turn sideways. He laughed and said something to Rat Kiley. Then he took a peculiar half step, moving from shade into bright sunlight, and the booby-trapped 105 round blew him into a tree. The parts were just hanging there, so Dave Jensen and I were ordered to shinny up and peel him off. I remember the white bone of an arm. I remember pieces of skin and something wet and yellow that must've been the intestines. The gore was horrible, and stays with me. But what wakes me up twenty years later is Dave Jensen singing "Lemon Tree" as we threw down the parts.

You can tell a true war story by the questions you ask. Somebody tells a story, let's say, and afterward you ask, "Is it true?" and if the answer matters, you've got your answer.

For example, we've all heard this one. Four guys go down a trail. A grenade sails out. One guy jumps on it and takes the blast and saves his three buddies.

Is it true?

The answer matters.

You'd feel cheated if it never happened. Without the grounding reality, it's just a trite bit of puffery, pure Hollywood, untrue in the way all such stories are untrue. Yet even if it did happen—and maybe it did, anything's possible—even then you know it can't be true, because a true war story does not depend upon that kind of truth. Absolute occurrence is irrelevant. A thing may happen and be a total lie; another thing may not happen and be truer than the truth. For example: Four guys go down a trail. A grenade sails out. One guy jumps on it and takes the blast, but it's a killer grenade and everybody dies anyway. Before they die, though, one of the dead guys says, "The fuck you do *that* for?" and the jumper says, "Story of my life, man," and the other guy starts to smile but he's dead. That's a true story that never happened.

Twenty years later, I can still see the sunlight on Lemon's face. I can see him turning, looking back at Rat Kiley, then he laughed and took that curious half step from shade into sunlight, his face suddenly brown and shining, and when his foot touched down, in that instant, he must've thought it was the sunlight that was killing him. It was not the sunlight. It was a rigged 105 round. But if I could ever get the story right, how the sun seemed to gather around him and pick him up and lift him high into a tree, if I could somehow re-create the fatal whiteness of that light, the quick glare, the obvious cause and effect, then you would believe the last thing Curt Lemon believed, which for him must've been the final truth.

Now and then, when I tell this story, someone will come up to me afterward and say she liked it. It's always a woman. Usually it's an older woman of kindly temperament and humane politics. She'll explain that as a rule she hates war stories; she can't understand why people want to wallow in all the blood and gore. But this one she liked. The poor baby buffalo, it made her sad. Sometimes, even, there are little tears. What I should do, she'll say, is put it all behind me. Find new stories to tell.

I won't say it but I'll think it.

I'll picture Rat Kiley's face, his grief, and I'll think, *You dumb cooze*. Because she wasn't listening. It wasn't a *war* story. It was a *love* story.

But you can't say that. All you can do is tell it one more time, patiently, adding and subtracting, making up a few things to get at the real truth. No Mitchell Sanders, you tell her. No Lemon, no Rat Kiley. No trail junction. No baby buffalo. No vines or moss or white blossoms. Beginning to end, you tell her, it's all made up. Every goddamn detail— the mountains and the river and especially that poor dumb baby buffalo. None of it happened. *None* of it. And even if it did happen, it didn't happen in the mountains, it happened in this little village on the Batangan Peninsula, and it was raining like crazy, and one night a guy named Stink Harris woke up screaming with a leech on his tongue. You can tell a true war story if you just keep on telling it.

And in the end, of course, a true war story is never about war. It's about sunlight. It's about the special way that dawn spreads out on a river when you know you must cross the river and march into the mountains and do things you are afraid to do. It's about love and memory. It's about sorrow. It's about sisters who never write back and people who never listen.

The Dentist

When Curt Lemon was killed, I found it hard to mourn. I knew him only slightly, and what I did know was not impressive. He had a tendency to play the tough soldier role, always posturing, always puffing himself up, and on occasion he took it way too far. It's true that he pulled off some dangerous stunts, even a few that seemed plain crazy, like the time he painted up his body and put on a ghost mask and went out trick- or-treating on Halloween. But afterward he couldn't stop bragging. He kept replaying his own exploits, tacking on little flourishes that never happened. He had an opinion of himself, I think, that was too high for his own good. Or maybe it was the reverse. Maybe it was a low opinion that he kept trying to erase.

In any case, it's easy to get sentimental about the dead, and to guard against that I want to tell a quick Curt Lemon story.

In February we were working an area of operations called the Rocket Pocket, which got its name from the fact that the enemy sometimes used the place to launch rocket attacks on the airfield at Chu Lai. But for us it was like a two-week vacation. The AO lay along the South China Sea, where things had the feel of a resort, with white beaches and palm trees and friendly little villages. It was a quiet time. No casualties, no contact at all. As usual, though, the higher-ups couldn't leave well enough alone, and one afternoon an Army dentist was choppered in to check our teeth and do minor repair work. He was a tall, skinny young captain with bad breath. For a half hour he lectured us on oral hygiene, demonstrating the proper flossing and brushing techniques, then afterward he opened up shop in a small field tent and we all took turns going in for personal exams. At best it was a very primitive setup. There was a battery- powered drill, a canvas cot, a bucket of sea water for rinsing, a metal suitcase full of the various instruments. It amounted to assembly-line dentistry, quick and impersonal, and the young captain's main concern seemed to be the clock.

As we sat waiting, Curt Lemon began to tense up. He kept fidgeting, playing with his dog tags. Finally somebody asked what the problem was, and Lemon looked down at his hands and said that back in high school he'd had a couple of bad experiences with dentists. Real sadism, he said. Torture chamber stuff. He didn't mind blood or pain—he actually enjoyed combat—but there was something about a dentist that just gave him the creeps. He glanced over at the field tent and said, "No way. Count me out. Nobody messes with *these* teeth."

But a few minutes later, when the dentist called his name, Lemon stood up and walked into the tent. It was over fast. He fainted even before the man touched him.

Four of us had to hoist him up and lay him on the cot. When he came to, there was a funny new look on his face, almost sheepish, as if he'd been caught committing some terrible crime. He wouldn't talk to anyone. For the rest of the day he stayed off by himself, sitting alone under a tree, just staring down at the field tent. He seemed a little dazed. Now and then we could hear him cussing, bawling himself out. Anyone else would've laughed it off, but for Curt Lemon it was too much. The embarrassment must've turned a screw in his head. Late that night he crept down to the dental tent. He switched on a flashlight, woke up the young captain, and told him he had a monster toothache. A killer, he said—like a nail in his jaw. The dentist couldn't find any problem, but Lemon kept insisting, so the man finally shrugged and shot in the Novocain and yanked out a perfectly good tooth. There was some pain, no doubt, but in the morning Curt Lemon was all smiles.

Sweetheart of the Song Tra Bong

Vietnam was full of strange stories, some improbable, some well beyond that, but the stories that will last forever are those that swirl back and forth across the border between trivia and bedlam, the mad and the mundane. This one keeps returning to me. I heard it from Rat Kiley, who swore up and down to its truth, although in the end, I'll admit, that doesn't amount to much of a warranty. Among the men in Alpha Company, Rat had a reputation for exaggeration and overstatement, a compulsion to rev up the facts, and for most of us it was normal procedure to discount sixty or seventy percent of anything he had to say. If Rat told you, for example, that he'd slept with four girls one night, you could figure it was about a girl and a half. It wasn't a question of deceit. Just the opposite: he wanted to heat up the truth, to make it burn so hot that you would feel exactly what he felt. For Rat Kiley, I think, facts were formed by sensation, not the other way around, and when you listened to one of his stories, you'd find yourself performing rapid calculations in your head, subtracting superlatives, figuring the square root of an absolute and then multiplying by maybe.

Still, with this particular story, Rat never backed down. He claimed to have witnessed the incident with his own eyes, and I remember how upset he became one morning when Mitchell Sanders challenged him on its basic premise.

"It can't happen," Sanders said. "Nobody ships his honey over to Nam. It don't ring true. I mean, you just can't import your own personal poontang."

Rat shook his head. "I saw it, man. I was right there. This guy did it."

"His girlfriend?"

"Straight on. It's a fact." Rat's voice squeaked a little. He paused and looked at his hands. "Listen, the guy sends her the money. Flies her over. This cute blonde—just a kid, just barely out of high school—she shows up with a suitcase and one of those plastic cosmetic bags. Comes right out to the boonies. I swear to God, man, she's got on culottes. White culottes and this sexy pink sweater. There she is."

I remember Mitchell Sanders folding his arms. He looked over at me for a second, not quite grinning, not saying a word, but I could read the amusement in his eyes.

Rat saw it, too.

"No lie," he muttered. "Culottes."

When he first arrived in-country, before joining Alpha Company, Rat had been assigned to a small medical detachment up in the mountains west of Chu Lai, near the village of Tra Bong, where along with eight other enlisted men he ran an aid station that provided basic emergency and trauma care. Casualties were flown in by helicopter, stabilized, then shipped out to hospitals in Chu Lai or Danang. It was gory work, Rat said, but predictable. Amputations, mostly—legs and feet. The area was heavily mined, thick with Bouncing Betties and homemade booby traps. For a medic, though, it was ideal duty, and Rat counted himself lucky. There was plenty of cold beer, three hot meals a day, a tin roof over his head. No humping at all. No officers, either. You could let your hair grow, he said, and you didn't have to polish your boots or snap off salutes or put up with the usual rear-echelon nonsense. The highest ranking NCO was an E-6 named Eddie Diamond, whose pleasures ran from dope to Darvon, and except for a rare field inspection there was no such thing as military discipline.

As Rat described it, the compound was situated at the top of a flat-crested hill along the northern outskirts of Tra Bong. At one end was a small dirt helipad; at the other end, in a rough semicircle, the mess hall and medical hootches overlooked a river called the Song Tra Bong. Surrounding the place were tangled rolls of concertina wire, with bunkers and reinforced firing positions at staggered intervals, and base security was provided by a mixed unit of RFs, PFs, and ARVN infantry. Which is to say virtually no security at all. As soldiers, the ARVNs were useless; the Ruff-and-Puffs were outright dangerous. And yet even with decent troops the place was clearly indefensible. To the north and west the country rose up in thick walls of wilderness, triple-canopied jungle, mountains unfolding into higher mountains, ravines and gorges and fast-moving rivers and waterfalls and exotic butterflies and steep cliffs and smoky little hamlets and great valleys of bamboo and elephant grass. Originally, in the early 1960s, the place had been set up as a Special Forces outpost, and when Rat Kiley arrived nearly a decade later, a squad of six Green Berets still used the compound as a base of operations. The Greenies were not social animals. Animals, Rat said, but far from social. They had their own hootch at the edge of the perimeter, fortified with sandbags and a metal fence, and except for the bare essentials they avoided contact with the medical detachment. Secretive and suspicious, loners by nature, the six Greenies would sometimes vanish for days at a time, or even weeks, then late in the night they would just as magically reappear, moving like shadows through the moonlight, filing in silently from the dense rain forest off to the west. Among the medics there were jokes about this, but no one asked questions.

While the outpost was isolated and vulnerable, Rat said, he always felt a curious sense of safety there. Nothing much ever happened. The place was never mortared, never taken under fire, and the war seemed to be somewhere far away. On occasion, when casualties came in, there were quick spurts of activity, but otherwise the days flowed by without incident, a smooth and peaceful time. Most mornings were spent on the volleyball court. In the heat of midday the men would head for the shade, lazing away the long afternoons, and after sundown there were movies and card games and sometimes all-night drinking sessions.

It was during one of those late nights that Eddie Diamond first brought up the tantalizing possibility. It was an offhand comment. A joke, really. What they should do, Eddie said, was pool some bucks and bring in a few mama-sans from Saigon, spice things up, and after a moment one of the men laughed and said, "Our own little EM club," and somebody else said, "Hey, yeah, we pay our fuckin' dues, don't we?" It was nothing serious. Just passing time, playing with the possibilities, and so for a while they tossed the idea around, how you could actually get away with it, no officers or anything, nobody to clamp down, then they dropped the subject and moved on to cars and baseball.

Later in the night, though, a young medic named Mark Fossie kept coming back to the subject. "Look, if you think about it," he said, "it's not that crazy. You could actually do it."

"Do what?" Rat said.

"You know. Bring in a girl. I mean, what's the problem?" Rat shrugged. "Nothing. A war."

"Well, see, that's the thing," Mark Fossie said. "No war *here*. You could really do it. A pair of solid brass balls, that's all you'd need."

There was some laughter, and Eddie Diamond told him he'd best strap down his dick, but Fossie just frowned and looked at the ceiling for a while and then went off to write a letter.

Six weeks later his girlfriend showed up.

The way Rat told it, she came in by helicopter along with the daily resupply shipment out of Chu Lai. A tall, big-boned blonde. At best, Rat said, she was seventeen years old, fresh out of Cleveland Heights Senior High. She had long white legs and blue eyes and a complexion like strawberry ice cream. Very friendly, too.

At the helipad that morning, Mark Fossie grinned and put his arm around her and said, "Guys, this is Mary Anne."

The girl seemed tired and somewhat lost, but she smiled.

There was a heavy silence. Eddie Diamond, the ranking NCO, made a small motion with his hand, and some of the others murmured a word or two, then they watched Mark Fossie pick up her suitcase and lead her by the arm down to the hootches. For a long while the men were quiet.

"That fucker," somebody finally said.

At evening chow Mark Fossie explained how he'd set it up. It was expensive, he admitted, and the logistics were complicated, but it wasn't like going to the moon. Cleveland to Los Angeles, LA to Bangkok, Bangkok to Saigon. She'd hopped a C-130 up to Chu Lai and stayed overnight at the USO and the next morning hooked a ride west with the resupply chopper.

"A cinch," Fossie said, and gazed down at his pretty girlfriend. "Thing is, you just got to *want* it enough."

Mary Anne Bell and Mark Fossie had been sweethearts since grammar school. From the sixth grade on they had known for a fact that someday they would be married, and live in a fine gingerbread house near Lake Erie, and have three healthy yellow-haired children, and grow old together, and no doubt die in each other's arms and be buried in the same walnut casket. That was the plan. They were very much in love, full of dreams, and in the ordinary flow of their lives the whole scenario might well have come true.

On the first night they set up house in one of the bunkers along the perimeter, near the Special Forces hootch, and over the next two weeks they stuck together like a pair of high school steadies. It was almost disgusting, Rat said, the way they mooned over each other. Always holding hands, always laughing over some private joke. All they needed, he said, were a couple of matching sweaters. But among the medics there was some envy. It was Vietnam, after all, and Mary Anne Bell was an attractive girl. Too wide in the shoulders, maybe, but she had terrific legs, a bubbly personality, a happy smile. The men genuinely liked her. Out on the volleyball court she wore cut-off blue jeans and a black swimsuit top, which the guys appreciated, and in the evenings she liked to dance to music from Rat's portable tape deck. There was a novelty to it; she was good for morale. At times she gave off a kind of come-get-me energy, coy and flirtatious, but apparently it never bothered Mark Fossie. In fact he seemed to enjoy it, just grinning at her, because he was so much in love, and because it was the sort of show that a girl will sometimes put on for her boyfriend's entertainment and education.

Though she was young, Rat said, Mary Anne Bell was no timid child. She was curious about things. During her first days in-country she liked to roam around the compound asking questions: What exactly was a trip flare? How did a Claymore work? What was behind those scary green mountains to the west? Then she'd squint and listen quietly while somebody filled her in. She had a good quick mind. She paid attention. Often, especially during the hot afternoons, she would spend time with the ARVNs out along the perimeter, picking up little phrases of Vietnamese, learning how to cook rice over a can of Sterno, how to eat with her hands. The guys sometimes liked to kid her about it—our own little native, they'd say—but Mary Anne would just smile and stick out her tongue. "I'm here," she'd say, "I might as well learn something."

The war intrigued her. The land, too, and the mystery. At the beginning of her second week she began pestering Mark Fossie to take her down to the village at the foot of the hill. In a quiet voice, very patiently, he tried to tell her that it was a bad idea, way too dangerous, but Mary Anne kept after him. She wanted to get a feel for how people lived, what the smells and customs were. It did not impress her that the VC owned the place.

"Listen, it can't be that bad," she said. "They're human beings, aren't they? Like everybody else?"

Fossie nodded. He loved her.

And so in the morning Rat Kiley and two other medics tagged along as security while Mark and Mary Anne strolled through the ville like a pair of tourists. If the girl was nervous, she didn't show it. She seemed comfortable and entirely at home; the hostile atmosphere did not seem to register. All morning Mary Anne chattered away about how quaint the place was, how she loved the thatched roofs and naked children, the wonderful simplicity of village life. A strange thing to watch, Rat said. This seventeen-year-old doll in her goddamn culottes, perky and fresh-faced, like a cheerleader visiting the opposing team's locker room. Her pretty blue eyes seemed to glow. She couldn't get enough of it. On their way back up to the compound she stopped for a swim in the Song Tra Bong, stripping down to her underwear, showing off her legs while Fossie tried to explain to her about things like ambushes and snipers and the stopping power of an AK-47.

The guys, though, were impressed.

"A real tiger," said Eddie Diamond. "D-cup guts, trainer-bra brains." "She'll learn," somebody said.

Eddie Diamond gave a solemn nod. "There's the scary part. I promise you, this girl will most definitely learn."

In parts, at least, it was a funny story, and yet to hear Rat Kiley tell it you'd almost think it was intended as straight tragedy. He never smiled. Not even at the crazy stuff. There was always a dark, far-off look in his eyes, a kind of sadness, as if he were troubled by something sliding beneath the story's surface. Whenever we laughed, I remember, he'd sigh and wait it out, but the one thing he could not tolerate was disbelief. He'd get edgy if someone questioned one of the details. "She *wasn't* dumb," he'd snap. "I never said that. Young, that's all I said. Like you and me. A *girl*, that's the only difference, and I'll tell you something: it didn't amount to jack. I mean, when we first got here—all of us—we were real young and innocent, full of romantic bullshit, but we learned pretty damn quick. And so did Mary Anne."

Rat would peer down at his hands, silent and thoughtful. After a moment his voice would flatten out.

"You don't believe it?" he'd say. "Fine with me. But you don't know human nature. You don't know Nam."

Then he'd tell us to listen up.

A good sharp mind, Rat said. True, she could be silly sometimes, but she picked up on things fast. At the end of the second week, when four casualties came in, Mary Anne wasn't afraid to get her hands bloody. At times, in fact, she seemed fascinated by it. Not the gore so much, but the adrenaline buzz that went with the job, that quick hot rush in your veins when the choppers settled down and you had to do things fast and right. No time for sorting through options, no thinking at all; you just stuck your hands in and started plugging up holes. She was quiet and steady. She didn't back off from the ugly cases. Over the next day or two, as more casualties trickled in, she learned how to clip an artery and pump up a plastic splint and shoot in morphine. In times of action her face took on a sudden new composure, almost serene, the fuzzy blue eyes narrowing into a tight, intelligent focus. Mark Fossie would grin at this. He was proud, yes, but also amazed. A different person, it seemed, and he wasn't sure what to make of it.

Other things, too. The way she quickly fell into the habits of the bush. No cosmetics, no fingernail filing. She stopped wearing jewelry, cut her hair short and wrapped it in a dark green bandanna. Hygiene became a matter of small consequence. In her second week Eddie Diamond taught her how to disassemble an M-16, how the various parts worked, and from there it was a natural progression to learning how to use the weapon. For hours at a time she plunked away at C-ration cans, a bit unsure of herself, but as it turned out she had a real knack for it. There was a new confidence in her voice, a new authority in the way she carried herself. In many ways she remained naive and immature, still a kid, but Cleveland Heights now seemed very far away.

Once or twice, gently, Mark Fossie suggested that it might be time to think about heading home, but Mary Anne laughed and told him to forget it. "Everything I want," she said, "is right here."

She stroked his arm, and then kissed him.

On one level things remained the same between them. They slept together. They held hands and made plans for after the war. But now there was a new imprecision in the way Mary Anne expressed her thoughts on certain subjects. Not necessarily three kids, she'd say. Not necessarily a house on Lake Erie. "Naturally we'll still get married," she'd tell him, "but it doesn't have to be right away. Maybe travel first. Maybe live together. Just test it out, you know?"

Mark Fossie would nod at this, even smile and agree, but it made him uncomfortable. He couldn't pin it down. Her body seemed foreign somehow—too stiff in places, too firm where the softness used to be. The bubbliness was gone. The nervous giggling, too. When she laughed now, which was rare, it was only when something struck her as truly funny. Her voice seemed to reorganize itself at a lower pitch. In the evenings, while the men played cards, she would sometimes fall into long elastic silences, her eyes fixed on the dark, her arms folded, her foot tapping out a coded message against the floor. When Fossie asked about it one evening, Mary Anne looked at him for a long moment and then shrugged. "It's nothing," she said. "Really nothing. To tell the truth, I've never been happier in my whole life. Never."

Twice, though, she came in late at night. Very late. And then finally she did not come in at all.

Rat Kiley heard about it from Fossie himself. Before dawn one morning, the kid shook him awake. He was in bad shape. His voice seemed hollow and stuffed up, nasal-sounding, as if he had a bad cold. He held a flashlight in his hand, clicking it on and off.

"Mary Anne," he whispered, "I can't *find* her."

Rat sat up and rubbed his face. Even in the dim light it was clear that the boy was in trouble. There were dark smudges under his eyes, the frayed edges of somebody who hadn't slept in a while.

"Gone," Fossie said. "Rat, listen, she's sleeping with somebody. Last night, she didn't even . . . I don't know what to *do*."

Abruptly then, Fossie seemed to collapse. He squatted down, rocking on his heels, still clutching the flashlight. Just a boy—eighteen years old. Tall and blond. A gifted athlete. A nice kid, too, polite and good-hearted, although for the moment none of it seemed to be serving him well.

He kept clicking the flashlight on and off.

"All right, start at the start," Rat said. "Nice and slow. Sleeping with who?"

"I don't know who. Eddie Diamond." "Eddie?"

"Has to be. The guy's always there, always hanging on her."

Rat shook his head. "Man, I don't know. Can't say it strikes a right note, not with Eddie."

"Yes, but he's—"

"Easy does it," Rat said. He reached out and tapped the boy's shoulder. "Why not just check some bunks? We got nine guys. You and me, that's two, so there's seven possibles. Do a quick body count."

Fossie hesitated. "But I can't . . . If she's there, I mean, if she's with somebody—"

"Oh, Christ."

Rat pushed himself up. He took the flashlight, muttered something, and moved down to the far end of the hootch. For privacy, the men had rigged up curtained walls around their cots, small makeshift bedrooms, and in the dark Rat went quickly from room to room, using the flashlight to pluck out the faces. Eddie Diamond slept a hard deep sleep—the others, too. To be sure, though, Rat checked once more, very carefully, then he reported back to Fossie.

"All accounted for. No extras." "Eddie?"

"Darvon dreams." Rat switched off the flashlight and tried to think it out. "Maybe she just—I don't know—maybe she camped out tonight. Under the stars or something. You search the compound?"

"Sure I did."

"Well, come on," Rat said. "One more time."

Outside, a soft violet light was spreading out across the eastern hillsides. Two or three ARVN soldiers had built their breakfast fires, but the place was mostly quiet and unmoving. They tried the helipad first, then the mess hall and supply hootches, then they walked the entire six hundred meters of perimeter.

"Okay," Rat finally said. "We got a problem."

When he first told the story, Rat stopped there and looked at Mitchell Sanders for a time.

"So what's your vote? Where was she?" "The Greenies," Sanders said.

"Yeah?"

Sanders smiled. "No other option. That stuff about the Special Forces—how they used the place as a base of operations, how they'd glide in and out—all that had to be there for a *reason*. That's how stories work, man."

Rat thought about it, then shrugged.

"All right, sure, the Greenies. But it's not what Fossie thought. She wasn't sleeping with any of them. At least not exactly. I mean, in a way she was sleeping with *all* of them, more or less, except it wasn't sex or anything. They was just lying together, so to speak, Mary Anne and these six grungy weirded-out Green Berets."

"Lying down?" Sanders said. "You got it."

"Lying down how?"

Rat smiled. "Ambush. All night long, man, Mary Anne's out on fuckin'
ambush."

Just after sunrise, Rat said, she came trooping in through the wire, tired-looking but cheerful as she dropped her gear and gave Mark Fossie a brisk hug. The six Green Berets did not speak. One of them nodded at her, and the others gave Fossie a long stare, then they filed off to their hootch at the edge of the compound.

"Please," she said. "Not a word."

Fossie took a half step forward and hesitated. It was as though he had trouble recognizing her. She wore a bush hat and filthy green fatigues; she carried the standard M-16 automatic assault rifle; her face was black with charcoal.

Mary Anne handed him the weapon. "I'm exhausted," she said. "We'll talk later."

She glanced over at the Special Forces area, then turned and walked quickly across the compound toward her own bunker. Fossie stood still for a few seconds. A little dazed, it seemed. After a moment, though, he set his jaw and whispered something and went after her with a hard, fast stride.

"Not later!" he yelled. "Now!"

What happened between them, Rat said, nobody ever knew for sure. But in the mess hall that evening it was clear that an accommodation had been reached. Or more likely, he said, it was a case of setting down some new rules. Mary Anne's hair was freshly shampooed. She wore a white blouse, a navy blue skirt, a pair of plain black flats. Over dinner she kept her eyes down, poking at her food, subdued to the point of silence. Eddie Diamond and some of the others tried to nudge her into talking about the ambush—What was the feeling out there? What exactly did she see and hear?—but the questions seemed to give her trouble. Nervously, she'd look across the table at Fossie. She'd wait a moment, as if to receive some sort of clearance, then she'd bow her head and mumble out a vague word or two. There were no real answers.

Mark Fossie, too, had little to say.

"Nobody's business," he told Rat that night. Then he offered a brief smile. "One thing for sure, though, there won't be any more ambushes. No more late nights."

"You laid down the law?"

"Compromise," Fossie said. "I'll put it this way—we're officially engaged."

Rat nodded cautiously.

"Well hey, she'll make a sweet bride," he said. "Combat ready."

Over the next several days there was a strained, tightly wound quality to the way they treated each other, a rigid correctness that was enforced by repetitive acts of willpower. To look at them from a distance, Rat said, you would think they were the happiest two people on the planet. They spent the long afternoons sunbathing together, stretched out side by side on top of their bunker, or playing backgammon in the shade of a giant palm tree, or just sitting quietly. A model of togetherness, it seemed. And yet at close range their faces showed the tension. Too polite, too thoughtful. Mark Fossie tried hard to keep up a self-assured pose, as if nothing had ever come between them, or ever could, but there was a fragility to it, something tentative and false. If Mary Anne happened to move a few steps away from him, even briefly, he'd tighten up and force himself not to watch her. But then a moment later he'd be watching.

In the presence of others, at least, they kept on their masks. Over meals they talked about plans for a huge wedding in Cleveland Heights— a two-day bash, lots of flowers. And yet even then their smiles seemed too intense. They were too quick with their banter; they held hands as if afraid to let go.

It had to end, and eventually it did.

Near the end of the third week Fossie began making arrangements to send her home. At first, Rat said, Mary Anne seemed to accept it, but then after a day or two she fell into a restless gloom, sitting off by herself at the edge of the perimeter. She would not speak. Shoulders hunched, her blue eyes opaque, she seemed to disappear inside herself. A couple of times Fossie approached her and tried to talk it out, but Mary Anne just stared out at the dark green mountains to the west. The wilderness seemed to draw her in. A haunted look, Rat said—partly terror, partly rapture. It was as if she had come up on the edge of something, as if she were caught in that no-man's-land between Cleveland Heights and deep jungle. Seventeen years old. Just a child, blond and innocent, but then weren't they all?

The next morning she was gone. The six Greenies were gone, too.

In a way, Rat said, poor Fossie expected it, or something like it, but that did not help much with the pain. The kid couldn't function. The grief took him by the throat and squeezed and would not let go.

"Lost," he kept whispering.

It was nearly three weeks before she returned. But in a sense she never returned. Not entirely, not all of her.

By chance, Rat said, he was awake to see it. A damp misty night, he couldn't sleep, so he'd gone outside for a quick smoke. He was just standing there, he said, watching the moon, and then off to the west a column of silhouettes appeared as if by magic at the edge of the jungle. At first he didn't recognize her—a small, soft shadow among six other shadows. There was no sound. No real substance either. The seven silhouettes seemed to float across the surface of the earth, like spirits, vaporous and unreal. As he watched, Rat said, it made him think of some weird opium dream. The silhouettes moved without moving. Silently, one by one, they came up the hill, passed through the wire, and drifted in a loose file across the compound. It was then, Rat said, that he picked out Mary Anne's face. Her eyes seemed to shine in the dark—not blue, though, but a bright glowing jungle green. She did not pause at Fossie's bunker. She cradled her weapon and moved swiftly to the Special Forces hootch and followed the others inside.

Briefly, a light came on, and someone laughed, then the place went dark again.

Whenever he told the story, Rat had a tendency to stop now and then, interrupting the flow, inserting little clarifications or bits of analysis and personal opinion. It was a bad habit, Mitchell Sanders said, because all that matters is the raw material, the stuff itself, and you can't clutter it up with your own half-baked commentary. That just breaks the spell. It destroys the magic. What you have to do, Sanders said, is trust your own story. Get the hell out of the way and let it tell itself.

But Rat Kiley couldn't help it. He wanted to bracket the full range of meaning.

"I know it sounds far-out," he'd tell us, "but it's not like *impossible* or anything. We all heard plenty of wackier stories. Some guy comes back from the bush, tells you he saw the Virgin Mary out there, she was riding a goddamn goose or something. Everybody buys it. Everybody smiles and asks how fast was they going, did she have spurs on. Well, it's not like that. This Mary Anne wasn't no virgin but at least she was real. I saw it. When she came in through the wire that night, I was right there, I saw those eyes of hers, I saw how she wasn't even the same person no more. What's so impossible about that? She was a girl, that's all. I mean, if it was a guy, everybody'd say, Hey, no big deal, he got caught up in the Nam shit, he got seduced by the Greenies. See what I mean? You got these blinders on about women. How gentle and peaceful they are. All that crap about how if we had a pussy for president there wouldn't be no more wars. Pure garbage. You got to get rid of that sexist attitude."

Rat would go on like that until Mitchell Sanders couldn't tolerate it any longer. It offended his inner ear.

"The story," Sanders would say. "The whole tone, man, you're wrecking it."

"Tone?"

"The *sound*. You need to get a consistent sound, like slow or fast, funny or sad. All these digressions, they just screw up your story's *sound*. Stick to what happened."

Frowning, Rat would close his eyes.

"Tone?" he'd say. "I didn't know it was all that complicated. The girl joined the zoo. One more animal—end of story."

"Yeah, fine. But tell it right."

At daybreak the next morning, when Mark Fossie heard she was back, he stationed himself outside the fenced-off Special Forces area. All morning he waited for her, and all afternoon. Around dusk Rat brought him something to eat.

"She has to come out," Fossie said. "Sooner or later, she has to." "Or else what?" Rat said.

"I go get her. I bring her out."

Rat shook his head. "Your decision. I was you, though, no way I'd mess around with any Greenie types, not for nothing."

"It's Mary Anne in there."

"Sure, I know that. All the same, I'd knock real extra super polite."

Even with the cooling night air Fossie's face was slick with sweat. He looked sick. His eyes were bloodshot; his skin had a whitish, almost colorless cast. For a few minutes Rat waited with him, quietly watching the hootch, then he patted the kid's shoulder and left him alone.

It was after midnight when Rat and Eddie Diamond went out to check on him. The night had gone cold and steamy, a low fog sliding down from the mountains, and somewhere out in the dark they heard music playing. Not loud but not soft either. It had a chaotic, almost unmusical sound, without rhythm or form or progression, like the noise of nature. A synthesizer, it seemed, or maybe an electric organ. In the background, just audible, a woman's voice was half singing, half chanting, but the lyrics seemed to be in a foreign tongue.

They found Fossie squatting near the gate in front of the Special Forces area. Head bowed, he was swaying to the music, his face wet and shiny. As Eddie bent down beside him, the kid looked up with dull eyes, ashen and powdery, not quite in register.

"Hear that?" he whispered. "You *hear*? It's Mary Anne."

Eddie Diamond took his arm. "Let's get you inside. Somebody's radio, that's all it is. Move it now."

"Mary Anne. Just listen." "Sure, but—"

"Listen!"

Fossie suddenly pulled away, twisting sideways, and fell back against the gate. He lay there with his eyes closed. The music—the noise, whatever it was—came from the hootch beyond the fence. The place was dark except for a small glowing window, which stood partly open, the panes dancing in bright reds and yellows as though the glass were on fire. The chanting seemed louder now. Fiercer, too, and higher pitched.

Fossie pushed himself up. He wavered for a moment then forced the gate open.

"That voice," he said. "Mary Anne."

Rat took a step forward, reaching out for him, but Fossie was already moving fast toward the hootch. He stumbled once, caught himself, and hit the door hard with both arms. There was a noise—a short screeching sound, like a cat—and the door swung in and Fossie was framed there for an instant, his arms stretched out, then he slipped inside. After a moment Rat and Eddie followed quietly. Just inside the door they found Fossie bent down on one knee. He wasn't moving.

Across the room a dozen candles were burning on the floor near the open window. The place seemed to echo with a weird deep-wilderness sound—tribal music—bamboo flutes and drums and chimes. But what hit you first, Rat said, was the smell. Two kinds of smells. There was a topmost scent of joss sticks and incense, like the fumes of some exotic smokehouse, but beneath the smoke lay a deeper and much more powerful stench. Impossible to describe, Rat said. It paralyzed your lungs. Thick and numbing, like an animal's den, a mix of blood and scorched hair and excrement and the sweet-sour odor of moldering flesh—the stink of the kill. But that wasn't all. On a post at the rear of the hootch was the decayed head of a large black leopard; strips of yellow- brown skin dangled from the overhead rafters. And bones. Stacks of bones—all kinds. To one side, propped up against a wall, stood a poster in neat black lettering: assemble your own gook!!. free sample kit!!. The images came in a swirl, Rat said, and there was no way you could process it all. Off in the gloom a few dim figures lounged in hammocks, or on cots, but none of them moved or spoke. The background music came from a tape deck near the circle of candles, but the high voice was Mary Anne's.

After a second Mark Fossie made a soft moaning sound. He started to get up but then stiffened.

"Mary Anne?" he said.

Quietly then, she stepped out of the shadows. At least for a moment she seemed to be the same pretty young girl who had arrived a few weeks earlier. She was barefoot. She wore her pink sweater and a white blouse and a simple cotton skirt.

For a long while the girl gazed down at Fossie, almost blankly, and in the candlelight her face had the composure of someone perfectly at peace with herself. It took a few seconds, Rat said, to appreciate the full change. In part it was her eyes: utterly flat and indifferent. There was no emotion in her stare, no sense of the person behind it. But the grotesque part, he said, was her jewelry. At the girl's throat was a necklace of human tongues. Elongated and narrow, like pieces of blackened leather, the tongues were threaded along a length of copper wire, one overlapping the next, the tips curled upward as if caught in a final shrill syllable.

Briefly, it seemed, the girl smiled at Mark Fossie.

"There's no sense talking," she said. "I know what you think, but it's not . . . it's not *bad*."

"Bad?" Fossie murmured. "It's not."

In the shadows there was laughter.

One of the Greenies sat up and lighted a cigar. The others lay silent. "You're in a place," Mary Anne said softly, "where you don't belong."

She moved her hand in a gesture that encompassed not just the hootch but everything around it, the entire war, the mountains, the mean little villages, the trails and trees and rivers and deep misted-over valleys.

"You just don't *know*," she said. "You hide in this little fortress, behind wire and sandbags, and you don't know what it's all about. Sometimes I want to eat this place. Vietnam. I want to swallow the whole country—the dirt, the death—I just want to eat it and have it there inside me. That's how I feel. It's like . . . this appetite. I get scared sometimes—lots of times—but it's not *bad*. You know? I feel close to myself. When I'm out there at night, I feel close to my own body, I can feel my blood moving, my skin and my fingernails, everything, it's like I'm full of electricity and I'm glowing in the dark—I'm on fire almost—I'm burning away into nothing—but it doesn't matter because I know exactly who I am. You can't feel like that anywhere else."

All this was said softly, as if to herself, her voice slow and impassive. She was not trying to persuade. For a few moments she looked at Mark Fossie, who seemed to shrink away, then she turned and moved back into the gloom.

There was nothing to be done.

Rat took Fossie's arm, helped him up, and led him outside. In the darkness there was that weird tribal music, which seemed to come from the earth itself, from the deep rain forest, and a woman's voice rising up in a language beyond translation.

Mark Fossie stood rigid.

"Do something," he whispered. "I can't just let her go like that." Rat listened for a time, then shook his head.

"Man, you must be deaf. She's already gone."

Rat Kiley stopped there, almost in midsentence, which drove Mitchell Sanders crazy.

"What next?" he said. "Next?"

"The girl. What happened to her?"

Rat made a small, tired motion with his shoulders. "Hard to tell for sure. Maybe three, four days later I got orders to report here to Alpha Company. Jumped the first chopper out, that's the last I ever seen of the place. Mary Anne, too."

Mitchell Sanders stared at him. "You can't do that."

"Do what?"

"Jesus Christ, it's against the *rules*," Sanders said.

"Against human *nature*. This elaborate story, you can't say, Hey, by the way, I don't know the *ending*. I mean, you got certain obligations."

Rat gave a quick smile. "Patience, man. Up to now, everything I told you is from personal experience, the exact truth, but there's a few other things I heard secondhand. Thirdhand, actually. From here on it gets to be . . . I don't know what the word is."

"Speculation."

"Yeah, right." Rat looked off to the west, scanning the mountains, as if expecting something to appear on one of the high ridgelines. After a second he shrugged. "Anyhow, maybe two months later I ran into Eddie Diamond over in Bangkok—I was on R&R, just this fluke thing—and he told me some stuff I can't vouch for with my own eyes. Even Eddie didn't really see it. He heard it from one of the Greenies, so you got to take this with a whole shakerful of salt."

Once more, Rat searched the mountains, then he sat back and closed his eyes.

"You know," he said abruptly, "I loved her." "Say again?"

"A lot. We all did, I guess. The way she looked, Mary Anne made you think about those girls back home, how clean and innocent they all are, how they'll never understand any of this, not in a billion years. Try to tell them about it, they'll just stare at you with those big round candy eyes. They won't understand zip. It's like trying to tell somebody what chocolate tastes like."

Mitchell Sanders nodded. "Or shit."

"There it is, you got to taste it, and that's the thing with Mary Anne. She was *there*. She was up to her eyeballs in it. After the war, man, I promise you, you won't find nobody like her."

Suddenly, Rat pushed up to his feet, moved a few steps away from us, then stopped and stood with his back turned. He was an emotional guy.

"Got hooked, I guess," he said. "I loved her. So when I heard from Eddie about what happened, it almost made me . . . Like you say, it's pure speculation."

"Go on," Mitchell Sanders said. "Finish up."

What happened to her, Rat said, was what happened to all of them. You come over clean and you get dirty and then afterward it's never the same. A question of degree. Some make it intact, some don't make it at all. For Mary Anne Bell, it seemed, Vietnam had the effect of a powerful drug: that mix of unnamed terror and unnamed pleasure that comes as the needle slips in and you know you're risking something. The endorphins start to flow, and the adrenaline, and you hold your breath and creep quietly through the moonlit nightscapes; you become intimate with danger; you're in touch with the far side of yourself, as though it's another hemisphere, and you want to string it out and go wherever the trip takes you and be host to all the possibilities inside yourself. Not *bad*, she'd said. Vietnam made her glow in the dark. She wanted more, she wanted to penetrate deeper into the mystery of herself, and after a time the wanting became needing, which turned then to craving.

According to Eddie Diamond, who heard it from one of the Greenies, she took a greedy pleasure in night patrols. She was good at it; she had the moves. All camouflaged up, her face smooth and vacant, she seemed to flow like water through the dark, like oil, without sound or center. She went barefoot. She stopped carrying a weapon. There were times, apparently, when she took crazy, death-wish chances—things that even the Greenies balked at. It was as if she were taunting some wild creature out in the bush, or in her head, inviting it to show itself, a curious game of hide-and-go-seek that was played out in the dense terrain of a nightmare. She was lost inside herself. On occasion, when they were taken under fire, Mary Anne would stand quietly and watch the tracer rounds snap by, a little smile at her lips, intent on some private transaction with the war. Other times she would simply vanish altogether—for hours, for days.

And then one morning, all alone, Mary Anne walked off into the mountains and did not come back.

No body was ever found. No equipment, no clothing. For all he knew, Rat said, the girl was still alive. Maybe up in one of the high mountain villes, maybe with the Montagnard tribes. But that was guesswork.

There was an inquiry, of course, and a week-long air search, and for a time the Tra Bong compound went crazy with MP and CID types. In the end, however, nothing came of it. It was a war and the war went on. Mark Fossie was busted to PFC, shipped back to a hospital in the States, and two months later received a medical discharge. Mary Anne Bell joined the missing.

But the story did not end there. If you believed the Greenies, Rat said, Mary Anne was still somewhere out there in the dark. Odd movements, odd shapes. Late at night, when the Greenies were out on ambush, the whole rain forest seemed to stare in at them—a watched feeling—and a couple of times they almost saw her sliding through the shadows. Not quite, but almost. She had crossed to the other side. She was part of the land. She was wearing her culottes, her pink sweater, and a necklace of human tongues. She was dangerous. She was ready for the kill.

Stockings

Henry Dobbins was a good man, and a superb soldier, but sophistication was not his strong suit. The ironies went beyond him. In many ways he was like America itself, big and strong, full of good intentions, a roll of fat jiggling at his belly, slow of foot but always plodding along, always there when you needed him, a believer in the virtues of simplicity and directness and hard labor. Like his country, too, Dobbins was drawn toward sentimentality.

Even now, twenty years later, I can see him wrapping his girlfriend's pantyhose around his neck before heading out on ambush.

It was his one eccentricity. The pantyhose, he said, had the properties of a good-luck charm. He liked putting his nose into the nylon and breathing in the scent of his girlfriend's body; he liked the memories this inspired; he sometimes slept with the stockings up against his face, the way an infant sleeps with a flannel blanket, secure and peaceful. More than anything, though, the stockings were a talisman for him. They kept him safe. They gave access to a spiritual world, where things were soft and intimate, a place where he might someday take his girlfriend to live. Like many of us in Vietnam, Dobbins felt the pull of superstition, and he believed firmly and absolutely in the protective power of the stockings. They were like body armor, he thought. Whenever we saddled up for a late-night ambush, putting on our helmets and flak jackets, Henry Dobbins would make a ritual out of arranging the nylons around his neck, carefully tying a knot, draping the two leg sections over his left shoulder. There were some jokes, of course, but we came to appreciate the mystery of it all. Dobbins was invulnerable. Never wounded, never a scratch. In August, he tripped a Bouncing Betty, which failed to detonate. And a week later he got caught in the open during a fierce little firefight, no cover at all, but he just slipped the pantyhose over his nose and breathed deep and let the magic do its work.

It turned us into a platoon of believers. You don't dispute facts.

But then, near the end of October, his girlfriend dumped him. It was a hard blow. Dobbins went quiet for a while, staring down at her letter, then after a time he took out the stockings and tied them around his neck as a comforter.

"No sweat," he said. "The magic doesn't go away."

Church

One afternoon, somewhere west of the Batangan Peninsula, we came across an abandoned pagoda. Or almost abandoned, because a pair of monks lived there in a tar paper shack, tending a small garden and some broken shrines. They spoke almost no English at all. When we dug our foxholes in the yard, the monks did not seem upset or displeased, though the younger one performed a washing motion with his hands. No one could decide what it meant. The older monk led us into the pagoda. The place was dark and cool, I remember, with crumbling walls and sandbagged windows and a ceiling full of holes. "It's bad news," Kiowa said. "You don't mess with churches." But we spent the night there, turning the pagoda into a little fortress, and then for the next seven or eight days we used the place as a base of operations. It was mostly a very peaceful time. Each morning the two monks brought us buckets of water. They giggled when we stripped down to bathe; they smiled happily while we soaped up and splashed one another. On the second day the older monk carried in a cane chair for the use of Lieutenant Jimmy Cross, placing it near the altar area, bowing and gesturing for him to sit down. The old monk seemed proud of the chair, and proud that such a man as Lieutenant Cross should be sitting in it. On another occasion the younger monk presented us with four ripe watermelons from his garden. He stood watching until the watermelons were eaten down to the rinds, then he smiled and made the strange washing motion with his hands.

Though they were kind to all of us, the monks took a special liking for Henry Dobbins.

"Soldier Jesus," they'd say, "good soldier Jesus."

Squatting quietly in the cool pagoda, they would help Dobbins disassemble and clean his machine gun, carefully brushing the parts with oil. The three of them seemed to have an understanding. Nothing in words, just a quietness they shared.

"You know," Dobbins said to Kiowa one morning, "after the war maybe I'll join up with these guys."

"Join how?" Kiowa said. "Wear robes. Take the pledge."

Kiowa thought about it. "That's a new one. I didn't know you were all that religious."

"Well, I'm not," Dobbins said. Beside him, the two monks were working on the M-60. He watched them take turns running oiled swabs through the barrel. "I mean, I'm not the churchy type. When I was a little kid, way back, I used to sit there on Sunday counting bricks in the wall. Church wasn't for me. But then in high school, I started to think how I'd like to be a minister. Free house, free car. Lots of potlucks. It looked like a pretty good life."

"You're serious?" Kiowa said.

Dobbins shrugged his shoulders. "What's serious? I was a kid. The thing is, I believed in God and all that, but it wasn't the religious part that interested me. Just being nice to people, that's all. Being decent."

"Right," Kiowa said.

"Visit sick people, stuff like that. I would've been good at it, too. Not the brainy part—not sermons and all that—but I'd be okay with the people part."

Henry Dobbins was silent for a time. He smiled at the older monk, who was now cleaning the machine gun's trigger assembly.

"But anyway," Dobbins said, "I couldn't ever be a real minister, because you have to be super sharp. Upstairs, I mean. It takes brains. You have to explain some hard stuff, like why people die, or why God invented pneumonia and all that." He shook his head. "I just didn't have the smarts for it. And there's the religious thing, too. All these years, man, I still hate church."

"Maybe you'd change," Kiowa said.

Henry Dobbins closed his eyes briefly, then laughed.

"One thing for sure, I'd look spiffy in those robes they wear—just like Friar Tuck. Maybe I'll do it. Find a monastery somewhere. Wear a robe and be nice to people."

"Sounds good," Kiowa said.

The two monks were quiet as they cleaned and oiled the machine gun. Though they spoke almost no English, they seemed to have great respect for the conversation, as if sensing that important matters were being discussed. The younger monk used a yellow cloth to wipe dirt from a belt of ammunition.

"What about you?" Dobbins said. "How?"

"Well, you carry that Bible everywhere, you never hardly swear or anything, so you must—"

"I grew up that way," Kiowa said.

"Did you ever—you know—did you think about being a minister?" "No. Not ever."

Dobbins laughed. "An Indian preacher. Man, that's one I'd love to see.

Feathers and buffalo robes."

Kiowa lay on his back, looking up at the ceiling, and for a time he didn't speak. Then he sat up and took a drink from his canteen.

"Not a minister," he said, "but I do like churches. The way it feels inside. It feels good when you just sit there, like you're in a forest and everything's really quiet, except there's still this sound you can't hear."

"Yeah."

"You ever feel that?" "Sort of."

Kiowa made a noise in his throat. "This is all wrong," he said. "What?"

"Setting up here. It's wrong. I don't care what, it's still a church." Dobbins nodded. "True."

"A church," Kiowa said. "Just wrong."

When the two monks finished cleaning the machine gun, Henry Dobbins began reassembling it, wiping off the excess oil, then he handed each of them a can of peaches and a chocolate bar. "Okay," he said, "*didimau*, boys. Beat it." The monks bowed and moved out of the pagoda into the bright morning sunlight.

Henry Dobbins made the washing motion with his hands.

"You're right," he said. "All you can do is be nice. Treat them decent, you know?"

The Man I Killed

His jaw was in his throat, his upper lip and teeth were gone, his one eye was shut, his other eye was a star-shaped hole, his eyebrows were thin and arched like a woman's, his nose was undamaged, there was a slight tear at the lobe of one ear, his clean black hair was swept upward into a cowlick at the rear of the skull, his forehead was lightly freckled, his fingernails were clean, the skin at his left cheek was peeled back in three ragged strips, his right cheek was smooth and hairless, there was a butterfly on his chin, his neck was open to the spinal cord and the blood there was thick and shiny and it was this wound that had killed him. He lay face-up in the center of the trail, a slim, dead, almost dainty young man. He had bony legs, a narrow waist, long shapely fingers. His chest was sunken and poorly muscled—a scholar, maybe. His wrists were the wrists of a child. He wore a black shirt, black pajama pants, a gray ammunition belt, a gold ring on the third finger of his right hand. His rubber sandals had been blown off. One lay beside him, the other a few meters up the trail. He had been born, maybe, in 1946 in the village of My Khe near the central coastline of Quang Ngai Province, where his parents farmed, and where his family had lived for several centuries, and where, during the time of the French, his father and two uncles and many neighbors had joined in the struggle for independence. He was not a Communist. He was a citizen and a soldier. In the village of My Khe, as in all of Quang Ngai, patriotic resistance had the force of tradition, which was partly the force of legend, and from his earliest boyhood the man I killed would have listened to stories about the heroic Trung sisters and Tran Hung Dao's famous rout of the Mongols and Le Loi's final victory against the Chinese at Tot Dong. He would have been taught that to defend the land was a man's highest duty and highest privilege. He had accepted this. It was never open to question. Secretly, though, it also frightened him. He was not a fighter. His health was poor, his body small and frail. He liked books. He wanted someday to be a teacher of mathematics. At night, lying on his mat, he could not picture himself doing the brave things his father had done, or his uncles, or the heroes of the stories. He hoped in his heart that he would never be tested. He hoped the Americans would go away. Soon, he hoped. He kept hoping and hoping, always, even when he was asleep.

"Oh, man, you fuckin' trashed the fucker," Azar said. "You scrambled his sorry self, look at that, you *did*, you laid him out like Shredded fuckin' Wheat."

"Go away," Kiowa said.

"I'm just saying the truth. Like oatmeal." "Go," Kiowa said.

"Okay, then, I take it back," Azar said. He started to move away, then stopped and said, "Rice Krispies, you know? On the dead test, this particular individual gets A-plus."

Smiling at this, he shrugged and walked up the trail toward the village behind the trees.

Kiowa kneeled down.

"Just forget that crud," he said. He opened up his canteen and held it out for a while and then sighed and pulled it away. "No sweat, man. What else could you do?"

Later, Kiowa said, "I'm serious. Nothing *anybody* could do. Come on, stop staring."

The trail junction was shaded by a row of trees and tall brush. The slim young man lay with his legs in the shade. His jaw was in his throat. His one eye was shut and the other was a star-shaped hole.

Kiowa glanced at the body.

"All right, let me ask a question," he said. "You want to trade places with him? Turn it all upside down—you want that? I mean, be honest."

The star-shaped hole was red and yellow. The yellow part seemed to be getting wider, spreading out at the center of the star. The upper lip and gum and teeth were gone. The man's head was cocked at a wrong angle, as if loose at the neck, and the neck was wet with blood.

"Think it over," Kiowa said.

Then later he said, "Tim, it's a *war*. The guy wasn't Heidi—he had a weapon, right? It's a tough thing, for sure, but you got to cut out that staring."

Then he said, "Maybe you better lie down a minute."

Then after a long empty time he said, "Take it slow. Just go wherever the spirit takes you."

The butterfly was making its way along the young man's forehead, which was spotted with small dark freckles. The nose was undamaged. The skin on the right cheek was smooth and fine-grained and hairless. Frail-looking, delicately boned, the young man would not have wanted to be a soldier and in his heart would have feared performing badly in battle. Even as a boy growing up in the village of My Khe, he had often worried about this. He imagined covering his head and lying in a deep hole and closing his eyes and not moving until the war was over. He had no stomach for violence. He loved mathematics. His eyebrows were thin and arched like a woman's, and at school the boys sometimes teased him about how pretty he was, the arched eyebrows and long shapely fingers, and on the playground they mimicked a woman's walk and made fun of his smooth skin and his love for mathematics. The young man could not make himself fight them. He often wanted to, but he was afraid, and this increased his shame. If he could not fight little boys, he thought, how could he ever become a soldier and fight the Americans with their airplanes and helicopters and bombs? It did not seem possible. In the presence of his father and uncles, he pretended to look forward to doing his patriotic duty, which was also a privilege, but at night he prayed with his mother that the war might end soon. Beyond anything else, he was afraid of disgracing himself, and therefore his family and village. But all he could do, he thought, was wait and pray and try not to grow up too fast.

"Listen to me," Kiowa said. "You feel terrible, I know that." Then he said, "Okay, maybe I *don't* know."

Along the trail there were small blue flowers shaped like bells. The young man's head was wrenched sideways, not quite facing the flowers, and even in the shade a single blade of sunlight sparkled against the buckle of his ammunition belt. The left cheek was peeled back in three ragged strips. The wounds at his neck had not yet clotted, which made him seem animate even in death, the blood still spreading out across his shirt.

Kiowa shook his head.

There was some silence before he said, "Stop *staring*."

The young man's fingernails were clean. There was a slight tear at the lobe of one ear, a sprinkling of blood on the forearm. He wore a gold ring on the third finger of his right hand. His chest was sunken and poorly muscled—a scholar, maybe. His life was now a constellation of possibilities. So, yes, maybe a scholar. And for years, despite his family's poverty, the man I killed would have been determined to continue his education in mathematics. The means for this were arranged, perhaps, through the village liberation cadres, and in 1964 the young man began attending classes at the university in Saigon, where he avoided politics and paid attention to the problems of calculus. He devoted himself to his studies. He spent his nights alone, wrote romantic poems in his journal, took pleasure in the grace and beauty of differential equations. The war, he knew, would finally take him, but for the time being he would not let himself think about it. He had stopped praying; instead, now, he waited. And as he waited, in his final year at the university, he fell in love with a classmate, a girl of seventeen, who one day told him that his wrists were like the wrists of a child, so small and delicate, and who admired his narrow waist and the cowlick that rose up like a bird's tail at the back of his head. She liked his quiet manner; she laughed at his freckles and bony legs. One evening, perhaps, they exchanged gold rings.

Now one eye was a star. "You okay?" Kiowa said.

The body lay almost entirely in shade. There were gnats at the mouth, little flecks of pollen drifting above the nose. The butterfly was gone. The bleeding had stopped except for the neck wounds.

Kiowa picked up the rubber sandals, clapping off the dirt, then bent down to search the body. He found a pouch of rice, a comb, a fingernail clipper, a few soiled piasters, a snapshot of a young woman standing in front of a parked motorcycle. Kiowa placed these items in his rucksack along with the gray ammunition belt and rubber sandals.

Then he squatted down.

"I'll tell you the straight truth," he said. "The guy was dead the second he stepped on the trail. Understand me? We all had him zeroed. A good kill—weapon, ammunition, everything." Tiny beads of sweat glistened at Kiowa's forehead. His eyes moved from the sky to the dead man's body to the knuckles of his own hands. "So listen, you best pull your shit together. Can't just sit here all day."

Later he said, "Understand?"

Then he said, "Five minutes, Tim. Five more minutes and we're moving out."

The one eye did a funny twinkling trick, red to yellow. His head was wrenched sideways, as if loose at the neck, and the dead young man seemed to be staring at some distant object beyond the bell-shaped flowers along the trail.

The blood at the neck had gone to a deep purplish black. Clean fingernails, clean hair—he had been a soldier for only a single day. After his years at the university, the man I killed returned with his new wife to the village of My Khe, where he enlisted as a common rifleman with the 48th Vietcong Battalion. He knew he would die quickly. He knew he would see a flash of light. He knew he would fall dead and wake up in the stories of his village and people.

Kiowa covered the body with a poncho.

"Hey, you're looking better," he said. "No doubt about it. All you needed was time—some mental R&R." Then he said, "Man, I'm sorry."

Then later he said, "Why not talk about it?" Then he said, "Come on, man, talk."

He was a slim, dead, almost dainty young man of about twenty. He lay with one leg bent beneath him, his jaw in his throat, his face neither expressive nor inexpressive. One eye was shut. The other was a star- shaped hole.

"Talk," Kiowa said.

Ambush

When she was nine, my daughter Kathleen asked if I had ever killed anyone. She knew about the war; she knew I'd been a soldier. "You keep writing these war stories," she said, "so I guess you must've killed somebody." It was a difficult moment, but I did what seemed right, which was to say, "Of course not," and then to take her onto my lap and hold her for a while. Someday, I hope, she'll ask again. But here I want to pretend she's a grown-up. I want to tell her exactly what happened, or what I remember happening, and then I want to say to her that as a little girl she was absolutely right. This is why I keep writing war stories:

He was a short, slender young man of about twenty. I was afraid of him—afraid of something—and as he passed me on the trail I threw a grenade that exploded at his feet and killed him.

Or to go back:

Shortly after midnight we moved into the ambush site outside My Khe. The whole platoon was there, spread out in the dense brush along the trail, and for five hours nothing at all happened. We were working in two-man teams—one man on guard while the other slept, switching off every two hours—and I remember it was still dark when Kiowa shook me awake for the final watch. The night was foggy and hot. For the first few moments I felt lost, not sure about directions, groping for my helmet and weapon. I reached out and found three grenades and lined them up in front of me; the pins had already been straightened for quick throwing. And then for maybe half an hour I knelt there and waited. Very gradually, in tiny slivers, dawn began to break through the fog, and from my position in the brush I could see ten or fifteen meters up the trail. The mosquitoes were fierce. I remember slapping at them, wondering if I should wake up Kiowa and ask for some repellent, then thinking it was a bad idea, then looking up and seeing the young man come out of the fog. He wore black clothing and rubber sandals and a gray ammunition belt. His shoulders were slightly stooped, his head cocked to the side as if listening for something. He seemed at ease. He carried his weapon in one hand, muzzle down, moving without any hurry up the center of the trail. There was no sound at all—none that I can remember. In a way, it seemed, he was part of the morning fog, or my own imagination, but there was also the reality of what was happening in my stomach. I had already pulled the pin on a grenade. I had come up to a crouch. It was entirely automatic. I did not hate the young man; I did not see him as the enemy; I did not ponder issues of morality or politics or military duty. I crouched and kept my head low. I tried to swallow whatever was rising from my stomach, which tasted like lemonade, something fruity and sour. I was terrified. There were no thoughts about killing. The grenade was to make him go away—just evaporate—and I leaned back and felt my mind go empty and then felt it fill up again. I had already thrown the grenade before telling myself to throw it. The brush was thick and I had to lob it high, not aiming, and I remember the grenade seeming to freeze above me for an instant, as if a camera had clicked, and I remember ducking down and holding my breath and seeing little wisps of fog rise from the earth. The grenade bounced once and rolled across the trail. I did not hear it, but there must've been a sound, because the young man dropped his weapon and began to run, just two or three quick steps, then he hesitated, swiveling to his right, and he glanced down at the grenade and tried to cover his head but never did. It occurred to me then that he was about to die. I wanted to warn him. The grenade made a popping noise—not soft but not loud either—not what I'd expected—and there was a puff of dust and smoke—a small white puff—and the young man seemed to jerk upward as if pulled by invisible wires. He fell on his back. His rubber sandals had been blown off. There was no wind. He lay at the center of the trail, his right leg bent beneath him, his one eye shut, his other eye a huge star-shaped hole.

It was not a matter of live or die. There was no real peril. Almost certainly the young man would have passed by. And it will always be that way.

Later, I remember, Kiowa tried to tell me that the man would've died anyway. He told me that it was a good kill, that I was a soldier and this was a war, that I should shape up and stop staring and ask myself what the dead man would've done if things were reversed.

None of it mattered. The words seemed far too complicated. All I could do was gape at the fact of the young man's body.

Even now I haven't finished sorting it out. Sometimes I forgive myself, other times I don't. In the ordinary hours of life I try not to dwell on it, but now and then, when I'm reading a newspaper or just sitting alone in a room, I'll look up and see the young man coming out of the morning fog. I'll watch him walk toward me, his shoulders slightly stooped, his head cocked to the side, and he'll pass within a few yards of me and suddenly smile at some secret thought and then continue up the trail to where it bends back into the fog.

Style

There was no music. Most of the hamlet had burned down, including her house, which was now smoke, and the girl danced with her eyes half closed, her feet bare. She was maybe fourteen. She had black hair and brown skin. "Why's she dancing?" Azar said. We searched through the wreckage but there wasn't much to find. Rat Kiley caught a chicken for dinner. Lieutenant Cross radioed up to the gunships and told them to go away. The girl danced mostly on her toes. She took tiny steps in the dirt in front of her house, sometimes making a slow twirl, sometimes smiling to herself. "Why's she dancing?" Azar said, and Henry Dobbins said it didn't matter why, she just was. Later we found her family in the house. They were dead and badly burned. It wasn't a big family: an infant and an old woman and a woman whose age was hard to tell. When we dragged them out, the girl kept dancing. She put the palms of her hands against her ears, which must've meant something, and she danced sideways for a short while, and then backwards. She did a graceful movement with her hips. "Well, I don't get it," Azar said. The smoke from the hootches smelled like straw. It moved in patches across the village square, not thick anymore, sometimes just faint ripples like fog. There were dead pigs, too. The girl went up on her toes and made a slow turn and danced through the smoke. Her face had a dreamy look, quiet and composed. A while later, when we moved out of the hamlet, she was still dancing. "Probably some weird ritual," Azar said, but Henry Dobbins looked back and said no, the girl just liked to dance.

That night, after we'd marched away from the smoking village, Azar mocked the girl's dancing. He did funny jumps and spins. He put the palms of his hands against his ears and danced sideways for a while, and then backwards, and then did an erotic thing with his hips. But Henry Dobbins, who moved gracefully for such a big man, took Azar from behind and lifted him up high and carried him over to a deep well and asked if he wanted to be dumped in.

Azar said no.

"All right, then," Henry Dobbins said, "dance right."

Speaking of Courage

The war was over and there was no place in particular to go. Norman Bowker followed the tar road on its seven-mile loop around the lake, then he started all over again, driving slowly, feeling safe inside his father's big Chevy, now and then looking out on the lake to watch the boats and water-skiers and scenery. It was Sunday and it was summer, and the town seemed pretty much the same. The lake lay flat and silvery against the sun. Along the road the houses were all low-slung and split-level and modern, with big porches and picture windows facing the water. The lawns were spacious. On the lake side of the road, where real estate was most valuable, the houses were handsome and set deep in, well kept and brightly painted, with docks jutting out into the lake, and boats moored and covered with canvas, and neat gardens, and sometimes even gardeners, and stone patios with barbecue spits and grills, and wooden shingles saying who lived where. On the other side of the road, to his left, the houses were also handsome, though less expensive and on a smaller scale and with no docks or boats or gardeners. The road was a sort of boundary between the affluent and the almost affluent, and to live on the lake side of the road was one of the few natural privileges in a town of the prairie—the difference between watching the sun set over cornfields or over water.

It was a graceful, good-sized lake. Back in high school, at night, he had driven around and around it with Sally Kramer, wondering if she'd want to pull into the shelter of Sunset Park, or other times with his friends, talking about urgent matters, worrying about the existence of God and theories of causation. Then, there had not been a war. But there had always been the lake, which was the town's first cause of existence, a place for immigrant settlers to put down their loads. Before the settlers were the Sioux, and before the Sioux were the vast open prairies, and before the prairies there was only ice. The lake bed had been dug out by the southernmost advance of the Wisconsin glacier. Fed by neither streams nor springs, the lake was often filthy and algaed, relying on fickle prairie rains for replenishment. Still, it was the only important body of water within forty miles, a source of pride, nice to look at on bright summer days, and later that evening it would color up with fireworks. Now, in the late afternoon, it lay calm and smooth, a good audience for silence, a seven-mile circumference that could be traveled by slow car in twenty-five minutes. It was not such a good lake for swimming. After high school, he'd caught an ear infection that had almost kept him out of the war. And the lake had drowned his friend Max Arnold, keeping him out of the war entirely. Max had been one who liked to talk about the existence of God. "No, I'm not saying *that*," he'd argue against the drone of the engine. "I'm saying it's possible as an *idea*, even necessary as an idea, a final cause in the whole structure of causation." Now he knew, perhaps. Before the war they'd driven around the lake as friends, but now Max was just an idea, and most of Norman Bowker's other friends were living in Des Moines or Sioux City, or going to school somewhere, or holding down jobs. The high school girls were mostly gone or married. Sally Kramer, whose pictures he had once carried in his wallet, was one who had married. Her name was now Sally Gustafson and she lived in a pleasant blue house on the less expensive side of the lake road. On his third day home he'd seen her out mowing the lawn, still pretty in a lacy red blouse and white shorts. For a moment he'd almost pulled over, just to talk, but instead he'd pushed down hard on the gas pedal. She looked happy. She had her house and her new husband, and there was really nothing he could say to her.

The town seemed remote somehow. Sally was remarried and Max was drowned and his father was at home watching baseball on national TV.

Norman Bowker shrugged. "No problem," he murmured.

Clockwise, as if in orbit, he took the Chevy on another seven-mile turn around the lake.

Even in late afternoon the day was hot. He turned on the air conditioner, then the radio, and he leaned back and let the cold air and music blow over him. Along the road, kicking stones in front of them, two young boys were hiking with knapsacks and toy rifles and canteens. He honked going by, but neither boy looked up. Already he had passed them six times, forty-two miles, nearly three hours without stop. He watched the boys recede in his rearview mirror. They turned a soft grayish color, like sand, before finally disappearing.

He tapped down lightly on the accelerator.

Out on the lake a man's motorboat had stalled; the man was bent over the engine with a wrench and a frown. Beyond the stalled boat there were other boats, and a few water-skiers, and the smooth July waters, and an immense flatness everywhere. Two mud hens floated stiffly beside a white dock.

The road curved west, where the sun had now dipped low. He figured it was close to five o'clock—twenty after, he guessed. The war had taught him to tell time without clocks, and even at night, waking from sleep, he could usually place it within ten minutes either way. What he should do, he thought, is stop at Sally's house and impress her with this new time-telling trick of his. They'd talk for a while, catching up on things, and then he'd say, "Well, better hit the road, it's five thirty-four," and she'd glance at her wristwatch and say, "Hey! How'd you *do* that?" and he'd give a casual shrug and tell her it was just one of those things you pick up. He'd keep it light. He wouldn't say anything about anything. "How's it being married?" he might ask, and he'd nod at whatever she answered with, and he would not say a word about how he'd almost won the Silver Star for valor.

He drove past Slater Park and across the causeway and past Sunset Park. The radio announcer sounded tired. The temperature in Des Moines was eighty-one degrees, and the time was five thirty-five, and "All you on the road, drive extra careful now on this fine Fourth of July." If Sally had not been married, or if his father were not such a baseball fan, it would have been a good time to talk.

"The Silver Star?" his father might have said. "Yes, but I didn't get it. Almost, but not quite."

And his father would have nodded, knowing full well that many brave men do not win medals for their bravery, and that others win medals for doing nothing. As a starting point, maybe, Norman Bowker might then have listed the seven medals he did win: the Combat Infantryman's Badge, the Air Medal, the Army Commendation Medal, the Good Conduct Medal, the Vietnam Campaign Medal, the Bronze Star, and the Purple Heart, though it wasn't much of a wound and did not leave a scar and did not hurt and never had. He would've explained to his father that none of these decorations was for uncommon valor. They were for common valor. The routine, daily stuff—just humping, just enduring— but that was worth something, wasn't it? Yes, it was. Worth plenty. The ribbons looked good on the uniform in his closet, and if his father were to ask, he would've explained what each signified and how he was proud of all of them, especially the Combat Infantryman's Badge, because it meant he had been there as a real soldier and had done all the things soldiers do, and therefore it wasn't such a big deal that he could not bring himself to be uncommonly brave.

And then he would have talked about the medal he did not win and why he did not win it.

"I almost won the Silver Star," he would have said. "How's that?"

"Just a story."

"So tell me," his father would have said.

Slowly then, circling the lake, Norman Bowker would have started by describing the Song Tra Bong. "A river," he would've said, "this slow flat muddy river." He would've explained how during the dry season it was exactly like any other river, nothing special, but how in October the monsoons began and the whole situation changed. For a solid week the rains never stopped, not once, and so after a few days the Song Tra Bong overflowed its banks and the land turned into a deep, thick muck for a half mile on either side. Just muck—no other word for it. Like quicksand, almost, except the stink was incredible. "You couldn't even sleep," he'd tell his father. "At night you'd find a high spot, and you'd doze off, but then later you'd wake up because you'd be buried in all that slime. You'd just sink in. You'd feel it ooze up over your body and sort of suck you down. And the whole time there was that constant rain. I mean, it never stopped, not ever."

"Sounds pretty wet," his father would've said, pausing briefly. "So what happened?"

"You really want to hear this?" "Hey, I'm your *father*."

Norman Bowker smiled. He looked out across the lake and imagined the feel of his tongue against the truth. "Well, this one time, this one night out by the river . . . I wasn't very brave."

"You have seven medals." "Sure."

"Seven. Count 'em. You weren't a coward either."

"Well, maybe not. But I had the chance and I blew it. The stink, that's what got to me. I couldn't take that goddamn awful *smell*."

"If you don't want to say any more—" "I do want to."

"All right then. Slow and sweet, take your time."

The road descended into the outskirts of town, turning northwest past the junior college and the tennis courts, then past Chautauqua Park, where the picnic tables were spread with sheets of colored plastic and where picnickers sat in lawn chairs and listened to the high school band playing Sousa marches under the band shell. The music faded after a few blocks. He drove beneath a canopy of elms, then along a stretch of open shore, then past the municipal docks, where a woman in pedal pushers stood casting for bullheads. There were no other fish in the lake except for perch and a few worthless carp. It was a bad lake for swimming and fishing both.

He drove slowly. No hurry, nowhere to go. Inside the Chevy the air was cool and oily-smelling, and he took pleasure in the steady sounds of the engine and air-conditioning. A tour bus feeling, in a way, except the town he was touring seemed dead. Through the windows, as if in a stop-motion photograph, the place looked as if it had been hit by nerve gas, everything still and lifeless, even the people. The town could not talk, and would not listen. "How'd you like to hear about the war?" he might have asked, but the place could only blink and shrug. It had no memory, therefore no guilt. The taxes got paid and the votes got counted and the agencies of government did their work briskly and politely. It was a brisk, polite town. It did not know shit about shit, and did not care to know.

Norman Bowker leaned back and considered what he might've said on the subject. He knew shit. It was his specialty. The smell, in particular, but also the numerous varieties of texture and taste. Someday he'd give a lecture on the topic. Put on a suit and tie and stand up in front of the Kiwanis club and tell the fuckers about all the wonderful shit he knew. Pass out samples, maybe.

Smiling at this, he clamped the steering wheel slightly right of center, which produced a smooth clockwise motion against the curve of the road. The Chevy seemed to know its own way.

The sun was lower now. Five fifty-five, he decided—six o'clock, tops.

Along an unused railway spur, four workmen labored in the shadowy red heat, setting up a platform and steel launchers for the evening fireworks. They were dressed alike in khaki trousers, work shirts, visored caps, and brown boots. Their faces were dark and smudgy. "Want to hear about the Silver Star I almost won?" Norman Bowker whispered, but none of the workmen looked up. Later they would blow color into the sky. The lake would sparkle with reds and blues and greens, like a mirror, and the picnickers would make low sounds of appreciation.

"Well, see, it never stopped raining," he would've said. "The muck was everywhere, you couldn't get away from it."

He would have paused a second.

Then he would have told about the night they bivouacked in a field along the Song Tra Bong. A big swampy field beside the river. There was a ville nearby, fifty meters downstream, and right away a dozen old mama-sans ran out and started yelling. A weird scene, he would've said. The mama-sans just stood there in the rain, soaking wet, yapping away about how this field was bad news. Number ten, they said. Evil ground. Not a good spot for good GIs. Finally Lieutenant Jimmy Cross had to get out his pistol and fire off a few rounds just to shoo them away. By then it was almost dark. So they set up a perimeter, ate chow, then crawled under their ponchos and tried to settle in for the night.

But the rain kept getting worse. And by midnight the field turned into soup.

"Just this deep, oozy soup," he would've said. "Like sewage or something. Thick and mushy. You couldn't sleep. You couldn't even lie down, not for long, because you'd start to sink under the soup. Real clammy. You could feel the crud coming up inside your boots and pants."

Here, Norman Bowker would have squinted against the low sun. He would have kept his voice cool, no self-pity.

"But the worst part," he would've said quietly, "was the smell. Partly it was the river—a dead-fish smell—but it was something else, too. Finally somebody figured it out. What this was, it was a shit field. The village toilet. No indoor plumbing, right? So they used the field. I mean, we were camped in a goddamn *shit* field."

He imagined Sally Kramer closing her eyes.

If she were here with him, in the car, she would've said, "Stop it. I don't like that word."

"That's what it *was*."

"All right, but you don't have to use that word." "Fine. What should we call it?"

She would have glared at him. "I don't know. Just stop it."

Clearly, he thought, this was not a story for Sally Kramer. She was Sally Gustafson now. No doubt Max would've liked it, the irony in particular, but Max had become a pure idea, which was its own irony. It was just too bad. If his father were here, riding shotgun around the lake, the old man might have glanced over for a second, understanding perfectly well that it was not a question of offensive language but of fact. His father would have sighed and folded his arms and waited.

"A shit field," Norman Bowker would have said. "And later that night I could've won the Silver Star for valor."

"Right," his father would've murmured, "I hear you."

The Chevy rolled smoothly across a viaduct and up the narrow tar road. To the right was open lake. To the left, across the road, most of the lawns were scorched dry like October corn. Hopelessly, round and round, a rotating sprinkler scattered lake water on Dr. Mason's vegetable garden. Already the prairie had been baked dry, but in August it would get worse. The lake would turn green with algae, and the golf course would burn up, and the dragonflies would crack open for want of good water.

The big Chevy curved past Centennial Beach and the A&W root beer stand.

It was his eighth revolution around the lake.

He followed the road past the handsome houses with their docks and wooden shingles. Back to Slater Park, across the causeway, around to Sunset Park, as though riding on tracks.

The two little boys were still trudging along on their seven-mile hike.

Out on the lake, the man in the stalled motorboat still fiddled with his engine. The pair of mud hens floated like wooden decoys, and the water- skiers looked tanned and athletic, and the high school band was packing up its instruments, and the woman in pedal pushers patiently rebaited her hook for one last try.

Quaint, he thought.

A hot summer day and it was all very quaint and remote. The four workmen had nearly completed their preparations for the evening fireworks.

Facing the sun again, Norman Bowker decided it was nearly seven o'clock. Not much later the tired radio announcer confirmed it, his voice rocking itself into a deep Sunday snooze. If Max Arnold were here, he would say something about the announcer's fatigue, and relate it to the bright pink in the sky, and the war, and courage. A pity that Max was gone. And a pity about his father, who had his own war and who now preferred silence.

Still, there was so much to say.

How the rain never stopped. How the cold worked into your bones. Sometimes the bravest thing on earth was to sit through the night and feel the cold in your bones. Courage was not always a matter of yes or no. Sometimes it came in degrees, like the cold; sometimes you were very brave up to a point and then beyond that point you were not so brave. In certain situations you could do incredible things, you could advance toward enemy fire, but in other situations, which were not nearly so bad, you had trouble keeping your eyes open. Sometimes, like that night in the shit field, the difference between courage and cowardice was something small and stupid.

The way the earth bubbled. And the smell.

In a soft voice, without flourishes, he would have told the exact truth. "Late in the night," he would've said, "we took some mortar fire."

He would've explained how it was still raining, and how the clouds were pasted to the field, and how the mortar rounds seemed to come right out of the clouds. Everything was black and wet. The field just exploded. Rain and slop and shrapnel, nowhere to run, and all they could do was worm down into slime and cover up and wait. He would've described the crazy things he saw. Weird things. Like how at one point he noticed a guy lying next to him in the sludge, completely buried except for his face, and how after a moment the guy rolled his eyes and winked at him. The noise was fierce.

Heavy thunder, and mortar rounds, and people yelling. Some of the men began shooting up flares. Red and green and silver flares, all colors, and the rain came down in Technicolor.

The field was boiling. The shells made deep slushy craters, opening up all those years of waste, centuries worth, and the smell came bubbling out of the earth. Two rounds hit close by. Then a third, even closer, and immediately, off to his left, he heard somebody screaming. It was Kiowa—he knew that. The sound was ragged and clotted up, but even so he knew the voice. A strange gargling noise. Rolling sideways, he crawled toward the screaming in the dark. The rain was hard and steady. Along the perimeter there were quick bursts of gunfire. Another round hit nearby, spraying up shit and water, and for a few moments he ducked down beneath the mud. He heard the valves in his heart. He heard the quick, feathering action of the hinges.

Extraordinary, he thought. As he came up, a pair of red flares puffed open, a soft fuzzy glow, and in the glow he saw Kiowa's wide-open eyes settling down into the scum. Briefly, all he could do was watch. He heard himself moan. Then he moved again, crabbing forward, but when he got there Kiowa was almost completely under. There was a knee. There was an arm and a gold wristwatch and part of a boot.

He could not describe what happened next, not ever, but he would've tried anyway. He would've spoken carefully so as to make it real for anyone who would listen.

There were bubbles where Kiowa's head should've been.

The left hand was curled open; the fingernails were filthy; the wristwatch gave off a green phosphorescent shine as it slipped beneath the thick waters.

He would've talked about this, and how he grabbed Kiowa by the boot and tried to pull him out. He pulled hard but Kiowa was gone, and then suddenly he felt himself going, too. He could taste it. The shit was in his nose and eyes. There were flares and mortar rounds, and the stink was everywhere—it was inside him, in his lungs—and he could no longer tolerate it. Not here, he thought. Not like this. He released Kiowa's boot and watched it slide away. Slowly, working his way up, he hoisted himself out of the deep mud, and then he lay still and tasted the shit in his mouth and closed his eyes and listened to the rain and explosions and bubbling sounds.

He was alone.

He had lost his weapon but it did not matter. All he wanted was a bath. Nothing else. A hot soapy bath.

Circling the lake, Norman Bowker remembered how his friend Kiowa had disappeared under the waste and water.

"I didn't flip out," he would've said. "I was cool. If things had gone right, if it hadn't been for that smell, I could've won the Silver Star."

A good war story, he thought, but it was not a war for war stories, nor for talk of valor, and nobody in town wanted to know about the terrible stink. They wanted good intentions and good deeds. But the town was not to blame, really. It was a nice little town, very prosperous, with neat houses and all the sanitary conveniences.

Norman Bowker lit a cigarette and cranked open his window. Seven thirty-five, he decided.

The lake had divided into two halves. One half still glistened, the other was caught in shadow. Along the causeway, the two little boys marched on. The man in the stalled motorboat yanked frantically on the cord to his engine, and the two mud hens sought supper at the bottom of the lake, tails bobbing. He passed Sunset Park once again, and more houses, and the junior college and the tennis courts, and the picnickers, who now sat waiting for the evening fireworks. The high school band was gone. The woman in pedal pushers patiently toyed with her line.

Although it was not yet dusk, the A&W was already awash in neon lights.

He maneuvered his father's Chevy into one of the parking slots, let the engine idle, and sat back. The place was doing a good holiday business. Mostly kids, it seemed, and a few farmers in for the day. He did not recognize any of the faces. A slim, hipless young carhop passed by, but when he hit the horn, she did not seem to notice. Her eyes slid sideways. She hooked a tray to the window of a Firebird, laughing lightly, leaning forward to chat with the three boys inside.

He felt invisible in the soft twilight. Straight ahead, over the take-out counter, swarms of mosquitoes electrocuted themselves against an aluminum Pest-Rid machine.

It was a calm, quiet summer evening.

He honked again, this time leaning on the horn. The young carhop turned slowly, as if puzzled, then said something to the boys in the Firebird and moved reluctantly toward him. Pinned to her shirt was a badge that said EAT MAMA BURGERS.

When she reached his window, she stood straight up so that all he could see was the badge.

"Mama Burger," he said. "Maybe some fries, too."

The girl sighed, leaned down, and shook her head. Her eyes were as fluffy and airy-light as cotton candy.

"You blind?" she said.

She put out her hand and tapped an intercom attached to a steel post. "Punch the button and place your order. All I do is carry the dumb trays."

She stared at him for a moment. Briefly, he thought, a question lingered in her fuzzy eyes, but then she turned and punched the button for him and returned to her friends in the Firebird.

The intercom squeaked and said, "Order." "Mama Burger and fries," Norman Bowker said. "Affirmative, copy clear. No rootie-tootie?"

"Rootie-tootie?"

"You know, man—*root* beer. "A small one."

"Roger-dodger. Repeat: one Mama, one fries, one small beer. Fire for effect. Stand by."

The intercom squeaked and went dead. "Out," said Norman Bowker.

When the girl brought his tray, he ate quickly, without looking up. The tired radio announcer in Des Moines gave the time, almost eight-thirty. Dark was pressing in tight now, and he wished there were somewhere to go. In the morning he'd check out some job possibilities. Shoot a few buckets down at the Y, maybe wash the Chevy.

He finished his root beer and pushed the intercom button. "Order," said the tinny voice.

"All done." "That's *it*?" "I guess so."

"Hey, loosen up," the voice said. "What you really need, friend?" Norman Bowker smiled.

"Well," he said, "how'd you like to hear about—" He stopped and shook his head.

"Hear *what*, man?" "Nothing."

"Well, hey," the intercom said, "I'm sure as fuck not *going* anywhere.

Screwed to a post, for God sake. Go ahead, try me." "Nothing."

"You sure?" "Positive. All done."

The intercom made a light sound of disappointment. "Your choice, I guess. Over an' out."

"Out," said Norman Bowker.

On his tenth turn around the lake he passed the hiking boys for the last time. The man in the stalled motorboat was gone; the mud hens were gone. Beyond the lake, over Sally Gustafson's house, the sun had left a smudge of purple on the horizon. The band shell was deserted, and the woman in pedal pushers quietly reeled in her line, and Dr. Mason's sprinkler went round and round.

On his eleventh revolution he switched off the air-conditioning, opened up his window, and rested his elbow comfortably on the sill, driving with one hand.

There was nothing to say.

He could not talk about it and never would. The evening was smooth and warm.

If it had been possible, which it wasn't, he would have explained how his friend Kiowa slipped away that night beneath the dark swampy field. He was folded in with the war; he was part of the waste.

Turning on his headlights, driving slowly, Norman Bowker remembered how he had taken hold of Kiowa's boot and pulled hard, but how the smell was simply too much, and how he'd backed off and in that way had lost the Silver Star.

He wished he could've explained some of this. How he had been braver than he ever thought possible, but how he had not been so brave as he wanted to be. The distinction was important. Max Arnold, who loved fine lines, would've appreciated it. And his father, who already knew, would've nodded.

"The truth," Norman Bowker would've said, "is I let the guy go." "Maybe he was already gone." "He wasn't." "But maybe."

"No, I could feel it. He wasn't. Some things you can feel."

His father would have been quiet for a while, watching the headlights against the narrow tar road.

"Well, anyway," the old man would've said, "there's still the seven medals."

"I suppose." "Seven honeys." "Right."

On his twelfth revolution, the sky went crazy with color.

He pulled into Sunset Park and stopped in the shadow of a picnic shelter. After a time he got out, walked down to the beach, and waded into the lake without undressing. The water felt warm against his skin. He put his head under. He opened his lips, very slightly, for the taste, then he stood up and folded his arms and watched the fireworks. For a small town, he decided, it was a pretty good show.

Notes

"Speaking of Courage" was written in 1975 at the suggestion of Norman Bowker, who three years later hanged himself in the locker room of a YMCA in his hometown in central Iowa.

In the spring of 1975, near the time of Saigon's final collapse, I received a long, disjointed letter in which Bowker described the problem of finding a meaningful use for his life after the war. He had worked briefly as an automotive parts salesman, a janitor, a car wash attendant, and a short-order cook at the local A&W fast-food franchise. None of these jobs, he said, had lasted more than ten weeks. He lived with his parents, who supported him, and who treated him with kindness and obvious love. At one point he had enrolled in the junior college in his hometown, but the course work, he said, seemed too abstract, too distant, with nothing real or tangible at stake, certainly not the stakes of a war. He dropped out after eight months. He spent his mornings in bed. In the afternoons he played pickup basketball at the Y, and then at night he drove around town in his father's car, mostly alone, or with a six-pack of beer, cruising.

"The thing is," he wrote, "there's no place to go. Not just in this lousy little town. In general. My life, I mean. It's almost like I got killed over in Nam . . . Hard to describe. That night when Kiowa got wasted, I sort of sank down into the sewage with him . . . Feels like I'm still in deep shit."

The letter covered seventeen handwritten pages, its tone jumping from self-pity to anger to irony to guilt to a kind of feigned indifference. He didn't know what to feel. In the middle of the letter, for example, he reproached himself for complaining too much:

God, this is starting to sound like some jerkoff vet crying in his beer. Sorry about that. I'm no basket case—not even any bad dreams. And I don't feel like anybody mistreats me or anything, except sometimes people act *too* nice, too polite, like they're afraid they might ask the wrong question . . . But I shouldn't bitch. One thing I hate—really hate— is all those whiner-vets. Guys sniveling about how they didn't get any parades. Such absolute crap. I mean, who in his right mind wants a *parade*? Or getting his back clapped by a bunch of patriotic idiots who don't know jack about what it feels like to kill people or get shot at or sleep in the rain or watch your buddy go down underneath the mud? Who *needs* it?

Anyhow, I'm basically A-Okay. Home free!! So why not come down for a visit sometime and we'll chase pussy and shoot the breeze and tell each other old war lies? A good long bull session, you know?

I felt it coming, and near the end of the letter it came. He explained that he had read my first book, *If I Die in a Combat Zone*, which he liked except for the "bleeding-heart political parts." For half a page he talked about how much the book had meant to him, how it brought back all kinds of memories, the villes and paddies and rivers, and how he recognized most of the characters, including himself, even though almost all of the names were changed. Then Bowker came straight out with it:

What you should do, Tim, is write a story about a guy who feels like he got zapped over in that shithole. A guy who can't get his act together and just drives around town all day and can't think of any damn place to go and doesn't know how to get there anyway. This guy wants to talk about it, but he *can't* . . . If you want, you can use the stuff in this letter. (But not my real name, okay?) I'd write it myself except I can't ever find any words, if you know what I mean, and I can't figure out what exactly to say. Something about the field that night. The way Kiowa just disappeared into the crud. You were there—you can tell it.

Norman Bowker's letter hit me hard. For years I'd felt a certain smugness about how easily I had made the shift from war to peace. A nice smooth glide—no flashbacks or midnight sweats. The war was over, after all. And the thing to do was go on. So I took pride in sliding gracefully from Vietnam to graduate school, from Chu Lai to Harvard, from one world to another. In ordinary conversation I never spoke much about the war, certainly not in detail, and yet ever since my return I had been talking about it virtually nonstop through my writing. Telling stories seemed a natural, inevitable process, like clearing the throat. Partly catharsis, partly communication, it was a way of grabbing people by the shirt and explaining exactly what had happened to me, how I'd allowed myself to get dragged into a wrong war, all the mistakes I'd made, all the terrible things I had seen and done.

I did not look on my work as therapy, and still don't. Yet when I received Norman Bowker's letter, it occurred to me that the act of writing had led me through a swirl of memories that might otherwise have ended in paralysis or worse. By telling stories, you objectify your own experience. You separate it from yourself. You pin down certain truths. You make up others. You start sometimes with an incident that truly happened, like the night in the shit field, and you carry it forward by inventing incidents that did not in fact occur but that nonetheless help to clarify and explain.

In any case, Norman Bowker's letter had an effect. It haunted me for more than a month, not the words so much as its desperation, and I resolved finally to take him up on his story suggestion. At the time I was at work on a new novel, *Going After Cacciato*, and one morning I sat down and began a chapter titled "Speaking of Courage." The emotional core came directly from Bowker's letter: the simple need to talk. To provide a dramatic frame, I collapsed events into a single time and place, a car circling a lake on a quiet afternoon in midsummer, using the lake as a nucleus around which the story would orbit. As he'd requested, I did not use Norman Bowker's name, instead substituting the name of my novel's main character, Paul Berlin. For the scenery I borrowed heavily from my own hometown. Wholesale thievery, in fact. I lifted up Worthington, Minnesota—the lake, the road, the causeway, the woman in pedal pushers, the junior college, the handsome houses and docks and boats and public parks—and carried it all a few hundred miles south and transplanted it onto the Iowa prairie.

The writing went quickly and easily. I drafted the piece in a week or two, fiddled with it for another week, then published it as a separate short story.

Almost immediately, though, there was a sense of failure. The details of Norman Bowker's story were missing. In this original version, which I still conceived as part of the novel, I had been forced to omit the shit field and the rain and the death of Kiowa, replacing this material with events that better fit the book's narrative. As a consequence I'd lost the natural counterpoint between the lake and the field. A metaphoric unity was broken. What the piece needed, and did not have, was the terrible killing power of that shit field.

As the novel developed over the next year, and as my own ideas clarified, it became apparent that the chapter had no proper home in the larger narrative. *Going After Cacciato* was a war story; "Speaking of Courage" was a postwar story. Two different time periods, two different sets of issues. There was no choice but to remove the chapter entirely. The mistake, in part, had been in trying to wedge the piece into a novel. Beyond that, though, something about the story had frightened me—I was afraid to speak directly, afraid to remember—and in the end the piece had been ruined by a failure to tell the full and exact truth about our night in the shit field.

Over the next several months, as it often happens, I managed to erase the story's flaws from my memory, taking pride in a shadowy, idealized recollection of its virtues. When the piece appeared in an anthology of short fiction, I sent a copy off to Norman Bowker with the thought that it might please him. His reaction was short and somewhat bitter.

"It's not terrible," he wrote me, "but you left out Vietnam. Where's Kiowa? Where's the shit?"

Eight months later he hanged himself.

In August of 1978 his mother sent me a brief note explaining what had happened. He'd been playing pickup basketball at the Y; after two hours he went off for a drink of water; he used a jump rope; his friends found him hanging from a water pipe. There was no suicide note, no message of any kind. "Norman was a quiet boy," his mother wrote, "and I don't suppose he wanted to bother anybody."

Now, a decade after his death, I'm hoping that "Speaking of Courage" makes good on Norman Bowker's silence. And I hope it's a better story. Although the old structure remains, the piece has been substantially revised, in some places by severe cutting, in other places by the addition of new material. Norman is back in the story, where he belongs, and I don't think he would mind that his real name appears. The central incident—our long night in the shit field along the Song Tra Bong—has been restored to the piece. It was hard stuff to write. Kiowa, after all, had been a close friend, and for years I've avoided thinking about his death and my own complicity in it. Even here it's not easy. In the interests of truth, however, I want to make it clear that Norman Bowker was in no way responsible for what happened to Kiowa. Norman did not experience a failure of nerve that night. He did not freeze up or lose the Silver Star for valor. That part of the story is my own.

In the Field

At daybreak the platoon of eighteen soldiers formed into a loose rank and began wading side by side through the deep muck of the shit field. They moved slowly in the rain. Leaning forward, heads down, they used the butts of their weapons as probes, wading across the field to the river and then turning and wading back again. They were tired and miserable; all they wanted now was to get it finished. Kiowa was gone. He was under the mud and water, folded in with the war, and their only thought was to find him and dig him out and then move on to someplace dry and warm. It had been a hard night. Maybe the worst ever. The rains had fallen without stop, and the Song Tra Bong had overflowed its banks, and the muck had now risen thigh-deep in the field along the river. A low, gray mist hovered over the land. Off to the west there was thunder, soft little moaning sounds, and the monsoons seemed to be a lasting element of the war. The eighteen soldiers moved in silence. First Lieutenant Jimmy Cross went first, now and then straightening out the rank, closing up the gaps. His uniform was dark with mud; his arms and face were filthy. Early in the morning he had radioed in the MIA report, giving the name and circumstances, but he was now determined to find his man, no matter what, even if it meant flying in slabs of concrete and damming up the river and draining the entire field. He would not lose a member of his command like this. It wasn't right. Kiowa had been a fine soldier and a fine human being, a devout Baptist, and there was no way Lieutenant Cross would allow such a good man to be lost under the slime of a shit field.

Briefly, he stopped and watched the clouds. Except for some occasional thunder it was a deeply quiet morning, just the rain and the steady sloshing sounds of eighteen men wading through the thick waters. Lieutenant Cross wished the rain would let up. Even for an hour, it would make things easier.

But then he shrugged. The rain was the war and you had to fight it.

Turning, he looked out across the field and yelled at one of his men to close up the rank. Not a man, really—a boy. The young soldier stood off by himself at the center of the field in knee-deep water, reaching down with both hands as if chasing some object just beneath the surface. The boy's shoulders were shaking. Jimmy Cross yelled again but the young soldier did not turn or look up. In his hooded poncho, everything caked with mud, the boy's face was impossible to make out. The filth seemed to erase identities, transforming the men into identical copies of a single soldier, which was exactly how Jimmy Cross had been trained to treat them, as interchangeable units of command. It was difficult sometimes, but he tried to avoid that sort of thinking. He had no military ambitions. He preferred to view his men not as units but as human beings. And Kiowa had been a splendid human being, the very best, intelligent and gentle and quiet-spoken. Very brave, too. And decent. The kid's father taught Sunday school in Oklahoma City, where Kiowa had been raised to believe in the promise of salvation under Jesus Christ, and this conviction had always been present in the boy's smile, in his posture toward the world, in the way he never went anywhere without an illustrated New Testament that his father had mailed to him as a birthday present back in January.

A crime, Jimmy Cross thought.

Looking out toward the river, he knew for a fact that he had made a mistake setting up here. The order had come from higher, true, but still he should've exercised some field discretion. He should've moved to higher ground for the night, should've radioed in false coordinates. There was nothing he could do now, but still it was a mistake and a hideous waste. He felt sick about it. Standing in the deep waters of the field, First Lieutenant Jimmy Cross began composing a letter in his head to the kid's father, not mentioning the shit field, just saying what a fine soldier Kiowa had been, what a fine human being, and how he was the kind of son that any father could be proud of forever.

The search went slowly. For a time the morning seemed to brighten, the sky going to a lighter shade of silver, but then the rains came back hard and steady. There was the feel of permanent twilight.

At the far left of the line, Azar and Norman Bowker and Mitchell Sanders waded along the edge of the field closest to the river. They were tall men, but at times the muck came to midthigh, other times to the crotch.

Azar kept shaking his head. He coughed and shook his head and said, "Man, talk about irony. I bet if Kiowa was here, I bet he'd just laugh. Eating shit—it's your classic irony."

"Fine," said Norman Bowker. "Now pipe down."

Azar sighed. "Wasted in the waste," he said. "A shit field. You got to admit, it's pure world-class irony."

The three men moved with slow, heavy steps. It was hard to keep balance. Their boots sank into the ooze, which produced a powerful downward suction, and with each step they would have to pull up hard to break the hold. The rain made quick dents in the water, like tiny mouths, and the stink was everywhere.

When they reached the river, they shifted a few meters to the north and began wading back up the field. Occasionally they used their weapons to test the bottom, but mostly they just searched with their feet.

"A classic case," Azar was saying. "Biting the dirt, so to speak, that tells the story."

"Enough," Bowker said.

"Like those old cowboy movies. One more redskin bites the dirt." "I'm serious, man. Zip it shut."

Azar smiled and said, "Classic."

The morning was cold and wet. They had not slept during the night, not even for a few moments, and all three of them were feeling the tension as they moved across the field toward the river. There was nothing they could do for Kiowa. Just find him and slide him aboard a chopper. Whenever a man died it was always the same, a desire to get it over with quickly, no fuss or ceremony, and what they wanted now was to head for a ville and get under a roof and forget what had happened during the night.

Halfway across the field Mitchell Sanders stopped. He stood for a moment with his eyes shut, feeling along the bottom with a foot, then he passed his weapon over to Norman Bowker and reached down into the muck. After a second he hauled up a filthy green rucksack.

The three men did not speak for a time. The pack was heavy with mud and water, dead-looking. Inside were a pair of moccasins and an illustrated New Testament.

"Well," Mitchell Sanders finally said, "the guy's around here somewhere."

"Better tell the LT." "Screw him." "Yeah, but—"

"Some lieutenant," Sanders said. "Camps us in a toilet. Man don't *know* shit."

"Nobody knew," Bowker said.

"Maybe so, maybe not. Ten billion places we could've set up last night, the man picks a latrine."

Norman Bowker stared down at the rucksack. It was made of dark green nylon with an aluminum frame, but now it had the curious look of flesh.

"It wasn't the LT's fault," Bowker said quietly. "Whose then?"

"Nobody's. Nobody knew till afterward."

Mitchell Sanders made a sound in his throat. He hoisted up the rucksack, slipped into the harness, and pulled the straps tight. "All right, but this much for sure. The man knew it was raining. He knew about the river. One plus one. Add it up, you get exactly what happened." Sanders glared at the river. "Move it," he said. "Kiowa's waiting on us." Slowly then, bending against the rain, Azar and Norman Bowker and Mitchell Sanders began wading again through the deep waters, their eyes down, circling out from where they had found the rucksack.

First Lieutenant Jimmy Cross stood fifty meters away. He had finished writing the letter in his head, explaining things to Kiowa's father, and now he folded his arms and watched his platoon crisscrossing the wide field. In a funny way, it reminded him of the municipal golf course in his hometown in New Jersey. A lost ball, he thought. Tired players searching through the rough, sweeping back and forth in long systematic patterns. He wished he were there right now. On the sixth hole. Looking out across the water hazard that fronted the small flat green, a seven iron in his hand, calculating wind and distance, wondering if he should reach instead for an eight. A tough decision, but all you could ever lose was a ball. You did not lose a player. And you never had to wade out into the hazard and spend the day searching through the slime.

Jimmy Cross did not want the responsibility of leading these men. He had never wanted it. In his sophomore year at Mount Sebastian College he had signed up for the Reserve Officer Training Corps without much thought. An automatic thing: because his friends had joined, and because it was worth a few credits, and because it seemed preferable to letting the draft take him. He was unprepared. Twenty-four years old and his heart wasn't in it. Military matters meant nothing to him. He did not care one way or the other about the war, and he had no desire to command, and even after all these months in the bush, all the days and nights, even then he did not know enough to keep his men out of a shit field.

What he should've done, he told himself, was follow his first impulse. In the late afternoon yesterday, when they reached the night coordinates, he should've taken one look and headed for higher ground. He should've known. No excuses. At one edge of the field was a small ville, and right away a couple of old mama-sans had trotted out to warn him. Number ten, they'd said. Evil ground. Not a good spot for good GIs. But it was a war, and he had his orders, so they'd set up a perimeter and crawled under their ponchos and tried to settle in for the night. The rain never stopped. By midnight the Song Tra Bong had overflowed its banks. The field turned to slop, everything soft and mushy. He remembered how the water kept rising, how a terrible stink began to bubble up out of the earth. It was a dead-fish smell, partly, but something else, too, and then later in the night Mitchell Sanders had crawled through the rain and grabbed him hard by the arm and asked what he was doing setting up in a shit field. The village toilet, Sanders said. He remembered the look on Sanders's face. The guy stared for a moment and then wiped his mouth and whispered, "Shit," and then crawled away into the dark.

A stupid mistake. That's all it was, a mistake, but it had killed Kiowa.

Lieutenant Jimmy Cross felt something tighten inside him. In the letter to Kiowa's father he would apologize point-blank. Just admit to the blunders.

He would place the blame where it belonged. Tactically, he'd say, it was indefensible ground from the start. Low and flat. No natural cover. And so late in the night, when they took mortar fire from across the river, all they could do was snake down under the slop and lie there and wait. The field just exploded. Rain and slop and shrapnel, it all mixed together, and the field seemed to boil. He would explain this to Kiowa's father. Carefully, not covering up his own guilt, he would tell how the mortar rounds made craters in the slush, spraying up great showers of filth, and how the craters then collapsed on themselves and filled up with mud and water, sucking things down, swallowing things, weapons and entrenching tools and belts of ammunition, and how in this way his son Kiowa had been combined with the waste and the war.

My own fault, he would say.

Straightening up, First Lieutenant Jimmy Cross rubbed his eyes and tried to get his thoughts together. The rain fell in a cold, sad drizzle.

Off toward the river he again noticed the young soldier standing alone at the center of the field. The boy's shoulders were shaking. Maybe it was something in the posture of the soldier, or the way he seemed to be reaching for some invisible object beneath the surface, but for several moments Jimmy Cross stood very still, afraid to move, yet knowing he had to, and then he murmured to himself, "My fault," and he nodded and waded out across the field toward the boy.

The young soldier was trying hard not to cry.

He, too, blamed himself. Bent forward at the waist, groping with both hands, he seemed to be chasing some creature just beyond reach, something elusive, a fish or a frog. His lips were moving. Like Jimmy Cross, the boy was explaining things to an absent judge. It wasn't to defend himself. The boy recognized his own guilt and wanted only to lay out the full causes.

Wading sideways a few steps, he leaned down and felt along the soft bottom of the field.

He pictured Kiowa's face. They'd been close buddies, the tightest, and he remembered how last night they had huddled together under their ponchos, the rain cold and steady, the water rising to their knees, but how Kiowa had just laughed it off and said they should concentrate on better things. And so for a long while they'd talked about their families and hometowns. At one point, the boy remembered, he'd been showing Kiowa a picture of his girlfriend. He remembered switching on his flashlight. A stupid thing to do, but he did it anyway, and he remembered Kiowa leaning in for a look at the picture—"Hey, she's *cute*," he'd said— and then the field exploded all around them.

Like murder, the boy thought. The flashlight made it happen. Dumb and dangerous. And as a result his friend Kiowa was dead.

That simple, he thought.

He wished there were some other way to look at it, but there wasn't. Very simple and very final. He remembered two mortar rounds hitting close by. Then a third, even closer, and off to his left he'd heard somebody scream. The voice was ragged and clotted up, but he knew instantly that it was Kiowa.

He remembered trying to crawl toward the screaming. No sense of direction, though, and the field seemed to suck him under, and everything was black and wet and swirling, and he couldn't get his bearings, and then another round hit nearby, and for a few moments all he could do was hold his breath and duck down beneath the water.

Later, when he came up again, there were no more screams. There was an arm and a wristwatch and part of a boot. There were bubbles where Kiowa's head should've been.

He remembered grabbing the boot. He remembered pulling hard, but how the field seemed to pull back, like a tug-of-war he couldn't win, and how finally he had to whisper his friend's name and let go and watch the boot slide away. Then for a long time there were things he could not remember. Various sounds, various smells. Later he'd found himself lying on a little rise, face-up, tasting the field in his mouth, listening to the rain and explosions and bubbling sounds. He was alone. He'd lost everything. He'd lost Kiowa and his weapon and his flashlight and his girlfriend's picture. He remembered this. He remembered wondering if he could lose himself.

Now, in the dull morning rain, the boy seemed frantic. He waded quickly from spot to spot, leaning down and plunging his hands into the water. He did not look up when Lieutenant Jimmy Cross approached.

"Right here," the boy was saying. "Got to be right here."

Jimmy Cross remembered the kid's face but not the name. That happened sometimes. He tried to treat his men as individuals but sometimes the names just escaped him.

He watched the young soldier shove his hands into the water. "Right *here*," he kept saying. His movements seemed random and jerky.

Jimmy Cross waited a moment, then stepped closer. "Listen," he said quietly, "the guy could be anywhere."

The boy glanced up. "Who could?" "Kiowa. You can't expect—" "Kiowa's *dead*."

"Well, yes."

The young soldier nodded. "So what about Billie?" "Who?"

"My girl. What about her? This picture, it was the only one I had. Right here, I lost it."

Jimmy Cross shook his head. It bothered him that he could not come up with a name.

"Slow down," he said, "I don't—"

"Billie's *picture*. I had it all wrapped up, I had it in plastic, so it'll be okay if I can . . . Last night we were looking at it, me and Kiowa. Right here. I know for sure it's right here somewhere."

Jimmy Cross smiled at the boy. "You can ask her for another one. A better one."

"She won't *send* another one. She's not even my *girl* anymore, she won't . . . Man, I got to find it."

The boy yanked his arm free.

He shuffled sideways and stooped down again and dipped into the muck with both hands. His shoulders were shaking. Briefly, Lieutenant Cross wondered where the kid's weapon was, and his helmet, but it seemed better not to ask.

He felt some pity come on him. For a moment the day seemed to soften. So much hurt, he thought. He watched the young soldier wading through the water, bending down and then standing and then bending down again, as if something might finally be salvaged from all the waste.

Jimmy Cross silently wished the boy luck.

Then he closed his eyes and went back to working on the letter to Kiowa's father.

Across the field Azar and Norman Bowker and Mitchell Sanders were wading alongside a narrow dike at the edge of the field. It was near noon now.

Norman Bowker found Kiowa. He was under two feet of water.

Nothing showed except the heel of a boot. "That's him?" Azar said.

"Who else?"

"I don't know." Azar shook his head. "I don't know."

Norman Bowker touched the boot, covered his eyes for a moment, then stood up and looked at Azar.

"So where's the joke?" he said. "No joke."

"Eating shit. Let's hear that one." "Forget it."

Mitchell Sanders told them to knock it off. The three soldiers moved to the dike, put down their packs and weapons, then waded back to where the boot was showing. The body lay partly wedged under a layer of mud beneath the water. It was hard to get traction; with each movement the muck would grip their feet and hold tight. The rain had come back harder now. Mitchell Sanders reached down and found Kiowa's other boot, and they waited a moment, then Sanders sighed and said, "Okay," and they took hold of the two boots and pulled up hard. There was only a slight give. They tried again, but this time the body did not move at all. After the third try they stopped and looked down for a while. "One more time," Norman Bowker said. He counted to three and they leaned back and pulled.

"Stuck," said Mitchell Sanders. "I see that. Christ."

They tried again, then called over Henry Dobbins and Rat Kiley, and all five of them put their arms and backs into it, but the body was jammed in tight.

Azar moved to the dike and sat holding his stomach. His face was pale. The others stood in a circle, watching the water, then after a time somebody said, "We can't just leave him there," and the men nodded and got out their entrenching tools and began digging. It was hard, sloppy work. The mud seemed to flow back faster than they could dig, but Kiowa was their friend and they kept at it anyway.

Slowly, in little groups, the rest of the platoon drifted over to watch. Only Lieutenant Jimmy Cross and the young soldier were still searching the field.

"What we should do, I guess," Norman Bowker said, "is tell the LT."

Mitchell Sanders shook his head. "Just mess things up. Besides, the man looks happy out there, real content. Let him be."

After ten minutes they uncovered most of Kiowa's lower body. The corpse was angled steeply into the muck, upside down, like a diver who had plunged headfirst off a high tower. The men stood quietly for a few seconds. There was a feeling of awe. Mitchell Sanders finally nodded and said, "Let's get it done," and they took hold of the legs and pulled up hard, then pulled again, and after a moment Kiowa came sliding to the surface. A piece of his shoulder was missing; the arms and chest and face were cut up with shrapnel. He was covered with bluish green mud. "Well," Henry Dobbins said, "it could be worse," and Dave Jensen said, "How, man? Tell me *how*." Carefully, trying not to look at the body, they carried Kiowa over to the dike and laid him down. They used towels to clean off the scum. Rat Kiley went through the kid's pockets, placed his personal effects in a plastic bag, taped the bag to Kiowa's wrist, then used the radio to call in a dustoff.

Moving away, the men found things to do with themselves, some smoking, some opening up cans of C rations, a few just standing in the rain.

For all of them it was a relief to have it finished. There was the promise now of finding a hootch somewhere, or an abandoned pagoda, where they could strip down and wring out their fatigues and maybe start a hot fire. They felt bad for Kiowa. But they also felt a kind of giddiness, a secret joy, because they were alive, and because even the rain was preferable to being sucked under a shit field, and because it was all a matter of luck and happenstance.

Azar sat down on the dike next to Norman Bowker.

"Listen," he said. "Those dumb jokes—I didn't mean anything." "We all say things."

"Yeah, but when I saw the guy, it made me feel—I don't know—like he was listening."

"He wasn't."

"I guess not. But I felt sort of guilty almost, like if I'd kept my mouth shut none of it would've ever happened. Like it was my fault."

Norman Bowker looked out across the wet field. "Nobody's fault," he said. "Everybody's."

Near the center of the field First Lieutenant Jimmy Cross squatted in the muck, almost entirely submerged. In his head he was revising the letter to Kiowa's father. Impersonal this time. An officer expressing an officer's condolences. No apologies were necessary, because in fact it was one of those freak things, and the war was full of freaks, and nothing could ever change it anyway. Which was the truth, he thought. The exact truth.

Lieutenant Cross went deeper into the muck, the dark water at his throat, and tried to tell himself it was the truth.

Beside him, a few steps off to the left, the young soldier was still searching for his girlfriend's picture. Still remembering how he had killed Kiowa.

The boy wanted to confess. He wanted to tell the lieutenant how in the middle of the night he had pulled out Billie's picture and passed it over to Kiowa and then switched on the flashlight, and how Kiowa had whispered, "Hey, she's *cute*," and how for a second the flashlight had made Billie's face sparkle, and how right then the field had exploded all around them. The flashlight had done it. Like a target shining in the dark.

The boy looked up at the sky, then at Jimmy Cross. "Sir?" he said.

The rain and mist moved across the field in broad, sweeping sheets of gray. Close by, there was thunder.

"Sir," the boy said, "I got to explain something."

But Lieutenant Jimmy Cross wasn't listening. Eyes closed, he let himself go deeper into the waste, just letting the field take him. He lay back and floated.

When a man died, there had to be blame. Jimmy Cross understood this. You could blame the war. You could blame the idiots who made the war. You could blame Kiowa for going to it. You could blame the rain.

You could blame the river. You could blame the field, the mud, the climate. You could blame the enemy. You could blame the mortar rounds. You could blame people who were too lazy to read a newspaper, who were bored by the daily body counts, who switched channels at the mention of politics. You could blame whole nations. You could blame God. You could blame the munitions makers or Karl Marx or a trick of fate or an old man in Omaha who forgot to vote.

In the field, though, the causes were immediate. A moment of carelessness or bad judgment or plain stupidity carried consequences that lasted forever.

For a long while Jimmy Cross lay floating. In the clouds to the east there was the sound of a helicopter, but he did not take notice. With his eyes still closed, bobbing in the field, he let himself slip away. He was back home in New Jersey. A golden afternoon on the golf course, the fairways lush and green, and he was teeing it up on the first hole. It was a world without responsibility. When the war was over, he thought, maybe then he would write a letter to Kiowa's father. Or maybe not. Maybe he would just take a couple of practice swings and knock the ball down the middle and pick up his clubs and walk off into the afternoon.

Good Form

It's time to be blunt.

I'm forty-three years old, true, and I'm a writer now, and a long time ago I walked through Quang Ngai Province as a foot soldier.

Almost everything else is invented.

But it's not a game. It's a form. Right here, now, as I invent myself, I'm thinking of all I want to tell you about why this book is written as it is. For instance, I want to tell you this: twenty years ago I watched a man die on a trail near the village of My Khe. I did not kill him. But I was present, you see, and my presence was guilt enough. I remember his face, which was not a pretty face, because his jaw was in his throat, and I remember feeling the burden of responsibility and grief. I blamed myself. And rightly so, because I was present.

But listen. Even *that* story is made up.

I want you to feel what I felt. I want you to know why story-truth is truer sometimes than happening-truth.

Here is the happening-truth. I was once a soldier. There were many bodies, real bodies with real faces, but I was young then and I was afraid to look. And now, twenty years later, I'm left with faceless responsibility and faceless grief.

Here is the story-truth. He was a slim, dead, almost dainty young man of about twenty. He lay in the center of a red clay trail near the village of My Khe. His jaw was in his throat. His one eye was shut, the other eye was a star-shaped hole. I killed him.

What stories can do, I guess, is make things present.

I can look at things I never looked at. I can attach faces to grief and love and pity and God. I can be brave. I can make myself feel again.

"Daddy, tell the truth," Kathleen can say, "did you ever kill anybody?" And I can say, honestly, "Of course not."

Or I can say, honestly, "Yes."

Field Trip

A few months after completing "In the Field," I returned with my daughter to Vietnam, where we visited the site of Kiowa's death, and where I looked for signs of forgiveness or personal grace or whatever else the land might offer. The field was still there, though not as I remembered it. Much smaller, I thought, and not nearly so menacing, and in the bright sunlight it was hard to picture what had happened on this ground some twenty years ago. Except for a few marshy spots along the river, everything was bone dry. No ghosts—just a flat, grassy field. The place was at peace. There were yellow butterflies. There was a breeze and a wide blue sky. Along the river two old farmers stood in ankle-deep water, repairing the same narrow dike where we had laid out Kiowa's body after pulling him from the muck. Things were quiet. At one point, I remember, one of the farmers looked up and shaded his eyes, staring across the field at us, then after a time he wiped his forehead and went back to work.

I stood with my arms folded, feeling the grip of sentiment and time.

Amazing, I thought. Twenty years.

Behind me, in the jeep, my daughter Kathleen sat waiting with a government interpreter, and now and then I could hear the two of them talking in soft voices. They were already fast friends. Neither of them, I think, understood what all this was about, why I'd insisted that we search out this spot. It had been a hard two-hour ride from Quang Ngai City, bumpy dirt roads and a hot August sun, ending up at an empty field on the edge of nowhere.

I took out my camera, snapped a couple of pictures, then stood gazing out at the field. After a time Kathleen got out of the jeep and stood beside me.

"You know what I think?" she said. "I think this place stinks. It smells like . . . God, I don't even *know* what. It smells rotten."

"It sure does. I know that." "So when can we go?" "Pretty soon," I said.

She started to say something but then hesitated. Frowning, she squinted out at the field for a second, then shrugged and walked back to the jeep.

Kathleen had just turned ten, and this trip was a kind of birthday present, showing her the world, offering a small piece of her father's history. For the most part she'd held up well—far better than I—and over the first two weeks she'd trooped along without complaint as we hit the obligatory tourist stops. Ho Chi Minh's mausoleum in Hanoi. A model farm outside Saigon. The tunnels at Cu Chi. The monuments and government offices and orphanages. Through most of this, Kathleen had seemed to enjoy the foreignness of it all, the exotic food and animals, and even during those periods of boredom and discomfort she'd kept up a good-humored tolerance. At the same time, however, she'd seemed a bit puzzled. The war was as remote to her as cavemen and dinosaurs.

One morning in Saigon she'd asked what it was all about. "This whole war," she said, "why was everybody so mad at everybody else?"

I shook my head. "They weren't mad, exactly. Some people wanted one thing, other people wanted another thing."

"What did *you* want?" "Nothing," I said. "To stay alive."

"That's all?"

"Yes."

Kathleen sighed. "Well, I don't get it. I mean, how come you were even here in the first place?"

"I don't know," I said. "Because I had to be." "But *why*?"

I tried to find something to tell her, but finally I shrugged and said, "It's a mystery, I guess. I don't know."

For the rest of the day she was very quiet. That night, though, just before bedtime, Kathleen put her hand on my shoulder and said, "You know something? Sometimes you're pretty weird, aren't you?"

"Well, no," I said.

"You are *too*." She pulled her hand away and frowned at me. "Like coming over here. Some dumb thing happens a long time ago and you can't ever forget it."

"And that's bad?"

"No," she said quietly. "That's weird."

In the second week of August, near the end of our stay, I'd arranged for the side trip up to Quang Ngai. The tourist stuff was fine, but from the start I'd wanted to take my daughter to the places I'd seen as a soldier. I wanted to show her the Vietnam that kept me awake at night—a shady trail outside the village of My Khe, a filthy old pigsty on the Batangan Peninsula. Our time was short, however, and choices had to be made, and in the end I decided to take her to this piece of ground where my friend Kiowa had died. It seemed appropriate. And, besides, I had business here.

Now, looking out at the field, I wondered if it was all a mistake. Everything was too ordinary. A quiet sunny day, and the field was not the field I remembered. I pictured Kiowa's face, the way he used to smile, but all I felt was the awkwardness of remembering.

Behind me, Kathleen let out a little giggle. The interpreter was showing her magic tricks.

There were birds and butterflies, the soft rustlings of rural-anywhere. Below, in the earth, the relics of our presence were no doubt still there, the canteens and bandoliers and mess kits. This little field, I thought, had swallowed so much. My best friend. My pride. My belief in myself as a man of some small dignity and courage. Still, it was hard to find any real emotion. It simply wasn't there. After that long night in the rain, I'd seemed to grow cold inside, all the illusions gone, all the old ambitions and hopes for myself sucked away into the mud. Over the years, that coldness had never entirely disappeared. There were times in my life when I couldn't feel much, not sadness or pity or passion, and somehow I blamed this place for what I had become, and I blamed it for taking away the person I had once been. For twenty years this field had embodied all the waste that was Vietnam, all the vulgarity and horror.

Now, it was just what it was. Flat and dreary and unremarkable. I walked up toward the river, trying to pick out specific landmarks, but all I recognized was a small rise where Jimmy Cross had set up his command post that night. Nothing else. For a while I watched the two old farmers working under the hot sun. I took a few more photographs, waved at the farmers, then turned and moved back to the jeep.

Kathleen gave me a little nod.

"Well," she said, "I hope you're having fun." "Sure."

"Can we go now?"

"In a minute," I said. "Just relax."

At the back of the jeep I found the small cloth bundle I'd carried over from the States.

Kathleen's eyes narrowed. "What's *that*?" "Stuff," I told her.

She glanced at the bundle again, then hopped out of the jeep and followed me back to the field. We walked past Jimmy Cross's command post, past the spot where Kiowa had gone under, down to where the field dipped into the marshland along the river. I took off my shoes and socks.

"Okay," Kathleen said, "what's going on?" "A quick swim."

"Where?"

"Right here," I said. "Stay put."

She watched me unwrap the cloth bundle. Inside were Kiowa's old moccasins.

I stripped down to my underwear, took off my wrist-watch, and waded in. The water was warm against my feet. Instantly, I recognized the soft, fat feel of the bottom. The water here was eight inches deep.

Kathleen seemed nervous. She squinted at me, her hands fluttering. "Listen, this is stupid," she said, "you can't even hardly get *wet*. How can you swim out there?"

"I'll manage."

"But it's not . . . I mean, God, it's not even *water*, it's like mush or something."

She pinched her nose and watched me wade out to where the water reached my knees. Roughly here, I decided, was where Mitchell Sanders had found Kiowa's rucksack. I eased myself down, squatting at first, then sitting. There was again that sense of recognition. The water rose to midchest, a deep greenish brown, almost hot. Small water bugs skipped along the surface. Right here, I thought. Leaning forward, I reached in with the moccasins and wedged them into the soft bottom, letting them slide away. Tiny bubbles broke along the surface. I tried to think of something decent to say, something meaningful and right, but nothing came to me.

I looked down into the field.

"Well," I finally managed. "There it is."

My voice surprised me. It had a rough, chalky sound, full of things I did not know were there. I wanted to tell Kiowa that he'd been a great friend, the very best, but all I could do was slap hands with the water.

The sun made me squint. Twenty years. A lot like yesterday, a lot like never. In a way, maybe, I'd gone under with Kiowa, and now after two decades I'd finally worked my way out. A hot afternoon, a bright August sun, and the war was over. For a few moments I could not bring myself to move. Like waking from a summer nap, feeling lazy and sluggish, the world collecting itself around me. Fifty meters up the field one of the old farmers stood watching from along the dike. The man's face was dark and solemn. As we stared at each other, neither of us moving, I felt something go shut in my heart while something else swung open. Briefly, I wondered if the old man might walk over to exchange a few war stories, but instead he picked up a shovel and raised it over his head and held it there for a time, grimly, like a flag, then he brought the shovel down and said something to his friend and began digging into the hard, dry ground.

I stood up and waded out of the water.

"What a mess," Kathleen said. "All that gunk on your skin, you look like . . . Wait'll I tell Mommy, she'll probably make you sleep in the garage."

"You're right," I said. "Don't tell her."

I pulled on my shoes, took my daughter's hand, and led her across the field toward the jeep. Soft heat waves shimmied up out of the earth.

When we reached the jeep, Kathleen turned and glanced out at the field.

"That old man," she said, "is he mad at you or something?" "I hope not."

"He *looks* mad."

"No," I said. "All that's finished."

The Ghost Soldiers

I was shot twice. The first time, out by Tri Binh, it knocked me against the pagoda wall, and I bounced and spun around and ended up on Rat Kiley's lap. A lucky thing, because Rat was the medic. He tied on a compress and told me to ease back, then he ran off toward the fighting. For a long time I lay there all alone, listening to the battle, thinking *I've been shot, I've been shot*: all those Gene Autry movies I'd seen as a kid. In fact, I almost smiled, except then I started to think I might die. It was the fear, mostly, but I felt wobbly, and then I had a sinking sensation, ears all plugged up, as if I'd gone deep under water. Thank God for Rat Kiley. Every so often, maybe four times altogether, he trotted back to check me out. Which took courage. It was a wild fight, guys running and laying down fire and regrouping and running again, lots of noise, but Rat Kiley took the risks. "Easy does it," he told me, "just a side wound, no problem unless you're pregnant." He ripped off the compress, applied a fresh one, and told me to clamp it in place with my fingers. "Press hard," he said. "Don't worry about the baby." Then he took off. It was almost dark when the fighting ended and the chopper came to take me and two dead guys away. "Happy trails," Rat said. He helped me into the helicopter and stood there for a moment. Then he did an odd thing. He leaned in and put his head against my shoulder and almost hugged me. Coming from Rat Kiley, that was something new.

On the ride into Chu Lai, I kept waiting for the pain to hit, but in fact I didn't feel much. A throb, that's all. Even in the hospital it wasn't bad.

When I got back to Alpha Company twenty-six days later, in mid- December, Rat Kiley had been wounded and shipped off to Japan, and a new medic named Bobby Jorgenson had replaced him. Jorgenson was no Rat Kiley. He was green and incompetent and scared. So when I got shot the second time, in the butt, along the Song Tra Bong, it took the son of a bitch almost ten minutes to work up the nerve to crawl over to me. By then I was gone with the pain. Later I found out I'd almost died of shock. Bobby Jorgenson didn't know about shock, or if he did, the fear made him forget. To make it worse, he bungled the patch job, and a couple of weeks later my ass started to rot away. You could actually peel off chunks of skin with your fingernail.

It was borderline gangrene. I spent a month flat on my stomach; I couldn't walk or sit; I couldn't sleep. I kept seeing Bobby Jorgenson's scared-white face. Those buggy eyes and the way his lips twitched and that silly excuse he had for a mustache. After the rot cleared up, once I could think straight, I devoted a lot of time to figuring ways to get back at him.

Getting shot should be an experience from which you can draw some small pride. I don't mean the macho stuff. All I mean is that you should be able to *talk* about it: the stiff thump of the bullet, like a fist, the way it knocks the air out of you and makes you cough, how the sound of the gunshot arrives about ten years later, and the dizzy feeling, the smell of yourself, the things you think about and say and do right afterward, the way your eyes focus on a tiny white pebble or a blade of grass and how you start thinking, Oh man, that's the last thing I'll ever see, *that* pebble, *that* blade of grass, which makes you want to cry.

Pride isn't the right word. I don't know the right word. All I know is, you shouldn't feel embarrassed. Humiliation shouldn't be part of it.

Diaper rash, the nurses called it. An in-joke, I suppose. But it made me hate Bobby Jorgenson the way some guys hated the VC, gut hate, the kind of hate that stays with you even in your dreams.

I guess the higher-ups decided I'd been shot enough. At the end of December, when I was released from the 91st Evac Hospital, they transferred me over to Headquarters Company—S-4, the battalion supply section. Compared with the boonies it was cushy duty. We had regular hours. There was an EM club with beer and movies, sometimes even live floor shows, the whole blurry slow motion of the rear. For the first time in months I felt reasonably safe. The battalion firebase was built into a hill just off Highway 1, surrounded on all sides by flat paddy land, and between us and the paddies there were reinforced bunkers and observation towers and trip flares and rolls of razor-tipped barbed wire. You could still die, of course—once a month we'd get hit with mortar fire—but you could also die in the bleachers at Met Stadium in Minneapolis, bases loaded, Harmon Killebrew coming to the plate.

I didn't complain. In an odd way, though, there were times when I missed the adventure, even the danger, of the real war out in the boonies. It's a hard thing to explain to somebody who hasn't felt it, but the presence of death and danger has a way of bringing you fully awake. It makes things vivid. When you're afraid, really afraid, you see things you never saw before, you pay attention to the world. You make close friends. You become part of a tribe and you share the same blood—you give it together, you take it together. On the other hand, I'd already been hit with two bullets; I was superstitious; I believed in the odds with the same passion that my friend Kiowa had once believed in Jesus Christ, or the way Mitchell Sanders believed in the power of morals. I figured my war was over. If it hadn't been for the constant ache in my butt, I'm sure things would've worked out fine.

But it hurt.

At night I had to sleep on my belly. That doesn't sound so terrible until you consider that I'd been a back-sleeper all my life. I'd lie there all fidgety and tight, then after a while I'd feel a swell of anger come on. I'd squirm around, cussing, half nuts with pain, and pretty soon I'd start remembering how Bobby Jorgenson had almost killed me. Shock, I'd think—how could he forget to treat for shock?

I'd remember how long it took him to get to me, and how his fingers were all jerky and nervous, and the way his lips kept twitching under that ridiculous little mustache.

The nights were miserable. Sometimes I'd roam around the base. I'd head down to the wire and stare out at the darkness, out where the war was, and think up ways to make Bobby Jorgenson feel exactly what I felt. I wanted to hurt him.

In March, Alpha Company came in for stand-down. I was there at the helipad to meet the choppers. Mitchell Sanders and Azar and Henry Dobbins and Dave Jensen and Norman Bowker slapped hands with me and we piled their gear in my jeep and drove down to the Alpha hootches. We partied until chow time. Afterward, we kept on partying. It was one of the rituals. Even if you weren't in the mood, you did it on principle.

By midnight it was story time.

"Morty Phillips used up his luck," Bowker said.

I smiled and waited. There was a tempo to how stories got told.

Bowker peeled open a finger blister and sucked on it. "Go on," Azar said. "Tell him everything."

"Well, that's about it. Poor Morty wasted his luck. Pissed it away." "On *nothing*," Azar said. "The dummy pisses it away on *nothing*."

Norman Bowker nodded, started to speak, but then stopped and got up and moved to the cooler and shoved his hands deep into the ice. He was naked except for his shorts and dog tags. In a way, I envied him—all of them. Their deep bush tans, the sores and blisters, the stories, the in- it-togethemess. I felt close to them, yes, but I also felt a new sense of separation. My fatigues were starched; I had a neat haircut and the clean, sterile smell of the rear. They were still my buddies, at least on one level, but once you leave the boonies, the whole comrade business gets turned around. You become a civilian. You forfeit membership in the family, the blood fraternity, and no matter how hard you try, you can't pretend to be part of it.

That's how I felt—like a civilian—and it made me sad. These guys had been my brothers. We'd loved one another.

Norman Bowker bent forward and scooped up some ice against his chest, pressing it there for a moment, then he fished out a beer and snapped it open.

"It was out by My Khe," he said quietly. "One of those killer hot days, hot-hot, and we're all popping salt tabs just to stay conscious. Can't barely breathe. Everybody's lying around, just grooving it, and after a while somebody says, 'Hey, where's Morty?' So the lieutenant does a head count, and guess what? No Morty."

"Gone," Ealasaid. "Poof. Novocain' Morty."

Norman Bowker nodded. "Anyhow, we send out two search patrols. No dice. Not a trace." Pausing a second, Bowker poured a trickle of beer onto his blister and licked at it. "By then it's almost dark. Lieutenant Cross, he's ready to have a fit—you know how he gets, right?—and then, guess what? Take a guess."

"Morty shows," I said.

"You got it, man. Morty shows. We almost chalk him up as MIA, and then, bingo, he shows."

"Soaking wet," said Azar. "Hey, listen—"

"Okay, but *tell* it."

Norman Bowker frowned. "Soaking wet," he said. "Turns out the moron went for a swim. You believe that? All alone, he just takes off, hikes a couple klicks, finds himself a river and strips down and hops in and starts doing the goddamn breast stroke or some such fine shit. No security, no nothing. I mean, the dude goes skinny dipping."

Azar giggled. "A hot day."

"Not that hot," said Dave Jensen. "Hot, though."

"Get the picture?" Bowker said. "This is My Khe we're talking about, dinks everywhere, and the guy goes for a *swim*."

"Crazy," I said.

I looked across the hootch. Twenty or thirty guys were there, some drinking, some passed out, but I couldn't find Morty Phillips among them.

Bowker smiled. He reached out and put his hand on my knee and squeezed.

"That's the kicker, man. No more Morty." "No?"

"Morty's luck gets all used up," Bowker said. His hand still rested on my knee, very lightly. "A few days later, maybe a week, he feels real dizzy. Pukes a lot, temperature zooms way up. I mean, the guy's *sick*.

Jorgenson says he must've swallowed bad water on that swim. Swallowed a VC virus or something."

"Bobby Jorgenson," I said. "Where is he?" "Be cool."

"Where's my good buddy Bobby?"

Norman Bowker made a short clicking sound with his tongue. "You want to *hear* this? Yes or no?"

"Sure I do."

"So listen up, then. Morty gets sick. Like you never seen nobody so bad off. This is real kickass disease, he can't walk or talk, can't fart. Can't nothin'. Like he's paralyzed. Polio, maybe."

Henry Dobbins shook his head. "Not polio. You got it wrong." "*Maybe* polio."

"No way," said Dobbins. "Not polio."

"Well, hey," Bowker said, "I'm just saying what Jorgenson says. Maybe fuckin' polio. Or that weird elephant disease. Elephantiasshole or whatever."

"Yeah, but not polio."

Across the hootch, sitting off by himself, Azar grinned and snapped his fingers. "Either way," he said, "it goes to show you. Don't throw away luck on little stuff. Save it up."

"There it is," said Mitchell Sanders. "Morty was due," Dave Jensen said. "Overdue," Sanders said.

Norman Bowker nodded solemnly. "You don't mess around like that.

You just don't fritter away all your luck." "Amen," said Sanders.

"Fuckin' polio," said Henry Dobbins.

We sat quietly for a time. There was no need to talk, because we were thinking the same things: about Morty Phillips and the way luck worked and didn't work and how it was impossible to calculate the odds. There were a million ways to die. Getting shot was one way. Booby traps and land mines and gangrene and shock and polio from a VC virus.

"Where's Jorgenson?" I said.

Another thing. Three times a day, no matter what, I had to stop whatever I was doing. I had to go find a private place and drop my pants and smear on this antibacterial ointment. The stuff left stains on the seat of my trousers, big yellow splotches, and so naturally there were some jokes. There was one about rear guard duty. There was another one about hemorrhoids and how I had trouble putting the past behind me. The others weren't quite so funny.

During the first full day of Alpha's stand-down, I didn't run into Bobby Jorgenson once. Not at chow, not at the EM club, not even during our long booze sessions in the Alpha Company hootch. At one point I almost went looking for him, but my friend Mitchell Sanders told me to forget it.

"Let it ride," he said. "The kid messed up bad, for sure, but you have to take into account how green he was. Brand-new, remember? Thing is, he's doing a lot better now. I mean, listen, the guy knows his shit. Say what you want, but he kept Morty Phillips alive."

"And that makes it okay?"

Sanders shrugged. "People change. Situations change. I hate to say this, man, but you're out of touch. Jorgenson—he's *with* us now."

"And I'm not?"

Sanders looked at me for a moment. "No," he said. "I guess you're not."

Stiffly, like a stranger, Sanders moved across the hootch and lay down with a magazine and pretended to read.

I felt something shift inside me. It was anger, partly, but it was also a sense of pure and total loss: I didn't fit anymore. They were soldiers, I wasn't. In a few days they'd saddle up and head back into the bush, and I'd stand up on the helipad to watch them march away, and then after they were gone I'd spend the day loading resupply choppers until it was time to catch a movie or play cards or drink myself to sleep. A funny thing, but I felt betrayed.

For a long while I just stared at Mitchell Sanders. "Loyalty," I said. "Such a pal."

In the morning I ran into Bobby Jorgenson. I was loading Hueys up on the helipad, and when the last bird took off, while I was putting on my shirt, I looked over and saw him leaning against my jeep, waiting for me. It was a surprise. He seemed smaller than I remembered, a little squirrel of a guy, short and stumpy-looking.

He nodded nervously. "Well," he said.

At first I just looked down at his boots. Those boots: I remembered them from when I got shot. Out along the Song Tra Bong, a bullet inside me, all that pain, but for some reason what stuck to my memory was the smooth unblemished leather of his fine new boots. Factory black, no scuffs or dust or red clay. The boots were one of those vivid details you can't forget. Like a pebble or a blade of grass, you just stare and think, Dear Christ, there's the last thing on earth I'll ever see.

Jorgenson blinked and tried to smile. Oddly, I almost felt some pity for him.

"Look," he said, "can we talk?"

I didn't move. I didn't say a word. Jorgenson's tongue flicked out, moving along the edge of his mustache, then slipped away.

"Listen, man, I fucked up," he said. "What else can I say? I'm sorry. When you got hit, I kept telling myself to move, move, but I couldn't *do* it, like I was full of drugs or something. You ever feel like that? Like you can't even move?"

"No," I said, "I never did." "But can't you at least—" "Excuses?"

Jorgenson's lip twitched. "No, I botched it. Period. Got all frozen up, I guess. The noise and shooting and everything—my first firefight—I just couldn't handle it . . . When I heard about the shock, the gangrene, I felt like . . . I felt miserable. Nightmares, too. I kept seeing you lying out there, heard you screaming, but it was like my legs were filled up with sand, they didn't *work*. I'd keep trying but I couldn't make my goddamn *legs* work."

He made a small sound in his throat, something low and feathery, and for a second I was afraid he might bawl. That would've ended it. I would've patted his shoulder and told him to forget it. But he kept control. He swallowed whatever the sound was and forced a smile and tried to shake my hand. It gave me an excuse to glare at him.

"It's not that easy," I said.

"Tim, I can't go back and do things over." "My ass."

Jorgenson kept pushing his hand out at me. He looked so earnest, so sad and hurt, that it almost made me feel guilty. Not quite, though. After a second I muttered something and got into my jeep and put it to the floor and left him standing there.

I hated him for making me stop hating him.

Something had gone wrong. I'd come to this war a quiet, thoughtful sort of person, a college grad, Phi Beta Kappa and summa cum laude, all the credentials, but after seven months in the bush I realized that those high, civilized trappings had somehow been crushed under the weight of the simple daily realities. I'd turned mean inside. Even a little cruel at times. For all my education, all my fine liberal values, I now felt a deep coldness inside me, something dark and beyond reason. It's a hard thing to admit, even to myself, but I was capable of evil. I wanted to hurt Bobby Jorgenson the way he'd hurt me. For weeks it had been a vow—*I'll get him, I'll get him*—it was down inside me like a rock. Granted, I didn't hate him anymore, and I'd lost some of the outrage and passion, but the need for revenge kept eating at me. At night I sometimes drank too much. I'd remember getting shot and yelling out for a medic and then waiting and waiting and waiting, passing out once, then waking up and screaming some more, and how the screaming seemed to make new pain, the awful stink of myself, the sweat and fear, Bobby Jorgenson's clumsy fingers when he finally got around to working on me. I kept going over it all, every detail. I remembered the soft, fluid heat of my own blood. *Shock*, I thought, and I tried to tell him that, but my tongue wouldn't make the connection. I wanted to yell, "You jerk, it's shock—I'm *dying*" but all I could do was whinny and squeal. I remembered that, and the hospital, and the nurses. I even remembered the rage. But I couldn't feel it anymore. In the end, all I felt was that coldness down inside my chest. Number one: the guy had almost killed me. Number two: there had to be consequences.

That afternoon I asked Mitchell Sanders to give me a hand.

"No pain," I said. "Basic psychology, that's all. Mess with his head a little."

"Negative," Sanders said.

"Spook the fucker."

Sanders shook his head. "Man, you're sick." "All I want is—"

"Sick."

Quietly, Sanders looked at me for a second and then walked away. I had to get Azar in on it.

He didn't have Mitchell Sanders's intelligence, but he had a keener sense of justice. After I explained the plan, Azar gave me a long white smile.

"Tonight?" he said.

"Just don't get carried away." "Me?"

Still smiling, Azar flicked an eyebrow and started snapping his fingers. It was a tic of his. Whenever things got tense, whenever there was a prospect for action, he'd do that snapping thing. Nobody cared for him, including myself.

"Understand?" I said.

Azar winked. "Roger-dodger. Only a game, right?"

We called the enemy ghosts. "Bad night," we'd say, "the ghosts are out." To get spooked, in the lingo, meant not only to get scared but to get killed. "Don't get spooked," we'd say. "Stay cool, stay alive." Or we'd say: "Careful, man, don't give up the ghost." The countryside itself seemed spooky—shadows and tunnels and incense burning in the dark. The land was haunted. We were fighting forces that did not obey the laws of twentieth-century science. Late at night, on guard, it seemed that all of Vietnam was alive and shimmering—odd shapes swaying in the paddies, boogiemen in sandals, spirits dancing in old pagodas. It was ghost country, and Charlie Cong was the main ghost. The way he came out at night. How you never really saw him, just thought you did. Almost magical—appearing, disappearing. He could blend with the land, changing form, becoming trees and grass. He could levitate. He could fly. He could pass through barbed wire and melt away like ice and creep up on you without sound or footsteps. He was scary. In the daylight, maybe, you didn't believe in this stuff. You laughed it off. You made jokes. But at night you turned into a believer: no skeptics in foxholes.

Azar was wound up tight. All afternoon, while we made the preparations, he kept chanting, "Halloween, Halloween." That, plus the finger snapping, almost made me cancel the whole operation. I went hot and cold. Mitchell Sanders wouldn't speak to me, which tended to cool it off, but then I'd start remembering things. The result was a kind of numbness. No ice, no heat. I just went through the motions, rigidly, by the numbers, without any heart or real emotion. I rigged up my special effects, checked out the terrain, measured distances, collected the ordnance and equipment we'd need. I was professional enough about it, I didn't make mistakes, but somehow it felt as if I were gearing up to fight somebody else's war. I didn't have that patriotic zeal.

If there had been a dignified way out, I might've taken it. During evening chow, in fact, I kept staring across the mess hall at Bobby Jorgenson, and when he finally looked up at me, almost nodding, I came very close to calling it quits. Maybe I was fishing for something. One last apology—something public. But Jorgenson only gazed back at me. It was a strange gaze, too, straight on and unafraid, as if apologies were no longer required. He was sitting there with Dave Jensen and Mitchell Sanders and a few others, and he seemed to fit in very nicely, all smiles and group rapport.

That's probably what cinched it.

I went back to my hootch, showered, shaved, threw my helmet against the wall, lay down for a while, got up, prowled around, talked to myself, applied some fresh ointment, then headed off to find Azar.

Just before dusk, Alpha Company stood for roll call.

Afterward the men separated into two groups. Some went off to write letters or party or sleep; the others trooped down to the base perimeter, where, for the next eleven hours, they would pull night guard duty. It was SOP—one night on, one night off.

This was Jorgenson's night on. I knew that in advance, of course. And I knew his bunker assignment: Bunker Six, a pile of sandbags at the southwest corner of the perimeter. That morning I'd scouted out every inch of his position; I knew the blind spots and the little ripples of land and the places where he'd take cover in case of trouble. But still, just to guard against freak screw-ups, Azar and I tailed him down to the wire. We watched him lay out his poncho and connect his Claymores to their firing devices. Softly, like a little boy, he was whistling to himself. He tested his radio, unwrapped a candy bar, then sat back with his rifle cradled to his chest like a teddy bear.

"A pigeon," Azar whispered. "Roast pigeon on a spit. I smell it sizzling."

"Except this isn't for real."

Azar shrugged. After a second he reached out and clapped me on the shoulder, not roughly but not gently either. "What's real?" he said. "Eight months in fantasyland, it tends to blur the line. Honest to God, I sometimes can't remember what real is."

Psychology—that was one thing I knew. You don't try to scare people in broad daylight. You wait. Because the darkness squeezes you inside yourself, you get cut off from the outside world, the imagination takes over. That's basic psychology. I'd pulled enough night guard to know how the fear factor gets multiplied as you sit there hour after hour, nobody to talk to, nothing to do but stare into the big black hole at the center of your own sorry soul. The hours go by and you lose your gyroscope; your mind starts to roam. You think about dark closets, madmen, murderers under the bed, all those childhood fears. Gremlins and trolls and giants. You try to block it out but you can't. You see ghosts. You blink and shake your head. Bullshit, you tell yourself. But then you remember the guys who died: Curt Lemon, Kiowa, Ted Lavender, a half-dozen others whose faces you can't bring into focus anymore. And then pretty soon you start to ponder the stories you've heard about Charlie's magic. The time some guys cornered two VC in a dead-end tunnel, no way out, but how, when the tunnel was fragged and searched, nothing was found except a pile of dead rats. A hundred stories. Ghosts wiping out a whole Marine platoon in twenty seconds flat. Ghosts rising from the dead. Ghosts behind you and in front of you and inside you. After a while, as the night deepens, you feel a funny buzzing in your ears. Tiny sounds get heightened and distorted. The crickets talk in code; the night takes on a weird electronic tingle. You hold your breath. You coil up and tighten your muscles and listen, knuckles hard, the pulse ticking in your head. You hear the spooks laughing. No shit, *laughing*. You jerk up, you freeze, you squint at the dark. Nothing, though. You put your weapon on full automatic. You crouch lower and count your grenades and make sure the pins are bent for quick throwing and take a deep breath and listen and try not to freak. And then later, after enough time passes, things start to get bad.

"Come on," Azar said, "let's *do* it," but I told him to be patient. Waiting was the trick. So we went to the movies, *Barbarella* again, the eighth straight night. A lousy movie, I thought, but it kept Azar occupied. He was crazy about Jane Fonda. "Sweet Janie," he kept saying. "Sweet Janie boosts a man's morale." Then, with his hand, he showed me which part of his morale got boosted. It was an old joke. Everything was old. The movie, the heat, the booze, the war. I fell asleep during the second reel—a hot, angry sleep—and forty minutes later I woke up to a sore ass and a foul temper.

It wasn't yet midnight.

We hiked over to the EM club and worked our way through a six-pack. Mitchell Sanders was there, at another table, but he pretended not to see me.

Around closing time, I nodded at Azar. "Well, goody gumdrop," he said.

We went over to my hootch, picked up our gear, and then moved through the night down to the wire. I felt like a soldier again. Back in the bush, it seemed. We observed good field discipline, not talking, keeping to the shadows and joining in with the darkness. When we came up on Bunker Six, Azar lifted his thumb and peeled away from me and began circling to the south. Old times, I thought. A kind of thrill, a kind of dread.

Quietly, I shouldered my gear and crossed over to a heap of boulders that overlooked Jorgenson's position. I was directly behind him. Thirty-two meters away, exactly. Even in the heavy darkness, no moon yet, I could make out the kid's silhouette: a helmet, a pair of shoulders, a rifle barrel. His back was to me. He gazed out at the wire and at the paddies beyond, where the danger was.

I knelt down and took out ten flares and unscrewed the caps and lined them up in front of me and then checked my wristwatch. Still five minutes to go. Edging over to my left, I groped for the ropes I'd set up that afternoon. I found them, tested the tension, and checked the time again. Four minutes. There was a light feeling in my head, fluttery and taut at the same time. I remembered it from the boonies. Giddiness and doubt and awe, all those things and a million more. You wonder if you're dreaming. It's like you're in a movie. There's a camera on you, so you begin acting, you're somebody else. You think of all the films you've seen, Audie Murphy and Gary Cooper and the Cisco Kid, all those heroes, and you can't help falling back on them as models of proper comportment. On ambush, curled in the dark, you fight for control. Not too much fidgeting. You rearrange your posture; you try for a grin; you measure out your breathing. Eyes open, be alert—old imperatives, old movies. It all swirls together, cliches mixing with your own emotions, and in the end you can't tell one from the other.

There was that coldness inside me. I wasn't myself. I felt hollow and dangerous.

I took a breath, fingered the first rope, and gave it a sharp little jerk. Instantly there was a clatter outside the wire. I expected the noise, I was even tensed for it, but still my heart took a hop.

Now, I thought. Now it starts.

Eight ropes altogether. I had four, Azar had four. Each rope was hooked up to a homemade noisemaker out in front of Jorgenson's bunker—eight ammo cans filled with rifle cartridges. Simple devices, but they worked. I waited a moment, and then, very gently, I gave all four of my ropes a little tug. Delicate, nothing loud. If you weren't listening, listening hard, you might've missed it. But Jorgenson was listening. At the first low rattle, his silhouette seemed to freeze.

Another rattle: Azar this time. We kept at it for ten minutes, staggering the rhythm—noise, silence, noise—gradually building the tension.

Squinting down at Jorgenson's position, I felt a swell of immense power. It was a feeling the VC must have. Like a puppeteer. Yank on the ropes, watch the silly wooden soldier jump and twitch. It made me smile. One by one, in sequence, I tugged on each of the ropes, and the sounds came flowing back at me with a soft, indefinite formlessness: a rattlesnake, maybe, or the creak of a trap door, or footsteps in the attic— whatever you made of it.

In a way I wanted to stop myself. It was cruel, I knew that, but right and wrong were somewhere else. This was the spirit world.

I heard myself laugh.

And then presently I came unattached from the natural world. I felt the hinges go. Eyes closed, I seemed to rise up out of my own body and float through the dark down to Jorgenson's position. I was invisible; I had no shape, no substance; I weighed less than nothing. I just drifted. It was imagination, of course, but for a long while I hovered there over Bobby Jorgenson's bunker. As if through dark glass I could see him lying flat in his circle of sandbags, silent and scared, listening. Rubbing his eyes. Telling himself it was all a trick of the dark. Muscles tight, ears tight—I could see it. Now, at this instant, he'd glance up at the sky, hoping for a moon or a few stars. But no moon, no stars. He'd start talking to himself. He'd try to bring the night into focus, willing coherence, but the effort would only cause distortions. Out beyond the wire, the paddies would seem to swirl and sway; the trees would take human form; clumps of grass would glide through the night like sappers. Funhouse country: trick mirrors and curvatures and pop-up monsters. "Take it easy," he'd murmur, "easy, easy, easy," but it wouldn't get any easier.

I could actually see it.

I was down there with him, inside him. I was part of the night. I was the land itself—everything, everywhere—the fireflies and paddies, the moon, the midnight rustlings, the cool phosphorescent shimmer of evil— I was atrocity—I was jungle fire, jungle drums—I was the blind stare in the eyes of all those poor, dead, dumbfuck ex-pals of mine—all the pale young corpses, Lee Strunk and Kiowa and Curt Lemon—I was the beast on their lips—I was Nam—the horror, the war.

"Creepy," Azar said. "Wet pants an' goose bumps." He held a beer out to me, but I shook my head. We sat in the dim light of my hootch, boots off, listening to Mary Hopkin on my tape deck.

"What next?" "Wait," I said. "Sure, but I mean—"

"Shut up and *listen*."

That high elegant voice. Someday, when the war was over, I'd go to London and ask Mary Hopkin to marry me. That's another thing Nam does to you. It turns you sentimental; it makes you want to hook up with girls like Mary Hopkin. You learn, finally, that you'll die, and so you try to hang on to your own life, that gentle, naive kid you used to be, but then after a while the sentiment takes over, and the sadness, because you know for a fact that you can't ever bring any of it back again. You just can't. Those were the days, she sang.

Azar switched off the tape.

"Shit, man," he said. "Don't you got *music*?"

And now, finally, the moon was out. We slipped back to our positions and went to work again with the ropes. Louder now, more insistent. Starlight sparkled in the barbed wire, and there were curious reflections and layerings of shadow, and the big white moon added resonance. There was no wind. The night was absolute. Slowly, we dragged the ammo cans closer to Bobby Jorgenson's bunker, and this, plus the moon, gave a sense of approaching peril, the slow belly-down crawl of evil.

At 0300 hours Azar set off the first trip flare.

There was a light popping noise, then a sizzle out in front of Bunker Six. The night seemed to snap itself in half. The white flare burned ten paces from the bunker.

I fired off three more flares and it was instant daylight.

Then Jorgenson moved. He made a short, low cry—not even a cry, really, just a short lung-and-throat bark—and there was a blurred sequence as he lunged sideways and rolled toward a heap of sandbags and crouched there and hugged his rifle and waited.

"There," I whispered. "Now you know."

I could read his mind. I was there with him. Together we understood what terror was: you're not human anymore. You're a shadow. You slip out of your own skin, like molting, shedding your own history and your own future, leaving behind everything you ever were or wanted or believed in. You know you're about to die. And it's not a movie and you aren't a hero and all you can do is whimper and wait.

This, now, was something we shared.

I felt close to him. It wasn't compassion, just closeness. His silhouette was framed like a cardboard cutout against the burning flares.

In the dark outside my hootch, even though I bent toward him, almost nose to nose, all I could see were the glossy whites of Azar's eyes.

"Enough," I said. "Oh, sure."

"Seriously."

Azar gave me a small, thin smile.

"Serious?" he said. "That's way too serious for me—I'm your basic fun lover."

When he smiled again, I knew it was hopeless, but I tried anyway. I told him the score was even. We'd made our point, I said, no need to rub it in.

Azar stared at me.

"Poor, poor boy," he said. The rest was inflection and white eyes.

An hour before dawn we moved in for the last phase. Azar was in command now. I tagged after him, thinking maybe I could keep a lid on.

"Don't take this personal," Azar said softly. "It's my own character flaw. I just like to finish things."

I didn't look at him. As we approached the wire, Azar put his hand on my shoulder, guiding me over toward the boulder pile. He knelt down and inspected the ropes and flares, nodded to himself, peered out at Jorgenson's bunker, nodded once more, then took off his helmet and sat on it.

He was smiling again.

"You know something?" he said. His voice was wistful. "Out here, at night, I almost feel like a kid again. The Vietnam experience. I mean, wow, I *love* this shit."

"Let's just—"

"Shhhh."

Azar put a finger to his lips. He was still smiling at me, almost kindly. "This here's what you wanted," he said. "Displaying war, right? That's

all this *is*. A cute little backyard war game. Brings back memories, I bet—

those happy soldiering days. Except now you're a has-been. One of those American Legion types, guys who like to dress up in a nifty uniform and go out and play at it. Pitiful. It was me, I'd rather get my ass blown away for real."

My lips had a waxy feel, like soapstone. "Come on," I said. "Just quit."

"Pitiful."

"Azar, for Christ sake."

He patted my cheek. "Purely pitiful," he said.

We waited another ten minutes. It was cold now, and damp. Squatting down, I felt a sudden brittleness come over me, a hollow sensation, as if someone could reach out and crush me like a Christmas tree ornament. It was the same feeling I'd had out along the Song Tra Bong. Like I was losing myself, everything spilling out. I remembered how the bullet had made a soft puffing noise inside me. I remembered lying there for a long while, listening to the river, the gunfire and voices, how I kept calling out for a medic but how nobody came and how I finally reached back and touched the hole. The blood was warm like dishwater. I could feel my pants filling up with it. All this blood, I thought—I'll be *hollow*. Then the brittle sensation hit me. I passed out for a while, and when I woke up the battle had moved farther down the river. I was still leaking. I wondered where Rat Kiley was, but Rat Kiley was in Japan. There was rifle fire somewhere off to my right, and people yelling, except none of it seemed real anymore. I smelled myself dying. The round had entered at a steep angle, smashing down through the hip and colon. The stench made me jerk sideways. I turned and clamped a hand against the wound and tried to plug it up. Leaking to death, I thought. And then I felt it happen. Like a genie swirling out of a bottle—like a cloud of gas—I was drifting upward out of my own body. I was half in and half out. Part of me still lay there, the corpse part, but I was also that genie looking on and saying, "There, there," which made me start to scream. I couldn't help it. When Bobby Jorgenson got to me, I was almost gone with shock. All I could do was scream. I tightened up and squeezed, trying to stop the leak, but that only made it worse, and Jorgenson punched me and told me to knock it off. Shock, I thought. I tried to tell him that. I tried to say, "Shock," but it wouldn't come out right. Jorgenson flipped me over and pressed a knee against my back, pinning me there, and I kept trying to say, "Shock, man, treat for shock." I was lucid—things were clear—but my tongue wouldn't fit around the words. Then I slipped under for a while. When I came back, Jorgenson was using a knife to cut off my pants. He shot in the morphine, which scared me, and I shouted something and tried to wiggle away, but he kept pushing down hard on my back. Except it wasn't Jorgenson now—it was that genie—he was smiling down at me, and winking, and I couldn't buck him off. Later on, things clicked into slow motion. The morphine, maybe. I focused on Jorgenson's brand-new boots, then on a pebble, then on my own face floating high above me—the last things I'd ever see. I couldn't look away. It occurred to me that I was witness to something rare.

Even now, in the dark, there were indications of a spirit world. Azar said, "Hey, you awake?" I nodded.

Down at Bunker Six, things were silent. The place looked abandoned.

Azar grinned and went to work on the ropes. It began like a breeze, a soft sighing sound. I hugged myself. I watched Azar bend forward and fire off the first illumination flare. "Please," I almost said, but the word snagged, and I looked up and tracked the flare over Jorgenson's bunker. It exploded almost without noise: a soft red flash.

There was a whimper in the dark. At first I thought it was Jorgenson. "Please?" I said.

I bit down and folded my hands and squeezed. I had the shivers.

Twice more, rapidly, Azar fired up red flares. At one point he turned toward me and lifted his eyebrows.

"Timmy, Timmy," he said. "Such a specimen." I agreed.

I wanted to do something, stop him somehow, but I crouched back and watched Azar pick up a tear-gas grenade and pull the pin and stand up and throw. The gas puffed up in a thin cloud that partly obscured Bunker Six. Even from thirty meters away I could smell it and taste it.

"Jesus, *please*," I said, but Azar lobbed over another one, waited for the hiss, then scrambled over to the rope we hadn't used yet.

It was my idea. I'd rigged it up myself: a sandbag painted white, a pulley system.

Azar gave the rope a quick tug, and out in front of Bunker Six, the white sandbag lifted itself up and hovered there in a misty swirl of gas.

Jorgenson began firing. Just one round at first, a single red tracer that thumped into the sandbag and burned.

"Oooo!" Azar murmured.

Quickly, talking to himself, Azar hurled the last gas grenade, shot up another flare, then snatched the rope again and made the white sandbag dance.

"Oooo!" he was chanting. "Starlight, star bright!"

Bobby Jorgenson did not go nuts. Quietly, almost with dignity, he stood up and took aim and fired once more at the sandbag. I could see his profile against the red flares. His face seemed relaxed, no twitching or screams. He stared out into the dark for several seconds, as if deciding something, then he shook his head and smiled. He stood up straight. He seemed to brace himself for a moment. Then, very slowly, he began marching out toward the wire; his posture was erect; he did not crouch or squirm or crawl. He walked upright. He moved with a kind of grace. When he reached the sandbag, Jorgenson stopped and turned and shouted out my name, then he placed his rifle muzzle up against the white sandbag.

"O'Brien!" he yelled, and he fired. Azar dropped the rope.

"Well," he muttered, "show's over." He looked down at me with a mixture of contempt and pity. After a second he shook his head. "Man, I'll tell you something. You're a sorry, sorry case."

I was trembling. I kept hugging myself, rocking, but I couldn't make it go away.

"Disgusting," Azar said. "Sorriest fuckin' case I ever seen."

He looked out at Jorgenson, then at me. His eyes had the opaque, polished surface of stone. He moved forward as if to help me up. Then he stopped and smiled. Almost as an afterthought, he kicked me in the head.

"Sad," he murmured, then he turned and headed off to bed.

"No big deal," I told Jorgenson. "Leave it alone."

But he led me down to the bunker and used a towel to wipe the gash at my forehead. It wasn't bad, really. I felt some dizziness, but I tried not to let it show.

It was almost dawn now, a hazy silver dawn. For a while we didn't speak.

"So," he finally said. "Right."

We shook hands. Neither of us put much emotion into it and we didn't look at each other's eyes. Jorgenson pointed out at the shot-up sandbag.

"That was a nice touch," he said. "It almost had me—" He paused and squinted out at the eastern paddies, where the sky was beginning to color up. "Anyway, a nice dramatic touch. You've got a real flair for it. Someday maybe you should go into the movies or something."

I nodded and said, "That's an idea."

"Another Hitchcock. *The Birds*—you ever see it?" "Scary stuff," I said.

We sat for a while longer, then I started to get up, except I was still feeling the wobbles in my head. Jorgenson reached out and steadied me.

"We're even now?" he said. "Pretty much."

Again, I felt that human closeness. Almost war buddies. We nearly shook hands again but then decided against it. Jorgenson picked up his helmet, brushed it off, and looked back one more time at the white sandbag. His face was filthy.

Up at the medic's hootch, he cleaned and bandaged my forehead, then we went to chow. We didn't have much to say. I told him I was sorry; he told me the same thing.

Afterward, in an awkward moment, I said, "Let's kill Azar." Jorgenson smiled. "Scare him to death, right?"

"Right," I said. "What a movie!"

I shrugged. "Sure. Or just kill him."

Night Life

A few words about Rat Kiley. I wasn't there when he got hurt, but Mitchell Sanders later told me the essential facts. Apparently he lost his cool.

The platoon had been working an AO out in the foothills west of Quang Ngai City, and for some time they'd been receiving intelligence about an NVA buildup in the area. The usual crazy rumors: massed artillery and Russian tanks and whole divisions of fresh troops. No one took it seriously, including Lieutenant Cross, but as a precaution the platoon moved only at night, staying off the main trails and observing strict field SOPs. For almost two weeks, Sanders said, they lived the night life. That was the phrase everyone used: the night life. A language trick. It made things seem tolerable. How's the Nam treating you? one guy would ask, and some other guy would say, Hey, one big party, just living the night life.

It was a tense time for everybody, Sanders said, but for Rat Kiley it ended up in Japan. The strain was too much for him. He couldn't make the adjustment.

During those two weeks the basic routine was simple. They'd sleep away the daylight hours, or try to sleep, then at dusk they'd put on their gear and move out single file into the dark. Always a heavy cloud cover. No moon and no stars. It was the purest black you could imagine, Sanders said, the kind of clock-stopping black that God must've had in mind when he sat down to invent blackness. It made your eyeballs ache. You'd shake your head and blink, except you couldn't even tell you were blinking, the blackness didn't change. So pretty soon you'd get jumpy. Your nerves would go. You'd start to worry about getting cut off from the rest of the unit—alone, you'd think—and then the real panic would bang in and you'd reach out and try to touch the guy in front of you, groping for his shirt, hoping to Christ he was still there. It made for some bad dreams. Dave Jensen popped special vitamins high in carotene. Lieutenant Cross popped NoDoz. Henry Dobbins and Norman Bowker even rigged up a safety line between them, a long piece of string tied to their belts. The whole platoon felt the impact.

With Rat Kiley, though, it was different. Too many body bags, maybe.

Too much gore.

At first Rat just sank inside himself, not saying a word, but then later on, after five or six days, it flipped the other way. He couldn't stop talking. Weird talk, too. Talking about bugs, for instance: how the worst thing in Nam was the goddamn bugs. Big giant killer bugs, he'd say, mutant bugs, bugs with fucked-up DNA, bugs that were chemically altered by napalm and defoliants and tear gas and DDT. He claimed the bugs were personally after his ass. He said he could hear the bastards homing in on him.

Swarms of mutant bugs, billions of them, they had him bracketed. Whispering his name, he said—his actual name—all night long—it was driving him crazy.

Odd stuff, Sanders said, and it wasn't just talk. Rat developed some peculiar habits. Constantly scratching himself. Clawing at the bug bites. He couldn't quit digging at his skin, making big scabs and then ripping off the scabs and scratching the open sores.

It was a sad thing to watch. Definitely not the old Rat Kiley. His whole personality seemed out of kilter.

To an extent, though, everybody was feeling it. The long night marches turned their minds upside down; all the rhythms were wrong. Always a lost sensation. They'd blunder along through the dark, willy-nilly, no sense of place or direction, probing for an enemy that nobody could see. Like a snipe hunt, Sanders said. A bunch of dumb Cub Scouts chasing the phantoms. They'd march north for a time, then east, then north again, skirting the villages, no one talking except in whispers. And it was rugged country, too. Not quite mountains, but rising fast, full of gorges and deep brush and places you could die. Around midnight things always got wild. All around you, everywhere, the whole dark countryside came alive. You'd hear a strange hum in your ears. Nothing specific; nothing you could put a name on. Tree frogs, maybe, or snakes or flying squirrels or who-knew-what. Like the night had its own voice—that hum in your ears—and in the hours after midnight you'd swear you were walking through some kind of soft black protoplasm, Vietnam, the blood and the flesh.

It was no joke, Sanders said. The monkeys chattered death-chatter.

The nights got freaky.

Rat Kiley finally hit a wall.

He couldn't sleep during the hot daylight hours; he couldn't cope with the nights.

Late one afternoon, as the platoon prepared for another march, he broke down in front of Mitchell Sanders. Not crying, but up against it. He said he was scared. And it wasn't normal scared. He didn't know *what* it was: too long in-country, probably. Or else he wasn't cut out to be a medic. Always policing up the parts, he said. Always plugging up holes. Sometimes he'd stare at guys who were still okay, the alive guys, and he'd start to picture how they'd look dead. Without arms or legs—that sort of thing. It was ghoulish, he knew that, but he couldn't shut off the pictures.

He'd be sitting there talking with Bowker or Dobbins or somebody, just marking time, and then out of nowhere he'd find himself wondering how much the guy's head weighed, like how *heavy* it was, and what it would feel like to pick up the head and carry it over to a chopper and dump it in.

Rat scratched the skin at his elbow, digging in hard. His eyes were red and weary.

"It's not right," he said. "These pictures in my head, they won't quit. I'll see a guy's liver. The actual fucking *liver*. And the thing is, it doesn't scare me, it doesn't even give me the willies. More like curiosity. The way a doctor feels when he looks at a patient, sort of mechanical, not seeing the real person, just a ruptured appendix or a clogged-up artery."

His voice floated away for a second. He looked at Sanders and tried to smile.

He kept clawing at his elbow.

"Anyway," Rat said, "the days aren't so bad, but at night the pictures get to be a bitch. I start seeing my own body. Chunks of myself. My own heart, my own kidneys. It's like—I don't know—it's like staring into this huge black crystal ball. One of these nights I'll be lying dead out there in the dark and nobody'll find me except the bugs—I can see it—I can see the goddamn bugs chewing tunnels through me—I can see the mongooses munching on my bones. I swear, it's too much. I can't keep seeing myself dead."

Mitchell Sanders nodded. He didn't know what to say. For a time they sat watching the shadows come, then Rat shook his head.

He said he'd done his best. He'd tried to be a decent medic. Win some and lose some, he said, but he'd tried hard. Briefly then, rambling a little, he talked about a few of the guys who were gone now, Curt Lemon and Kiowa and Ted Lavender, and how crazy it was that people who were so incredibly alive could get so incredibly dead.

Then he almost laughed.

"This whole war," he said. "You know what it is? Just one big banquet.

Meat, man. You and me. Everybody. Meat for the bugs." The next morning he shot himself.

He took off his boots and socks, laid out his medical kit, doped himself up, and put a round through his foot.

Nobody blamed him, Sanders said.

Before the chopper came, there was time for goodbyes. Lieutenant Cross went over and said he'd vouch that it was an accident. Henry Dobbins and Azar gave him a stack of comic books for hospital reading. Everybody stood in a little circle, feeling bad about it, trying to cheer him up with bullshit about the great night life in Japan.

The Lives of the Dead

But this too is true: stories can save us. I'm forty-three years old, and a writer now, and even still, right here, I keep dreaming Linda alive. And Ted Lavender, too, and Kiowa, and Curt Lemon, and a slim young man I killed, and an old man sprawled beside a pigpen, and several others whose bodies I once lifted and dumped into a truck. They're all dead. But in a story, which is a kind of dreaming, the dead sometimes smile and sit up and return to the world.

Start here: a body without a name. On an afternoon in 1969 the platoon took sniper fire from a filthy little village along the South China Sea. It lasted only a minute or two, and nobody was hurt, but even so Lieutenant Jimmy Cross got on the radio and ordered up an air strike. For the next half hour we watched the place burn. It was a cool bright morning, like early autumn, and the jets were glossy black against the sky. When it ended, we formed into a loose line and swept east through the village. It was all wreckage. I remember the smell of burnt straw; I remember broken fences and torn-up trees and heaps of stone and brick and pottery. The place was deserted—no people, no animals—and the only confirmed kill was an old man who lay face-up near a pigpen at the center of the village. His right arm was gone. At his face there were already many flies and gnats.

Dave Jensen went over and shook the old man's hand. "How-dee- doo," he said.

One by one the others did it too. They didn't disturb the body, they just grabbed the old man's hand and offered a few words and moved away.

Rat Kiley bent over the corpse. "Gimme five," he said. "A real honor." "Pleased as punch," said Henry Dobbins.

I was brand-new to the war. It was my fourth day; I hadn't yet developed a sense of humor. Right away, as if I'd swallowed something, I felt a moist sickness rise up in my throat. I sat down beside the pigpen, closed my eyes, put my head between my knees.

After a moment Dave Jensen touched my shoulder.

"Be polite now," he said. "Go introduce yourself. Nothing to be afraid about, just a nice old man. Show a little respect for your elders."

"No way."

"Maybe it's too real for you?" "That's right," I said. "Way too real."

Jensen kept after me, but I didn't go near the body. I didn't even look at it except by accident. For the rest of the day there was still that sickness inside me, but it wasn't the old man's corpse so much, it was that awesome act of greeting the dead. At one point, I remember, they sat the body up against a fence. They crossed his legs and talked to him. "The guest of honor," Mitchell Sanders said, and he placed a can of orange slices in the old man's lap. "Vitamin C," he said gently. "A guy's health, that's the most important thing."

They proposed toasts. They lifted their canteens and drank to the old man's family and ancestors, his many grandchildren, his newfound life after death. It was more than mockery. There was a formality to it, like a funeral without the sadness.

Dave Jensen flicked his eyes at me.

"Hey, O'Brien," he said, "you got a toast in mind? Never too late for manners."

I found things to do with my hands. I looked away and tried not to think.

Late in the afternoon, just before dusk, Kiowa came up and asked if he could sit at my foxhole for a minute. He offered me a Christmas cookie from a batch his father had sent him. It was February now, but the cookies tasted fine.

For a few moments Kiowa watched the sky.

"You did a good thing today," he said. "That shaking hands crap, it isn't decent. The guys'll hassle you for a while—especially Jensen—but just keep saying no. Should've done it myself. Takes guts, I know that."

"It wasn't guts. I was scared." Kiowa shrugged. "Same difference."

"No, I couldn't *do* it. A mental block or something . . . I don't know, just creepy."

"Well, you're new here. You'll get used to it." He paused for a second, studying the green and red sprinkles on a cookie. "Today—I guess this was your first look at a real body?"

I shook my head. All day long I'd been picturing Linda's face, the way she smiled.

"It sounds funny," I said, "but that poor old man, he reminds me of . . . I mean, there's this girl I used to know. I took her to the movies once. My first date."

Kiowa looked at me for a long while. Then he leaned back and smiled. "Man," he said, "that's a bad date."

Linda was nine then, as I was, but we were in love. And it was real. When I write about her now, three decades later, it's tempting to dismiss it as a crush, an infatuation of childhood, but I know for a fact that what we felt for each other was as deep and rich as love can ever get. It had all the shadings and complexities of mature adult love, and maybe more, because there were not yet words for it, and because it was not yet fixed to comparisons or chronologies or the ways by which adults measure such things.

I just loved her.

She had poise and great dignity. Her eyes, I remember, were deep brown like her hair, and she was slender and very quiet and fragile- looking.

Even then, at nine years old, I wanted to live inside her body. I wanted to melt into her bones—*that* kind of love.

And so in the spring of 1956, when we were in the fourth grade, I took her out on the first real date of my life—a double date, actually, with my mother and father. Though I can't remember the exact sequence, my mother had somehow arranged it with Linda's parents, and on that damp spring night my dad did the driving while Linda and I sat in the back seat and stared out opposite windows, both of us trying to pretend it was nothing special. For me, though, it was very special. Down inside I had important things to tell her, big profound things, but I couldn't make any words come out. I had trouble breathing. Now and then I'd glance over at her, thinking how beautiful she was: her white skin and those dark brown eyes and the way she always smiled at the world—always, it seemed—as if her face had been designed that way. The smile never went away. That night, I remember, she wore a new red cap, which seemed to me very stylish and sophisticated, very unusual. It was a stocking cap, basically, except the tapered part at the top seemed extra long, almost too long, like a tail growing out of the back of her head. It made me think of the caps that Santa's elves wear, the same shape and color, the same fuzzy white tassel at the tip.

Sitting there in the back seat, I wanted to find some way to let her know how I felt, a compliment of some sort, but all I could manage was a stupid comment about the cap. "Jeez," I must've said, "what a *cap*."

Linda smiled at the window—she knew what I meant—but my mother turned and gave me a hard look. It surprised me. It was as if I'd brought up some horrible secret.

For the rest of the ride I kept my mouth shut. We parked in front of the Ben Franklin store and walked up Main Street toward the State Theater. My parents went first, side by side, and then Linda in her new red cap, and then me tailing along ten or twenty steps behind. I was nine years old; I didn't yet have the gift for small talk. Now and then my mother glanced back, making little motions with her hand to speed me up.

At the ticket booth, I remember, Linda stood off to one side. I moved over to the concession area, studying the candy, and both of us were very careful to avoid the awkwardness of eye contact. Which was how we knew about being in love. It was pure knowing. Neither of us, I suppose, would've thought to use that word, love, but by the fact of not looking at each other, and not talking, we understood with a clarity beyond language that we were sharing something huge and permanent.

Behind me, in the theater, I heard cartoon music.

"Hey, step it up," I said. I almost had the courage to look at her. "You want popcorn or what?"

The thing about a story is that you dream it as you tell it, hoping that others might then dream along with you, and in this way memory and imagination and language combine to make spirits in the head. There is the illusion of aliveness. In Vietnam, for instance, Ted Lavender had a habit of popping four or five tranquilizers every morning. It was his way of coping, just dealing with the realities, and the drugs helped to ease him through the days. I remember how peaceful his eyes were. Even in bad situations he had a soft, dreamy expression on his face, which was what he wanted, a kind of escape. "How's the war today?" somebody would ask, and Ted Lavender would give a little smile to the sky and say, "Mellow—a nice smooth war today." And then in April he was shot in the head outside the village of Than Khe. Kiowa and I and a couple of others were ordered to prepare his body for the dustoff. I remember squatting down, not wanting to look but then looking. Lavender's left cheekbone was gone. There was a swollen blackness around his eye. Quickly, trying not to feel anything, we went through the kid's pockets. I remember wishing I had gloves. It wasn't the blood I hated; it was the deadness. We put his personal effects in a plastic bag and tied the bag to his arm. We stripped off the canteens and ammo, all the heavy stuff, and wrapped him up in his own poncho and carried him out to a dry paddy and laid him down.

For a while nobody said much. Then Mitchell Sanders laughed and looked over at the green plastic poncho.

"Hey, Lavender," he said, "how's the war today?" There was a short quiet.

"Mellow," somebody said.

"Well, that's good," Sanders murmured, "that's real, real good. Stay cool now."

"Hey, no sweat, I'm mellow."

"Just ease on back, then. Don't need no pills. We got this incredible chopper on call, this once in a lifetime mind-trip."

"Oh, yeah—mellow!"

Mitchell Sanders smiled. "There it is, my man, this chopper gonna take you up high and cool. Gonna relax you. Gonna alter your whole perspective on this sorry, sorry shit."

We could almost see Ted Lavender's dreamy blue eyes. We could almost hear him.

"Roger that," somebody said. "I'm ready to fly."

There was the sound of the wind, the sound of birds and the quiet afternoon, which was the world we were in.

That's what a story does. The bodies are animated. You make the dead talk. They sometimes say things like, "Roger that." Or they say, "Timmy, stop crying," which is what Linda said to me after she was dead.

Even now I can see her walking down the aisle of the old State Theater in Worthington, Minnesota. I can see her face in profile beside me, the cheeks softly lighted by coming attractions.

The movie that night was *The Man Who Never Was*. I remember the plot clearly, or at least the premise, because the main character was a corpse. That fact alone, I know, deeply impressed me. It was a World War Two film: the Allies devise a scheme to mislead Germany about the site of the upcoming landings in Europe. They get their hands on a body—a British soldier, I believe; they dress him up in an officer's uniform, plant fake documents in his pockets, then dump him in the sea and let the currents wash him onto a Nazi beach. The Germans find the documents; the deception wins the war. Even now, I can remember the awful splash as that corpse fell into the sea. I remember glancing over at Linda, thinking it might be too much for her, but in the dim gray light she seemed to be smiling at the screen. There were little crinkles at her eyes, her lips open and gently curving at the corners. I couldn't understand it. There was nothing to smile at. Once or twice, in fact, I had to close my eyes, but it didn't help much. Even then I kept seeing the soldier's body tumbling toward the water, splashing down hard, how inert and heavy it was, how completely dead.

It was a relief when the movie finally ended.

Afterward, we drove out to the Dairy Queen at the edge of town. The night had a quilted, weighted-down quality, as if somehow burdened, and all around us the Minnesota prairies reached out in long repetitive waves of corn and soybeans, everything flat, everything the same. I remember eating ice cream in the back seat of the Buick, and a long blank drive in the dark, and then pulling up in front of Linda's house. Things must've been said, but it's all gone now except for a few last images. I remember walking her to the front door. I remember the brass porch light with its fierce yellow glow, my own feet, the juniper bushes along the front steps, the wet grass, Linda close beside me. We were in love. Nine years old, yes, but it was real love, and now we were alone on those front steps. Finally we looked at each other.

"Bye," I said.

Linda nodded and said, "Bye."

Over the next few weeks Linda wore her new red cap to school every day. She never took it off, not even in the classroom, and so it was inevitable that she took some teasing about it. Most of it came from a kid named Nick Veenhof. Out on the playground, during recess, Nick would creep up behind her and make a grab for the cap, almost yanking it off, then scampering away. It went on like that for weeks: the girls giggling, the guys egging him on. Naturally I wanted to do something about it, but it just wasn't possible. I had my reputation to think about. I had my pride. And there was also the problem of Nick Veenhof. So I stood off to the side, just a spectator, wishing I could do things I couldn't do. I watched Linda clamp down the cap with the palm of her hand, holding it there, smiling over in Nick's direction as if none of it really mattered.

For me, though, it did matter. It still does. I should've stepped in; fourth grade is no excuse. Besides, it doesn't get easier with time, and twelve years later, when Vietnam presented much harder choices, some practice at being brave might've helped a little.

Also, too, I might've stopped what happened next. Maybe not, but at least it's possible.

Most of the details I've forgotten, or maybe blocked out, but I know it was an afternoon in late spring, and we were taking a spelling test, and halfway into it Nick Veenhof held up his hand and asked to use the pencil sharpener. Right away the kids laughed. No doubt he'd broken the pencil on purpose, but it wasn't something you could prove, and so the teacher nodded and told him to hustle it up. Which was a mistake. Out of nowhere Nick developed a terrible limp. He moved in slow motion, dragging himself up to the pencil sharpener and carefully slipping in his pencil and then grinding away forever. At the time, I suppose, it was funny. But on the way back to his seat Nick took a short detour. He squeezed between two desks, turned sharply right, and moved up the aisle toward Linda.

I saw him grin at one of his pals. In a way, I already knew what was coming.

As he passed Linda's desk, he dropped the pencil and squatted down to get it. When he came up, his left hand slipped behind her back. There was a half-second hesitation. Maybe he was trying to stop himself; maybe then, just briefly, he felt some small approximation of guilt. But it wasn't enough. He took hold of the white tassel, stood up, and gently lifted off her cap.

Somebody must've laughed. I remember a short, tinny echo. I remember Nick Veenhof trying to smile. Somewhere behind me, a girl said, "Uh," or a sound like that.

Linda didn't move.

Even now, when I think back on it, I can still see the glossy whiteness of her scalp. She wasn't bald. Not quite. Not completely. There were some tufts of hair, little patches of grayish brown fuzz. But what I saw then, and keep seeing now, is all that whiteness. A smooth, pale, translucent white. I could see the bones and veins; I could see the exact structure of her skull. There was a large Band-Aid at the back of her head, a row of black stitches, a piece of gauze taped above her left ear.

Nick Veenhof took a step backward. He was still smiling, but the smile was doing strange things.

The whole time Linda stared straight ahead, her eyes locked on the blackboard, her hands loosely folded at her lap. She didn't say anything. After a time, though, she turned and looked at me across the room. It lasted only a moment, but I had the feeling that a whole conversation was happening between us. *Well?* she was saying, and I was saying, *Sure, okay.*

Later on, she cried for a while. The teacher helped her put the cap back on, then we finished the spelling test and did some fingerpainting, and after school that day Nick Veenhof and I walked her home.

It's now 1990. I'm forty-three years old, which would've seemed impossible to a fourth grader, and yet when I look at photographs of myself as I was in 1956, I realize that in the important ways I haven't changed at all. I was Timmy then; now I'm Tim. But the essence remains the same. I'm not fooled by the baggy pants or the crew cut or the happy smile—I know my own eyes—and there is no doubt that the Timmy smiling at the camera is the Tim I am now. Inside the body, or beyond the body, there is something absolute and unchanging. The human life is all one thing, like a blade tracing loops on ice: a little kid, a twenty-three- year-old infantry sergeant, a middle-aged writer knowing guilt and sorrow.

And as a writer now, I want to save Linda's life. Not her body—her life.

She died, of course. Nine years old and she died. It was a brain tumor. She lived through the summer and into the first part of September, and then she was dead.

But in a story I can steal her soul. I can revive, at least briefly, that which is absolute and unchanging. In a story, miracles can happen. Linda can smile and sit up. She can reach out, touch my wrist, and say, "Timmy, stop crying."

I needed that kind of miracle. At some point I had come to understand that Linda was sick, maybe even dying, but I loved her and just couldn't accept it. In the middle of the summer, I remember, my mother tried to explain to me about brain tumors. Now and then, she said, bad things start growing inside us. Sometimes you can cut them out and other times you can't, and for Linda it was one of the times when you can't.

I thought about it for several days. "All right," I finally said. "So will she get better now?"

"Well, no," my mother said, "I don't think so." She stared at a spot behind my shoulder. "Sometimes people don't ever get better. They die sometimes."

I shook my head. "Not Linda," I said.

But on a September afternoon, during noon recess, Nick Veenhof came up to me on the school playground. "Your girlfriend," he said, "she kicked the bucket."

At first I didn't understand.

"She's dead," he said. "My mom told me at lunch-time. No lie, she actually kicked the goddang *bucket*."

All I could do was nod. Somehow it didn't quite register. I turned away, glanced down at my hands for a second, then walked home without telling anyone.

It was a little after one o'clock, I remember, and the house was empty.

I drank some chocolate milk and then lay down on the sofa in the living room, not really sad, just floating, trying to imagine what it was to be dead. Nothing much came to me. I remember closing my eyes and whispering her name, almost begging, trying to make her come back. "Linda," I said, "please." And then I concentrated. I willed her alive. It was a dream, I suppose, or a daydream, but I made it happen. I saw her coming down the middle of Main Street, all alone. It was nearly dark and the street was deserted, no cars or people, and Linda wore a pink dress and shiny black shoes. I remember sitting down on the curb to watch. All her hair had grown back. The scars and stitches were gone. In the dream, if that's what it was, she was playing a game of some sort, laughing and running up the empty street, kicking a big aluminum water bucket.

Right then I started to cry. After a moment Linda stopped and carried her water bucket over to the curb and asked why I was so sad.

"Well, God," I said, "you're dead."

Linda nodded at me. She was standing under a yellow streetlight. A nine-year-old girl, just a kid, and yet there was something ageless in her eyes—not a child, not an adult—just a bright ongoing everness, that same pinprick of absolute lasting light that I see today in my own eyes as Timmy smiles at Tim from the graying photographs of that time.

"Dead," I said.

Linda smiled. It was a secret smile, as if she knew things nobody could ever know, and she reached out and touched my wrist and said, "Timmy, stop crying. It doesn't *matter*."

In Vietnam, too, we had ways of making the dead seem not quite so dead. Shaking hands, that was one way. By slighting death, by acting, we pretended it was not the terrible thing it was. By our language, which was both hard and wistful, we transformed the bodies into piles of waste. Thus, when someone got killed, as Curt Lemon did, his body was not really a body, but rather one small bit of waste in the midst of a much wider wastage. I learned that words make a difference. It's easier to cope with a kicked bucket than a corpse; if it isn't human, it doesn't matter much if it's dead. And so a VC nurse, fried by napalm, was a crispy critter. A Vietnamese baby, which lay nearby, was a roasted peanut. "Just a crunchie munchie," Rat Kiley said as he stepped over the body.

We kept the dead alive with stories. When Ted Lavender was shot in the head, the men talked about how they'd never seen him so mellow, how tranquil he was, how it wasn't the bullet but the tranquilizers that blew his mind. He wasn't dead, just laid-back. There were Christians among us, like Kiowa, who believed in the New Testament stories of life after death. Other stories were passed down like legends from old-timer to newcomer. Mostly, though, we had to make up our own. Often they were exaggerated, or blatant lies, but it was a way of bringing body and soul back together, or a way of making new bodies for the souls to inhabit. There was a story, for instance, about how Curt Lemon had gone trick-or-treating on Halloween. A dark, spooky night, and so Lemon put on a ghost mask and painted up his body all different colors and crept across a paddy to a sleeping village—almost stark naked, the story went, just boots and balls and an M-16—and in the dark Lemon went from hootch to hootch—ringing doorbells, he called it—and a few hours later, when he slipped back into the perimeter, he had a whole sackful of goodies to share with his pals: candles and joss sticks and a pair of black pajamas and statuettes of the smiling Buddha. That was the story, anyway. Other versions were much more elaborate, full of descriptions and scraps of dialogue. Rat Kiley liked to spice it up with extra details: "See, what happens is, it's like four in the morning, and Lemon sneaks into a hootch with that weird ghost mask on. Everybody's asleep, right? So he wakes up this cute little mama-san. Tickles her foot. 'Hey, Mama-san,' he goes, real soft like. 'Hey, Mama-san—trick or treat!' Should've seen her *face*. About freaks. I mean, there's this buck naked ghost standing there, and he's got this M-16 up against her ear and he whispers, 'Hey, Mama-san, trick or fuckin' treat!' Then he takes off her pj's. Strips her right down. Sticks the pajamas in his sack and tucks her into bed and heads for the next hootch."

Pausing a moment, Rat Kiley would grin and shake his head. "Honest to God," he'd murmur. "Trick or treat. Lemon—there's one class act."

To listen to the story, especially as Rat Kiley told it, you'd never know that Curt Lemon was dead. He was still out there in the dark, naked and painted up, trick-or-treating, sliding from hootch to hootch in that crazy white ghost mask. But he was dead.

In September, the day after Linda died, I asked my father to take me down to Benson's Funeral Home to view the body. I was a fifth grader then; I was curious. On the drive downtown my father kept his eyes straight ahead. At one point, I remember, he made a scratchy sound in his throat. It took him a long time to light up a cigarette.

"Timmy," he said, "you're sure about this?"

I nodded at him. Down inside, of course, I wasn't sure, and yet I had to see her one more time. What I needed, I suppose, was some sort of final confirmation, something to carry with me after she was gone.

When we parked in front of the funeral home, my father turned and looked at me. "If this bothers you," he said, "just say the word. We'll make a quick getaway. Fair enough?"

"Okay," I said.

"Or if you start to feel sick or anything—" "I *won't*," I told him.

Inside, the first thing I noticed was the smell, thick and sweet, like something sprayed out of a can. The viewing room was empty except for Linda and my father and me. I felt a rush of panic as we walked up the aisle. The smell made me dizzy. I tried to fight it off, slowing down a little, taking short, shallow breaths through my mouth. But at the same time I felt a funny excitement. Anticipation, in a way—that same awkward feeling when I walked up the sidewalk to ring her doorbell on our first date. I wanted to impress her. I wanted something to happen between us, a secret signal of some sort. The room was dimly lighted, almost dark, but at the far end of the aisle Linda's white casket was illuminated by a row of spotlights up in the ceiling. Everything was quiet. My father put his hand on my shoulder, whispered something, and backed off. After a moment I edged forward a few steps, pushing up on my toes for a better look.

It didn't seem real. A mistake, I thought. The girl lying in the white casket wasn't Linda. There was a resemblance, maybe, but where Linda had always been very slender and fragile-looking, almost skinny, the body in that casket was fat and swollen. For a second I wondered if somebody had made a terrible blunder. A technical mistake: like they'd pumped her too full of formaldehyde or embalming fluid or whatever they used. Her arms and face were bloated. The skin at her cheeks was stretched out tight like the rubber skin on a balloon just before it pops open. Even her fingers seemed puffy. I turned and glanced behind me, where my father stood, thinking that maybe it was a joke—hoping it was a joke—almost believing that Linda would jump out from behind one of the curtains and laugh and yell out my name.

But she didn't. The room was silent. When I looked back at the casket, I felt dizzy again. In my heart, I'm sure, I knew this was Linda, but even so I couldn't find much to recognize. I tried to pretend she was taking a nap, her hands folded at her stomach, just sleeping away the afternoon. Except she didn't *look* asleep. She looked dead. She looked heavy and totally dead.

I remember closing my eyes. After a while my father stepped up beside me.

"Come on now," he said. "Let's go get some ice cream."

In the months after Ted Lavender died, there were many other bodies. I never shook hands—not that—but one afternoon I climbed a tree and threw down what was left of Curt Lemon. I watched my friend Kiowa sink into the muck along the Song Tra Bong. And in early July, after a battle in the mountains, I was assigned to a six-man detail to police up the enemy KIAs. There were twenty-seven bodies altogether, and parts of several others. The dead were everywhere. Some lay in piles. Some lay alone. One, I remember, seemed to kneel. Another was bent from the waist over a small boulder, the top of his head on the ground, his arms rigid, the eyes squinting in concentration as if he were about to perform a handstand or somersault. It was my worst day at the war. For three hours we carried the bodies down the mountain to a clearing alongside a narrow dirt road. We had lunch there, then a truck pulled up, and we worked in two-man teams to load the truck. I remember swinging the bodies up. Mitchell Sanders took a man's feet, I took the arms, and we counted to three, working up momentum, and then we tossed the body high and watched it bounce and come to rest among the other bodies. The dead had been dead for more than a day. They were all badly bloated. Their clothing was stretched tight like sausage skins, and when we picked them up, some made sharp burping sounds as the gases were released. They were heavy. Their feet were bluish green and cold. The smell was terrible. At one point Mitchell Sanders looked at me and said, "Hey, man, I just realized something."

"What?"

He wiped his eyes and spoke very quietly, as if awed by his own wisdom.

"Death sucks," he said.

Lying in bed at night, I made up elaborate stories to bring Linda alive in my sleep. I invented my own dreams. It sounds impossible, I know, but I did it. I'd picture somebody's birthday party—a crowded room, I'd think, and a big chocolate cake with pink candles—and then soon I'd be dreaming it, and after a while Linda would show up, as I knew she would, and in the dream we'd look at each other and not talk much, because we were shy, but then later I'd walk her home and we'd sit on her front steps and stare at the dark and just be together.

She'd say amazing things sometimes. "Once you're alive," she'd say, "you can't ever be dead."

Or she'd say: "Do I *look* dead?"

It was a kind of self-hypnosis. Partly willpower, partly faith, which is how stories arrive.

But back then it felt like a miracle. My dreams had become a secret meeting place, and in the weeks after she died I couldn't wait to fall asleep at night. I began going to bed earlier and earlier, sometimes even in bright daylight. My mother, I remember, finally asked about it at breakfast one morning. "Timmy, what's *wrong*?" she said, but all I could do was shrug and say, "Nothing. I just need sleep, that's all." I didn't dare tell the truth. It was embarrassing, I suppose, but it was also a precious secret, like a magic trick, where if I tried to explain it, or even talk about it, the thrill and mystery would be gone. I didn't want to lose Linda.

She was dead. I understood that. After all, I'd seen her body, and yet even as a nine-year-old I had begun to practice the magic of stories. Some I just dreamed up. Others I wrote down—the scenes and dialogue. And at nighttime I'd slide into sleep knowing that Linda would be there waiting for me. Once, I remember, we went ice skating late at night, tracing loops and circles under yellow floodlights. Later we sat by a wood stove in the warming house, all alone, and after a while I asked her what it was like to be dead. Apparently Linda thought it was a silly question. She smiled and said, "Do I *look* dead?"

I told her no, she looked terrific. I waited a moment, then asked again, and Linda made a soft little sigh. I could smell our wool mittens drying on the stove.

For a few seconds she was quiet.

"Well, right now," she said, "I'm *not* dead. But when I am, it's like . .. I don't know, I guess it's like being inside a book that nobody's reading."

"A book?" I said.

"An old one. It's up on a library shelf, so you're safe and everything, but the book hasn't been checked out for a long, long time. All you can do is wait. Just hope somebody'll pick it up and start reading."

Linda smiled at me.

"Anyhow, it's not so bad," she said. "I mean, when you're dead, you just have to be yourself." She stood up and put on her red stocking cap. "This is stupid. Let's go skate some more."

So I followed her down to the frozen pond. It was late, and nobody else was there, and we held hands and skated almost all night under the yellow lights.

And then it becomes 1990. I'm forty-three years old, and a writer now, still dreaming Linda alive in exactly the same way. She's not the embodied Linda; she's mostly made up, with a new identity and a new name, like the man who never was. Her real name doesn't matter. She was nine years old. I loved her and then she died. And yet right here, in the spell of memory and imagination, I can still see her as if through ice, as if I'm gazing into some other world, a place where there are no brain tumors and no funeral homes, where there are no bodies at all. I can see Kiowa, too, and Ted Lavender and Curt Lemon, and sometimes I can even see Timmy skating with Linda under the yellow floodlights. I'm young and happy. I'll never die. I'm skimming across the surface of my own history, moving fast, riding the melt beneath the blades, doing loops and spins, and when I take a high leap into the dark and come down thirty years later, I realize it is as Tim trying to save Timmy's life with a story.

Mother Tongue

by Amy Tan

I am not a scholar of English or literature. I cannot give you much more than personal opinions on the English language and its variations in this country or others.

I am a writer. And by that definition, I am someone who has always loved language. I am fascinated by language in daily life. I spend a great deal of my time thinking about the power of language—the way it can evoke an emotion, a visual image, a complex idea, or a simple truth. Language is the tool of my trade. And I use them all—all the Englishes I grew up with.

Recently, I was made keenly aware of the different Englishes I do use. I was giving a talk to a large group of people, the same talk I had already given to half a dozen other groups. The nature of the talk was about my writing, my life, and my book, *The Joy Luck Club*. The talk was going along well enough, until I remembered one major difference that made the whole talk sound wrong. My mother was in the room. And it was perhaps the first time she had heard me give a lengthy speech, using the kind of English I have never used with her. I was saying things like, "The intersection of memory upon imagination" and "There is an aspect of my fiction that relates to thus-and-thus'—a speech filled with carefully wrought grammatical phrases, burdened, it suddenly seemed to me, with nominalized forms, past perfect tenses, conditional phrases, all the forms of standard English that I had learned in school and through books, the forms of English I did not use at home with my mother.

Just last week, I was walking down the street with my mother, and I again found myself conscious of the English I was using, the English I do use with her. We were talking about the price of new and used furniture and I heard myself saying this: "Not waste money that way." My husband was with us as well, and he didn't notice any switch in my English. And then I realized why. It's because over the twenty years we've been together I've often use d that same kind of English with him, and sometimes he even uses it with me. It has become our language of intimacy, a different sort of English that relates to family talk, the language I grew up with.

So you'll have some idea of what this family talk I heard sounds like, I'll quote what my mother said during a recent conversation which I videotaped and then transcribed. During this conversation, my mother was talking about a political gangster in Shanghai who had the same last name as her family's, Du, and how the gangster in his early years wanted to be adopted by her family, which was rich by comparison. Later, the gangster became more powerful, far richer than my mother's family, and one day showed up at my mother's wedding to pay his respects. Here's what she said in part: "Du Yusong having business like fruit stand. Ike off the street kind. He is Du like Du Zong — but not Tsung-ming Island people. The local people call putong, the river east side, he belong to that side local people. That man want to ask Du Zong father take him in like become own family. Du Zong wasn't look down on him, but didn't take seriously, until that man big like become a mafia. Now important person, very hard to inviting him. Chinese way, came only to show respect, don't stay for dinner. Respect for making big celebration, he shows up. Mean gives lots of respect. Chinese custom. Chinese social life that way. If too important won't have to stay too long. He come to my wedding. I didn't see, I heard it. I gone to boy's side, they have YMCA dinner. Chinese age I was nineteen."

You should know that my mother's expressive command of English belies how much she actually understands. She reads the Forbes report, listens to Wall Street Week, converses daily with her stockbroker, reads all of Shirley MacLaine's books with ease—all kinds of things I can't begin to understand. Yet some of my friends tell me they understand 50 percent of what my mother says. Some say they understand 80 to 90 percent. Some say they understand none of it, as if she were speaking pure Chinese. But to me, my mother's English is perfectly clear, perfectly natural. It's my mother tongue. Her language, as I hear it, is vivid, direct, full of observation and imagery. That was the language that helped shape the way I saw things, expressed things, made sense of the world.

Lately, I've been giving more thought to the kind of English my mother speaks. Like others, I have described it to people as "broken" or "fractured" English. But I wince when I say that. It has always bothered me that I can think of no way to describe it other than "broken," as if it were damaged and needed to be fixed, as if it lacked a certain wholeness and soundness. I've heard other terms used, "limited English," for example. But they seem just as bad, as if everything is limited, including people's perceptions of the limited English speaker.

I know this for a fact, because when I was growing up, my mother's "limited" English limited my perception of her. I was ashamed of her English. I believed that her English reflected the quality of what she had to say. That is, because she expressed them imperfectly her thought were imperfect. And I had plenty of empirical evidence to support me: the fact that people in department stores, at banks, and at restaurants did not take her seriously, did not give her good service, pretended not to understand her, or even acted as if they did not hear her.

My mother has long realized the limitations of her English as well. When I was fifteen, she used to have me call people on the phone to pretend I was she. In this guise, I was forced to ask for information or event to complain and yell at people who had been rude to her. One time it was a call to her stockbroker in New York. She had cashed out her small portfolio and it just so happened we were going to go to New York the next week, our very first trip outside California. I had to get on the phone and say in an adolescent voice that was not very convincing, "This is Mrs. Tan."

And my mother was standing in the back whispering loudly, "Why he don't send me check, already two weeks late. So mad he lie to me, losing me money."

And then I said in perfect English, "Yes, I'm getting rather concerned. You had agreed to send the check two weeks ago, but it hasn't arrived."

Then she began to talk more loudly. "What he want, I come to New York to tell him front of his boss, you cheating me?" And I was trying to calm her down, make her be quiet, while telling the stockbroker, "I can't tolerate any more excuses. If I don't receive the check immediately, I am going to have to speak to your manager when I'm in New York next week." And sure enough, the following week there we were in front of this astonished stockbroker, and I was sitting there red-faced and quiet, and my mother, the real Mrs. Tan, was shouting at his boss in her impeccable broken English.

We used a similar routine just five days ago, for a situation that was far less humorous. My mother had gone to the hospital for an appointment, to find out about a benign brain tumor a CAT scan had revealed a month ago. She said she had spoken very good English, her best English, no mistakes. Still, she said, the hospital did not apologize when they said they had lost the CAT scan and she had come for nothing. She said they did not seem to have sympathy when she told them she was anxious to know the exact diagnosis, since her husband and son had both died of brain tumors. She said they would not give her any more information until the next time and she would have to make another appointment for that. So she said she would not leave until the doctor called her daughter. She wouldn't budge. And when the doctor finally called her daughter, me, who spoke in perfect English — lo and behold — we had assurances the CAT scan would be found, promises that a conference call on Monday would be held, and apologies for any suffering my mother had gone through for a most regrettable mistake.

I think my mother's English almost had an effect on limiting my possibilities in life as well. Sociologists and linguists probably will tell you that a person's developing language skills are more influenced by peers. But I do think that the language spoken in the family, especially in immigrant families which are more insular, plays a large role in shaping the language of the child. And I believe that it affected by results on achievement tests, I.Q. tests, and the SAT. While my English skills were never judged as poor, compared to math, English could not be considered by strong suit. In grade school I did moderately well, getting perhaps B's, sometimes B-pluses, in English and scoring perhaps in the sixtieth or seventieth percentile on achievement tests. But those scores were not good enough to override the opinion that my true abilities lay in math and science, because in those areas I achieved A's and scored in the ninetieth percentile or higher.

This was understandable. Math is precise; there is only one correct answer. Whereas, for me at least, the answers on English tests were always a judgment call, a matter of opinion and personal experience. Those tests were constructed around items like fill-in-the-blank sentence completion, such as, "Even though Tom was, Mary thought he was —." And the correct answer always seemed to be the most bland combinations of thoughts, for example, "Even though Tom was shy, Mary thought he was charming:' with the grammatical structure "even though" limiting the correct answer to some sort of semantic opposites, so you wouldn't get answers like, "Even though Tom was foolish, Mary thought he was ridiculous:' Well, according to my mother, there were very few limitation as to what Tom could have been and what Mary might have thought of him. So I never did well on tests like that.

The same was true with word analogies, pairs of words in which you were supposed to find some sort of logical, semantic relationship — for example, "Sunset is to nightfall as is to." And here you would be presented with a list of four possible pairs, one of which showed the same kind of relationship: red is to stoplight, bus is to arrival, chills is to fever, yawn is to boring: Well, I could never think that way. I knew what the tests were asking, but I could not block out of my mind the images already created by the first pair, "sunset is to nightfall"—and I would see a burst of colors against a darkening sky, the moon rising, the lowering of a curtain of stars. And all the other pairs of words —red, bus, stoplight, boring—just threw up a mass of confusing images, making it impossible for me to sort out something as logical as saying: "A Sunset precedes nightfall" is the same as " a chill precedes a fever." The only way I would have gotten that answer right would have been to imagine as associative situation, for example, my being disobedient and staying out past sunset, catching a chill at night, which turns into feverish pneumonia as punishment, which indeed did happen to me.

I have been thinking about all this lately, about my mother's English, about achievement tests. Because lately I've been asked, as a writer, why there are not more Asian Americans represented in American literature. Why are there few Asian Americans enrolled in creative writing programs? Why do so many Chinese students go into engineering! Well, these are broad sociological questions I can't begin to answer. But I have noticed in surveys — in fact, just last week — that Asian students, as a whole, always do significantly better on math achievement tests than in English. And this makes me think that there are other Asian-American students whose English spoken in the home might also be described as "broken" or "limited." And perhaps they also have teachers who are steering away from writing and into math and science. Which is what happened to me.

Fortunately, I happen to be rebellious in nature and enjoy the challenge of disproving assumptions made about me. I became an English major my first year in college, after being enrolled as pre-med. I started writing nonfiction as a freelancer the week after I was told by my former boss that writing was my worst skill and I should hone my talents toward account management.

But it wasn't until 1985 that I finally began to write fiction. And at first I wrote using what I thought to be wittily crafted sentences, sentences that would finally prove I had mastery over the English language. Here's an example from the first draft of a story that later made its way into *The Joy Luck Club*, but without this line: "That was my mental quandary in its nascent state." A terrible line, which I can barely pronounce.

Fortunately, for reasons I won't get into today, I later decided I should envision a reader for the stories I would write. And the reader I decided upon was my mother, because these were stories about mothers. So with this reader in mind — and in fact she did read my early drafts — I began to write stories using all the Englishes I grew up with: the English I spoke to my mother, which for lack of a better term might be described as "broken"; my translation of her Chinese, which could certainly be described as "watered down"; and what I imagined to be her translation of her Chinese if she could speak in perfect English, her internal language, and for that I sought to preserve the essence, but neither nor a Chinese structure. I wanted to capture what language ability tests can never reveal: her intent, her passion, her imagery, the rhythms of her speech and the nature of her thoughts.

Apart from what any critic had to say about my writing, I knew I had succeeded where it counted when my mother finished reading my book and gave me her verdict: "So easy to read."

Once More to the Lake

by E.B. White

One summer, along about 1904, my father rented a camp on a lake in Maine and took us all there for the month of August. We all got ringworm from some kittens and had to rub Pond's Extract on our arms and legs night and morning, and my father rolled over in a canoe with all his clothes on; but outside of that the vacation was a success and from then on none of us ever thought there was any place in the world like that lake in Maine. We returned summer after summer—always on August 1st for one month. I have since become a salt-water man, but sometimes in summer there are days when the restlessness of the tides and the fearful cold of the sea water and the incessant wind which blows across the afternoon and into the evening make me wish for the placidity of a lake in the woods. A few weeks ago this feeling got so strong I bought myself a couple of bass hooks and a spinner and returned to the lake where we used to go, for a week's fishing and to revisit old haunts.

I took along my son, who had never had any fresh water up his nose and who had seen lily pads only from train windows. On the journey over to the lake I began to wonder what it would be like. I wondered how time would have marred this unique, this holy spot—the coves and streams, the hills that the sun set behind, the camps and the paths behind the camps. I was sure that the tarred road would have found it out and I wondered in what other ways it would be desolated. It is strange how much you can remember about places like that once you allow your mind to return into the grooves which lead back. You remember one thing, and that suddenly reminds you of another thing. I guess I remembered clearest of all the early mornings, when the lake was cool and motionless, remembered how the bedroom smelled of the lumber it was made of and of the wet woods whose scent entered through the screen. The partitions in the camp were thin and did not extend clear to the top of the rooms, and as I was always the first up I would dress softly so as not to wake the others, and sneak out into the sweet outdoors and start out in the canoe, keeping close along the shore in the long shadows of the pines. I remembered being very careful never to rub my paddle against the gunwale for fear of disturbing the stillness of the cathedral. The lake had never been what you would call a wild lake. There were cottages sprinkled around the shores, and it was in farming although the shores of the lake were quite heavily wooded. Some of the cottages were owned by nearby farmers, and you would live at the shore and eat your meals at the farmhouse. That's what our family did. But although it wasn't wild, it was a fairly large and undisturbed lake and there were places in it which, to a child at least, seemed infinitely remote and primeval.

I was right about the tar: it led to within half a mile of the shore But when I got back there, with my boy, and we settled into a camp near a farmhouse and into the kind of summertime I had known, I could tell that it was going to be pretty much the same as it had been before—I knew it, lying in bed the first morning, smelling the bedroom, and hearing the boy sneak quietly out and go off along the shore in a boat. I began to sustain the illusion that he was I, and therefore, by simple transposition, that I was my father. This sensation persisted, kept cropping up all the time we were there. It was not an entirely new feeling, but in this setting it grew much stronger. I seemed to be living a dual existence. I would be in the middle of some simple act, I would be picking up a bait box or laying down a table fork, or I would be saying something, and suddenly it would be not I but my father who was saying the words or making the gesture. It gave me a creepy sensation.

We went fishing the first morning. I felt the same damp moss covering the worms in the bait can, and saw the dragonfly alight on the tip of my rod as it hovered a few inches from the surface of the water. It was the arrival of this fly that convinced me beyond any doubt that everything was as it always had been, that the years were a mirage and there had been no years. The small waves were the same, chucking the rowboat under the chin as we fished at anchor, and the boat was the same boat, the same color green and the ribs broken in the same places, and under the floor boards the same freshwater leavings and debris—the dead helgramite, the wisps of moss, the rusty discarded fishhook, the dried blood from yesterday's catch. We stared silently at the tips of our rods, at the dragonflies that came and wells. I lowered the tip of mine into the water, tentatively, pensively dislodging the fly, which darted two feet away, poised, darted two feet back, and came to rest again a little farther up the rod. There had been no years between the ducking of this dragonfly and the other one—the one that was part of memory. I looked at the boy, who was silently watching his fly, and it was my hands that held his rod, my eyes watching. I felt dizzy and didn't know which rod I was at the end of.

We caught two bass, hauling them in briskly as though they were mackerel, pulling them over the side of the boat in a businesslike manner without any landing net, and stunning them with a blow on the back of the head. When we got back for a swim before lunch, the lake was exactly where we had left it, the same number of inches from the dock, and there was only the merest suggestion of a breeze. This seemed an utterly enchanted sea, this lake you could leave to its own devices for a few hours and come back to, and find that it had not stirred, this constant and trustworthy body of water. In the shallows, the dark, water-soaked sticks and twigs, smooth and old, were undulating in clusters on the bottom against the clean ribbed sand, and the track of the mussel was plain. A school of minnows swam by, each minnow with its small, individual shadow, doubling the attendance, so clear and sharp in the sunlight. Some of the other campers were in swimming, along the shore, one of them with a cake of soap, and the water felt thin and clear and insubstantial. Over the years there had been this person with the cake of soap, this cultist, and here he was. There had been no years.

Up to the farmhouse to dinner through the teeming, dusty field, the road under our sneakers was only a two-track road. The middle track was missing, the one with the marks of the hooves and the splotches of dried, flaky manure. There had always been three tracks to choose from in choosing which track to walk in; now the choice was narrowed down to two. For a moment I missed terribly the middle alternative. But the way led past the tennis court, and something about the way it lay there in the sun reassured me; the tape had loosened along the backline, the alleys were green with plantains and other weeds, and the net (installed in June and removed in September) sagged in the dry noon, and the whole place steamed with midday heat and hunger and emptiness. There was a choice of pie for dessert, and one was blueberry and one was apple, and the waitresses were the same country girls, there having been no passage of time, only the illusion of it as in a dropped curtain—the waitresses were still fifteen; their hair had been washed, that was the only difference—they had been to the movies and seen the pretty girls with the clean hair.

Summertime, oh summertime, pattern of life indelible, the fade proof lake, the woods unshatterable, the pasture with the sweet fern and the juniper forever and ever, summer without end; this was the background, and the life along the shore was the design, the cottages with their innocent and tranquil design, their tiny docks with the flagpole and the American flag floating against the white clouds in the blue sky, the little paths over the roots of the trees leading from camp to camp and the paths leading back to the outhouses and the can of lime for sprinkling, and at the souvenir counters at the store the miniature birch-bark canoes and the post cards that showed things looking a little better than they looked. This was the American family at play, escaping the city heat, wondering whether the newcomers at the camp at the head of the cove were "common" or "nice," wondering whether it was true that the people who drove up for Sunday dinner at the farmhouse were turned away because there wasn't enough chicken.

It seemed to me, as I kept remembering all this, that those times and those summers had been infinitely precious and worth saving. There had been jollity and peace and goodness. The arriving (at the beginning of August) had been so big a business in itself, at the railway station the farm wagon drawn up, the first smell of the pine-laden air, the first glimpse of the smiling farmer, and the great importance of the trunks and your father's enormous authority in such matters, and the feel of the wagon under you for the long ten-mile haul, and at the top of the last long hill catching the first view of the lake after eleven months of not seeing this cherished body of water. The shouts and cries of the other campers when they saw you, and the trunks to be unpacked, to give up their rich burden. (Arriving was less exciting nowadays, when you sneaked up in your car and parked it under a tree near the camp and took out the bags and in five minutes it was all over, no fuss, no loud wonderful fuss about trunks.)

Peace and goodness and jollity. The only thing that was wrong now, really, was the sound of the place, an unfamiliar nervous sound of the outboard motors. This was the note that jarred, the one thing that would sometimes break the illusion and set the years moving. In those other summertimes, all motors were inboard; and when they were at a little distance, the noise they made was a sedative, an ingredient of summer sleep. They were one-cylinder and two-cylinder engines, and some were make-and-break and some were jump-spark, but they all made a sleepy sound across the lake. The one-lungers throbbed and fluttered, and the twin-cylinder ones purred and purred, and that was a quiet sound too. But now the campers all had outboards. In the daytime, in the hot mornings, these motors made a petulant, irritable sound; at night, in the still evening when the afterglow lit the water, they whined about one's ears like mosquitoes. My boy loved our rented outboard, and his great desire was to achieve single-handed mastery over it, and authority, and he soon learned the trick of choking it a little (but not too much), and the adjustment of the needle valve. Watching him I would remember the things you could do with the old one-cylinder engine with the heavy flywheel, how you could have it eating out of your hand if you got really close to it spiritually. Motor boats in those days didn't have clutches, and you would make a landing by shutting off the motor at the proper time and coasting in with a dead rudder. But there was a way of reversing them, if you learned the trick, by cutting the switch and putting it on again exactly on the final dying revolution of the flywheel, so that it would kick back against compression and begin reversing. Approaching a dock in a strong following breeze, it was difficult to slow up sufficiently by the ordinary coasting method, and if a boy felt he had complete mastery over his motor, he was tempted to keep it running beyond its time and then reverse it a few feet from the dock. It took a cool nerve, because if you threw the switch a twentieth of a second too soon you would catch the flywheel when it still had speed enough to go up past center, and the boat would leap ahead, charging bull-fashion at the dock.

We had a good week at the camp. The bass were biting well and the sun shone endlessly, day after day. We would be tired at night and lie down in the accumulated heat of the little bedrooms after the long hot day and the breeze would stir almost imperceptibly outside and the smell of the swamp drift in through the rusty screens. Sleep would come easily and in the morning the red squirrel would be on the roof, tapping out his gay routine. I kept remembering everything, lying in bed in the mornings—the small steamboat that had a long rounded stern like the lip of a Ubangi, and how quietly she ran on the moonlight sails, when the older boys played their mandolins and the girls sang and we ate doughnuts dipped in sugar, and how sweet the music was on the water in the shining night, and what it had felt like to think about girls then. After breakfast we would go up to the store and the things were in the same place—the minnows in a bottle, the plugs and spinners disarranged and pawed over by the youngsters from the boys' camp, the fig newtons and the Beeman's gum. Outside, the road was tarred and cars stood in front of the store. Inside, all was just as it had always been, except there was more Coca Cola and not so much Moxie and root beer and birch beer and sarsaparilla. We would walk out with a bottle of pop apiece and sometimes the pop would backfire up our noses and hurt. We explored the streams, quietly, where the turtles slid off the sunny logs and dug their way into the soft bottom; and we lay on the town wharf and fed worms to the tame bass. Everywhere we went I had trouble making out which was I, the one walking at my side, the one walking in my pants.

One afternoon while we were there at that lake a thunderstorm came up. It was like the revival of an old melodrama that I had seen long ago with childish awe. The second-act climax of the drama of the electrical disturbance over a lake in America had not changed in any important respect. This was the big scene, still the big scene. The whole thing was so familiar, the first feeling of oppression and heat and a general air around camp of not wanting to go very far away. In mid-afternoon (it was all the same) a curious darkening of the sky, and a lull in everything that had made life tick; and then the way the boats suddenly swung the other way at their moorings with the coming of a breeze out of the new quarter, and the premonitory rumble. Then the kettle drum, then the snare, then the bass drum and cymbals, then crackling light against the dark, and the gods grinning and licking their chops in the hills. Afterward the calm, the rain steadily rustling in the calm lake, the return of light and hope and spirits, and the campers running out in joy and relief to go swimming in the rain, their bright cries perpetuating the deathless joke about how they were getting simply drenched, and the children screaming with delight at the new sensation of bathing in the rain, and the joke about getting drenched linking the generations in a strong indestructible chain. And the comedian who waded in carrying an umbrella. When the others went swimming my son said he was going in too. He pulled his dripping trunks from the line where they had hung all through the shower, and wrung them out. Languidly, and with no thought of going in, I watched him, his hard little body, skinny and bare, saw him wince slightly as he pulled up around his vitals the small, soggy, icy garment. As he buckled the swollen belt suddenly my groin felt the chill of death.

The Struggle to Be an All American Girl

by Elizabeth Wong

It's still there, the Chinese school on Yale Street where my brother and I used to go. Despite the new coat of paint and the high wire fence, the school I knew 10 years ago remains remarkably, stoically the same.

Every day at 5 P.M., instead of playing with our fourth and fifth grade friends or sneaking out to the empty lot to hunt ghosts and animal bones, my brother and I had to go to Chinese school. No amount of kicking, screaming, or pleading could dissuade my mother, who was solidly determined to have us learn the language or our heritage.

Forcibly, she walked us the seven long, hilly blocks from our home to school, deposing our defiant tearful faces before the stern principal. My only memory of him is that he swayed on his heels like a palm tree, and he always clasped his impatient twitching hands behind his back. I recognized him as a repressed maniacal child killer, and knew that if we ever saw his hands we would be in big trouble.

We all sat in little chairs in an empty auditorium. The room smelled like Chinese medicine, an important faraway mustiness. Like ancient mothballs or dirty closets. I hated that smell. I favored crisp new scents. Like the soft French perfume that my American teacher wore in public school.

There was a stage far to the right, flanked by an American flag and the flag of the Nationalist Republic of China, which was also red, white and blue but not as pretty.

Although the emphasis at the school was mainly language - speaking, reading, and writing - the lessons always began with an exercise in politeness. With the entrance of the teacher, the best student would tap a bell and everyone would get up, kowtow, and chant, "Sing san ho," the phonetic for "How are you, teacher?"

Being ten years old, I had better things to learn than ideographs copied painstakingly in lines that ran right to left from the tip of a *moc but*, a real ink pen that had to be held in an awkward way if blotches were to be avoided. After all, I could do the multiplication tables, name the satellites of Mars, and write reports on "Little Women" and "Black Beauty." Nancy Drew, my favorite book heroine, never spoke Chinese.

The language was a source of embarrassment. More times than not, I had tried to disassociate myself from the nagging loud voice that followed me wherever I wandered in the nearby American supermarket outside Chinatown. The voice belonged to my grandmother, a fragile woman in her seventies who could outshout the best of the street vendors. Her humor was raunchy, her Chinese rhythmless, pattern less. It was quick, it was loud, and it was unbeautiful. It was not like the quiet, lilting romance of French or the gentle refinement of the American South. Chinese sounded pedestrian. Public.

In Chinatown, the comings and goings of hundreds of Chinese on their daily tasks sounded chaotic and frenzied. I did not want to be thought of as mad, as talking gibberish. When I spoke English, people nodded at me, smiled sweetly, and said encouraging words. Even the people in my culture would cluck and say that I would do well in life. "My, doesn't she move her lips fast," they would say, meaning that I would be able to keep up with the world outside Chinatown.

My brother was even more fanatical than I about speaking English. He was especially hard on my mother, criticizing her, often cruelly, for her pidgin speech-smatterings of Chinese scattered like chop suey in her conversation. "It's not ' what it is,' Mom," he would say in exasperation. "It is "What is it, what is it, what is it!" Sometimes Mom might leave out an occasional "the" or "a" or perhaps a verb of being. He would stop her in mid-sentence: "Say it again, Mom. Say it right." When he tripped over his own tongue, he'd blame it on her. "See, Mom, it is all your fault. You set a bad example."

What infuriated my mother was when my brother cornered her on her consonants, especially "r." My father had played a cruel joke on Mom by assigning her an American name that her tongue would not allow her to say. No matter how hard she tried, "Ruth" always ended up "Luth" or "Roof."

After two years of writing with a *moc but* and reciting words with multiples of meanings, I finally was granted a cultural divorce. I was permitted to stop Chinese school. I thought of myself as multicultural. I preferred tacos to egg rolls; I enjoyed Cinco de Mayo more than Chinese New Year. At last I was one of you; I was not one of them. Sadly, I still am.

2

Education

Sex. Math. Violence

Public service ad sponsored by the American School Counselor Association and created by Jill Applebaum, Young and Rubicam, New York (2002)

SEX. MATH. VIOLENCE.

PHYSICS. ALCOHOL. GYM. RACISM.

ENGLISH. DRUGS. HISTORY.

WHAT ARE YOUR KIDS REALLY LEARNING?

As a parent, one of your greatest dreams is to see that your children achieve theirs.

As school counselors, we are trained to help your children teach their full potential. There is a common misconception that the only role of the school counselor is to help students get into college.

But these are countless situations we can help them get out of. Every day, students face challenges. Tough courses, peer pressure, eating disorders, depression, school violence.

It's a long list. And even the best parents with the best intentions don't always know what's on their children's minds. Often, children are more willing to open up to someone who doesn't have the power to ground them or to grade them. Someone who exists purely to guide them.

It's been said that life is a journey, so make sure your kids have a guide. A collaborative relationship with your children's school counselor can reinforce that they have are heading in the right direction.

We don't pretend to have all of the answers, but we do have infinite resources.

Give your child's school counselor a call. Because there is a textbook for everything. Except life.

America Skips School: Why We Talk so Much About Education and Do so Little

by Barber, Benjamin R.

Harper's Magazine, 0017789X, Nov93, Vol. 287, Issue 1722

On September 8, the day most of the nation's children were scheduled to return to school, the Department of Education Statistics issued a report, commissioned by Congress, on adult literacy and numeracy in the United States. The results? More than 90 million adult Americans lacked simple literacy. Fewer than 20 percent of those surveyed could compare two metaphors in a poem; not 4 percent could calculate the cost of carpeting at a given price for a room of a given size, using a calculator. As the DOE report was being issued, as if to echo its findings, two of the nation's largest school systems had delayed their openings: in New York, to remove asbestos from aging buildings; in Chicago, because of a battle over the budget.

Inspired by the report and the delays, pundits once again began chanting the familiar litany of the education crisis. We've heard it all many times before: 130,000 children bring guns along with their pencils and books

to school each morning; juvenile arrests for murder increased by 85 percent from 1987 to 1991; more than 3,000 youngsters will drop out today and every day for the rest of the school year, until about 600,000 are lost by June—in many urban schools, perhaps half the enrollment. A lot of the dropouts will end up in prison, which is a surer bet for young black males than college: one in four will pass through the correctional system, and at least two out of three of those will be dropouts.

In quiet counterpoint to those staggering facts is another set of statistics: teachers make less than accountants, architects, doctors, lawyers, engineers, judges, health professionals, auditors, and surveyors. They can earn higher salaries teaching in Berlin, Tokyo, Ottawa, or Amsterdam than in New York or Chicago. American children are in school only about 180 days a year, as against 240 days or more for children in Europe or Japan. The richest school districts (school financing is local, not federal) spend twice as much per student as poorer ones do. The poorer ones seem almost beyond help: children with venereal disease or AIDS (2.5 million adolescents annually contract a sexually transmitted disease), gangs in the schoolyard, drugs in the class room, children doing babies instead of homework, playground firefights featuring Uzis and Glocks.

Clearly, the social contract that obliges adults to pay taxes so that children can be educated is in imminent danger of collapse. Yet for all the astonishing statistics, more astonishing still is that no one seems to be listening. The education crisis is kind of like violence on television: the worse it gets the more inert we become, and the more of it we require to rekindle our attention. We've had a "crisis" every dozen years or so at least since the launch of Sputnik, in 1457, when American schools were accused of falling behind the world standard in science education. Just ten years ago, the National Commission on Excellence in Education warned that America's pedagogical inattention was putting America "at risk." What the commission called "a rising tide of mediocrity" was imperiling "our very future as a Nation and a people." What was happening to education was an "act of war."

Since then, countless reports have been issued decrying the condition of our educational system, the DOE report being only the most recent. They have come from every side, Republican as well as Democrat, from the private sector as well as the public. Yet for all the talk, little happens. At times, the schools look more like they are being dismantled than rebuilt. How can this be? If Americans over a broad political spectrum regard education as vital, why has nothing been done?

I have spent thirty years as a scholar examining the nature of democracy, and even more as a citizen optimistically celebrating its possibilities, but today I am increasingly persuaded that the reason for the country's inaction is that Americans do not really care about education—the country has grown comfortable with the game of "let's pretend we care."

As America's educational system crumbles, the pundits, instead of looking for solutions, search busily for scapegoats. Some assail the teachers—those "Profscam" pedagogues trained in the licentious Sixties who, as aging hippies, are supposedly still subverting the schools—for producing a dire illiteracy. Others turn on the kids themselves, so that at the same moment as we are transferring our responsibilities to the shoulders of the next generation, we are blaming them for our own generation's most conspicuous failures. Allan Bloom was typical of the many recent critics who have condemned the young as vapid, lazy, selfish, complacent, self-seeking, materialistic, small-minded, apathetic, greedy, and, of course, illiterate. E. D. Hirsch in his Cultural Literacy and Diane Ravitch and Chester E. Finn Jr. in their What Do Our Seventeen-Year-Olds Know? have lambasted the schools, the teachers, and the children for betraying the adult generation from which they were to inherit, the critics seemed confident, a precious cultural legacy.

How this captious literature reeks of hypocrisy! How sanctimonious all the hand-wringing over still another "education crisis" seems. Are we ourselves really so literate? Are our kids stupid or smart for ignoring what we preach and copying what we practice? The young, with their keen noses for hypocrisy, are in fact adept readers—but not of books. They are society-smart rather than school-smart, and what they read so acutely are the social signals emanating from the world in which they will have to make a living. Their teachers in that world, the nation's true pedagogues, are television, advertising, movies, politics, and the celebrity domains they define. We prattle about deficient schools and the gullible youngsters they turn out, so vulnerable to the siren song of drugs, but think nothing of letting the advertisers into the classroom to fashion what an Advertising Age essay calls "brand and product loyalties through classroom-centered, peer-powered lifestyle patterning."

Our kids spend 900 hours a year in school (the ones who go to school) and from 1,200 to 1,800 hours a year in front of the television set. From which are they likely to learn more? Critics such as Hirsch and Ravitch want to find out what our seventeen-year-olds know, but it's really pretty simple; they know exactly what our forty-seven- year-olds know and teach them by example—on television, in the boardroom, around Washington, on Madison Avenue, in Hollywood. The very first lesson smart kids learn is that it is much more important to heed what society teaches implicitly by its deeds and reward structures than what school teaches explicitly in its lesson plans and civic sermons. Here is a test for adults that may help reveal what the kids see when they look at our world.

REAL WORLD CULTURAL LITERACY

1. According to television, having fun in America means
    a. going blond
    b. drinking Pepsi
    c. playing Nintendo
    d. wearing Air Jordans
    e. reading Mark Twain
2. A good way to prepare for a high-income career and to acquire status in our society is to
    a. win a slam-dunk contest
    b. take over a company and sell off its assets
    c. start a successful rock band
    d. earn a professional degree
    e. become a kindergarten teacher
3. Book publishers are financially rewarded today for publishing
    a. mega-cookbooks
    b. mega—cat books
    c. megabooks by Michael Crichton
    d. megabooks by John Grisham
    e. mini-books by Voltaire
4. A major California bank that advertised "no previous credit history required" in inviting Berkeley students to apply for Visa cards nonetheless turned down one group of applicants because
    a. their parents had poor credit histories
    b. they had never held jobs
    c. they had outstanding student loans
    d. they were "humanities majors"
5. Colleges and universities are financially rewarded today for
    a. supporting bowl-quality football teams
    b. forging research relationships with large corporations
    c. sustaining professional programs in law and business
    d. stroking wealthy alumni
    e. fostering outstanding philosophy departments
6. Familiarity with Henry IV, Part II is likely to be of vital importance in
    a. planning a corporate takeover
    b. evaluating budget cuts in the Department of Education
    c. initiating a medical-malpractice lawsuit
    d. writing an impressive job resume
    e. taking a test on what our seventeen-year-olds know
7. To help the young learn that "history is a living thing," Scholastic, Inc., a publisher of school magazines and paperbacks, recently distributed to 40,000 junior and senior high school classrooms
    a. a complimentary video of the award-winning series The Civil War
    b. free copies of Plato's Dialogues
    c. an abridgment of Alexis de Tocqueville's Democracy in America
    d. a wall size Periodic Table of the Elements
    e. gratis copies of Billy Joel's hit single "We Didn't Start the Fire"(which recounts history via a vaguely chronological list of warbled celebrity names)

My sample of forty-seven-year-olds scored very well on the test. Not surprisingly, so did their seventeen- year-old children. (For each question, either the last entry is correct or all responses are correct except the last one.) The results of the test reveal again the deep hypocrisy that runs through our lamentations about education. The illiteracy of the young turns out to be our own reflected back to us with embarrassing force. We honor ambition, we reward greed, we celebrate materialism, we worship acquisitiveness, we cherish success, and we commercialize the classroom—and then we bark at the young about the gentle arts of the spirit. We recommend history to the kids but rarely consult it ourselves. We make a fuss about ethics but are satisfied to see it taught as an "add on," as in "ethics in medicine" or "ethics in business"—as if Sunday morning in church could compensate for uninterrupted sinning from Monday to Saturday.

The children are onto this game. They know that if we really valued schooling, we'd pay teachers what we pay stockbrokers; if we valued books, we'd spend a little something on the libraries so that adults could read, too; if we valued citizenship, we'd give national service and civic education more than pilot status; if we valued children, we wouldn't let them be abused, manipulated, impoverished, and killed in their beds by gang-war cross fire and stray bullets. Schools can and should lead, but when they confront a society that in every instance tells a story exactly opposite to the one they are supposed to be teaching, their job becomes impossible. When the society undoes each workday what the school tries to do each school day, schooling can't make much of a difference.

Inner-city children are not the only ones who are learning the wrong lessons. TV sends the same messages to everyone, and the success of Donald Trump, Pete Rose, Henry Kravis, or George Steinbrenner makes them potent role models, whatever their values. Teen dropouts are not blind; teen drug sellers are not deaf; teen college students who avoid the humanities in favor of pre-business or pre law are not stupid. Being apt pupils of reality, they learn their lessons well. If they see a man with a rubber arm and an empty head who can throw a ball at 95 miles per hour pulling down millions of dollars a year while a dedicated primary-school teacher is getting crumbs, they will avoid careers in teaching even if they can't make the major leagues. If they observe their government spending up to $35,000 a year to keep a young black behind bars but a fraction of that to keep him in school, they will write off school (and probably write off blacks as well).

Our children's illiteracy is merely our own, which they assume with commendable prowess. They know what we have taught them all too well: there is nothing in Homer or Virginia Woolf, in Shakespeare or Toni Morrison, that will advantage them in climbing to the top of the American heap. Academic credentials may still count, but schooling in and of itself is for losers. Bookworms. Nerds. Inner-city rappers and fraternity-house wise guys are in full agreement about that. The point is to start pulling down the big bucks. Some kids just go into business earlier than others. Dropping out is the national pastime, if by dropping out we mean giving up the precious things of the mind and the spirit in which America shows so little interest and for which it offers so little payback.

While the professors argue about whether to teach the ancient history of a putatively white Athens or the ancient history of a putatively black Egypt, the kids are watching televised political campaigns driven by mindless image mongering and inflammatory polemics that ignore history altogether. Why, then, are we so surprised when our students dismiss the debate over the origins of civilization, whether Eurocentric or Afrocentric, and concentrate on cash-and-carry careers? Isn't the choice a tribute not to their ignorance but to their adaptive intelligence? Although we can hardly be proud of ourselves for what we are teaching them, we should at least be proud of them for how well they've learned our lessons.

Not all Americans have stopped caring about the schools, however. In the final irony of the educational endgame, cynical entrepreneurs like Chris Whittle are insinuating television into the classroom itself, bribing impoverished school boards by offering free TV sets on which they can show advertising for children—sold to sponsors at premium rates. Whittle, the mergers and acquisitions mogul of education, is trying to get rich off the poverty of public schools and the fears of parents. Can he really believe advertising in the schools enhances education? Or is he helping to corrupt public schools in ways that will make parents even more anxious to use vouchers for private schools—which might one day be run by Whittle's latest entrepreneurial venture, the Edison Project.

According to Lifetime Learning Systems, an educational-software company, "kids spend 40 percent of each day . . . where traditional advertising can't reach them." Not to worry, says Lifetime Learning in an Advertising Age promo: "Now, you can enter the classroom through custom-made reaming materials created with your specific marketing objectives in mind. Communicate with young spenders directly and, through them, their teachers and families as well." If we redefine young learners as "young spenders," are the young really to be blamed for acting like mindless consumers? Can they become young spenders and still become young critical thinkers, let alone informed citizens? If we are willing to give TV cartoons the government's imprimatur as "educational television" (as we did a few years ago, until the FCC changed its mind), can we blame kids for educating themselves on television trash?

Everyone can agree that we should educate our children to be something more than young spenders molded by "lifestyle patterning." But what should the goals of the classroom be? In recent years it has been fashionable to define the educational crisis in terms of global competition and minimal competence, as if schools were no more than vocational institutions. Although it has talked sensibly about education, the Clinton Administration has leaned toward this approach, under the tutelage of Secretary of Labor Robert Reich.

The classroom, however, should not be merely a trade school. The fundamental task of education in a democracy is what Tocqueville once called the apprenticeship of liberty: learning to be free. I wonder whether Americans still believe liberty has to be reamed and that its skills are worth learning. Or have they been deluded by two centuries of rhetoric into thinking that freedom is "natural" and can be taken for granted?

The claim that all men are born free, upon which America was founded, is at best a promising fiction. In real life, as every parent knows, children are born fragile, born needy, born ignorant, born unformed, born weak, born foolish, born dependent—born in chains. We acquire our freedom over time, if at all. Embedded in families, clans, communities, and nations, we must learn to be free. We may be natural consumers and born narcissists, but citizens have to be made. Liberal-arts education actually means education in the arts of liberty; the "servile arts" were the trades reamed by unfree men in the Middle Ages, the vocational education of their day. Perhaps this is why Thomas Jefferson preferred to memorialize his founding of the University of Virginia on his tombstone rather than his two terms as president; it is certainly why he viewed his Bill for the More GeneralDiffusion of Knowledge in Virginia as a centerpiece of his career (although it failed passage as legislation—times were perhaps not so different). John Adams, too, boasted regularly about Massachusett's high literacy rates and publicly funded education.

Jefferson and Adams both understood that the Bill of Rights offered little protection in a nation without informed citizens. Once educated, however, a people was safe from even the subtlest tyrannies. Jefferson's democratic proclivities rested on his conviction that education could turn a people into a safe refuge—indeed "the only safe depository" for the ultimate powers of society. "Cherish therefore the spirit of our people," he wrote to Edward Carrington in 1787, "and keep alive their attention. Do not be severe up on their errors, but reclaim them by enlightening them. If once they become inattentive to public affairs, you and I and Congress and Assemblies, judges and governors, shall all become wolves."

The logic of democracy begins with public education, proceeds to informed citizenship, and comes to fruition in the securing of rights and liberties. We have been nominally democratic for so long that we presume it is our natural condition rather than the product of persistent effort and tenacious responsibility. We have decoupled rights from civic responsibilities and severed citizenship from education on the false assumption that citizens just happen. We have forgotten that the "public" in public schools means not just paid for by the public but procreative of the very idea of a public. Public schools are how a public—a citizenry—is forged and how young, selfish individuals turn into conscientious, community-minded citizens.

Among the several literacies that have attracted the anxious attention of commentators, civic literacy has been the least visible. Yet this is the fundamental literacy by which we live in a civil society. It encompasses the competence to participate in democratic communities, the ability to think critically and act with deliberation in a pluralistic world, and the empathy to identify sufficiently with others to live with them despite conflicts of interest and differences in character. At the most elementary level, what our children suffer from most, whether they're hurling racial epithets from fraternity porches or shooting one another down in schoolyards, is the absence of civility. Security guards and metal detectors are poor surrogates for civility, and they make our schools look increasingly like prisons (though they may be less safe than prisons). Jefferson thought schools would produce free men: we prove him right by putting dropouts in jail.

Civility is a work of the imagination, for it is through the imagination that we render others sufficiently like ourselves for them to become subjects of tolerance and respect, if not always affection. Democracy is anything but a "natural" form of association. It is an extraordinary and rare contrivance of cultivated imagination. Give the uneducated the right to participate in making collective decisions, and what results is not democracy but, at best, mob rule: the government of private prejudice once known as the tyranny of opinion. For Jefferson, the difference between the democratic temperance he admired in agrarian America and the rule of the rabble he condemned when viewing the social unrest of Europe's teeming cities was quite simply education. Madison had hoped to "filter" out popular passion through the device of representation. Jefferson saw in education a filter that could be in' stalled within each individual, giving to each the capacity to rule prudently. Education creates a ruling aristocracy constrained by temperance and wisdom; when that education is public and universal, it is an aristocracy to which all can belong. At its best, the American dream of a free and equal society governed by judicious citizens has been this dream of an aristocracy of everyone.

To dream this dream of freedom is easy, but to secure it is difficult as well as expensive. Notwithstanding their lamentations, Americans do not appear ready to pay the price. There is no magic bullet for education. But I no longer can accept that the problem lies in the lack of consensus about remedies—in a dearth of solutions. There is no shortage of debate over how to repair our educational infrastructure. National standards or more local control?

Vouchers or better public schools? More parental involvement or more teacher autonomy? A greater federal presence (only 5 or 6 percent of the nation's education budget is federally funded) or fairer local school taxes? More multicultural diversity or more emphasis on what Americans share in common? These are honest disputes. But I am convinced that the problem is simpler and more fundamental. Twenty years ago, writer and activist Frances Moore Lappe captured the essence of the world food crisis when she argued that starvation was caused not by a scarcity of food but by a global scarcity in democracy. The education crisis has the same genealogy. It stems from a dearth of democracy: an absence of democratic will and a consequent refusal to take our children, our schools, and our future seriously.

Most educators, even while they quarrel among themselves, will agree that a genuine commitment to any one of a number of different solutions could help enormously. Most agree that although money can't by itself solve problems, without money few problems can be solved. Money also can't win wars or put men in space, but it is the crucial facilitator. It is also how America has traditionally announced, We are serious about this!

If we were serious, we would raise teachers' salaries to levels that would attract the best young professionals in our society: starting lawyers get from $70,000 to $80,000—why don't starting kindergarten teachers get the same? Is their role in vouchsafing our future less significant? And although there is evidence suggesting that an increase in general educational expenditures doesn't translate automatically into better schools, there is also evidence that an increase aimed specifically at instructional services does. Can we really take in earnest the chattering devotion to excellence of a country so wedded in practice to mediocrity, a nation so ready to relegate teachers—conservators of our common future—to the professional backwaters?

If we were serious, we would upgrade physical facilities so that every school met the minimum standards of our better suburban institutions. Good buildings do not equal good education, but can any education at all take place in leaky, broken-down habitats of the kind described by Jonathan Kozol in his Savage Inequalities?? If money is not a critical factor, why are our most successful suburban school districts funded at nearly twice the level of our inner-city schools? Being even at the starting line cannot guarantee that the runners will win or even finish the race, but not being even pretty much assures failure. We would rectify the balance not by penalizing wealthier communities but by bringing poorer communities up to standard, perhaps by finding other sources of funding for our schools besides property taxes.

If we were serious, we'd extend the school year by a month or two so that learning could take place throughout the year. We'd reduce class size (which means more teachers) and nurture more cooperative learning so that kids could become actively responsible for their own education and that of their classmates. Perhaps most important; we'd raise standards and make teachers and students responsible for them. There are two ways toe breed success: to lower standards so that everybody "passes" in a way that loses all meaning in the real world; and to raise standards and then meet them, so that school success translates into success beyond the classroom. From Confucian China to Imperial England, great nations have built their success in the world upon an education of excellence. The challenge in a democracy is to find a way to maintain excellence while extending educational opportunity to everyone.

Finally, if we were serious, parents, teachers, and students would be the real players while administrators, politicians, and experts would be secondary, at best advisers whose chief skill ought to be knowing when and how to facilitate the work of teachers and then get out of the way. If the Democrats can clean up federal government bureaucracy (the Gore plan), perhaps we can do the same for educational bureaucracy. In New York up to half of the city's teachers occupy jobs outside the classroom. No other enterprise is run that way: Half the soldiers at company headquarters? Half the cops at stationhouse desks? Half the working force in the assistant manager's office? Once the teachers are back in the classroom, they will need to be given more autonomy, more professional responsibility for the success or failure of their students. And parents will have to be drawn in not just because they have rights or because they are politically potent but because they have responsibilities and their children are unlikely to learn without parental engagement. How to define the parental role in the classroom would become serious business for educators.

Some Americans will say this is unrealistic. Times are tough, money's short, and the public is fed up with almost all of its public institutions: the schools are just one more frustrating disappointment. With all the goodwill in the world, it is still hard to know how schools can cure the ills that stem from the failure of so many other institutions. Saying we want education to come first won't put it first.

America, however, has historically been able to accomplish what it sets its mind to. When we wish it and will it, what we wish and will has happened. Our successes are willed; our failures seem to happen when will is absent. There are, of course, those who benefit from the bankruptcy of public education and the failure of democracy. But their blame is no greater than our own: in a world where doing nothing has such dire consequences,, complacency has become a greater sin than malevolence.

In wartime, whenever we have known why we were fighting and believed in the cause, we have prevailed.

Because we believe in profits, we are consummate salespersons and efficacious entrepreneurs. Because we love sports, ours are the dream teams. Why can't a Chicago junior high school be as good as the Chicago Bulls? Because we cherish individuality and mobility, we have created a magnificent (if costly) car culture and the world's largest automotive consumer market. Even as our lower schools are among the worst in the Western world, our graduate institutions are among the very best—because professional training in medicine, law, and technology is vital to our ambitions and because corporate America backs up state and federal priorities in this crucial domain. Look at the things we do well and observe how very well we do them: those are the things that as a nation we have willed.

Then observe what we do badly and ask yourself, Is it because the challenge is too great? Or is it because, finally, we aren't really serious? Would we will an end to the carnage and do whatever it took—more cops, state militias, federal marshals, the Marines?—if the dying children were white and middle class? Or is it a disdain for the young—white, brown, and black—that inures us to the pain? Why are we so sensitive to the retirees whose future (however foreshortened) we are quick to guarantee—don't worry, no reduced cost-of-living allowances, no taxes on social security except for the well-off—and so callous to the young? Have you noticed how health care is on every politician's agenda and education on no one's?

To me, the conclusion is inescapable: we are not serious. We have given up on the public schools because we have given up on the kids; and we have given up on the kids because we have given up on the future—perhaps because it looks too multicolored or too dim or too hard. "Liberty," said Jean-Jacques Rousseau, "is a food easy to eat but hard to digest." America is suffering from a bad case of indigestion. Finally, in giving up on the future, we have given up on democracy. Certainly there will be no liberty, no equality, no social justice without democracy, and there will be no democracy without citizens and the schools that forge civic identity and democratic responsibility. If I am wrong (I'd like to be), my error will be easy to discern, for before the year is out we will put education first on the nation's agenda. We will put it ahead of the deficit, for if the future is finished before it starts, the deficit doesn't matter. Ahead of defense, for without democracy, what liberties will be left to defend? Ahead of all the other public issues and public goods, for without public education there can be no public and hence no truly public issues or public goods to advance. When the polemics are spent and we are through hyperventilating about the crisis in education, there is only one question worth asking: are we serious? If we are, we can begin by honoring that old folk homily and put our money where for much too long our common American mouth has been. Our kids, for once, might even be grateful.

A Nation Still at Risk

by Chester E. Finn

Six years ago, a blue-ribbon commission studying our education system declared us a "nation at risk." Our students were not studying the right subjects, were not working hard enough, were not learning enough. Their schools suffered from slack and uneven standards. Many of their teachers were ill-prepared. "If an unfriendly foreign power had attempted to impose on America the mediocre educational performance that exists today," the panel said, "we might well have viewed it as an act of war." And, it soberly warned, if the United States did not promptly set matters right, our social structure would crack, our culture erode, our economy totter, our national defenses weaken.

To be sure, panels of this sort practically always forecast dire consequences if drastic improvements are not speedily made. But the National Commission on Excellence in Education did not exaggerate. And its voice was not a lone one. An avalanche of studies and reports in the early 1980's drew the same conclusions. It was a time of searching appraisals of American education, and the verdicts were almost uniformly grim.

Nor did they go unheard. Largely thanks to the leadership of crusading "education governors," gutsy state legislators, worried business leaders, and other non-educators, we have had at least a half-decade of efforts to change the practices of the education system in the hope of strengthening its results. Many call this reform wave the "excellence movement." Actually, it is heir to the smaller "back-to-basics" movement of the late 70's, a time when, alarmed by evidence of illiterate high-school graduates, some states adopted "minimum-competency" laws and other measures designed to ensure that those getting diplomas from the public schools would possess at least rudimentary skills in the three R's.

This concern with the output of the education system has proved more durable than anyone expected, and some of the actions taken in its name have been imaginative, more than a few of them courageous. Such terms as

"accountability" have gained currency. One state after another has enacted "comprehensive" education-reform legislation, adding to graduation requirements, installing a kindergarten level, shrinking the average class size, obliging teachers to take literacy exams, making students pass all manner of tests, rearranging the rules for teacher licensing, experimenting with "school site management," revamping administrative arrangements, and more.

Such changes cost money, and as a nation we have been paying generously. We have also been raising teacher salaries nearly everywhere. Though impoverished schools can be found here and there, and although occasionally a school levy is rejected, the average per-pupil expenditure in American public education this year is about $4,800, some $1,500 higher than when A Nation at Risk was released. Today we are spending roughly twice as much per student in real terms as in the mid-60's, and nearly three times the level of the mid-50's.

In early 1988, a half-decade after the appearance of A Nation at Risk, President Reagan asked then-Education Secretary William J. Bennett to prepare a progress report. It was in Bennett's interest to paint as rosy a picture as possible. He was, after all, summing up developments on his and Reagan's watch. Yet here is what he reported:

> American education has made some undeniable progress in the last few years. . . . We are doing better than we were in 1983.
>
> But we are certainly not doing well enough, and we are not doing well enough fast enough. We are still at risk. The absolute level at which our improvements are taking place is unacceptably low. Too many students do not graduate from our high schools, and too many of those who do graduate have been poorly educated. Our students know too little, and their command of essential skills is too slight. . . . And the entire project of American education—at every level—remains insufficiently accountable for the result that matters most: student learning.

The long and short of it is that when gauged in terms of student learning—the only outcome that ultimately counts, all else being means to that end—the results of the excellence movement to date have been scant. The average student continues to emerge from the typical school in possession of mediocre skills and skimpy knowledge.

To be sure, as Bennett suggested, all is not entirely bleak. We are not doing badly at the bottom end. Rudimentary skills are nearly universal. Among those who remain in school and graduate, few today are wholly illiterate. The gap between white youngsters' scores and those of black and Hispanic children has narrowed. We can thus take passing satisfaction from our progress in getting "back to the basics."

Moreover, as always in the vastness of American education with its 100,000 schools, 3,400 colleges, and 58 million students, there are many fine schools and high-achieving youngsters. When the results of the Westinghouse science-talent search come out each winter, a few high schools do wonderfully well. Of the 300 semi-finalists in 1989, Virginia's Thomas Jefferson High School for Science and Technology accounted for 15; New York City schools claimed 105, mainly at the selective Bronx Science and Stuyvesant high schools.

But all this is the exception, and hardly constitutes a plateau to rest on. More typical are recent findings of the National Assessment of Educational Progress and similar barometers:

- Just 5 percent of seventeen-year-old high-school students can read well enough to understand and use information found in technical materials, literary essays, and historical documents.
- Barely 6 percent of them can solve multi-step math problems and use basic algebra. That means correctly answering questions at this level of difficulty: "Christine borrowed $850 for one year from the Friendly Finance Company. If she paid 12 percent simple interest on the loan, what was the total amount she repaid?"
- Only 7 percent are able to infer relationships and draw conclusions from detailed scientific knowledge. Sixty percent of eleventh-graders do not know why The Federalist papers were written; three-quarters cannot say when Lincoln was President; just one in five knows what "Reconstruction" was about. Most high-school students cannot explain what a "government budget deficit" is; two-thirds do not know what "profits" mean.

So how, it is fair to ask, are we doing? What have we to show for these sizable infusions of treasure, energy, and concern? Are we any less at risk?

- Given a blank map of Europe and asked to identify particular countries, young American adults (ages eighteen to twenty-four) typically give the correct answer less than one time in four. Twenty-six percent spot Greece, 37 percent France, just 10 percent Yugoslavia. Asked to do the same thing with American states, fewer than half locate New York and only one in four properly labels Massachusetts.

Such examples are painfully familiar nowadays. We often encounter them in the morning papers and on the evening news. In fact, however, they are but the tip of an iceberg of ignorance. Note, too, that most of the reports from which they are drawn describe young people who have stayed in school and are soon to graduate, those commonly deemed to be "succeeding" in our education system. Excluded from the data is the quarter of the teenage population that drops out, slows down, or defers completion of high school.

Looking overseas for points of reference, we find even greater reason for dismay. Every year or so, we get the results of another international study. The most recent, reported by the Educational Testing Service in January, compares the performance of thirteen-year-olds in mathematics and science in six countries. In math, ours came in dead last. In science, American girls and boys were tied for last place (with Ireland a provinces). Korea led in both subjects, and the United States was also bested in both by England, Spain, and three other Canadian provinces.

- The Southern Regional Education Board recently asked colleges and universities in its fifteen states how many of their entering freshmen were academically unready for higher education. Thirty percent of the institutions reported that this was the case with at least half their new students; on 60 percent of the campuses, remedial work was indicated for at least a third of the freshmen.
- New Jersey administers a basic-skills placement test to all students entering its state colleges and universities. In 1987, just 27 percent of them were found "proficient" in verbal skills, 31 percent in "computation," and only 15 percent in elementary algebra. Even at Rutgers, the flagship, barely half the freshmen could handle elementary algebra and nearly two in five lacked verbal skills.

One might surmise that students unprepared for college at age eighteen will not have acquired a full-fledged
"higher" education four years later. Though hard data are scarce, such information as we have suggests that this is indeed the case. Our campuses are conferring degrees on many people whose intellectual skills are still shaky. Reports the National Center for Education Statistics, after analyzing various forms of "literacy" among young adults in 1985:

> Among the most highly educated young adults in the nation—those with a four-year college degree—one-half of white young adults and more than 8 out of 10 black young adults were unable to perform at the 350 level of the scales. Tasks characteristic of this level include stating in writing the argument made in a long newspaper column, using a bus schedule to select the bus for given departures and arrivals, and calculating a tip in a restaurant given the tip percentage and the bill.

Although my main focus here is on the elementary and secondary schools, the implications for higher education are profound. More than half of our secondary-school graduates enter college right away (and 70 percent commence some sort of post-secondary education within six years). In the population aged twenty-five to thirty-five, the United States now boasts many more college graduates than high-school dropouts, a demographic milestone reached in the 1970's. We award more than 1.8 million additional degrees each year. The scale of our higher-education system is staggering—and unprecedented in the world. But for how many of the young people who swarm into it does "participation in post-secondary education," or even earning a degree, mean acquiring a real "higher" education? The evidence is not encouraging:

Finally, if students entering college are inadequately prepared, so are those young Americans who head into jobs rather than through university gates at the end of their secondary schooling. Many employers report acute difficulty hiring skilled and even semiskilled workers. New York Telephone Company, for example, has grown accustomed to a 20-percent pass rate on its test for telephone operators. Motorola has found about the same proportion succeeding on its seventh-grade-level English composition and fifth-grade math tests. By some estimates, companies are spending as much as $60 billion a year on employee training, a huge fraction of this not on specialized job-related techniques but on equipping workers with essential intellectual skills and knowledge, the kind they did not get in school.

Foreign visitors to American schools are often struck favorably by the geniality and helpfulness of the students they meet. Unfortunately, affability is not a sufficient outcome of formal education. To persist on our present course is to continue producing high-school graduates who are amiable but ignorant. It is to keep turning many colleges into remedial high schools, and to continue pouring into the job market millions of young people who do not have what it takes to handle the jobs available to them. And this, of course, means continuing as a nation to fall behind our European and Asian allies, enemies, and rivals.

Why are we not getting better results? Why have so many sincere efforts at reform yielded so little? It is not for lack of concern, not for lack of national self-reproach, and not for want of money. Instead, we have been foundering on three large obstacles, and are on the verge of colliding with a fourth that is the most formidable of all.

American parents are reasonably content, too. Harold W. Stevenson of the University of Michigan has spent years comparing the educational performance of elementary-school students in the U.S. with that of youngsters in Taiwan, Japan, and China. The American children lag way behind the others in reading and math. But one would never known this from their mothers' attitudes and opinions. Here are some of Stevenson's findings:

> Not only did American mothers generally have the most favorable evaluations of their children, they also were the most satisfied with their child's current academic performance. . . . Mothers also were asked to evaluate the effectiveness of the schools in educating their children. American mothers were very positive: 91 percent judge the schools as doing an "excellent" or "good" job. This was more than double the percentage of Chinese mothers (42 percent) and Japanese mothers (39 percent) who chose these categories.

Professional educators contribute to the general complacency. Beginning with a generalized "t'ain't so" reaction to A Nation at Risk, the profession has spent a fair portion of its energy these past six years arguing that things are not really so bad—and citing data contrived to prove the point. As John J. Cannell has demonstrated, virtually every state and locality in the land that uses standardized tests (i.e., essentially all of them) has managed to find its own students "above average"—and improving. Immediately dubbed the "Lake Woebegon effect," this statistical fantasy results from shrewd test selection, from not "renorming" on a regular basis, from slipshod test security, and perhaps from a bit of plain old cheating.

The first of the obstacles is widespread denial. Most Americans appear to agree that the nation as a whole is experiencing some sort of educational meltdown, but simultaneously persist in believing that they and their children are doing satisfactorily. One of the questions asked by the international math and science study cited above was whether the thirteen-year-olds who took the test considered themselves "good at mathematics." The American youngsters, while trailing their agemates everywhere in terms of actual proficiency, led the pack when it came to self-regard. Sixty-eight percent answered this question affirmatively, as opposed to just 23 percent in high-scoring Korea.

When denial fails, educators sometimes resort to scapegoating. Thus, when Secretary Bennett issued his five-year appraisal in 1988, the National Education Association promptly termed it a "cover-up for the Reagan administration's failure to help improve America's schools." Ernest Boyer of the Carnegie Foundation for the Advancement of Teaching said Bennett's "divisiveness" was "really sad, if not tragic." Frank Newman of the Education Commission of the States dubbed the report a "major disservice." Gordon Ambach of the Council of Chief State School Officers sniffed that it was a "reheated wall chart out front of the Secretary's rehashed personal agenda." "Did he expect that there was going to be some overnight miracle or something?" fumed Hartford's school superintendent.

The public has thus been lulled for years into thinking that the schools are in pretty decent shape and getting better, if not in the country at large then certainly in their own community. This is surely why the Gallup poll annually shows people giving higher marks to their children's school than to schools-in-general. What is more, the signals parents get from their local schools nearly always indicate that their own children are doing satisfactorily—passing grades on their report cards, regular promotion to the next grade. Little do parents know that the standards themselves are lax, that doing well in school is not necessarily the same as learning much, and that it is an article of faith among American educators that "retaining" children is evil.

In education, as in any enterprise that strives to turn one thing into another, the normal way to begin is by describing as clearly as possible the product one proposes to create. With specifications in hand, it then becomes possible to design a system that will yield the desired result. If we are clear about the skills, knowledge, habits, and attitudes a young person should possess upon emerging from school into adulthood, practically everything else can be fitted into place: the detailed curriculum, the allocation of resources, the choice of textbooks, the requisites for teaching, the amount of time (which will surely vary) individuals must spend in order to progress through the subordinate levels that accumulate into the eventual result.

A basic failing of education-reform efforts in recent years is that they have tried to work the other way around. We have tinkered endlessly with the production system—its resources, processes, organizational arrangements, and employees—without pausing to specify the product we want to emerge at the other end. The consequence has been a lot of wasted motion.

With goals, of course, must come standards and expectations, or the goals will never be achieved. Most young people learn pretty much what they are obliged to learn by parents and teachers—and in matters academic, not a great deal more. That is why educational norms are so important, especially for disadvantaged youngsters. And that is why uncommonly demanding teachers—like Jaime Escalante, recently portrayed in the movie Stand and Deliver and the book Escalante: The Best Teacher in America—succeed.

Obvious though this maxim sounds, we have not taken it to heart. A look at the transcripts of the high-school graduating class of 1987—the youngsters who entered high school in the autumn the nation was declared "at risk"—reveals that only 30 percent of them actually took four years of English and three years each of math, science, and social studies. And even this minimalist core was unevenly distributed, with more than half of Asian-American but fewer than a quarter of black and Hispanic youngsters toiling through it.

Second, our reform efforts to date have lacked any coherent sense of exactly what results we are seeking to achieve.

Third, in the absence of clear goals, it has been easy to ignore the primordial finding both of educational research and of common sense: people tend to learn that which they study, and to learn it in rough proportion to the amount of time they spend at the task.

We know perfectly well that learning takes time and perspiration, yet in our high schools important academic subjects—history, chemistry, foreign languages—are commonly studied for just a single year, while in other countries they are part of every year's curriculum. Moreover, our children have shorter school days and school years than their peers in most of the rest of the industrialized world; they spend far fewer hours doing homework; and big chunks of the typical American school day and class period are given over to nonacademic pursuits, ranging from assembly programs to the time spent passing out and collecting materials.

It is no mystery what needs doing. It is, rather, a matter of the will to do it. But here we come smack up against the fourth obstacle—the one now being rolled into place by the education profession itself.

It begins with the warning, trumpeted by professional educators and their advocates in every medium at their command, that "top-down" changes of the sort urged by commissions, designed by governors, and enacted by legislatures, cannot yield significant gains in student learning, and that such moves actually worsen matters by curbing the professional discretion of teachers and turning them into tightly controlled educational mechanics. Instead, we are instructed, the way to make progress is to "empower" teachers and principals to do pretty much as they see fit, school building by school building.

Accompanying these notions is—no real surprise—a demand for still more money for education. The additional outlays are to go mainly for higher salaries and for hiring more teachers, the latter proposal often justified by the desire to reduce class size, begin school at a younger age, and provide more "services," especially for "children at risk."

It is obvious why educators should warm to this set of suggestions—collectively termed the "second reform movement" by Albert Shanker, president of the American Federation of Teachers—and why they have already become the conventional wisdom within the profession, filling the journals, the annual conventions, many union contract negotiations, and myriad faculty meetings at colleges of education. Less clear is why they have caught the eye of a number of elected officials, lay policy-makers, newspaper editorialists, and even business leaders. Perhaps these people have become disheartened by the slow pace of reform; or perhaps they are growing weary of policy combat with the professionals, and are disposed to step aside. In any event, if the new agenda is followed, it will assuredly lead to greater public expenditures on education, endless palaver, and myriad reports and studies. It will also serve to enlarge the professional education industry. But will it do any good for students? Will they actually learn more? No one has the faintest idea, though worthwhile experiments are under way in such places as Miami, San Diego, and Rochester that may eventually shed some light on this question.

Certainly, there is much to be said in principle for cutting back the stultifying central-office bureaucracies of school systems, for recognizing the individual school as the essential unit of educational activity (and accountability), for encouraging schools to distinguish themselves from one another, and for allowing families to choose those that will best serve their children. In these respects, the "second reform movement" contains ideas that ought not to be dismissed. But we dare not romanticize the capacity of the average school, turned loose on its own, rapidly to bring about marked gains in the

---

These three failings are grave. Unchanged, they will keep us from making significant educational gains. Setting them right will be arduous, maybe harder than we have the stomach for. But they are not beyond our capacities to resolve. We can, if we choose, accept the fact that it is our children, and the school down the street, that are "at risk." We can become clear about what we desire the education system to produce, and settle upon a satisfactory minimum level of attainment. (Several states and a number of localities are already demonstrating what a core curriculum might look like, and so is the Thatcher government in England.) And we can become much more exacting about performance standards, and more generous with the amount of time and instruction devoted to meeting them.

skills and knowledge of its students. Neither is it prudent to dash off in hot pursuit of an unproven strategy until we have corrected the mistakes in our present plan of attack.

But the biggest reason we ought not to follow the advice of the education profession is that its ideas about the goals of schooling are mostly wrong.

Simply put, the underlying problem we confront as we set about to produce more knowledgeable citizens is that few of our educators have much use for knowledge. The same is true of those who prepare them for classroom teaching, and, by and large, it is also true of the intellectual elites now propounding their own notions of how to fix the schools. This is the condition most menacing to the hopes and prospects of school reform.

American education is dominated by the conviction that it is not really important to know anything in particular. Facts are out. What is in is exemplified by this recent episode:

A fourth grader is assigned by the teacher to write a report about the Navaho. The teacher's instructions carefully set forth the aspects of Indian life that the students are to cover, such as dress, food, housing, rituals, and transportation.

The boy seeks assistance from his mother, who sensibly begins by asking what era the report is to describe. Spanning the entire history of the Navaho people over the millennia seems a bit much for the fourth grade; to the mother, it is plain that a report will differ enormously according to whether one is looking at the 15th century, the 19th century, or last month.

The boy does not know. The teacher has not said. So mother calls teacher to inquire about this elementary but—she thinks—fundamental feature of the class assignment. What historical period does the teacher have in mind?

The teacher, it emerges, not only has no answer, she does not think the question appropriate. The report, she says, is intended to be about Indians, not about any particular time period. "We teach the process method," she explains.

This is what E.D. Hirsch, the author of last year's best-selling Cultural Literacy, calls "educational formalism." According to this way of viewing the learning enterprise, it is not the knowledge entering one's head but the act of thinking that matters. So long as one can analyze, it is not important what is being analyzed. Knowing how to read is important, but what one reads is not. In general, it is not the role of educators to tell youngsters what they should know. It is their solemn obligation to help them "think critically."

How to teach "higher-order cognitive skills" is the stuff of hundreds of education workshops and "in-service days" every month. Yet for all its trendiness, the notion is also of a piece with the long-prevailing philosophy of education schools and journals. This is the philosophy of progressive education, according to which the role of the teacher is not to dominate but to facilitate, and thinking creatively, being imaginative, and solving problems are preferable to following rules, internalizing traditions, and assimilating knowledge.

This emphasis on intellectual skills—"higher-order cognitive skills" is today's term of art—eases all sorts of pedagogical dilemmas. "Thinking critically" avoids the relativist's agony of having to designate "right" and

"wrong" answers. It skirts those endless disputes about "canons" and about "what knowledge is of greatest value," the kind of thing that can tie up a faculty committee for months. It sidesteps the clash between supporters of a common culture and partisans of cultural pluralism (while awarding sure victory to the pluralists, since no common culture consists wholly of "reasoning skills"). It helps educators deal with the thorny issue of

"values"—a term which, when used by the education establishment, signifies something one examines and at times "clarifies" rather than something one absorbs from elders, spiritual leaders, or teachers.

This strand of thought has wound through American education for a good part of the century, and by now has assumed the status of an orthodoxy. As one might expect, it is not without an implicit and sometimes explicit political component. Consider, for example, the enraged response of the education community to Hirsch's Cultural Literacy, a deeply liberal treatise which argues that disadvantaged and minority youngsters, and those from tattered families and bad neighborhoods, are ill-served by schools which fail to equip all their students with the essential background information needed for success in modern society. This work has been dismissed as elitist, as culturally hidebound, as an arid "list of facts," as the ravings of a latter-day Gradgrind, as a handbook to the game of Trivial Pursuit, as a plea for "rote learning," and as a harsh rejection of individual differences and ethnic diversity. Hirsch also stands accused of the crime of nationalism—as in, "He perpetuates the nation-state as the world's most fundamental political unit" (Catherine R. Stimpson, dean of the graduate school at Rutgers).

Thus do contemporary politics enter the educational debate, often clad in progressive pedagogical garb. One might have supposed facts to be ideologically inert, elements that all might agree on even while battling furiously over explanations and interpretations. But that is not true of American education today. My colleague Diane Ravitch and I have often cited with concern the astonishing finding that only a third of the eleventh-grade students surveyed for our 1987 book What Do Our Seventeen-Year-Olds Know? could place the Civil War in the correct half-century. Yet here is how Professor Stimpson dismisses that concern: "We would be more literate if at least two-thirds of those kids could pin the tail of time more accurately on the donkey of war." And here is former Weatherman William Ayers—a professor of, needless to say, education—on our book:

> They are not interested in teaching as an activity that empowers the young to ask their own questions and seek their own answers. They are not concerned with teaching for self-determination, teaching for invention, teaching for transformation. They are not interested in teaching as a dialectical interplay of content and experience, past and present.

> We had no exams, no report cards, and no training in English grammar. We were taught to "write as we feel" and to write naturally. We had no specific history classes, but a sort of hodgepodge amalgam of sociology, civics, history combined. We concentrated on different periods of history, but never did achieve a consecutive chronology of events . . . all of which left me with only a vague notion of history.

Half a century ago, there was still a price to be paid for ignorance: the college my mother wanted to attend informed her she was inadequately prepared, and would first have to go somewhere else and accumulate "some grades they could examine." Today, it is unlikely that any college in the land would signal directly that one's prior education was flawed—and even less likely that a paucity of English grammar or historical chronology would be deemed evidence of a problem grave enough to inconvenience a student displaying it.

And where English and history have led the way, mathematics and science, once regarded as the solidest parts of the school curriculum, are today not far behind. Here, too, we are now being told, there are no right answers. Here, too, the role of educators is to help students seek their own path.

In math education, among today's avant-garde the rage is for "problem solving," usually with the help of electronic calculators. "Drill and practice" are deemed archaic, and computation—those long rows of fractions to multiply and six-digit numbers to divide—is thought tiresome, hence dispensable. Nor is precision highly valued: getting the "right answer" is less important than devising a "creative" strategy for attacking the problem.

The curricular effects of "teaching for invention, teaching for transformation" have not changed much over the decades. My mother, for instance, attended a progressive school on the campus of Ohio State University in the mid-1930's. Here is how she once described it in a letter:

This is the view of the National Council of Teachers of Mathematics, which in March laid before the nation a whole new approach to math education. It is a view shared by the National Academy of Sciences, which has just published its own glossy tome entitled "Everybody Counts: A Report to the Nation on the Future of Mathematics Education." The panel that assembled it reads like a who's who of American education. Financial support came from four private foundations and five federal agencies. Here is a representative passage:

> Unfortunately, as children become socialized by school and society, they begin to view mathematics as a rigid system of externally dictated rules governed by standards of accuracy, speed, and memory. . . . A mathematics curriculum that emphasizes computation and rules is like a writing curriculum that emphasizes grammar and spelling: both put the cart before the horse. . . . Teachers . . . almost always present mathematics as an established doctrine to be learned just as it was taught. This "broadcast" metaphor for learning leads students to expect that mathematics is about right answers rather than about clear creative thinking. . . .

One wonders how many of Jaime Escalante's poor Hispanic students in East Los Angeles would pass Advanced Placement calculus if their teacher scorned "standards of accuracy, speed, and memory"—or how many middle-class adults could hope to balance their own checkbooks.

> One difference is that boundaries between traditional subject-matter categories are softened and connections are emphasized. . . .
>
> A second difference is that the amount of detail that students are expected to retain is considerably less than in traditional science, mathematics, and technology courses. Ideas and thinking skills are emphasized at the expense of specialized vocabulary and memorized procedures. . . .

And here are some of the classroom precepts for teachers as set forth in the AAAS report: "do not separate knowing from finding out"; "deemphasize the memorization of technical vocabulary"; "use a team approach"; "reward creativity"; "encourage a spirit of healthy questioning"; "avoid dogmatism"; "promote aesthetic responses"; "emphasize group learning"; "counteract learning anxieties."

This is not advice for teaching cooking, or even sociology. Nor are these the words of an eccentric fringe. This broadside emanates from a panel co-chaired by the former head of Bell Labs and the dean of undergraduate instruction of MIT, and including, besides the ubiquitous Albert Shanker, the former editor of Scientific American and the distinguished Harvard statistician Frederick Mosteller. The advice of this elevated group would certainly have fallen on friendly ears in my mother's progressive school of the 1930's. That it is being proffered in 1989 as a solution to our educational problems is, to say the least, remarkable—so remarkable that even the editors of the Washington Post were compelled to ask a simple question:

> It's all very interesting, but will it do anything to address the much-documented inability of American students to answer international test questions on which way a plant will turn in the presence of sunlight? Not a thing. . . .

Indeed, nothing we have learned about education, past or present, at home or abroad, gives us any grounds for believing that the "process method," however elegantly refined, will ever produce people who know anything. This may seem a minor defect to educators, for whom specific knowledge

---

As for science, millions of dollars are now being spent in a highly publicized effort by the American Association for the Advancement of Science (AAAS) and its allies to revamp the nation's entire educational approach to the subject. The plan differs in two large ways from customary approaches. In the words of the panel:

is an unfashionable commodity. But it is also, finally, the reason why civilian control of education remains absolutely essential. We do not allow soldiers free rein with the "shooting method," doctors with the "surgery method," or bus drivers with the

"honking method." Experts have their place. They also have their interests, and their severe limitations as shapers of policy. Left to follow their own norms, professional educators and their kindred organizations and think tanks will not just preserve the legacy of progressivism, they will enshrine the "process method" in larger, and emptier, cathedrals than ever before imagined.

Most Americans, when asked, say they want their children to know more than they do, and are appalled by the prospect that the next generation will know less. Yet so long as today's professional norms and beliefs hold sway, so long as they shape what actually occurs in the classroom, that is precisely the future that awaits our children. Changing the culture of any large enterprise is far more difficult than altering the specific policies by which it operates. But that is the central task confronting us—and also, one might add, confronting the man who would be our "education President."

America Needs Its Nerds

by Leonid Fridman

Becoming Educated

by Barbara Charline Jordan

So I was at Boston University in this new and strange and different world, and it occurred to me that if I was going to succeed at this strange new adventure, I would have to read longer and more thoroughly than my colleagues at law school had to read. I felt that in order to compensate for what I had missed in earlier years, I would have to work harder, and study longer, than anybody else. I still had this feeling that I did not want my colleagues to know what a tough time I was having understanding the concepts, the words, the ideas, the process. I didn't want them to know that. So I did my reading not in the law library, but in a library at the graduate dorm, upstairs where it was very quiet, because apparently nobody else there studied. So I would go there at night after dinner. I would load my books under my arm and go to the library, and I would read until the wee hours of the morning and then go to bed. I didn't get much sleep during those years. I was lucky if I got three or four hours a night, because I had to stay up. I had to. The professors would assign cases for the next day, and these cases had to be read and understood or I would be behind, further behind than I was.

I was always delighted when I would get called upon to recite in class. But the professors did not call on the "ladies" very much. There were certain favored people who always got called on, and then on some rare occasions a professor would come in and would announce: "We're going to have Ladies Lady today." And he would call on the ladies. We were just tolerated. We weren't considered really top drawer when it came to the study of the law.

At some time in the spring, Bill Gibson, who was dating my new roommate, Norma Walker, organized a black study group, as we blacks had to form our own. This was because we were not invited into any of the other study groups. There were six or seven in our group—Bill, and Issie, and I think Maynard Jackson—and we would just gather and talk it out and hear ourselves do that. One thing I learned was that you had to talk out the issues, the facts, the cases, the decisions, the process. You couldn't just read the cases and study alone in your library as I had been doing; and you couldn't get it all in the classroom. But once you had talked it out in the study group, it flowed more easily and made a lot more sense.

And from time to time I would go up to the fourth floor at 2 Rawley Street to check on how Louise was doing. She was always reading *Redbook*. I don't know how she could do that. She was not prepared in class when the professors would call on her to discuss cases, but that did not bother her. Whereas it was a matter of life and death with me. I had to make law school. I just didn't have any alternatives. I could not afford to flunk out. That would have been an unmitigated disaster. So I real all the time I was not in class.

Finally I felt I was really learning things, really going to school. I felt that I was getting educated, whatever that was. I became familiar with the process of thinking. I learned to think things out and reach conclusions and defend what I had said.

In the past I had got along by spouting off. Whether you talked about debates or oratory, you dealt with speechifying. Even in debate it was pretty much canned because you had, in your little three-by-five box, a response for whatever issue might be raised by the opposition. The format was structured to that there was no opportunity for independent thinking. (I really had not had my ideas challenged ever.) But I could no longer orate and let that pass for reasoning. Because there was not any demand for an orator in Boston University Law School. You had to think and read and understand and reason. I had learned at twenty-one that you couldn't just say a thing is so because it might not be so, and somebody brighter, smarter, and more thoughtful would come out and tell you it wasn't so. Then, if you still thought it was, you had to prove it. Well, that was a new thing for me. I cannot, I really cannot describe what that did to my insides and to my head. I thought: I'm being educated finally.

Read a more current and contemporary account about the struggles of beginning college by Jennine Capo Crucet, a first-generation college student, who felt alone and confused her first days of college: "Taking My Parents to College" at

[www] https://www.nytimes.com/2015/08/23/opinion/sunday/taking-my-parents-to-college.html

The Big Score

by Daniel McGinn

Inside Chicago's top-ranked Whitney Young High School, the posters started appearing last December. LET'S BE #1! GIVE IT 110%! Usually this sort of rah-rah propaganda supports the basketball team, but this campaign by the principal had a different aim: urging kids to score high on the Illinois Goal Assessment Program, a standardized test that students would take in February. Tests are nothing new to the kids at Whitney Young—they already take three other batteries of standardized exams each year. But for a group of high-achieving 11th graders, the pressure was just too much. These kids say real learning is being shoved aside as teachers focus on boosting test scores. Creative writing? Forget it. Instead, they say, teachers emphasize a boilerplate essay format that exam scorers prefer. So on Feb. 2, eight juniors purposely failed the social-studies portion of the test. The next day 10 failed the science test. Then they sent a letter to the principal: "We refuse to feed into this test-taking frenzy."

As rebellions go, it wasn't exactly the Boston Tea Party. But it's a small sign of the growing anxiety among parents, teachers and kids over the proliferation of standardized tests. Fill-in-the-bubble exams have been part of classroom life for decades, but for most of their history they were no big deal. Scores were tucked in students' folders; at most, they were used to segregate kids into higher- and lower-level classes. That's changed dramatically in the last decade as reformers try to improve school quality by holding educators accountable for learning. Every state has a different testing scheme, but many state legislatures are writing new standards for what kids should learn in each grade and mandating tough new "high stakes" tests to gauge progress. Unlike such old-style standardized tests as the Iowas or Metropolitans, many of the new exams are linked to the curriculum and feature essays and short answers, not just multiple choice. The biggest difference: low scores can bring real pain. Kids can be held back, forced into summer school or, under rules in 26 states, denied a diploma. Educators can lose pay or be fired; schools can face state takeover. In polls, the tests win wide public support, and more states are jumping on the bandwagon.

Yet there is no easy answer to the most basic question: do these tests help kids learn? As the testing movement has grown, opposing experts have churned out a mountain of conflicting research. Fans of the tests say they're as necessary to schooling as a scale is to dieting. Ideally, they're diagnostic tools, letting teachers know Jack doesn't understand two-digit multiplication and Jill needs help with subject-verb agreement. Yes, it's sad that a single exam might keep a child from graduating, but most European countries already use exit exams, and some U.S. students are kept from graduating for lesser offenses, like flunking gym or cutting too many classes. And as schools ask for money to hire teachers and cut class size, taxpayers have every right to expect a measurable payback. Supporters of the new exams point to encouraging results in Texas, one of the first states to implement this type of reform plan.

Despite those arguments, a growing number of critics say this testing inevitably leads to dumbed-down teaching. "Every hour that teachers feel compelled to try to raise test scores is an hour not spent helping kids become critical, creative, curious thinkers," says Alfie Kohn, author of "The Schools Our Children Deserve." It's those skills, after all, that put the United States ahead of world competitors in areas like entrepreneurship. Last fall the National Research Council warned Congress that schools should refrain from basing important decisions like who gets promoted or graduates solely on test scores, and called for more exploration of the unintended consequences of high-stakes exams. Teachers in the inner cities, where many children are being held back for failing the tests, worry that these exams are overwhelming their already overcrowded and understaffed classrooms. Suburban homeowners have more bottom-line concerns; they fear that dismal test scores will lower home values. For now, those worries will persist. Testing opponents have scored small victories in places like Wisconsin, but momentum is on the side of reformers. As kids return to classrooms this fall, the new exams will be part of the curriculum.

At Madison High School in Houston, the tests have already brought an innovation that makes teenagers cringe: Saturday classes. In 1990 Texas replaced its old tests with a tough new one (its acronym: TAAS); students who failed wouldn't graduate. Early results were abysmal. Madison principal Warner Ervin remembers when dozens of seniors failed. Students were crushed, parents were irate, teachers embarrassed. "It was difficult for everyone," Ervin says. So in 1997, Ervin began requiring every failing kid to attend tutoring sessions, some held on Saturday. The year before the tutoring began, 57 seniors failed; last spring the whole class passed. Results are also improving statewide. Last spring 78 percent of Texas students passed the test, up from 53 percent in 1994. Education is certain to be a key issue in the presidential race, so expect Gov. George W. Bush to tout this track record.

Other states can boast of their own success stories. Take 9-year-old Steven Ip of Brooklyn, one of 17,591 third graders who failed the high-stakes test given to New York City kids for the first time last winter. Steven, whose parents emigrated from China, has solid math skills, but because of his limited English ability, he scored in the 11th percentile on the reading test. So like a record 37,000 New York City kids, he faced mandatory summer school; if he failed his retest in August, he'd be forced to repeat third grade. During five sweaty weeks in a classroom at P.S. 241, teacher Maria Teresa Maisano worked with Steven and seven other students. They read books in class and for homework, learning how to ask questions and find key ideas. When test day arrived, Steven felt prepared. Like roughly 60 percent of the summer students, he passed the exam and can start fourth grade. The city's school chancellor, Rudolph Crew, has been blasted for retaining kids and mandating summer school, but he's standing firm. "This is high anxiety—it's not for the meek of heart," he says. "But I think it's the right thing to do."

Other educators aren't so enthusiastic. At Santa Monica Boulevard Elementary in Los Angeles, the lilting sounds of Spanish fill the playground. But in teacher David Levinson's fifth grade, as in all other California schools, classes must be taught in English. For 31 of his 32 students, English is a second language. "The scores for most of these kids are low and it's not too hard to figure out why," says Levinson. "These tests are extremely unfair." But they're the law, and as a consequence they're beginning to drive the curriculum. "We spend a lot more time teaching to the test and a lot less on the kind of hands-on, learn-by-doing teaching we did in the past," says the school's longtime principal, Albert Arnold. "My teachers are very frustrated, and kids pick up on that." They'll be more frustrated next year when, for the first time, students who fail the test are held back.

California's on-again, off-again testing regimen shows just how messy the transition to exam-driven reform can be. Until the late '80s, California's schools were topnotch. Then in the early '90s, a sinking economy, political bickering over education reform and a growing immigrant population set them back. So the state devised a new test, the California Learning Assessment System. But critics attacked essay questions as too subjective to be fairly graded, and reformers who favor a back-to-basics approach lobbied for more focus on the three Rs. By 1994, the CLAS was dead, and students went untested for three years as legislators debated new standards. Most experts urged them to design a customized exam that tests exactly the skills the state's kids should be learning, instead of an off-the-shelf national exam. When standards, curriculum and tests are aligned through the made-to-order tests many states are adopting, "teaching to the test" can become a positive technique, experts say. But California's leaders couldn't wait for a custom exam, so they opted to use a generic test in the interim. Experts say that's been a weak link in their reform plan. "The system in California is imperfect," says Stanford professor Kenji Hakuta. "What's needed are tests that more closely line up to instruction." This disparity is a recurring theme: experts favor a gradual, methodical transition, but political realities often force quick, crude steps to try to show improvement before the next election.

As testing spreads, experts aren't the only ones parsing the quality of exams. When Wisconsin Gov. Tommy Thompson proposed a statewide graduation exam in 1997, he had wide public support. Then parents saw sample questions. "It scared the heck out of them," says state Sen. Bob Jauch. "They weren't sure they could pass it themselves." A strange coalition of opponents emerged, consisting of parents concerned that the tests were too tough, educators who resented the state's giving orders to locally run schools and legislators who'd rather spend the $10 million testing budget on a tax cut. By June, Wisconsin's new test was dead.

Tales like that one give hope to the Chicago kids at Whitney Young who bucked the test last winter. Over the summer they rounded up like-minded students from other schools and named themselves the Organized Students of Chicago. They've already passed out leaflets denouncing the city's testmania; now they're planning teach-ins. The focus on the exams "just seems so totally excessive," says Will Tanzman, 17. Eli Presser, an 18-year-old who graduated last spring but is still active in the group, says the rising number of tests makes students feel "like they're under constant jeopardy—like every single test was going to influence their life." Principal Joyce Kenner ordered the students to perform 10 hours of community service for refusing to take last year's exam. So far, they haven't served it, and may rally more students to boycott the exams this winter.

School officials are sympathetic to charges that they're giving too many tests. "Nobody wants to be test crazy . . . We don't want you to be drones," says Chicago school board president Gery Chico. But like administrators around the country, he says schools need to face the reality that the status quo, in which thousands of kids languished in classes with virtually no instruction, couldn't continue. Parents like Jay Rehak, who's also a Whitney Young teacher, worry their kids are suffering for the sake of the system. When his daughter faced her first high-stakes exam two years ago, "she came home panicked every night," he says. But University of Chicago researcher Melissa Roderick, who's followed 100 students at five schools through Chicago's pass-the-test-or-stay-back program, says the get-tough approach is needed, the same way financiers impose harsh, short-term measures to stabilize troubled economies. "The tests are getting us moving," Roderick says. "Over time we'll look to other things."

Perhaps. Or maybe this new breed of exam will become a defining part of school days well into the next century. Most states are only beginning to get their curriculum in sync with the new tests, so experts say it will be years before we see whether they deliver improvements dramatic enough to justify the investment. "We're in the middle of the maelstrom—it's very difficult to see which way it's going to go," says Judith Mathers, a policy analyst at the Education Commission of the States. Until then, pencils in hand, we all plunge ahead.

Remarks by the First Lady at Topeka School District Senior Recognition Day

by Michelle Obama

MRS. OBAMA: Thank you, guys. Thank you so much. Wow! (Applause.) Look at you guys. (Applause.) All right, you all rest yourselves. You've got a big day tomorrow. I want you guys to be ready.

It is beyond a pleasure and an honor, truly, to be with you here today to celebrate the class of 2014. Thank you so much for having me. I'm so proud of you guys. (Applause.) Days like this make me think of my own daughters, so forgive me if a get a little teary. You guys look great.

We have a great group of students here. We have students from Highland Park High School. (Applause.) We have Hope Street Academy students here today. (Applause.) Topeka High School is in the house. (Applause.) And of course, we have Topeka West High School in the house. (Applause.)

Tomorrow will be a big day for all of you. You all have worked so hard, I know—I can tell. You've come so far. And as you walk across that stage tomorrow to get your diploma, know that I'm going to be thinking of you all. I am so proud of you all and all that you've achieved thus far.

And you have got so many people here who are proud of you tonight. Your families are here, your teachers and counselors, your principals, your coaches, everyone who has poured their love and hope into you over these many, many years. So, graduates, let's just take a moment to give a round of applause to those folks, as well. Tonight is their night, too. Yes! (Applause.)

Now, I want to start by thanking Lauren for that amazing introduction. (Applause.) Yes, indeed. Well done, Lauren. I want to thank a few other people here—of course, Secretary Sebelius. As you know, my husband and I are so grateful for all that she has done, her wonderful service. (Applause.) And I'm so glad that she and her family could join us tonight.

And of course, I want to recognize Congresswoman Jenkins, Governor Brownback, and Mayor Wolgast, as well as Superintendent Ford, School Board President Johnson, and all of your great principals—Principals Carton, New, Noll and Wiley. (Applause.) Yay!

And finally, to our fantastic student speakers—Alisha, Rosemary and Noah -- just hearing your backgrounds makes me feel like an underachiever, so thank you so much for your remarks about Brown vs. Board of Ed.. I know Noah is coming. You have approached this issue past, present and future.

And I think it's fitting that we're celebrating this historic Supreme Court case tonight, not just because Brown started right here in Topeka or because Brown's 60th anniversary is tomorrow, but because I believe that all of you -- our soon-to-be-graduates -- you all are the living, breathing legacy of this case. Yes. (Applause.)

I mean, just look around at this arena. Not only are you beautiful and handsome and talented and smart, but you represent all colors and cultures and faiths here tonight. (Applause.) You come

From https://obamawhitehouse.archives.gov by First Lady Michelle Obama, 5/17/2014.

from all walks of life, and you've taken so many different paths to reach this moment. Maybe your ancestors have been here in Kansas for centuries. Or maybe, like mine, they came to this country in chains. Or maybe your family just arrived here in search of a better life.

But no matter how you got here, you have arrived at this day together. For so many years, you all have studied together in the same classrooms, you've played on the same teams, attended the same parties—hopefully you behaved yourselves at those parties. (Laughter.) You've debated each other's ideas, hearing every possible opinion and perspective. You've heard each other's languages in the hallways, English, Spanish and others, all mixed together in a uniquely American conversation. You've celebrated each other's holidays and heritages—in fact, I was told that at one of your schools so many students who aren't black wanted to join the black students club that you decided to call it the African American Culture Club so everyone would feel welcome. Way to go. (Applause.)

So, graduates, it is clear that some of the most important parts of your education have come not just from your classes, but from your classmates. And ultimately, that was the hope and dream of Brown. That's why we're celebrating here tonight, because the fact is that your experience here in Topeka would have been unimaginable back in 1954, when Brown v. Board of Education first went to the Supreme Court. This would not be possible.

As you all know, back then, Topeka, like so many cities, was segregated. So black folks and white folks had separate restaurants, separate hotels, separate movie theaters, swimming pools, and, of course, the elementary schools were segregated, too. So even though many black children lived just blocks away from their white schools in their neighborhoods, they had to take long bus rides to all-black schools across town. So eventually, a group of black parents got tired of this arrangement—and they decided to do something about it.

Now, these were ordinary folks. Most of them were not civil rights activists, and some of them were probably nervous about speaking up, worried they might cause trouble for themselves and their families. And the truth is, while the black schools were far away, the facilities were pretty decent, and the teachers were excellent.

But eventually, these parents went to court to desegregate their children's schools because, as one of the children later explained as an adult, she said, "We were talking about the principle of the thing."

Now, think about that for a moment. Those folks had to go all the way to the Supreme Court of the United States just to affirm the principle that black kids and white kids should be able to attend school together. And today, 60 years later, that probably seems crazy to all of you in this graduating class, right? You all take the diversity you're surrounded by for granted. You probably don't even notice it. And that's understandable, given the country you have grown up in—with a woman Governor, a Latina Supreme Court Justice, a black President. (Applause.)s

You have seen Latino singers win Grammys, black coaches win Super Bowls. You've watched TV shows in—characters of every background. So when you watch a show like the "The Walking Dead," you don't think it's about a black guy, a black woman, an Asian guy, a gay couple and some white people—you think it's about a bunch of folks trying to escape some zombies, right? Period. (Laughter.)

And then when some folks got all worked up about a cereal commercial with an interracial family, you all were probably thinking, really, what's the problem with that? When folks made a big deal about Jason Collins and Michael Sam coming out as gay, a lot of kids in your generation thought, what is the issue here? (Applause.) And if someone were to say something racist on Twitter, well, I imagine that many of you would tweet right back, letting them know that's just not cool.

You see, when you grow up in a place like Topeka, where diversity is all you've ever known, the old prejudices just don't make any sense. Seems crazy to think that folks of the same race or ethnicity all think or act the same way—because you actually know those folks. They're your teammates, your lab partner, your best friend. They're the girl who's obsessed with the Jayhawks but loves computer science programming; the guy who loves the Wildcats and dreams of being an artist. (Applause.) That's the world you've grown up in.

But remember, not everyone has grown up in a place like Topeka. See, many districts in this country have actually pulled back on efforts to integrate their schools, and many communities have become less diverse as folks have moved from cities to suburbs.

So today, by some measures, our schools are as segregated as they were back when Dr. King gave his final speech. And as a result, many young people in America are going to school largely with kids who look just like them. And too often, those schools aren't equal, especially ones attended by students of color which too often lag behind, with crumbling classrooms and less experienced teachers. And even in schools that seem integrated according to the numbers, when you look a little closer, you see students from different backgrounds sitting at separate lunch tables, or tracked into different classes, or separated into different clubs or activities.

So while students attend school in the same building, they never really reach beyond their own circles. And I'm sure that probably happens sometimes here in Topeka, too. And these issues go well beyond the walls of our schools. We know that today in America, too many folks are still stopped on the street because of the color of their skin—(applause)—or they're made to feel unwelcome because of where they come from, or they're bullied because of who they love. (Applause.)

So, graduates, the truth is that Brown vs. Board of Ed. isn't just about our history, it's about our future. Because while that case was handed down 60 years ago, Brown is still being decided every single day -- not just in our courts and schools, but in how we live our lives.

Now, our laws may no longer separate us based on our skin color, but nothing in the Constitution says we have to eat together in the lunchroom, or live together in the same neighborhoods. There's no court case against believing in stereotypes or thinking that certain kinds of hateful jokes or comments are funny.

So the answers to many of our challenges today can't necessarily be found in our laws. These changes also need to take place in our hearts and in our minds. (Applause.) And so, graduates, it's up to all of you to lead the way, to drag my generation and your grandparents' generation along with you.

And that's really my challenge to all of you today. As you go forth, when you encounter folks who still hold the old prejudices because they've only been around folks like themselves, when you meet folks who think they know all the answers because they've never heard any other viewpoints, it's up to you to help them see things differently.

And the good news is that you probably won't have to bring a lawsuit or go all the way to the Supreme Court to do that. You all can make a difference every day in your own lives simply by teaching others the lessons you've learned here in Topeka.

Maybe that starts simply in your own family, when grandpa tells that off-colored joke at Thanksgiving, or you've got an aunt talks about "those people." Well, you can politely inform them that they're talking about your friends. (Applause.)

Or maybe it's when you go off to college and you decide to join a sorority or fraternity, and you ask the question, how can we get more diversity in our next pledge class? Or maybe it's years from now, when you're on the job and you're the one who asks, do we really have all the voices and viewpoints we need at this table? Maybe it's when you have kids of your own one day, and you go to your school board meeting and insist on integrating your children's schools and giving them the resources they need.

But no matter what you do, the point is to never be afraid to talk about these issues, particularly the issue of race. Because even today, we still struggle to do that. Because this issue is so sensitive, is so complicated, so bound up with a painful history. And we need your generation to help us break through. We need all of you to ask the hard questions and have the honest conversations, because that is the only way we will heal the wounds of the past and move forward to a better future. (Applause.)

And here's the thing—the stakes here simply couldn't be higher, because as a nation, we have some serious challenges on our plate -- from creating jobs, to curing diseases, to giving every child in this country a good education. And we know—we don't even know where the next new breakthrough, the next great discovery will come from.

Maybe the solution to global warming will come from that girl whose parents don't speak a word of English, but who's been acing her science classes since kindergarten. (Applause.) Maybe the answer to poverty will come from the boy from the projects who understands this issue like no one else. So we need to bring everyone to the table. We need every voice in our national conversation.

So, graduates, that is your mission: to make sure all those voices are heard, to make sure everyone in this country has a chance to contribute.

And I'm not going to lie to you, this will not be easy. You might have to ruffle a few feathers, and believe me, folks might not always like what you have to say. And there will be times when you'll get frustrated or discouraged. But whenever I start to feel that way, I just take a step back and remind myself of all the progress I've seen in my short lifetime.

I think about my mother, who, as a little girl, went to segregated schools in Chicago and felt the sting of discrimination. I think about my husband's grandparents, white folks born and raised right here in Kansas, products themselves of segregation. (Applause.) Good, honest people who helped raise their bi-racial grandson, ignoring those who would criticize that child's very existence. (Applause.) And then I think about how that child grew up to be the President of the United States, and how today—(applause)—that little girl from Chicago is helping to raise her granddaughters in the White House. (Applause.)

And finally, I think about the story of a woman named Lucinda Todd who was the very first parent to sign on to Brown vs. Board of Education. See, Lucinda's daughter, Nancy, went to one of the all-black schools here in Topeka, and Mrs. Todd traveled across this state raising money for the case, determined to give her daughter -- and all our sons and daughters -- the education they deserve. And today, six decades later, Mrs. Todd's grandniece, a young woman named Kristen Jarvis, works as my right-hand woman in the White House. She is here with me today. (Applause.) She has traveled with me around the world.

So if you ever start to get tired, if you ever think about giving up, I want you to remember that journey from a segregated school in Topeka all the way to the White House. (Applause.) I want you to think about folks like Lucinda Todd—folks who, as my husband once wrote, decided that "a principle is at stake," folks who "make their claim on this community we call America" and "choose our better history."

Every day, you have the power to choose our better history—by opening your hearts and minds, by speaking up for what you know is right, by sharing the lessons of Brown v. Board of Education—the lessons you all learned right here in Topeka—wherever you go for the rest of your lives. And I know you all can do it.

I am so proud of all that you've accomplished. This is your day. I am here because of you. And I cannot wait to see everything you will achieve in the years ahead.

So congratulations, once again, to the class of 2014. I love you. Godspeed on your journey ahead. Thank you, all. God bless you. I love you. (Applause.)

Blue Collar Brilliance

by Mike Rose

My mother, Rose Meraglio Rose (Rosie), shaped her adult identity as a waitress in coffee shops and family restaurants. When I was growing up in Los Angeles during the 1950s, my father and I would occasionally hang out at the restaurant until her shift ended, and then we'd ride the bus home with her. Sometimes she worked the register and the counter, and we sat there; when she waited booths and tables, we found a booth in the back where the waitresses took their breaks.

There wasn't much for a child to do at the restaurants, and so as the hours stretched out, I watched the cooks and waitresses and listened to what they said. At mealtimes, the pace of the kitchen staff and the din from customers picked up. Weaving in and out around the room, waitresses warned *behind you* in impassive but urgent voices. Standing at the service window facing the kitchen, they called out abbreviated orders. *Fry four on two*, my mother would say as she clipped a check onto the metal wheel. Her tables were *deuces*, *four-tops*, or *six-tops* according to their size; seating areas also were nicknamed. The *racetrack*, for instance, was the fast-turnover front section. Lingo conferred authority and signaled know-how.

Rosie took customers' orders, pencil poised over pad, while fielding questions about the food. She walked full tilt through the room with plates stretching up her left arm and two cups of coffee somehow cradled in her right hand. She stood at a table or booth and removed a plate for this person, another for that person, then another, remembering who had the hamburger, who had the fried shrimp, almost always getting it right. She would haggle with the cook about a returned order and rush by us, saying, *He gave me lip, but I got him*. She'd take a minute to flop down in the booth next to my father. *I'm all in*, she'd say, and whisper something about a customer. Gripping the outer edge of the table with one hand, she'd watch the room and note, in the flow of our conversation, who needed a refill, whose order was taking longer to prepare than it should, who was finishing up.

I couldn't have put it in words when I was growing up, but what I observed in my mother's restaurant defined the world of adults, a place where competence was synonymous with physical work. I've since studied the working habits of blue-collar workers and have come to understand how much my mother's kind of work demands of both body and brain. A waitress acquires knowledge and intuition about the ways and the rhythms of the restaurant business. Waiting on seven to nine tables, each with two to six customers, Rosie devised memory strategies so that she could remember who ordered what. And because she knew the average time it took to prepare different dishes, she could monitor an order that was taking too long at the service station.

Reprinted from *The American Scholar, Volume 78, No. 3, Summer 2009*. Copyright © 2009 by Mike Rose. Reprinted by permission.

Like anyone who is effective at physical work, my mother learned *to work smart*, as she put it, *to make every move count*. She'd sequence and group tasks: What could she do first, then second, then third as she circled through her station? What tasks could be clustered? She did everything on the fly, and when problems arose—technical or human—she solved them within the flow of work, while taking into account the emotional state of her co-workers. Was the manager in a good mood? Did the cook wake up on the wrong side of the bed? If so, how could she make an extra request or effectively return an order?

And then, of course, there were the customers who entered the restaurant with all sorts of needs, from physiological ones, including the emotions that accompany hunger, to a sometimes complicated desire for human contact. Her tip depended on how well she responded to these needs, and so she became adept at reading social cues and managing feelings, both the customers' and her own. No wonder, then, that Rosie was intrigued by psychology. The restaurant became the place where she studied human behavior, puzzling over the problems of her regular customers and refining her ability to deal with people in a difficult world. She took pride in *being among the public*, she'd say. *There isn't a day that goes by in the restaurant that you don't learn something.*

My mother quit school in the seventh grade to help raise her brothers and sisters. Some of those siblings made it through high school, and some dropped out to find work in railroad yards, factories, or restaurants. My father finished a grade or two in primary school in Italy and never darkened the schoolhouse door again. I didn't do well in school either. By high school I had accumulated a spotty academic record and many hours of hazy disaffection. I spent a few years on the vocational track, but in my senior year I was inspired by my English teacher and managed to squeak into a small college on probation.

My freshman year was academically bumpy, but gradually I began to see formal education as a means of fulfillment and as a road toward making a living. I studied the humanities and later the social and psychological sciences and taught for 10 years in a range of situations—elementary school, adult education courses, tutoring centers, a program for Vietnam veterans who wanted to go to college. Those students had socioeconomic and educational backgrounds similar to mine. Then I went back to graduate school to study education and cognitive psychology and eventually became a faculty member in a school of education.

Intelligence is closely associated with formal education—the type of schooling a person has, how much and how long—and most people seem to move comfortably from that notion to a belief that work requiring less schooling requires less intelligence. These assumptions run through our cultural history, from the post–Revolutionary War period, when mechanics were characterized by political rivals as illiterate and therefore incapable of participating in government, until today. More than once I've heard a manager label his workers as "a bunch of dummies." Generalizations about intelligence, work, and social class deeply affect our assumptions about ourselves and each other, guiding the ways we use our minds to learn, build knowledge, solve problems, and make our way through the world.

Although writers and scholars have often looked at the working class, they have generally focused on the values such workers exhibit rather than on the thought their work requires—a subtle but pervasive omission. Our cultural iconography promotes the muscled arm, sleeve rolled tight against biceps, but no brightness behind the eye, no image that links hand and brain.

One of my mother's brothers, Joe Meraglio, left school in the ninth grade to work for the Pennsylvania Railroad. From there he joined the Navy, returned to the railroad, which was already in decline, and eventually joined his older brother at General Motors where, over a 33-year career, he moved from working on the assembly line to supervising the paint-and-body department. When I was a young man, Joe took me on a tour of the factory. The floor was loud—in some places deafening—and when I turned a corner or opened a door, the smell of chemicals knocked my head back. The work was repetitive and taxing, and the pace was inhumane.

Still, for Joe the shop floor provided what school did not; it was *like schooling*, he said, a place where *you're constantly learning*. Joe learned the most efficient way to use his body by acquiring a set of routines that were quick and preserved energy. Otherwise he would never have survived on the line.

As a foreman, Joe constantly faced new problems and became a consummate multi-tasker, evaluating a flurry of demands quickly, parceling out physical and mental resources, keeping a number of ongoing events in his mind, returning to whatever task had been interrupted, and maintaining a cool head under the pressure of grueling production schedules. In the midst of all this, Joe learned more and more about the auto industry, the technological and social dynamics of the shop floor, the machinery and production processes, and the basics of paint chemistry and of plating and baking. With further promotions, he not only solved problems but also began to find problems to solve: Joe initiated the redesign of the nozzle on a paint sprayer, thereby eliminating costly and unhealthy overspray. And he found a way to reduce energy costs on the baking ovens without affecting the quality of the paint. He lacked formal knowledge of how the machines under his supervision worked, but he had direct experience with them, hands-on knowledge, and was savvy about their quirks and operational capabilities. He could experiment with them.

In addition, Joe learned about budgets and management. Coming off the line as he did, he had a perspective of workers' needs and management's demands, and this led him to think of ways to improve efficiency on the line while relieving some of the stress on the assemblers. He had each worker in a unit learn his or her co-workers' jobs so they could rotate across stations to relieve some of the monotony. He believed that rotation would allow assemblers to get longer and more frequent breaks. It was an easy sell to the people on the line. The union, however, had to approve any modification in job duties, and the managers were wary of the change. Joe had to argue his case on a number of fronts, providing him a kind of rhetorical education.

Eight years ago I began a study of the thought processes involved in work like that of my mother and uncle. I catalogued the cognitive demands of a range of blue-collar and service jobs, from waitressing and hair styling to plumbing and welding. To gain a sense of how knowledge and skill develop, I observed experts as well as novices. From the details of this close examination, I tried to fashion what I called "cognitive biographies" of blue-collar workers. Biographical accounts of the lives of scientists, lawyers, entrepreneurs, and other professionals are rich with detail about the intellectual dimension of their work. But the life stories of working-class people are few and are typically accounts of hardship and courage or the achievements wrought by hard work.

Our culture—in Cartesian fashion—separates the body from the mind, so that, for example, we assume that the use of a tool does not involve abstraction. We reinforce this notion by defining intelligence solely on grades in school and numbers on IQ tests. And we employ social biases pertaining to a person's place on the occupational ladder. The distinctions among blue, pink, and white collars carry with them attributions of character, motivation, and intelligence. Although we rightly acknowledge and amply compensate the play of mind in white-collar and professional work, we diminish or erase it in considerations about other endeavors—physical and service work particularly. We also often ignore the experience of everyday work in administrative deliberations and policymaking.

But here's what we find when we get in close. The plumber seeking leverage in order to work in tight quarters and the hair stylist adroitly handling scissors and comb manage their bodies strategically. Though work-related actions become routine with experience, they were learned at some point through observation, trial and error, and, often, physical or verbal assistance from a co-worker or trainer. I've frequently observed novices talking to themselves as they take on a task, or shaking their head or hand as if to erase an attempt before trying again. In fact, our traditional notions of routine performance could keep us from appreciating the many instances within routine where quick decisions and adjustments are made. I'm struck by the thinking-in-motion that some work requires, by all the mental activity that can be involved in simply getting from one place to another: the waitress rushing back through her station to the kitchen or the foreman walking the line.

The use of tools requires the studied refinement of stance, grip, balance, and fine-motor skills. But manipulating tools is intimately tied to knowledge of what a particular instrument can do in a particular situation and do better than other similar tools. A worker must also know the characteristics of the material one is engaging—how it reacts to various cutting or compressing devices, to degrees of heat, or to lines of force. Some of these things demand judgment, the weighing of options, the consideration of multiple variables, and, occasionally, the creative use of a tool in an unexpected way.

In manipulating material, the worker becomes attuned to aspects of the environment, a training or disciplining of perception that both enhances knowledge and informs perception. Carpenters have an eye for length, line, and angle; mechanics troubleshoot by listening; hair stylists are attuned to shape, texture, and motion. Sensory data merge with concept, as when an auto mechanic relies on sound, vibration, and even smell to understand what cannot be observed.

Planning and problem solving have been studied since the earliest days of modern cognitive psychology and are considered core elements in Western definitions of intelligence. To work is to solve problems. The big difference between the psychologist's laboratory and the workplace is that in the former the problems are isolated and in the latter they are embedded in the real-time flow of work with all its messiness and social complexity.

Much of physical work is social and interactive. Movers determining how to get an electric range down a flight of stairs require coordination, negotiation, planning, and the establishing of incremental goals. Words, gestures, and sometimes a quick pencil sketch are involved, if only to get the rhythm right. How important it is, then, to consider the social and communicative dimension of physical work, for it provides the medium for so much of work's intelligence.

Given the ridicule heaped on blue-collar speech, it might seem odd to value its cognitive content. Yet, the flow of talk at work provides the channel for organizing and distributing tasks, for troubleshooting and problem solving, for learning new information and revising old. A significant amount of teaching, often informal and indirect, takes place at work. Joe Meraglio saw that much of his job as a supervisor involved instruction. In some service occupations, language and communication are central: observing and interpreting behavior and expression, inferring mood and motive, taking on the perspective of others, responding appropriately to social cues, and knowing when you're understood. A good hair stylist, for instance, has the ability to convert vague requests (*I want something light and summery*) into an appropriate cut through questions, pictures, and hand gestures.

Verbal and mathematical skills drive measures of intelligence in the Western Hemisphere, and many of the kinds of work I studied are thought to require relatively little proficiency in either. Compared to certain kinds of white-collar occupations, that's true. But written symbols flow through physical work.

Numbers are rife in most workplaces: on tools and gauges, as measurements, as indicators of pressure or concentration or temperature, as guides to sequence, on ingredient labels, on lists and spreadsheets, as markers of quantity and price. Certain jobs require workers to make, check, and verify calculations, and to collect and interpret data. Basic math can be involved, and some workers develop a good sense of numbers and patterns. Consider, as well, what might be called material mathematics: mathematical functions embodied in materials and actions, as when a carpenter builds a cabinet or a flight of stairs. A simple mathematical act can extend quickly beyond itself. Measuring, for example, can involve more than recording the dimensions of an object. As I watched a cabinetmaker measure a long strip of wood, he read a number off the tape out loud, looked back over his shoulder to the kitchen wall, turned back to his task, took another measurement, and paused for a moment in thought. He was solving a problem involving the molding, and the measurement was important to his deliberation about structure and appearance.

In the blue-collar workplace, directions, plans, and reference books rely on illustrations, some representational and others, like blueprints, that require training to interpret. Esoteric symbols—visual jargon—depict switches and receptacles, pipe fittings, or types of welds. Workers themselves often make sketches on the job. I frequently observed them grab a pencil to sketch something on a scrap of paper or on a piece of the material they were installing.

Though many kinds of physical work don't require a high literacy level, more reading occurs in the blue-collar workplace than is generally thought, from manuals and catalogues to work orders and invoices, to lists, labels, and forms. With routine tasks, for example, reading is integral to understanding production quotas, learning how to use an instrument, or applying a product. Written notes can initiate action, as in restaurant orders or reports of machine malfunction, or they can serve as memory aids.

True, many uses of writing are abbreviated, routine, and repetitive, and they infrequently require interpretation or analysis. But analytic moments can be part of routine activities, and seemingly basic reading and writing can be cognitively rich. Because workplace language is used in the flow of other activities, we can overlook the remarkable coordination of words, numbers, and drawings required to initiate and direct action.

If we believe everyday work to be mindless, then that will affect the work we create in the future. When we devalue the full range of everyday cognition, we offer limited educational opportunities and fail to make fresh and meaningful instructional connections among disparate kinds of skill and knowledge. If we think that whole categories of people—identified by class or occupation—are not that bright, then we reinforce social separations and cripple our ability to talk across cultural divides.

Affirmation of diverse intelligence is not a retreat to a softhearted definition of the mind. To acknowledge a broader range of intellectual capacity is to take seriously the concept of cognitive variability, to appreciate in all the Rosies and Joes the thought that drives their accomplishments and defines who they are. This is a model of the mind that is worthy of a democratic society.

3

Literacy and Language

The Joy of Reading and Writing: Superman and Me

by Sherman Alexie

I learned to read with a Superman comic book. Simple enough, I suppose. I cannot recall which particular Superman comic book I read, nor can I remember which villain he fought in that issue. I cannot remember the plot, nor the means by which I obtained the comic book. What I can remember is this: I was 3 years old, a Spokane Indian boy living with his family on the Spokane Indian Reservation in eastern Washington state. We were poor by most standards, but one of my parents usually managed to find some minimum-wage job or another, which made us middle-class by reservation standards. I had a brother and three sisters. We lived on a combination of irregular paychecks, hope, fear and government surplus food.

My father, who is one of the few Indians who went to Catholic school on purpose, was an avid reader of westerns, spy thrillers, murder mysteries, gangster epics, basketball player biographies and anything else he could find. He bought his books by the pound at Dutch's Pawn Shop, Goodwill, Salvation Army and Value Village. When he had extra money, he bought new novels at supermarkets, convenience stores and hospital gift shops. Our house was filled with books. They were stacked in crazy piles in the bathroom, bedrooms and living room. In a fit of unemployment-inspired creative energy, my father built a set of bookshelves and soon filled them with a random assortment of books about the Kennedy assassination, Watergate, the Vietnam War and the entire 23-book series of the Apache westerns. My father loved books, and since I loved my father with an aching devotion, I decided to love books as well.

I can remember picking up my father's books before I could read. The words themselves were mostly foreign, but I still remember the exact moment when I first understood, with a sudden clarity, the purpose of a paragraph. I didn't have the vocabulary to say "paragraph," but I realized that a

---

A smart Indian is a dangerous person, widely feared and ridiculed by Indians and non-Indians alike. I fought with my class-mates on a daily basis. They wanted me to stay quiet when the non-Indian teacher asked for answers, for volunteers, for help. We were Indian children who were expected to be stupid. Most lived up to those expectations inside the classroom but subverted them on the outside. They struggled with basic reading in school but could remember how to sing a few dozen powwow songs. They were monosyllabic in front of their non-Indian teachers but could tell complicated stories and jokes at the dinner table. They submissively ducked their heads when confronted by a non-Indian adult but would slug it out with the Indian bully who was 10 years older. As Indian children, we were expected to fail in the non-Indian world. Those who failed were ceremonially accepted by other Indians and appropriately pitied by non-Indians.

paragraph was a fence that held words. The words inside a paragraph worked together for a common purpose. They had some specific reason for being inside the same fence. This knowledge delighted me. I began to think of everything in terms of paragraphs. Our reservation was a small paragraph within the United States. My family's house was a paragraph, distinct from the other paragraphs of the LeBrets to the north, the Fords to our south and the Tribal School to the west. Inside our house, each family member existed as a separate paragraph but still had genetics and common experiences to link us. Now, using this logic, I can see my changed family as an essay of seven paragraphs: mother, father, older brother, the deceased sister, my younger twin sisters and our adopted little brother.

At the same time I was seeing the world in paragraphs, I also picked up that Superman comic book. Each panel, complete with picture, dialogue and narrative was a three-dimensional paragraph. In one panel, Superman breaks through a door. His suit is red, blue and yellow. The brown door shatters into many pieces. I look at the narrative above the picture. I cannot read the words, but I assume it tells me that "Superman is breaking down the door." Aloud, I pretend to read the words and say, "Superman is breaking down the door." Words, dialogue, also float out of Superman's mouth. Because he is breaking down the door, I assume he says, "I am breaking down the door." Once again, I pretend to read the words and say aloud, "I am breaking down the door" In this way, I learned to read.

This might be an interesting story all by itself. A little Indian boy teaches himself to read at an early age and advances quickly. He reads "Grapes of Wrath" in kindergarten when other children are struggling through "Dick and Jane." If he'd been anything but an Indian boy living on the reservation, he might have been called a prodigy. But he is an Indian boy living on the reservation and is simply an oddity. He grows into a man who often speaks of his childhood in the third-person, as if it will somehow dull the pain and make him sound more modest about his talents.

I refused to fail. I was smart. I was arrogant. I was lucky. I read books late into the night, until I could barely keep my eyes open. I read books at recess, then during lunch, and in the few minutes left after I had finished my classroom assignments. I read books in the car when my family traveled to powwows or basketball games. In shopping malls, I ran to the bookstores and read bits and pieces of as many books as I could. I read the books my father brought home from the pawnshops and secondhand. I read the books I borrowed from the library. I read the backs of cereal boxes. I read the newspaper. I read the bulletins posted on the walls of the school, the clinic, the tribal offices, the post office. I read junk mail. I read auto-repair manuals. I read magazines. I read anything that had words and paragraphs. I read with equal parts joy and desperation. I loved those books, but I also knew that love had only one purpose. I was trying to save my life.

Despite all the books I read, I am still surprised I became a writer. I was going to be a pediatrician. These days, I write novels, short stories, and poems. I visit schools and teach creative writing to Indian kids. In all my years in the reservation school system, I was never taught how to write poetry, short stories or novels. I was certainly never taught that Indians wrote poetry, short stories and novels. Writing was something beyond Indians. I cannot recall a single time that a guest teacher visited the reservation. There must have been visiting teachers. Who were they? Where are they now? Do they exist? I visit the schools as often as possible. The Indian kids crowd the classroom. Many are writing their own poems, short stories and novels. They have read my books. They have read many other books. They look at me with bright eyes and arrogant wonder. They are trying to save their lives. Then there are the sullen and already defeated Indian kids who sit in the back rows and ignore me with theatrical precision. The pages of their notebooks are empty. They carry neither pencil nor pen. They stare out the window. They refuse and resist. "Books," I say to them. "Books," I say. I throw my weight against their locked doors. The door holds. I am smart. I am arrogant. I am lucky. I am trying to save our lives.

Learning to Write

by Russell Baker

When our class was assigned to Mr. Fleagle for third-year English I anticipated another grim year in that dreariest of subjects. Mr. Fleagle was notorious among City students for dullness and inability to inspire. He was said to be stuffy, dull, and hopelessly out of date. To me he looked to be sixty or seventy and prim to a fault. He wore primly severe eyeglasses, his wavy hair was primly cut and primly against the collar buttons of his primly starched white shirts. He had a primly pointed jaw, a primly straight nose, and a prim manner of speaking that was so correct, so gentlemanly, that he seemed a comic antique.

I anticipated a listless, unfruitful year with Mr. Fleagle and for a long time was not disappointed. We read *Macbeth*. Mr. Fleagle loved *Macbeth* and wanted us to love it too, but he lacked the gift of infecting others with his own passion. He tried to convey the murderous ferocity of Lady Macbeth one day by reading aloud the passage that concludes

. . . I have given suck, and now

How tender 'tis to love the babe that milks me.

I would, while it was smiling in my face,

Have plucked my nipple from his boneless gums . . .

The idea of prim Mr. Fleagle plucking his nipple from boneless gums was too much for the class. We burst into gasps of irrepressible snickering. Mr. Fleagle stopped.

"There is nothing funny, boys, about giving suck to a babe. It is the—the very essence of motherhood, don't you see."

He constantly sprinkled his sentences with "don't you see." It wasn't a question but an exclamation of mild surprise at our ignorance. "Your pronoun needs an antecedent, don't you see," he would say, very primly. "The purpose of the Porter's scene, boys, is to provide comic relief from the horror, don't you see."

Late in the year we tackled the informal essay. "The essay, don't you see, is the . . . "My mind went numb. Of all forms of writing, none seemed so boring as the essay. Naturally we would have to write informal essays.

Mr. Fleagle distributed a homework sheet offering us a choice of topics. None was quite so simpleminded as "What I Did on My Summer Vacation," but most seemed to be almost as dull. I took the list home and dawdled until the night before the essay was due. Sprawled on the sofa, I finally

---

faced up to the grim task, took the list out of my notebook, and scanned it. The topic on which my eye stopped was "The Art of Eating Spaghetti."

This title produced an extraordinary sequence of mental images. Surging up out of the depths of memory came a vivid recollection of a night in Belleville when all of us were seated around the supper table—Uncle Allen, my mother, Uncle Charlie, Uncle Hal—and Aunt Pat served spaghetti for supper. Spaghetti was an exotic treat in those days. Neither Doris nor I had ever eaten spaghetti, and none of the adults had enough experience to be good at it. All the good humor of Uncle Allen's house reawoke in my mind as I recalled the laughing arguments we had that night about the socially respectable method for moving spaghetti from plate to mouth.

Suddenly I wanted to write about that, about the warmth and good feeling of it, but I wanted to put it down simply for my own joy, not for Mr. Fleagle. It was a moment I wanted to recapture and hold for myself. I wanted to relive the pleasure of an evening at New Street. To write it as I wanted, however, would violate all the rules of formal composition I'd learned in school, and Mr. Fleagle would surely give it a failing grade. Never mind. I would write something else for Mr. Fleagle after I had written this thing for myself.

When I finished it the night was half gone and there was no time left to compose a proper, respectable essay for Mr. Fleagle. There was no choice next morning, but to turn in my private reminiscence of Belleville. Two days passed before Mr. Fleagle returned the graded papers, and he returned everyone's but mine. I was bracing myself for a command to report to Mr. Fleagle immediately after school for discipline when I saw him lift my paper from his desk and rap for the class's attention.

"Now, boys," he said, "I want to read you an essay. This is titled 'The Art of Eating Spaghetti.'"

And he started to read. My words! He was reading *my words* out loud to the entire class. What's more, the entire class was listening. Listening attentively. Then somebody laughed, then the entire class was laughing, and not in contempt and ridicule, but with openhearted enjoyment. Even Mr. Fleagle stopped two or three times to repress a small prim smile.

I did my best to avoid showing pleasure, but what I was feeling was pure ecstasy at this startling demonstration that my words had the power to make people laugh. In the eleventh grade, at the eleventh hour as it were, I had discovered a calling. It was the happiest moment of my entire school career. When Mr. Fleagle finished he put the final seal on my happiness by saying, "Now that, boys, is an essay, don't you see. It's—don't you see—it's of the very essence of the essay, don't you see. Congratulations, Mr. Baker."

How I Learned to Read and Write

by Frederick Douglass

I lived in Master Hugh's family about seven years. During this time, I succeeded in learning to read and write. In accomplishing this, I was compelled to resort to various stratagems. I had no regular teacher. My mistress, who had kindly commenced to instruct me, had, in compliance with the advice and direction of her husband, not only ceased to instruct, but had set her face against my being instructed by any one else. It is due, however, to my mistress to say of her, that she did not adopt this course of treatment immediately. She at first lacked the depravity indispensable to shutting me up in mental darkness. It was at least necessary for her to have some training in the exercise of irresponsible power, to make her equal to the task of treating me as though I were a brute.

My mistress was, as I have said, a kind and tender-hearted woman; and in the simplicity of her soul she commenced, when I first went to live with her, to treat me as she supposed one human being ought to treat another. In entering upon the duties of a slaveholder, she did not seem to perceive that I sustained to her the relation of a mere chattel, and that for her to treat me as a human being was not only wrong, but dangerously so. Slavery proved as injurious to her as it did to me. When I went there, she was a pious, warm, and tender-hearted woman. There was no sorrow or suffering for which she had not a tear. She had bread for the hungry, clothes for the naked, and comfort for every mourner that came within her reach. Slavery soon proved its ability to divest her of these heavenly qualities. Under its influence, the tender heart became stone, and the lamb-like disposition gave way to one of tiger-like fierceness. The first step in her downward course was in her ceasing to instruct me. She now commenced to practise her husband's precepts. She finally became even more violent in her opposition than her husband himself. She was not satisfied with simply doing as well as he had commanded; she seemed anxious to do better. Nothing seemed to make her more angry than to see me with a newspaper. She seemed to think that here lay the danger. I have had her rush at me with a face made all up of fury, and snatch from me a newspaper, in a manner that fully revealed her apprehension. She was an apt woman; and a little experience soon demonstrated, to her satisfaction, that education and slavery were incompatible with each other.

From this time I was most narrowly watched. If I was in a separate room any considerable length of time, I was sure to be suspected of having a book, and was at once called to give an account of myself. All this, however, was too late. The first step had been taken. Mistress, in teaching me the alphabet, had given me the inch, and no precaution could prevent me from taking the ell.

The plan which I adopted, and the one by which I was most successful, was that of making friends of all the little white boys whom I met in the street. As many of these as I could, I converted into

---

From *Narrative of the Life of Frederick Douglass, an American Slave* by Frederick Douglass, 1845.

teachers. With their kindly aid, obtained at different times and in different places, I finally succeeded in learning to read. When I was sent of errands, I always took my book with me, and by going one part of my errand quickly, I found time to get a lesson before my return. I used also to carry bread with me, enough of which was always in the house, and to which I was always welcome; for I was much better off in this regard than many of the poor white children in our neighborhood. This bread I used to bestow upon the hungry little urchins, who, in return, would give me that more valuable bread of knowledge. I am strongly tempted to give the names of two or three of those little boys, as a testimonial of the gratitude and affection I bear them; but prudence forbids: -not that it would injure me, but it might embarrass them; for it is almost an unpardonable offence to teach slaves to read in this Christian country. It is enough to say of the dear little fellows, that they lived on Philpot Street, very near Durgin and Bailey's ship-yard. I used to talk this matter of slavery over with them. I would sometimes say to them, I wished I could be as free as they would be when they got to be men. "You will be free as soon as you are twenty-one, but I am a slave for life! Have not I as good a right to be free as you have?" These words used to trouble them; they would express for me the liveliest sympathy, and console me with the hope that something would occur by which I might be free.

I was now about twelve years old, and the thought of being a slave for life began to bear heavily upon my heart. Just about this time, I got hold of a book entitled "The Columbian Orator." Every opportunity I got, I used to read this book. Among much of other interesting matter, I found in it a dialogue between a master and his slave. The slave was represented as having run away from his master three times. The dialogue represented the conversation which took place between them, when the slave was retaken the third time. In this dialogue, the whole argument in behalf of slavery was brought forward by the master, all of which was disposed of by the slave. The slave was made to say some very smart as well as impressive things in reply to his master-things which had the desired though unexpected effect; for the conversation resulted in the voluntary emancipation of the slave on the part of the master.

In the same book, I met with one of Sheridan's mighty speeches on and in behalf of Catholic emancipation. These were choice documents to me. I read them over and over again with unabated interest. They gave tongue to interesting thoughts of my own soul, which had frequently lashed through my mind, and died away for want of utterance. The moral which I gained from the dialogue was the power of truth over the conscience of even a slaveholder. What I got from Sheridan was a bold denunciation of slavery, and a powerful vindication of human rights. The reading of these documents enabled me to utter my thoughts, and to meet the arguments brought forward to sustain slavery; but while they relieved me of one difficulty, they brought on another even more painful than the one of which I was relieved. The more I read, the more I was led to abhor and detest my enslavers. I could regard them in no other light than a band of successful robbers, who had left their homes, and gone to Africa, and stolen us from our homes, and in a strange land reduced us to slavery. I loathed them as being the meanest as well as the most wicked of men. As I read and contemplated the subject, behold! that very discontentment which Master Hugh had predicted would follow my learning to read had already come, to torment and sting my soul to unutterable anguish. As I writhed under it, I would at times feel that learning to read had been a curse rather than a blessing. It had given me a view of my wretched condition, without the remedy. It opened my eyes to the horrible pit, but to no ladder upon which to get out. In moments of agony, I envied my fellow-slaves for their stupidity. I have often wished myself a beast. I preferred the condition of the meanest reptile to my own. Any thing, no matter what, to get rid of thinking! It was this everlasting thinking of my condition that tormented me. There was no getting rid of it. It was pressed upon me by every object within sight or hearing, animate or inanimate. The silver trump of freedom had roused my soul to eternal wakefulness. Freedom now appeared, to disappear no more forever. It was heard in every sound, and seen in every thing. It was ever present to torment me with a sense of my wretched condition. I saw nothing without seeing it, I heard nothing without hearing it, and felt nothing without feeling it. It looked from every star, it smiled in every calm, breathed in every wind, and moved in every storm.

I often found myself regretting my own existence, and wishing myself dead; and but for the hope of being free, I have no doubt but that I should have killed myself, or done something for which I should have been killed. While in this state of mind, I was eager to hear any one speak of slavery. I was a ready listener. Every little while, I could hear something about the abolitionists. It was some time before I found what the word meant. It was always used in such connections as to make it an interesting word to me. If a slave ran away and succeeded in getting dear, or if a slave killed his master, set fire to a barn, or did any thing very wrong in the mind of a slaveholder; it was spoken of as the fruit of abolition. Hearing the word in this connection very often, I set about learning what it meant. The dictionary afforded me little or no help. I found it was "the act of abolishing"; but then I did not know what was to be abolished. Here I was perplexed. I did not dare to ask any one about its meaning, for I was satisfied that it was something they wanted me to know very little about. After a patient waiting, I got one of our city papers, containing an account of the number of petitions from the north, praying for the abolition of slavery in the District of Columbia, and of the slave trade between the States. From this time I understood the words abolition and abolitionist, and always drew near when that word was spoken, expecting to hear something of importance to myself and fellow-slaves. The light broke in upon me by degrees. I went one day down on the wharf of Mr. Waters; and seeing two Irishmen unloading a scow of stone, I went, unasked, and helped them. When we had finished, one of them came to me and asked me if I were a slave. I told him I was. He asked, "Are ye a slave for life?" I told him that I was. The good Irishman seemed to be deeply affected by the statement. He said to the other that it was a pity so fine a little fellow as myself should be a slave for life. He

said it was a shame to hold me. They both advised me to run away to the north; that I should find friends there, and that I should be free. I pretended not to be interested in what they said, and treated them as if I did not understand them; for I feared they might be treacherous. White men have been known to encourage slaves to escape, and then, to get the reward, catch them and return them to their masters. I was afraid that these seemingly good men might use me so; but I nevertheless remembered their advice, and from that time I resolved to run away. I looked forward to a time at which it would be safe for me to escape. I was too young to think of doing so immediately; besides, I wished to learn how to write, as I might have occasion to write my own pass. I consoled myself with the hope that I should one day find a good chance. Meanwhile, I would learn to write.

The idea as to how I might learn to write was suggested to me by being in Durgin and Bailey's ship-yard, and frequently seeing the ship carpenters, after hewing, and getting a piece of timber ready for use, write on the timber the name of that part of the ship for which it was intended. When a piece of timber was intended for the larboard side, it would be marked thus-"L." When a piece was for the starboard side, it would be marked thus-"S." A piece for the larboard side forward, would be marked thus-"L. F." When a piece was for starboard side forward, it would be marked thus-"S. F." For larboard aft, it would be marked thus-"L. A." For starboard aft, it would be marked thus-"S. A." I soon learned the names of these letters, and for what they were intended when placed upon a piece of timber in the ship-yard. I immediately commenced copying them, and in a short time was able to make the four letters named. After that, when I met with any boy who I knew could write, I would tell him I could write as well as he. The next word would be, "I don't believe you. Let me see you try it." I would then make the letters which I had been so fortunate as to learn, and ask him to beat that. In this way I got a good many lessons in writing, which it is quite possible I should never have gotten in any other way. During this time, my copy-book was the board fence, brick wall, and pavement; my pen and ink was a lump of chalk. With these, I learned mainly how to write. I then commenced and continued copying the Italics in Webster's Spelling Book, until I could make them all without looking on the book. By this time, my little Master Thomas had gone to school, and learned how to write, and had written over a number of copy-books. These had been brought home, and shown to some of our near neighbors, and then laid aside. My mistress used to go to class meeting at the Wilk Street meetinghouse every Monday afternoon, and leave me to take care of the house. When left thus, I used to spend the time in writing in the spaces left in Master Thomas's copy-book, copying what he had written. I continued to do this until I could write a hand very similar to that of Master Thomas. Thus, after a long, tedious effort for years, I finally succeeded in learning how to write.

The Watcher at the Gates

by Gail Godwin

I first realized I was not the only writer who had a restraining critic who lived inside me and sapped the juice from green inspirations when I was leafing through Freud's "Interpretation of Dreams" a few years ago. Ironically, it was my "inner critic" who had sent me to Freud. I was writing a novel, and my heroine was in the middle of a dream, and then I lost faith in my own invention and rushed to "an authority" to check whether she could have such a dream. In the chapter on dream interpretation, I came upon the following passage that has helped me free myself, in some measure, from my critic and has led to many pleasant and interesting exchanges with other writers.

Freud quotes Schiller, who is writing a letter to a friend. The friend complains of his lack of creative power. Schiller replies with an allegory. He says it is not good if the intellect examines too closely the ideas pouring in at the gates. "In isolation, an idea may be quite insignificant, and venturesome in the extreme, but it may acquire importance from an idea which follows it. . . . In the case of a creative mind, it seems to me, the intellect has withdrawn its watchers from the gates, and the ideas rush in pell-mell, and only then does it review and inspect the multitude. You are ashamed or afraid of the momentary and passing madness which is found in all real creators, the longer or shorter duration of which distinguishes the thinking artist from the dreamer . . . you reject too soon and discriminate too severely."

So that's what I had: a Watcher at the Gates. I decided to get to know him better. I discussed him with other writers, who told me some of the quirks and habits of their Watchers, each of whom was as individual as his host, and all of whom seemed passionately dedicated to one goal: rejecting too soon and discriminating too severely.

It is amazing the lengths a Watcher will go to keep you from pursuing the flow of your imagination. Watchers are notorious pencil sharpeners, ribbon changers, plant waterers, home repairers and abhorrers of messy rooms or messy pages. They are compulsive looker-uppers. They are superstitious scaredy-cats. They cultivate self-important eccentricities they think are suitable for "writers." And they'd rather die (and kill your inspiration with them) than risk making a fool of themselves.

My Watcher has a wasteful penchant for 20-pound bond paper above and below the carbon of the first draft. "What's the good of writing out a whole page," he whispers begrudgingly, "if you just have to write it over again later? Get it perfect the first time!" My Watcher adores stopping in the middle of a morning's work to drive down to the library to-check on the name of a flower or a World

---

War Il battle or a line of metaphysical poetry. "You can't possibly go on till you've got this right!" he admonishes. I go and get the car keys.

Other Watchers have informed their writers that:

"Whenever you get a really good sentence you should stop in the middle of it and go on tomorrow. Otherwise you might run dry."

"Don't try and continue with your book till your dental appointment is over. When you're worried about your teeth, you can't think about art."

Another Watcher makes his owner pin his finished pages to a clothesline and read them through binoculars "to see how they look from a distance." Countless other Watchers demand "bribes" for taking the day off: lethal doses of caffeine, alcoholic doses of Scotch or vodka or wine.

There are various ways to outsmart, pacify, or coexist with·your Watcher. Here are some I have tried, or my writer friends have tried, with success:

Look for situations when he's likely to be off-guard. Write too fast for him in an unexpected place, at an unexpected time. (Virginia Woolf captured the "diamonds in the dustheap" by writing at a "rapid haphazard gallop" in her diary.) Write when very tired. Write in purple ink on the back of a Master Charge statement. Write whatever comes into your mind while the kettle is boiling and make the steam whistle your deadline. (Deadlines are a great way to outdistance the Watcher.)

Disguise 'what you are writing. If your Watcher refuses to let you get on with your story or novel, write a "letter" instead, telling your "correspondent" what you are going to write in your story or next chapter. Dash off a "review" of your own unfinished opus. It will stand up like a bully to your Watcher the next time he throws obstacles in your path. If you write yourself a good one.

Get to know your Watcher. He's yours. Do a drawing of him (or her). Pin it to the wall of your study and turn it gently to the wall when necessary. Let your Watcher feel needed. Watchers are excellent critics after inspiration has been captured; they are dependable, sharp-eyed readers of things already set down. Keep your Watcher in shape and he'll have less time to keep you from shaping. If he's really ruining your whole working day, sit down, as Jung did with his personal demons, and write him a letter. On a very bad day I once wrote my Watcher a letter. "Dear Watcher," I wrote, "What is it you're so afraid I'll do?" Then I held his pen for him, and he replied instantly with a candor that has kept me from truly despising him.

"Fail," he wrote back.

Shitty First Drafts

by Anne Lamott

Now, practically even better news than that of short assignments is the idea of shitty first drafts. All good writers write them. This is how they end up with good second drafts and terrific third drafts. People tend to look at successful writers who are getting their books published and maybe even doing well financially and think that they sit down at their desks every morning feeling like a million dollars, feeling great about who they are and how much talent they have and what a great story they have to tell; that they take in a few deep breaths, push back their sleeves, roll their necks a few times to get all the cricks out, and dive in, typing fully formed passages as fast as a court reporter. But this is just the fantasy of the uninitiated. I know some very great writers, writers you love who write beautifully and have made a great deal of money, and not one of them sits down routinely feeling wildly enthusiastic and confident. Not one of them writes elegant first drafts. All right, one of them does, but we do not like her very much. We do not think that she has a rich inner life or that God likes her or can even stand her. (Although when I mentioned this to my priest friend Tom, he said you can safely assume you've created God in your own image when it turns out that God hates all the same people you do.)

Very few writers really know what they are doing until they've done it. Nor do they go about their business feeling dewy and thrilled. They do not type a few stiff warm-up sentences and then find themselves bounding along like huskies across the snow. One writer I know tells me that he sits down every morning and says to himself nicely, "It's not like you don't have a choice, because you do—you can either type, or kill yourself." We all often feel like we are pulling teeth, even those writers whose prose ends up being the most natural and fluid. The right words and sentences just do not come pouring out like ticker tape most of the time. Now, Muriel Spark is said to have felt that she was taking dictation from God every morning—sitting there, one supposes, plugged into a Dictaphone, typing away, humming. But this is a very hostile and aggressive position. One might hope for bad things to rain down on a person like this.

For me and most of the other writers I know, writing is not rapturous. In fact, the only way I can get anything written at all is to write really, really shitty first drafts.

The first draft is the child's draft, where you let it all pour out and then let it romp all over the place, knowing that no one is going to see it and that you can shape it later. You just let this childlike part of you channel whatever voices and visions come through and onto the page. If one of the characters wants to say, "Well, so what, Mr. Poopy Pants?," you let her. No one is going to see it. If the kid wants to get into really sentimental, weepy, emotional territory, you let him. Just get it all down on paper because there may be something great in those six crazy pages that you would never have gotten to by more rational, grown-up means. There may be something in the very last line of the very last paragraph on page six that you just love, that is so beautiful or wild that you now know what you're supposed to be writing about, more or less, or in what direction you might go—but there was no way to get to this without first getting through the first five and a half pages.

I used to write food reviews for *California* magazine before it folded. (My writing food reviews had nothing to do with the magazine folding, although every single review did cause a couple of canceled subscriptions. Some readers took umbrage at my comparing mounds of vegetable puree with various ex-presidents' brains.) These reviews always took two days to write. First I'd go to a restaurant several times with a few opinionated, articulate friends in tow. I'd sit there writing down everything anyone said that was at all interesting or funny. Then on the following Monday I'd sit down at my desk with my notes and try to write the review. Even after I'd been doing this for years, panic would set in. I'd try to write a lead, but instead I'd write a couple of dreadful sentences, XX them out, try again, XX everything out, and then feel despair and worry settle on my chest like an x-ray apron. It's over, I'd think calmly. I'm not going to be able to get the magic to work this time. I'm ruined. I'm through. I'm toast. Maybe, I'd think, I can get my old job back as a clerk-typist. But probably not. I'd get up and study my teeth in the mirror for a while. Then I'd stop, remember to breathe, make a few phone calls, hit the kitchen and chow down. Eventually I'd go back and sit down at my desk, and sigh for the next ten minutes. Finally I would pick up my one-inch picture frame, stare into it as if for the answer, and every time the answer would come: all I had to do was to write a really shitty first draft of, say, the opening paragraph. And no one was going to see it.

So I'd start writing without reining myself in. It was almost just typing, just making my fingers move. And the writing would be terrible. I'd write a lead paragraph that was a whole page, even though the entire review could only be three pages long, and then I'd start writing up descriptions of the food, one dish at a time, bird by bird, and the critics would be sitting on my shoulders, commenting like cartoon characters. They'd be pretending to snore, or rolling their eyes at my overwrought descriptions, no matter how hard I tried to tone those descriptions down, no matter how conscious I was of what a friend said to me gently in my early days of restaurant reviewing. "Annie," she said, "it is just a piece of chicken. It is just a bit of cake."

But because by then I had been writing for so long, I would eventually let myself trust the process—sort of, more or less. I'd write a first draft that was maybe twice as long as it should be, with a self-indulgent and boring beginning, stupefying descriptions of the meal, lots of quotes from my black-humored friends that made them sound more like the Manson girls than food lovers, and no ending to speak of The whole thing would be so long and incoherent and hideous that for the rest of the day I'd obsess about getting creamed by a car before I could write a decent second draft. I'd worry that people would read what I'd written and believe that the accident had really been a suicide, that I had panicked because my talent was waning and my mind was shot.

The next day, I'd sit down, go through it all with a colored pen, take out everything I possibly could, find a new lead somewhere on the second page, figure out a kicky place to end it, and then write a second draft. It always turned out fine, sometimes even funny and weird and helpful. I'd go over it one more time and mail it in.

Then, a month later, when it was time for another review, the whole process would start again, complete with the fears that people would find my first draft before I could rewrite it.

Almost all good writing begins with terrible first efforts. You need to start somewhere. Start by getting something—anything—down on paper. A friend of mine says that the first draft is the down draft—you just get it down. The second draft is the up draft—you fix it up. You try to say what you have to say more accurately. And the third draft is the dental draft, where you check every tooth, to see if it's loose or cramped or decayed, or even, God help us, healthy.

The Love of Books

by Gloria Naylor

Any life amounts to "organized chaos": biologically we are more space than matter and that matter consists of careening atoms always in flux; psychologically we are minute electrical charges, running from the brain to the spinal cord, the organs, the hormonal systems. Sitting apart from that is a consciousness tat orders, to our specific preferences, any given reality at any given time. A long way of saying: our lives are what we make them. And definitely our "writing lives," which is miming life in both its execution and its product. And so to make sense of the senseless, writers reach for metaphors to explain-to themselves and others—exactly what it is that they do. Those metaphors and the resultant explanation are value-laden; they spring from our specific culture and our personal politics.

Why do I write? The truth, the unvarnished truth, is that I haven't a clue. The answer to that question lies hidden in the same box that holds the origin of human creativity, our imperative need as a species to communicate; and to be touched. Many minds for many years have busied themselves trying to unlock that box, and writers, for the most part, are quite happy to allow the literary critics, anthropologists, psychologists, and biologists to argue interdiscipline and intradiscisipline while, they stay out of the fray. And when writers are invited in, they'll reach for some shorthand, some metaphor, to throw quickly into the ring so they can get back to doing—for whatever reason—what they do best.

I normally reach for a poem called "The Unclaimed," by Nikky Finney, a young African-American woman who evokes the spirit of all the women in her past "whose names do not ripple in neon lights or whose distinctiveness has yet to be embedded on printed paper." These women, the poet tells us, were never allowed time to pamper themselves in front of mirrors or even time to cry. They were women who sang over stovetops and washtubs; scribbled poems on bits of paper and dinner napkins—women who acted out the drama of their lives unsung and forgotten. And so she concludes:

> for all that you were
> for all that you wanted to be
> each time i sign my name
> know that it is for a thousand like you
> who could not hold a pen
> but who instead held me

---

and rocked me gently

to the creative rhythms

i now live by

I elect to trace the untraceable, my passionate love of book and my affair with the written word, back to my mother, who was also an avid lover of books. She and my father were from sharecropping families and grew up in the 1930s in Mississippi. She was not allowed to use the public libraries; and purchasing books was out of the question for her. What many young people tend to forget today, in the age of excessiveness and of almost ingrained waste that we have in consumerist America, is that books were once a luxury for people until the advent of the ten-cent novel which eventually evolved into the paperback. Most people, especially working-class and poor people, were not able to buy books so they depended on the public libraries. That is why Ben Franklin instituted the free lending library, hoping to give the children of the working class at least a competitive edge with the children of the upper class, who could afford to have books.

My mother was one of eight children and her family worked collectively on a farm from Monday to Friday to bring in the requisite crop—for them it was cotton. Since this was in the South. in the Bible Belt, it meant that Sunday was spent in church—all day. Saturday was then the only free time my mother had. So while her sisters and brothers went off to town spend their time, she would hire herself out in someone else's field on her tree Saturdays. For that labor, she received fifty cents a day—but it was her fifty cents. At the end of the month she had two dollars and she would take that two dollars and send away to book clubs. And that's how she got her reading material.

She made a vow to herself that she would never raise a child in the South. lt is ironic that when my parents, in 1949, moved north to New York City, they left behind a region that would eventually become a place much more conducive for African-Americans to hold power than the place to which they fled. But who was to know the future? My mother only knew her past and her history spoke loud and clear: if you were poor, and if you were black in Tunica County, you were not going to read. She always told my sisters and me that she was not ashamed of her background—it was no sin to be poor. Bur the greatest sin is to keep people from learning to dream. And my mother believed that books taught the young how to dream. She knew, of course, that she would not be eradicating racism from her life by moving, as Malcolm X said, "from down South to up South." But she was aware that, in New York City at least, her tax dollars would go to support public institutions that would be open to her children.

Because we grew up without much money and a whole lot of dreams, we spent a great deal of time in the public libraries. The law in New York was that a child had to be able to write their name in order to get a juvenile library card. But before my sisters and I had even attained the age of literacy, mv mother would take us on these pilgrimages to the library. They live in my mind as small dark rooms with heavy bookcases and the heavy desks of the librarian, who looked Olive Oyl. My mother would say, "Do you see all these books? Once you can write your name, all of these books will be yours. For two weeks. But yours."

I had to get much older to understand why she took us on those pilgrimages. While indeed it was to educate us, i think it was also to heal some place within herself. For me it made the library a place that was quite familiar, a place that was even welcoming. I was eager to be able to qualify to enter those doors. I was eager to discover whatever mystery was within the ink upon that paper, because also within me—and this had to be genetic—was a fascination with the written word. I used to love the feel and the heft of a book. In those days, they were made with a certain kind of glue and when you broke the binding you could smell that special glue. I'm not saying I was getting high off that glue. There was just this wonderful, earthy smell to it.

My mother didn't know then and, of course, at four and five l didn't know that i was on my way to being a very shy and very repressed adolescent. Books were to be my only avenue out of the walls my emotions built around me in those years. I felt trapped within my home and trapped within school, and it was through the pages of books that l was released into other worlds. I literally read my way from the A's to the Z's in the children's section of the library. I can still see that two-shelf row of books, and it ran the whole length of the room. Louisa May Alcott's, l recall, was the first set of books—*Little Women*, and *Little Men*, and *Jo's Boys*, and Under the Umbrella—she wrote a whole slew of books: following those young women from adolescence into adulthood. I can remember reading all the way through to the last author because there was another set of books by Laura Ingalls Wilder—*Little House on the Prairie*, *Little House in the Big Woods*, *Those Happy Golden Years*. Once again following a young girl in her coming of age from adolescence all the way into adulthood and marriage. It was the world through which I lived.

I don't believe this would have been enough to have created a writer, although most begin as avid readers. But a writer needs something else—a conscious connection between the validity of their personal experience and the page. My shyness kept me from communicating verbally to the point that my teachers thought perhaps I was slow. The theory of education in those years—the fifties and early sixties—held that a well-rounded child participated in class. That meant raising your hand, which for a child like me meant to break out in a cold sweat. The idea that I had to step forth and give voice to something was a nightmare.

My mother, seeing that l was not a talker and understanding that indeed I was, of the three girls, perhaps her most gifted child (the teachers came to understand that later as well because I always excelled in the written tests), went out to Woolworth's and bought me one of those white plastic diaries. I think they went for something like ninety-nine cents in those days, and stamped on it in gold leaf was "One Year Diary"—the kind with the cheap lock your sister could open with a bobby pin. My mother said, "You know, Gloria, I'll bet there are a lot of things going on in the world you don't understand and I'm sure there are even things going on in here in our home that might be troubling you, but since you can't seem to talk to your father and me about these things. why don't you write them down in here." She threw the book on the bed and was wise enough to leave the room, and not belabor the point. I picked up the· diary and I did just that, l proceeded to write down all the things that I could not say.

From the age of twelve I made the vital connection between inarticulate feeling and the written word. Whatever went into those original pages are not eternal keepsakes, they are not classic thoughts, but they were my feelings, it was my pain, and the pain was real to me at twelve years old. And we wonder about the rise in teenage suicides. It is because adults resist believing that whatever the demons are, if they're twelve-year-old, thirteen-year-old, fourteen-year-old demons they are *real*. I know; I had them.

Through the luck of the draw of having a very wise and perceptive mother who happened to match what I needed with the gift of that diary, my life was saved. Because those feelings were going to come out. I was goi.ng to speak one day. But the horrifying question is, in what language those feelings have been expressed? I paraphrase Toni Morrison in *Sula*: An artist without an art form is a dangerous thing. It is probably one of the most dangerous things on this earth. And being a female in the 1960s, I would have, I think, directed that destruction inward as opposed to outward. But instead, l filled up that diary, and then proceeded to fill up the spare pages in my loose-leaf notebook at the end of the school year with my ramblings that slowly turned into poems. The poems slowly evolved into *Twilight Zone-type* short stories—I have always been enamored somehow with the mystical and the idea of alternative realities, and began writing supernatural stories even as an adolescent.

But it took until I was twenty-seven years old for me to believe that I had the faintest chance of being a writer. I went through my adolescence and young adulthood being told that black people did not write books. How did this come about? I was a kid who read to the tune of a book a day, who had been "discovered" by her middle school teachers who plied me with extra reading, which I would take home on the weekends. In those hundreds of texts that I read, there was nothing about black Americans or by black Americans. Those authors weren't on the shelves in the public libraries in New York City, and they definitely weren't on my standard junior high school or high school curriculum. If black people had written books, would I not have read them? Would I not have been taught them? If Gwendolyn Brooks had indeed won the Pulitzer Prize the year she did, 1950 (ironically the year I was born), should she not qualify as a talented enough American writer to be on my syllabus?

We do not say to our children, "You are nothing." We don't have to stand up in an auditorium, on a parade ground, and blatantly shout out to them, "You have nothing to give." We have done this much more effectively, through silence, through what they do *not* see, through what is *not* there when we parade before them what we declare is worthy. It is a very effective message. It was the one that I received. And I received it from well-meaning people, who thought I was bright, I had a future. I had promise. It took the unrest in the sixties and the kids then in their late teens and early twenties, who were willing to put their careers on the line, their lives on the line—and some lost them at Jackson and Kent State—in order to give birth to the educational institutions that began to exist in the mid seventies. Ones which taught what America really was, that provided an education that edified and represented the entire citizenry. This was the gift that they gave me. And so by the time I entered Brooklyn College, once again an institution supported by public funds, there was an Africana Studies Department, a Women's Studies Program, Chicano Studies (as they were called in those years), Asian Studies. And I then was able to encounter the words of Ralph Ellison, Toni Morrison, Nikki Giovanni, James Baldwin, Richard Wright, Zora Neale Hurston. . . the list goes on and on. We're not talking about people who deserved a Black Literature Day or a Black Literature Hour in our curriculums. These are names that will be here in the year 3000, because they have helped to define not only American literature, but world literature. I owe those young people who spilled their blood in the sixties a huge debt of gratitude, because by learning that there was this heritage of writers behind me, and specifically black female writers, when I looked in the mirror there was the image I desperately needed to see. What I had see previously was no image. Slowly, by completing my diet with these books, an outline was filled in. And that outline did not say that black was beautiful, it did not say that black was ugly. It said simply: you are. You exist. It reverberated enough to give me the courage to pick up the pen. And it's what finally validated me.

My first novel, *The Women of Brewster Place*, literally began that very semester at Brooklyn College when I discovered that there was a whole history of black writing in America; and that I had the foremothers an forefathers who stood behind me with the ghosts of their excellence. And I was determined that if I had only one novel in me, I was going to write about what I had not had, in those twenty-some odd years of literacy, the privilege to read about. I was going to write all about me. And I knew that if I just chose one female character, one protagonist, she would not do justice to the diversity of the black female experience in America. One woman couldn't do it all. So I hit upon the structure of having different chapters devoted to the lives of different women. I can remember making a mental list of how they would differ. They were to vary, beginning with something as superficial as their skin colors. I know it's not currently in vogue but I do like the word "colored." Because when I look around, that's what I see—colored people—pink on up in the European American; then moving from alabaster to ebony in the black female. We also range from being devotedly religious to almost irreligious. We are young and old. We are political, nonpolitical.

We even differ in our sexual preferences. So on this dead-end street, I had hoped to create a whole panorama of what it meant to be black and female in America. To claim and to validate as many lives as I possibly could. To give them each the dignity that I felt they each deserved. To this day I still call that book—which not fifteen years old—my love letter to the black woman in America. But it first began as a love letter to myself. And by beginning with what was indeed a very visceral and personal it had reverberated and touched women all over the world. I have received letters from as far away as Japan, from Korean women who inform me that they are a minority within that society. They saw their own grandparents and aunts on that dead-end street.

Every writer must articulate from the specific. They must reach down where they stand, because there is nothing else from which to draw. Therefore were I to go along with the traditional view that Western literature began with Homer (a good argument to the contrary is the subject of another essay)—Homer didn't write about the Romans, nor the Phoenicians, nor about the Huns. He wrote about the Greeks because that's what he was. Shakespeare wrote about Elizabethan Englishmen. He put them in the Caribbean, he put them in Denmark, he put them in Verona—but they were all Elizabethan Englishmen. Joyce wrote about the Irish; Philip Roth writes about the Jews, Maxine Hong Kingston about Chinese-Americans. You write where you are. It's the only thing you have to give. And if you are fortunate enough, there is a spark that will somehow ignite a work so that it touches almost anyone who reads it, although it is about a very specific people at a very specific time. And so that's what I attempt to do with my work—to reach down where I am and to articulate those lives. I could spend my entire life, what I have left of a natural life span, writing only about the Brewster Places in America and never exhaust that which is universal to it.

What I plan to do though with the rest of my life is indeed to communicate with images. They will not always be written images. I love working for the stage. I will write for film. I will always have stories to tell. They may not be good stories, they may not be bad stories. But I would like to believe that I will always tell honest stories and that to the lives that come to me I will somehow do them justice.

The Lonely, Good Company of Books

by Richard Rodriguez

From an early age I knew that my mother and father could read and write both Spanish and English. I had observed my father making his way through what, I now suppose, must have been income tax forms. On other occasions I waited apprehensively while my mother read onion paper letters air-mailed from Mexico with news of a relative's illness or death. For both my parents, however, reading was something done out of necessity and as quickly as possible. Never did I see either of them read an entire book. Nor did I see them read for pleasure. Their reading consisted of work manuals, prayer books, newspapers, recipes. . . .

In our house each school year would begin with my mother's careful instruction: "Don't write in your books so we can sell them at the end of the year." The remark was echoed in public by my teachers, but only in part: "Boys and girls, don't write in your books. You must learn to treat them with great care and respect."

OPEN THE DOORS OF YOUR MIND WITH BOOKS, read the red and white poster over the nun's desk in early September. It soon was apparent to me that reading was the classroom's central activity. Each course had its own book. And the information gathered from a book was unquestioned. READ TO LEARN, the sign on the wall advised in December. I privately wondered: What was the connection between reading and learning? Did one learn something only by reading it? Was an idea only an idea if it could be written down? In June, CONSIDER BOOKS YOUR BEST FRIENDS. Friends? Reading was, at best, only a chore. I needed to look up whole paragraphs of words in a dictionary. Lines of type were dizzying, the eye having to move slowly across the page, then down, and across. . . . The sentences of the first books I read were coolly impersonal. Toned hard. What most bothered me, however, was the isolation reading required. To console myself for the loneliness I'd feel when I read, I tried reading in a very soft voice. Until: "Who is doing all that talking to his neighbor?" Shortly after, remedial reading classes were arranged for me with a very old nun.

At the end of each school day1 for newly six months, I would meet with her in the tiny room that served as the school's library but was actually only a storeroom for used textbooks and a vast collection of *National Geographics*. Everything about our sessions pleased me: the smallness of the room; the noise of the janitor's broom hitting the edge of the long hallway outside the door; the green of the sun, lighting the wall; and the old woman's face blurred white with a beard. Most of the time we took turns. I began with my elementary text. Sentences of astonishing simplicity seemed to me lifeless and drab: "The boys ran from the rain. . . . She wanted to sing. . . . The kite rose in the blue." Then the old nun would read from her favorite books, usually biographies of early American presidents. Playfully she ran through complex sentences, calling the words alive with her voice, making it seem that the author somehow was speaking directly to me. I smiled just to listen to her. I sat there and sensed for the very first time some possibility of fellowship between a reader and a writer, a communication, never *intimate* like that I heard spoken words at home convey, but one nonetheless *personal*.

One day the nun concluded a session by asking me why I was so reluctant to read by myself. I tried to explain; said something about the way written words made me feel all alone—almonst, I wanted to add but didn't, as when I spoke to myself in a room just emptied of furniture. She studied my face as I spoke; she seemed to be watching more than listening. In an uneventful voice she replied that I had nothing to fear. Didn't I realize that reading would open up whole new worlds? A book could open doors for me. It could introduce me to people and show me places I never imagined existed. She gestured toward the bookshelves. (Bare-breasted African women danced, and the shiny hubcaps of automobiles on the back covers of the *Geographic* gleamed in my mind.) I listened with respect. But her words were not very influential. I was thinking then of another consequence of literacy, one I was too shy to admit but nonetheless trusted. Books were going to make me "educated." *That* confidence enabled me, several months later, to overcome my fear of the silence.

In fourth grade I embarked on a grandiose reading program. "Give me the names of important books," I would say to startled teachers. They soon found out that I had in mind "adult books." I ignored their suggestion of anything I suspected was written for children. (Not until I was in college, as a result, did I read *Huckleberry Finn* or *Alice's Adventures in Wonderland*.) Instead, I read *The Scarlet Letter* and Franklin's *Autobiography*. And whatever I read I read for extra credit. Each time I finished a book, I reported the achievement to a teacher and basked in the praise my effort earned. Despite my best efforts, however, there seemed to be more and more books I needed to read. At the library I would literally tremble as I came upon whole shelves of books I hadn't read. So I read and I read and I read: *Great Expectations*; all the short stories of Kipling; *The Babe Ruth Story*; the entire first volume of the *Encyclopaedia Britannica* (A-ANSTEY); the *Iliad*; *Moby Dick*; *Gone with the Wind*; *The Good Earth*; *Ramona*; *Forever Amber*; *The Lives of the Saints*; *Crime and Punishment*; *The Pearl*. . . . Librarians who initially frowned when I checked out the maximum ten books at a time started saving books they thought I might like. Teachers would say to the rest of the class, "I only wish the rest of you took reading as seriously as Richard obviously does."

But at home I would hear my mother wondering, "What do you see in your books?" (Was reading a hobby like her knitting? Was so much reading even healthy for a boy? Was it the sign of "brains"? Or was it just a convenient excuse for not helping around the house on Saturday mornings?) Always, "What do you see. . .?"

What *did* I see in my books? I had the idea that they were crucial for my academic success, though I couldn't have said exactly how or why. In this sixth grade I simply concluded that what gave a book its value was some major idea or theme it contained. If that core essence could be mined and memorized, I would become learned like my teachers. I decided to record in a notebook the themes of the books that I read. After reading *Robinson Crusoe*, I wrote that it is theme was "the value of learning to live by oneself." When I completed *Wuthering Heights*, I noted the danger of "letting emotions get out of control." Rereading these brief moralistic appraisals usually left me disheartened. I couldn't believe that they were really the source of rending's value. But for many years, they constituted the only means I had of describing to myself the educational value of books.

In spite of my earnestness, I found reading a pleasurable activity. l came to enjoy the lonely, good company of books. Early on weekday mornings, I'd read in my bed. I'd feel a mysterious comfort then, reading in the dawn quiet—the blue-gray silence interrupted by the occasional churning of the refrigerator motor a few rooms away or the more distant sounds of a city bus beginning its run. On weekends I'd go to the public library to read, surrounded by old men and women. Or, if the weather was fine, I would take my books to the park and read in the shade of a tree. Neighbors would leave for vacation and I would water their lawns. I would sit through the twilight on the front porches or in backyards, reading to the cool, whirling sounds of the sprinklers.

I also had favorite writers. But often those writers I enjoyed most I was least able to value. When I read William Saroyan's *The Human Comedy*, I was immediately pleased by the narrator's warmth and the charm of his story. But as quickly I became suspicious. A book so enjoyable to read couldn't be very "important." Another summer I determined to read all the novels of Dickens. Reading his fat novels, I loved the feeling I got—after the first hundred pages—of being at home in a fictional world where I knew the names of the characters and cared about what was going to happen to them. And it bothered me that I was forced away at the conclusion, when the fiction closed tight, like a fortune-teller's fist—the futures of all the major characters neatly resolved. I never knew how to take such feelings seriously, however. Nor did I suspect that these experiences could be part of a novel's meaning. Still, there were pleasures to sustain me after I'd finish my books. Carrying a volume back to the library, I would be pleased by its weight. I'd run my fingers along the edge of the pages and marvel at the breadth of my achievement. Around my room, growing stacks of paperback books reinforced my assurance.

I entered high school having read hundreds of books. My habit of reading made me a confident speaker and writer of English. Reding also enabled me to sense something of the shape, the major concerns, of Wester thought. (I was able to say something about Dante and Descartes and Engels and James Baldwin in my high school term papers.) In these various ways, books brought me to academic success as I hoped that they would. But I was not a good reader. Merely bookish, I lacked a point of view when I read. Rather, I read in order to acquire a point of view. I vacuumed books for epigrams, scarps of information, ideas, themes—anything to fill the hollow within me and make me feel educated. When one of my teachers suggested to his drowsy tenth-grade English class that person could not have a "complicated idea" until he had read at least two thousand books, I heard the remark without detecting either its irony or its very complicated truth. I merely determined to compile a list of all the books I had ever read. Harsh with myself, I included only once a title I might have read several times. (How, after all, could one read a book more than once?) And I included only those books over a hundred pages in length. (Could anything shorter be a book?)

There was yet another high school list I compiled. One day I came across a newspaper article about the retirement of an English professor at a nearby state college. The article was accompanied by a list of the "hundred most important books of Western Civilization." "More than anything else in my life," the professor told the reporter with finality, "these books have made me all that I am." That was the kind of remark I couldn't ignore. I clipped out the list and kept it for the several months it took me to read all of the titles. Most books, of course, I barely understood. While reading Plato's *Republic*, for instance, I needed to keep looking at the book jacket comments to remind myself what the text was about. Nevertheless, with the special patience and superstition of a scholarship boy, I looked at every word of the text. And by the time I reached the last word, relieved, I convinced myself that I had read *The Republic*. In a ceremony of great pride, I solemnly crossed Plato off my list.

One Writer's Beginnings

by Eudora Welty

I learned from the age of two or three that any room in our house, at any time of day, was there to read in, or to be read to. My mother read to me. She'd read to me in the big bedroom in the mornings, when we were in her rocker together, which ticked in rhythm as we rocked, as though we had a cricket accompanying the story. She'd read to me in the diningroom on winter afternoons in front of the coal fire, with our cuckoo clock ending the story with "Cuckoo," and at night when I'd got in my own bed. I must have given her no peace. Sometimes she read to me in the kitchen while she sat churning, and the churning sobbed along with *any* story. It was my ambition to have her read to me while I churned; once she granted my wish, but she read off my story before I brought her butter. She was an expressive reader. When she was reading "Puss in Boots," for instance, it was impossible not to know that she distrusted all cats.

It had been startling and disappointing to me to find out that story books had been written by *people*, that books were not natural wonders, coming up of themselves like grass. Yet regardless of where they came from, I cannot remember a time when I was not in love with them—with the books themselves, cover and binding and the paper they were printed on, with their smell and their weight and with their possession in my arms, captured and carried off to myself. Still illiterate, I was ready for them, committed to all the reading I could give them.

Neither of my parents had come from homes that could afford to buy many books, but though it must have been something of a strain on his salary, as the youngest officer in a young insurance company, my father was all the while carefully selecting and ordering away for what he and Mother thought we children should grow up with. They bought first for the future.

Besides the bookcase in the livingroom, which was always called "the library," there were the encyclopedia tables and dictionary stand under windows in our diningroom. Here to help us grow up arguing around the diningroom table were the Unabridged Webster, the Columbia Encyclopedia, Compton's Pictured Encyclopedia, the Lincoln Library of Information, and later the Book of Knowledge. And the year we moved into our new house, there was room to celebrate it with the new 1925 edition of the Britannica, which my father, his face always deliberately turned toward the future, was of course disposed to think better than any previous edition.

In "the library," inside the mission-style bookcase with its three diamond-latticed glass doors, with my father's Morris chair and the glass-shaded lamp on its table beside it, were books I could soon begin on—and I did, reading them all alike and as they came, straight down their rows, top shelf

---

to bottom. There was the set of Stoddard's Lectures, in all its late nineteenth-century vocabulary and vignettes of peasant life and quaint beliefs and customs, with matching halftone illustrations: Vesuvius erupting, Venice by moonlight, gypsies glimpsed by their campfires. I didn't know then the clue they were to my father's longing to see the rest of the world. I read straight through his other love-from-afar: the Victrola Book of the Opera, with opera after opera in synopsis, with portraits in costume of Melba, Caruso, Galli-Curci, and Geraldine Farrar, some of whose voices we could listen to on our Red Seal records.

My mother read secondarily for information; she sank as a hedonist into novels. She read Dickens in the spirit in which she would have eloped with him. The novels of her girlhood that had stayed on in her imagination, besides those of Dickens and Scott and Robert Louis Stevenson, were *Jane Eyre, Trilby, The Woman in White, Green Mansions, King Solomon's Mines*. Marie Corelli's name would crop up but I understood she had gone out of favor with my mother, who had only kept *Ardath* out of loyalty. In time she absorbed herself in Galsworthy, Edith Wharton, above all in Thomas Mann of the *Joseph* volumes.

St. Elmo was not in our house; I saw it often in other houses. This wildly popular Southern novel is where all the Edna Earles in our population started coming from. They're all named for the heroine, who succeeded in bringing a dissolute, sinning roué and atheist of a lover (St. Elmo) to his knees. My mother was able to forgo it. But she remembered the classic advice given to rose growers on how to water their bushes long enough: "Take a chair and *St. Elmo*."

To both my parents I owe my early acquaintance with a beloved Mark Twain. There was a full set of Mark Twain and a short set of Ring Lardner in our bookcase, and those were the volumes that in time united us all, parents and children.

Reading everything that stood before me was how I came upon a worn old book without a back that had belonged to my father as a child. It was called *Sanford and Merton*. Is there anyone left who recognizes it, I wonder? It is the famous moral tale written by Thomas Day in the 1780s, but of him no mention is made on the title page of *this* book; here it is *Sanford and Merton in Words of One Syllable* by Mary Godolphin. Here are the rich boy and the poor boy and Mr. Barlow, their teacher and interlocutor, in long discourses alternating with dramatic scenes—danger and rescue allotted to the rich and the poor respectively. It may have only words of one syllable, but one of them is "quoth." It ends with not one but two morals, both engraved on rings: "Do what you ought, come what may," and "If we would be great, we must first learn to be good."

This book was lacking its front cover, the back held on by strips of pasted paper, now turned golden, in several layers, and the pages stained, flecked, and tattered around the edges; its garish illustrations had come unattached but were preserved, laid in. I had the feeling even in my heedless childhood that this was the only book my father as a little boy had had of his own. He had held onto it, and might have gone to sleep on its coverless face: he had lost his mother when he was seven. My father had never made any mention to his own children of the book, but he had brought it along with him from Ohio to our house and shelved it in our bookcase.

My mother had brought from West Virginia that set of Dickens; those books looked sad, too—they had been through fire and water before I was born, she told me, and there they were, lined up—as I later realized, waiting for me.

I was presented, from as early as I can remember, with books of my own, which appeared on my birthday and Christmas morning. Indeed, my parents could not give me books enough. They must have sacrificed to give me on my sixth or seventh birthday—it was after I became a reader for myself—the ten-volume set of Our Wonder World. These were beautifully made, heavy books I would lie down with on the floor in front of the diningroom hearth, and more often than the rest volume 5, *Every Child's Story Book*, was under my eyes. There were the fairy tales—Grimm, Andersen, the

English, the French, "Ali Baba and the Forty Thieves"; and there was Aesop and Reynard the Fox; there were the myths and legends, Robin Hood, King Arthur, and St. George and the Dragon, even the history of Joan of Arc; a whack of *Pilgrim's Progress* and a long piece of *Gulliver.* They all carried their classic illustrations. I located myself in these pages and could go straight to the stories and pictures I loved; very often "The Yellow Dwarf" was first choice, with Walter Crane's Yellow Dwarf in full color making his terrifying appearance flanked by turkeys. Now that volume is as worn and backless and hanging apart as my father's poor *Sanford and Merton.* The precious page with Edward Lear's "Jumblies" on it has been in danger of slipping out for all these years. One measure of my love for Our Wonder World was that for a long time I wondered if I would go through fire and water for it as my mother had done for Charles Dickens; and the only comfort was to think I could ask my mother to do it for me.

I believe I'm the only child I know of who grew up with this treasure in the house. I used to ask others, "Did you have Our Wonder World?" I'd have to tell them The Book of Knowledge could not hold a candle to it.

I live in gratitude to my parents for initiating me—and as early as I begged for it, without keeping me waiting—into knowledge of the word, into reading and spelling, by way of the alphabet. They taught it to me at home in time for me to begin to read before starting to school. I believe the alphabet is no longer considered an essential piece of equipment for traveling through life. In my day it was the keystone to knowledge. You learned the alphabet as you learned to count to ten, as you learned "Now I lay me" and the Lord's Prayer and your father's and mother's name and address and telephone number, all in case you were lost.

My love for the alphabet, which endures, grew out of reciting it but, before that, out of seeing the letters on the page. In my own story books, before I could read them for myself, I fell in love with various winding, enchanting-looking initials drawn by Walter Crane at the heads of fairy tales. In "Once upon a time," an "O" had a rabbit running it as a treadmill, his feet upon flowers. When the day came, years later, for me to see the Book of Kells, all the wizardry of letter, initial, and word swept over me a thousand times over, and the illumination, the gold, seemed a part of the word's beauty and holiness that had been there from the start.

Learning stamps you with its moments. Childhood's learning is made up of moments. It isn't steady. It's a pulse.

In a children's art class, we sat in a ring on kindergarten chairs and drew three daffodils that had just been picked out of the yard; and while I was drawing, my sharpened pencil and the cup of the yellow daffodil gave off whiffs just alike. That the pencil doing the drawing should give off the same smell as the flower it drew seemed a part of the art lesson—as shouldn't it be? Children, like animals, use all their senses to discover the world. Then artists come along and discover it the same way, all over again. Here and there, it's the same world. Or now and then we'll hear from an artist who's never lost it.

In my sensory education I include my physical awareness of the *word.* Of a certain word, that is; the connection it has with what it stands for. At around age six, perhaps, I was standing by myself in our front yard waiting for supper, just at that hour in a late summer day when the sun is already below the horizon and the risen full moon in the visible sky stops being chalky and begins to take on light. There comes the moment, and I saw it then, when the moon goes from flat to round. For the first time it met my eyes as a globe. The word "moon" came into my mouth as though fed to me out of a silver spoon. Held in my mouth the moon became a word. It had the roundness of a Concord grape Grandpa took off his vine and gave me to suck out of its skin and swallow whole, in Ohio.

This love did not prevent me from living for years in foolish error about the moon. The new moon just appearing in the west was the rising moon to me. The new should be rising. And in early childhood the sun and moon, those opposite reigning powers, I just as easily assumed rose in east and west respectively in their opposite sides of the sky, and like partners in a reel they advanced, sun from the east, moon from the west, crossed over (when I wasn't looking) and went down on the other side. My father couldn't have known I believed that when, bending behind me and guiding my shoulder, he positioned me at our telescope in the front yard and, with careful adjustment of the focus, brought the moon close to me.

The night sky over my childhood Jackson was velvety black. I could see the full constellations in it and call their names; when I could read, I knew their myths. Though I was always waked for eclipses, and indeed carried to the window as an infant in arms and shown Halley's Comet in my sleep, and though I'd been taught at our diningroom table about the solar system and knew the earth revolved around the sun, and our moon around us, I never found out the moon didn't come up in the west until I was a writer and Herschel Brickell, the literary critic, told me after I misplaced it in a story. He said valuable words to me about my new profession:

"Always be sure you get your moon in the right part of the sky."

My mother always sang to her children. Her voice came out just a little bit in the minor key. "Wee Willie Winkie's" song was wonderfully sad when she sang the lullabies.

"Oh, but now there's a record. She could have her own record to listen to," my father would have said. For there came a Victrola record of "Bobby Shafftoe" and "Rock-a-Bye Baby," all of Mother's lullabies, which could be played to take her place. Soon I was able to play her my own lullabies all day long.

Our Victrola stood in the diningroom. I was allowed to climb onto the seat of a diningroom chair to wind it, start the record turning, and set the needle playing. In a second I'd jumped to the floor, to spin or march around the table as the music called for—now there were all the other records I could play too. I skinned back onto the chair just in time to lift the needle at the end, stop the record and turn it over, then change the needle. That brass receptable with a hole in the lid gave off a metallic smell like human sweat, from all the hot needles that were fed it. Winding up, dancing, being cocked to start and stop the record, was of course all in one the act of *listening*—to "Overture to *Daughter of the Regiment*," "Selections from *The Fortune Teller*," "Kiss Me Again," "Gypsy Dance from *Carmen*,"

"Stars and Stripes Forever," "When the Midnight Choo-Choo Leaves for Alabam," or whatever came next. Movement must be at the very heart of listening.

Ever since I was first read to, then started reading to myself, there 24 has never been a line read that I didn't *hear*. As my eyes followed the sentence, a voice was saying it silently to me. It isn't my mother's voice, or the voice of any person I can identify, certainly not my own. It is human, but inward, and it is inwardly that I listen to it. It is to me the voice of the story or the poem itself. The cadence, whatever it is that asks you to believe, the feeling that resides in the printed word, reaches me through the reader-voice. I have supposed, but never found out, that this is the case with all readers—to read as listeners—and with all writers, to write as listeners. It may be part of the desire to write. The sound of what falls on the page begins the process of testing it for truth, for me. Whether I am right to trust so far I don't know. By now I don't know whether I could do either one, reading or writing, without the other.

My own words, when I am at work on a story, I hear too as they go, in the same voice that I hear when I read in books. When I write and the sound of it comes back to my ears, then I act to make my changes. I have always trusted this voice.

PART *II*

WRITING INSTRUCTION

The Writing Instruction section focuses on two key tenets: writing as a process and the inextricable connection between reading and writing. It is organized chronologically, taking instructors and students throughout the semester, beginning with personal-based essays and concluding with text-based essays. This section offers tutorials beginning with detail, description, narration and basic academic essay structure and culminating with activities in critical reading, summary writing and integration of borrowed material resulting in meaningful engagement with texts. Activities and lessons directly correspond to the formal essay/paper (Task Paper) assignments in the Instructor's Resource Guide but can also be used on their own.

Introduction for Student Writers

In the Text

The Table of Contents is set up to help you easily find the information you need. Take a minute and browse the Table of Contents and you will find that it is organized by questions you may ask when confused or searching for guidance and information.

This first part of the Writing Instruction section guides you through the entire writing process with assignments that focus on writing about personal experiences. In this section, you will find writing prompts that will help you to formulate and expand upon ideas and topics for writing, exercises that will help you to develop detail and description, lessons that will help you to organize your ideas and formulate and develop paragraphs, student samples that you will use as models for your own writing and revision exercises that will guide you in strengthening and refining your writing. If you wish to produce the most effective, thesis-driven, reader-based writing you can, it is vital that you actively participate in all of these exercises and lessons for they have been created with the sole purpose of helping you with your essays.

This second part of the Writing Instruction section continues to guide you through the writing process with exercises in establishing content, organization and development; however, this section goes beyond these areas and introduces you to text-based writing. As a result, you will read about and participate in lessons on writing summary and analysis, paraphrasing, incorporating and explaining borrowed material in your own writing and MLA format and documentation. Text-based essays will be more difficult than previous assignments and are the assignments that truly prepare you for your next composition class and all other college classes; therefore, it is vital that you begin these papers as soon as possible, carefully complete each stage of the writing process, participate in all activities and revision exercises and ask your Instructor and peers for instruction and guidance.

This third part of the Writing Instruction section covers key areas in grammar and sentence structure to help you understand the parts of speech and how each part of a sentence truly works. Information on how to locate and correct fragment and run-on sentences and refine your sentence structure, helpful lists such as "Do's and Don'ts" and exercises at the end of each chapter direct you in competent, correct and clear writing.

This final part of the Writing Instruction section offers a Writer's Workshop model for the writing classroom. Studies indicate that students who fully participate in Supplemental Instruction, like Writer's Workshop with the use of peer tutors and mentors, have improved motivation, retention rates and course grades. If you are in a Writer's Workshop, pay careful attention to the rules and policies of the workshop for they will determine your success in this course.

Discovering the Student, Discovering the Self is structured to help take you through the writing process for different types of reading and writing assignments in a new way. With its series of smaller activities, lessons, practice assignments, outlines and models, your formal writing assignments will not seem so overwhelming. Please realize that these activities are not "busy work" but necessary activities that will guide you in approaching and completing not only the reading and writing assignments in this course but in other courses as well. You can move back and forth among these activities, internalizing and adapting these activities and processes to your own needs and the needs of each assignment.

IIa. Getting Started: Reflecting on Who You Are as a Reader and Writer and Finding Your Own Writing Process

Getting Started: If you wish to improve your reading and writing abilities and skills this semester, it is important that you first do an inventory of your experiences and attitudes regarding reading and writing. Is there something that has happened to you in the past that affects your attitudes towards reading and writing today? Perhaps your mean 5th grade English teacher has made you hate all reading and writing. Or, perhaps, you still remember the sweet and calming sound of your mother's voice as she read to you at bedtime and that is why you love to read. Are you afraid of sharing what you write? Are you afraid that your reader or teacher will not like your piece or you may get a bad grade? Or do you get a rush when standing up in front of a group of people and reading? Your feelings about reading and writing can impact your ability, but not in the ways you may think. Just because you do not enjoy writing does not mean you are not good at it. However, one of the goals of this course is to increase your enjoyment when reading and writing and have you view these activities as pleasurable and meaningful. If you are not there yet, that is OK. We will work on it. If you already enjoy reading and writing, then you can only add to those feelings.

Writing Prompts

Write: Choose (at least) one set of questions from each section—A, B and C—and write your responses to them. Please be honest and detailed. Tell stories for each set of questions.

A.

As a young child, do you remember being read to by your teacher, parent, older sibling, family member, etc.? If so, did you enjoy it? What books and authors do you recall? As a child, did you have a favorite book or character? If you were not read to, what activities replaced reading?

Describe your elementary classroom. What items were on the walls, shelves, desks and floors? Do you recall the overall mood or atmosphere of the room as well as of the teacher and children?

Was there a particular person (family member, friend, teacher) who helped or hindered your reading when young? How and why? Tell a story. Did your family members and friends like to read/write or not?

B.

How much reading and writing did you do in elementary, middle and high school? What types of assignments did teachers require? How did the assignments change? What were your least and most favorites? Tell a story.

What kinds of writing have you done in the past year both inside and outside of the classroom? In addition to school writing, do you write letters, journals, lyrics, poetry, blogs, etc.? Do you write for your job/workplace? Explain and describe.

C.

When you have a writing task ahead of you, what do you do before you start to write? Do you have a writing process? Do you have any "rituals" you follow? Do you plan ahead and give yourself time or do you procrastinate and wait until the last minute? Do you dread and fear the task or look forward to it? Why? Tell a story.

Discuss: After you have written thoughtful responses to the questions you have chosen, please share them with your classmates, Instructor and/or Writer's Workshop Leader/Student Tutor. Your Instructor and/or Writer's Workshop Leader/Student Tutor should also share their responses and experiences.

Reading, Response and Reflection: Gail Godwin's "The Watcher at the Gates"

Introduction: During the course of this semester, in both class and workshop, you will be discussing and practicing the writing process. In fact, no one just sits down and writes a perfect text. Effective writing occurs in stages and is a complex and recursive (back and forth) process. In this course, you will be learning about your own writing process and how to refine it so you can write more easily and effectively. For example, you must be able to realize your own obstacles and struggles when writing in order to overcome them. Keep all of this in mind as you read Gail Godwin's essay "The Watcher at the Gates" and take the Writing Apprehension Survey.

Read: Gail Godwin's essay "The Watcher at the Gates" in *Discovering the Student, Discovering the Self*. Please take notes while reading. Be prepared to discuss the essay and how you can relate to it.

Write: Answers to the questions below.

1. To what does the title of the essay refer? Who or what is the "watcher"?
2. Reread paragraphs 2 and 3. What is the meaning of each paragraph? What is the danger in having a "watcher"?
3. Are there also advantages to having a "watcher"?
4. How would you describe the author and the tone of this piece? How does she make you, the reader, feel?
5. Now, try to relate this essay to your own life and to your own writing process. Do you have a "watcher"? Describe your watcher and what he/she makes you do. Do you procrastinate? Do you have certain "rituals" you carry out when you write? Think about and share your writing process.
6. What did you think of the very last line? How does it make you feel? Have you or your "watcher" ever felt this way? Why?

Discuss: After you have written thoughtful responses to the questions above (or other prompts that may be assigned), please share them with your classmates, Instructor and/or Writer's Workshop Leader/Student Tutor.

· ·

Writing Apprehension Test

Complete Test:

1. 1. This survey, which is on the next page, measures your attitude towards writing; it measures how much apprehension, anxiety or nervousness you have in regard to the writing process. Please note that this survey does **not** measure your writing skill or ability.
2. Answer all questions completely and honestly.
3. Calculate your "score."

Discuss:

4. Discussion Part I: Did your score surprise you or is it what you expected? Did this survey accurately measure your attitude towards writing? Make connections between this survey and the essay "The Watcher at the Gates."
5. Discussion Part II: What questions did you answer with a 1 or 5? Why did you feel so strongly about these statements? Explain and use a story/example for support and illustration.

At the end of the semester, you will retake the test and compare your results.

Name_____   **Date** _____

The following is a series of statements about writing. Because there are no right or wrong answers, please indicate as honestly as possible how you feel about each statement by circling the appropriate number according to the following scale:

Please go to the following site to print out and complete the Writing Apprehension Test.
http://www.as.wvu.edu/~richmond/measures/wat.pdf

The Writing Process

As you reflect on your past writing experiences, assess your present-day attitudes towards language and writing and prepare for new experiences this semester, let's review the writing process. All successful writers understand the process, as a whole, but then also create their own that works for them. This is what Gail Godwin writes about in "The Watcher at the Gates" and Anne Lamott writes of in "Shitty First Drafts." When you answered earlier questions about your writing rituals, this is all part of the writing process. So whether you realize it or not, you already have one. One of the purposes of this course is to aid you in developing and refining that process. In fact, the activities that you will complete in this textbook carry you through that process. More importantly, you want to wholly understand and internalize this process and all of the activities and lessons within each stage, so you can then apply this knowledge when writing for other classes. One day, when sitting in class, at your desk, and the instructor proclaims, "Here is your writing assignment. It is due in 2 weeks. You must complete it on your own," you will be prepared to do so.

The writing process has an order but it is also a process that is recursive, which means that you can go back and forth between the stages. That is why every person has a slightly different process. And you may find that your specific progression of steps and stages differs depending upon the task and assignment.

Throughout *Discovering the Student, Discovering the Self*, you will come across statements like "no one just sits down and writes the perfect paper" and "writing is a series of choices." To help you write that (almost) "perfect" paper and to help you with those choices, we have the writing process:

Prewriting

> "He [Schiller] says it is not good if the intellect examines too closely the ideas pouring in at the gates" (Gail Godwin, "The Watcher at the Gates").

Have you ever exclaimed, "I don't know what to write!" or "I know what I want to say but I don't know where to begin!" If so, you need this stage of prewriting. Prewriting, like the name explains, comes before the actual writing of a draft. Prewriting allows you to get ideas down on paper and find the inspiration you are looking for. However, you must be patient. When you freewrite, do not censor or edit yourself and do not think about your "watcher." As Godwin claims, you may need to outsmart your "watcher" and "write too fast for him in an unexpected place . . . write whatever comes into your mind while the kettle is boiling and make the steam whistle your deadline . . . Disguise what you are writing . . . write a letter instead, telling your 'correspondent' what you are going to write in your story or next chapter." Do not worry about form and correctness. Just write and write and write some more. Your first and second sentence or idea may not be great, but that is OK—because that first and second "shitty" idea will eventually lead to a better third idea and even better fourth idea. Nancy Sommers says, "From writing emerges writing." What she means is that writing is a meaning-making process; writing will clarify and develop our ideas and help us to make sense of our writing and ourselves. Prewriting can include freewriting, brainstorming, clustering, listing and outlining. You may need to try a variety of activities or you may realize that some types work better with specific types of assignments. You may also discover that you need to revisit your prewriting activities throughout the writing process to perfect and polish your ideas and content. You want to experiment with a variety of prewriting exercises and find what works best for you. In fact, throughout *Discovering the Student, Discovering the Self*, you will experiment with different kinds of prewriting, including freewriting, listing, outlining and writing prompts.

Drafting

"All good writers write them [shitty first drafts]. This is how they end up with good second drafts and terrific third drafts . . . In fact, the only way I can get anything written at all is to write really, really shitty first drafts."

"The first draft is the down draft—you just get it down."

(Anne Lamott, "Shitty First Drafts")

Once you have established some ideas and focus, you have a starting point for the drafting process. In this stage, you will typically write a series of drafts of your essay/paper. The first draft is a rough draft where you organize those ideas into something that resembles an essay/paper but requires multiple drafts through the stage of revision. Throughout *Discovering the Student, Discovering the Self*, you will find various activities, such as outlines, worksheets and models, to help you create a rough draft.

Revising

But because by then I had been writing for so long, I would eventually let myself trust the process—sort of more or less . . . The next day, I'd sit down, go through it all with a colored pen, take out everything I possibly could, find a new lead somewhere on the second page, figure out a kicky place to end it, and then write a second draft."

"The second draft is the up draft—you fix it up."

(Anne Lamott, "Shitty First Drafts")

This is an essential, painstaking and demanding stage of the writing process and, unfortunately, it is a stage many students misunderstand. Oftentimes, instructors conclude that students do not willingly revise or are too lazy to do so when, frequently, students do not have the information and strategies to successfully revise. *Discovering the Student, Discovering the Self* provides you with both the information and strategies to meaningfully revise.

So what is revision? If you take apart the word, you will see the two parts: "re" meaning "to do again" and "vision" meaning "to see." So, to revise, you must see again—you must see your essay/paper draft in a new and more profound light. And what will you be seeing again in your essay? In this stage, you will focus on content and organization. In terms of content, you want to assess your topic and claim. Is your argument sound and developed? Have you offered support for that argument? Do you have relevant and significant details, description and narration in your personal experience essays? Do you have support and evidence from the text in your text-based essays? Is that support and evidence explained and connected to your argument? Have you answered the readers' questions? Revision requires not only adding information but may also require deleting information that is not relevant or moving around information to a more practical place in your essay/paper. Revising is difficult because you may need to take apart and reform your essay/paper. In terms of organization, you want to assess introduction and conclusion cohesion, paragraph structure and patterns of organization. Is the order of your essay easy to follow and is there a discernable pattern of organization? Do you have focused and supported body paragraphs? Does your introduction and thesis provide both interest and focus? Is your conclusion satisfying? You can see that this is a challenging stage and as you formulate questions and rethink your essay/paper, you may need to go back to the prewriting or drafting stages; this is what is meant by the writing process being recursive and not linear. According to Nancy Sommers, "The experienced writers see their revision process as a recursive process—a process with significant recurring activities—with different levels of attention and different agenda for each cycle . . . As their [experienced writers'] ideas change, revision becomes an attempt to make their writing consonant [consistent/compatible/in agreement] with that changing vision." Writing is a meaning-making process and the act of revision will help you to make that meaning deeper and clearer. If you thought that revision was just correcting sentences and punctuation, then pay careful attention to the revision strategies and exercises as well as student essay models to correctly guide you through this stage. Because revision is vital, much of *Discovering the Student, Discovering the Self* is dedicated to this stage and provides a multitude of lessons, assignments, informal and formal peer response activities and models to help you ask the important questions and make the important changes.

Editing

"And the third draft is the dental draft, where you check every tooth, to see if it's loose or cramped or decayed, or even, God help us, healthy" (Anne Lamott, "Shitty First Drafts").

"Watchers are excellent critics after inspiration has been captured; they are dependable, sharp-eyed readers of things already set down" (Gail Godwin, "Watcher at the Gates").

Once you are satisfied with the content and organization of your essay/paper, you can focus on sentence-level concerns of your essay/paper, including grammar, sentence structure, vocabulary and punctuation, and the overall "polishing" of your paper. If you focus on these areas of concern too early, you may run into "writer's block" and the problems Gail Godwin writes of in "The Watcher at the Gates." Although this stage is the "final" stage of the writing process, it is still a very important stage. Students, oftentimes, do not save enough time for this stage and, as a result, their writing suffers. Content, form and style work together to create an effective, well-defined and even powerful message and even if only one aspect is weak, then the whole message is weakened. It is always best to step away from your essay/paper after revision is complete in order to obtain distance and objectivity. Putting aside the essay/paper for a day or two is most helpful. However, if you are under a tight deadline, then step away for even an hour, do something that will get your mind off your essay/paper and then return to begin the editing stage. The Grammar Instruction and Sentence Construction sections in *Discovering the Student, Discovering the Self* will aid you in the editing stage.

Finding Your Writing Process

Now that you have read about and discussed the writing process and the individual processes of Gail Godwin and Anne Lamott, it is time to reflect on your own writing process. What do you do to start writing? Where do you think and write? Do you write multiple drafts or just one? Is your process linear or recursive? How do you feel when you write? To answer these questions, explain and chart your writing process through drawing. Represent your process, surroundings and emotions in pictures and images. Be creative and have fun!

Share and discuss: When done, compare/contrast your drawing with those of your peers/classmates. Are there aspects/features of your writing processes that you share? What are the differences? Are you surprised by others' drawings?

IIb. Personal-Based Writing

Thesis-Driven, Reader-Based Prose

If your Instructor asks you to write about a significant person, place or event, this may, at first, seem easy. You just have to tell a story. However, there is much more to this kind of assignment when you are writing it for a college writing class. Yes, you will tell a story. But you must go beyond just telling a story. What does an effective story include? One of the purposes of this kind of college writing assignment is to introduce you to college-level writing, which means your writing must be thesis-driven and reader-based. A thesis-driven essay is one that focuses on a specific claim or argument. In this case, you must persuade your reader that your person, place or event is significant. How did this person, place or event impact and change you? How did it shape and change your personality, values and beliefs? How did it help you evolve? What did you learn? You will answer these questions in your thesis and throughout your paper. This will also be a demonstration of your critical thinking skills. The stories you tell must illustrate and prove your claim. They must help to persuade your reader that this person, place or event is important to you. Furthermore, your reader does not know you and does not know who/what you are writing about, so you must be detailed in your description and narration, helping to bring this person, place or event to life and answering questions your reader may have. This is reader-based writing, where your reader, your audience, is a focus. You are no longer just writing for yourself (writer-based prose). Writing is a series of conscious decisions, so the decisions you make, from prewriting to final essay, must be guided by these concepts.

Writing Prompts to Find a Meaningful Topic

Write: Each is a separate activity/prompt that will help you to find a meaningful topic and get started on your essay/paper/Task Paper. Choose the activity/prompt that corresponds with your paper and respond.

Person: For this activity, write a letter or conversation to a specific person in your life (a person you directly know). Address it to someone with whom you would like to speak and to whom you have something important to say. The person can be alive or dead, from your past or present. Speak honestly. Tell that person what is important and what is on your mind and heart. It can be positive or negative. Perhaps you want to say thank you or you are angry and hurt and want to express those feelings.

Tell a detailed story that illustrates the relationship you have with one of your parents (or the person who has acted as a parent, mentor or support in your life).

Event: Make a list of your character traits, personality and words used to describe yourself. Now connect each of these to an event in your life. What happened that helped to create or illustrate a trait or facet of your personality?

Create/draw a timeline of important events in your life.

- Does one stand out? This event can be either good or bad (often bad events are more significant than good events). Choose one event and write about it. Be sure to include descriptions about emotions and other characteristics. Explain what it is about this event that makes it so significant. How would your life be different if this had not happened?

OR

- Are these events connected in some way? Do they show an evolution or progression? Do they reveal how you have grown and changed? Are they connected by certain people? Specific feelings? Tell a story.

Place: Where do you come from? Where do you feel safe? Where do you feel like you belong? How do you define "home"? Write about where you feel most at home. Describe it in such detail that you feel you're there. In your mind, take a walk through this place and begin with that description. If you have pictures of this place, use them to help you with detail and description.

Write about a place where you (and/or your family) have vacationed. In your response, describe the physical place and then explain why this place is memorable and what it means to you and your family. Tell stories from that place and use vivid detail and description.

Write about a place where stories are told or where a specific group of people gather to talk, to feel safe, to escape, to bond, etc. In your response, describe your physical place, what happens there and then explain its significance and meaning. Tell stories about people in that place.

Write about a place from where you have escaped or wish to escape. First describe the place, conveying your feelings about the place and the mood the place evokes. Then tell a story connected to the place and answers why you left or why you want to leave.

Discuss: After writing, read aloud your freewrite so your peers, Instructor and/or Writer's Workshop Leader/Student Tutor can respond. Every student will respond to the following questions: What do you like best? What is the most vivid description? What question do you have for the writer? What do you wish the writer would develop?

Using a Response Model to Develop Writing in a Meaningful Way

Throughout the semester, any time in this class, whenever you write, it is important to get feedback and then reflect and act upon that feedback in order to strengthen your writing. Furthermore, the act of providing feedback to others can also help you to improve upon your own writing. Here is one quick and easy model for the first stage of this process—giving feedback (and it works for most types of writing and writing assignments). After you have read or listened to the piece of writing, respond to the following questions (verbally or in writing):

Praise: Give one point of praise to the writer. What did you like best about the text?

Question: What is one question you have for the writer? Is there something you did not understand? Do you need more information? Is something confusing? Tell the writer.

Wish: What do you wish the writer would do next? Does the writer need to develop information? Take out or clarify information? Can you give a suggestion or direction to the writer?

As a member of the E-Team behind National Writing Project's E-Anthology, Brian Slusher discovered this effective response strategy in his article, "Praising, Questioning, Wishing: An Approach to Responding to Writing" at **https://www.nwp.org/cs/public/print/resource/2868**

Description and Detail: Reading and Writing Exercise

Description is vital in your writing and for it to be effective and impactful it must be both vivid and significant. Vivid means your description must create a specific image in the reader's mind; it must bring to life the person, place or event you are writing about and must utilize the senses. Significance means your description and detail must convey the importance of your person, place or event to the reader. Through your description and detail, your reader can understand the impact your person, place or event has had upon you.

Introduction: Let's look at a piece of the student essay, "A Year in the Bricks," by James A. Garrison. What do you think of his writing, specifically his description and detail?

Read: Excerpt from "A Year in the Bricks" by James A. Garrison

When I first arrived at Clinton County, I had a few minutes to take the place in. It was built in 1974, on the same site where two previous court houses had burned to the ground, and one would imagine it hadn't been touched since. The jail is in the "basement" of the court house, and is very much like a dungeon. All cold metal, and slick, gray, lacquered floors and walls giving the appearance of perpetual wetness. There are two wings in the jail with a small third wing set up for the female inmates. All three wings are separated by heavy, solid, metal doors with only a small, one foot by one foot barred window facing into the main kitchen and intake area. Each of the two main wings, ideally, holds up to 28 inmates with 7 sets of cells excluding the drunk tank/solitary cell, containing 4 beds each. Even in the middle of summer, somehow, it is freezing cold.

The beds are made of rusting steel and painted with layers of green paint, now flaking with age. They are bolted to the one foot thick, concrete walls with large, rusty lag bolts one bunk above another. The whole place never stops stinking of human waste as the only bathrooms are 1 per cell and completely out in the open. The toilets are connected to a water fountain sink abomination made from shiny, beat up steel. The mattresses on the bed are made up of some sort of green, woven canvas and if you have the bottom bunk you can usually stare up as you lay there and read all kinds of graffiti on the underside of the bunk above. Everything from tick marks counting down days, to threats to the guards, to perverted jokes, to claims of faith and promises to god about what will change if he will "just get me out of this!"

Once a week, barring any incidents, you get to go to visitation down the hall. The visiting room is more like a small, dead end hallway than a room. It has 5, semi partitioned, sections each with an old, rusty, lopsided, metal chair in it. There is a small quarter counter that runs the length of the bays in front of the chairs. In each bay there is a large, bullet proof window with a set of small, concentric circles cut into them in the middle. The glass is smeared and chipped from years of inmate temper tantrums and hands being pressed against the smooth glass, reaching out to loved ones on the other side. On the right hand side of each bay there is an old fashioned phone receiver connected to the wall with a shiny, metal cord used to communicate to the visitor through the glass. Everything in this room is painted with cold, white, chipped paint that flakes off and floats onto the counter like some mockery of snow. Appearing to those on the other side of the glass, in my mind at least, as if they were staring into some sort of terrible, slow motion, snow globe.

The whole place gave the impression that the whole building was elderly and depressed and ready to crawl back into the earth and die at any second.

Discuss: Is the description and detail vivid? What are his first impressions of the jail? How does he feel? How does this paragraph make you feel? What senses does he use? What is your favorite description/ sentence/word(s) and why? Use specific examples from the text.

Write: Now, choose a person, place or event in your life to describe. How can you attach most/all of your senses to this person, place or event? When writing your description, think about why you have chosen this, how it makes you feel and what you remember most vividly.

Discuss: If time allows, share your descriptions with classmates, Instructor and/or Writer's Workshop Leader/Student Tutor and have your classmates answer the same questions they did at the start of this lesson.

Narration: Reading and Writing Exercise

Telling a good story may be harder than you think. In fact, you do not want to spend all of your time telling; rather you want to spend your time showing as well. An effective piece of writing/storytelling has a balance between showing and telling. You might think that it is better to tell the reader something rather than showing him/her, but a reader gets more fulfillment figuring out things on his/her own. Plus, as you will see, you can get more information when showing than you might even intend. An effective narrator or storyteller uses detail and description that will further the meaning and significance of his/her topic and will possess a unique voice and create a presence on the page. Through these, the reader will come to understand the writer and why he/she is writing.

Introduction: Let's look at another piece of the student essay, "A Year in the Bricks," by James A. Garrison. He tells the story of observing inmates as they first enter prison.

Read: Excerpt from "A Year in the Bricks" by James A. Garrison

Over my 365 days, I learned that human nature, when given the right set of circumstances, can be funny, sad, predictable and even mystifying. I was ushered back into the cell area and shown what 10 × 10 dark, damp, and stinking corner I was going to share with 4 other grown men for the next year. I slid onto a paper thin, green canvas mattress, kicked my feet up and laid back on my small bundle of provided possessions. I have always been the type of person who sits back and observes, letting events, and people, flow around me like a river. I fell back into that habit here, and haven't seen anything quite like it since, short of television. As new inmates were admitted, I came to notice they went through 3 phases over what was usually a 2- week period. When they arrived they would be angry usually, desperate, willing to do anything to get out. Demanding the guards let them use the phone so they could call everyone they could think of. Trying to get friends and relatives on the outside to sell cars, houses, and electronics, anything so they could just make bail and get out of this pit. They would bang on the door to the cell block until a guard would finally come over, and they would proceed to tell them all kinds of stories about how they shouldn't be here and someone had made a mistake. As if, if the story was good enough, the guard would say, "Oh my god what have they done!?" and open the door and set them free. After they had banged, screamed, and sometimes cried themselves out, they would enter the second phase. This phase, was a phase of depression. Usually they would stop eating, not speaking to anyone, and sleep for, what was sometimes, days. The third phase was acceptance. Once they realized they were here for the long haul, and they had a chance to fall into the rhythm of the daily cycle, they would fall back into, what I assume to be, their usual selves, and personalities. How people of all backgrounds, race, personality, integrity, would all sink into the exact same cycle always mystified me.

Discuss: What is your favorite (most powerful, surprising, etc.) passage and why? Find one example of telling and one example for showing. Through this story and the writer's description, what does he learn about these men, the prison and human nature overall? What does the reader learn about the writer? What would you suggest to the writer to improve this story/paragraph? What questions do you have for the writer?

Write: Application to your essay/paper/Task Paper: Now, tell a story about your person, place or event. Use detail to enhance the reader's experience as well as to establish your own voice and purpose for the narrative. Use who, what, when, where and why to describe and narrate. Think about why you have chosen this topic, what you remember most vividly. If time allows, share your descriptions and have your classmates answer the same questions they did at the start of this lesson.

Stretching a Paragraph

"I think new writers are too worried that it has all been said before.
Sure it has, but not by you" —Asha Dornfest

Introduction: Effective writers have the ability to connect their personal experiences to others. Detailed stories and specifics are crucial for the paper to come alive and be powerful. Vague anecdotes, observations or memories will not be enough to convince the reader of your topic's significance.

Examples: Below are student descriptions that helped them to stretch a paragraph. To what senses do the writers appeal? What significance is conveyed by these descriptions? What do we learn about the event, place and person? Is there both a physical and psychological or emotional description offered by the writers?

- The sun was just rising in Taji, Iraq, and like every other day in Taji, the smell of burning trash and spent ammunition filled our noses and slowly chopped away at our souls. Our patrol base was located on the premises of an old meat processing plant. A scene of buildings you would expect to see from old World War II footage; standing but torn inside out by war, not unlike the souls of men. As usual, my crew was preparing for another long patrol.

- At Bridgewater, we tromped through the woods getting caught in thorns and fallen branches. We were laughing and talking having a great time. Then he shushed me, so I asked him, "What, did you hear something?" I took a second to listen and realized that what he had heard was moving water. We both got so excited! We had no idea there was a body of water out here, so we followed the sound of the water. We thought it was a pond but what we discovered was far from a pond. We found the 102 River. I started my way down the slippery, muddy cliff like hill. When I got to the bottom, John came down next. When we got down we saw that there was a rock bed we could stand on that allowed us to be on the river without being in water. The hills around the river were immaculate. We skipped rocks and talked for what seemed like hours. The sunset was just starting and the sun was just over the top of those hills; the sky was a canvas of color. It had pink, orange, red, yellow, and purple and it painted its way across the sky and created uneven shadows across the land.

- Shirley was five foot six inches tall, very round and had a turkey neck. Have you ever noticed that extra skin under a turkey's neck? Shirley had it. Her hair resembled that of a poodle, white and gray with super tight curls. Her round glasses sat on the end of her nose, which made her gray, squinty eyes stand out even more. She reminded me of an old librarian that was scolding you for being too loud in the library. She was wearing her work uniform which consisted of black work pants and a white shirt; however she also wore a black puffy sleeveless vest. The vest wasn't uniform standard but she always said, "I like to stand out."

Write: Your job is to transform one of the vague sentences below by adding as much as you can to create a realistic visual and mental scene. Such details that mimic the five senses (taste, sight, touch, smell and sound) would be the first step to jumpstart the expansion process when moving from one box to the next.

Step One: Pick a sentence from below.
1. I walked across the busy New York City street.
2. Every day, after school, I take the same route home, walking through my suburban neighborhood.
3. One time, I avoided the embarrassment of reading aloud by saying I had to go the bathroom and never came back.
4. Jerry was the mechanic at the service station.

Step Two: Add more detail to your chosen sentence to fill this box.

_____

_____

_____

Step Three: Add even more detail from the above, to fill this larger box.

_____

_____

_____

_____

_____

_____

_____

Discuss: After you have written thoughtful responses to the questions you have chosen, please share them with your classmates, Instructor and/or Writer's Workshop Leader/Student Tutor and record feedback and comments.

Write (Application to your essay/paper/Task Paper): Choose a vague sentence from your own essay/paper/Task Paper draft and complete the same exercise.

Courtesy of Dawn Terrick and Erica Cook, Copyright © Kendall Hunt Publishing Company

Academic Essay Structure: Introduction, Thesis Statement and Conclusion

For this course, the focus is on the structure of the academic essay, which, simply, is an introduction with a thesis statement, focused body paragraphs and a conclusion. This structure will be expected by most, if not all, of your instructors on campus and for most, if not all, college essays. Since this is the beginning of the semester and you may have questions and concerns about structure and organization, we will begin with a basic academic structure model that you can apply to most courses and essays. This model is referred to as the pyramid or triangle model and provides a plan or framework for the entire academic essay. Although this is just one model, it is effective for many different types of assignments and it is a useful "first" model when you are a beginner or just struggle with organization and structure. Once you learn the basic model and components, you can develop each component and revise it to the given assignment.

Pyramid or Triangle Model

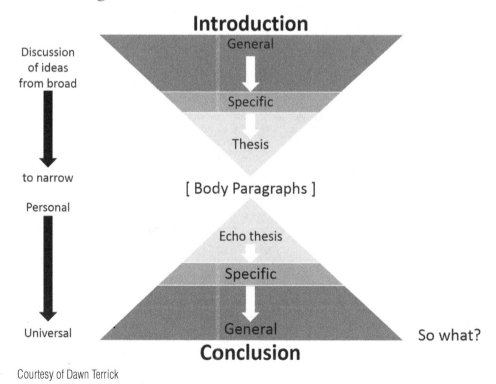

Courtesy of Dawn Terrick

Introduction

Most writing/texts have some sort of introduction, whether it is explicit or implicit, that grounds and engages the reader. A writer's introduction strategy depends upon the assignment, topic/subject, genre, audience and purpose. A writer has many options to choose from to begin his/her text but can only choose one word and one sentence to begin. This is why it can be difficult to begin and why many writers say, "I know what I want to say but I don't know how to start."

Look at how your favorite author begins his/her book or how the journalist began the news article you read this morning. How did they begin? Was it an effective start? Why or why not? The more you read, the better writer you will become because reading allows you to build your repertoire of ideas, possibilities and models for writing.

For this course, the focus is on the academic essay and the introduction in the academic essay comes with its own set of rules but even within this set, there are various options for the writer. In an academic essay, the introduction is usually the first paragraph of your paper; however, it can sometimes be longer than one paragraph and may be the first two paragraphs (depending upon the assignment, the amount of information needed, the development of the "hook" or attention-getter at the start, etc.). For this model, we will establish the first paragraph as the introduction. At this point, it is recommended to use the "general to specific" format for your introduction. Try imagining your introduction as an inverted pyramid or triangle. Begin with an attention-getter, then add a few general sentences about your subject and then become more specific with your information as you end the paragraph with your most specific sentence(s)—the thesis statement. Although this is just one model, it is effective for many different types of assignments and it is a useful "first" model when you are a beginner or just struggle with organization and structure. Once you learn the basic model and components, you can develop each component and revise it to the given assignment. As you become more confident in your writing, you can begin to look for other models in what you read and in what your Instructor provides.

"Hook" or Attention-Getter

When writing an introduction, it is important to find a way to draw your reader in. Listed below are a few common ways to grab your reader's attention. These can all be effective if used correctly. Take the time and thought to experiment with different ideas and models. Be sure your "hook" or attention-getter is appropriate to your assignment, topic/subject, genre, audience and purpose.

1. Pose a question
2. Begin with a quotation
3. Provide a surprising statistic/fact
4. Begin the paragraph with a brief description, scene, anecdote or dialogue
5. Define a problem
6. Provide background information about your subject/topic/conversation you are joining

Thesis Statement

Explanation

Have you ever seen a trailer for a movie and gotten every excited. The action, the romance, the comedy! Then, after you pay for the movie, you find out it is nothing like the trailer. The trailer was misleading or it only focused on a small aspect of the movie or just one character. You leave the theater disappointed and angry. You do not want to leave your readers disappointed and angry.

So, create a trailer—a thesis—that will both get your readers' attention (so they want to experience your essay) and leave your readers with a clear expectation and understanding of what is to come. However, in your thesis, do not "announce" or write, "In this paper I will discuss," or any similar statement.

Thesis Statement Definition and Components

A thesis statement is more than just a statement that tells what your essay is about. An effective thesis statement provides the following:

- Topic
- Claim/assertion/argument
- Focus/direction
- Mood

Examples:

Topic: For your topic, be specific. If you are writing about the farm you lived on, tell your reader where the farm is located, the name of the farm (if applicable) and when you lived there. If you are writing about standardized testing, be specific and explain what kind of standardized tests and for what grade/level of schooling.

Claim/Assertion/Argument: Your thesis must include more than your topic of the farm you lived in as a child, and must also include a claim/argument about the farm and its significance. Why do you remember that farm? What lessons did you learn on that farm? Do those lessons and experience still impact and drive you today? Into what kind of person did the farm shape you? An answer to one of these questions can be turned into an argument that you will then need to prove. Your thesis must include more than the topic of standardized testing in school. What is your claim/argument? What is your stance on standardized testing? Is it helpful or hurtful to students' intellectual and social skills and why?

Focus/Direction: In addition to your topic and claim, the thesis must provide your reader with some sort of scope, timeframe or direction. If you are arguing that the farm you lived on as a child impacted you, will you just focus on that childhood and/or your life after your childhood, after you left the farm? Will your paper cover your entire life or just a small event or portion of it? If you are arguing for a change in testing in our educational system, will you discuss only elementary school or the entire public school system from elementary school to high school? Will you discuss the impact of testing just while students are in school or the impact on their lives after school as well?

Mood: An effective thesis should also create a dominant mood, feeling or impression. Was life on the farm difficult and did it force you to do backbreaking work or was it a life of freedom in which you immersed yourself in nature? Are your experiences within the educational system positive or negative? Constructive or damaging? This mood can be furthered by your language and word choice.

An effective and engaging thesis must do a lot, so if you need to use more than one sentence for your thesis, that should be fine.

Thesis Statement Activity 1

In the following thesis statement, identify topic and claim:

Thesis: Pauly's Barbershop in South Philly was my sanctuary, where I soaked up vast amounts of knowledge that kept me off the streets and molded me into the person I am today.

Topic:

Claim/Assertion/Argument:

In the following revised thesis statement, identify evidence, direction/focus and mood:

Revised thesis: Pauly's Barbershop in South Philly was my sanctuary where, as a kid, I soaked up vast amounts of knowledge and advice that kept me off the unforgiving streets and molded me into the attentive and protective, yet honest, father I am today.

Evidence:

Direction/focus:

Mood:

Thesis Statement Activity 2

Write (Application to your essay/paper/Task Paper): Write a thesis statement for your essay/paper, following the steps listed below:

1. Write down your topic (person, place, event, etc.).
2. Write down your feelings/opinions about the topic.
3. Make a claim/argument/assertion about the topic. What do you want to prove and persuade?
4. List evidence to support the claim.
5. Rewrite the sentence, incorporating the claim and the evidence.

Discuss: Share and discuss your thesis statements as a group, answering the following questions:

1. Are they doubtable, making a claim that requires evidence?
2. What are the possible advantages and disadvantages of writing thesis statements at the start of your writing process/paper?
3. What do you do if you finish writing your paper and realize that your evidence actually supports a different thesis statement?
4. What do you do if you change your mind about the evidence you need to support the claim or the order in which it will appear?
5. How do you know if you have written a "good" thesis statement?

Conclusion

For the conclusion, you will turn around or rotate your inverted pyramid or triangle to an upright pyramid or triangle and, thus, "flip" your model. For the conclusion, you will begin more specifically and then move towards more general statements at the end. As a result, you can begin the conclusion with a focused statement or a restatement of your thesis (however, do not just copy and paste the thesis). Then, if you like, you can include a brief summary of your main points/argument/claim. This will help with the cohesion of your introduction and conclusion and, therefore, the cohesion of the entire essay. However, an effective conclusion must go beyond just a restatement of the essay. Your conclusion must answer the question, "So what?" You do not want your readers to conclude your essay and ask themselves, "Why did I just read this? "Who cares?" "Why is this important to me?" If you are writing about a personal experience, you must then move from the personal to the universal. What can your readers learn from your experiences and opinions? What can your experiences tell the readers about human nature and shared experiences? In your conclusion, like in your introduction/thesis, do not "announce" or write statements like, "In conclusion . . ."

Cohesion

Sticking together, forming a whole, everything fits, connects, supports or matches.

An effective essay/paper is cohesive because all of the parts (thesis and introduction, topic sentences and body paragraphs and conclusion) form a whole and your thoughts complete a full circle. All aspects of your essay/paper should connect and support each other. Specifically, the pyramid or triangle model focuses on the cohesion between your introduction and conclusion. In order to create cohesion between your introduction and conclusion, consider the following options for your conclusion:

1. If you are writing about a current event or social issue, in the conclusion you can place it in a larger context for your readers and explain how it effects them either directly or indirectly, how they can have an impact on the event or issue, etc.
2. If you posed a question in the introduction, you can answer it in the conclusion.
3. If you began with a scene or dialogue, come back to it and "complete" it, providing readers with a sense of closure, satisfaction, reflection and/or analysis in the conclusion.

Patterns of Organization: Chronological Order and "Before and After"

To effectively communicate with your reader, you must have a well-organized essay and that means you must choose the most effective pattern of organization for your assignment, topic, genre, purpose and audience. In most situations, people seek out order and patterns to help make sense of information and to more clearly understand and analyze that information. When readers are unable to locate a pattern that makes sense, they become confused. This frustrates readers and distracts them from your message. A sign of an ineffective essay/paper is that it takes too much effort on the part of your readers to make sense of your essay. There are many patterns of organization from which to choose and there is no one right pattern to choose. In fact, more than one pattern can be used in an essay and you may have a major and a minor organizational pattern. It is important that you carefully think about the genre as well as your claim, purpose and audience in order to locate the patterns that make the most sense in clearly and persuasively conveying your information to the readers. Writing is a series of choices and this is yet another choice to carefully consider.

Chronological Order: When writing about a personal experience, autobiographical incident, memoir or narrative, chronological order is usually the most effective because when we tell a story, we usually follow the order in which events occur. Chronological order follows the order in which the events occur. This would include an essay/Paper/Task Paper in which you write about a significant person, place or event in your life. Chronological order arranges information in the order of occurrence or according to a progression of time (from beginning to end or earliest to latest). When using a chronological pattern, each section or chunk (this can be one or more than one paragraph for each) of information represents a particular period of time.

"Before and After" Pattern: A variation of this organizational pattern involves dividing a topic into "before-during-after" sections or chunks (again, this can be one or more than one paragraph for each). Examples:

Topic: The neighborhood you moved to when you were 10 years old and lived in for the next 8 years.

Claim: The neighborhood (those who lived there, the events that happened there and the physical space itself) taught you the importance of helping others as well as the need for everyone to have a refuge from the larger, harsher world.

Order: Your major or overarching pattern of organization would be chronological order and within that larger pattern, you could then use the more specific pattern of "before, during and after."

Before: You were a selfish and sheltered person before the move to the neighborhood. During: Through description of the place and people, anecdotes/stories and examples, you illustrate how you learned about hardship and struggle and the importance of a community helping each other. After: Now, you are a selfless person with a broader worldview who helps the less fortunate.

Explanation: This pattern is a way to persuade your readers of the impact this place had upon you. If a place has changed you, it is important to explain to your readers how you were before and after this place as a way to illustrate that you grew and changed as a person, your worldview evolved and you learned new traits and attributes.

Topic Sentences and Body Paragraphs

Like the thesis statement, topic sentences are crucial to developing a successful college essay/paper. The **topic sentence** is a statement of the main idea of each paragraph. For beginning writers, most topic sentences appear at the beginning of the paragraph and are explicit (directly stated). The topic sentence, like the thesis, should include a topic and a claim and provide your purpose for the paragraph. A topic sentence can answer questions such as, "What is this paragraph about?" "Why did you write this paragraph?" "What do you want the reader to learn from this paragraph?" "What are you trying to prove in this paragraph?" "What is your support/evidence for your thesis?" The thesis statement in the introduction and the topic sentences in the body paragraphs are like the skeleton or framework of the essay and all are connected and support each other for cohesion. Topic sentences will help both the reader and writer find focus, purpose and cohesion.

In order to construct a developed and focused (or unified) paragraph, use the acronym **TEE** to serve as a guide. Each paragraph should contain: **T**opic sentence, **E**xample and **E**xplanation. Your topic sentence must be directly supported, developed and clarified by the use of examples and explanation. Be sure that you end your paragraph by explaining to readers how the example relates to your claim. Remember, you want to have a balance between showing and telling. This is the hardest part and the part that many writers forget. If you find yourself beginning or ending a paragraph with a quote, you know you are not doing your job. You must introduce and "frame" your examples and paragraphs. Remember, when "framing," the beginning and end of the body paragraph should come from you.

As you become a more sophisticated writer, you will be able to experiment a bit more with your use of implicit topic sentences and the placement of topic sentences elsewhere in the paragraph. But, remember, you cannot break the rules until you first understand how to follow and incorporate them. And do not be alarmed if your body paragraphs are lengthy or a single support stretches into more than one body paragraph. This means that your thoughts are becoming more complex and that is what we want. As long as you follow the TEE format, you will be fine.

Here is another way to understand a paragraph. In paragraph 3 of Sherman Alexie's "Superman and Me," he recalls when he grasped the purpose of a paragraph:

"I didn't have the vocabulary to say 'paragraph,' but I realized that a paragraph was a fence that held words. The words inside the paragraph worked together for a common purpose. They had some specific reason for being inside the same fence. The knowledge delighted me. I began to think of everything in terms of paragraphs. Our reservation was a small paragraph within the United States. My family's house was a paragraph, distinct from the other paragraphs of the LeBrets to the north, the Fords to our South and the Tribal school to the west. Inside our house, each family member existed as a separate paragraph but still had genetics and common experiences to link us. Now, using this logic, I can see my changed family as an essay of seven paragraphs: mother, father, older brother, the deceased sister, my younger twin sisters, and our adopted little brother."

Discuss: What do you think of Alexie's metaphor? Can you create your own? Describe and/or explain a paragraph to your peers.

Write: For this exercise, create effective paragraphs, beginning with a strong topic sentence (topic and claim), following with a detailed example and finishing with an explanation and connection back to the topic sentence. Follow the TEE model for a paragraph. It may be helpful to also use a chronological pattern of organization. *You can complete the entire activity or for a shortened activity, you can create just one fully developed body paragraph.

1. As a group/class/workshop, select a topic for this activity (or your Instructor or Workshop Leader/Tutor may select one for you). You can use a topic directly related to your writing assignment/ essay/paper/Task Paper. However, if you wish, choose a fun or "crazy" topic and be creative! Once a topic is chosen, briefly discuss the topic and the argument you wish to make about it. Have a student take notes and write ideas on the board/computer. Then craft a "working" thesis statement and place it on the board/computer as well.

2. Then, each student will be provided with a sheet of paper. At the top of each sheet of paper, write an effective topic sentence that supports the thesis. Remember that the topic sentence should have both topic/focus and claim/purpose. A topic sentence can be more than one sentence.

3. Pass your sheet one person to the right. Now, look at the sheet you have been given, read the topic sentence your classmate has written and add (at least) one sentence to the developing paragraph. If the topic sentence is vague, then revise or add to the topic sentence before starting an example.

4. Pass the sheet to the right again. Look at this new sheet you have received, read the topic sentence and the sentence(s) that has been added and add (at least) one sentence to this developing paragraph. As you are doing this, you should be writing and continuing an example (i.e., a detailed story).

5. Pass the sheet on again, and repeat this process until your OWN original sheet makes it back to you. Pass the sheet around again if your group is small. When it comes back to you, read your topic sentence and the paragraph that has been written, and then add concluding sentences to finish the paragraph (your explanation).

6. Your Instructor and/or Workshop Leader/Student Tutor will write the paragraph(s) on the board or computer screen. Listen carefully to the paragraph as it is read. Discuss the strengths and weaknesses of the paragraph and ways to revise. First look at the topic sentence: Is it specific enough and does it have both a topic and clear claim? Is the purpose clear? Then look at the example sentences: Is the example fully developed with details and description? If it is a story, is it complete and engaging? Does the example support and illustrate the topic sentence? Then look at the explanation sentences: Do they connect back to the example and offer an explanation that is more than superficial? Do they connect back to the thesis statement you wrote on the board/computer? If you answered no to any of the above questions, then discuss ways to revise and improve upon the paragraph.

Application to your own essay/paper/Task Paper: Take out your draft and focus on one body paragraph, applying what you just learned. Answer the above questions for your own paragraph. Do you have a strong topic sentence and focused, fully developed paragraph? If not, how can you revise it?

Note: This activity can be done for every Task Paper, so plan to return to it and revise it as needed.

● ●

Five-Minute Essay Outline

Complete the following outline (just jot down ideas; do not use complete sentences yet) before you draft in order to find focus and ensure that your ideas and paragraphs are developed and before you revise in order to focus, refine and develop your essay. If you cannot fill in every line, then go back and review your choices.

- Topic of the paper (person, place or event): _____
- Claim/assertion (What's the significance?): _____

Introduction

Attention-getter/hook:

Thesis statement (topic plus claim/assertion from above):

Body Paragraph One

Topic sentence/s (topic and claim):

Example/personal story:

Explanation (significance/connection to thesis)

Body Paragraph Two

Topic sentence/s:

Example/personal story:

Explanation:

Body Paragraph Three

Topic sentence/s:

Example/ personal story:

Explanation:

Body Paragraph Three

Topic sentence/s:

Example/personal story:

Explanation:

Conclusion

Restate the thesis and main points:

One powerful/important point:

Review the Structure of an Academic Essay: Workshopping a Student Essay

Read: The student essay "Freedom on the Farm" by Laura Sapp. This essay is about a significant place. Does the student prove the farm is significant to her and her family? How well does her essay fit the academic content and structure we reviewed in this section?

Living in a small town in rural Missouri would be considered uncomplicated and simple to most people. Small towns are known for their close-knit, and most are believed to be normal and safe. And there are always those few poor families who give the local landowners a steady income by renting their old worn out houses. Humansville, Missouri, had approximately a dozen rentals and my family lived in every one of them. Some were known for their special attributes such as the mouse house, the haunted house and the house on the hill. The summer I turned 16 we went beyond the city limits and moved to an old farm house about three miles west of town. That farm, dilapidated and sadly lacking in modern amenities, was the best, most liberating place we ever lived.

My father was career Army, and during my early childhood, we went where he was stationed. We went to Germany just before I turned two and then on to Louisiana when I was four. By the time I began school at 6 years old, we were back in Missouri. My father did two tours of Korea and Vietnam each. While he was out fighting wars, we settled into my mother's home town Humansville, Missouri.

We called it Human Misery as a joke, but there were times that it really felt like misery. My father was a very troubled alcoholic and my mother thought she had to take the abuse he mete out, both physical and verbal, as part of her marriage vow. While my parents were married, we got an allotment check from the Army. It was barely enough to pay the living expenses for our growing family but did afford the better rentals in town. In the early days we had more bedrooms and yard space for gardening and playing. Life was pretty normal when Dad wasn't around; my mother stayed at home and took care of us. When dad came home on leave, things went beyond normal. Invariably, there would be a happy reunion with presents for us children, kisses for mother and a few days of good times. Then the drinking and arguing would start. It wasn't long until actual fighting would break out with screaming, cursing and fists swinging. Usually the town sheriff would come and then dad would leave. Mother would cry for a while and 9 months later a new baby would come join the already crowded household. That was the routine until I was 11 years old and there were eight children with one more on the way. When mother lost the ninth child and had to have a hysterectomy, my dad left and never came back.

After my parent's divorce, the places we lived became smaller and starker; we were severely overcrowded. Mother was always looking for a cheaper, more affordable place for us to live. Often there were only one or two bedrooms, a small living room and kitchen. Every room but the kitchen was filled with boxes of clothes and beds. It was common for us to sleep three and four to a bed. The houses were usually in poor repair, drafty and prone to heating and plumbing problems. Having frozen water pipes in the winter was a way of life. We used a wood stove for heating and always tacked plastic on the windows to help keep the cold out. Mother had gone to work in a factory after dad left and we did get assistance from welfare, but that wasn't always enough. We often had our utilities turned off for lack of payment. We coped with it by hauling water or using candles and oil lamps until we could pay the bill and be reconnected.

Renting homes that were somewhat worn out and without any desirable attributes, seemed to be a way of life for my family. We moved into the mouse house immediately after my dad left. It had two bedrooms and a large living room with a sleeper sofa. The mice would come out at night and get into everything. Mother would set up traps with cheese or peanut butter to catch them and we would be awakened with the snap of the trap and know that there would be the body of some poor innocent mouse to bury or flush the next morning.

There was the haunted house that had a water stain that looked like the outline of a woman's head. My older sister Susan, told us stories about the woman and her tragic death; how she wandered the house and yard at night because she couldn't rest in peace as long as the house stood. We were all terrified until Susan admitted that it was all made up. The rain that caused the stain eventually drove us to another rental, as the leaky roof created a misery of its own.

The summer I turned 16 my mother remarried and we moved to the farm outside town that my stepfather rented for $15 a month. The owners were farmers and had cattle in the fields surrounding the property. They wanted the house occupied, so they rented it cheap. The first time I saw the place was when we went out to clean it up before we moved into it. We drove two miles out route CC and turned right onto a gravel road. We traveled a mile, then turned left onto a lane that lead over a creek and ended at a circle drive that went around an old fruit cellar; which had a chimney that stuck out of a big cement hump. The house was two stories with a front porch that faced the lane. The paint on the house was almost gone and grayish from age. The windows were blank and grayish with no curtains. The house was gray, the barn was gray, the old well and out-buildings were all gray but the trees and grass were green and wonderful! The late spring earth smelled damp from rain and the air was full of the sound of birds. There wasn't another house in sight, which meant no snoopy neighbors to watch us and tell mom on us when they thought we were out of line.

The inside was a typical old farm house. The first floor had the living-room, a large front bedroom, the kitchen with an open outside porch that faced the garden and creek. The old-fashioned well was at the bottom of the stairs that led off the porch. There was another closed-in back porch on the other side of the kitchen that had been finished into a bedroom, with an outside door that led to the outhouse. The rooms downstairs were wallpapered with old fashioned designs that had faded and were unnoticed for the most part. The floors had worn linoleum on them which required constant sweeping and mopping. The stairs that led to the second floor were enclosed and steep. The long room upstairs had a pitched ceiling; the chimney divided the space in half. The floors were unfinished wood that was dry and splintered. The windows, which were at both ends of the room, were drafty and unfinished, like someone had forgotten to put frames around them. We were excited about all of the space inside and outside. The lack of a bathroom didn't really bother us until we actually moved in and had to go out there in the dark. We had electricity in the house, barn and a yard light. We also had a phone with a party-line, which was a great source of entertainment to us. We thought we were moving to heaven!

Our first summer was an adventure of learning a new way of life. Because we had no indoor plumbing we had to draw water from the well outside the kitchen. My stepfather, Russell, thought he was purifying the water by pouring a gallon of bleach into it; but the well was shallow and a gallon was way too much. We could only use the well water for washing clothes after that. We hauled water from the area springs or from Humansville's water tower in five gallon milk cans. We took baths in an old tub on the back porch where we fashioned an area for privacy next to our own little port-a-potty, a five gallon bucket and a partition. When rain came we all ran for the soap and shampoo to take showers under the roof downspout.

Caring for the animal life on the farm was a great learning experience for us. We learned to respect the cattle that were grazing in the fields around us. Being chased by a bull weighing a half ton was not a desired past time. We ordered a hundred baby chicks and got a hundred free to fill the old chicken house. They had to stay in our kitchen in pens for a couple of weeks until they were big enough to move outside. The smell of chicken poop and the sound of two hundred cheeping chicks just about drove us all out of the house. Caring for the chickens, two dogs, two cats and the horse that Russell won in a poker game was a chore we all shared and enjoyed. The horse, Red, was green broke and a wild ride. We took turns riding and caring for him. He would take off on a wild run with one of us on his back and all we could do was hold on. It's a wonder we survived some of those rides.

My mother grew up on a farm and was familiar with living in the country and the self-sufficiency it demanded. When she came home from work in the evening, she was more relaxed and fun to be around. She showed us how to have cow chip fights, how to watch for snakes in the creek while we swam and how to plant the biggest garden we ever had. We planted plenty for fresh produce all summer and then she taught us to can what was left for the winter. I learned to cook fresh vegetables and once the chickens got big enough for laying eggs and slaughtering, we felt rich. To be able to feed ourselves without assistance from an outside source was a matter of great pride. We older girls took turns learning new recipes, which gave mother more time to spend with the family.

Each season had its share of hardships that had to be overcome or at least dealt with. When school started in the fall, we felt that our freedom had been severely encroached upon. We had to catch the bus at 6:30 a.m. We were the first on the bus in the morning and the last off the bus in the afternoon. For the first time in our lives we were able to invite friends to our home without shame. The house wasn't perfect, especially without indoor plumbing, but we were proud of what we had and excited to share it. Winter brought its own challenges, but we had the satisfaction and reward of being prepared. We had spent the summer stacking long rows of wood alongside the house. The wood stove was in the living room and our primary source of heat. The propane oven in the kitchen helped take the chill off, but not very effectively. The bedrooms got so cold that if you left a glass of water by your bed at night, it would freeze solid. On the coldest nights we would move our mattresses into the living room and camp out on the floor. When spring came it was like nature was awakening and we eagerly looked forward to discovering the changing sights and smells.

The passing seasons brought changes in each of us. We quickly grew to love living in the country where we had the freedom to spread out and actually breathe our own air. Being cramped in small houses and constantly under the eye of judgmental neighbors had stunted our growth in a way that is hard to explain. There had always been a sense of shame that colored every aspect of our lives. The trust we had for others was limited; we didn't have a lot of close friends. From the distance of time I can look back and see how the alcohol, divorce, poverty and all the abuses that go with those things, had built a prison around us, at least in our minds. The experience of learning to be self-sufficient and self- respecting was what was liberating. The place of this discovery just happened to be an old farm.

Write and Discuss: After you have read "Freedom on the Farm", respond to the following questions. After you write your responses, you will discuss with your peers, Instructor and/or Writer's Workshop Leader/Student Tutor.

Write out the thesis and explain its components. Is the thesis effective? What is the significance of the farm? Does it control the essay? Does she prove her thesis throughout the paper? Do you like the rest of her introduction? Do her first sentences get your attention? Why or why not?

Discuss detail, description and anecdotes in the body paragraphs. What do you like? Find specific descriptions, words and passages. What stands out? Can you picture these places?

Discuss the overall order/organization of the body paragraphs? What organizational pattern does she use? Although her essay is about the farm, the student writer does not write about the experiences at that specific farm until paragraph 6. This is a thought out and effective strategy—why?

Choose a specific body paragraph that uses the TEE model. Highlight the specific topic sentence(s) in one color and the example(s) in another color. Does the student writer have clear and direct ending sentences that explain the meaning and significance? Does she show rather than tell? Find specific examples.

Think about the conclusion. Does it both restate the essay and answer the question, "So what?" What did the student writer learn about herself, her family and life/human nature in general? Is there anything that you can take away from this essay? What is emotion of the three last sentences? What feelings does this conclusion evoke?

Application to your own essay/paper/Task Paper: For this activity, you will need your draft and a set of highlighters in different colors.

For Introduction:

- Highlight your thesis in one color

For Body Paragraphs:

- Highlight all of your topic sentences in another color
- Highlight all of your examples (example, story/anecdote, detail, description) in another color
- Highlight all of your explanations in another color

For Conclusion:

- Highlight the most powerful and definitive statement in another color

Now, look at your paper and make sure that you have used all of your colors. For body paragraphs, do you have a balance between the examples and explanations? Is there anything you need to develop? Switch drafts with a partner and see if he/she agrees with what you have highlighted. Discuss any places of disagreement.

Peer Response Activities

Peer Revision Sheet—Writing about personal experience

Student Writer_____ **Student Responder** _____

Directions: Switch papers with your partner, read his/her paper and write your responses below. Do this at the same time and when you are both done, read over your partner's responses and discuss your papers.

What did you like best about the paper?

The presentation of the place: Is there enough background information on the place? Has the writer effectively described the place with vivid detail, using the senses and creating imagery? Yes or Somewhat or No
What is your favorite piece of description? Write here:

Suggestions and comments:

The thesis: Is there a specific thesis that provides the topic (specific place) and the claim (significance)? Does it meet the criteria for thesis that we discussed in class? Yes or Somewhat or No
Write thesis here:

Suggestions and comments:

Go through each paragraph and list a strength, weakness and question for each. Be as specific as possible and provide suggestions where you can. Look for content and structure/organization (TEE for body paragraphs, cohesion, triangle format for introduction/conclusion). Use the back of this sheet and additional paper if needed.

Peer Revision Sheet—Writing about personal experience

Student Writer_____ **Student Responder** _____

Directions: Please circle responses to all questions and provide detailed suggestions for each. You can use a separate sheet of paper and write on draft as well.

What did you like best about the paper?

The presentation of the person, place or event: Is there enough background information on the person, place or event? Has the writer effectively described the person, place or event? Yes or Somewhat or No
Suggestions:

The significance of the person, place or event:

- Does the writer make the significance clear to the reader? Does the writer provide meaningful examples, anecdotes and details to illustrate the significance of this person, place or event? Does the writer answer the reader's questions about his/her life and the person, place or event? Yes or Somewhat or No

Suggestions:

Organizational plan:

Introduction:

- Does it have clear, logical organization? Yes or Somewhat or No
- Does it have a clear and specific thesis that controls the entire paper? Yes or Somewhat or No

Write thesis here:

Suggestions:

Body paragraphs:

- Does each paragraph have one clear topic and follow TEE? Yes or Somewhat or No
- Are the paragraphs developed and do they have adequate support (details, examples, excerpts, etc.)?

Yes or Somewhat or No

- Do the paragraphs refer back to the thesis/focus/main idea? Yes or Somewhat or No
- Are the paragraphs easy to follow? Yes or Somewhat or No

Suggestions:

Conclusion:

- Does it cohere to the introduction and to the rest of the paper? Yes or Somewhat or No
- Does it move from the personal to the universal? Answer, "So what?" Yes or Somewhat or No

Suggestions:

Are there any grammatical, sentence structure or mechanical errors that distract the reader? Yes or Somewhat or No Is the essay well edited and proofread? Yes or Somewhat or No
Suggestions:

IIc. Interviewing Techniques and Writing

The Importance of the Interview and Interview Paper

In a world that is so frantic, diverse and, sometimes, divisive, the concept of listening to people's stories, understanding their lives and having empathy and compassion are vital. We must realize that stories are history and the recording of that history is important for present and future generations. For example, if you visit the Densho website, you will hear the tales of Japanese Americans who survived the internment camps during World War II, an event in American history that is not widely spoken about and taught. What happens as these victims and heroes die? Who is left to tell their stories and help ensure that the United States does not repeat this unjust act to another group? Moreover, in a world where we are constantly bombarded with images and ideas and sometimes forget to pick up our heads from our phones, the art of conversation seems lost. How does one truly listen and engage in a conversation? What is a truly meaningful conversation and relationship? The interview process answers these questions and provides documentation and comprehension of real people's lives in all their glory and tragedy, humor and sadness.

The interview and interview paper also teach critical thinking, reading and writing skills. From the start, as you write effective questions for your interview subject, you are taking part in critical thinking. This first step can be challenging for there are many aspects to consider such as the content, wording and organization/order of your questions as well as the purpose of your interview and why you chose this particular subject. The act of the interview is also an act in critical thinking. Engaging and sustaining meaningful conversation relies on careful listening, quick response and the ability to maintain a focused dialogue and to ask follow-up questions. This skill will be even further honed as you transcribe, analyze and evaluate your interview. Thoughtful reading of the interview is essential. Since this assignment requires more than just a transcript of the interview, you must decide the focus and purpose, find a "thread" that connects the entire interview and integrate your responses and reflections into the paper. And, just think, you have not even begun to write the paper yet! Writing the paper requires you to apply all that you have learned so far about academic essay content and structure. This paper is not written as a "Q and A" but, rather, will be written like any other academic essay with an introduction/thesis, body paragraphs and conclusion. Similar to writing about your own experiences, you will be required to include detail, description and anecdotes; however, in this interview paper, stories and examples will be from your interview subject. In addition, you must now begin to think about how to effectively incorporate the words and ideas of your interview subject into your paper. Where will you summarize, paraphrase and use direct quotes? How do you ensure that your reader knows what information is from your interview subject and what is from you? This paper introduces you to these aspects of writing and researching and provides the "bridge" or transition into text-based essays/papers.

Because this assignment embodies the foundational skills of college and the workplace, you may find that various instructors in various classes and disciplines will assign an interview and interview paper. And, although, you will be asked to interview different kinds of people for different reasons, the skills you learn and the processes you complete for this assignment will be applicable to those future assignments as well.

Write: A response to the question, "Why is interviewing someone important?"

Watch: YouTube Video: TED Talk, "10 Ways to Have a Better Conversation" by Celeste Headlee, May 2015: https://www.ted.com/talks/celeste_headlee_10_ways_to_have_a_better_conversation?language=en [www]

Visit and Listen: StoryCorps: https://storycorps.org/listen/ [www]

According to the StoryCorps' website: "NPR's StoryCorps' mission is to preserve and share humanity's stories in order to build connections between people and create a more just and compassionate world. We do this to remind one another of our shared humanity, to strengthen and build the connections between people, to teach the value of listening, and to weave into the fabric of our culture the understanding that everyone's story matters. At the same time, we are creating an invaluable archive for future generations."

Go to the website and listen to some of the thousands of interviews and stories from people all around the country. You can choose random interviews and stories or search by "collections" or put in your own search subject. Get lost in their stories of hope and tragedy, humor and sadness, strength and compassion. What is most engaging about these stories and why? How did they impact you? How can you learn to write interview questions and engage in conversation from just listening?

Visit and Read: Humans of New York: http://www.humansofnewyork.com/ [www]

According to Brandon Stanton, creator of Humans of New York, "Humans of New York began as a photography project in 2010. The initial goal was to photograph 10,000 New Yorkers on the street, and create an exhaustive catalogue of the city's inhabitants . . . Somewhere along the way, I began to interview my subjects in addition to photographing them. And alongside their portraits, I'd include quotes and short stories from their lives . . . Taken together, these portraits and captions became the subject of a vibrant blog. HONY now has over 20 million followers on social media, and provides a worldwide audience with daily glimpses into the lives of strangers on the streets of New York City. Over the past 5 years, it has also expanded to feature stories from over 20 different countries."

Visit and Listen: Densho: Preserving Stories of the Past for Generations of Tomorrow: https://densho.org/ [www]

According to the Densho website, "Densho's mission is to preserve the testimonies of Japanese Americans who were unjustly incarcerated during World War II before their memories are extinguished. We offer these irreplaceable firsthand accounts and interviews, coupled with historical images and teacher resources, to explore principles of democracy, and promote equal justice for all."

Discuss: After you have watched the TED Talk and discussed some interviews and conversations from StoryCorps, Humans of New York and Densho, revisit the question, "Why is interviewing someone important?" Has your answer stayed the same, changed or just developed? If it has changed, how and why? As a class/group, make a list of reasons. How can you apply this discussion to your Interview Essay/Paper/Task Paper.

Visit these sites to help you organize your interview questions and notes

Visit: https://storycorps.org/participate/storycorps-app/: This StoryCorps App will allow you to store your interview questions as well as record and post/share your interview and photos. You will also find resources to help with writing interview questions. Check out the following links:

Getting Started Instruction Sheet:

https://storycorpsme.s3.amazonaws.com/uploads/2015/10/Getting-Started.pdf

Handouts on topics like writing good interview questions:
https://storycorps.me/about/resources/

Keywords:
https://storycorpsme.s3.amazonaws.com/uploads/2015/05/StoryCorps-App_Interview-Keywords
-form_v.5.pdf [www]

· ·

The Interview Process

Planning:

- Person-centered interview: To find out about person's likes, dislikes, background, experiences, opinions, etc. Possible interview subject(s) include family members who can provide you with interesting and engaging stories and experiences. Seek out people who are good storytellers. Remember, the stories can be positive or negative, happy or sad, serious or humorous, etc.
- Subject-centered interview: To find out about a specific topic, issue, event. Possible interview subjects include authorities in a specific academic discipline (such as a professor) and/or in a specific career (such as a law enforcement officer).
- Preparing interview questions. First ask yourself what is the purpose of your interview. Then make a list of specific questions. What about the subject's experiences would you like to learn? Begin questioning at a general level (gather background information first) and then move to the more specific. Make sure that you have open-ended questions and NOT questions with yes or no answers in order to get the subject talking. Also keep in mind the kinds of information an interview can provide better than other sources like anecdotes, strong quotes and descriptive material. Be sure you go into the interview prepared and focused.

Types of interviews: For this assignment, you will conduct face-to-face interviews (if this is impossible, then talk to your Instructor).

Setting Up Interview: Through phone call, email or face-to face interaction, fully explain your project/purpose. Set up your interview ASAP. To record the interview, ask permission prior to interview.

During the interview: Interviews are conversations so do not be alarmed if you end up not using all of your questions. Think of your questions as a guide but since an interview is a conversation, be prepared to ask follow- up questions and to just talk to your subject. Be a good conversationalist. Demonstrate to your subject that you really want to learn from him/her.

After the interview: End the interview by verifying your information. Ask if you can contact him/her with follow-up questions. Make sure that you have noted direct quotes. And always thank your subject.

Note-taking: You must use both a recorder and a notepad because a combination of both is most effective. Furthermore, you must submit a recording of the interview with your essay. We will practice, in class, note-taking techniques. Practicing on your own and devising abbreviations and shortcuts for words and phrases are also helpful. If you are organized prior to the interview and prepared with writing utensils, a list of questions, etc., note-taking will be easier.

Analyzing the interview and preparing to write the paper:

- What are the most important things you learned?
- What, if anything, surprised you?
- Can you relate to anything your subject discussed? Have you had similar or different experiences?
- What does the interview contribute to your understanding of a specific topic, issue, event, etc.?
- What questions does the interview raise?
- What information and/or direct quotes were most powerful or important?
- What do you want your readers to learn from this?

Writing Effective Interview Questions

Types of questions:

- Open-ended questions: Allow for more information, explanation, anecdotes, etc.
- Closed questions: "Yes" or "No"

Instead of asking a yes or no question like "Do you like school?" you can ask, "What past experiences, classes and teachers have led to your feelings about school?" You want to hear detailed stories and descriptions.

- Biased or leading questions: Questions that encourage a certain answer—do NOT ask these types of questions. For example, instead of asking, "Why is school so boring?" ask, "What is your opinion of school—do you find it interesting or boring?" Then, when you get a response, follow up with questions that will elicit more detail, etc.
- Questions for multiple subjects: Ask the same *main* questions.
- Wording of questions: Choose wording of each question carefully—be specific and precise with word choice.
- Fact or opinion: Do you want a fact or an opinion? Be sure to make clear in question. For example, ask, "Do you know" (for fact) and "What do you think" (for opinion).
- Write and ask questions in a specific and logical order (chronological, sorted by topics, etc.). You may want to write and ask questions in the order they will appear in your essay. Write approximately 20 questions.

- Begin with background questions: Establish that your subject is an "authority" and is credible; you may need information like age, class, race, family history if you are conducting a person-centered interview where authority is based upon experience.
- Open-ended questions that will elicit stories, experiences, facts and opinions
- Insightful and analytical questions that require reflection and explanation
- Concluding questions: Ask subject what he/she learned, what advice he/she has to give, etc.

One of the most important things you must remember during an interview is to listen. You want to not only appear interested, but actually be focused, interested and hear everything that your subject is saying. This will put your subject at ease and will impel him/her to share more with you.

You must also listen so that you can ask follow-up questions, ask your subject to clarify something you did not understand or expand upon something you think is important to the assignment. In order to do this, you must ask open questions that help elicit your subject's perspective and opinions, allow for a conversation and encourage your subject to tell detailed stories. You must also be willing and prepared to change your questions or ask new questions as the conversation moves in different directions.

*Some general open questions that encourage the subject to share experiences:

- Tell me more about the time when . . .
- Describe the people who were most important to . . .
- Describe the first time . . .
- Tell me about the person who taught you . . .
- Describe a typical day of . . .

*Some general open questions that encourage the subject to share reflection, analysis and advice:

- What stands out for you when you remember . . . ?
- How did you feel then and how do you feel now about . . . ?
- What is the most important thing you have learned from . . .
- What is the one thing you want your reader to know/one misconception you want to clarify . . .
- What advice do you have for others who have experienced something similar or know someone who has experienced something similar . . . ?
- How/why has your life, beliefs, relationships, etc. changed . . . ?

When thinking of questions to ask, make your subject your teacher. You want to learn about his/her experiences, knowledge, opinions and point of view. Think of your interview as a conversation!

Write your specific questions here:

Interview Questions Activity
After you have a draft of all of your interview questions, work with a partner on this peer response activity.

Student Writer_____ **Student Responder** _____

Read all of the student's questions first then answer: What topic did the student choose? Do you see a focus/purpose/significance emerging from the questions? Do you have any general questions for the student? Yes or Somewhat or No Write here:

- Does the student have the four types of questions (Background, Open Ended, Insightful/Analytical, Concluding)? Yes or Somewhat or No What is missing? Write here:

- Are the questions sufficient and detailed? Will they elicit enough detailed responses and stories? Are there enough open-ended questions? Yes or Somewhat or No. Provide suggestions. Can you reword/rewrite questions? Can you add questions? Write here:

- Are they in the correct/logical order? What pattern of organization has been used? Are the types of questions grouped together? Yes or Somewhat or No Help reorganize if needed. Write here:

- What other information/detail/facts/stories/questions may the student want? What else do you want to know from this interview? List here:

- Do you feel like this interview/story will interest you? Yes or Somewhat or No Why or why not? Explain and provide guidance.

Interview Practice: In-class Exercise on Interviewing

Today, you will try out your interviewing skills in class. In this interview you will be gathering information in response to these questions: What is the purpose of a college education and what goal does assigning grades serve? Are knowledge and grades connected? Your interview subject, an authority because he/she is a student and part of the education process, will provide you with one perspective on this issue of education and grades.

1. Each student will compose a short list of questions. When writing down your questions think about what kinds of questions will elicit the most helpful information. You want your questions to be pointed, but you do not want to "lead" your interview subject. You want to devise open-ended questions. Perhaps you also want to devise questions that will encourage your interview subject to tell you stories about his/her own experiences in the classroom, with professors and with grades.

2. Be sure to get relevant background information from your subject (name, year in school, major, etc.)
3. After you have a short list of questions, interview a classmate. Be sure to listen and follow up your subject's responses. *Write down at least one direct quote. Be as accurate as possible.
4. Switch roles and do the same.

As you reflect on this brief experience, respond to the following questions:

- What questions were most effective? Did they provide the responses you were looking for?
- Did you follow your list of questions? Why or why not? Did you have a discussion with your interview subject?
- Was it difficult to take accurate notes while asking questions, discussing and listening to your interview subject? Did you use abbreviations or other note-taking strategies? Would you do the same next time?
- Did you get down all information? Did you write down direct quotes? Was it accurately done? Was it an effective quote?
- From your questions and the answers you received, would you be able to write an interesting and accurate essay on your subject's view of education and grades?
- What did you learn about your interview subject and the issue of education and grades?
- What did you learn about the interview process? Was it easier or more difficult than you thought?

Interview Worksheets and Outlines

Student Writer_____

This worksheet has two parts. Complete the first part before and the second part after the interview. The first part will help you to organize and focus yourself before the interview and will help you to create the most effective questions. The second part (on the back of the sheet) will help you to organize your interview material and aid you in writing a structured, in-depth and reflective essay/paper/Task Paper on the interview.

Before the Interview: Answer these questions first. Then start to write out your interview questions. Be specific.
List your interview subject(s)—full name and relation:

Why are you going to interview this person(s)? What is your purpose? What do you hope to learn about your topic of education, successes and failures, subcultures, etc.?

How do you plan to conduct the interview? How will you record and take notes during the interview? What kind of notes and what information and details will you write down?

What are the age, background, gender, social, cultural and family background of the interviewee? How might this person's background influence his/her views?

What are your expectations for this interview?

After the Interview:
Compare/contrast your expectations of the interviewee's responses to his/her actual responses.

Where did the interview lead you? What did you learn? Did it bring up new issues? Did it help you understand more about your topic of education, successes and failures, subcultures, etc.? Be specific.

How do you plan to incorporate the information gathered in this interview into your paper? How will you organize it? What is the thesis of the paper?

What direct quotations are the most powerful and telling? Which do you want to use in the paper. List here.

Do you feel that you are missing any information, any information is underdeveloped or you have any unanswered questions? Do you need to return to your interview subject for a follow-up?

Review the Interview Essay: Workshopping a Student Essay

Questions, Responses and Activities

Carefully listen to your interview and read over your notes. Before you draft, complete this outline.

What relevant background information do you have on your subject? Organize this information and place in your introduction. If there is a lot of information, perhaps devote the first body paragraph to background information.

What are the themes, issues, topics that are discussed in your interview? List each here:

If your discussion was in chronological order and/or about an event (i.e., someone's life story about her addiction to drugs), create a timeline. Perhaps use a "before, during, after" timeline.

Can each of the themes/issues/topics and/or events be its own paragraph? Yes or No To determine this, answer the following questions:

- Is there enough information for each paragraph?
- Are there enough details in the responses or do you need to go back and ask follow-up questions?
- Could certain themes/issues/topics be grouped together in one paragraph?

Now that you have organized your interview, create "working" topic sentences for each body paragraph. Make sure your topic sentences contain a topic and claim. Remember, your interview essay must go beyond just a transcript of your interview. You must explain what you learned from this interview and include your own responses in the body paragraphs. Do NOT begin body paragraphs with a quote or an interview question. List "working" topic sentences here.

Body P1

Body P2

Body P3

Body P4

Body P5

Now, look over your topic sentences (and body paragraphs) and write a "working" thesis statement. What is the connecting thread throughout the interview? What did you learn from this interview? This must be addressed in the thesis statement.

Now, develop the idea of what you learned. What do you want your readers to learn? How can you make this person's story relevant to all of your readers? Answer the question, "So what?" This information will appear in your **conclusion.**

. . . .

Review the Interview Essay: Workshopping a Student Essay

Student Essay, "Transgender Metamorphosis"

Read: The student interview essay, "Transgender Metamorphosis," by Tori Kibbe. How can this lesson help you with your own interview and interview paper?

"I just remember going to bed that night and praying to God that while I slept, he would fix the mistake and when I woke up that I'd be the boy I knew I was supposed to be," Derrick says to me. At six-years-old, he feels like he was born in the wrong body, but at that age, he didn't even know what transgender (a person whose gender identity does not correspond to that person's biological sex assigned at birth) meant. Early on he wanted to wear what the boys got to wear when going swimming, though he wasn't allowed because his mother explains to him that he was a girl. Struggling with self-conflict is hard enough, and it is even harder when someone is struggling with gender identity issues on top of that. We all have something about ourselves that other people don't always like, but being able to be who we are truly meant to be takes a tremendous amount of courage and willpower.

Derrick, being transgender female-to-male (FTM), talked to me openly about the struggle he and his family had in his early years. He explained to me how difficult it is not being able to express these feelings clearly when he was a child. "There were just a lot of disagreements during my younger years, because what my family wanted and what I wanted was vastly different from each other and I had no way of communicating my feelings in a way for them to understand," he states. He began having a difficult time around the age that children start to form their own sense of style and are more verbal about how they feel. A six or seven-year-old Derrick, found him-self fighting with the strong women in his life. He fought with his mother and grandmother about his clothes, hair, and activities in which he would partake. He said, "Being born female and living in a small town . . . where people don't really know much about the LGBTQ+ (lesbian, gay, bisexual, transgender, and questioning) community, they wanted me to dress the way a little girl should dress." It wasn't easy for him knowing he was different. The self-conflict issues alone were hard enough, but adding his family into the situation made it even more difficult. His mother wanted to see him happy, but it is hard for a parent to grasp such a big change in their child. This proves his point that it's not just hard to be a transgender child, but its also hard being the parent of a transgender child and not knowing what they need to feel comfortable in life and with themselves.

People identify in many ways. In middle School, friends start asking questions about who is cute and that's usually when kids start to figure out where they are and how they fit in socially in society, this is just one way we identify ourselves. Growing up Trans makes it harder to label who we are. Most Trans people first identify as something else before their transition because just five years ago, being transgender was not widely publicized. Derrick tells me of the time that he becomes aware of his feelings for women, "Once I reached 7th grade and began noticing the feeling of attraction, I noticed that I'd rather sit with the boys and look at the girls. I realized then that I was attracted to women and I began identifying as Lesbian. He was living in Texas When he met someone for the first time that identified as transgender. Meeting this person was the turning point in how he viewed himself and how he would from then on out identify. Getting older made it more difficult to correctly identify himself and to be who he was, until he could transition on his own around the age eighteen. During this time, he started considering a name change. Derrick narrowed down his list to, two names and would introduce himself in the mirror with each one separately. Ultimately he states, "The name chose me and the meaning of the name Derrick, means a lot to me. I believe my name defines me as a person and my struggle."

The meaning of his name is defender and protector of men, which I feel like it fits him well. He is someone who wants to protect Trans men and women alike, while defending the LGBTQ+ altogether. Finally, being able to correctly identify/ label himself made such a huge difference.

Someone Transgender today leaves them subjected to discrimination and assault of many different forms. Someone who is transgender can become a victim/survivor of physical, mental, and sexual assault. They also have to deal with discrimination when it comes to finding a job, shopping at the store, being provided medical care, and can even be subjected to death. Derrick tells me, "I feel an incredible amount of pressure to keep it a secret or on a need to know basis because of all the risks of being openly transgender. I need to make a living and support myself and my family and I certainly don't want to lose my life." When I hear the percentage rates of the crimes against the transgender community, I can't believe what I'm hearing. Knowing that he wants to be a spokesman, to educate and inspire others outside of his Trans community, even when the death of a transgender person is 50% higher than others of the LBGTQ+ is overwhelming. He states, "I believe that transgender people should have the right to have their stories publicized. I think it's time that this country begins to understand that there aren't just two genders and that not everything is black and white." Derrick has been a survivor of being refused medical attention; he has been discriminated against, and he even had his civil rights violated by the police when his life was threatened and he was physically assaulted. The police officers said there are no laws in place, in Missouri, to protect people of "his kind'. He says to me with a quivering rasp in his voice, "The most hurtful part of today's society, is the willingness to murder someone's loved one simply because they are transgender." After someone that is Trans is murdered, they are often called the wrong name and have their gender labeled incorrectly, and then as a nation, we humiliate them even after death.

Taking action and educating our local areas helps people understand what being transgender really means, as a whole. To inform others that being a transgender person doesn't make a person any different than cis-gender (someone who's personal identity is that of their gender assigned at birth) people, they just want to be considered as an equal, just like the rest of the cis-gender population. With heavy breath Derrick passionately tells me, "The first step to resolving the ignorance of a subject is education. If I could change one view of the transgender community, it would be to help people understand that we arent freaks. To know that we are not just lesbians and gay men trying to fit in to normal society or trick people." Having him in my life I have never felt any differently about him. When I first met Derrick, I was unaware that he was transgender. To me he was and still is a man. Even after he opened up to me about himself. I never felt anything but honor to know him on a deeper level. I was happy that he was able to confide in me about his transition.

Derrick has successfully navigated through some rough experiences while going through his transition. Some advice that has helped him get through his transitioning stages is that, everyone experiences their transition differently; not one person will transition like another.

Knowing this allowed him to see that just because one person's results were one way didn't mean his would be. He needed to be comfortable with his results because his transition is his own. I wanted to know specifically what being Trans has taught him about himself. One thing he said that grabbed at me was, "Me being transgender doesn't change who I am as a person, it's my personality and my morals that makes me who I am, not being transgender." Just because

Derrick is transgender it does not make him any less human, or does it make him any less than the rest of us. His inspirational words for others of the transgender community were, "You are not alone. In me you will always have an ally, someone you can count on to try to help you through the emotional toll transitioning can take on someone." I love the way he can continue to be strong for himself and other people going through tough self-identity issues.

For me, knowing Derrick gives me more willpower and courage to continue my journey being a cis-gender Pan-sexual (someone who is open to members of all sexual orientations or gender identities). In no way, have I or will I go through as much scrutiny as he has or will. My experience with self-identity was different because even though I may get disapproving looks or people who do not agree with me, I don't have people scrutinizing me in the ways he has. The way he has overcome so much adversity to be himself provides me the reassurance I need to help him in his own journey to make our community aware of such a controversial topic. Something we both feel strongly about is that everyone deserves to feel happiness and to be comfortable with who they are. If you need support reach out, not everyone in the world is full of hate for the LGBTQ+ community. Keep fighting and if it gets hard just remember you deserve a good life as much as the next person. No one should struggle with self-identity issues alone. We all have something about us that could be a scrutinized topic in tomorrow's news.

Write: In response to all of the following questions about "Transgender Metamorphosis."

Before you conduct your interview:

- Why do you think the person interviewed was chosen? What kind of information did the interviewer want and get? What makes the interview significant? What do you like best? Do his/her experiences and struggles come to life?

- Make a list of questions you think the interviewer asked. What changes would you make? Would you add any questions?

After you conduct your interview:

Part I:

- What do we learn from introduction? Is there enough information? What is writer's thesis? Is it effective? Why or why not?

- Find the example/anecdote/detail that you like, that struck you the most, etc., and explain why.

- Find one instance where the student writer uses a direct quote and write it down. Is this a good quote? Effective and helpful?

- Find one instance where the student writer uses an introductory/signal/attribution phrase for the quote and write it down. Is it effective? Could it be more detailed?

- Does the student writer have a balance between quotes and summary/paraphrase?

- Map the essay. How are the body paragraphs organized? What is the purpose of each body paragraph? Does each paragraph follow TEE (topic sentence, example, explanation)? Is there a balance between information from the interview subject and the student writer? Is there enough information in each paragraph?

- Explain the strengths and weaknesses of the conclusion. Discuss cohesion between introduction and conclusion.

- Overall, is this an effective and engaging essay? What are the strengths and weaknesses of this interview and essay? What suggestions do you have for the writer?

Part II: Highlight different parts of the essay in different colors: 1. Thesis 2. Topic sentences 3. Quotes, summary/paraphrase and 4. Student commentary/response.

Application to your essay/paper/Task Paper: Students, now do the same with your drafts: Ask the above questions and complete the above highlighting exercise. You can also apply the Five-Minute Essay Outline to the student paper and then to your own drafts.

Note: For instruction and lessons on how to effectively incorporate interview material, consult the next section.

Peer Response Sheet for Interview Paper

Read paper and answer <u>all</u> questions. You can use a separate s heet of paper to write suggestions. Then return to student writer.

Student Writer_____ **Student Responder** _____

Getting Started:

- **What do you like best about paper? What got your attention? Do you get insight into person?**

Content of Interview:

- Is there some useful background information on the interview subject? Yes or Somewhat or No
- Can you tell what questions were asked and the responses received? Is it clear who says what?
- Is there a balance between paraphrase and quote? Yes or Somewhat or No
- Is there enough information provided by the subject? Yes or Somewhat or No

*Write here one instance where it is unclear who says what:

*Write here where there is not enough information or detail:

Introduction:

Is there a thesis statement in introduction that states the person interviewed, why and what learned? Yes or Somewhat or No

*Write thesis here and give suggestions if needed:

Structure/Organization of Body:

Does each paragraph have one clear topic and topic sentences? Yes or Somewhat or No

Do the paragraphs refer back to thesis/focus/main idea? Yes or Somewhat or No

Does writer comment and respond? Yes or Somewhat or No

Are the paragraphs easy to follow to interview subject? Yes or Somewhat or No

*Please give some suggestions for a paragraph with weak organization:

Conclusion:

Did the writer/interviewer sum up what was learned or gained from this interview/interview subject? Yes or Somewhat or No

Grammar and Sentence Structure: Is the essay free of grammatical and/or mechanical errors that are distracting to reader? Yes or Somewhat or No *List ONE weakness the writer has in this area:

IId. Text-Based Writing

Overview

We are now making the shift to academic, text-based writing, the type of writing you will do in almost all of your college classes. Text-based writing, or writing in response to a text (something you have read, watched or listened to), is the foundation for college work. As a result, these assignments for the remainder of the semester are vital. If you cannot successfully navigate this type of writing, you will not be successful in college. More importantly, the critical thinking, reading and writing skills you need for these types of assignments will aid you in life outside of college as well. In today's world of technology and social media, we are bombarded with opinions, ideas, stories and facts. But what is really true? What information, ideas, policies and actions will truly help us? How do we not allow ourselves to be manipulated? How do we discern between real and fake news? To be able to critically think through an argument or a problem will ensure that we will make wise decisions, we will not be exploited and we will be able to clearly formulate and support our own ideas and opinions. Learning how to critically think, read and write poses new challenges to all students and that is why we will spend much time practicing these skills, even before we write our formal text-based papers.

Responses to Reading: Summary, Analysis and Evaluation

Summary: Perhaps the most important step in understanding and evaluating what you read is to summarize it. Summarizing means to discuss the work's main ideas in your own words. A detailed summary should take the place of the text; the reader should, by just reading a summary, understand the author's argument and evidence. A summary is also proof to your reader that you have completely understood the text and the author's claim. An effective summary requires condensing a work into a briefer restatement of main points that does not misrepresent or distort the author's ideas. A summary does not include your opinions or personal responses. In writing a summary, be careful to use your own words and sentence structure rather than the author's in order to avoid paraphrase plagiarism. If, during a point in your summary, you do decide to use the author's words, be sure to use quotation marks. The ability to summarize is a reflection of both solid reading and writing skills. Some guidelines to follow:

- Include the title and author of the work
- Begin with the writer's thesis (in your own words) and then present additional key points (usually) following the order of the work you are summarizing

- Combine main ideas into fewer sentences than were used in the original text
- Be careful of your word choice—use specific, accurate words; avoid vagueness
- Offer no opinion

Analysis: To analyze a work is to break it down into smaller parts, to examine and understand these smaller parts and then to discover how all these parts relate to each other and form a whole piece. After you have come to understand the author's main points, you want to examine, more closely, the author's purpose, audience and language. Some possible questions to ask when engaging in analysis:

- Who is the author's audience?
- What are the author's purpose and intentions?
- How well does the author accomplish the purpose and intentions?
- Is the supporting evidence convincing? Is it reliable? Is it sufficient? Is it relevant? Is it biased in any way?
- Does the author appeal to the audience's emotions and/or reason/logic? Does the author provide facts, statistics, quotes from authority, stories? What sources does the author use? If no sources are used, then why?
- How would you characterize the author's tone? What language is used?
- Did the author address opposing ideas or views?

Evaluation: When you evaluate a work, you consider its value for yourself as a reader. Evaluation consists essentially of two different kinds of assessment: 1) a judgment about the work's achievement, including the power and validity of its ideas, and 2) a consideration of the values the work reflects or endorses. Evaluation also involves analysis.

In this course, your writings will be responses and reactions to texts. Consequently, a good habit to begin is taking notes (or annotating) while reading a text. This act will increase your involvement in and your understanding of a text. Always read with a pen or pencil in hand so that you can make marginal notes, jot down immediate questions and responses, mark what you do not understand so that you can return to it later, etc.

Steps in Responding to a Text

Step 1: Before you can offer any personal response to or analysis of a text, you must be certain you have wholly understood the author's claim and evidence. Oftentimes, it is more fun to begin with your own opinions and experiences, but when we do this, we are likely to miss some key points of the text and even some subtler claims. It is important to use a step-by-step process to ensure that you have fully understood the author so that your questions, challenges and analysis are valid. With practice and repetition, you will begin to internalize the steps and it will become easier and more organic to respond to anything you read, listen to or watch. When writing a <u>detailed summary</u> (for a critical response journal, formal assignment, etc.) follow these steps:

1. Begin with title (and specific chapter if applicable), author and specific thesis in your own words: What is the purpose of this essay/text/chapter? What is the author's argument/claim? This can be more than one sentence.
2. Include main points of argument, story, etc. being sure to explain and connect them.
3. Assume your reader has not read this essay/text, so provide background and be specific.

4. Be accurate; do not misrepresent the author and his/her claims.

5. Use at least one direct quote; introduce with signal/introductory/attribution phrase and follow it with explanation.

6. Do not commit paraphrase plagiarism; if you are rewording a statement from the author, you need to change both the vocabulary and the sentence structure but NOT the idea. The sentence(s) should sound like you but relay the author's point because you are borrowing the idea and not the words.

7. Conclude with definitive point (that connects back to thesis).

Step 2: After you complete a summary, you can complete a <u>personal response</u> to the text. You can provide your reaction to the text in terms of agreement and/or disagreement as well as a comparison and/or contrast between you and your ideas and experiences and those of the text/author. Be sure to use the text for support and illustration.

Step 3: Now you are ready to complete a formal <u>analysis and evaluation</u> of the text. Refer to the explanation and questions on the previous page. Be sure to use the text for support and illustration.

These steps are crucial for successfully completing text-based writing essays/papers/Task Papers.

Blended Paragraph Exercise—Part I

To prepare for upcoming text-based writing (i.e., Task Three), we must review and practice a number of skills: 1. Critical reading 2. Note-taking and choosing effective quotes 3. Integration of the reading/text with your own ideas and experiences. As a result, our first activity will be to write a "blended" paragraph in which you blend or integrate the ideas and words of another with your own. This process and paragraph will then provide models for you when you write an entire essay. If you can successfully write one blended paragraph, then you will be able to write multiple body paragraphs for your text-based essays. Once again, we will break down this process into smaller parts so that you can more easily comprehend and master each step and, ultimately, the entire essay/paper/Task Paper.

Effective text-based writing is *not* the act of just dropping a quote or two from an author into your own writing. Students often, incorrectly, approach these assignments by writing an essay that focuses on their opinions and stories first and then flipping through the text to find some quotes from the author to drop into their paper. To write an effective text-based essay, you must first truly comprehend the argument/claim and the evidence of the author. You can do this by first engaging with the text through annotation and taking notes. Then you can begin to make connections to that author's ideas and claims as well as question the author. You are only now ready to begin writing.

This is a complicated process, so to guide you, we will attack this entire process through a comprehensive "blended paragraph" exercise. This will then provide a model for your thinking, reading and writing processes for any text-based academic writing assignment.

Lesson One

Read: Barbara Jordan's "Becoming Educated" and annotate/take notes.

Write: Respond to the following questions and then discuss.

1. Before reading the essay, please read the blurb about the author and when this essay was written. How does learning about the author and date of publication impact your reading?

In what context will you place this essay? How do you expect her experiences to be similar to or vary from your experiences?

2. What is the thesis of this essay, that is, what is the author's claim/argument? What did Jordan learn and what does she want you to learn?

3. Summarize Jordan's law school experiences. What is the significance of "Ladies Day" and the black study group?

4. Choose one "important" quote, write it down, explain it in your own words/place it in the context of the story and then respond to it, explaining if you agree or disagree, etc.

5. What is Jordan's definition of "becoming educated"? What does she believe you truly must have and do to be educated and knowledgeable? What does she not see as being educated?

6. What is your response to this essay? Do you agree with Jordan's definition of "becoming educated"? What are your feelings towards the teaching and learning processes in high school and college? What is the role of the teacher and the student?

7. Can you parallel this story to any in your educational experience? Have you had similar struggles in learning and succeeding in college? Do you feel unprepared now that you are in college? How have you been treated by teachers in the classroom? Due to Jordan's race and gender, she faced obstacles and, oftentimes, was alienated in the classroom and by her professor. Have you ever felt or experienced something similar for similar or different reasons?

Discuss: After you have written thoughtful responses to the questions above, please share them with your classmates, Instructor and/or Writer's Workshop Leader/Student Tutor.

Lesson Two

Discuss: What is it you want to say in response to Jordan? Do you want to focus on her struggles in law school? Do you want to focus on issues of race and/or gender? Do you want to discuss the definition of "being educated" and the purpose of higher education? Write at least one fully developed blended paragraph where you address one of the above questions (or come up with your own) by blending information from the text with your own explanation and response. Use the previous questions and discussion to guide your writing. You can agree and/or disagree with Jordan; you can compare and/or contrast her experiences with your own experiences. Be sure to include the following:

1. Topic sentence(s) with claim
2. Title (in quotation marks) and author
3. Background/summary information on the essay (assume your reader has not read this essay)
4. One direct quote <u>with</u> introductory/signal/attribution phrase
5. Explanation of quote
6. Your response, opinion and experience/story
7. End paragraph with a note of analysis or explanation, restatement of the connection between you and story, etc. Be sure that the final sentence(s) of the paragraph "wraps up" the paragraph

Note: We will review parenthetical documentation later; for this assignment we will focus on content and structure first.

This paragraph will provide the foundation for the critical thinking, reading and writing you will need to accomplish in your text-based writing assignments for this class and for any text-based writing you do in college.

Review: Blended paragraph practice lessons (Parts II and III) and quoting exercises on next pages

Write: Blended paragraph

Discuss: When done, share your paragraphs. Read aloud and discuss; revise as a group; peer response with partner (PQW). Do not rush through this activity.

Blended Paragraph Exercise—Part II

Introduction: This is a very weak blended paragraph. Although this paragraph is in response to a different essay, working with this paragraph illustrates what to do and not to do when writing this blended paragraph or any type of text-based writing paragraph/essay/paper/Task Paper.

Read: The following blended paragraph

Write and Discuss: 1. Make notes on the paragraph 2. Write down a point of praise/a strength of the paragraph 3. Write down a question you have 4. Make a list of what you want the writer to work on 5. Write a response to the writer to help her revise. Use the guidelines from the blended paragraph lesson to help you.

I agree with Anna Quindlen that Connie Heerman should not have been fired for helping her students. *The Freedom Writer's Diary* by Erin Gruwell is an excellent book and it really helped her students so she should have been allowed to use the book with her class. The school board was wrong. "The members of that board were outraged by alleged insubordination when they should have been outraged by the glacial pace of decision-making by their top administrators." This reminds me a lot of my high school. Mrs. Doakes was my favorite teacher and she was always coming up with creative assignments for us to do. The entire class loved her. And it was the only class I liked. But then her boss told her that she was not teaching the right material and she needed to prepare us for the MAP tests. After that, class became boring and we spent a lot of time talking about the tests we had to take. I don't remember anything else from that class. Schools and administrators can be unfair to students and teachers because they don't listen to what they really want to do and learn.

Write responses below:

Now that you have shared your responses about the example blended paragraph, compare your responses to the instructor's response below.

Read: The instructor's comments below.

Dear student,

I can see that you are passionate about your topic and that is always important in your writing. You also have two examples that effectively parallel each and begin to illustrate the unfairness of the school system, so the foundation of your argument is valid. However, I still have many questions and you need to develop this paragraph and your argument if this blended paragraph is to be successful. First of all, what is your claim/argument for this paragraph? Your paragraph starts abruptly and confuses the reader for she does not know who Connie Heerman is. I suggest you look to your last sentence and echo that idea in your opening sentences. I would also like you to think about why it is important for school administrators to listen to teachers and students? How will this ensure learning and make our educational system more effective? If you want to go one step further, you can even make the parallel/connection between your story and the story in Quindlen's article in your opening sentences. You must also assume that your reader has not read Quindlen's "Write and Wrong" so in addition to introducing the author and title, you must provide some background/summary on the article and Heerman. Moreover, you need to explain how *The Freedom Writer's Diary* really helped Gruwell's and Heerman's students. This is a good place to add a specific story/example and quote from the article in your paragraph. What topics were the students reading and writing about? How did this help them in life and in school? You must answer those questions for the reader and to support your claim that this book is helpful. I liked the quote you chose, but, remember, every quote must be introduced, placed in context and explained. How does the quote support your claim that the school board was wrong? What does "subordination" to refer to? What did Heerman do? And what was wrong with the "glacial pace of decision-making" by the administrators. Please explain this to your readers. Once you do that then you can transition to your own story. Using your own experiences can be powerful but only if you use specific examples and vivid detail. What were the assignments Mrs. Doakes used? What class was this? Did her class go beyond just fun? What specifically did you learn? You must use details and answer these questions. Convince me that Mrs. Doakes was a great teacher who inspired her students and that without her own lessons, you did not learn as much. You make a good point in the last sentence, but I would like you to develop and clarify it. Why is it important that administrators listen to teachers and students? Will this increase learning and student engagement? Help students in their lives? Connect back to the idea of education, learning and knowledge. Moreover, at the end of the paragraph, you can come back to the connection between your experience and Heerman's experience. Clarify that because of both your experiences, your argument is valid.

Discuss: What are the similarities and differences between the instructor's comments and your comments? What can you learn from this exercise to help you with your own blended paragraph and writing for your text-based writing/essay/paper/Task Paper?

Blended Paragraph Exercise—Part III

Read: The *revised* blended paragraph below.

Public school administrators should be more flexible with school curriculum and allow high school teachers flexibility so they can better teach and inspire their students with relevant, "real world" lessons. In "Write and Wrong," Anna Quindlen writes about a teacher, Connie Heerman, who was fired for using *The Freedom Writer's Diary* without the school board's permission. Connie Heerman attended a teaching seminar with Erin Gruwell who spoke about her book *The Freedom Writer's Diary* and the success she had with it. The book chronicles how Gruwell had her students keep diaries where they could write about their challenges and problems, like drug use and abuse, and as they continued to write in their diaries, their writing improved and they became more interested in school. Quindlen argues, "The students in Gruwell's classes started out believing they might not survive high school—literally. By the end of the book, they're heading to college" (45). Heerman saw how the students' lives were changed both inside and outside of the classroom. As a result, Heerman found funds to buy the books and told her principal she would be starting this lesson. He told her to wait; she did but when she had not received any other response, she had her students begin. Heerman passed out permission slips to parents and most signed them. The students were excited. She then told the administration that she would be starting the project. However, the administration told her to collect the books and resign. I believe *The Freedom's Writer Diary* and the lessons that go with it were reaching her students and made them feel valuable and worthwhile. In fact, they all kept the book. According to Quindlen, one of Heerman's students wrote, "Who would have thought of the at-risk kids making it this far? But we did, even though the educational system desperately tried to hold us down" (qtd. in Quindlen 45). *By thinking, discussing and writing about their problems and current issues like violence, drugs, abuse and racism, students found strength and courage to be good people and students. It is unfair of anyone to deny them of this hope.* Qunidlen sums up the problem by saying, "But it's a cautionary tale about what's too often the ruling principle in American public education: the timidity and inefficiency of powerful bureaucracies far removed from the daily lives of either teachers or kids" (45). *I agree with Quindlen and think the key is the last part of the sentence. The focus should be on the kids and what they need. Do the administrators know what happens in the classroom every day? Do they know what it takes to interest kids today? Do they know they need to talk and write about these issues? No. But teachers do. When teachers are allowed to make decisions, like Gruwell, students will thrive and succeed.* **Heerman's story reminds me a lot of my high school and how it was run.** In sophomore English class, Mrs. Doakes had us read *Tuesdays with Morrie* and then she brought us to a nursing home to interview the older citizens. Louis was a fascinating man and I could not wait to write about all I learned from him. The entire class felt like me. However, when the principal found out, Mrs. Doakes had to stop the project and focus on preparing us for the MAP test. I was angry, frustrated and lost interest in class and preparing for MAP. I resisted. *Like Heerman's students and I learned, administrators can be unfair to students and teachers. If students could do work that was relevant to their lives, to their struggles and questions, they would be more interested in learning. There are many ways to teach reading and writing and administrators need to recognize this. If you want students to value and further their education, you must show them its relevance and power. Administrators should be open to new ideas and provide opportunities for teachers to test them out. Even if one student's life changes for the better, it is worth it.*

Write and discuss:

How is this revision better? What changes were made? What are the strengths of this paragraph?

What advice from the teacher did the student take? Did it help the paragraph? Did she ignore any advice? Why do you think?

What questions, advice and suggestions do you have for the writer?

Outline of Blended Paragraph:

First sentence has topic and claim/topic sentence

Full title and author of text

Summary of text and all of the key characters in the story

All quotes are introduced (underlined) and explained (italicized)

Transition between Quindlen's essay and writer's personal experience (boldfaced)

Writer makes clear what is from author and what is from her

Concludes with definitive point/claim/argument from writer and connects to topic sentence and examples (italicized)

Verbs Used in MLA Introductory/Signal/Attribution Phrases

There are many words/verbs available when choosing an introductory/signal/attribution phrase to introduce a quote. The key to good writing is to use a variety of words. The following are some words you can use to help your paper sound more academic:

Author is Neutral	Author infers or Suggests	Author Argues	Author is Uneasy or Disparaging	Author Agrees
Comments	Analyzes	Alleges	Belittles	Admits
Describes	Asks	Claims	Bemoans	Agrees
Explains	Assesses	Contends	Complains	Concedes
Illustrates	Concludes	Defends	Condemns	Concurs
Notes	Considers	Disagrees	Deplores	Grants
Observes	Finds	Holds	Deprecates	Accepts
Points out	Predicts	Insists	Derides	Affirms
Records	Proposes	Maintains	Laments	Describes
Relates	Reveals	Believes	Warns	Explains
Reports	Shows	Claims	Admits	Indicates
Says	Speculates	Confirms	Mentions	Reports
Sees	Suggests	Declares	Submits	Testifies
Thinks	Supposes	Insists	Regards	Verifies
Writes	Brings to Light	Makes Clear		
Adds	Reveals	Proposes		
Comments	Suggests	Points Out		

Quoting Exercises

Choosing "Good" or "Effective" Quotes

When writing a text-based essay/paper/Task Paper, it is vital that you not only incorporate some direct quotes into your writing but also choose effective quotes. But what does that mean? What is an effective, important or good quote? A direct quote offers evidence and support for your argument, expresses a message, theme or significance of the text/author, establishes your own credibility as a reader, writer and researcher and captures the voice, style and passion of the author. Do not waste a direct quote with basic, factual information that can be paraphrased or summarized.

Choosing just the right quotes that will establish your credibility, persuade and engage your reader and articulate the claims of the author can be challenging because it is a demonstration of your critical thinking, reading and writing skills. As a result, being able to do so means that you must start this process before writing the paper and start when reading the text. As you read, it is vital to annotate the text and take part in a conversation with the text. Highlight important passages, write notes in the margins, record questions and challenges you have about the text, make notes of ideas and words you do not understand and make connections to other texts and/or larger issues. These notes and highlighted passages can create a starting point for your writing. Furthermore, as you engage with the text, you will begin to understand it more clearly. And this will make the actual writing assignment easier.

Read: The ten most highlighted lines, on the Kindle, from the *Harry Potter* series are as follows:

1. "It is our choices, Harry, that show what we truly are, far more than our abilities." (*Harry Potter and the Chamber of Secrets*)
2. "After all, to the well-organized mind, death is but the next great adventure." (*Harry Potter and the Sorcerer's Stone*)
3. "Harry, there is never a perfect answer in this messy, emotional world. Perfection is beyond the reach of humankind, beyond the reach of magic. In every shining moment of happiness is that drop of poison: the knowledge that pain will come again. Be honest to those you love, show your pain. To suffer is as human as to breathe." (*Harry Potter and the Cursed Child—Parts One and Two*)
4. "To have been loved so deeply, even though the person who loved us is gone, will give us some protection forever." (*Harry Potter and the Sorcerer's Stone*)
5. "Always use the proper name for things. Fear of a name increases fear of the thing itself." (*Harry Potter and the Sorcerer's Stone*)
6. "Humans do have a knack of choosing precisely those things that are worst for them." (*Harry Potter and the Sorcerer's Stone*)
7. "There is no good and evil, there is only power, and those too weak to seek it." (*Harry Potter and the Sorcerer's Stone*)
8. "Youth cannot know how age thinks and feels. But old men are guilty if they forget what it was to be young." (*Harry Potter and the Order of the Phoenix*)
9. "Indifference and neglect often do much more damage than outright dislike." (*Harry Potter and the Order of the Phoenix*)
10. "The truth is a beautiful and terrible thing, and should therefore be treated with great caution." (*Harry Potter and the Cursed Child—Parts One and Two*)

Discuss: Whether you have read the books or not, why do you think these are the most highlighted lines? Why were readers drawn to these lines and want to remember them? What do all of these passages have in common? What are they about or to what do they reference (and not reference)? If you have read the books, are you surprised/not surprised by these choices? Do you remember any of these passages? Would you have chosen these or others? If you have not read the books, do they help you to understand something about the books (their messages, characters, author, audience, etc.)? How do these quotes transcend the books as well? Which is your "favorite" line and why?

Application to your reading and writing process for a text-based writing assignment. Essay/ paper/Task Paper:

Discuss: A. How does this lesson apply to your own critical thinking, reading and writing processes? How can thinking about these quotes help you when 1. annotating a text, 2. analyzing a text, and 3. choosing "important" quotes for your own writing assignments? B. Create a definition for an effective, important or good quote.

Write: Refer back to a text that you have recently read or choose a new text. Write down five "good" quotes. When you are done, share the list with your peers, Instructor and/or Writer's Workshop Leader; explain why you chose these specific quotes and/or how they could be used to develop a text-based essay/paper/Task Paper. What do they have in common with the list above? If you and a peer read the same text, did you choose the same or different quotes? Why? Are all the quotes "good" or are some better than others? Why?

Watch an excerpt from one of the *Harry Potter* movies and discuss how the plot and characters embody one of the quotes from this assignment. [www]

How to Effectively Incorporate a Quote: IQAA

I: Introduce the Quote

Q: Quote the Quote

A: Analyze the Quote

A: Apply the Quote (to your evidence, life or thesis)

Read: "Shitty First Drafts" by Anne Lamott. Find a quote that is relevant to your writing/writing process, that sticks out to you and/or that you like.

Write:

- *Introduce* the quote (In her essay, "Shitty First Drafts," Anne Lamott asserts . . .).
- *Quote* and write down **accurately** the quote you want to use. Be sure to quote exactly!
- *Analyze* by immediately following the quote with an explanation of the quote in your own words.
- *Apply* the quote to an anecdote in your own life or apply the quote to a bigger idea.

Example: In her essay "Shitty First Drafts" Anne Lamott states, "People tend to look at successful writers who are getting their books published and maybe even doing well financially and think that they sit down at their desks every morning feeling like a million dollars, feeling great about who they are and how much talent they have and what a great story they have to tell . . . But this is just the fantasy of the uninitiated." Anne Lamott is talking about the lie that discourages so many novice writers. The lie that we are either talented in writing or we are not. I feel this way at the beginning of every semester when I would sit down to write my first paper for the class. I think about all of the great essays I've read in the past or I think about the examples that the teacher used in class from past students that really stood out. I think to myself that I am no good at writing and I should just try a different career. I start to write and immediately erase everything I have written because it does not sound anything like what I view as "good writing."

Suggestion: Use introductory phrases like, "Anne Lamott suggests," "Anne Lamott reveals" or "Anne Lamott implies." Try to avoid writing, "Anne Lamott says. . . ." Be creative. Refer to the chart in this textbook.

Discuss: Each student will share what he/she wrote and the rest of the group/class will provide response and suggestions.

- Is the quote chosen important/significant? Does it capture Lamott's argument, passion, purpose, etc.?
- Is there an effective introduction to the quote?
- Do the analysis and application/anecdote fit the quote?
- Is the anecdote detailed and engaging? Does it connect to Lamott's quote and her overall essay? (Remember, a connection can be a point of comparison and/or contrast.)

Courtesy of Dawn Terrick and Erica Cook, Copyright © Kendall Hunt Publishing Company

Academic Essay Structure for Text-Based Essays: Introduction, Thesis Statement and Conclusion for Text-Based Essays

Whether writing a personal or text-based college essay, your essay structure and organization should remain mostly unchanged. This is why it is important to understand, internalize and use the information and models presented in this textbook because they will aid you as you write essays and papers throughout your college career. However, as assignments and classes evolve, so will your writing's structure and organization. With text-based writing, you are adding another component—the text—to your essay or paper. For this course and its text-based papers, you can continue to use the pyramid or triangle model for your introduction and conclusion and the TEE model for your body paragraphs, but you will find that you must stretch your models to accommodate this new information. But don't worry. If you remember the basic structure, this will be easier than you think.

If your essay/paper/Task Paper is focusing on a text (i.e., a book, article or essay), use the following guidelines to help you with structure and organization:

Introduction: You can still follow the inverted pyramid or triangle model, but you may find it helpful to also include some information about the text in your introduction. If you assume your reader has not read the text, then a brief summary of the text aids in grounding and focusing your readers. For example, after your attention-getting opening, you can introduce the topic of your essay/paper and then offer a brief discussion of text.

Thesis: If you follow the inverted pyramid model, after a brief summary of the text, you need to narrow your discussion and focus in the introduction and then end the introduction with the thesis statement. One way to accomplish this is to include the text in your thesis: title and author, claim about the issue and connection (agree and/or disagree, compare and/or contrast) to the text. Your thesis should still have the four components (topic, claim, focus/direction, mood) explained earlier in the textbook. This may take you more than one sentence and it is acceptable to experiment with this.

Read: The introduction from Chris Bennett in his essay, "Literacy in Hi-Fi," and label all of the parts of this introduction and thesis. Does this introduction get your interest? Is this an effective and focused introduction and thesis? How does he adhere to the model?

Some would venture to say that education is a product of literacy abilities. That the amount of education that we possess, our desire to possess, is singlehandedly attributed to how much and what we read. In a powerful quote regarding reading, by the late, great, Carl Sagan once said "One glance at a book and you hear the voice of another person, perhaps someone dead for 1,000 years. To read is to voyage through time." However, how does one ascertain a passion, love, or desire to read when they are not shown by their parents what the benefits can be? What if the very thought of reading scares them due to the erroneous feelings of isolation? In the narrative essay entitled "The Lonely, Good Company of Books,", excerpted from the autobiography, *Hunger of Memory: The Education of Richard Rodriguez*, Rodriguez, who at one point held jobs from that of a teacher to a journalist, who is arguably one of the more contentious writers of his time, based upon his views of affirmative action and bilingual education, recounts overcoming these impediments and finding his passion for reading. Like that of Rodriguez in his essay, "The Lonely, Good Company of Books," I was not shown the benefits of reading by my parents. However, unlike Rodriguez, I never acquired a desire to read books. Although our journeys in literacy are similar, they differ in the way that we obtained knowledge and differ in the aspect that he learned through books, and I through the polar opposite, music.

Conclusion: If you follow the pyramid or triangle model for the conclusion and want to ensure coherence in your essay/paper and between your introduction and conclusion, be sure to come back to the text. One simple way to achieve this is to restate the title and author. And as you move to the more general or universal, you still must answer the question, "So what?" What does the event or issue discussed in the text and in your own essay/paper have to do with your readers? Why should they care about this event or issue? Either directly or indirectly, you must connect this event or issue to your readers and place it in a context they can understand. For example, if you are arguing against the use of standardized tests in high school, then how will a reader who is not in school connect with this issue? For those who have children in school you can make a more personal argument. For those who do not, you can place testing in a larger context involving education. Does standardized testing hinder students' intellectual growth and thus hinder their performances as employees and citizens? These discussions will persuade *all* readers to see that they should care because this issue effects them in some way.

Read: The conclusion from the essay "Read with Purpose" and label all of the parts of this conclusion. Does she come back to the text? Does she answer the question, "So what?" How does she adhere to the model?

In the essay, "The Love of Books" by Gloria Naylor, fortunately for her she found her niche. Having the ability to read opened up writing for her as a means of expression and communication. The very simple beginning of rambling in a diary showed her the way to touch thousands of people through her writings. Her first novel, *The Women of Brewster Place*, was "first written about herself and then as a love letter to the Black Woman in America," but the book transcended across the world to other minority women including those in Japan and Korea. Naylor suggests, "You write where you are. It's the only thing that you have to give" (230). That statement speaks volumes to me as I finish my last writing task for this class and look toward the next level of writing that awaits me. The challenge is taking the time to read respectable literature, but it is vital to us as individuals and as a country. Although I may not have learned that at an early age, I am grateful for the opportunity to have learned it in college; and to learn that writing can simply be a matter of just telling your story in a way that will touch people's lives. Our aim or intention in reading should be to aspire to learn more about someone or something, and to relate to what you have learned.

Topic Sentences and Body Paragraphs for Text-Based Essays/Papers/Task Papers

Focus and cohesion in body paragraphs are even more important in text-based essays/papers due to the fact that you are now incorporating more information and material into your writing. In addition to your experiences and opinions, you must now also include the experiences, examples, stories and opinions of the text and author. In order to maintain focus and cohesion, you can still use the TEE model yet in an expanded version. Within this TEE model, you will once again choose an organizational pattern(s) that will effectively convey all of this information to your reader in a structured and meaningful way.

Patterns of Organization: Comparison/Contrast and Point by Point

If you are **comparing and/or contrasting** your experiences and opinions with one of the authors/texts, you can use a **block or a point-by-point (or alternating) organizational pattern** for your body paragraphs. Here, the focus will be on the **point-by-point method**. With the point-by-point or alternating pattern, you, the writer, move back and forth between the two things, in this case the text and you. The two things are compared and contrasted point by point or characteristic by characteristic.

Model 1:

Body Paragraph: Topic or Point 1

Text

You

Body Paragraph: Topic or Point 2

Text

You

OR

Model 2:

Body Paragraph: Topic or Point 1

      Text

Body Paragraph: Topic or Point 1

      You

Body Paragraph: Topic or Point 2

      Text

Body Paragraph: Topic or Point 2

      You

  If you use a point-by-point organizational pattern for your paper, be sure to be consistent and, within the paper, always use the same model (all body paragraphs contain information from both you and the text OR all body paragraphs keep the information from you and the text separate) and the same order (if the first body paragraph begins with information from the text, then each, subsequent body paragraph should as well).

TEE Using the Point-By-Point Model 1:

Topic Sentence:	Topic or Point 1 with claim
Example:	Example from the text and example from you (as detail, evidence and support)
Explanation:	Explain the significance of the topic and claim AND the connection between you and the text/author
Topic Sentence:	If you want to take this model one step further, you can develop the topic sentence to include both the topic and claim AND the connection between you and the text/author.

Example of Model 1:

  <u>(T) Masculinity is a social construct and, therefore, is learned. Unfortunately, in our American society, masculinity is commonly defined as strong, violent, overprotective and emotionless. One way males learn this stereotype of being a "real" man is through role models they look up to in their life. My father made bad decisions as a result of living up to male stereotypes embodied by a family member much like Wes 2.</u> **(Example from writer)** My father revealed to me that most of what he learned about being a man was what he saw his father do growing up. My father learned to never back down, like Wes 2, but that resulted in my father solving his problems with violence. As a child, my father witnessed his father's angry outbursts whenever someone questioned or challenged him. One day, in elementary school, a classmate made fun of me and I went home and told my dad. The next night, we went over to the kid's house and I watched as my dad beat up the boy's father as a way to teach him a lesson to never disrespect his family. My father was proud of this and told me that is the way a man protects his family. Because my father witnessed violence in the family as a child, that violence continued when he had his own family. **(Example from text)** Similarly, the other Wes, in the book *The Other Wes Moore*, emulated his big brother Tony because he didn't have a father around. Tony was a cruel and powerful drug dealer. Tony could have anything he wanted and was well respected in the streets. The author explains, "Tony's dead-eyed ruthlessness inspired fear" (Moore 27). Wes 2 thought of Tony as a "certified gangsta" and a real man who got everything he wanted (Moore 27). Moore tells us that Tony got into a shooting with some boys over a corner and

needless to say it became his corner. Wes saw Tony's power, freedom and wealth as the equivalent to being a "man" and Wes wanted to be a man as well. The author explains, "Tony was the closest thing Wes had to a role model, but the more he tried to be like his brother, the more his brother rejected him" (Moore 72). Even though Tony encouraged Wes to attend school and find his own path, Wes 2 followed Tony's path of drugs and violence. According to the author, Moore, "[Tony's] façade is just a way to hide a deeper pain" (28). This pain is Tony's struggle with what it means to be a man. And Wes's actions prove that the actions of role models are powerful; for males this is one way they learn about masculinity and what they think it means to be a man. **(Explanation)** Just like my father's father, Tony was not a good role model to show Wes how to be a positive and productive man. For a male to do better, he needs positive role models who challenge the traditional idea of masculinity. These negative traits of masculinity, when passed down and learned, can be harmful and lead someone to go down a dangerous path.

TEE Using the Point-By-Point Model 2:

Topic Sentence:	Topic or Point 1 with claim
Example:	Example from the text (as detail, evidence and support)
Explanation:	Explain the significance of the topic and claim (and the connection between you and the text/author)
Topic Sentence:	Topic or Point 1 with claim
Example:	Example from you (as detail, evidence and support)
Explanation:	Explain the significance of the topic and claim (and the connection between you and the text/author)

Example of Model 2:

(T)For Wes 1, the author, having **a strong support system** and positive aspects in his life resulted in his success. With the support of the Valley Forge Military School, he made a turn for the good. **(Example from text)** As Wes states, "With the support of people like Cadet Captain Hill and the others in my chain of command and on the faculty, I'd actually started to enjoy military school" (Moore 115). Wes 1 looks up to Cadet Captain Hill as a role model because he was the one who took Wes under his wing and showed him respect and trust. Wes admired him for commanding respect of the other cadets and for acting like a mature adult. With Wes underneath Captain Hill's wing, Wes began to excel in academic life as well as the ranks of military school. Wes explains that he gets this book called the *Fab Five* by Mitch Albom. It's about five freshman starters who made it all the way to the national championship game. This was Wes 1's favorite book and he now enjoyed reading. Wes 1 states, "Just as military school had slowly grown on me, so had academic life" (Moore 130). Even though it's a book it gives him the courage to continue to do well, so he can have a future. **(Explanation)**With the support offered by military school and all of those people and opportunities within the school, Wes completes a turning point and is now headed in a successful and positive direction.

(T)However, the other Wes (Wes 2), **lacks positive support systems** and this ultimately leads to his destruction. **(Example from text)** Wes 2 began to get heavier into the drug game. He got his girlfriend Alicia pregnant and considering he didn't have any father figure in his life, he didn't really yearn for a relationship with his girlfriend and baby. Wes 2 left his first girlfriend Alicia and went to another woman named Cheryl and had two more babies, but he left her because she began to do drugs. Then Wes 2 got out the drug game and went to Job Corps. As Wes states, "After agonizing over it, Wes decided to go with Levy to his final Job Corps interview. While there, Wes sat down with a counselor and began a conversation" (Moore 140). Because his job wasn't supporting him financially, Wes did not have the patience to wait and he couldn't make ends meet and live off the low budget job. Even though he earned his degree, he decided to go back to the drug game, because he had no positive role models and no support from family and friends. He did not see anyone in his family or neighborhood with a "real" job or anyone who worked hard and struggled for an honest life. He followed in the footsteps of his drug dealing, gang member brother. Tony and Wes 2 decided to rob a jewelry store. Then they ended up killing a police officer. Then Wes 2 and his brother Tony ended up going on trial for murder. **(Explanation)** Because Wes 2 didn't have any support system and had no one to help him make good decisions, he ended up in jail for the rest of his life.

<u>(T)When I was a freshman in high school, I began to get in trouble and got into some altercations with my peers. But I had a guidance counselor, Ms. Patten, who would talk to me and help me to understand why I was resorting to fighting and how I could find more productive ways to deal with my anger. She was **my support system**</u>. **(Example from writer)** I had a lot going on at that time in my life and my family issues were affecting my behavior and my school work. I remember sitting in Ms. Patten's cluttered but comforting office as she explained to me, "Your mother is always going to be your mother, so that means you will have to deal with her for the rest of your life regardless if you like it or not. It will not only help you now but in the future if you learn positive ways to cope with your arguments rather than resorting to violence. Talking to someone like me or, perhaps, writing in a journal, are constructive things you can do. These will help you to understand the differences between you and your mother and how to resolve them." With the help of Ms. Patten, I stopped fighting and even began to do better in school. She is one of my role models and the reason I am in college. **(Explanation)** Without her, I may have given in to the negative people and pressures in my life and never learned to process my anger. Her guidance, support and desire to truly listen and help me have resulted in my successes in high school and now in college.

Framing: All quotes and paraphrases from the text/author should be framed, which means that they are part of the example and placed in context and explained by your topic sentence(s) and explanation. You should never begin or end a body paragraph with a quote.

For another way to envision a paragraph, see **the Paragraph Sandwich Model**:
https://www.google.com/search?q=paragraph+sandwich+understanding+rhetoric&rlz=1C1RUCY_en US708US708&tbm=isch&tbo=u&source=univ&sa=X&ved=0ahUKEwix6eT7sM_UAhUFyoMKH WhJDi4QsAQIMw&biw=1600&bih=794#imgrc=K9YFLRc8SENwhM:

Practice with Topic Sentences, Body Paragraphs and Patterns for Organization for Text-Based Essay/Papers/Task Papers

Discuss: Since the quotes and facts are about plastic surgery, discuss the topic of plastic surgery (different kinds, reasons for it, your views/stance, what is says about our culture/society, importance of appearance and youth in today's society, etc.) to help generate ideas and insights about the topic as well as possible approaches and claims for your body paragraph.

Write: For this exercise, create a fully developed paragraph (refer to the TEE and blended paragraph models) using the quotes and facts provided (you do not have to use all). Students must create a topic sentence(s) that states a claim/argument that connects the quotes, then provide a lead in and introductory/signal/attribution phrase for each quote. An explanation must follow each quote as well. Also include your own opinions, reactions and relevant experiences. To conclude the paragraph, students must end with a closing statement(s) that echoes the topic sentence, makes a claim/argument and "wraps up" the entire paragraph.

This activity can be done like the topic sentence activity from earlier in the semester (one student writes the first sentence, then passes it onto the next student who writes the second sentence, etc., until the paragraph is complete) or can be completed individually or even with a partner.
Note: Students can make up/add to the information (name, title, source, etc.) for the introductory/signal/attribution phrases. Be detailed and creative! Have fun!
From "All I Want for Christmas is a Brand-New Face" by Rebecca Dana on page 47.

Quotes:

from a plastic surgeon: "Plastic surgery may allow you to stay competitive. A lot of people feel like at least it allows them to make money and stay in the game."

from another plastic surgeon: "My calendar is booked for 3 months and in a 4-week period, I'll perform a dozen breast augmentations, 11 liposuctions and eight tummy tucks."

a 59-year-old who received plastic surgery: "There are pressures to look young in the workplace."

a 24-year-old who is getting a tummy tuck: "I want a new life, a new abdomen and a new self-image. I'll just feel very svelte and happy."

Facts:

Between 2009 and 2010, Americans spent 3.8 percent less on food, 2 percent less on housing, 1.4 percent less on clothes and 7 percent less on entertainment. At the same time, 5.1 percent more on lipo, 8.1 percent more on eyelid surgery and a whopping 24.4 percent more on butt lifts.

The average American income during this time period fell 0.6 percent.

Discuss: When done, the completed paragraph(s) will be posted on the board/computer screen and discussed.

• •

Getting Started for a Text-Based Writing Assignment: Joining a Conversation

Introduction: For your text-based writing assignment, you will need to make an argument regarding a specific topic/issue that you have read about from at least one of the authors, using the text(s) and your own experiences as evidence for your argument. What conversation do you want to join? Answer the following questions in a thoughtful manner, being as specific as possible and using examples where needed. If you need help getting started, see the example that follows.

Write: Respond to all of the following questions:

What topic/issue do you wish to explore in your paper and why?

What are your views/claims on this topic/issue?

From where are you getting your views and claims? From your own experiences, news articles and shows, books, magazines, social media, family, friends? Be specific. Which sources are the most credible?

What text(s) will you use? What does the author (or authors) claim about this topic/issue? Find examples and passages in the text. Do you agree and/or disagree with the author? Are your experiences and observations similar and/or different?

Note: If you cannot decide upon a text, write in response to multiple texts and use this activity to help you decide and find a focus.

Example:

Read: The example below.

What topic/issue do you wish to explore in your paper and why? I wish to explore the topic of gender inequality, gender stereotypes and how girls and young women are treated differently than boys and young men. I have three brothers and as I was growing up, they had way more freedom than I had. I was very restricted as to the kinds of toys I could play with, the TV shows I could watch, the books I could read. My parents would say things like, "Sports are not appropriate for a young girl. Don't you want to stay home and stay clean and pretty?" My brothers were able to explore and have fun. Now that we are all grown up, they are fearless, travel and went away to college. I am shy, live at home with my parents and go to college in my hometown.

What are your views/claims on this topic/issue? I think that gender stereotypes are very unfair and limit both boys and girls in different ways. I think that teachers and parents need to be more open minded and let all children explore different books, opportunities, activities and places. I think media and advertising are to blame too.

From where are you getting your views and claims? From your own experiences, news articles and shows, books, magazines, social media, family, friends? Be specific. Which sources are the most credible? I am using a lot of my own stories and experiences (and the experiences of my brothers as well). I read an article in *People* magazine about how the tabloids shame female celebrities when they gain weight or get plastic surgery. The article said the press does not do this as much with male celebrities and they do not make as much money off of the male celebrities. I also just read an article on *Huffington Post* about the gender wage gap and that one of the reasons women earn less than men for the same job is that women are afraid or do not know how to negotiate their salaries or stand up for themselves and I can see that I would not be able to do those things either. Of course, on social media, there are a lot of gender stereotypes, shaming girls for being a slut or being fat. My family's views are different than mine and my friends have a lot of different views. News articles and statistics on wages and jobs would be the most credible. I am still figuring out what news articles and shows are the most reliable. I know social media is crazy.

What does the author (or authors) claim about this topic/issue? Find examples and passages in the text. Do you agree and/or disagree with the author? Are your experiences and observations similar and/or different? The essay I am using is Curtis Sittenfeld's "Your Life as a Girl." I agree with the author and have similar experiences to those in the essay. I relate to the confusion about growing up, becoming a woman, having sex and listening to rude comments about women. The yearbook story is an example of slut shaming. I can also relate to her going on diets and being angry and confused when her teacher didn't want her to talk so much in class. In the essay, when writing about going to boarding school, Sittenfeld writes that girls need to "make sure you're acting appropriately" and this reminds me of what my parents always told me. Another quote I relate to is "you're careful to station yourself in the back, or at the edges." I think her essay sums up a lot of girls' lives and these things continue into adulthood and make us afraid.

The Importance of the Literacy Autobiography

A literacy autobiography can be a story about one's journey with language, reading and writing and this story has many possibilities. In literacy autobiographies, people tell of their love or hate for reading and/or writing or how they learned to read and/or write. People can write about their favorite books, authors and literary characters. However, these stories do not have to be limited to the classroom and, in many instances, one's experiences with and attitude towards reading and writing have much to do with circumstances outside of the classroom. These stories include the personal but also the social, political and historical. Oftentimes, writers of these autobiographies have a contentious relationship with literacy. Literacy autobiographies can also include authors' definition of literacy in their own lives and what literacy has meant to them. In the professional literacy autobiographies you will read in your textbook, authors explain how they became writers or how learning to read and write shaped and saved their lives. You may not, at first, understand how literacy can be empowering and life saving, but once you read these stories, you will begin to comprehend these ideas in the specific and the abstract. Furthermore, to reflect our digital world, literacy autobiographies can also address questions about both traditional and modern digital literacy and what our digital world says about the different ways we communicate, think, teach, learn, read and write.

In order to be a successful college student, it is vital that you reflect upon not only the experiences that have shaped you in the past few months but also all of your past experiences, both good and bad, that have shaped you as a reader, writer, student and learner. In order to be a successful citizen, it is vital to think about literacy beyond the personal and in terms of the social, political and historical. As a result, the literacy autobiography, in many forms, is a very popular assignment from grade school to graduate school and this course and assignment encourage you to be part of this important conversation.

Literacy Autobiography—Joining a Conversation

Activity 1: What is literacy?

Discuss:

What is your definition of literacy and why is literacy important/not important?

In the digital age, has the traditional definition of literacy changed? Why or why not?

Are there other types of literacies and knowledge? Other ways to communicate, learn of current events and convey feelings and emotions? What has replaced traditional books for entertainment and information?

Do factors such as family, community and identity affect the definition, purpose and importance of literacy?

What is your favorite book (and/or type of book) and why?

What do you read other than books? Challenge yourself with this question and broadly apply the word "read" and go beyond just written texts.

Activity 2: Watch: YouTube Videos: Go to YouTube and find a Literacy Autobiography (use search term "literacy autobiography"). Then show it to your class and explain why you chose it. What is the importance of the video and of what the student is saying about his/her literacy? Can you compare/contrast your experiences and opinions to those in the video? What is engaging and enlightening? Can you apply the video to your own literacy autobiography essay/paper/Task Paper? Did the information in this video connect to any of your responses or your peers' responses to the above questions?

Activity 3: One of the things that Task Four asks you to do is to tell stories, stories about your past educational life and your journey to literacy:

- Do you remember when and how you learned to read? Did a family member, like your mother, grandmother or big brother, read to you?
- Do you remember your favorite book as a child? What was it and why?
- Did your room and house have a lot of books, newspapers and reading materials? If so, describe.
- What about that evil, scary looking grade school teacher you had that made you hate reading and writing? What did she look and sound like?

- What obstacles did you face as a youngster in learning to read and/or write? OR What is your crowning moment of glory in learning to read and/or write? Tell this story.
- Did you have reading time in grade school? What class and teacher? What did you do? Did you enjoy it? Tell this story.
- Do you have a true passion or fierce dislike for reading and writing? Think back on your childhood and find the moment when this formed. Tell about it, using details and description.

Write: Go back into your memories and find a story regarding literacy that you vividly remember. What specific details do you remember? Is it serious or funny? What emotions do you want to evoke from your audience with this story? Feel free to use the questions/prompts above.

Discuss: After writing, read aloud your freewrite so your peers, Instructor and/or Writer's Workshop Leader/ Student Tutor can respond. Every student will respond to the following questions: What do you like best? What is the most vivid description? What question do you have for the writer? What do you wish the writer would develop? In turn, the student writer will explain the significance of this memory and why he/she thinks he/she remembered this specific story?

Making Connections with the Text for Your Literacy Autobiography

Summary: Write a 2–3 sentence summary for each of the literacy autobiographies/essays you have read. Some are listed below. If you have read others, add them to the list.
"How I Learned to Read and Write":
"The Lonely, Good Company of Books":
"One Writer's Beginnings":
"The Watcher at the Gates":
"The Love of Books":
"Superman and Me":

Connections Chart: Create a chart to help you make connections among the essays and between you and the essays. Use the following criteria to help and feel free to add your own. For each topic, list what each author said/experienced and then list your own ideas and experiences for the topic as well.

Topics: Author 1   Author 2 . . .   You
Literacy and parents/family
Literacy and childhood/elementary school
Literacy and high school
Literacy as an adult
How learned to read?
What read and why?
Definition of reading, writing, literacy and significance

Five-Minute Essay Outline: Text-Based Essay—Comparison/Contrast

Author and title of the text:
Topic:
Claim:

I: Introduction:

Attention-getter:

Introduction of the text: will include the author's name, the title of the text and general summary:

Thesis Sentence: (topic of your paper, claim you are making, connection between you and text)

II: Body Paragraph One:

Topic Sentence (topic and claim/connection between you and text):

Example from text:

   Quote from text:

Example from your life/experience/opinion:

Explanation: significance; connection between text and you:

III: Body Paragraph Two:

Topic Sentence:

Example from text:

   Quote from text:

Example from you:

Explanation:

IV: Body Paragraph Three:

Topic Sentence:

Example from text:

   Quote from text:

Example from you:

Explanation:

V: Body Paragraph Four:

Topic Sentence:

Example from text:

   Quote from text:

Example from you:

Explanation:

VI: Body Paragraph Five (and so on):

Topic Sentence:

Example from text:

   Quote from text:

Example from you:

Explanation:

V: Conclusion

Restatement of thesis:

Review your main points:

One powerful point/statement:

So what?:

Review the Content and Structure of a Text-Based Essay: Workshopping a Student Essay

Read: The student essay "It's Our Choice" by Au'sha Ramirez-Quevado. This is a text-based essay in response to the book *The Other Wes Moore*.

We didn't ask to be on this earth, some random bodies decided to work together and bring forth a human being. Was it for selfish reasons, to see a little hint of himself and herself all in one little body? Was it to be loved unconditionally, but not one thought about the conditions for that promised love? Or was bringing a child into the world an accident? Two consenting adults indulging in one another, not thinking about all the people involved, you, your partner, along with the unexpected life. Nevertheless, we are now on this earth, never given a choice, a choice to choose our care takers, our environment and our skin. We are products of choices made. *The Other Wes Moore* by Wes Moore is a book about personal responsibilities and decision making, how your free will to make decisions can affect those around you, as well as your fate for the good or the bad. I certainly find this to be true, for I have had to live with the choices made by others, along with the decisions I've personally made. Yet, just like the character Wes, the author, I've taken responsibility for the actions I've made; if I didn't who knows where I would be today.

The Other Wes Moore by Wes Moore is about two boys who share the same name. Along with the same name these boys have a similar life style, being that they both live in the same neighborhood. These boys are 3 years apart, and they both don't have a father in their lives. Wes one's father had passed away when Wes one was 6 years old, leaving young Wes with a few memories. As for Wes two's father, he was an alcoholic, his father did not really care to make an appearance in his life. These young boys came across similar peer pressure, academic struggles, as well as run-ins with the law. Yet as they grew up their identical paths began to change. Wes one became successful, his success, as well as hard work allowed him the freedom to explore new places, people, and learn unbelievable lessons and culture. On the other hand, Wes two course led him to life in prison for a robbery and a murder. *The Other Wes Moore* by Wes Moore writes about what the world gave these boys to start with and how they used and abused what they had, and if and how they learned from their mistakes.

As children we have slim to none independence to make important choices. All of the possible courses of action are up to our care takers. I believe Wes two's father's choice to be a ghost in his life gave Wes two the mind set to not truly care about being a part of his children's lives. Moore assesses this further by stating, "Wes's nonexistent relationship with his father probably contributed to his seeming indifference about becoming a farther himself. All he knew was his mom. He had no idea what his role would be in this new situation—he wasn't even sure he had a role" (Moore 100). His dad's lack of responsibility and inability to be a father was a choice, and, in turn, a similar choice Wes Two made. Wes Two being a recipient of a fatherless life style possibly made him think that that life style was the only option. Ultimately, Wes became that same man he didn't know. He is now known as a ghost that is never seen and rarely felt by his children, just like his 'father' was to him. Similarly to Wes Two, I grew up with not knowing my father due to his deportation back to South America. Although he was in a different country, he did have the information needed to contact both my sister and l, but he never did. My mom would always say, "Your dad's family has my number, so there's no excuse as to why you guys don't hear from him. I've had the same number for years.' My mom was right there is no excuse, if you truly want something or someone you'll take extreme measures to see that you get what you want or who you want, but that was not the case with my dad. Like Wes Two, I imagined my family with no father, just myself as the head, the tail, and the back bone of the family. My sister Kami and I would talk about how it was unusual to think like that, yet that vision of no father in the home was okay for us. After all who needed a man? Looking at our neglectful dad and incompetent step dad as examples of a "father," we figured fatherless children would be the least of our worries. Later I came to realize that a father is what a child needs, both parents is what a child needs. To know who you come from is a great thing to have, to have both parents teach you how to become an adult is a necessity in life. I assume that is why I'm so picky when it comes to men and relationships. I'm aware of the mistakes made and the situation I was brought up in. I had decided I didn't want to relive the same life my parents lived, nor do I want my kids to live the same life I did as a child. The biggest difference between Wes Two and myself is our outlook. Wes two didn't grasp the cause and effect due to his father's mistakes, so he didn't think to do the opposite of his father's actions. As for myself, I made it a priority to learn from the mistakes of my parents and others. That little saying, "Children are like sponges" is quite true; unwillingly and unknowingly children can become their surroundings by observing the actions that play out before their eyes. Their decisions can affect their path for the positive or negative.

In the book the characters Wes one and two are growing. As they grow they're making rash decisions for themselves, causing their parents to have to choose for them in hopes to get them on the right track. If you were lucky, you may have received an intervention, like the characters and myself. This was apparent for Wes one. He was getting out of hand, he was ditching school, his grades were plummeting, and he was getting caught up by the cops, due to tagging. At this point Wes's mom Joy was getting fed-up, "She was devastated. She was losing her son, and she was not sure how to turn the tide" (Moore 89). Wes's mother finally had chosen to send her son to military school. The move to military school resulted into an attitude from Wes one, then his attitude grew into rebellion. Wes one's strike included disobeying the leading sergeant in his corridor and running away; Wes one had run away four times within a 4-day period of being there. Wes's last attempt of running away ended with him getting sent to the office to have a talk with Officer Colonel Batt. After Wes one and the officers conversation, along with a 5-minute wakeup call—literally—Wes one decided to give the place another shot. Wes one then realized what military school had to offer him, "It was a different psychological environment, where my normal expectations were invert, where leadership was honored and class clowns were ostracized" (Moore). He had realized that military school was a place where your actions determined whether or not you'll get respect and succeed. This observation gave Wes one a new perspective on his choices. In like fashion, I was ditching school, running away, and just plain bad. This outrageous behavior of mine added extreme amounts of stress to my mom. In turn, she held the same disappointment in me, as Joy did for Wes one. My mom had reached her breaking point. She didn't know what to do with me, so she would confide in my cousin asking for help or suggestions. Later my mom, along with my cousin, had agreed to send me to California to attend high school there. I genuinely wanted to start fresh and better myself, so unlike Wes one I didn't really have a problem with moving from my home town (Denver). Still after the move, it was hard for me to get used to the new rules and surroundings I was now in. Yet, I must say the new high school in Lakeport, Ca and living with my well educated, older cousins Diana and her husband George gave me a new outlook on life. I learned to be more open to people. My cousins showed me what getting an education could get you: a well off job, allow you the freedom to travel, and they also taught me that learning new things could open up door to multiple worlds with in this one. As I lived in California, I also realized what I didn't want— a small minded mentality toward different people and their cultures. Similar to Wes one's new outlook, I, too, came to terms with my actions. I became aware of the choices made. If it wasn't for both Wes one's mother and mine stepping in when our judgment was cloudy, our perception of life may have never changed for the better. Even as we grow old enough to know wrong from right and are able to choose our actions, we still need someone's help at times to guide us to a less destructive path. The guidance of others can be a great thing, but it is ultimately up to us to choose whether or not we want to work toward improving ourselves, or hinder ourselves from growth.

Becoming an adult is becoming one hundred percent responsible for yourself, which includes all that you do. There isn't always going to be someone to catch you when you fall. There's not always going to be someone to correct your mistakes, especially as an adult. As you become independent in all aspects of the word, you now must tread carefully within your decision making. Wes one found this out when he attend military school his high school year. Wes one along with his friend Dalio had decided to leave campus for a bite to eat. In the middle of their excursion they came across a couple of people in a car, who seemed to be under the influence of liquor, so Wes one and Dalio ignored these people. Soon after the run in with the drunken fools, Wes as well as his friend became a moving target for the people behind the wheel. Once again Wes and Dalio brushed it off and continued to move toward their desired destination. To both Wes one and Dalio's surprise, the guys in the car were sitting and waiting for them. Before they even noticed the ambush, one of the drunks in the car threw something hard at Wes's face, causing his tooth to become loss and his mouth bloody. Along with the violent act came an obscene remark, "Go home n*****!" (Moore 121). Wes one truly wanted to react—who could blame him—yet he decided against it. The author goes in to depth as to why Wes one withheld himself from retaliating, " . . . I had to let this go. I had to look at the bigger picture," " . . . I thought about my mother and how she would feel if this escalated any further. I thought about my father and the name [Watende-meaning "revenge will not be sought"] he chose for me" (Moore 121). With those thoughts Wes and his friend had quickly made a detour back to their school. Wes one was extremely head strong and wise when he made the decision to turn the other cheek. He not only thought about the long term effects his choice to retaliate would bring, but he also thought about the people involved, those who put their energy into his wellbeing. He also put aside the teachings of the Bronx Streets, acknowledging that what they taught did not apply to him nor the situation brought to him. He ignored the stereotypes of what a black man or any man should do in a situation like his-to fight back, but fight twice as hard. The fact that he thought about the outcome and the people he may effect, because of his actions, made him a man. In an ironic, sad way I can relate to this situation Wes one was in. During my attendance at the high School in California, I came across a lot of students who were ignorant toward race. One day in particular, I had happened to hear a female student say, "I rather be broke than black." She had repeated herself to my face twice, but I decided to ignore her—I tried. Throughout the school day all I kept hearing in my head was her words, feelings of shock, hurt and embarrassment due to the fact that I didn't do anything filled my thoughts. So I devised a plan; I was going to fight her on the school bus. My plan was successful;

she had gotten a bloody nose, and she was now hurt and embarrassed as much as I was. After the altercation I had gotten sent home (my cousin's places). I had received some advice from my cousin's husband. He told me about how he had come across racial situations in the military and responded how I had acted, then went on to say, "You can't fight everyone who disrespects you." My cousin's sound advice had come too late. Unlike Wes one, I didn't think about the outcome of my actions before acting upon them, but when I did it was too late. My decision lead me to get suspended, which defeated the purpose as to why I was living in California. I was there to better myself, yet my actions said different. I didn't think of what would have happened if I didn't come out of the fight on top. I was too busy being worried of proving to everyone that this black girl didn't take no shit—like a black girl "supposed" to do. I didn't want to look weak, nor did I want her to get away with what she said. I let expectations of what "strong" looked like rule my actions. I let limitations of how should be and act limit my options on how I could've better handled the situation. Wes one and I chose different ways to handle the disrespect thrown at us. This obviously led to different end results. The choice Wes one made didn't set him back or drastically change his path, as for me the situation put a hold on my education. Nevertheless, one thing we both learned is once you free yourself from the chains of society's pressure on how you should be, that is when you become an adult.

Life is not as simple as just black and white, there are grey areas. Our choices being a part of the grey area at times, whether our choices were made because of where we are from, the people that play the role as an example, or maybe we simply didn't know better at that moment. Nonetheless, the reality is no one will take the time to understand why we make the choices we make. When we grow older the tolerance of another's understanding will wear-thin. Our excuses or our reasoning for our choices will no longer matter. In result our second chances will dissipate, no longer having a safety net in which we had at the start of our unrequested journey in life. All you have is the great and failed examples and the lessons learned to influence the choices made, said early on in this essay, "It is ultimately up to us to choose whether or not we want to work toward improving ourselves, or hinder ourselves from growth." firmly stand by this. At the end of everyone's day our world revolves around our choices. The child you tuck in bed every night was created due to a choice, the job you clock-in at was due to a choice, and the people you hang around was due to a choice. Granted there are obvious elements in our lives that we had no say in, but it is up to use to make the decision on whether or not will make our set back in life be just that, a setback. In *The Other Wes Moore* it is clear that the ultimate factor in these men's lives was their choices and no one else's. These men started at the same line in the race of life, yet one gave up and the other prevailed. Wes one made the choice to beat all odds and to change his strategy in life, when the race was looking bleak. As for Wes two, he failed to see that finish line and called it quits. No one "great" became great by not running the race of life, they became great by enduring the race of life. The greats made the choice to push and persevere, no one chose for them. No one chose for me. And no one will chose for you. Ultimately our actions and our choice of actions are up to us.

Introduction to Writing and Discussion Activities: Writing a text-based essay in which you compare/contrast your experiences with those of the author is challenging for you have a lot to do in the essay. In addition to telling your own detailed stories, you must do the same in regard to the text. You must assume your reader has not read the text, so you must provide enough summary and background information on the text to enable the reader to follow along. Furthermore, you must draw clear connections and parallels to the text by comparing and/or contrasting and/or agreeing and/or disagreeing with the author. As we have also reviewed, you must choose and use your quotes carefully. Be certain the quotes are significant and capture the author's ideas, arguments, passion and voice. Also be certain that there is a balance between you and the text.

Write: Responses to all questions below in response to "It's Our Choice."

What background/summary information does the writer provide? Where does she provide it? Why is it helpful to the reader?

Choose one body paragraph and "map" it. Highlight in one color the topic sentence(s), in another color the examples and in another color the explanation/connection to the author. Are the examples and explanations developed? Is there a balance between the examples from the text and from the writer's life?

Choose one quote the author integrates into her essay. Is it a well-chosen quote? Is it placed within the context of the text or a story from the text? Does she explain it and make a relevant connection to it?

What is the writer's thesis and her overall argument? Is it valid? Is it a claim that you can apply to your own life or learn from it?

What is the impact of the conclusion? Does it answer, "So what?" Does her essay, overall, explore and grapple with an important issue or lesson?

What suggestions and advice do you have for the writer?

Review the Content and Structure of the Literacy Autobiography Essay: Workshopping a Student Essay

Read: The student essay, "Literacy in Hi-Fi," by Chris Bennett.

Some would venture to say that education is a product of literacy abilities. That the amount of education that we possess, our desire to possess, is singlehandedly attributed to how much and what we read. In a powerful quote regarding reading, by the late, great, Carl Sagan once said "One glance at a book and you hear the voice of another person, perhaps someone dead for 1,000 years. To read is to voyage through time." However, how does one ascertain a passion, love, or desire to read when they are not shown by their parents what the benefits can be? What if the very thought of reading scares them due to the erroneous feelings of isolation? In the narrative essay entitled "The Lonely, Good Company of Books," excerpted from the autobiography, *Hunger of Memory: The Education of Richard Rodriguez*, Rodriguez, who at one point held jobs from that of a teacher to a journalist, who is arguably one of the more contentious writers of his time, based upon his views of affirmative action and bilingual education, recounts overcoming these impediments and finding his passion for reading. Like that of Rodriguez, I was not shown the benefits of reading by my parents. However, unlike Rodriguez, I never acquired a desire to read books. Although our journeys in literacy are similar, they differ in the way that we obtained knowledge and differ in the aspect that he learned through books, and I through the polar opposite, music.

Growing up, Richard Rodriguez was faced with many hurdles in his journey in literacy and his eventual hunger and aspiration for reading. One of these hurdles was that of his parents' unattractive thoughts of reading. Recounting memories of his parents', Rodriguez tells us that for them, ". . . reading was something done out of necessity and as quickly as possible. Never did I see them read an entire book. Nor did I see them read for pleasure" (293). Like Rodriguez, I never saw my mother read for pleasure. The only thing that I can recollect that she would read, other than mail that was addressed to her, was the daily newspaper. Conversely, the only section that she would read was the classifieds, for at the time she was searching for a new job before she got diagnosed with multiple sclerosis and was no longer able to work. I feel as though this had a negative impact on my personal excursion in literacy. Had Rodriguez and myself been raised in a home that taught the importance of reading, our trip may not have been as rough as it was.

Rodriguez's path, with the help of the older nun, enabled him to establish his passion. Reading list after list of top books, reading any type of book that he could get his hands on. Rodriguez went on to become a teacher and later on, a writer. He received his M.A. from Columbia University in 1966. While his path took him on a course to education, my path has just recently been discovered. Unlike that of Rodriguez, I took a slight detour on my path. My path took me to places and experiences that I would not even wish upon my enemies. However, after nearly 14 years, my path has once again veered toward education, and possibly the path towards a degree in either education or journalism. I have yet to decide on which one but being that I have only recently started college I have a little bit of time to decide on which one. I have always known that education is important and without it you are not only hurting yourself but you are also hurting your children by not being the positive role model that all parents should strive to be. This is where my path and Rodriguez's meet again. We both feel that education is important.

Unlike myself, Rodriguez had more to battle than just his parents' joyless approach to reading. Rodriguez had to overcome his erroneous feeling that reading was nothing more than a labored chore, not unlike that of a child having to do the dishes or take the trash out the night before trash was collected. To this he also had to combat is inner mental state of isolation and loneliness I regards to the way he felt when he would read. Rodriguez tells of his time of being placed in a remedial reading class and that with the help of an older nun, he was able to learn that there was nothing to fear in regards to reading and his feelings of loneliness and isolation. Rodriguez recounts ". . . I was thinking of another consequence of literacy. . .Books were going to make me 'educated'. That confidence enabled me, several months later, to overcome my fear of the silence" (295). I never had the issues that he did in regards to remedial reading. Unfortunately, I never had someone to show me the possible jubilation that comes with reading. The only positive memories that I can remember, in regards to reading, are of my early childhood when my mother would read to me at night before bed. By the time that I turned 7 years old, they all but abruptly ceased. My mother never suggested for me to pick up a book and read, she however, would make me look up a word in the dictionary, if I were to ever ask her how to spell a word.

To the average person, reading books is how most procure a more academically thought-provoking vocabulary and superior comprehension skills. Conversely, I achieved my intellectually eloquent grasp of the English language through a different approach to reading. I did not sit around my dwellings reading books, venturing off to faraway places in my imagination that I had never seen or experienced. I did, however, sit around my room with a pair of black, Sony headphones that were attached to my portable CD player. While I was listening to my favorite band, whichever one that may have been at the time, I would read the lyrics from the CD insert. If I didn't know what a word meant, I would go to my dictionary to find the meaning of the word. I would do this until I was able to decipher, like that of a cryptologist finally unlocking a code that could change the world, what the meaning of the song was. From the time that I started to do this, which was around the time that I entered the fourth grade, to this very day, I still continue with these habits. Rodriguez recounts a sign that hung above the nun's desk in his fourth grade classroom that read, "Open the Doors of Your Mind with Books" (293). With this quote, the orthodox that learned through reading books would most likely agree. To the unorthodox, who learned through music, like I did, the following quote is from that of not only a brilliant actor, but also that of a musician, Johnny Depp. Johnny Depp explains that "Music touches us emotionally, where words alone can't."

To say that music is not a key to open up one's mind would not only be ignorant, but also unreservedly naïve. See, music and books share something in common that most people fail to realize. Books tell, through complex dialogue, vivid descriptions, and many of pages a story. Now stop and compare a song to a book. Does a song not tell a story from beginning to end? Are there not emotions that are felt depending upon the type of song, just like there are emotions felt when reading a book, too, depending upon the style of the book? Can they not both enable a person to learn? The only real difference between the story in a book and the story told through music is the way we input them into our mind. With books, our minds are grouping shapes and lines into letters, and then to that of words for us to soak up, whereas music is sent through the air in the form of frequencies to our ears, then sent to our brain for processing, and yes, just like that with books, we soak it up.

Books and music can both have the same effects in one's endless quest through literacy and education. Regardless of whether or not I ever found a desire to read, as Rodriguez did, which I have not, makes no difference. However, what is important is that I found a way to educate myself. My way is to use a different sense than Rodriguez. Whether it's our similarities in regards to our parents, or how we are different in terms of our literacy passion, one thing that I feel we both hold close is that without literacy, we can have no education; without education, we will have no future.

Write:

What do you like best about this essay? Be specific.

What is your favorite music/song/lyrics and why? Does it touch you emotionally? Or impact you in a different way?

In this essay, the writer is making connections, connections between himself and the author Richard Rodriguez and between books and music. What are those connections? What are the similarities and differences between the student writer and Rodriguez? What are the similarities and differences between books and music? Have you thought about this connection before? Is it valid? Provide examples from the essay.

Does the writer provide enough information about his own life as well as Rodriguez's life for the reader to understand both and to be engaged in the stories? Provide examples from the text and suggestions.

What is the thesis? Is it effective? Why or why not?

How does the writer construct his body paragraphs? Underline his topic sentences and the transitions sentences (sentences he uses to transition from writing about the author to writing about himself). Are these effective? Can you suggest another way he construct his body paragraphs and topic sentences?

Find one place where the writer could develop a story/anecdote.

Reread paragraph 5. Do you have suggestions for revision of the paragraph? How does this structure not match the previous body paragraphs? Where could he develop?

Reread the last two paragraphs, his conclusion. Does it cohere to the rest of the essay? How does his conclusion answer the question, "So what?" What can you learn from his conclusion? What are your final thoughts?

Discuss: After you have written thoughtful responses to the questions above, please share them with your classmates, Instructor and/or Writer's Workshop Leader/Student Tutor.

Application to your essay/paper/Task Paper: How can this exercise help you with your essay/paper/Task Paper? How can you use this student essay to help you formulate your own ideas about literacy and get started? How can this student essay help you to focus and develop your own body paragraphs? How can this student essay help you to answer, "So what?" for your own essay/paper/Task Paper?

Peer Response Activities

Peer Response Questions for Text-Based Essay/Paper/Task Paper

Student Writer_____ **Student Responder** _____

What do you like best about the paper? Be specific.

The thesis statement: <u>Underline the thesis statement</u>: Does it establish a link between the student writer and essay/book? Does it state title/author and topic, claim, argument, experience? Does it control the paper? Yes or Somewhat or No *Suggestions:*

The discussion: What topic(s)/issue(s) in the book is student writer discussing? *Write here:*

- Is there background/summary of essay/book? Yes or Somewhat or No
- Does the writer discuss his/her experiences and/or opinions regarding the topic and link it to the essay/book and character(s) of Wes? Yes or Somewhat or No
- Does the writer provide supporting material from the essay/book (quotes, examples, stories)? Yes or Somewhat or No
- Is there a <u>balance</u> between the text and the student writer? Yes or Somewhat or No

Write down one paragraph that needs development and explain why and how to improve:

The body paragraphs:

- <u>**Underline each topic sentence:**</u> Do the paragraphs have clear topic sentences and clear focus? Yes or Somewhat or No
- Are the paragraphs developed and have adequate support (details, examples, anecdotes, passages/quotes from the text, etc.) and explanation? Yes or Somewhat or No
- How does student writer organize paper/body paragraphs? *Explain here:*

Find one strong and one weak paragraph and explain why. Give suggestions for weak paragraph:

Documentation: Does the writer use the following:

- Introductory phrases for all quotes? Yes or Somewhat or No
- Explanation after each quote and example/story? Yes or Somewhat or No
- Parenthetical documentation? Yes or Somewhat or No

Suggestions:

Style and Mechanics: Are there any grammatical or mechanical errors that distract the reader? Yes or Somewhat or No *Explain and provide suggestions:*

Peer Response Questions for Text-Based Literacy Autobiography

Student Writer_____ **Student Responder(s)**_____

Content and fulfillment of assignment

What do you like best about the paper? Write it down. Did the essay contain engaging stories from the student writer? Be specific.

The thesis statement: Does it state the connection between the writer and the author(s) or the connection (i.e., comparison or contrast) between the essays/authors? Does it state title(s)/ author(s) and claim, argument, experience? Does Yes or Somewhat or No
Write thesis here:

Suggestions:

The identification of issue, experience and/or opinion: Is there enough background information on writer and author/essay in regard to literacy and life? Yes or Somewhat or No
Suggestions:

The discussion: Does the writer discuss his/her educational/literacy stories and experiences and link it to one or more of the essays?

- Does the writer provide detailed and interesting examples and anecdotes? Yes or Somewhat or No
- Does the writer express significance and reflection? Yes or Somewhat or No
- Does the writer provide supporting material from an outside source and directly connect that material to him/her? Is all borrowed information clearly explained? Yes or Somewhat or No
Suggestions:

Consider the body paragraphs:

- Do the paragraphs have clear topic sentences and clear focus? Yes or Somewhat or No
- Are the paragraphs developed and have adequate support (details, examples, anecdotes, passages/quotes from the text, etc.)? Yes or Somewhat or No
- Do the paragraphs refer back to thesis/focus/main idea? Yes or Somewhat or No

Write down the strongest paragraph and why:

Write down the weakest paragraph and why:

Documentation:

- Is it clear what are the student writer's words and ideas and what is borrowed information? Yes or Somewhat or No
- Does the writer use introductory phrases to integrate borrowed material and then explain that material? Yes or Somewhat or No
- Does the writer correctly document use of sources in text by using parenthetical documentation? Yes or Somewhat or No

Suggestions:

PART III

USING AND DOCUMENTING SOURCES ACCORDING TO MLA (MODERN LANGUAGE ASSOCIATION)

" . . . [S]tudents produce research projects by piecing together passages quoted verbatim and stitched together with a few introductory or transitional words. They assemble research as patchwork quilts rather than weaving a fabric of new knowledge. The practice of patchwork research highlights the difference between information and knowledge. They "recall" and "summarize" but do not "analyze," "synthesize," or "evaluate." They do not construct new knowledge. . . . [T]hese students have used other people's words and ideas to commit a conceptual, inadvertent form of plagiarism."

—from Janice Cooper, "Patchwork Plagiarism"

Terms and Definitions

Plagiarism

Using others' ideas or words as if they were your own. Paraphrases, direct quotes, statistics, research and facts that are not common knowledge must have parenthetical documentation and a corresponding entry on the Works Cited page in order to avoid plagiarism. Direct quotes must also have quotation marks around the material directly quoted from the source. Inadequate or incorrect parenthetical documentation and attribution phrases are types of unintentional plagiarism. Lack of parenthetical documentation and attribution phrases are types of intentional plagiarism. In addition, turning in someone else's work (whether a whole work or just part of a work) or obtaining a paper/essay, lesson, notes, journals, etc. from someone else or the internet is intentional plagiarism. You must also be careful when receiving help and feedback on your papers. Too much help can be considered a form of plagiarism if the paper is influenced more by the person helping you than yourself. It is always best to only receive feedback from your Instructor, your classmates in a guided manner and tutoring services on campus. To avoid plagiarism, take careful notes when reading, citing all information and ideas that are not yours. Take notes in your own words/language and when you come across a passage or language that is important and powerful, be certain to use quotation marks and write down the corresponding author and page number. Make it clear in your notes and essay/paper what has been paraphrased and what is a direct quote.

Summary

Condenses (a lot briefer than original) and restates. You extract only the main points from a passage, a few passages or even an entire work and convert them into your own words. Although you are restating the author's ideas and opinions, your summary should be written in your own language, voice and style. You leave out your opinion.

Paraphrase

Restatement of an original passage. Saying in your own words, in about the same length as the author, what you understand the author to mean in a particular sentence/passage. Borrowing a person's idea or argument means **significantly** rephrasing it in your own words. Use your own vocabulary and sentence structure. Because a paraphrase is not originally your own idea, you must use documentation and give credit to the person whose idea it is.

Paraphrase Plagiarism

When you have not sufficiently changed vocabulary and sentence structure in a paraphrase. You are borrowing only ideas not language, so do not rely too heavily on the source. A paraphrase should have the author's idea but sound like you. You must also have parenthetical documentation for all paraphrases. Most paraphrase plagiarism is an example of unintentional or inadvertent plagiarism.

Direct Quote

Citing "word for word" what the author has said/written. In order to present technical words, to capture an effective, powerful or interesting sentence and to enhance your credibility as a reader, writer and researcher, you can use direct quotes (but use them sparingly). Be sure to use the exact wording, quotation marks, introductory/signal/attribution phrase and parenthetical documentation.

Parenthetical Documentation (in-text citation)

Using MLA guidelines, after **each** paraphrase and direct quote, you must inform reader from where this information came by providing information, in parentheses, after the end of each sentence. If there are quotation marks, they go before the parenthetical documentation but the punctuation/period is placed after the parenthetical documentation. Place the author's last name and page number in parentheses, followed by punctuation. If you state the author in the sentence then just put the page number in parentheses. If there is no author, then use the title. If there is no page number (electronic source, website, HTML full text), then use a paragraph number (i.e., par. 7). If your source/author is quoting someone else, you need to clarify this by placing the name of the actual person being quoted in the introductory/signal/attribution phrase and the source/author in the parenthetical documentation along with (qtd. in). A source cited in another source is often referred to as an indirect source and "qtd. in" is used to indicate the source you actually consulted.

Examples:

"   " (Moore 37).
According to Wes Moore, "   "(37).
"   " ("The Problem with Standardized Testing" 75).
"   " (Smith, par. 4).
According to Dr. John Williams, History Professor at Syracuse University, "   " (qtd. in Smith 56).

Works Cited Page: Using MLA guidelines, you must have a works cited page that gives full bibliographic information on each work that is cited in your paper. A Works Cited page is the last, separate page of your essay (that does NOT count toward page length) that is titled, double-spaced and alphabetized.

MLA Guidelines, Rules and Usage

Formatting Quotes

- **Ellipses** (a set of three spaced dots . . .) can replace wordy or irrelevant information that you wish to omit in a quote. If a quote is too long and you wish to use only part of it, you can use the ellipsis to denote what information/words/phrases you have omitted. You must be certain that the omitted words do not change the meaning of the sentence and that the sentence still makes sense to the reader.
- **Brackets** [ ] allow you to add explanatory words to clarify the quotation. If you need to add a word or phrase in order to add an explanation or make the sentence make sense, you can do this by placing the added words in brackets.
- **Block/Long Quote:** If a quote is longer than four lines, you need to block it or set it off. This requires that you make some changes in how you will set up and punctuate your quote: Indent the quote 10 spaces (2 tabs), do not use quotation marks and place your punctuation before the parenthetical documentation. When you introduce the quote, use a colon rather than a comma after the introductory phrase.
- **Introductory/Signal/Attribution Phrases:** *Every* quotation you use should be blended into your text and you can use an introductory phrase to achieve this. An introductory/signal/ attribution phrase can create a bridge or transition to your information, as well as inform the reader from where the quote came, who said it and why it is a valid piece of information. Phrases can include title, author and background information. Basic examples of integration:

  According to Dr. Smith, a psychologist at Blake University, " . . ."

  A study by an Ohio University medical team in 2017 claims, " . . ."

  James Bell, a scientist at Jones Laboratories of NY, states, " . . ."

  James T. Baker in "How Do We Find the Student" asserts, " . . ."

- **Explaining Borrowed Information:** When incorporating *any* kind of borrowed information be sure not only to document it but also to place it in context, explain it, analyze it and/or tell your reader how it "fits" into your paper or argument. You must balance borrowed material with your own material and ideas. It is your paper and must have your voice, ideas and opinions as well as outside information. For this specific assignment, you should have your own experiences, opinions and voice.

Examples:

Original source: "The children are onto this game. They know that if we really valued schooling, we'd pay teachers what we pay stockbrokers; if we valued books, we'd spend a little something on the libraries so that adults could read, too; if we valued citizenship, we'd give national service and civic education more than pilot status; if we valued children, we wouldn't let them be abused, manipulated, impoverished, and killed in their beds by gang-war cross fire and stray bullets." This quote is from Benjamin R. Barber's "America Skips School" in *Discovering the Student, Discovering the Self.*

Paraphrase: It is evident to American school children that we do not care about their education, their participation in our communities or their safety for if we did, then we would be funneling more money into our schools and teachers' salaries as well as into programs that would help impoverished areas and inner cities to combat crime, increase jobs and support families (Barber 232).

Quote with an introductory/signal/attribution phrase: In the essay, "America Skips School," Benjamin R. Barber argues, "The children are onto this game. They know that if we really valued schooling, we'd pay teachers what we pay stockbrokers; if we valued books, we'd spend a little something on the libraries so that adults could read, too; if we valued citizenship, we'd give national service and civic education more than pilot status; if we valued children, we wouldn't let them be abused, manipulated, impoverished, and killed in their beds by gang-war cross fire and stray bullets" (232).

Quote with ellipsis: "The children are onto this game. They know that if we really valued schooling, we'd pay teachers what we pay stockbrokers; if we valued books, we'd spend a little something on the libraries so that adults could read, too; if we valued citizenship, we'd give national service and civic education more than pilot status; if we valued children, we wouldn't let them be abused, manipulated, impoverished, and killed . . . " (Barber 232).

Quote with brackets: " They [children] know that if we really valued schooling, we'd pay teachers what we pay stockbrokers; if we valued books, we'd spend a little something on the libraries so that adults could read, too; if we valued citizenship, we'd give national service and civic education more than pilot status; if we valued children, we wouldn't let them be abused, manipulated, impoverished, and killed in their beds by gang-war cross fire and stray bullets" (Barber 232).

Block Quote Example:
In the essay, "America Skips School," Benjamin R. Barber argues:

> The children are onto this game. They know that if we really valued schooling, we'd pay teachers what we pay stockbrokers; if we valued books, we'd spend a little something on the libraries so that adults could read, too; if we valued citizenship, we'd give national service and civic education more than pilot status; if we valued children, we wouldn't let them be abused, manipulated, impoverished, and killed in their beds by gang-war cross fire and stray bullets. (232)

Formatting an Essay, Paper or Manuscript According to MLA Guidelines

MLA (Modern Language Association) Format is used for almost all college papers in the Humanities. MLA format covers documenting sources within the paper and formatting a works cited/consulted page that comes after the paper. In addition, MLA covers the main format of the paper. Below are the MLA page format requirements. Review these, but also be sure to check with your Instructor for each instructor can alter this format to fit the needs of each assignment and class.

1. The entire paper should be double spaced.
2. The font should be a standard, easily readable typeface and type size (e.g., an 11 or 12 point Times New Roman font).
3. The margins should be set at 1".
4. New paragraphs should be indented 5 spaces or 1 "tab".
5. The heading should be on the left side of the first page that gives your full name, your professor's name, the class and the date (each on a separate line; heading may be single spaced).
6. The title of the paper should be the same font as the rest of your paper, should be centered and should not be underlined or boldfaced.

7. The paper should be numbered consecutively in the upper right-hand corner. Type your last name before the page number; this is a header. Word processing programs will allow you to automatically number pages and create running headers.

8. The titles of major works (books, newspapers, magazines, etc.) should be underlined or italicized. The titles of minor works (essays in a book/anthology, articles in a newspaper or magazine, poem, etc.) should be placed within quotation marks.

Formatting a Works Cited Page According to MLA Guidelines

Once you have written a paper using words and ideas from outside sources and have cited those sources within your text, you will still need to compile a list of works cited that will appear as the last page of your text and will be titled "Works Cited." If you have more than one source to list, cite the items in alphabetical order using the first word of your entry. The first part of your parenthetical documentation should always match the first piece of information in your Works Cited entry. The Works Cited page is important because it gives detailed information so readers can locate and read your sources. Your paper needs this information because it is proof that what you quoted is correct and real. It supports your paper and gives it credibility.

Checklist for Works Cited Page

- Begin Works Cited page on a new/separate sheet of paper
- Number the Works Cited page (but it does not count toward page length requirements)
- Center the title Works Cited at the top of the page
- Alphabetize each entry by the first word of each entry
- Double space the entire page
- Indent the second and third line of an entry 5 spaces/1 tab
- Place a period at the end of each entry

Works Cited Entries

In your citation, the elements should be listed in the following order:

1. Author.   (last name, first name)
2. Title of source.
3. Title of container,   (larger work)
4. Other contributors,   (editor in an anthology or textbook, translator, etc.)
5. Version,
6. Number,
7. Publisher,
8. Publication date,
9. Location.   (page numbers, URL, etc.)

Each element should be followed by the punctuation mark shown.

Note: This information is from the most recent eighth edition of MLA. Earlier editions of the handbook included the place of publication, and required punctuation such as journal editions in parentheses, and colons after issue numbers. In the current version, punctuation is simpler (just commas and periods separate the elements), and information about the source is kept to the basics.

Examples:

Book: Moore, Wes. *The Other Wes Moore.* Spiegel and Grau, 2011.
Essay from textbook: Naylor, Gloria. "The Love of Books." *Discovering the Student, Discovering the Self,* Edited by Dawn Terrick, Kendall Hunt, 2018, pp.
Personal Interview: Smith, Jones. Personal interview. 10 October 2017.
Article from magazine: Quindlen, Anna. "Write and Wrong." *Newsweek*, 21 July 2008, p. 68.
Online text: Wheelis, Mark. "Investigating Disease Outbreaks Under a Protocol to the Biological and Toxin Weapons Convention." *Emerging Infectious*

    Diseases, vol. 6, no. 6, 2000, pp. 595-600, wwwnc.cdc.gov/eid/article/6/6/00-0607_article. Accessed 8 Feb. 2009.

For more detailed information on the MLA Works Cited page and examples of various entries, consult: https://owl
.english.purdue.edu/owl/resource/747/01/
https://www.mla.org/MLA-Style

Practice with Quoting and MLA Documentation

You can complete this exercise multiple times as you choose different essays, quotes and signal phrases,
develop your explanations, correct your errors, etc.

- Choose one quote from the essay you are using (or have used) for a text-based writing
  assignment and write it here. Be exact.
- Now using the quote above, answer the following questions.
  1. Use a detailed signal phrase using the author and title to introduce the quote and
     also include correct punctuation and parenthetical documentation. Choose an
     appropriate verb from the list in textbook.
     Write another signal phrase using background information and context.
  2. Write a paraphrase of the quote being certain to use your own language/
     vocabulary as well as your own sentence structure. Remember, you are borrowing
     the idea and not the language. Your paraphrase should sound like you and not
     the author. Compare your paraphrase, side by side, to the original passage and
     be certain you have changed the vocabulary and sentence structure. Also include
     correct parenthetical documentation.
- Choose a long quote (more than four typed lines) from the same essay and 1. introduce
  it, 2. set if off with correct formatting, punctuation and documentation, 3. follow it with
  explanation. Write this as it would appear in your paper.
- Write a Works Cited entry as it would appear in your essay/paper/Task Paper.

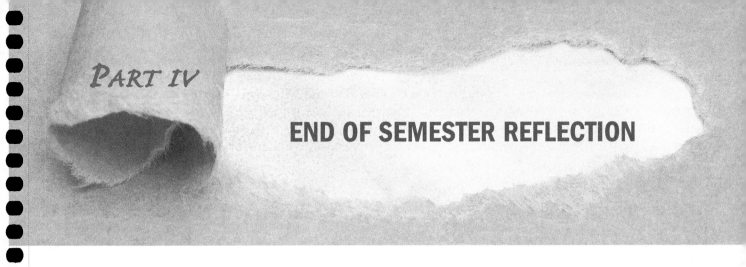

PART IV

END OF SEMESTER REFLECTION

Activity 1 - The Challenges and Rewards of the Semester

Write: Many aspects of this course have been challenging and I would like you to tell me about this. Which were most challenging for you and why? Many aspects were rewarding. Which did you find most rewarding and why? And in meeting all of these challenges, what class activities and lessons helped you the most and least?

Finally, now that you have completed your final essay for this course, how satisfied are you with your writing and writing process? Have you learned anything about yourself as a reader, writer, learner and student? What are your greatest strengths and improvements in writing at the end of this semester? What would you like to still change and improve?

What do you think you can take away from this course and semester that will help you in your next writing class and in other college courses?

Activity 2 - Writing Apprehension Test, Revisited

Write: At the start of the semester, you completed writings and a survey regarding your attitude towards writing. Now, retake the Writing Apprehension Test/Survey. Carefully reread the responses and writings you completed during the first weeks regarding your experiences with and opinions on reading and writing. Compare/contrast the survey from the first week of class to today's survey. Do you see any changes? If so, what are they? If there are no changes, explain why you think this is. Have you grown or learned? Be specific. Were your expectations for this course met? Why or why not?

Activity 3 - Finding Your Writing Process, Revisited

At the beginning of the semester, you "drew" your writing process. Now, create a drawing that reflects your writing process today. Represent your process, surroundings and emotions in pictures and images. Be creative and have fun!

Share and discuss: Once again, compare/contrast your drawing with those of your classmates/ peers. In addition, compare/contrast today's drawing with the one you completed at the start of the semester. What are the similarities and differences? Do you think these changes are for the better or worse? How will you carry over this process in other classes and assignments?

● ●

Activity 4 - Group Reflection: What Have You Learned This Semester?

Discuss: As a group/class, generate a list of all that you have learned this semester in regard to thinking, reading and writing. You can list specific terms/definitions, models, class readings/essays, grammar/sentence structure lessons, study skills, etc. Have someone record all items on the board/ computer screen.

Write: Then, individually, choose the five most significant items to you and explain why.

Discuss: After you have written thoughtful responses to the questions above, please share them with your classmates, Instructor and/or Writer's Workshop Leader/Student Tutor.

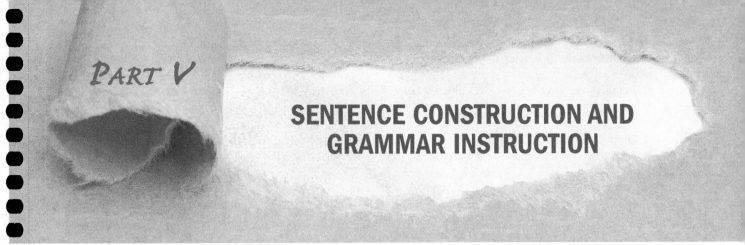

PART V

SENTENCE CONSTRUCTION AND GRAMMAR INSTRUCTION

PARTS OF SPEECH

Students often forget the parts of speech that are used in writing. These are integral to understanding how sentences are correctly written. Students must know the terms.

Noun: a person, place, or thing. These can be common nouns such as *man*, or proper nouns such as *Mr. Smith*.

Pronouns: take the place of a noun. There are personal pronouns like *I*, *me*, *we*, or *us*. There are indefinite pronouns such as *one*, *many*, *several*, *both*, *everybody*, *anyone*, *nobody*, or *someone*. There are also possessive pronouns such as *his*, *hers*, *my*, *mine*, or *our*.

Verbs: Verbs come in two types: action and linking/state of being. Action verbs are words like *run*, *skip*, *hop*, *push*, or *jump*. Linking verbs are words such as *is*, *are*, *was*, *were*, and *am*.

Example: We ran, skipped, and hopped. (action)

                She is tall. (links "tall" with the word it describes)

Adjectives: words that describe/modify nouns or pronouns.

Example: The tall girl walked by.

                ("tall" describes the girl)

                She is tall.

                ("tall" describes the pronoun "she")

Adverbs: words that describe/modify verbs, adjectives, and other adverbs.

Describing a verb: He walked slowly.

                ("slowly" tells how he walked)

Describing an adverb: He walked very slowly.

                ("very" describes how slowly)

From *Basics in Writing* by Georgia Turner. Copyright © 2016 by Georgia Turner. Reprinted by permission.

Describing an adjective: The very tall girl walked by us.

>> ("very" describes how tall)

Prepositions: words introducing phrases regarding time and space that end with nouns or pronouns. Some common prepositions are *over, under, around, through, across, below, beneath, above, on, with, by, of, among,* and *for.* Prepositions are always followed by a phrase such as *over the bridge, under the bridge, around the bridge, across the bridge, below the bridge,* or *by the bridge.*

An example of time: Before the storm, we were outdoors.
An example of space: We looked behind the door.

Conjunctions: joiners/connectors of words, phrases, and sentences.
These words include *and, but, or, for, nor, yet,* and *so* (coordinating)

Example: Jim **and** John went fishing.
Example: We looked in the closet **and** under the bed.
Example: Dan went to the store, **so** he bought groceries.

The coordinating conjunction used for connecting two sentences to make a compound **must be preceded by a comma** as in the third example.

PREPOSITIONS: INSTRUCTION AND EXERCISES

Don't Abuse Innocent Prepositions

Prepositions are the baby seals of the grammar world. They're small, they're cute, they're cuddly, and they get brutally killed on a regular basis.

Okay, maybe they aren't actually cuddly. Or cute. But they are small. And they do get massacred regularly. And this in spite of the fact that they're such useful words. We use prepositions all the time: in fact, without them, most of our sentences would just fall apart. So be kind—study this section thoroughly, and save the prepositions from slaughter.

What the Heck Are Prepositions, Anyway?

Prepositions are officially part of a larger class of words called "adpositions," which includes both prepositions and postpositions, and there's a whole lot of linguistic mumbo-jumbo to go along with that already fairly complicated definition. So let's try to simplify:

First off, examples of prepositions include words like *of, on, over, with, through, above, below, throughout,* and dozens of others. Simply put, prepositions show relationships between parts of your sentence. That relationship might be physical and tell you where the objects are in relation to each other, like this:

The pancake sat *on* the bunny's head.

The kung fu master put his fist *through* the wall.

Or the relationship can relate to time:

I saw the alien spacecraft *before* anyone else did.

It landed *during* the presidential inauguration.

They can also show things like direction:

I put the essay *into* the garbage disposal.

And other general relationships:

I descended into the smoking, monster-infested pit *with* her.

There are about 150 prepositions in English, and there are dozens of websites out there to help you find complete lists. But now that you have learned something about this endangered part of speech, let's learn how to protect it in its wild environment—your writing.

Save the Prepositions

Prepositions are actually the most common word type in the English language—so there's plenty of opportunity for you to go completely wrong.

The difficult part is that prepositions are often based on what grammar experts call "usage." That is, the way we use them is just the way we use them, and there's no general principle guiding which one you should choose in situation A and which one in situation B. So the best way to really learn them is just to read—a lot. Read newspapers, books, cereal boxes, whatever you can find.

If you're a native speaker of English, a lot of preposition use will come to you fairly naturally. But there are still a few trouble spots, so read and understand the following rules to make sure you're not committing any of them yourself.

Multi-Word Prepositions

Some prepositions include more than one word to get the point across. Some of the most important of these will be covered below, but examples include "up to" and "instead of."

Expressing Time

Remember to use "since" when we're talking about something that started at a particular point in time and goes up to the present. But use "for" when you're talking about a specific period of time:

WRONG: He has been playing *World of Warcraft* since sixteen hours.

RIGHT: He has been playing *World of Warcraft* since 4:00 a.m.

RIGHT: He has been playing *World of Warcraft* for sixteen hours.

Showing Preference

When you want to show that something is better, bigger, more, or stronger than something else, you are making a comparison. Most comparisons use "than," not "to":

WRONG: My dog is bigger *to* that Chihuahua.

RIGHT: My dog is bigger *than* that Chihuahua.

WRONG: The aliens are smarter *to* the zombies.

RIGHT: The aliens are smarter *than* the zombies.

Note that you also use this pattern when you have another word in between your comparing word and the preposition:

The zombies, however, are a greater threat *than* the aliens.

Some comparisons, however, do use "to." When you compare two things using words like "superior," "inferior," "senior," or "junior," use the word "to" instead:

WRONG: Our firepower is inferior than the aliens.

RIGHT: Our firepower is inferior to the aliens.

WRONG: The zombies' numbers are superior than our own.

RIGHT: The zombies' numbers are superior to our own.

WRONG: My boss is senior than me.

RIGHT: My boss is senior to me.

Between

Always follow "between" with the word *and*, not with "against":

WRONG: The tournament fight will be between Jeanry "the Mountain" *against* Nathan "the Hobbit."

RIGHT: The tournament fight will be between Johnny "the Mountain" *and* Nathan "the Hobbit."

WRONG: The tournament is scheduled take place between 10 a.m. *to* 4 p.m.

RIGHT: The tournament is scheduled take place between 10 a.m. *and* 4 p.m.

Between and During

When talking about time, use "between [date] and [date]" when you want to specify a starting and ending date or time. Do not use "during" in these circumstances.

WRONG: The interview was held *during* 6–7 on Friday.

RIGHT: The interview was held *between* 6 and 7 p.m. Friday.

WRONG: In World War II, there was a fight with good and evil.

RIGHT: In World War II, there was a fight between good and evil.

Use "during" instead when you're referring to a named, specific span of time:

Some of the worst movies were made *during* the Seventies.

At and To

"At" refers to where something is. "To" refers to another location:

WRONG: Godzilla has arrived *to* Times Square.

RIGHT: Godzilla has arrived *at* Times Square.

WRONG: Next, he will go *at* Manhattan.

RIGHT: Next, he will go *to* Manhattan.

In

Use "in" when you want to talk about cities, towns, countries, or regions. Avoid "at" or "on" in these contexts:

WRONG: The general arrived *at* the Pacific Northwest to investigate claims of Canadian aggression.

RIGHT: The general arrived *in* the Pacific Northwest to investigate claims of Canadian aggression.

WRONG: The plane arrived *on* Vancouver yesterday.

RIGHT: The plane arrived *in* Vancouver yesterday.

Addresses

Addresses and specific places use "at." When speaking only of a street, however, use "on":

WRONG: He works *on* LAX.

RIGHT: He works *at* LAX.

WRONG: The Munsters live on 1313 Elm Street.

RIGHT: The Munsters live *at* 1313 Elm Street.

RIGHT: The Munsters' house is *on* Elm Street.

Dates and Times

When giving a general period of time, use "in":

I have Jiu-Jitsu class *in* the morning.

We usually go *to* the international tournament in the summer.

For specific dates and times, use "at":

My Jiu-Jitsu class starts *at* 7 a.m.

For specific days, use "on":

This year's tournament is *on* Monday.

About, Around, and Up To

Use these when you want to approximate an amount, location, or time, along with a number of other things:

Joe weighs *about* 475 pounds.

His doctor says he should lose *up to* 300 pounds of that weight.

He will need to lose it in *around* two years.

Phrases with Prepositions

There are some phrases in English that require prepositions, and some that will sound funny if you use them. Here are a few that need to have a preposition to make sense:

Love of/Love for

Hatred of

Fear of

Afraid of

Concern/Concerned for

Worry about

Test for

Study for

At the same time, you should avoid adding prepositions where they aren't grammatically necessary. Though they may not technically make the sentence incorrect, adding too many prepositions sounds wordy and immature:

WRONG: Get this clown nose *off of* me.

RIGHT: Get this clown nose *off* me.

WRONG: Where is *my jacket at*?

RIGHT: Where is *my jacket*?

WRONG: I need to *meet up with* my instructor for some additional help.

RIGHT: I need to *meet with* my instructor for some additional help.

Prepositions with "Ask"

When you want to use ask someone to give you something, you need to use "for" with the word "ask":

WRONG: I *asked* the ray gun, so I could shoot the alien.

RIGHT: I *asked for* the ray gun, so I could shoot the alien.

In the first example, it sounds like you're literally asking the ray gun a question, rather than asking to be given it.

If you want someone to *do* something, on the other hand, leave out the preposition:

WRONG: I *asked for* him to shoot the alien with the ray gun.

RIGHT: I *asked* him to shoot the alien with the ray gun.

Prepositions with "Meet"

Though it's not technically incorrect grammatically, avoid using the preposition "with" after the word "meet." It sounds wordy and makes your sentences unnecessarily bulky:

I will meet with you tomorrow on the field of battle.

I will meet you tomorrow on the field of battle.

Prepositions with "Prevent"

When using the word "prevent," you will usually use the preposition "from" and a verb with an "-ing" ending:

WRONG: Godzilla must be *prevented to smash* downtown L.A.

RIGHT: Godzilla must be *prevented from smashing* downtown L.A.

Prepositions with "Go"

There are several common ways to use the word *go*. If you mean to say you want to go do something, especially something athletic or outdoorsy, don't use any preposition—instead, just use the verb you want with the "-ing" ending:

We want *to go swimming*.

We're *going hiking* tomorrow.

However, people frequently turn the activity into a noun instead, such as "a swim" or "a hike." In these cases, use "for":

We want *to go for a swim*.

We're *going for a hike tomorrow*.

In slang, "go" is also often used with "for" to mean "attempt to reach a goal."

I'm going to go for my certification in underwater basket weaving, but I need a scuba certification.

Prepositions with "Insist"

Don't use "to" after "insist." Instead, use "on":

WRONG: I insist to face the dragon with you.

RIGHT: I insist on facing the dragon with you.

Using Prepositions in Consecutive Phrases

If you're using two phrases in a row that need a preposition, you can skip the second one so long as it would be the same preposition:

WRONG: I use my video game skills both in games and in real life.

RIGHT: I use my video game skills both in games and real life.

However, if the two prepositions need to be different, both need to be present for the sentence to work:

WRONG: I use my video game skills both *in* games and the road.

RIGHT: I use my video game skills both *in* games and *on* the road.

Can I Use a Preposition at the End of a Sentence?

Yes. People who still say you can't are following an outdated and kind of silly rule that never made sense for English in the first place. That rule only exists because the first people to write down the grammar rules were monks and scholars, and back then, monks and scholars thought Latin was the best language ever. So they made English rules follow Latin rules—and in Latin, it's *impossible* to put a preposition at the end of a sentence.

So, long story short: Ignore them. Put your prepositions where you want them.

EXERCISE

- -

IDENTIFYING PREPOSITIONS

In the following passage, underline or circle all of the prepositions. Remember that prepositions are words that show various kinds of relationships between other words.

Interestingly, the vampire we see in movies today has not always been the vampire that the public would recognize. In fact, vampire lore goes back thousands of years, and includes types of blood-sucking monsters that the modern moviegoer has never dreamed of.

Most modern Americans think of Dracula when they think of vampires—suave, debonaire, handsome, but a little creepy. Dracula was a man in appearance, but able to turn into a bat or a wolf or, in some cases, a vapor. But the legend of Dracula is relatively recent, based on Vlad Tepez, or Vlad the Impaler, known as the Little Dragon, or "Dracul-a" (his father was known as Dracul—the dragon). Vlad was so feared that legends grew up around him, explaining his extreme cruelty by claiming he was undead. Though he is a spectacular figure, he is far from the first vampire.

In Cambodia, for example, a vampire called an "ab" is a floating head wrapped in intestines, and thorn bushes might have been used to prevent an attack, as they feared catching their delicate intestines in them. Chinese vampires, or Jiang Shi, were reanimated corpses that hopped from place to place and drained their victims' life forces.

There are many dozens of other examples, but the vast majority does not resemble the sexy, humanlike vampires most of us have come to expect. Instead, most are hideous, deformed, or animalistic, making the vampire much more a monster—and much less a teen idol.

- -

CHOOSING THE CORRECT PREPOSITION

In the following sentences, insert the correct preposition. If no preposition is needed, put an "X" in the blank.

1. The president lives _____ Pennsylvania Ave.
2. _____ about an hour, the pot roast will be done.
3. Whenever I call, Samantha never seems to be _____ home.
4. I will respond to your question _____ another question.
5. The city will react to your request for a new stoplight _____ doing nothing.
6. Broccoli is good _____ you.
7. My grandmother was always very good _____ people.
8. What kind of meat did you use _____ this stew?
9. I never answer that question—people have an easier time without that information _____ their heads.
10. Some people spend all of their time _____ the phone.
11. The dealer was selling his drugs _____ the corner of 5th and Main when the cops arrested him.
12. I will stay with you _____ you're ready to go.

13. Since the student was too afraid to talk to her teacher, she had her mom call _____ her.
14. I am interested _____ many different hobbies.
15. The professor talked _____ biological anthropology.

PREPOSITION MISTAKES

Fix the following errors with prepositions.
1. He has been driving the bus since fourteen hours.
2. My Irish wolfhound is bigger to your German Shepherd which is bigger to her Chihuahua.
3. The duel between Count Orlock against Edward Cullen ended badly for poor old Ed.
4. Registration for the Professional Cake-Off will be held during 5–6.
5. When your cake arrives to the convention center, make sure that it is labeled with your name.
6. We also allow no snacking because of what happened at Hoboken.
7. They live on 241 Macaroon Road.
8. Their neighbors all live at Macaroon Road, as well.
9. I worry over the test I just took.
10. I have allergies against cats.

PUNCTUATION: INSTRUCTION AND EXERCISES

The Terrors of Punctuation

Getting punctuation right can really be a chore. Like most aspects of English, the rules never work all the time; there are always lots of exceptions, and frequently, it seems like what you just used in the last sentence won't work in this sentence. What's more, people who "get" punctuation tend to laugh at you when you put a comma in the wrong place or use a colon when you need a semicolon.

So how's a learning writer to avoid looking bad? Fortunately, punctuation isn't nearly as hard as it seems. In this section, we'll lay out simple rules for using each piece of punctuation, and we'll try to help you get a handle on those pesky exceptions. Punctuation isn't really as hard as it seems—it's just that nobody has told you how to avoid the particular don'ts you have to look out for.

Understanding Sentences As Chunks

To really get your punctuation under control, you want to start looking at sentences as puzzles. Each sentence can be broken down to a number of different sections, and each section, or "chunk," can be either a complete sentence or an incomplete sentence (for more information on this concept, see the book *Building Blocks* by this author).

So look at the following sentence:

When Joe started snoring, I reached for the ejection seat button.

There are two clear chunks of thought here:

[When Joe started snoring,] [I reached for the ejection seat button.]

Your job is to decide which is a complete sentence by itself, and which isn't. In this case, the first half by itself is incomplete, and the second half is complete. If we wanted to make an "equation" out of this sentence, it would look like this:

IS, CS

to show we have an incomplete sentence (IS) followed by a complete sentence (CS). We will use this trick of making "equations" to check your punctuation in several places throughout this chapter, most notably when dealing with connecting sentences or ideas.

Punctuation Marks: An Overview

If you're intimidated by the idea of punctuation, then take heart: there are actually only fourteen punctuation marks in English for you to master. Considering that some of them are fairly simple, that's really not that much.

So what are the punctuation marks?

Apostrophe	'
Braces	{ }
Brackets	[ ]
Colon	:
Comma	,
Dash	—
Ellipsis	. . .
Exclamation point	!
Hyphen	-

Parentheses	( )
Question mark	?
Quotation mark	" " or ' '
Period	.
Semicolon	;

Punctuation Play By Play

So let's approach these one by one, and you'll see that punctuation isn't as bad as you might have thought. Once you understand the principles, the application is easy.

Apostrophes (')

Apostrophes have two uses: showing possession and creating contractions.

Showing Possession

Regular Nouns

The apostrophe-s ending after a regular noun shows that the next word in the sequence belongs to that noun:

> That is Joe's axe.

> The axe's edge is dull.

With Words Ending in "S"

If the word already ends in an "s," but is still only one thing, then just follow it with an postrophe. This is often the case with names:

> Jesus' restaurant has the best Mexican food.

> Thomas' greatest enemy was named Smith.

In general, do the same thing when you want to show that something belongs to a group:

> The seagulls' main intention was to eat anything they could find.

> The Smiths' dog is so fat that he gets stuck in the doggie door.

Plural Words Spelled the Same as the Singular

Some words, like "fish," "deer," or "sheep" don't necessarily change spelling to become plural—you just use the same word for both. In these cases, add the apostrophe-s.

Sheep → Sheep's

Deer → Deer's

Fish → Fish's

In this case, it may seem confusing because both the singular and the plural look the same. However, context should make this clear in most cases:

> That deer's antlers have twelve points.

> The deer's habitats are disappearing.

Words That Are Already Plural

Words like "children" or "men" are *already* plural, so just add the apostrophe-s. *Don't* add the "s" first, as if you need to make it plural, and then add the apostrophe after:

> WRONG: The childrens' room is too messy.

> RIGHT: The children's room is messy.

WRONG: Ma'am, the mens' room is across the hall.

RIGHT: Ma'am, the men's room is across the hall.

Contractions

The other use for apostrophes is to form contractions. *Contractions* are shortened versions of words that use fewer letters and are easier and faster to say.

The title of this book includes a common contraction: "don't." Don't is short for "do not." The apostrophe shows that a letter has been taken out between the "n" and the "t":

Do not → don[o]t → don't

This is how it works with all contractions—the apostrophe shows you where something's been cut out. Usually, the apostrophe takes the place of those letters, but occasionally there will be additional missing letters that aren't fully reflected:

Cannot → can[no]t → can't

Should not → shouldn[o]t → shouldn't

But

Shall not → sha[ll]n[o]t → shan't

Or, to include a slightly different type of contraction—and one we used earlier in this section:

Something has → Something[ha]s → Something's

In these last two cases, multiple letters are removed, but only one apostrophe is used to signal that the word is contracted.

Also remember that a few words will change spelling slightly in contracted form:

Will not → w[ill]n[o]t → w[o]nt → won't

Braces ({})

Braces are pretty darn unusual. It's likely that you'll never really need to use them, but even so, it's best to know what they're for; at least you can avoid using them wrong.

With Choices

Braces can be used to denote options or choices:

There are four colors to choose from {Rhubarb, Ebony, Morning Mist, and Twilight}, but most customers prefer to simply call them red, black, silver, and blue.

This usage of the brace is fairly rare, as parentheses work just as well in virtually all circumstances (see below).

There are occasional other uses for braces, but in general, they fall under its use as a mathematical symbol.

Brackets ([])

Brackets are often used identically to parentheses, but they shouldn't be. They have their own uses, and keeping them separate makes writing clearer and more effective.

Brackets explain or include information that the editor or author wants the reader to have.

Adding Explanation to Clarify a Sentence

Use brackets to add information that isn't normally included in the sentence. Parentheses could be used effectively in this circumstance, but it's really the brackets' job:

The boss was staying at the hotel [the Four Seasons] when I got a call about the deal.

Adding or Replacing Words

When you're quoting someone, you might find that he or she has naturally used a word that will make the quote confusing for the reader. For example, if you've been talking about the mayor with a friend for half an hour, he or she might say something like this:

"I even had to go to his daughter's dance recital for him; he was too busy to go himself."

Out of context, your reader won't know who "he" is, so you use your trusty brackets to make it clear:

"I even had to go to [the mayor's] daughter's dance recital; he was too busy to go himself."

Alternatively, you can just leave the original word in and add the explanation after it:

"John and Barry got in a fistfight, and before the security guard could intervene, John broke his [Barry's] nose."

Similarly, you can add words the speaker left out completely if the quoted sentence might be confusing without them:

"The explosion was fourteen miles from the base, but only two [miles] from the train station."

In general, any time you modify a quote, put the modification in brackets.

All of these uses can be summed up in one equation:

CS Part 1 [Clarification] CS Part 2.

Using [sic]

Brackets are also useful on the occasion that you have to quote something exactly, but there's a mistake in the quote that you don't want people to think is yours. "Sic" is a Latin word that represents the phrase "sic erat scriptum," or "Thus was it written." It's really a fancy way of saying "The guy I'm quoting screwed this one up—don't blame me."

If you choose to use [*sic*], remember two things:

1. It's pointing out a mistake in someone else's work, so make sure you're right and that it actually *is* an error.
2. You may come off as somewhat insulting.

When using [*sic*], italicize the word but not the brackets.

Colons (:)

Colons are usually associated with lists, but they have a number of other uses as well. Remember the following rule:

GIGA-IMPORTANT COLON RULE: A colon must *always* be preceded by a complete sentence. What comes after the colon can be anything at all, so long as it says something about the sentence before the colon.

To put it in simpler terms:

relates back

CS: [Anything]

This is the basic rule you'll want to remember. Here are some specific applications of colons.

To Introduce Lists

Colons can introduce lists but only after a complete sentence:

WRONG: I bought: a pound of butter, a deep-fat fryer, and twelve Snickers bars.

RIGHT: I bought the following: a pound of butter, a deep-fat fryer, and twelve Snickers bars.

To Draw a Conclusion or Complete a Thought

If you've set up a conclusion in your complete sentence before your colon, you may want to state that conclusion after the colon. This conclusion can be a complete sentence, a single word, even a single letter, so long as it relates back to the complete sentence.

Cartman was dedicated to his goal: he wanted to get Kyle's money.

Cartman had only one thing on his mind: ham.

Cartman's episode of his show was brought to you by one letter: A.

With Subtitles

If your title has a subtitle, set it off with a colon and a new line:
Deconstructing the Semiotics of Sesame Street:
When is a Grouch not a Grouch?

Spacing

Use only one space after a colon.

Capitalizing after Colons

If what comes after the colon is a complete sentence in its own right, it's generally better to capitalize the first letter. If not, keep it lowercase.

I was really tired: When I got home, I fell immediately into bed.
When I looked up I saw them: flying saucers.

Commas (,)

Commas are probably the most misunderstood punctuation mark in the English language. Mostly this is because they have so many different uses.

There are two primary rules you'll need to remember to get down probably 90% of all your commas. Once you have those under your belt, the rest of the uses are just exceptions.

Commas with FANBOYS

The FANBOYS are a group of words grammar people call "coordinating conjunctions." FANBOYS is an acronym:

For
And
Nor

But
Or
Yet
So

All of these words behave alike when it comes to commas, and not understanding this behavior accounts for a sizable chunk of writers' comma mistakes—even experienced writers.

COMMA RULE OF THUMB #1: If what comes after a FANBOY is a complete sentence, then use a comma before the FANBOY. If what comes after it isn't, then don't.

Or to put it more simply:

CS, [FANBOY] CS

CS [FANBOY] IS

Take a look at these examples:

WRONG: I saw the clown and I was scared. (Complete sentence after: use a comma)

RIGHT: I saw the clown, and I was scared.

WRONG: I saw the clown, and was scared (Incomplete sentence after: no comma)

RIGHT: I saw the clown and was scared.

When Linking Ideas

The other really important rule of thumb regards using commas to link ideas together:

COMMA RULE OF THUMB #2: If a complete sentence is followed by an incomplete sentence, do not use a comma. If an incomplete sentence is followed by a complete sentence, use a comma.

And in equation form:

CS IS

IS, CS

Understanding and applying this rule will get you through almost all of the rest of your comma confusion. Take a look at these examples:

With my controller in hand, I entered the Halo tournament. (IS, CS)

I entered the Halo tournament with my controller in hand. (CS IS)

After that unfortunate experience, I never looked at snails the same way. (IS, CS)

I never looked at snails the same way after that unfortunate experience. (CS IS)

There are lots of different types of incomplete sentence chunks, but this rule will generally hold true for all of them.

And there you have it—in those two rules, you'll find the answer to over 90% of your comma problems. The remaining 10% are covered in a handful of exceptions.

Exception 1: With Lists

Separate lists of more than two elements with commas:

I brought a machete, a shotgun, and a power bar.

But

I brought a machete and a power bar.

Though different sources disagree over whether to use a comma before the final list item in a series, in general, it is clearer to use one than not. If space isn't an issue, and if you haven't been told otherwise (by your in-house style guide, your boss, or your teacher), then use it.
In equation form, it looks like this:

[Item 1], [Item 2], . . . [Item *n*], and [Final Item].

Exception 2: With Insertions

When you want to put something into the middle of a longer sentence, you can use commas to enclose it. This is called a "parenthetical" in fancy grammar terms, but we'll just call it an "insertion."

When inserting with commas, the information you're including needs to be nonessential to the sentence. Transitional words like "however" or "of course" qualify for nonessential when they're inserted into the middle of a sentence, as does any information that isn't crucial to your meaning:

If you keep driving without a license, *of course*, you'll eventually go to jail.

Mbizi, *however*, was not as sure that Yuri would be punished.

My friend, who was nineteen at the time, got us both put in jail.

In the last example, you can see that the added information, the age of the writer's friend, isn't crucial to the main sentence, which really deals with his friend getting them put in jail. That qualifies it for nonessential information status.
A simpler way to look at this rule is this:

CS Part 1, [Nonessential Information], CS Part 2

Remember that *essential* information doesn't get commas, because the commas signal that you don't need that part. This is often a slippery concept to grasp, but look at these two examples:

My sister, who has brown hair, likes to get her hair done.

My sister who has brown hair likes to get her hair done.

Both versions are correct, depending on the circumstances: if the speaker has only one sister, then her hair color isn't essential for identifying which sister he's talking about. If he has more than one sister, and only one has brown hair, then the hair color becomes a necessary part of the sentence, and so doesn't take the commas.

Exception 3: With Nonessential Information at the End of a Sentence

Frequently, you'll find that your nonessential information comes at the end of your sentence. This information might be anything you would treat as an insertion, above, or it can include tag questions like "don't you" or "should I":

She's a survivor, like me.

I don't think I should invest in that Colorado oceanfront development, do you?

So:

CS, [Nonessential Information].

Exception 4: With Series of Adjectives

When a series of adjectives are describing the same word, use a comma between them if they are equal in importance. These are called "coordinate adjectives." But how can you tell when you have coordinate adjectives? There are two tests:

1. Reverse the order and see if they still mean the same thing.
2. See if you can put "and" in between them and the sentence still reads smoothly.

Try it with the following examples:

We saw a kind, wise lady.

CHECK #1: We saw a wise, kind lady.

CHECK #2: We saw a wise (and) kind lady.

This sentence checks out: the comma is necessary. But some sentences aren't so lucky:

We saw a kind, old lady.

CHECK #1: We saw an old, kind lady. (Doesn't mean quite the same thing)

CHECK #2: We saw a kind and old lady. (Doesn't fit smoothly)

In this case, the two words aren't really reversible, and the "and" makes the sentence sound weird. In this case, the comma is incorrect.

RIGHT: We saw a kind old lady.

Exception 5: With Quotes

When setting a quote apart from who said it, use a comma if the two are side-by-side:

Joe said, "Hey, why is that guy over there sparkling in the sunlight?"

John said, "Because he's a dork."

Use this outline to help understand commas with quotations:

"[Quoted Matter]," [Attribution].

[Attribution], "[Quoted Matter]."

Omit this comma with *inline quotations*. Inline quotes are quotes that are worked into the grammar of the sentence. In these cases, what was said and who said it generally aren't side-by-side:

The mayor said that his staff "is ready and able" to help the earthquake victims.

Or:

CS Part 1 "CS Part 2" CS Part 3.

Note in this last case that the third complete sentence section is optional—the sentence can just as well end immediately after the quotation.

Exception 6: In Dates

Use commas to separate days, months, and years if using the standard "American" format of day, month, year:

Monday, April 30, 2012

Do not use them, however, in European formatted dates, which are also military and MLA format:

30 April 2012

Exception 7: With Numbers

Use commas to divide large numbers into sets of three digits, starting from the right:

> 100
>
> 1,000
>
> 10,000
>
> 100,000
>
> 1,000,000

However, do not use these commas if the number is an address or the year in a date:

> 4242 Douglas Lane
>
> The date was April 30, 2012. Walpurgisnacht.

Exception 8: With Cities and States

Separate cities from states or countries with a comma:

> The Professor lives in Arkham, Massachusetts.
>
> He once worked at the library in Buenos Aires, Argentina.

Exception 9: With Degrees or Other Titles

If you need to write out someone's formal name, you'll usually want to include their titles and degrees after it, at least if they're relevant to the topic under discussion. Set these degrees off with commas, even if you have more than one:

> Dr. Jonas Merrifield, Ph.D.
>
> Bill Baggins, M.D., Ph.D., D.O., C.P.A.

Dashes (—)

Dashes are not the same as hyphens (see below). Hyphens are shorter and generally used within words; dashes are used at the sentence level.

Dashes are handy, but don't get carried away using them because they get overwhelming fast. Dashes can be used to mark an interruption or change in thought, to draw a conclusion, or to insert:

Interruption or Change in Thought

Use the dash to signify that some thought has been interrupted, whether by another thought or by an outside influence. This is particularly useful when trying to imitate natural speech:

> "I don't know how to approach this new experiment," Sally said. It's just—"
>
> "Too hard?" Janice interrupted.

Drawing a Conclusion

When drawing a conclusion from a sentence, treat the dash much as you would a colon (see above), but don't use it to start a list:

> There is only one best weapon for zombie slaying—the chainsaw.
>
> Seal Team Six trains constantly—they are the best at what they do.

CS—[Conclusion]

In Insertions

Use the dash to insert information in the same way you would use parentheses (see below): to insert information into another sentence:

I opened the box—it was unlocked—to find my grandfather's photo album inside.

And in equation form:

CS—[Insertion]—CS

Ellipses (. . .)

Ellipses show your reader that you've removed something from a longer piece of writing. Most readers recognize this as "trailing off":

"Then the tanker caught fire, and I thought all was lost. . . ."

In general, an ellipsis is three periods in a row. Normally, you can just put three periods into your word processor and the program will replace them with a special ellipsis character consisting of three periods with special spacing. If your word processor doesn't make this change for you, the next best thing is to put a space between your periods; don't use the newspaper style of putting three periods close together with one space on either side:

WRONG: It was the . . . worst of times.

RIGHT: It was the . . . worst of times.

The ellipsis signals that something has been removed from the sentence, but is generally only used in quoted writing. In fact, in formal writing, the "trailing off" effect is inappropriate, so in your academic papers, use ellipses *only* to show that you have removed something from a quote. For example, a long sentence like this one could be shortened:

The mayor said he had had enough, was tired of, and generally was disgusted by these hooligans spray painting graffiti on the walls of City Hall.

With an ellipse, it becomes much more readable:

The mayor said he . . . was disgusted by these hooligans spray painting graffiti on the walls of City Hall.

There are two simple tips to keep in mind when using ellipses:

1. If you use ellipses at the end of the sentence, add a period *after* the ellipse—three periods for the removed words, and one for the end of the sentence.
2. Don't overuse ellipses—they become annoying when there's more than a few of them on the page.

Exclamation Points (!)

Exclamation points act much like periods: they signal the end of the sentence. But instead of a simple stop, the exclamation point says, "Look at me! This sentence is exciting and surprising!"

The problem is that, if you've done your job well as a writer, you should never *need* an exclamation point. The words you used should get that point across just fine. Take a look at this example:

I came into the bathroom to find that an elephant had torn the wall off the side of my house!

I came into the bathroom to find that an elephant had torn the wall off the side of my house.

In this case, the period is fine—the surprise and shock should register from the story itself, not from the exclamation point. Similarly, don't try to add excitement by throwing around exclamation points—they aren't generally well-respected punctuation marks, and most readers will find them annoying.

In Dialog

The exception to this rule is in dialog, where the exclamation point is used to convey that someone has raised his or her voice or has said something with volume or intensity:

"Khan!" James said.

Hyphens (-)

Hyphens are not the same as dashes—dashes are much longer and are used at the sentence level, while hyphens are short and used generally within words.

Hyphens are used to show a connection between words. They can be used to split words that don't fit on a single line, to connect adjectives that are working together, and to show that words separated in the sentence are still meant to function together:

With Word Breaks at Ends of Lines

If a word won't fit on the line, and you don't want to put it on the next line, you can use a hyphen to break that word into two halves. Remember to break the word between syllables, not in the middle of a syllable:

WRONG: When Indiana picked up the golden idol, he looked at the bottom. The in scription read "Made in China."

RIGHT: When Indiana picked up the golden idol, he looked at the bottom. The inscription read "Made in China."

With Adjectives That Work Together

Sometimes, you need to use two adjectives together to get your meaning across. Grammary people call these "compound adjectives." If you need both adjectives to be read together for it to make the sense you want, you probably have a compound adjective.

Use hyphens to show that the two words work together to modify the noun and come *before* the noun:

The *five-minute* version of the story is that space Nazis are invading the country.

Since this isn't a "five version of the story" or a "minute version of the story," you have to use both of the words together for it to make sense: it takes five minutes, so it is a "fiveminute" version.

Other examples of this phenomenon include ice-cold water, red-hot coals, and drop-dead gorgeous. If the descriptive words come after the noun, don't bother to hyphenate:

I served them ice-cold water.

The water I served them was ice cold.

Suspended Hyphenation

Sometimes, you may have two compound adjectives that have the same second word:

The **rat-infested** and **cockroach-infested** building was condemned.

Instead of writing it this way—which is clunky and sounds weird—you can just remove the first "infested" and leave the hyphen hanging at the end of the word. This signals your reader that both words go with the word "infested," not just the second one:

The **rat-** and **cockroach-infested** building was condemned.

This process is called "suspended hyphenation."

Parentheses (())

Parentheses are used to insert things into sentences.

To Add Nonessential Information

Parentheses show your reader that you want to pull him or her aside and add information that may be interesting or useful, but that isn't crucial.

Fortunato (he was the one who liked wine) seemed closed off last I talked to him.

Avoid parentheses unless you really don't feel the information you're adding is crucial: many readers skip over parentheses as unimportant. If you want to ensure your reader reads what you put in your insertions, use dashes (above).

Boiled down to its most basic elements, it looks like this:

CS Part 1 (Nonessential Information) CS Part 2

In Citations

In MLA and some other styles, page numbers for citations are put in parentheses:

According to Yankovic, "Everything you know is wrong" (23).

"Everything you know is wrong" (Yankovic 23).

Question Marks (?)

Question marks signify (big surprise) questions.

With Standard Questions

In any regular question, end the sentence with a question mark:

Should we allow this to continue?

Where's my dog?

Do *not* use a question mark with indirect questions, which report or explain a question rather than asking it:

WRONG: Every time I wear my fedora, people ask me where I got it?

RIGHT: Every time I wear my fedora, people ask me where I got it.

Quotation Marks (" "/' ')

Usually, quotation marks show your reader that you're quoting someone or something word for word—but that's only part of the equation.

Regular Quotes

In regular quotes, the exact words someone says or writes—and only their exact words—are put in quotes. Remember to set off the quote itself from who said it with a comma (see Commas, p. 54).

WRONG: The mayor said, "My opponent is an idiot." But he didn't use the word "idiot."

RIGHT: The mayor said, "My opponent doesn't know how to run the city."
OR
RIGHT: The mayor said words to the effect that his opponent is incompetent.

Quotes within Quotes

When you're in the middle of the quote and want to quote someone else, use single quotes, not double quotes, for the inner quote:

WRONG: The sergeant said, "The guy just kept yelling the word "cheese" over and over again."

RIGHT: The sergeant said, "The guy just kept yelling the word 'cheese' over and over again."

If both quotes end in the same place, just use the single quotes followed by the double, with the punctuation inside *all three* quotes:

The sergeant said, "I'm annoyed by the prisoner in Cell Eight who keeps yelling, 'cheese.'"

With Titles

Use quotation marks to signify that something is the title of a short work or a part of another work. For long works like novels, use italics. Works that take quotation marks include chapters, poems, songs, and magazine articles:

WRONG: The article was published in "Forbes" magazine.

RIGHT: The article was published in *Forbes* magazine.

WRONG: The article was entitled Four Ways to Make a Million.

RIGHT: The article was entitled "Four Ways to Make a Million."

RIGHT: The song was called "Midnight Ride" and it was on the album *Born Yesterday*.

Punctuation with Quotation Marks

Whether using single or double quotation marks, follow these rules:

1. Periods, commas, and exclamation points *always* go *inside* your quotation marks.

   Ash said, "This is my boom stick!"

   "This is my boom stick," Ash said.

   "Apparently," said Ash, "You haven't met my boom stick yet."

2. Question marks go inside your quotation marks when used with standard quotes, but not when using quotation marks to show titles. Question marks inside title quotes mean that the question mark is part of the title:

   Roger said, "Have you read that story?"

   BUT

   Isn't that story's title "For a Breath I Tarry"?

   OR

   That poem's title is "Shall I Compare Thee to a Summer's Day?"

   Note that in this last case, no period is necessary; the question mark serves double duty, even though the sentence itself isn't a question.

3. Semicolons, colons, and dashes go outside quotation marks.

   The music critic said that *Born Yesterday* was "quite an album"; this is why it sold so well.

   The music critic said that *Born Yesterday* was "quite an album": this is why it sold so well.

   The music critic said that *Born Yesterday* was "quite an album"— this is why it sold so well.

4. In most cases, you put a comma between the *quote* and *who said the quote*. (see "Commas," above).

> Robert Neville said, "I hate zombies."
> "We're vampires," the vampires said.

1. In-Line Quotations

   Quotations that flow into the grammar of a sentence are called "in-line quotations," and they don't need a comma:

   Joe the barber said cutting my hair was "like trimming a thorn bush."

   Joe said he was "going to need gardening shears" to get through my tangles.

2. For Sarcasm or Nonliteral Meanings

   Quotes can show that something is meant to be taken either *sarcastically* or *nonliterally*. This is why you should *never* use quotation marks in an attempt to emphasize something.

   RIGHT: We spent three hours at the "party." (Implies that the party was either not really a party, as in being in a group project at work, or that the party wasn't much fun.)

   RIGHT: "Breakfast" was a cup of coffee and half a cookie. (The speaker doesn't consider this breakfast.)

   RIGHT: "This created a "domino effect" in the crowd. (There are no literal dominoes, but the speaker is using a figure of speech.)

   WRONG: Here at EZ-Mart, we have "great" service. (Implies that the service isn't actually great at all.)

Periods

Period are used to end sentences:

> This is the end of the sentence.

> In general, they can be followed by one or two spaces, though currently the preference leans toward one.

> There are, however, other uses of periods.

Periods in Acronyms

Acronyms are groups of letters that stand in for groups of words in order to save time:

NATO → North Atlantic Treaty Organization

MBA → Master of Business Administration

LSD → Lysergic Acid Diethylamide

Though periods were traditionally used between the letters of an acronym, the current trend is to omit them and use simple capitals, like we've done in the examples.

Periods in Initials

Though you can omit the periods in acronyms, do *not* do so with people's initials:

> WRONG: HP Lovecraft
> RIGHT: H.P. Lovecraft

Other Abbreviations

Non-acronym abbreviations generally need periods:

Tues.

Homeowners' assn.

Periods after Initials and Abbreviations

Do not use both periods if a sentence ends immediately after someone's initials or an abbreviation:

WRONG: The man's initials were J.R.R..

This confuses your reader, making him or her wonder if you meant to use an ellipse (see Skill 5.1) but forgot a period. It also just plain looks silly. Instead, use only one period in these places, letting the single period do "double duty" for both the initials and the end of the sentence:

RIGHT: The man's initials were J.R.R.

Periods with Parentheses

If you have the whole sentence inside the parentheses, put the period inside, too. If the parentheses are only part of a longer sentence, then put the period outside.

Whole sentence inside: I love bunnies. (They're so cute.)

Part of sentence inside: I was tired (it was really late) so I fell asleep in the car.

Part of sentence inside, at end: Falling asleep in the car was a bad idea (I was driving).

Periods with Quotation Marks

When the end of a quotation comes at the end of a sentence, *always* put the period inside. No exceptions.

WRONG: Sam said the music was "funkadelic".

RIGHT: Sam said the music was "funkadelic."

Semicolons (;)

Semicolons look like a weird hybrid of a comma and a period—which is what they are. Semicolons create a pause that's right between a comma's brief break and a period's full stop. They are used to connect complete, related sentences and to separate complex lists.

Connecting Complete Sentences

If you have two complete sentences that are related, use a semicolon to connect them:

I saw the UFO land on Godzilla's head; he was confused by its choice of landing pad.

Remember, though, that the sentences have to be related for a semicolon to work:

RIGHT: I saw the UFO land on Godzilla's head; he swatted at it with his tail.

WRONG: I saw the UFO land on Godzilla's head; I hate asparagus.

As an equation:

CS; CS

In Complex Lists

In complex lists, semicolons can act as "supercommas," showing the divisions between list items that already contain commas. This makes your list much clearer:

WRONG: The three groups consisted of Crichton, Aeryn, and Ka; Darth, Boba, and Palpatine, and Mal, Wash, and River.

RIGHT: The three groups consisted of Crichton, Aeryn, and Ka; Darth, Boba, and Palpatine; and Mal, Wash, and River.

As you can see, the semicolon forms a kind of a "wall" that separates the groups from each other and clarifies them without the reader having to look for the "ands" and backengineer your meaning from there.

So essentially, the semicolon is what you use when making a list of smaller lists, or when you feel the need to list phrases or sentences that already contain commas. This distills down to the following equation:

[Complex List Item 1], [Complex List Item 2], . . . [Complex List Item n], and [Final Complex List Item]

EXERCISES

SECTION 1: BREAKING DOWN SENTENCES INTO CHUNKS

In order to make correct decisions about punctuation, we need to understand how sentences can be viewed as "chunks" of information, and each "chunk" must be designated as either a complete or an incomplete sentence if it were to be taken on its own.

For the following sentences, break down each into logical chunks—ideas that seem to hang together. Draw brackets around these chunks, and then label each as a Complete Sentence (CS) or an Incomplete Sentence (IS). Remember that for these designations, you are not looking at the *entire* sentence, but only its individual pieces.

1. The play is called *Rosencrantz and Guildenstern Are Dead*, and the movie version features the song "Seamus" by Pink Floyd.
2. The play tells the story of *Hamlet* through the eyes of minor characters.
3. It's one of those weird movies that questions the nature of reality itself.
4. Many of its actors are famous: Gary Oldman and Richard Dreyfuss, for example.
5. Frequently, the characters are seen passing the time while parts of the original play go on around them.

SECTION 2: USING PUNCTUATION

Often, people learn best by following what is called "anticipation and repetition," in which they try to remember the answer to a question, get as much as they can, and then go back to review the parts they missed. For the following questions, you will follow this process by writing in under each punctuation mark all the rules you can remember on using them. Then go back and review what you missed. You may even want to copy a blank answer sheet before you begin, so that you can go through this process several times. Before you know it, the rules of punctuation will be a part of you.

1. Apostrophe

    _____

2. Braces

    _____

3. Brackets

    _____

4. Colon

    _____

5. Comma

    _____

6. Dash

    _____

7. Ellipsis

_____

8. Exclamation Point

_____

9. Hyphen

_____

10. Parentheses

_____

11. Question Mark

_____

12. Quotation Mark

_____

13. Period

_____

14. Semicolon

_____

SECTION 3: TESTING THE RULES OF PUNCTUATION

The following sentences contain errors involving the punctuation mark specified. Note that this section deals only with the most important rules of the most important punctuation marks. Identify and fix the errors, using the rules listed above. Some sentences may be correct as-is.

Apostrophes:
1. This Carlos's car.
2. The fishes's habitats are disappearing.
3. This is the Fullerton Mens' Choir.

Colons
1. The reasons the movie sucked are: poor acting, poor writing, and bad special effects.
2. Godzilla attacked the town, crushing all before him: I hate rap.

Commas
1. The mayor wasn't very bright and he usually made poor decisions.
2. INGSOC is the name for "English Socialism" in _1984_, but not in real life.
3. I told the student he was failing for he had shown up only twice.
4. I was surprised, when the clown hit me in the face with a stapler.
5. I feared the clown, for it was creepy.
6. I bought a new car; it was shiny and fast but it didn't go.
7. When the UFO landed on Godzilla's head the monster was confused.
8. I ate an entire pizza and threw up.

Ellipses
1. Then the airlock closed behind them, and they thought all was lost . . .
2. The old man said, "Hey you [expletive] punks, get the [expletive] off my lawn!" (replace editorial remarks in brackets with properly formatted ellipses.

327

Parentheses

1. As Ellis ran along the track, he had to keep shooting behind him (there were zombies.) (This made it a bad day).

Question Marks

1. Have you read the "Declaration of Independence?"

Quotation Marks

1. The cop said, "Well, the mayor had a meeting yesterday, and he said, "I will tolerate no more spitting on the sidewalk!""
2. The president of the company said that sales were, "lackluster."

Semicolons

1. I ran to the store; and bought a pound of bacon.
2. I went with three groups of three: Joe, Sarah, and John, Bill, Cletus, and Biff, and Zorg, Buzz and Woody. (Note: add semicolons where needed)
3. I think there are UFOs circling the earth right now; I like cherries.

SECTION 4: APPLYING THE RULES OF PUNCTUATION

Fix the punctuation errors in the following sentences. Some sentences have more than one error. Repair the errors or rewrite the sentences to solve the problems.

1. Kragnar the Barbarian was only five years old when first he held his father's sword.
2. The sword was named Longarm, for it was what the Kings of the barbarians used to punish wrongdoers.
3. The blade was longer than Kragnar himself (it was almost six feet long.)
4. As Kragnar held it aloft (struggling with its weight), the boy's father said to him, "I was but your age when my own father gave me this sword, and said "go forth, and punish evil"."
5. As he grew into manhood, Kragnar took to his job eagerly-he sought out those who mistreated the poor and the destitute, and he brought them to justice.
6. His "weapon" eventually became the image of his might among the barbarians of the tribe of Broken Kneecap.
7. When his father chose to step down, Kragnar took the throne, the change of leadership was peaceful and the people were greatly pleased.
8. As he left the throne room for the last time, the old king said "Obey my son.............he will watch over you."
9. All of this is according to the History of Kragnar [a Work of Epic Fiction] by Cletus Daggenworth.
10. The author himself said, "I feel that (Kragnar) is a hero for all ages, swinging his mighty sword and felling dragons and giants for the good of the land."
11. The guy was screaming at me, yelling "get of my lawn you (punk)."

SENTENCE CONSTRUCTION: INSTRUCTION WITH EXERCISES

Definition: A sentence is a group of words, which contains a subject and a verb that can stand alone. Another name for a sentence is an **independent clause** because it can stand on its own.

Definition: A **subordinate clause** is a group of words that contains a subject and a verb but cannot stand alone. It has to be connected/attached to an independent clause.

Types of Sentences

A **simple sentence** is an independent clause containing no subordinate clauses.

Example: Jim and John went fishing and hunting.

A **compound sentence** is a sentence that contains two independent clauses connected by a semicolon or a comma plus a conjunction.

Example: I went to the store, but I forgot to buy milk.

                 I went to the store; I forgot to buy milk.

A **complex sentence** is a sentence containing an independent clause plus one or more subordinate clauses.

Example: Because he was tall, he played basketball.

He played basketball because he was tall.

A **compound/complex sentence** is a compound sentence that also has a subordinate clause in one of the two sentences.

Example: I went to the store, and I bought extra canned goods because they were on sale.

Active Voice

Active voice in sentences: Active verbs are preferred over *be* verbs and passive verbs. Active verbs express stronger meaning.

Example of passive voice: The wallpaper was hung by me.

Example of active voice: I hung the wallpaper.

Parallelism

In sentence writing, two or more ideas should be written using the same grammatical form.

Example: People walked, jogged, and sprinted during the race.

                 (words are all past tense verbs)

Example: I searched around the house and in my car.

                 (two prepositional phrases)

From *Basics in Writing* by Georgia Turner. Copyright © 2016 by Georgia Turner. Reprinted by permission.

Example: Many stores are reducing prices and extending sales to increase profits.

(pairing words with -*ing* endings)

Shift in Point of View

Informational essays **should be written in either first or third person.** This means to **avoid second person,** which is the use of you/your/understood or implied you (command). Choose one point of view, either first or third person, and stay with it.

Example: I have a new job. The company I work for gave me a credit card for expenses. You get to buy gas with it.

*Do *you* get to buy gas with the card? No, *I* do.

Shift in Tense

A writer must maintain consistent verb tense—either staying in present or past tense. If an essay is started in present tense, then the essay must be completely in present tense. Conversely, if the essay is begun in past tense, then the essay must be completed in past tense.

Example: I ran a marathon yesterday. Just as I came toward the finish line, another runner comes to the line and wins the race.

Correction: I ran a marathon yesterday. Just as I came toward the finish line, another runner came to the line and won the race.

*Start in *past* tense. Stay in *past* tense.

Wordiness

Wordiness comes in redundancies and empty/inflated phases. Here are some examples and how to make them more concise. In informational essays, it is best to write as concisely as possible.

Wordy phrase	Concise
due to the fact that	because
at the current time	now, currently
in spite of the fact that	although
in order to	to
in the event that	if
in this day and age	now
until such a time	until
red of color	red

Activities: Change the words/phrases in these sentences to show conciseness.

1. The boy played basketball for the reason he was tall.
2. We will go the accountant in order to get our taxes done.
3. In the event of a power outage, people should have candles.
4. My new dress is blue of color.
5. I agree with my opponent at the present time.
6. I will return back the book to the library.
7. A large number of people came to the rally.
8. Most people have a computer in this day and age.
9. The baby slept during the time that his parents were driving.
10. The more wore a shirt big in size.

Don't Slaughter Your Sentences

Don't Promulgate Verbose Superfluity (Don't Be Wordy)

When you first read that title up there, your immediate response was probably "What the heck?" And that's a logical response—the first title is way too fancy to get the point across; in fact, a lot of people won't understand it at all without the translation below it.

This is called wordy writing. In general, it means using more words than you need to get the job done. But it goes a little beyond that: It also means using excessively fancy words (like these), making your sentences too complicated, or using verbs that unnecessarily obscure your meaning. All these mistakes are big don'ts because they get between you and your reader; they slow down your writing and keep people from getting what you're trying to tell them.

Don't Be Redundant

Redundancy is using more than one word or phrase to say the same thing, or saying something that's clearly implied:

> WORDY: The disgusting and gross mess in the dirty refrigerator grossed me out.
>
> REVISION: ~~The disgusting and gross~~ [**I was disgusted by the**] mess in the ~~dirty~~ refrigerator ~~grossed me out.~~
>
> REVISED: I was disgusted by the mess in the refrigerator.

In the first sentence, words like *disgusting* and *gross* and *gross me out* all do the same thing, so reduce it to only one use. Also, if you're disgusted by the mess in the fridge, then you don't really need to tell your reader that it's "dirty."

Pointless Words and Phrases

Don't fall victim to the temptation to "dress up" your writing with extra words:

> WORDY: In my opinion, there is absolutely no reason to continue working on the project in spite of the fact that we have invested our money in it. The reason is because it will never work.
>
> REVISION: ~~In my opinion,~~ there is ~~absolutely~~ no reason to continue ~~working on~~ the project ~~in spite of the fact that~~ [**even though**] we have invested our money in it. The reason is because it will never work.
>
> REVISED: There is no reason to continue the project even though we have invested in it. It will never work.

Passive Wording

Some ways of talking about actions get straight to the point, wasting no time, while others beat around the bush. These are called *active* and *passive voice*.

In active voice, the subject of the sentence is the one doing the action:

> ACTIVE: I kicked the spy.

While in passive voice, the subject of the sentence is the one that has the action done *to* it:

> PASSIVE: The spy was kicked by me.

As you can see, passive phrases are wordier, and therefore weaker, than active ones. It gets even more complicated if you want to add more details to your sentence:

From *The Little Book of Don't's* by Jason M. Taylor. Copyright © 2012 by Jason M. Taylor. Reprinted by permission.

PASSIVE: The spy was kicked in the head by me.

In general, you'll make your sentences more readable by using active voice:

ACTIVE: I kicked the spy in the head.

It is better to avoid passive voice on the whole—but it isn't required. On some occasions, it may be necessary or even sound better; just remember to limit your use of it as much as possible.

Inflated Diction

Some writers don't just want to add words—they want to add the *coolest* words. When a simple, readily recognized word will work, don't use a fancy one from the bowels of your dictionary. In general, if most of your readers would have to look it up, don't use it.

INFLATED: I am cognizant of the manifold outcomes of my exploits.

REVISED: I know the many consequences of my actions.

In the revised version, the overly fancy words get dropped and replaced with more normal vocabulary, and the result is a cleaner, more understandable sentence.

Don't Get Shifty

Readers have a hard time following you if you keep changing up the game on them. So when you're writing, make sure that you don't make unexpected shifts in the way you're talking.

Tense Shifts

These are some of the most common—and distracting—errors. Be sure that you keep your tenses consistent: if you're talking about past events, stay in the past. If you're talking about present events, use the present. But whatever you do, don't go back and forth.

WRONG: When I was fourteen, I went to Medieval Times for the first time. I had tickets from my grandmother. So we sit down, and the fighting starts, and everyone starts yelling.

So which is it? Present or past? Since it's a story, this writer should stick to past tense:

RIGHT: When I was fourteen, I went to Medieval Times for the first time. I had tickets from my grandmother. So we sat down, and the fighting started, and everyone started yelling.

Point of View Shifts

"Point of view" means who's telling the story. First person point of view is told using "I," while third is told using "he" or "she." Second person, one of the most problematic points of view, is told using "you."

Figure out what the most logical point of view is and stick with it. Most often, the mistake writers make is to shift into "you," which is itself wrong (see Things You Should Never Do, p. 93).

WRONG: I was on a show called *American Ninja Super Master Fighter*. To win, *you* had to do obstacle courses and not fall off into the water.

RIGHT: I was on a show called *American Ninja Super Master Fighter*. To win, *I* had to do obstacle courses and not fall off into the water.

Don't Dangle Your Modifiers

Modifiers *modify* or describe other parts of the sentence. They can come in a number of places and can be single words, phrases, or *prepositional phrases*, which is just a fancy term for phrases that begin with prepositions. Modifiers always modify the nearest word they can find. For more information on modifiers, see *Building Blocks*).

Exhausted, I trudged into the safe room. (Modifier describes "I")

(With his machete in hand), Cletus faced the wilderness.

Misplaced Modifiers

Modifiers describing the wrong word make your sentence sound like it says something different than you meant. Revise these sentences to keep the modifier as close as possible to what you want it to describe:

WRONG: The girl watched the airplane take off in a short skirt. (Means the airplane is wearing the skirt).

REVISED: The girl in a short skirt watched the airplane take off.

OR

REVISED: In a short skirt, the girl watched the airplane take off.

Dangling Modifiers

Sometimes, the modifier gets "left hanging," because the word it's supposed to describe isn't even in the sentence. Put the word you really want described back in the sentence:

WRONG: With a grim smile on his face, the machete slashed through the underbrush. (The machete can't smile.)

RIGHT: With a grim smile on his face, Cletus slashed his machete through the underbrush.

Squinting Modifiers

Squinting modifiers are confused—they have two perfectly good words they could describe, but there's no way to tell which one they go with:

WRONG: Dogs that shed occasionally make good watchdogs.

It's unclear whether the writer means that dogs that shed sometimes make particularly good watchdogs, or that dogs that shed make good watchdogs only some of the time.

To avoid this confusing problem, do what you do with all modifiers: put it right next to the word you want it to modify—and make sure it's not just as close to another word it could go with:

RIGHT: Occasionally, dogs that shed make good watchdogs.

RIGHT: Dogs that shed make good watchdogs occasionally.

RIGHT: Occasionally, good watchdogs can be made of dogs that shed.

Don't Tangle Your Tenses

Verb tenses specify *when* things happen. In grade school, you most likely learned how the past tense happened before now, the future after now, and the present, now. But there's more to getting your tenses right.

Present Tense
With Facts
Use present tense to discuss facts, even if the subject is something that happens over time:

> "Every year, hundreds of thousands of people text while driving."

Scheduled Events
Anything scheduled ahead of time or on a regular basis takes present tense, even though it may take place in the future:

> *Castle* comes on every Monday at 10 p.m.

> Paleography 101 starts next semester.

Summarizing Plots
Use present tense, not past, to describe the plots of stories, books, movies, and so forth:

> In the book *Frankenstein*, Victor Frankenstein creates a monster—and then becomes a whiny loser.

Past Tense
With Sequences of Events
Use past tense when a number of events happen in rapid succession in the past. Don't worry about using the tense to show what order they happened in—just list them in that order:

> Once Jim *got* a copy of World of Warcraft, he *got* addicted, *lost* his girlfriend, *lost* his job, *lost* his car, *lost* his house, and *ended up* on the streets.

Future Tense
With Expected Future Events
Aside from things that will happen, future tense can refer to things that the speaker *assumes* will happen:

> If the virus hits this state, the zombies will eat our brains.

With Sudden Decisions
Use future tense when a speaker comes to a sudden decision:

> I know! I will do the fandango!

Other Tenses
Showing the Past Tense of a Past Tense
When you want to show that something happened in the past before another event in the past, use the form "had [verb]ed." This is called the "past perfect":

> He *went* for his dagger, but Tex *had drawn* his gun already.

The second verb form isn't actually past tense, even though it looks like the past. It's a verb form called a *past participle*, which frequently looks like a past tense, but often has a slightly different spelling:

> PAST TENSE: I *drank* a bottle of Sunset Sarsaparilla.

> PAST PERFECT WITH PAST PARTICIPLE: I *had drunk* a bottle of Sunset Sarsaparilla.

You should be able to remember which is the correct form by saying to yourself "I have . . . ." And then seeing which verb form sounds correct. However, to be positive, you should use a dictionary for any word you are unclear on.

Showing Past Events with Current Impact

Use the form "has [verb]ed" when you want to show that something started in the past but is still continuing now. This is called the *present perfect* tense.

> I have worked on this project for hours already. Can you take over?

Also use present perfect when you're talking about an event that happened in the past that has a direct impact on what you're talking about now:

> I have seen *Twilight*. Once was more than enough.

Showing Continuous Events

Use the form "is [verb]ing" to show that an action is occurring in the present, but that it also has just occurred in the immediate past, and will continue to occur in the immediate future. This is called the *present progressive*.

> He is fixing my watch while I wait.

> I *am yawning* every few minutes because he *is taking* so long.

Aside from these meanings, the present progressive can also express a couple of other ideas: Something planned to occur in the future:

> I am driving to Buffalo next week.

Something happening for a limited period of time:

> They are showing *Manos: Hands of Fate* until Wednesday afternoon.

GRAMMATICAL STRUCTURE OF SENTENCES

Don't Be Disagreeable

In grammar, "agreement" just means "making words match." There are two main kinds of agreement that readers get wrong: *subject-verb*, and *number*.

Subject-Verb Agreement

Make sure that plural subjects have plural verbs, and that singular ones have singular verbs:

> WRONG: We is.

> RIGHT: We are.

> This may be an obvious mistake, but in many cases, it's much harder to tell if you have a mismatch or not.

Separated Subjects and Verbs

Don't confuse the nearest noun to your verb with your actual subject.

> WRONG: The authors of the paper, each of whom has studied extensively at the university, *explains* how the vampire myth got started.

The real subject is "authors," but the verb matches the closer noun, "university," even though the university doesn't actually explain anything. Make the verb match the real subject, "authors":

> RIGHT: The authors of the paper, each of whom has studied extensively at the university, *explain* how the vampire myth got started.

From *Basics in Writing* by Georgia Turner. Copyright © 2016 by Georgia Turner. Reprinted by permission.

Backwards Sentences

Sometimes, sentence structures get reversed. If dealing with a sentence like this, remember that the subject comes *after* the verb, not before it:

WRONG: There is three types of vampires we know about in the greater Transylvanian Metropolitan Area.

RIGHT: There are three types of vampires we know about in the greater Transylvanian Metropolitan Area.

In this sentence, the subject is "types," not "there," as many writers mistakenly think.

To make sure it's right, flip it around and put the verb after the subject:

CHECK: Three types of vampires are . . . .

Use this pattern with sentences starting with "there is," "here is," there are," and so forth, and for sentences that reverse order for style reasons:

WRONG: On the table **is** the last brownies. ("Brownies is . . . .")

RIGHT: On the table **are** the last brownies. ("Brownies are . . . .")

Confusing Words

Some words can seem like they should be plural but are actually singular.

Use singular with words that end in "-body," "-either," "-thing," or "-one," and the word "each," even if the word seems like it should be plural. Use plural for "some."

WRONG: Everybody know that ninjas are better than dinosaurs.

RIGHT: Everybody knows that ninjas are better than dinosaurs.

WRONG: Some sees the danger of the projected earthquake.

RIGHT: Some see the danger of the projected earthquake.

With Who, Which, and That

Who, which, and that can be singular or plural, depending on what they refer back to in the sentence. Look back to that word to decide if you need a singular or a plural:

They just hired new officers **who are** all Jackie Chan fans. ("Officers" is plural).

The new officers each get a special shotgun, which is autographed by Jackie himself. ("Shotgun" is singular.)

Subjects with Multiple Words

With a subject with more than one word in it, follow these rules:

1. With two things, singular or plural, linked by "and," the verb is plural.
   Cletus and Buford shopped for ammunition.
2. With two singular things linked by "or" or "nor," the verb is singular.
   Eliza or Charlotte bought a puppy.
   Neither Eliza nor Charlotte bought a puppy.
3. If you have a singular and a plural linked by "or" or "nor," make the verb agree with the word closest to it.
   The alligator or the cannibals were going to eat Indiana.
   The cannibals or the alligator was going to eat Indiana.

Number Agreement

Number agreement refers to keeping the same number—again, singular or plural—when you're talking about the same things. This is most commonly a problem that occurs when writers use pronouns:

WRONG: Every ninja has their own favorite weapon.

In this sentence, the word "ninja" is singular, but the word that refers back to it again—"their"—is plural. Most often this is because the writer knows the group has both males and females in it, and so wants to avoid the use of "his," which would be inaccurate and sound sexist.

Instead, use "he or she," "his or her" and so forth:

RIGHT: Every ninja has his or her own favorite weapon.

In general, avoid "his/her." Do not use "s/he," as it has no matching form for "his or her."

EXERCISES

SECTION 1: CUTTING OUT WORDINESS

Use simpler language to restate the following sentences. If you don't know some of the words, use a dictionary. Feel free to simplify the sentences themselves, as well. Note that these sentences are extreme versions of what you might normally need to correct in your own writing.

1. My central appellation is Joseph.
2. I'm fatigued from excessive exertion, so I will now ensconce myself on the sofa and watch TV.
3. My dog is generally sedentary and obtuse.
4. My corpulent brother overflowed his elephantine fleshiness over onto my seat on the airplane.
5. Your Lilliputian vocabulary is no match for my Brobdingnagian lexicon.
6. I am tired and weary of your tendency to go on and on about your missing Legos.
7. In mine and in the opinions of my brethren here on the council, there is no good reason to extend the tax, and there is every good reason to make shorter its time.
8. The town was burned when fi re was breathed on it by the dragon
9. The dragon was made dead by Kragnar using the sword of his father.
10. The altercation was long, of high volume, and filled with angry outbursts.

SECTION 2: TENSE AND POINT OF VIEW SHIFTS

Correct tense and point of view shifts in the following paragraph.

My cousin Bubba and I went to MIT together. Bubba majored in applied nuclear technology, and I studied electrical engineering. At the end of our first semester, Bubba's teacher comes to him and suggests that he should take his class project and turn it into a real product. I was happy to help him, because you need to help friends in need—especially if they can make some money.

SECTION 3: MODIFIER ERRORS

The following sentences contain dangling, misplaced, or squinting modifiers. Reword the sentences so that these errors are removed.

1. Running ahead of the crowd, my backpack squeaked with every step.
2. Zombies that bark and drool occasionally eat people.
3. I ran to the window frightened by the storm outside.
4. I strolled down the street listening to the music.
5. Seeing the accident develop, my arm instinctively reached out to the handbrake.

SECTION 4: VERB TENSES

For each of the following verbs, write out the present perfect, past perfect, and present progressive forms.

1. Run

   _____

2. Walk

   _____

3. Sing

   _____

4. Eat

   _____

5. Sleep

   _____

6. Drink

   _____

7. Dive

   _____

8. Fly

   _____

9. Be

   _____

10. Breed

   _____

SECTION 5: AGREEMENT

For the following questions, choose the correct form of the word to ensure that the subject and the verb agree.

1. There is/are four oranges in the fridge.
2. On the pages of the book is/are the greatest tale ever told.
3. Somebody is/are watching me.
4. Everybody is/are watching me.
5. The miners, each of whom has to protect his stake in the mine, is/are concerned about the cave-in.
6. Buford and Mary-Lou buy/buys Cletus a present.
7. Buford or Mary-Lou wrap/wraps the present.
8. Cletus or his four friends unwrap/unwraps the gift.
9. Neither the four friends nor Cletus owns/own one already
10. We, who witnessed the giving of the gift, is/are now ready to eat cake.

Understanding the Don'ts: Instruction with Exercises

Don't Write Mindlessly: Conscious Writing Will Get You Halfway There

Any of you who've taken a class in study skills has heard the term *active reading*. Active reading is the process of paying attention, asking questions, and really thinking through what you're reading. It's how you read most effectively for studying. But not too many books talk about *active writing*.

Active writing is the process of writing *mindfully*, really paying attention to every detail and trying at every possible point in the writing process to improve your work. Good writing doesn't just "happen" by luck—good writing is work, and work you'll have to do. So when you sit down to pick up your pen (or pencil, or keyboard), don't expect to just "fill up the pages." That might get you the 3 to 5 page limit you need, but it won't be *writing*. At best, it will be filling up blank space with words and hoping your reader will believe you when you say it's writing.

So how do you write actively? The tools are before you in the rest of this book. You can apply all of the don'ts to improve your writing significantly, but you have to be paying attention to do it.

So as you continue through the rest of this guide, try to add each new element to your mental checklist of things to avoid. Pay attention. Write like you read—as actively as possible—and soon you'll find that your sentences are crisper, your ideas clearer, and your work stronger. And what's more, your readers will take you much more seriously.

The Biggest Don't Of All: Don't Forget Your Audience

Audience is one of the most important aspects of writing. In some ways, it's *the* most important aspect. It's so important that I'm putting it first in an *entire book* of stuff you shouldn't mess up. That should tell you something.

It's so important because your audience will tell you how to approach the rest of your piece of writing, no matter what it is. You can know exactly what you want to say, the points you want to use to support it, and even some of the words you want to use, but if you don't know your audience, you've got nothing.

Audience is just the first and most important part of an entire concept that people who sit around and come up with theories about writing call the "rhetorical situation." The rhetorical situation, they will tell you, includes three primary components: your assignment, your purpose, and (there it is again) that all-important *audience*.

So really, it's a fancy way of saying "what you're writing and who you're writing it to." But let's take a look at each of them anyhow.

Assignment

Your **assignment** includes all of the things that you'd usually ask your college English professor if he told you there was a paper due tomorrow. That list would include things such as

- How long is it?
- How do I format it?
- What's my topic?
- How long does it have to be?
- What kinds of examples should I use?
- Do I need to include charts or graphs?
- Are you sure it has to be *that* long?

All kidding aside, the *assignment* is all the requirements for the piece of writing you're doing. Usually, this is all decided by someone else: your teacher, your boss, your publisher. But sometimes, it's set by you—for example, if you decide to write a novel about evil ninja hamsters invading the United States by way of Canada, you'd be calling the shots on how long it would be, how many chapters you would use, the point of view you want, how many hamsters you want to make invade Kansas, and so on. That is, you'd be calling the shots until you tried to get it published, and then you'd have a publisher telling you all those things, as well as probably telling you that nobody wants to read about evil ninja hamsters, anyway. (Evil ninja chinchillas are way more engaging.)

Everything you write has an assignment, one way or another. Part of your job as a writer is to figure out what that assignment is and then follow it.

Purpose

Your **purpose** is the reason you're putting yourself through all this in the first place. Okay, the reason is *probably* because your teacher or your boss made you, but even in that case, you at least have to be making an effort to accomplish something in your writing. That something is your *purpose*.

You can write for all kinds of purposes: to entertain, to persuade, to inform, to analyze, to compare. We don't need to go into them here—suffice it to say that your purpose is what you're trying to get done in the writing work you're doing.

Audience

And that brings us back to the cornerstone of all this: your *audience*. Your audience is important because, even if you have the same assignment and purpose, everything you do in your writing will change based on your audience. It's like you're building a house: the assignment might be the walls and doors, and the purpose might be the windows or the chimney. But the audience is the foundation itself, and without that slab of concrete underneath it, your house will slide right down the hill and onto Interstate 10.

Let's look at an example: you're writing a letter asking for money to invest in a business. In this case, your purpose and assignment are pretty well established: you're writing a letter, for which much of the formatting requirements and general length are established by social convention, and your purpose is also preordained: you wouldn't be writing if you didn't need the money. You want to convince your reader to send you some cash so that you can put it into whatever harebrained business scheme you've cooked up this time.

But watch how changing the audience still changes everything about the way you write it. (And I mean *everything*.)

Example 1: Writing to a Friend

Say you're writing that letter to a friend of yours. For argument's sake, let's say the business you're writing about has something to do with the medical field. Your friend is an electrician in Newark, where you both grew up. You've been friends for 25 years, and you used to call him Stinky when you were kids. Would you start that letter this way?

> Dear Sir,
>
> I submit for your perusal the following business proposal. Please examine it at your leisure and get back to me at your earliest convenience . . . .

Probably not. Why? Because the likely response to that letter would be this one:

> Dude,
>
> Someone hacked your account. Deal with it so I don't have to block you.
>
> Stinky

Because you haven't addressed Stinky in the tone he expects from a good friend, he's not even necessarily going to assume it's you—your calling card, which is your writing, has misled him into mistaking you for someone else, probably a spammer.

If he *does* figure out it's you, you might be in even worse trouble—because now you've approached a close friend as if he were some random person you're asking for money. It's too formal, and it's likely to insult him—sort of like if you started suddenly referring to a longtime friend as "Mr. Anderson," in very formal tones. People know where they're supposed to stand with you socially, and when you break those expectations, you can upset them.

Instead, you might start that same letter like this:

Hey man,

I know you said you were interested in finding some investment opportunities, so I thought I'd send this your way. It's my business—no pressure; just let me know what you think.

If you feel comfortable doing it, you might even address him as "Hey Stinky," depending on how much he hated being called that when you were kids.

Example 2: Writing to a Business Investor

Okay, so now let's say we write the same assignment to a venture capitalist—the guy who gives you money to invest for your business in return for a share of the profits. Do you think it'd be wise to start off like this?

Hey Dood,

Check out my bizness proposal below. It's the best thing you'll see this year! When you dicide to give me the money give me a hollah at my home number.

You probably wouldn't even get a response to this one. It might catch the investor's eye, but only on the way to the trash can in the corner of his or her office. Let's look at how to do this better:

Dear Mr. Smith

Attached please find the brief entitled "Medical Device Project Abstract." I believe you will find everything you need there to make a decision about investing in the project. I am confident in my design, and so I hope that you will choose to support it. Please pay special attention to the quarterly profit predictions and the production tooling schedule, and I believe you will see that this is an investment that will earn great profits for you and your company in the long term.

Sincerely,

Thomas Anderson

This version does a few things differently. For one, it approaches the investor with a far more formal and polite tone. Also, while expressing hope that the reader will decide in the writer's favor, it doesn't *assume* that he or she will do so.

Something else you might notice here is that our Mr. Anderson uses business language—he knows how to use words like "brief" and "abstract" in a business sense. This is "talking the talk"—if your audience expects you to use certain terms, you'd better know how, or you're going to find your way to that trash can no matter how good your ideas are.

Example 3: Writing to a Medical Group

What if you wanted to write to a group of doctors about your new medical device? Would you use the same letter you wrote for the venture capitalist?

In a word, no. The venture capitalist is interested in what investments will make money for him- or herself and for his or her company. Medical doctors don't want to lose money, of course, but they're probably interested in other aspects of the project:

Dear Arkham Massachusetts Psychiatric Care Team,

Please examine the following project proposal and technical specifications for "Medical Device." I have included the entire medical analysis of the device's operation, as well as a prospectus on the kinds of therapies you can expect to achieve using this breakthrough piece of equipment. I am confident that you will agree with me that this is one piece of technology that the public should have access to in their health care decisions. As you examine the papers, I hope that you will provide your financial support to the project in the form of an investment, which, of course, I am confident will pay off extremely well in the long term.

I hope to hear from you soon,

Dr. Wingate Peasley

Here we see the same ideas transformed into something new. Now the focus is on something doctors *should* at least be more interested in—effective therapies for their patients. It doesn't ignore the issue of money, but it downplays it while assuring them that there will be a healthy profit involved.

In this case, notice also how much technical information the writer is attaching: the entire medical analysis and therapeutic prospectus. The writer here is aware that he's speaking to doctors, and realizes that he can't just promise them that something medical will work as planned; they'll want to judge that for themselves. He uses his awareness of what the audience wants and expects to make the best impression possible, and the best impression means the best chance at getting what the writer wants—a new investment in his project.

As you can see, audience is in fact a pretty big part of writing. Everything relies on it—so before you start any project, be sure you ask not just *what* you're writing, but *who* you're writing it to. That will tell you *how* you're supposed to write it.

The Academic Audience

This brings us to one important question—in a classroom setting, who exactly *are* you writing to?

You might be tempted to say "my teacher," but that's too easy. Your teacher is only one person, and an essay isn't like a letter—it shouldn't be written with only one person in mind. That's why college classes use what's called the "academic audience." The academic audience is who you write to in college, and it consists of your instructor *plus* your classmates. By assuming that you're writing to everyone in your class, you have to make sure you make your ideas clear even to the people who aren't familiar with your topic or need more help following your arguments.

If your teacher is really into video games, for example, and you were as well, you could write all day about the games you liked and how much you hated "TKing" and "camping" and how in "l4d2" you wished Rochelle was a more engaging character, but your teacher would be one of the few people who would get it. You need to broaden out your essay for the nonenthusiast, and if you're using specialized terms from your field, that means spelling them out for the yokels.

Don't Hand in Your First Draft: One Simple Step to Fix All Your Writing Problems

This should be self-explanatory, but it isn't. So here goes:

When you're done writing something, *read it again and fix it*. Really. I know a lot of you out there think that when you finish a piece of writing, it's so amazingly super-giga-awesome that you don't have to ever look at it again, that you can hand it in to your teacher and receive high praise and great marks for it.

Wrong.

Once in a while, you can get lucky and escape unscathed from a first-draft submission, but most of the time, you're going to get hammered. It's just too hard to find all the mistakes you might be making without reading over your work, and reading it over again, and again, and maybe even again.

Even really good writers, experts in the field, have to revise. In fact, most will tell you that good writing *is* revision—that the first draft is just a stepping-stone to a final product. And they're absolutely right. You need to revise to be able to find your mistakes, the little don'ts this book is talking about. If you're too confident or too lazy to do that, then you're going to miss stuff, and some of that stuff will cost you—either in points in school or in credibility outside of school.

The key to this step of the writing process is *time management*. I know, I know, you've probably been told about that by teachers and parents and bosses and whomever else for years. But there's a reason all those people tell you about time management: because it's important.

For example, if you're writing a paper for a college class, and that paper is due on Wednesday, starting to write it on Tuesday night is poor time management. Even starting it Saturday morning, though better, isn't all that good.

So when should you start? Give yourself a week or two. Write a rough draft, then set it aside for a day or two so you can come back to it with a fresh eye. Reread it for mistakes, for sentences that sound weird or clunky, and for any don'ts you have a special problem with. Once you're done, set it aside, and repeat, until you're either happy with the result or out of time.

And that's how the pros do it—revise, revise, and revise some more. Only if you do that can you expect to put your best foot forward when you're communicating in writing, and that's important, because people will judge you based on what you're willing to show them in writing. Make sure they're judging you on a fair sample of your abilities.

Don't Confuse Your Don'ts

Not all don'ts are created equal. In fact, though most people think of all the mistakes they make in writing as "grammar errors," grammar is only a small portion of the actual mistakes they make. In fact, there are a wide variety of errors everyone makes, and to learn these errors better, it's best to understand how to categorize them.

Grammar

Grammar errors involve mistakes in the structure of the language. For example, if you say "I is" to someone, you're making a grammar error—the proper form is "I am." The same thing goes for the sentence, "Seeing the stop sign, my foot went down on the brake." Your foot didn't literally see the stop sign, but that's what your sentence means according to the rules of the language—so this is a grammar error. If you say "I have many lucks this year," you're applying a number to a non-count noun, so, you guessed it, grammar error.

Most native English speakers don't have too much trouble with these, but second- language English speakers often have tremendous difficulty in resolving them.

Mechanics

Mechanics errors are mistakes made in putting the language itself on paper. Two types of problems crop up under mechanics:

Orthography: Mistakes in spelling or capitalization, and

Punctuation: Mistakes involving the use (or misuse) of punctuation marks. Most of what the average English student thinks is grammar is, in fact, punctuation.

Usage

These are errors in which the writer uses a word or phrase incorrectly. This can mean having a correctly spelled word, but using it the wrong way, as follows:

I drove too the store.

Or it can mean using a word in a way that's not normal for English:

I insist you to go with me.

And a variety of other possibilities. Usage errors come in all shapes and sizes, but the basic principle is that, in some way, the language is being applied incorrectly.

Style

Style errors refer to mistakes that aren't exactly incorrect language, but that disrupt the reader's expectations, make the sentence confusing, or don't follow the rules of clear communication. Style errors are also often confused for grammar errors. Take a look at the following example:

The moon is in close proximity to the Earth.

What's wrong here? Well, grammatically, nothing. But the word *proximity* implies closeness—so close proximity is redundant. Instead, say simply that the moon is "in proximity to" the Earth. Or try this example:

Use of limburger cheese on your burger is generally to be avoided.

Again, nothing really wrong here. But it does sound a little off. That's because this sentence is in passive voice, which means it's a wordier version of the sentence you want:

Generally, avoid using limburger cheese on your burger.

The corrected version is much easier to understand. Once again, this is a style error—nothing about it is wrong *per se*, but it could be said better.

And that concludes our whirlwind tour. Now, as you go through the book, try to fit each of the don'ts into one of these categories—it'll help you to remember them, and therefore, to commit fewer of them.

EXERCISES

SECTION 1: KNOWING YOUR AUDIENCE

1. On the following lines, reflect on the most unusual or difficult audience you've had to write for. Reflect on how you approached that audience. What special accommodations did you have to make to ensure that your point came across? And if you didn't use any, which ones should you have made? Either way, what was the outcome of that writing situation, and did you feel you got across what you could have? Could you have improved what you did in any way?

    _____

    _____

    _____

    _____

    _____

2. Imagine that you are a mayoral candidate running for office in your local town. You haven't got much money, so you need to get as many votes personally as you can—and that means getting in touch with voter groups directly. On a separate page (or a computer) write a series of short (roughly one-page) business letters to the following groups asking them to support your candidacy for mayor. Make sure you take into account the kinds of expectations and requirements they may have to take you seriously. Be creative—you can address any issues that are really (or not really) facing your home community right now.

    a. Group 1: The police officers' union in your town. Remember that members of the police force tend to have very strong feelings about law and order, funding for police department salaries and equipment, and local laws regarding how the police may or may not interact with the public.

    b. Group 2: A local retirement community. Remember that most of the individuals reading this letter will be over 65. Take into account the values that senior citizens generally find important: good family structures, low crime, continued access to Social Security, effective health care, available jobs for the younger generation, and so forth.

    c. Group 3: The local men's social club, similar to the Elks or the Masons in many communities. These groups generally consist of grown men with jobs, families, and mortgages. They will be concerned about taking care of their families as well as issues such as property taxes, local school budgets, and public projects such as building new stoplights. *Note:* Though the men's versions of these groups are the most well known, there are women's groups with very similar characteristics and issues, as well as co-ed groups. Feel free to write to one of these.

    d. Group 4: A local gamers' group. Most members of this group will be young, often college aged, and very involved in social media and their preferred hobbies, generally role-playing games, video games, and the like.

e. Group 5: The local Renaissance Fair: This is a business with a handful of individuals at the top who organize a yearly event at the community park. They have a vested interest in your views on park usage and park fees. Also, they have a great many individuals working for them, most notably actors, many of whom cross over with the members of Group 4.

- -

SECTION 2: KNOW YOUR DON'TS

In the following questions, determine what kind of don't each boldfaced mistake falls under, and then fix the mistake (if you know how). Feel free to use the rest of the book as a resource; it will get you familiar with the material and give you an overview of the kinds of errors you may encounter in real life.

1. The **council are** going to decide on that issue tomorrow. _____
2. I looked over at my friend and realized that her **Fiancee** had turned into a zombie. _____
3. When the **Pirates** hit **the,** coast, they began to plunder. _____
4. Over **their** is where the aliens landed. _____
5. The **whiches** stirred the cauldron and cast a spell. _____
6. I put the book **to** the table. _____
7. The book was called the *Necronomicon*, and I was **to** scared **too** open it. _____
8. As I approached the door, **it was opened by** the bouncers. _____
9. I **was being born** on the 4th of **july**. _____
10. I wish you **many good thing** this year. _____

Common Errors: Instruction with Exercises

Don't Round Up the Usual Suspects: A Grab Bag of Common Errors

Up to this point in the book, we've covered the nuts and bolts of English, trying to help you avoid the "don'ts" that cause writers so much trouble. But there are a handful of errors that most teachers of English run into all the time, and it's also helpful for you to know their names and how to fix them, because they don't neatly fit into any of the sections we've covered above. After the titles of each, we've included some of the common ways teachers and editors may mark these mistakes in your writing, to help you navigate them if you need to.

Cliché

Avoid old, overused phrases. There are dozens of these, but here are a few examples of clichés. If you use these, find another way to say it:

Avoid something like the plague.

Ugly as sin.

Fighting tooth and nail.

Avoiding something by the skin of your teeth.

All's fair in love and war.

Comma Splices (C/S)

This is probably one of the most common beginner's errors. A comma is a weak piece of punctuation, so it can't separate two complete sentences:

WRONG: The dog wagged its tail at me, it probably wanted to go out.

This throws readers off because they don't expect to read a complete sentence after the comma. Then they have to go back and reread to understand your point—you don't want to make them do that.

Use semicolons, a comma and a FANBOY, or a period to fix this problem:

RIGHT: The dog wagged its tail at me; it probably wanted to go out.

RIGHT: The dog wagged its tail at me, so it probably wanted to go out.

RIGHT: The dog wagged its tail at me. It probably wanted to go out.

Run-On Sentences (Ro)

A run-on sentence is almost identical to a comma splice, except it doesn't have a comma in it to divide the thoughts at all, making it much more jarring to the reader:

WRONG: The kid played with the new action figure he really liked it a lot.

Readers expect the "he" in this sentence to start a description of the action figure, like "the action figure **he got for Christmas**" or something similar. A new sentence makes them go back and try again.

Since the errors are almost identical, fix them identically: use a semicolon, a FANBOY with a comma, or a period.

RIGHT: The kid played with the new action figure; he really liked it a lot.

RIGHT: The kid played with the new action figure, and he really liked it a lot.

RIGHT: The kid played with the new action figure. He really liked it a lot.

Do not try to fix a run-on with a comma; if you do that, you just turn it into a comma splice error—see above.

Sentence Fragments (Frag.)

These are sentences that don't have all the parts they need—subject, verb, and complete thought—to be a complete sentence, but that have been punctuated and capitalized as if they were.

Any sentence missing one of those three elements is a sentence fragment, but the most common and difficult to see is the sentence missing the complete thought, because it has a subject and a verb and *looks* complete at first glance:

WRONG: If I see a dolphin.

There's a subject and verb, but no complete idea—if you see a dolphin, *what?* Most writers make this mistake because the sentences next to the fragment make the idea seem complete:

WRONG: If I see a dolphin. I'll take a picture of it.

Find the nearby sentence that goes with your fragment and attach the two using the rules for linking sentences (see Commas, p. 54).

RIGHT: If I see a dolphin, I'll take a picture of it.

Things You Should Never Do

The following is a list of things you should *always* avoid in your writing. Note that many of these issues have been covered elsewhere in the book; however, this section is meant to serve as a quick reference guide to some of the most common style, grammar, punctuation, spelling, and clarity errors. If you are prone to any of these mistakes, keep the book nearby, open to this page, as you are writing.

- Using "that" instead of "who": "who" is the proper form when referring to people. Do not use "that" unless referring to things.

  WRONG: He is the teacher *that* I felt had the most impact on me.

  RIGHT: He is the teacher *who* I felt had the most impact on me.
- Using "literally" incorrectly: "literally" means "how it is written." Whatever you say is supposed to be an exact description of real life. It does *not* intensify figurative language (figures of speech, slang terms, etc.)

  WRONG: He literally hit the roof. [Means he literally reached up and punched it.]

  RIGHT: He hit the roof **OR** He was very angry.
- Misspelling "nowadays": Not "now days," "now a days," "now in days," "now and days," or any other variation. But as a cliché, it should probably be avoided anyway: "**In the current** *state* of American politics . . ." or "The way our industry stands **now** . . ." or simply "**today**. . . ."
- Using the word "anyways": The proper word is "anyway."
- Using two words in a row that mean the same thing:

  WRONG: He had many ways and ideas to solve the problem. ["Ways" and "ideas" mean the same thing.]

  RIGHT: He had many ideas for solving the problem. [Pick one and rewrite as necessary.]
- Using the word "irregardless": It is not a cool form of "regardless." It isn't a real word at all. If you want something that sounds neater than "regardless," use "irrespective."

  WRONG: The play will go on *irregardless* of our problems so far.

  RIGHT: The play will go on *irrespective* of our problems so far.

- Using "so" instead of "very": "So" does not to make your describing words stronger. It can only be used in front of an adjective if you say "**So** scared **that** I yelled out loud" or a similar construction.

WRONG: I was *so* excited.

RIGHT: I was *so* excited *that* I jumped up and down.

RIGHT: I was *very* excited.

- Using the general "you": "You" is for direct addresses to your reader. Do not use it instead of "everyone," "someone," "people," or "you."

WRONG: You shouldn't steal because it's wrong, as I found out. [So is stealing okay for everyone else?]

RIGHT: People shouldn't steal because it's wrong, as I found out. [Revised to include everybody, not just the reader.]

- Confusing "their," "there," and "they're":

There: I left it over there. ["There" usually refers to place.]

Their: That's not my cat. That's their cat. ["Their" refers to possession by more than one.]

They're: They're going to regret going to see *Event Horizon*. ["They're" is a contraction of "They are."]

- Confusing "To," "Two," and "Too."

To: I went to the store. ["To" is a preposition showing the direction of an action.]

Too: Really? Why, I hate cats, too! ["Too" means "also".]

Two: I have two dozen eggs in the fridge. ["Two" is a number.]

- Confusing "Your" and "You're": "Your" is possessive, while "you're" *always* means "you are."

Your: Is that your dog? [Something that belongs to "you."]

You're: You're going to be sorry if you don't let him out soon. [You're = "you are."]

- Using "it's" instead of "its": "Its" is possessive, while "it's" is *always* "it is":

The dinosaur has its meaty bone to chew on.

I'm not sure how long it's going to be eating it.

- Using apostrophes to show plurals: Never use the apostrophe-s to show plurals. "Air conditioner's for sale" means the air conditioner is selling something.
- Using "of" instead of "have": Because of common pronunciation, phrases like "could have" or "should have" are often written as "could of" or "should of," mainly because they are spoken with a contraction: "could've."

WRONG: I could *of* told you that myself.

RIGHT: I could *have* told you that myself.

Name_____ Date _____

EXERCISES

Much of the work for this section has been covered elsewhere—in Chapter 2, you practiced avoiding clichés and misused reflexive forms. In Chapter 4, you learned to avoid agreement errors. But Chapter 6 covers a few errors you'll want to study separately, which is why they have been separated out.

Section 1: Sentence Boundaries (Comma Splices, Run-Ons, and Fragments)

Fix the errors in the following sentences.
1. If you tell me to. I'll rewrite the proposal.
2. Comma splices are an error that is easy to fix, there may be one in this sentence.
3. I like blue Jell-o it tastes like raspberries.
4. I hate it when an employer bribes his or her favorites. With vacation time.
5. Two men entered that dome, only one man is coming back out.
6. Try Neosporin on that cut. With a band aid.
7. I reloaded twice it was a particularly tough zombie.
8. On the fourteenth level of World of Warcraft I have a mage his name is Swordpunk1337.
9. Driving without a license is a very bad idea, you can lose your car.
10. The Porta-Potty tipped over I realized I was going to need more Purell.

Section 2: Things You Should Never Do

Fix the following sentences.
1. I was so scared.
2. We saw and were aware of the approaching ninjas before they thought we were.
3. Irregardless of your careful setting of the alarm clock, I believe that we will wake up late tomorrow.
4. That burger was so bad it literally killed me.
5. I could of gotten a refund for the really bad movie I saw yesterday.
6. From that experience, I learned that you shouldn't steal.
7. You're going to have to take me too the store.
8. These model's are for sale.
9. Mr. Harrison is the teacher that influenced my life the most.
10. I was so confused that my head was literally spinning.
11. I could of fixed my car if I'd had the time.
12. Means and methods for winning are available to me.
13. Irregardless of your education, my use of words is still better than yours.
14. Now of days, we have to be aware of potential dangers at the workplace.

15. I was so tired.
16. There limo is over there and they're waiting.
17. Egg's for sale.
18. I want to vote anyways.
19. My cat is over their; I call it "Rations."
20. I could of gotten a better deal on that car.

PART VI

Student Essays

This section includes real student essays from students in the ENG 100 program from Missouri Western State University. The essays below were chosen for publication. These essays have not been edited or revised.

On The Move

by Debra Anderson

"The more that you read, the more things you will know.
The more that you learn, the more places you'll go."
I Can Read With My Eyes Shut!
Dr. Seuss

I grew up in a family with parents who hadn't completed more than the 6th and 8th grades. We didn't have money for vacations and didn't spend any real-time with grandparents or cousins. We moved often, either to a new place in the same town or down the road to another small town. At one point my younger brother and I attended five different schools in two years. The one constant for me was school and more importantly, the library and the escape books gave me. Whether it was a school library, a public library, or a bookmobile, a library always felt like a safe place when things were chaotic and unpredictable at home.

Early on I found that libraries, with their quiet calm atmosphere and sense of order, were reassuring. My earliest memory of a library was in the Clarkfield elementary school. Once a week we walked single file down the long hallway to the library. It had, what seemed, shelves and shelves of books all the way to the ceiling. The librarian's large wooden desk sat in front of a cinder block wall with windows that overlooked the playground. Heavy dark drapes hung on both sides of the windows and would be closed on hot days in the fall and spring. In one corner was a two-tiered metal cart on wheels with the reel to reel movie projector. Lined up in neat rows were little rectangular tables with tan tops and with appropriately sized brightly colored chairs of red, blue, yellow, and green. I loved the sounds of pages turning, hushed voices, and of feet hurrying across the carpet to find the right book before it was time to go. There were the giggles of the girls at another table and the librarians shush when they were too loud. We could only check out three books. Once we had found our treasures we stood in line to check them out with the librarian. We would remove the little card from the pocket inside the back cover and neatly print our first and last names with a little pencil. The librarian would then stamp the due date on the slip inside the book and on the card with our name. I would take the books home and read them over and over until the following week when I could check out three more.

In the fourth grade, Mrs. Stanford read out loud to us after recess. She would read a chapter or maybe two if they were short. She was the one who introduced me to Laura Ingalls Wilder when she read *Farmer Boy* to us. As we settled down there were desks opening and closing and paper rattling by those who wanted to draw while she read. This was my favorite part of the day. I usually preferred to put my head down on my desk, close my eyes, and just listen. I didn't have to wonder if any of my classmates knew my secrets like how much my parents fought or that my Dad was drunk a lot.

The move to Echo in October of fifth grade was the first in a series of moves that would leave me isolated, and looking back, depressed. Before this, I had been a pretty good student, shy and self-conscious, but I always had at least one friend. At first, everyone is your friend when you are the new kid. When they realize you are shy and poor the novelty wears off pretty quickly. During this time money was more of an issue than usual for our family so second-hand clothes and free lunches at school became the norm. My classmates were now old enough to notice these things and in a small town everyone knows everyone else's business, so my family's situation was always common knowledge. Eating alone or having someone be nice to you so they could find a way to embarrass you were common.

The calm atmosphere of the library and its books became even more of an escape during this time. The school buildings in these towns were old and their libraries reflected that. When entering you were greeted by high ceilings, dark wood shelves, windows that looked dirty, and that musty smell that comes from old books and magazines unused for too many years. None of that mattered to me. What mattered was that it was ok to sit quietly by yourself because it didn't make you different or stand out. What mattered was that there were Nancy Drew Mysteries that I hadn't read many times for me to escape to when my dad was on a drunken rant, blaming his wife and four children for all of his problems.

As I moved through elementary school the school library was the one place I felt comfortable and safe. When everything else was scary and uncertain I could count on the library to have books that felt like home (Nancy Drew, Laura Ingalls Wilder, Judy Blume) and new ones that could take me to new places and become new friends. In most of these small rural towns that I lived in, with their Mom & Pop grocery stores that carried milk and bread and cans of soup or boxes of cereal that looked like their expiration dates were long past, public libraries were already a thing of the past or had never been. Bookmobiles filled that void for many in these towns. Young mothers with preschool children and the old were their patrons and in the summer I joined them on the sidewalk waiting for these small RVs with books lining their walls to arrive and open their doors to the library on wheels. In the summer when my classmates were hanging out with their friends I was hanging out with mine: Nancy, Laura, and Judy.

In the spring of my sixth-grade year, we moved to a new town for the last time. Five towns in two years were enough for my mother; if my father wanted to move again he would do so alone. I felt a sense of relief. Marshall, population 10,000, was the biggest town I had ever lived in and the public library, oh the library. The building was new with large clean windows, bright lights, and a separate children/teen section on the second floor. I was there often, especially in the summer, retreating to its calm quiet atmosphere as a break from the continuing tensions at home. Some things were better. Money was less of an issue and I had found a friend who loved reading almost as much as I did. I was doing better in school again thanks, in part, to a teacher who encouraged me to come out of my shell. But the library would continue to be an important part of my life. By the time I was a freshman I noticed a couple of girls from high school putting away books and helping to check them out. Up until then, I had never imagined, that as a student, I could get paid to work in the library, surrounded by books and other people who loved them. The summer before my junior year I worked up enough courage to apply for a part-time job at the library.

For the next four years, my job at the library would provide a sense of community that had been lacking in my life. I developed some confidence in myself as I learned how to interact with people I didn't know by talking to the people who visited the library regularly. There is a connection that happens between strangers who share a love of something. It makes it easier for strangers to become friends. The women who worked there would become my aunts and big sisters, they were the ones I shared my ups and downs with. It was their advice I sought out on issues with school, friends, and boys. When my first boyfriend broke my heart it was Linda's shoulder that I cried on. In time I would share the secrets of my home life with them. I began to see that it wasn't necessary to hide my home life from everyone. While libraries had always provided a sense of calm and escape for me, the four years I worked at the Marshall-Lyon County Library helped me to start to overcome my shyness and feel less isolated and more confident.

As I moved from grade to grade and town to town and went from reading the *Little House on the Prairie* series, Nancy Drew mysteries, and I'm embarrassed to say, Harlequin Romance novels the library and its books provided an escape from living in a dysfunctional home with an alcoholic father and a mother, who grew up with an abusive alcohol father, struggling to do better for her children. Over time the library would provide a sense of community and family that I had only experienced from the outside looking in. I began to understand that being shy didn't mean you didn't need interactions with real people. As Winnie the Pooh said, "You can't stay in your corner of the forest waiting for others to come to you. You have to go to them sometimes." The people skills I began to develop while working there would help me develop the confidence to reach out to others, in particular, those who I sensed were struggling as I had. Even after all these years later when I walk into a library a sense of calm and security comes over me and it feels a little bit like home.

The One and Only Shirley A. Milbourn

by Nora Cogdill

Sometimes it's the people that we trust the most in our lives that are the first ones to deceive and hurt us. Most of us generally trust those that we've been around for a long period of time and why wouldn't we, as long as they have never given us any reason not to. We like to believe that those we spend time with are telling us the truth. However, that may not always be the case. No matter how long you have known someone, you should always question their motives and their stories. Not everyone is who they appear to be.

I met Shirley Milbourn on May 4,1999. It was a bright, beautiful, warm, sunny day. It was my first day on the job at the St. Jo Frontier Casino. She was a fifty-nine-year-old Security Guard and I was a 19-year-old Guest Service Representative. I was just a kid entering the adult world and Shirley took me under her wing and showed me the ropes. My first image of her was very vivid. She was five foot six inches tall, very round and had a turkey neck. Have you ever noticed that extra skin under a turkey's neck? Shirley had it. Her hair resembled that of a poodle, white and gray with super tight curls. Her round glasses sat on the end of her nose, which made her gray, squinty eyes stand out even more. She reminded me of an old librarian that was scolding you for being too loud in the library. She was wearing her work uniform which consisted of black work pants and a white shirt, however she also wore a black puffy sleeveless vest. The vest wasn't uniform standard but she always said, "I like to stand out", which she had no problem doing. When she walked, there was a skip in her step, as if she was carefree with no place in the world to be. Several people thought she was mean, because she would tell you exactly what she thought of you, not caring if she hurt your feelings. I thought she was entertaining and enjoyed being around her.

I worked with Shirley eight hours a day, five days a week, so we became very close pretty quickly. We'd spend hours just talking about work and life. She enjoyed talking, especially when it came to her grandson Michael Jr., whom she was raising. I asked her several times about the boy's mother and she always had negative things to say about her. She would say things such as, "She walked out on him when he was a baby", and "She was nothing but an alcoholic and druggy." She would also say that she would call from time to time just to ask for money. She truly disliked her. That should have been a sign, but who was I to judge someone? I thought it was awesome that Shirley helped her son Michael raise him. There was nothing she wouldn't do for him. She worked extra hours just to help pay for school trips, she'd take him on elaborate vacations, such as Disney World and the Grand Canyon. She was the picture of an ideal grandma.

Shirley also taught me a great work ethic. She use to always say, "If you aren't at least fifteen minutes early, then you are already late.", which to this day I still arrive early everywhere I go. She was always very reliable and never called in to work. She'd say, "Can't pay the bills if you're not here to earn the money." That's why when she didn't show up to work one morning, we all were concerned. Several of us attempted to contact her numerous times; I even stopped by her house on the way home that day and no one was there. It wasn't until the next day that I received a call that informed me Shirley had been arrested and was on the front page of the newspaper. I ran down the street to the closest newspaper stand and couldn't believe what I was seeing.

The *Saint Joseph News-Press* articles and television reporters stated that Shirley was being charged with a murder. Not just any murder, but the murder of her daughter-in-law that took place twenty-four years ago at the time of her arrest. I was baffled. There was no way that this woman I had worked so closely with for the last six years could be responsible for something so disturbing and vile. How could she keep such a secret? I had so many questions, but, yet no answers. I started questioning every conversation that her and I had ever had.

As the story unfolded more, the *Saint Joseph News-Press* stated that on November 28, 1981, Shirley's daughter-n-law, Rhonda Burgess, the mother to the grandson whom she was raising, stopped by her house on Mitchell Avenue and got into an argument with Shirley's son Michael. Rhonda threated to take Michael Jr and leave town, which didn't set very well with Shirley, so she walked to the bedroom, picked up a shot gun that was hidden in the closet and returned to the kitchen to find them both still arguing. That's when Shirley pointed the shotgun at Rhonda and pulled the trigger. Not just once but twice.

If that wasn't bad enough, Shirley and her son, Michael, waited for it to get dark then loaded Rhonda's body into their van, drove up to Andrew County and buried her on the property that they owned there. After that they returned home and cleaned up the mess in the kitchen. They made a promise to never speak of that day again, but somewhere along the line one of them broke that promise and spoke about it in front of others. It was one of Shirley's granddaughters that ratted her out. Shirley's granddaughter Meghan had been arrested and called Grandma Shirley for bail money but when grandma refused to bail her out, Meghan then spilled the beans about the murder that took place long ago. Immediately detectives took action and located the remains of the body exactly where Meghan had said it would be. DNA proved that it was in fact the remains of twenty-two-year-old Rhonda Burgess who had disappeared back in 1981. Detectives and Crime Scene Investigators requested a search warrant and searched Shirley's house; even after twenty-four years, they still found some of Rhonda's DNA in the kitchen. Special equipment was brought in and located blood splatter that was wiped cleaned and covered with new wallpaper and deep in the cracks of the hard-wood floor, they still found traces of her blood as well. Shirley and Michael both were arrested at that time.

On January 27, 2006, Shirley A. Milbourn was sentenced to thirty years in prison for second degree murder and her son Michael was sentenced to eight years for the disposal of the body and destroying evidence. I haven't spoken to Shirley since the day before she got arrested. My last words to her were, "Have a great night." I can't help but think about Michael Jr., who obviously is now an adult, but what about all those years that he spent with his father and grandmother telling him that his mother walked out on him. How many lies did they tell that poor incident child? Would his mother ever had changed? That's something we will never know. Shirley destroyed that chance the day she pulled that trigger. Maybe Rhonda had seen a dark side in Shirley and Michael and just wanted to get her son away from them, or maybe what Shirley had said about Rhonda was true. Maybe Rhonda was a horrible mom who liked to drink and do drugs. That still did not give Shirley the right to do such a vicious thing. There are so many questions that I would love to ask, but I know I will never have that chance too. Yes, I could write her letters, but I want to remember her the way I knew her, that happy go lucky security guard, that skipped everywhere she went and not as a convicted murderer.

If it weren't for meeting Shirley, there is a good chance that I would still be naive and trust people that I shouldn't. She taught me that it's not only strangers that you should worry about, it's also those closest to you. Just because they are family, or a close friend, doesn't mean they won't lie, hurt, betray, or even kill you. We all have deep dark secrets that we would like to keep hidden, granted it's fair to say that most of ours isn't murder. Just remember that no matter how long you have known someone, or how well you think you know them, you should always question peoples motives and stories. I wish I would have.

A Year in the Bricks

by James A. Garrison

In the Fall of 2000, I was sentenced to two, back to back, 5 year sentences to be suspended, 1 year in Clinton County Jail, and 500 hours of community service. With a slam of the gavel I was off to begin my 1 year sentence. The next year of my life showed me a lot about man kinds' true nature, pushed the physical and mental limits of what most people typically endure, and gave me a window into my future if I did not veer quickly from my current path.

When I first arrived at Clinton County, and after the whole booking process, I had a few minutes to take the place in. It was built in 1974, on the same site where two previous court houses had burned to the ground, and one would imagine it hadn't been touched since. The jail is in the "basement" of the court house, and is very much like a dungeon. All cold metal, and slick, gray, lacquered floors and walls giving the appearance of perpetual wetness. There are two wings in the jail with a small third wing set up for the female inmates. All three wings are separated by heavy, solid, metal doors with only a small, one foot by one foot barred window facing into the main kitchen and intake area. Each of the two main wings, ideally, holds up to 28 inmates with 7 sets of cells excluding the drunk tank/ solitary cell, containing 4 beds each. Even in the middle of Summer, somehow, it is always freezing cold. The beds are made of rusting steel and painted with layers of green paint, now flaking with age. They are bolted to the one foot thick, concrete walls with large, rusty lag bolts one bunk above another. The whole place never stops stinking of human waste as the only bathrooms are 1 per cell and completely out in the open. The toilets are connected to a water fountain sink abomination made from shiny, beat up steel. The mattresses on the bed are made up of some sort of green, woven canvas and if you have the bottom bunk you can usually stare up as you lay there and read all kinds of graffiti on the underside of the bunk above. Everything from tick marks counting down days, to threats to the guards, to perverted jokes, to claims of faith and promises to god about what will change if he will "just get me out of this!". Once a week, barring any incidents, you get to go to visitation down the hall. The visiting room is more like a small, dead end hallway then a room. It has 5, semi partitioned, sections each with an old, rusty, lopsided, metal chair in it. There is a small quarter counter that runs the length of the bays in front of the chairs. In each bay there is a large, bullet proof window with a set of small, concentric circles cut into them in the middle. The glass is all smeared, and chipped from years of inmate temper tantrums, and hands being pressed against the smooth glass, reaching out to loved ones on the other side. On the right hand side of each bay there is an old fashioned phone receiver connected to the wall with a shiny, metal cord used to communicate to the visitor through the glass. Everything in this room is painted with cold, white, chipped paint that flakes off and floats onto the counter like some mockery of snow. Appearing to those on the other side of the glass, in my mind at least, as if they were staring into some sort of terrible, slow motion, snow globe. The whole place gave the impression that the whole building was elderly and depressed and ready to crawl back into the earth and die at any second.

Over my 365 days, I learned that human nature, when given the right set of circumstances, can be a funny thing. I was ushered back into the cell area and shown what 10 x 10 dark, damp, and stinking corner I was going to share with 4 other grown men for the next year. I slid onto a paper thin, green canvas mattress, kicked my feet up and laid back on my small bundle of provided possessions. I have always been the type of person who sits back and observes, letting events, and people, flow around me like a river. I fell back into that habit here, and haven't seen anything quite like it since, short of television. As new inmates were admitted, I came to notice they went through 3 phases over what was usually a two week period. When they arrived they would be angry usually, desperate, willing to do anything to get out. Demanding the guards let them use the phone so they could call everyone they could think of. Trying to get friends and relatives on the outside to sell cars, houses, electronics, anything so they could just make bail and get out of this pit. They would bang on the door to the cell block until a guard would finally come over, and they would proceed to tell them all kinds of stories about how they shouldn't be here and someone had made a mistake. As if, if the story was good enough, the guard would say "oh my god what have they done!?" and open the door and set them free. After they had banged, screamed, and sometimes cried themselves out, they would enter the second phase. This phase, was a phase of depression. Usually they would stop eating, not speaking to anyone, and sleep for, what was sometimes, days. The third phase was acceptance. Once they realized they were here for the long haul, and they had a chance to fall into the rhythm of the daily cycle, they would fall back into, what I assume to be, their usual selves, and personalities. How people of all backgrounds, race, personality, integrity, would all sink into the exact same cycle always mystified me.

As I am a very antisocial person, with A.D.H.D. and a decent temper, being thrown in with a bunch of violent strangers definitely tested the limits of my endurance. To make matters worse, the conditions were subhuman to be sure. There was one uncovered light in each cell, it was never shut off even at night. There was always this one, unblinking, yellow eye glaring down on you, cutting through your eye lids as you tried to sleep. All of the inmates would yell back and forth through all hours of the night. Screaming nonsense sometimes, sometimes threats, sometimes just a conversation. It would wear on my nerves until I just wanted to rivet their mouths shut. It took all my self-control not to start anything as I knew it could add another year to my sentence if it escalated to a full on fight. So I just kept my mouth shut most of the time and squeezed my forearms over my ears until I passed out from pure exhaustion. I tend to over think things a lot, and in there it was compounded at least ten fold. Especially when it came down to what time of day I would mark that particular day off my calendar. I know it doesn't seem like much now, but if I marked it off in the morning I would usually forget by evening and all day think that I had spent one more day then I actually had. At night when I discovered what had happened, it was incredibly depressing. In the winter it got terribly cold. The walls being made of gray concrete and old, chipped windows with ill-fitting bars didn't do much to keep out the freezing temperatures from outside. Everyone was sick constantly, all we were issued was one scratchy, very thin blanket, and sick or not that was all you got. I would basically divide my day into meal times, which was the only thing to look forward to, and broke up the monotony of the day. I dealt with my time in there much the way I hear AA tells alcoholics to deal with their issues. By not looking too far down the road, but only making it to that next meal, then on to the next one, and so on.

My time in Clinton County opened my eyes to how I would live a very large chunk of my life if I did not immediately transition away from my life style. It showed me how easily something that seemed so small at the time, could have such a very large impact on my quality of life. I realized very quickly that I wanted a big house, not a 10 x 10 cell with 4 uninvited roommates. I didn't want people telling me what to do every second, how to dress, when to eat, what to eat. I gave a guy a ride and I was in the same cells as murderers and rapists. There was this guy named Joe who, I found out after playing several hands of cards with the 19 year old, stabbed his girlfriend 27 times in front of their 6 month old son. Or a guy they shipped in named Billy, that swung his 1 year old son by his ankles, head first, into a concrete wall until he was dead. I also saw people that had made one small mistake, a mistake that I could easily have made myself with my temper, and my tendency to drink vodka, that sent them away for decades at a time. Like a guy I met named Ray, who after finding out his wife was seeing someone else, downed a case of beer and went and found the guy. Inevitably, one thing led to another, and they started swinging. Ray got one unlucky shot off and the guy drops dead. I saw Ray get 30 years for 2nd degree murder and wondered how many drunken fist fights had I been in over some girl. How close had I been to that very same thing. How long would my luck hold until the judge would just replace Ray with James, and I would be getting 30 years? I knew what I had to do now, and I knew how to do it. I was determined to make that guard that always jeered at people when they got released, saying "You'll be back! They always come back!" into a liar this time.

In the end, that year is one that I would never give back. I learned more about human kind then I ever wanted to. About how any random acquaintance I may know, appearing perfectly normal in every way, could be hiding a killer, or a rapist, or a thief, behind those surprisingly average looking eyes. I gained a lot of inner strength from enduring the boredom, solitude, fights, and mental stress. Proving, in my mind, that old adage "Whatever doesn't kill you makes you stronger". It also gave me all the tools, and inspiration I would ever need, to never find myself in that position ever again. That year is one I would never wish on anyone, and at the same time, one I wouldn't give up for anything.

Sanctuary at Bridgewater

by Nikki Groom

I have a place that holds a lot of important memories that involves my brother John and I. It's a beautiful, quiet place surrounded by trees and pathways. There's a lot of animals that you hear and see. It's a place that's very important to me and its name is Bridgewater. Bridgewater is important to me because it holds the memories of the things my brother and I did before he died and it makes me feel closer to him. Also because it's my place to escape reality.

At Bridgewater, John and I loved walking down the pathways in the forest and looking at the animals and listening to the way all the sounds fit together. We heard crickets, bees birds chirping, leaves moving in the wind, squirrels climbing up and down trees. There were animals walking over leaves and sticks, we even noticed a faint sound of water flowing over rocks. When we listened to the sounds not only did it relax us, but we also noticed that it created a beautiful symphony. All the sounds just tied together and made the most magical music we had ever heard.

John and I had a lot of adventures at Bridgewater together that brought us even closer than before. The one thing during that day that both of us never wanted to forget was the group of fallen trees we found. At first we just decided to climb up and sit down on them, then we started to get a little restless. I was sitting there thinking if we could climb and jump from upright trees with no problem, then why can't we with fallen down trees? So once again John and I decided to do something incredibly dangerously stupid that somehow always managed to work out in our favor. We jumped from tree to tree and after awhile that got to be boring so we upped the stakes a bit and decided to play tree tag, which is very similar to regular tag but in tree tag you have to stay in or on trees. I'm honestly surprised that neither one of us got hurt. The fallen trees we found turned out to be a great place that we went just to sit down and talk, but little did we know that the fallen trees we loved so much and thought to be the best place in the world was about to become second best. One time when we were up at Bridgewater we decided to take a little adventure and diverge from the path and into the woods. We tromped through the woods getting caught in thorns and fallen branches. We were laughing and talking having a great time. Then he shushed me, so I asked him, "What, did you hear something?" He looked at me and asked if I heard that noise. I took a second to listen and realized that what he had heard was moving water. We both got so excited! We had no idea there was a body of water out here, so we followed the sound of the water. We thought it was a pond but what we discovered was far from a pond. We found a river, it was the 102 river. We were so excited we both loved rivers! We only had one problem, the only way to get down to the river was a very steep and muddy hill. So we decided one of us should stay up until the other got down in case one of us ended up hurt. We did rock-paper-scissors in order to see who went down first, and of course I lost. So I started my way down the slippery, muddy cliff like hill. When I got to the bottom, John came down next. He made it down with ease just like I did. We loved climbing, so stuff like this was easy for us. When we got down we saw that there was a rock bed we could stand on that allowed us to be on the river without being in water. The view was amazing. We could see up the river to where it cut off in a different direction, the hills around the river where it turned were immaculate. We could see down the river as well but it was nothing like the view up river. We decided it would be fun to have a rock skipping contest. John always beat me, but I was always close behind. We skipped rocks and talked for what seemed like hours. We even went swimming and we would continue to come to the river for the rest of the times we came back. The sunset was just starting to happen and the sun was just over the top of those hills, the sky was a canvas of color. It had pink, orange, red, yellow, and purple and it painted its way across the sky and created uneven shadows across the land. In that moment I knew that this place this awe-inspiring river and rock bed would always be our own place for each other. This was now and forever our place.

Bridgewater became the most important place in the world to me on May 21st, 2014, the day my brother drowned in the Skidmore river. I never realized how important a place could be and how many memories one place could hold until the day I could never make new memories with my brother there again. For the longest time after my brother died, all I did when I was alone, was drive to Bridgewater. Most of the time people thought I was with someone or out running errands, but I wasn't. I was out at Bridgewater trying desperately to understand why it had to be my brother. I couldn't even bring myself to get out of my car for the first week after he had died, but on the second week I decided to get out and go to the river. At first it felt wrong walking down this path without my brother. I felt like I was betraying him somehow. But as I got deeper into the pathway and closer to our spot I started to feel like someone was walking right beside me. I felt a hand grab my hand and I looked to where he would usually walk and I saw him there, not physically saw him but I knew he was here with me, walking down that pathway to our spot. I knew then in that moment that he wanted this to remain our spot, forever. When I got to the river I started to skip rocks. Then the memories started flowing back so fast and hard I got light headed and weak, I ended up falling down. I was so razed but I had no emotions; I was so verklempt. I sat there for what seemed like minutes but was actually hours just staring at the water, and when I finally looked up I noticed that the sunset was just starting and it looked exactly like the first time we discovered the river. That's when my body finally registered what was really happening and my eyes started to rain, and I don't mean a nice pleasant rain, I mean like a heavy down pour with a flash flood warning. After about 10 minutes I felt like someone was trying to wrap their arms around me and stand me up, so I stood up and stared at the sunset. I started thinking about how much more special Bridgewater is to me now that my brother is gone, and how much more meaning it has, because of the memories I got to share with my brother in this heavenly place.

Now that my brother is gone, I use Bridgewater as a sanctuary, a place to think, escape my life sucking job and my obnoxious family I call reality. When I'm stressed and need to get away, I go to the quite serenity of the river John and I found together. When I go to the river it helps me feel closer to my brother and sometimes I feel like he's there standing right next to me. Feeling closer to John helps me remember to appreciate every second I have of my life because the one person I thought I'd never lose was taken from me, and it made me realize that living life desultory is not good enough. Sometimes when I need to think I will go to the fallen trees we found and climb to the tallest one and just sit up there for hours thinking about my life or whatever is going on with me in that moment. I think about my family and my friends, I think about all the things that went wrong in my life and how I managed to get back up and be where I am today, I think about what's stressing me out and how I can fix it. Like the time I went to Bridgewater when the doctors told me they thought I might have a brain tumor. I was so scared and nervous I couldn't handle life at that particular moment. So I went to Bridgewater to calm myself down and think about what I could do. I thought about what I was going to do with my life, but mostly I thought about the memories I shared with John at Bridgewater, and how different things might be if we hadn't found this special place to share together. Every time I go to Bridgewater it reminds me that no matter what has happened to someone there will always be a place where you feel them around you.

When I first started going back I thought it would be a little weird, but surprisingly everything basically seemed the same. The fishy smell of the river didn't change, the mossy smell of the rivers rocks didn't change, the wildflowers and pollen still smelled amazing, the smells still all harmonized together. The sounds were the same too, the river flowing over the rocks, the wind blowing through the trees, sticks getting stepped on by animals, it all sounded the same and for some reason it shocked me that they weren't different. I'm not entirely sure why I expected things to be so different but they weren't that different at all. I still do some of the things me and John used to do together. I still went to the river and skipped rocks, climbed trees, swam, walk the paths, and I still mushroom hunted. Sometimes I will go walking around looking for random junk like John and I used to do. One time when I was walking through the woods I found a toilet, and my first reaction wasn't your typical reaction. The highly logical reaction would be "Why would someone put a toilet out here?" But that wasn't my first reaction, my first thought was, "That's pretty funny, someone actually just randomly decided that the best place to dump your old used toilet was in the middle of no where," and all I could do was laugh. I had no idea why it was so funny I just thought it was extremely comical that someone would actually dump a toilet out here. Going to Bridgewater makes me feel a lot of emotions, sometimes it gives me a happy feeling, other times I get sad because I want John here with me. Sometimes all I feel is relaxed, and sometimes I get anxious because I'm worrying to much and have to slow down and breath to stop myself from having a anxiety attack where no one can help me. I'm never sure which emotion is going to pop up but either way to me it's a sign that he still lives within me.

We didn't realize it back then, but that was our spot, the place where we told all our secrets and confided in each other. The place where we could be ourselves with no one to judge us. Every time we needed to talk about something that was relatively deep, Bridgewater was the place we went. Like the time I needed to talk about how my ex husband had been treating me. I needed a safe place to tell my brother just how bad he had physically hurt me, and Bridgewater was that place. The place to confide in John, the place to let all my emotional baggage out.

There's a lot of people who have to deal with death in troubling ways. They never had that one person or that special place that made it all a little easier, which in some cases could lead to them becoming reckless and destructive. I'm lucky I had Bridgewater to help me through it all because without that place I would probably be one of those reckless and destructive people. Spending time at Bridgewater after my brother died helped me though his death. It helped me remember that even though he's gone I can hold him and his memories in my heart. All the memories I have with John, and all the memories I made when he was gone has made Bridgewater so special and meaningful to me. Without Bridgewater I would be a completely different person. I wouldn't have learned how to deal with my brother's death, and I wouldn't be where I am today as a person. That is why Bridgewater means so much to me.

Why Queer Isn't a Bad Word

by Debra Anderson

When your children are born you have all of these hopes and dreams for them. You want them to be healthy and grew up to be happy successful adults. I think most parents also want them to have it easier than they did. While you know there will be challenges for your children you hope they will be the typical challenges that will help them grow and become stronger. What you don't hope for is them being the target of misconceptions, discrimination, hatred, and even violence because of who they are. When your child is bi-sexual their road to becoming happy, healthy, successful adults is longer and paved with challenges that most people will never experience. My daughter Brittany is bisexual. What that means is she is attracted to both men and women. I have known that she is bi-sexual for few years and she shares the details of her life with me on a regular basis but we have never sat down and talked about her journey to self-acceptance and its challenges from the beginning. I wanted to interview her to help others understand the challenges members of the L.G.B.T. community face, dispel some misconceptions by making it more personal through her story, and help others who may be on this journey.

When you are L.G.B.T. (lesbian, gay, bi-sexual, transgender) coming to terms with one's sexuality when you are surrounded by people who basically look and sound alike and whose values and beliefs are based on the Judeo-Christian heritage is a confusing and painful process. We lived in a town in southwestern Minnesota, population 1,300. Cottonwood was a conservative rural community. It was a single parent household that included me (her mom), Brittany, and her younger brother Dalton. While their father wasn't around much they had extended family in the area including grandparents with whom they spent time on a regular basis. According to Brittany, this was a good place to grow up in, "The whole fabric of the community was knit together, whether it was school activities or church activities, or whatever town stuff was going on! Yah, everyone was everywhere." Despite all these great things about growing up in a small town, the truth was, if she had come out while still in school many of these caring supportive people would have shunned her or worse.

Puberty is always a difficult time, but for someone who is also grappling with their sexual identity, there is another layer of confusion. Brittany's first sense that she might be different was in the sixth grade. She had a dream about kissing a girl and it "freaked" her out. Certain situations began to make her feel self-conscious, like the girl's locker room. Her friendships with other girls were often intense. Growing up Brittany had a close group of friends who, "when we were watching movies and stuff always wanted to cuddle and they would all pile together on the couch and I always felt weird about that. I would never join them, um, or at sleepovers, if everybody piled on the bed I would choose to sleep on the floor." There wasn't one incident telling her she was different, but rather a gradual increase in discomfort as she moved from junior high to high school.

At barely 18, Brittany headed off to college in New York City but that didn't mean she suddenly could put a name to her feelings. During her freshman year, many of her new friends were gay men. There was this saying "gay by May" to convey the process of coming out for many of the gay men at college. They would come to college identifying as straight but would gradually identify as bi-sexual and finally by the end of the year openly gay. According to these "experts" bi-sexuality wasn't real, but a step before admitting to being gay. This added to her confusion about her attraction to both men and women.

The first time someone opens up about their sexuality, it usually isn't a full blown coming out. In Brittany's case, during the fall of her sophomore year, she shared with a straight friend at college that she thought she had a crush on a co-worker named Belinda. She chose Kate, who was part of the circle of friends that included gay men, but that didn't remove the anxiety or confusion. For Brittany, is was the "first time I expressed out loud, um, that, that it was a possibility. I wouldn't say that it was me coming out necessarily but it was like testing the waters, for sure." At this point, she hadn't identified herself as either a lesbian or bi-sexual and it would be about two more years before she would make that leap.

The decision to come out isn't the end of the journey to self-acceptance but merely a big step forward, and for Brittany, it would be a gradual process over several years. She had become friends with Aaron, who was gay and like a big brother to her. She was in an on-again-off-again relationship with a woman and struggling with uncertainty and fear. As Brittany said, "I wasn't identifying as anything." but just trying to figure out what it meant to be bi-sexual because her images of what it meant to be bi-sexual were from awful reality shows and she kept thinking "that's not me." Telling Aaron was the first time she had said to another person that she was bi-sexual and as she said with a hesitant laugh, "saying the words, like, I'm bi-sexual, it was so hard but was such a relief." The door was now open to having an actual open relationship with a woman, at least in New York City.

Brittany's first serious relationship with a woman would be the push for her to tell me that she was bi-sexual. We are close and she said it felt weird to keep that part of her life from me. Brittany told me when she was back home for a friend's wedding. We were in the car and while I don't remember her exact words, it took me a few seconds to comprehend what she had just said. For her it was a "big step in my identity shifting", but for me it was heartbreaking. All I could think was if only I had known when she was a teenager I could have been there for her. When she was confused and struggling I could have put my arms around her, told her I loved her, and that she was perfect just as she was. As her mother, I still get emotional thinking about how confused and scared she must have been and that she had faced that alone.

First loves are always intense and exciting and Brittany's was no different. While there had been a couple of other relationships with men and women this was the first one that was serious. Brittany met Cindy during training for residence hall staff. Describing it, Brittany said, "I fell madly in love, um, and it was just, it was great. It was really great. I mean it was like a hard relationship, but it was really exciting to fall for someone and have it feel, just like, that natural." While Brittany had come out to me and had introduced Cindy to me via Skype, Cindy was adamant that she couldn't tell her family because of their extreme homophobia. She would be disowned and lose her financial support. This left Brittany feeling like Cindy was "ashamed" of her. The strain would play a major part in their break up.

When you're living in the melting pot of New York City you would expect there to be less open harassment and hostility towards members of the L.G.B.T. community, but Brittany and Cindy discovered this to be far from true. One day they were walking down the street holding hands and a homeless man sitting in front of a Starbucks started chasing them, screaming that he was going to rape them. On another occasion a man starting following them, getting right behind them and began describing very graphically what sexual acts he wanted to do to them. The worst incident may have been when they were riding on the subway, chatting about their day, when a man got on and came and stood over them and started simulating masturbating and grunting. The subway was crowded so there wasn't anywhere for them to move to. They were scared, but tried to ignore it and relieved when he got off at the next stop. Not once did anyone try to stop these people from harassing them or even ask them if they were all right when the incidents were over. Adding to Brittany's general sense of fear and anxiety were a couple of incidents of gay men being shot and the murder of a transsexual woman in New York City. These incidents combined with something happening back in Minnesota would push Brittany to come out sooner than she probably would have.

In May of 2013, there was a bill in the Minnesota Legislature legalizing gay marriage. Chris Swedzinski, the representative from Southwestern Minnesota, was interviewed by the local newspaper on the amendment. His response began Brittany's short journey to needing to share her sexual orientation with her grandparents and other family members. Brittany and Cindy had begun to talk about getting married someday. Brittany had been following the progress of the gay marriage amendment back home in Minnesota. The measure was going to pass, but Chris Swedzinski said he would be voting no because being gay was sinful and gay marriage was not part of the family values of his constituents. This hurt because he was a person of authority, an elected official, and he was saying she wasn't welcome in his district. She said "I didn't choose this," and "one of the reasons I think I ultimately needed to get out of there was the feeling that I would be burned at the stake," she said with nervous laughter. To deal with her feelings she wrote a letter explaining how hurtful and destructive his statements were not only to her but to L.G.B.T. individuals living in his district. She sent it to friends, including Rayne, who was interning at the Huffington Post. She hadn't intended for it to be published but he responded almost immediately asking if they could publish it in their on-line edition. With the vote coming up in the next day or two, they wanted to do so right away. He gave her a couple of hours to make a decision. She knew if she said yes that would mean coming out to everyone in a very public way. With her brother and I no longer living in Cottonwood it felt safer to open up about this. It also meant that she could no long put off telling her father and grandparents if she didn't want them to find out from someone else.

Coming out to her dad and his family was one of the hardest parts of the journey for Brittany. When she had come out to me, her brother, and my side of the family she found mostly acceptance. She did find at least verbal acceptance from her father and her stepmother. The big question was how would her paternal grandparents react? They were conservative Christian farmers who had lived in southwestern Minnesota their whole lives. Brittany was their first grandchild and they put her on a "pedestal." In their world homosexuality was a sin. Her decision to allow the Huffington Post to publish her letter meant the phone call had to be made. Their reaction would be what she expected but not what she hoped for. The phone call to Grandma Anderson was "by far the scariest thing I've ever done," she said. Brittany had hoped they would be proud of her. She tried to explain that she was coming out in hopes of helping others and how when others shared their stories it helped her feel less alone. She had hoped the conversation would end on a semi-positive note but that would not be the case, instead, it ended with her grandmother expressing she was disappointed in Brittany. When Brittany hung up she wasn't sure if she would ever talk to her grandparents again. That night was also a big gala event and Brittany was the senior senator for Hunter College. There she was, sitting on a balcony on the Upper East Side overlooking Central Park, in a beautiful dress, crying her eyes out while friends held her. She thought to herself, "after everything I had accomplished for her to be disappointed. I hadn't killed anyone." Her grandmother called her a couple of weeks later to say

Brittany was still her granddaughter and she loved her. Since then there has been a lot of progress, but the relationship has never been quite the same.

Being bi-sexual creates its own set of dating challenges that, like me, most people probably have never considered. Some members of the L.G.B.T. community don't think bisexuality is real. According to Brittany, they think you are either confused or not ready to admit you are gay/lesbian. Women initially think you are a lesbian and then they start to worry you will leave them for a man. Straight men may initially think it's "hot" but then start to worry you will leave them for a woman. Also, most people assume she is straight even when, as she says, "My hair was really short and I had the most cliché' queer girl haircut." This even happens in gay bars. Some people assume they have a larger pool to pick from but both straight and homosexuals are uncomfortable with having to compete with additional individuals when dating someone who is bi-sexual.

Professionally there have been some unique challenges for her as well. Brittany works for a labor union so her co-workers and other members of the community tend to be progressive and it is politically acceptable in those circles. While she hasn't had to hide her sexual orientation there has been some resentment among the older "queers". They couldn't come out when they were her age for fear of hurting their careers or they did come out and suffered for it. It has also meant more work because as she says, "In a moment when suddenly like it's much more politically acceptable you get tokenized. I get tokenized a lot and I've used it to my advantage, but it's also really frustrating that I'm the token queer person who has to go to this and that, and represent, you know, it ends up being like more work for me because I'm the queer one." It also feels weird to have the people she interacts with on a professional level know her sexuality. Brittany has found ways to use this to her advantage and that has opened doors for her professionally.

I asked my daughter what advice would she give to those struggling with their sexuality or whether to come out. She said, "Be patient with yourself. Love yourself." According to Brittany, there has been so much progress in the last 5 years that is it already a different ball game and not just politically. It is less acceptable to be homophobic and technology, like blogs and Tumbler, has made it easier to connect and find a sense of community, even if it isn't in person. Feeling isolated and alone can be one of the biggest challenges for members of the L.G.B.T. community so having a support system is crucial to finding their way in the world.

I also asked her what advice would she give to family and friends and she again said "be patient" and also "don't make assumptions." Her grandmother is a good example of this. Over time she has begun to ask questions about things she wonders about or doesn't understand. She worried that she would say something wrong or ask a dumb question. Brittany has reassured her that she wants her to ask those questions. It is better to put yourself out there, by showing your vulnerability, it will make it easier for the L.G.B.T. person to open up to you.

My final question for my daughter was "What one thing would you want other people to know about you that would surprise them?" Brittany replied so softly I had to ask her to repeat what she said, "I am full of surprises." She then continued that she finds it funny that I won't call her queer. She understands for me it has negative connotations and that for most of my life terms like queer and fag were used in a derogatory way. Brittany explained that the term "bi-sexual" still feels 'icky' but she doesn't feel that way about the word queer. "Queer feels empowering." I realized I could hear the difference in her voice when she said each word. This was a surprise to me and I will have to work on it.

Since Brittany went off to New York City eight years ago I have watched her become this strong and fierce young woman. She puts herself out there all the time. When she was displaced by Hurricane Sandy and taken in by a friend's family she was so grateful for their generosity that she volunteered at a shelter for displaced disabled adults. After Ferguson, she became involved in the Black Lives Matter protests and before that she was involved in the Occupy Wall Street movement in New York City. When the shooting in the gay nightclub in Orlando happened it was a terrifying reminder that there are individuals out there that hate my daughter so much they are willing to shoot them like fish in a rain barrel. Shaken but not defeated, she continues to work for equality and justice for those whose voices are often forgotten.

It is still hard sometimes to have Brittany live so far away. She has overcome so much, but sometimes still struggles with navigating the world she lives in. I am so proud of who she has become and how brave she is in the face of discrimination, hostility and sometimes just ignorance. More than once she has called and said she is ready to give up and leave New York City. She has booked last minute flights to come home where there is fresh air, open spaces, and quiet. Being surrounded by people who love her, she is rejuvenated and returns to New York to "fight the good fight." I believe what most parents want, to paraphrase Martin Luther King Jr., is for the day when their child will be judged by who they are and what they have accomplished not by a label that the world has stuck on them.

Works Cited

Anderson, Brittany. Personal interview. 1 October 2016.

Transgender Metamorphosis

by Tori Kibbe

"I just remember going to bed that night and praying to God that while I slept, he would fix the mistake and when I woke up that I'd be the boy I knew I was supposed to be," Derrick says to me. At six-years-old, he feels like he was born in the wrong body, but at that age, he didn't even know what transgender (a person whose gender identity does not correspond to that person's biological sex assigned at birth) meant. Early on he wanted to wear what the boys got to wear when going swimming, though he wasn't allowed because his mother explains to him that he was a girl. Struggling with self-conflict is hard enough, and it is even harder when someone is struggling with gender identity issues on top of that. We all have something about ourselves that other people don't always like, but being able to be who we are truly meant to be takes a tremendous amount of courage and willpower.

Derrick, being transgender female-to-male (FTM), talked to me openly about the struggle he and his family had in his early years. He explained to me how difficult it is not being able to express these feelings clearly when he was a child. "There were just a lot of disagreements during my younger years, because what my family wanted and what I wanted was vastly different from each other and I had no way of communicating my feelings in a way for them to understand," he states. He began having a difficult time around the age that children start to form their own sense of style and are more verbal about how they feel. A six or seven-year-old Derrick, found him-self fighting with the strong women in his life. He fought with his mother and grandmother about his clothes, hair, and activities in which he would partake. He said, "Being born female and living in a small town . . . where people don't really know much about the LGBTQ+ (lesbian, gay, bisexual, transgender, and questioning) community, they wanted me to dress the way a little girl should dress." It wasn't easy for him knowing he was different. The self-conflict issues alone were hard enough, but adding his family into the situation made it even more difficult. His mother wanted to see him happy, but it is hard for a parent to grasp such a big change in their child. This proves his point that it's not just hard to be a transgender child, but its also hard being the parent of a transgender child and not knowing what they need to feel comfortable in life and with themselves.

People identify in many ways. In middle School, friends start asking questions about who is cute and that's usually when kids start to figure out where they are and how they fit in socially in society, this is just one way we identify ourselves. Growing up Trans makes it harder to label who we are. Most Trans people first identify as something else before their transition because just five years ago, being transgender was not widely publicized. Derrick tells me of the time that he becomes aware of his feelings for women, "Once I reached 7th grade and began noticing the feeling of attraction,

I noticed that I'd rather sit with the boys and look at the girls. I realized then that I was attracted to women and I began identifying as Lesbian. He was living in Texas When he met someone for the first time that identified as transgender. Meeting this person was the turning point in how he viewed himself and how he would from then on out identify. Getting older made it more difficult to correctly identify himself and to be who he was, until he could transition on his own around the age eighteen. During this time, he started considering a name change. Derrick narrowed down his list to, two names and would introduce himself in the mirror with each one separately. Ultimately he states, "The name chose me and the meaning of the name Derrick, means a lot to me. I believe my name defines me as a person and my struggle."

The meaning of his name is defender and protector of men, which I feel like it fits him well. He is someone who wants to protect Trans men and women alike, while defending the LGBTQ+ altogether. Finally, being able to correctly identify/ label himself made such a huge difference.

Someone Transgender today leaves them subjected to discrimination and assault of many different forms. Someone who is transgender can become a victim/survivor of physical, mental, and sexual assault. They also have to deal with discrimination when it comes to finding a job, shopping at the store, being provided medical care, and can even be subjected to death. Derrick tells me, "I feel an incredible amount of pressure to keep it a secret or on a need to know basis because of all the risks of being openly transgender. I need to make a living and support myself and my family and I certainly don't want to lose my life." When I hear the percentage rates of the crimes against the transgender community, I can't believe what I'm hearing. Knowing that he wants to be a spokesman, to educate and inspire others outside of his Trans community, even when the death of a transgender person is 50% higher than others of the LBGTQ+ is overwhelming. He states, "I believe that transgender people should have the right to have their stories publicized. I think it's time that this country begins to understand that there aren't just two genders and that not everything is black and white." Derrick has been a survivor of being refused medical attention; he has been discriminated against, and he even had his civil rights violated by the police when his life was threatened and he was physically assaulted. The police officers said there are no laws in place, in Missouri, to protect people of "his kind'. He says to me with a quivering rasp in his voice, "The most hurtful part of today's society, is the willingness to murder someone's loved one simply because they are transgender." After someone that is Trans is murdered, they are often called the wrong name and have their gender labeled incorrectly, and then as a nation, we humiliate them even after death.

Taking action and educating our local areas helps people understand what being transgender really means, as a whole. To inform others that being a transgender person doesn't make a person any different than cis-gender (someone who's personal identity is that of their gender assigned at birth) people, they just want to be considered as an equal, just like the rest of the cis-gender population. With heavy breath Derrick passionately tells me, "The first step to resolving the ignorance of a subject is education. If I could change one view of the transgender community, it would be to help people understand that we arent freaks. To know that we are not just lesbians and gay men trying to fit in to normal society or trick people." Having him in my life I have never felt any differently about him. When I first met Derrick, I was unaware that he was transgender. To me he was and still is a man. Even after he opened up to me about himself. I never felt anything but honor to know him on a deeper level. I was happy that he was able to confide in me about his transition.

Derrick has successfully navigated through some rough experiences while going through his transition. Some advice that has helped him get through his transitioning stages is that, everyone experiences their transition differently; not one person will transition like another.

Knowing this allowed him to see that just because one person's results were one way didn't mean his would be. He needed to be comfortable with his results because his transition is his own. I wanted to know specifically what being Trans has taught him about himself. One thing he said that grabbed at me was, "Me being transgender doesn't change who I am as a person, it's my personality and my morals that makes me who I am, not being transgender." Just because

Derrick is transgender it does not make him any less human, or does it make him any less than the rest of us. His inspirational words for others of the transgender community were, "You are not alone. In me you will always have an ally, someone you can count on to try to help you through the emotional toll transitioning can take on someone." I love the way he can continue to be strong for himself and other people going through tough self-identity issues.

For me, knowing Derrick gives me more willpower and courage to continue my journey being a cis-gender Pan-sexual (someone who is open to members of all sexual orientations or gender identities). In no way, have I or will I go through as much scrutiny as he has or will. My experience with self-identity was different because even though I may get disapproving looks or people who do not agree with me, I don't have people scrutinizing me in the ways he has. The way he has overcome so much adversity to be himself provides me the reassurance I need to help him in his own journey to make our community aware of such a controversial topic. Something we both feel strongly about is that everyone deserves to feel happiness and to be comfortable with who they are. If you need support reach out, not everyone in the world is full of hate for the LGBTQ+ community. Keep fighting and if it gets hard just remember you deserve a good life as much as the next person. No one should struggle with self-identity issues alone. We all have something about us that could be a scrutinized topic in tomorrow's news.

How Reading Changed My Life

by Debra Anderson

"Books are the plane, and the train, and the road.
They are the destination and the journey.
They are home." Anna Quindlen

I tell people I am a college student, I am engaged, and I am 55 years old. Often I get a laugh and or in the case of another non-traditional female student, a high-five. What am I doing sitting in a college classroom with a bunch of kids who are younger than both of my children? It is not the first time I have sat in a college classroom. It has been 30 years since I last sat in a college classroom and this is my third attempt at completing my college degree. I grew up in the age before cable TV and the internet. If I wanted to learn about something I had to go to the library, we didn't have money to buy books. I loved libraries, not only because I loved to read, but because their quiet calm atmosphere and sense of order were reassuring when much of my world wasn't. I am not unique because of my struggles. My story is long, it is painful, but not without good things. I was reminded of this as I read each of the authors' stories. Reading changed their lives and for some, may have literally saved them. In "The Lonely, Good Company of Books" by Richard Rodriquez, "The Joy of Reading and Writing: Superman and Me" by Sherman Alexie, and "One Writer's Beginnings" by Eudora Welty I found pieces of their stories that fit into my life's puzzle. My parents and Rodriquez's parents were similar, Alexie's determination to break down doors to a better life are similar to mine, and as a parent I was like Welty's parents. Books became windows to worlds and possibilities that I would never have realized existed and when I became a parent I worked hard to inspire a love of reading in my children. Learning to love reading changed the lives of these three authors and changed not only my life, but those of my children.

Like Richard Rodriquez, I didn't learn to love books from my parents. Reading was something you learned in school. They grew up in a time and place where the value of even a high school degree didn't seem necessary. My father completed the eight grade and my mother only sixth. Like Rodriquez's parents, "reading was something done out of necessity and as quickly as possible. Never did I see either of them read an entire book" (Rodriquez 293). In fact, outside of a newspaper or owner's manual, I never saw either of my parents pick up a book until I was an adult. The reality of trying to keep a roof over our heads and food on the table didn't leave time for reading. My father's free time was usually spent drinking and my mother's "free" time meant falling asleep in the recliner while watching TV. For years she worked the overnight shift going to bed after she got us off to school in the morning and getting up by noon to take care of cleaning, laundry, shopping, and cooking. After supper she would take another three-hour nap before her 11:00pm – 7:00am shift. Not only did they not read for their own pleasure they never read to their children.

Unlike Rodriquez, reading drew me in from the beginning. Books were an escape from a chaotic, uncertain home, and friends when real friends were not to be found. We are also different because unlike Rodriquez, who initially felt reading was "impersonal" and isolating, to me books were inviting, a friend who took me on trips to places far from the small towns I lived in, introducing me to people and ideas that gave me hope for a different future. Over time Rodriquez began to love reading and like him I was, "at home in a fictional world where I knew the names of the characters and cared about what was going to happen to them" (Rodriquez 296). I wanted to be part of the Ingalls family or smart and pretty helping Nancy Drew solve the next mystery. I not only wanted to be somewhere else, I wanted to be someone else.

Both Rodriquez and I began to associate reading with being educated. Rodriquez went so far so to make lists of important books he should read and then write down the themes of the books. As he said, "I had the idea that they were crucial for my academic success, though I couldn't have said exactly how or why" (Rodriquez 295). He thought that the value of a book was in finishing it and checking it off a list. I think because we both came from homes that didn't see value in reading for its own sake it took time for that connection to be made and even longer to understand why. When I looked at the people I knew who were respected and looked up to, teachers and librarians, they read books. Rodriquez's family didn't understand what he saw in books, he would hear his "mother wondering' What do you see in your books?' (Was reading a hobby like her knitting? Was so much reading even healthy for a boy? Was it the sign of "brains"? Or was it just a convenient excuse for not helping around the house on those Saturday mornings?) Always, "What do you see . . . .?" (Rodriquez). I don't think my family understood what I saw in all those books either, why they had to shake me because I didn't hear them calling me from the kitchen that supper was on the table. I knew that books were special and that getting an education offered hope that someday I would no longer be standing outside, looking through a window, and watching other people live the lives I desperately wanted to be a part of.

In the Native American students that Sherman Alexie works with he sees a door that separates them from a better life, for me, it feels more like a window, but just as tough to break through. Alexie and his students had to battle stereotypes of what Native Americans could be, "As Indian children, we were expected to fail in the non-Indian world. Those who failed were ceremonially accepted by other Indians and appropriately pitied by non-Indians." Alexie refused to fail and so he read anything he could get his hands on from books to cereal boxes to auto repair manuals. He kept banging against that door because as he said, "I was trying to save my life" (Alexie 14). Alexie knew he had to be his own Superman. I also read all the time. Weekends, breaks, and summers were spent reading. In those small libraries, when I ran out of different books I wanted to read I returned to old favorites. Alexie says he is lucky he made it out but he knows not everyone can make it without help so he spends time teaching at a reservation. There are students he has reached, "they look at me with bright eyes and arrogant wonder. They are trying to save their lives. Then there are the sullen and already defeated Indian kids who sit in the back rows and ignore me with theatrical precision" (Alexie 14). The bright-eyed students come into the classroom ready to learn, they are reading beyond what the classroom requires and writing. Alexie has shown them that a different future is possible and for those who embrace it, they have a chance to change their lives. The ones with the "empty notebooks" (Alexie 14) are the ones who still need a superman like Sherman Alexie to break down their door of fear and apathy.

Like Alexie, my family and for a long time most of my teachers didn't have expectations of college for me. That expectation wasn't because I didn't have the ability but because I came from a poor family with an alcoholic father and uneducated parents who worked menial jobs. About his family Alexie said, "We lived on a combination of irregular paychecks, hope, fear, and government surplus food." (Alexie 11). Expectations are usually low when you are poor no matter where you live. In my mind, an educated person was someone who had went to college and I thought it would be just a continuation of high school. Anything else I thought I knew about college came from books I had read or from what I saw on TV or in the movies and those portrayals were far from reality. The classmates I wanted to be like were going to college but I didn't think college was an option because we were too poor. During my senior year, I found out that there were grants and loans to help pay college. This meant I could go to college. Now I thought I had the key I that would open the window and I would no longer be on the outside looking in.

I was wrong. That key wasn't enough. I failed not once but twice. Why did I fail is a question I have asked myself many times? It wasn't a lack of intelligence, things didn't come easily, but I maintained a B average. Making friends was easier because you start with a clean slate. No one knows anything about your family unless you share it with them. I worked really hard at looking like I belonged there. I went to my classes and did my homework. When you grow with an alcoholic you learn that appearance is important. If you can appear to the outside world that things are fine, then you don't have to admit they're not. Admitting there is a problem means you have to do something even if it is choosing to do nothing. At first, I was sure I was on my way to breaking the window that separated me from where I wanted to be. Over the course of my freshman year this vague feeling that something was missing began to hang over my shoulder and continued to grow during my sophomore year. The first time I took a break from college was the spring of my 3rd year. I would return the following fall and when I was offered an internship in St. Paul that spring I took it. On the outside I still looked like I was doing fine. When the internship was over I simply never moved back. I was really close to finishing but felt like I didn't belonged there and I would never actually get my degree. For 25 years I lived 13 miles from SMSU and didn't do anything about finishing my degree. So, why am I finally trying to finish my degree? First it is now financially feasible. I have someone who has encouraged me to do this and is supporting me in any way he can. Secondly I am different. I can admit I don't always know what I am going and ask for help. I sometimes still feel like I am banging against that window but it has some pretty big cracks in it and with some help from the Robins in my life, I can be my own Superman and shatter that window.

Parents are the best role models and facilitators in creating a love of reading in their children and like Eudora Welty's parents, I was determined to be that kind of parent. I hoped, unlike me, my children would be able to break through the window. Welty's mother read to her all the time and in many different rooms of their house. Her mother read to her in the morning while sitting in a rocking chair in the bedroom and in the "dining room on winter afternoons in front of the coal fire, with our cuckoo clock ending the story with 'Cuckoo,' and at night when I'd got in my own bed" (Welty 298). Our house, like Welty's, had books everywhere. There was a bookcase in the playroom and in each of my children's bedrooms. When they were infants, I sat in the worn gold rocker with them on my lap and "read" to them the brightly colored plastic books, cloth books with textures, and then the hard cardboard ones. We read *Chicka Chicka Boom Boom* so often all three of us had it memorized. I read them the the Robert Munsch books, including *I'll Love You Forever* and the Little House books, and books about dinosaurs and big machines. I read to them every day until they could read by themselves and then I would lay on their beds with them and they would read to me. Like Welty's parents, I wanted my children to feel that books were communal, something to be shared with the people around them. When Welty wrote about her parents giving her books, "I was presented, from as early as I can remember, with books of my own, which appeared on my birthday and Christmas morning" (Welty 301). I was that parent. When my children brought home the Scholastic book orders I would sit down at the kitchen table with them and we would pick out the books they wanted. Books were always included in their presents at Christmas, Easter, and their birthdays. I didn't forget about the library which had been such an important place for me. In the summer and sometimes on a nice winter day we would walk the few blocks to the small library downtown. Both of my children grew to love reading the same way that I did. When my son and daughter were older and had money of their own it wasn't unusual for them to buy a book. As adults, my children have continued to be readers, but instead of giving them actual books I often give them a gift card to a bookstore. Books are a bond between us, a part of our shared memories that bring to mind a cozy warm feeling and sometimes laughter, that can never be broken.

Books provided me with a safe place to escape to and were friends when I didn't have them. They showed me there was a world beyond what I knew and gave me hope for a better future. Without them, I'm not sure if I would have ever thought there was more to life or even went to college at all. I know that I have more and have been to places my parents never even dreamed about because of my love of reading. I am proud to say that both of my children have post-secondary degrees. My daughter has a Bachelor's degree in Social Studies and my son has a two-year degree in HVAC and Plumbing. Richard Rodriquez, Sherman Alexie, and Eudora Welty became who they were because they read. It was their love of reading that began their journey to becoming writers. No matter who you are or how much money you have books can open doors in your mind and plant seeds that can grow and make not only your world better but your children's and the world around you.

Works Cited

Alexie, Sherman. "Superman and Me." *Writing about Writing: A College Reader*, edited by Elizabeth Wardle, Bedford St Martin's, 2014, pp. 11–14.

Rodriguez, Richard. "The Lonely, Good Company of Books," *Introduction to College Writing*, McGraw Hill Companies, Inc., 2010, pp. 293–297.

Welty, Eudora. "One Writer's Beginning." *Introduction to College Writing*, McGraw Hill Companies, Inc., 2008, pp. 298–303.

Literacy in Hi-Fi

by Chris Bennett

Some would venture to say that education is a product of literacy abilities. That the amount of education that we possess, our desire to possess, is singlehandedly attributed to how much and what we read. In a powerful quote regarding reading, by the late, great, Carl Sagan once said "One glance at a book and you hear the voice of another person, perhaps someone dead for 1,000 years. To read is to voyage through time." However, how does one ascertain a passion, love, or desire to read when they are not shown by their parents what the benefits can be? What if the very thought of reading scares them due to the erroneous feelings of isolation? In the narrative essay entitled "The Lonely, Good Company of Books,", excerpted from the autobiography, *Hunger of Memory: The Education of Richard Rodriguez*, Rodriguez, who at one point held jobs from that of a teacher to a journalist, who is arguably one of the more contentious writers of his time, based upon his views of affirmative action and bilingual education, recounts overcoming these impediments and finding his passion for reading. Like that of Rodriguez, I was not shown the benefits of reading by my parents. However, unlike Rodriguez, I never acquired a desire to read books. Although our journeys in literacy are similar, they differ in the way that we obtained knowledge and differ in the aspect that he learned through books, and I through the polar opposite, music.

Growing up, Richard Rodriguez was faced with many hurdles in his journey in literacy and his eventual hunger and aspiration for reading. One of these hurdles was that of his parents' unattractive thoughts of reading. Recounting memories of his parents', Rodriguez tells us that for them, ". . . reading was something done out of necessity and as quickly as possible. Never did I see them read an entire book. Nor did I see them read for pleasure" (293). Like Rodriguez, I never saw my mother read for pleasure. The only thing that I can recollect that she would read, other than mail that was addressed to her, was the daily newspaper. Conversely, the only section that she would read was the classifieds, for at the time she was searching for a new job before she got diagnosed with multiple sclerosis and was no longer able to work. I feel as though this had a negative impact on my personal excursion in literacy. Had Rodriguez and myself been raised in a home that taught the importance of reading, our trip may not have been as rough as it was.

Rodriguez's path, with the help of the older nun, enabled him to establish his passion. Reading list after list of top books, reading any type of book that he could get his hands on. Rodriguez went on to become a teacher and later on, a writer. He received his M.A. from Columbia University in 1966. While his path took him on a course to education, my path has just recently been discovered. Unlike that of Rodriguez, I took a slight detour on my path. My path took me to places and experiences that I would not even wish upon my enemies. However, after nearly fourteen years, my path has once again veered toward education, and possibly the path towards a degree in either education or journalism. I have yet to decide on which one but being that I have only recently started college I have a little bit of time to decide on which one. I have always known that education is important and without it you are not only hurting yourself but you are also hurting your children by not being the positive role model that all parents should strive to be. This is where my path and Rodriguez's meet again. We both feel that education is important.

Unlike myself, Rodriguez had more to battle than just his parents' joyless approach to reading. Rodriguez had to overcome his erroneous feeling that reading was nothing more than a labored chore, not unlike that of a child having to do the dishes or take the trash out the night before trash was collected. To this he also had to combat is inner mental state of isolation and loneliness I regards to the way he felt when he would read. Rodriguez tells of his time of being placed in a remedial reading class and that with the help of an older nun, he was able to learn that there was nothing to fear in regards to reading and his feelings of loneliness and isolation. Rodriguez recounts ". . . I was thinking of another consequence of literacy . . . Books were going to make me 'educated'. That confidence enabled me, several months later, to overcome my fear of the silence" (295). I never had the issues that he did in regards to remedial reading. Unfortunately, I never had someone to show me the possible jubilation that comes with reading. The only positive memories that I can remember, in regards to reading, are of my early childhood when my mother would read to me at night before bed. By the time that I turned seven years old, they all but abruptly ceased. My mother never suggested for me to pick up a book and read, she however, would make me look up a word in the dictionary, if I were to ever ask her how to spell a word.

To the average person, reading books is how most procure a more academically thought-provoking vocabulary and superior comprehension skills. Conversely, I achieved my intellectually eloquent grasp of the English language through a different approach to reading. I did not sit around my dwellings reading books, venturing off to faraway places in my imagination that I had never seen or experienced. I did, however, sit around my room with a pair of black, Sony headphones that were attached to my portable CD player. While I was listening to my favorite band, whichever one that may have been at the time, I would read the lyrics from the CD insert. If I didn't know what a word meant, I would go to my dictionary to find the meaning of the word. I would do this until I was able to decipher, like that of a cryptologist finally unlocking a code that could change the world, what the meaning of the song was. From the time that I started to do this, which was around the time that I entered the fourth grade, to this very day, I still continue with these habits. Rodriguez recounts a sign that hung above the nun's desk in his fourth grade classroom that read, "Open the Doors of Your Mind with Books" (293). With this quote, the orthodox that learned through reading books would most likely agree. To the unorthodox, who learned through music, like I did, the following quote is from that of not only a brilliant actor, but also that of a musician, Johnny Depp. Johnny Depp explains that "Music touches us emotionally, where words alone can't."

To say that music is not a key to open up one's mind would not only be ignorant, but also unreservedly naïve. See, music and books share something in common that most people fail to realize. Books tell, through complex dialogue, vivid descriptions, and many of pages a story. Now stop and compare a song to a book. Does a song not tell a story from beginning to end? Are there not emotions that are felt depending upon the type of song, just like there are emotions felt when reading a book, too, depending upon the style of the book? Can they not both enable a person to learn? The only real differences between the story in a book and the story told through music is the way we input them into our mind. With books, our minds are grouping shapes and lines into letters, and then to that of words for us to soak up, whereas music is sent through the air in the form of frequencies to our ears, then sent to our brain for processing, and yes, just like that with books, we soak it up.

Books and music can both have the same effects in one's endless quest through literacy and education. Regardless of whether or not I ever found a desire to read, as Rodriguez did, which I have not, makes no difference. However, what is important is that I found a way to educate myself. My way is to use a different sense than Rodriguez. Whether it's our similarities in regards to our parents, or how we are different in terms of our literacy passion, one thing that I feel we both hold close is that without literacy, we can have no education; without education, we will have no future.

Works Cited

Rodriguez, Richard. "The Lonely, Good Company of Books." <u>Introduction to College Writing</u>, Mc Graw Hill, 2010, pp. 232–235.

You Do Have a Choice

by Chris Bennett

Some people would venture to argue that in today's culture that choices are not made based upon free thought or free will. Instead those people that believe this are forced to pioneer down a path riddled with crime, broken homes and an absence of education and skills suitable to ascertain a career. Many people that walk this path in life end up in our penal system, not once, but more often than not, on a continuous cancerous cycle. A great example of this, would be that of *The Other Wes Moore: One Name, Two Faces.* This book was written by Wes Moore. He gives an intricate view into the lives of two different people with the same name, but with two completely different outcomes due to the choices they made. They both had run-ins with the police, except one learned from this while the other one would eventually return to the penal system, where he would spend the rest of his life. This can be attributed to the lack of rehabilitation and second chances once released from incarceration.

Jails and prisons were originally meant to be places, for those that were incarcerated, a structure designed to rehabilitate those who committed crimes. However, over time these places have become nothing more than a breeding ground for animosity, brutality, and the lack of personal accountability for one's own actions. Instead of being given the resources and tools to better their chances of not returning through what seems to be nothing more than revolving doors at a prison, the inmates are left to ruminate on the thoughts that no cares and that the reason they are incarcerated is everyone else's fault, rather than their own. Irvin Weathersby Jr., who at one time taught for a reentry program, in nothing short of a biased article, published by *The Atlantic* in February of 2015, entitled "A Second Chance," reports statistics and data on one demographic, that demographic being of young, black, formerly incarcerated Americans. His argument is clear and true in that the incarcerated should be given the means to better themselves to have a decent chance of not returning back to the path that led them there in the first place. However, Irvin states that "Formerly incarcerated men must learn to embrace methods of self-improvement, and we as Americans must learn to empathize and restore their citizenship." Most would agree that everyone needs to embrace methods to better improve themselves. What most would not agree with is the fact that we as Americans should empathize with people that have committed crimes. We shouldn't empathize, but rather give most of these men a second chance, judge them not by their past, but judge them by their current actions. One of the most simple, yet most powerful, things that we have control over in our life is our ability to decide what contributions we may bring to this world and what type of mark we decide to leave. Just because people may have made poor choices early on in life, does not mean they haven't a possibility of a future, and shouldn't be offered an opportunity to achieve more. Wes Moore, author and decorated Army veteran stated, in a simplistic, yet extremely powerful excerpt, from his book *The Other Wes Moore: One name, Two Fates*, "The choices that we make about the lives that we live determine the kinds of legacies we leave" (175) clearly showed that he understood the importance of how we live our lives and the effect we have on others in this world.

We as the human race tend to get lost in our own blithest behavior and not take into account Sir Isaac Newton's Third Law of Motion, published in the *Principia Mathematica Philospiae Naturalis* in 1686, which states that "for every action in nature, there is an equal and opposite reaction." This law is not only applicable to nature, but to actions of people as well. A prime example of choices and how they have an effect on others is when Wes was involved in the robbery that left an off duty police officer dead:

> "One of the people being held at gun point was Sergeant Bruce Prothero, a thirty-five year-old, thirteen-year veteran of the Baltimore County police department. Earlier that day, he'd left his wife and five children, ranging in age from two to six, t work his second job as a security guard at the jeweler's . . . Sergeant Prothero scampered behind the Delta 88 and began to lift his head, a black gloved hand reached out the window holding a handgun and let off three shots, striking Prothero at point-blank range." (147-148)

Those three shots ended up killing Sergeant Prothero. However, those three shots also affected other people who were not there, who knew nothing of the actions that were taking place. Like a pebble thrown into a pond, the ripples move further and further away from where the pebble has now become part of the pond. Metaphorically, the pebble would be that of the three shots fired that turned a wife into a widow, and left five children without a father, these resulting actions being the ripples. These choices will forever have an impact on not only Sergeant Prothero's family, but also that of Wes. Had Wes chose to remain at Job Corps, he never would have found himself in that situation. Like I have said, one little choice can and will affect the rest of your life. Sadly, Wes's impact that he will leave on this earth is that of anger and sadness. He was unable to break a cycle, and instead fell into the same cancerous void that many never get out of. By making the right, harder choices, Wes ultimately set a cycle that was also set for him. His father was never around, now Wes will no longer be around for his children.

Poverty, drugs, no education, missing fathers, lack of positive role models, and these can all be factors that place hurdles in one's life and make it seem as though there is no escape. I escaped poverty, drugs, a drug addicted and alcoholic father, a mentally abusive step-father, and drive-byes. My motivation was to not be like my father, to finish high school, and to obtain a college degree and when I had a child, to not walk out of their life regardless of the situation. My plans didn't quit follow through the way that I had thought they would. I realized that if I didn't make a choice to get out of the area I was living, make a choice to escape my step-father that I would fall into a cycle that my father fell victim to. So, instead of taking the easy way out and letting whatever happens happen, I took hold of my future and made a choice to join the Army. See, no matter what, every person has a choice to change.

The question is why can't people take a path towards a brighter future for themselves and their families? Fear of uncertainty, not being man enough, or is it just fear of failure? No one on this planet has ever gotten every little thing they have ever done right without failing. We are human, we make mistakes, but it's how we let these things affect us that determines whether or not we overcome and drive on, or retreat back to what it was we used to know. Wes Moore had something to say about failing: "Failing doesn't make us a failure, but not trying to do better, to be better, does make us fools." (185) Those that give up after failing once, those that don't try to do better, to be better, they truly are the definition of cowardly fools. Only cowards *choose* to not strive to do better. Cowards *choose* not to be better. Choices, we all have them, we all make them, and they all have everlasting implications for those around us. *Choose* to be better, *choose* to work harder, and *choose* to break any cycle that inhibits your ability to pursue what you want from life. Legacy, strive to leave one behind that has a positive impact, and remember that you, and only you, are responsible for your actions, and that those actions affect more than just you, but affect everyone around you.

Works Cited

Moore, Wes. <u>The Other Wes Moore</u>. Spiegel and Grau, 2011.

A Personal Evolution of Literacy

by James A. Garrison

As we change and grow from children into adulthood, literacy grows along with us, changing over time in its applications and utilities according to our needs. Literacy is incredibly fluid, and over the course of my own life has, and will have, taken on at least three very distinct forms that stand out to me. In most people's lives it will cover a wide spectrum from Eudora Welty's whimsical love affair with fiction as a child in "One Writer's Beginnings", to the more black and white knowledge based form of literacy as experienced by Richard Rodriguez in his essay "The Lonely, Good Company of Books", and eventually to Gloria Naylor's promise at the end of her essay "The Love of Books", to utilize literacy as a career. I shared the childhood experience of Welty so far as her experiences with fiction, and am now experiencing the second form of literacy, as experienced by Rodriguez, as I attend college, and I fully intend to keep Naylor's promise of using literacy to make a living in my near future.

Unlike Welty, as a child, my parents did not have books around the house. According to Welty, there were always books a-plenty in her home growing up, alluding later that they were a clue to her father's longing to see the world. She says, "There was the set of Stoddard's Lectures, in all its late nineteenth-century vocabulary and vignettes of peasant life and quaint beliefs and customs, with matching halftone illustrations: Vesuvius erupting, Venice by moonlight, gypsies glimpsed by their campfires. I didn't know then the clue they were to my father's longing to see the rest of the world."(183). In sharp contrast, my father was a preacher and the only books that he kept were all deeply religious books, and books on theology. These he kept locked away in his office across the street from our house in the small church where he preached on Sundays and Wednesday nights. We were strictly forbidden to handle those books for fear that we would tear the pages or scuff them up in some way. The closest I ever got to having my father read to me was in his sermons. My mother would gather myself and my two brothers up and we would all march across the street and sit in the front pew every Sunday morning, Sunday evening, and Wednesday evening. There my father would drone on in an even monotone reading from a prepared sermon he had written the week before.

Where my childhood reading experiences and Welty's become similar, is when my mother brought me the full box set of The Lion the Witch and the Wardrobe for my fourth birthday. That was my first true introduction to what literacy could be, and when I was initially thrust into what was to be the first manifestation that literacy took for me. Welty says, "It had been startling and disappointing to me to find out that story books had been written by people, that books were not natural wonders, coming up of themselves like grass."(182), I also experienced that same disappointment when I was young. At that age, I selfishly liked to think that the experience of reading and being thrust into another world or universe was something that was my own. Making it that much more spectacular and special to me. I think it was almost a pride thing even at that young, I didn't like the idea of someone else being able to manipulate my mind versus the thought that the universes and new realities I was reading about already existed in my mind and the books simply were the catalyst. Over the course of my preteen years, I read a great many books, obtaining them from all three of the schools libraries, and the public library. When the book fairs would come to our school twice a year, my mother would usually give me enough money to buy a couple books, and I ended up with quite an impressive collection of a teen horror series by R.L. Stine called Goosebumps. Over all, like Welty, growing up reading was a very magical experience for me, more like traveling then turning pages. I loved seeing new worlds, learning about exotic animals in faraway places, reading about the giant lizards of the past, and traveling to the center of the earth with Jules Vern. As I made the transition from teen to adult however, literacy transitioned with me and began to morph into a whole new entity.

This transition brought me to the form of literacy experienced by Rodriguez in his essay, it is the form of acquiring knowledge, and is a personal, and somewhat unique challenge for me. This form takes on a much more rigid, and far less enjoyable aspect. Having learned to live with severe A.D.H.D. there are some parts of it that I will never escape. In this college environment of remembering every little date, every obscure name mentioned in a marked up text book, it seems that I have to work twice as hard to obtain half the knowledge as my peers. This then leads to the grinding, mind numbing practice of repetitive reading, and writing and re-writing notes. Rodriguez writes "The sentences of the first books I read were coolly impersonal. Toned hard. What most bothered me, however, was the isolation reading required."(232-233). This is my world now, I have to tell my wife and children that I am going to my room, after spending 8 hours at school, because I can't concentrate on what I am reading if there is even the slightest of noises. I lay there on my bed, not spending any time with my family, trying to force every little detail into my brain so I can prepare for one test or another. It can best be described in one word, solitude. Reading, once my warm companion, is now my cold instructor. No more imagination, there are no new worlds here, nothing fantastic at all anymore. Only well-organized columns of cold facts to be absorbed through hours and days and weeks and years of effort. Literacy in these two contrasting forms is amazing to me. It's like two animals of the same species, all at once related, but so many differences. Rodriguez states "Books were going to make me "educated." That confidence enabled me, several months later, to overcome my fear of the silence."(233). Like Rodriguez, I too use the confidence that books will make me educated to push through this impersonal role that literacy has now stepped into in my life, and look forward to what I expect the third form of literacy to take for me.

Much like Naylor's statement, "What I plan to do though with the rest of my life is indeed to communicate with images."(231), my chosen line of education will, once again, require literacy to assume yet another role. I am studying now to be a computer programmer, the ways that I will use literacy in the future will bend it to my will, and make me a living. All of the various "languages" that I will use, all of the various symbols and syntax are all a form of literacy. Unlike the second form, however, this form excites me and brings with it all the joys of creation. I will have already put in the tedious work of memorizing these languages and symbols, and will be able to manipulate them to write programs that help move the gears of a virtual world. Like Naylor's statement "Every writer must articulate from the specific. They must reach down where they stand, because there is nothing else from which to draw."(230). That is exactly what I intend to do. I grew up in this technical environment, and somehow ended up with a knack for understanding its complex languages, and symbols. I plan to reach down into what I know, and draw from that knowledge to make literacy carry me into this new and exciting future.

In the end, I view all three forms that literacy has, and will have, in my life as equally important, and equally necessary to my success. Much like most things in our lives, this transformation is cyclical. We revisit these phases periodically as we move through the years, reading the books we read when we were children to our children, stopping in for a visit, going back to all those familiar, long lost worlds. Then again as we reach our twilight years, reading a book just for the sake of reading it to pass a warm afternoon on the front porch. Literacy is one of man-kinds most versatile, and powerful tools, and should be sought out in every form it takes.

Works Cited

Naylor, Gloria. "The Love of Books." <u>Introduction to College Writing</u>, Fifth Edition, McGraw Hill, 2010, pp. 225-231.

Rodriguez, Richard. "The Lonely, Good Company of Books." <u>Introduction to College Writing</u>, Fifth Edition, McGraw Hill, 2010, pp. 232–235.

Welty, Eudora. "One Writer's Beginnings." <u>Introduction to College Writing</u>, Fifth Edition, McGraw Hill, 2010, pp. 182–186.

I Do It with a Purpose

by Au'sha Ramirez-Quevado

If you know me well then you'd know that everything I do, I do for a greater purpose than the one assumed. One of the things I do that holds a great purpose is reading and writing. Like myself, Gloria Naylor and Fredrick Douglass wrote and read for and with a purpose. Each of these authors writes about their journey on how they became lovers of words, whether it was written for them or written by them. In "The Love of Books" by Gloria Naylor, she too writes about how she came across books and writing. She writes about what books, reading, and writing did for her. Naylor was born around the time African-American's lacked opportunities to gain education. Yet, in her story she is blessed to learn how to read and write. She also came to find her voice through writing as she states, "From the age of twelve I made the vital connection between inarticulate feeling and the written word" (Naylor 228). Naylor using her new found voice then decided to write a novel called *Women of Brewster Place*. Her intentions were to touch the heart of her fellow Black sisters, but in great astonishment her voice spoke to many women, of many nations, and races. As for Fredrick Douglass he wrote, "How I Learned to Read and Write." Douglass was a young slave when he was introduced to reading and writing. His slave master's (Mr. Auld) wife Mrs. Auld had taught Douglass the basics, but that quickly ended. Yet, that did not stop him from continuing to learn how to read and write. He went on to use clever tactics to further his education himself. The drive Fredrick Douglass had was because reading and writing were skills needed to free him, mentally and physically. Being that he was a slave, freedom was important to Douglass, so important in fact that he would risk his life to hold the knowledge of reading and writing. Reading these great authors' stories led me to think deeply about why I, too, read and write. Reading their stories got me to realize that these skills to read and write aren't just skills, they're life changing for me and those around me. Like these inspiring authors, I too read and write to show my respect of those invested in me, to share the knowledge that books hold, and to free myself from ignorance or a small minded mentality.

You know those memories that forever stick with you? The ones that may weigh on your character, as to why you love or do a certain thing? Well I have a few of those memories. One in particular are the times spent with my mom going to libraries. I remember seeing my mom's enthusiastic facial expression as we entered the library. She would glow as she explained to us what the plan was for today. "Okay", she would say, "Go get some books you would like me to read to you." My sister and I would gladly follow her request. We would then be back at home sitting on the couch huddled up, first listening to my mom's steady voice reading to us. Then we would take her place in reading a page or two. As we read aloud, with every word we got right she would startle us with her excitement, yelling something along the lines of, "Oh my babies are so smart!" Until this day I carry her positive vibes with me. To hear how well I was doing was very reassuring. To know that the time I put into books and my education was looked at in a positive light, was great. I believe she is one of my many reasons as to why I like to read and write. I think unconsciously I wanted her to continue to be proud of my efforts, so I applied myself to reading and writing throughout my life. Gloria Naylor and I are similar in this way. Naylor goes on to write, "But before my sister and I had even attained the age of literacy, my mother would take us on these pilgrimages to the library" (Naylor 227). Gloria Naylor's mother had lived in the South. Being that her mother was black she didn't receive an education, so when her mother had Naylor and her siblings' she went on to move to New York where African-Americans were opened to an education. That's where the library took play. Naylor's mother had opened a can of worms-in a good way. Naylor was now nose deep in all kinds of books as she states, "I was eager to discover what ever mystery was within the ink upon that paper, because also with in me- and this had to be genetic-was a fascination with the written word" (Naylor 227). Naylor and I both had been lucky girls to have had mothers that taught us the value of reading. Our mothers sharing the wonders between the covers of books, then gave us a purpose to further explore. In those new beginning moments in which we first learned how to read. our mission was to search for the many possibilities that reading had to offer.

Obtaining a skill requires patience, hard work and a strong will. At times you want to say "To hell with this!" But with those troubling times you've then built strength and learned something new about yourself, and you now hold a new skill. That skill you worked so hard for can now open many possibilities that may have been nonexistent before. Fredrick Douglass relates to this for he had tremendous hurdles while trying to obtain the skills he then later mastered. At the start of Douglass's journey to learning how to read and write, he was being taught to read by Mrs. Auld, Douglass's slave 'master's' wife. She soon had stopped teaching Douglass due to the persuasion of her husband Mr. Auld. Douglass restates the words overheard and shared between Mr. and Mrs. Auld, "A n**** should know nothing but to obey his master-to do as he is told to do. Learning would spoil the best n***** in the world" (Douglass 270). Douglass's 'owner' was one of many obstacles he now had to face. Auld was trying to keep Douglass ignorant. Auld had known once his 'property' held the skills to learn he would now be able to comprehend the right and the wrong done to the slaves. Auld was not having that. But, Douglass was not settling for ignorance. Auld's comment had stirred fire upon Douglass's belly. He now knew that reading and writing would reveal all the secrets Mr. Auld-and men like him-held. He goes on to write, "I now understood what had been to me a most perplexing difficulty-to wit, the white man's power to enslave the black man. It was a grand achievement, and I prized it highly. From that moment, I understood the pathway from slavery to freedom" (Douglass 270). This was the light bulb that flickered over Douglass's head. This was Douglass's drive to learn how to read and write. Young Douglass had devised a plan, to trick the neighborhood boys, preying on their egos by telling these young white boys that he-a black slave-was smarter than them. 'Impossible' I can imagine these young boys saying to Douglass. To these boy, it was impossible for a slave to be smart. So, they would flaunt their newly owned knowledge, thinking nothing of it. Little did they know Douglass was soaking up their knowledge like his melanin did the sun. Douglass continued to find numerous clever ways to teach himself. He wanted to break free from the ghostly chains and he wanted to break free from those iron shackles, and reading and writing would do that for him. Like Douglass, I have always had a thirst for knowledge. Every time I came across something new and interesting, I'd gravitate to it like a lion turning to an oasis after a long day of vigorous hunting. I remember conversing with people and not knowing exactly what they were talking about, feeling slightly stupid and shamed. I remember an associate of mine would have deep conversations about politics or race. When she spoke on these topics her voice and words would sound assertive of her opinions and facts. I remember how I would sometimes keep quiet during certain parts of the conversation, knowing that I didn't know much about what was being spoken of. And when I did speak my words would lack the confidence of knowing that my argument had a valid point, because after all my knowledge was just repeated words stolen from someone else's mouth. My facts or opinions got shot down or belittled with a laugh or a sarcastic remark, bruising my ego black and blue. At those moments I didn't have the knowledge to spit facts at her opposing argument. I didn't have the knowledge to even know if her 'facts' were merely made up opinions just perfectly worded to sound like facts. The lack of knowing had left me vulnerable and ignorant. Although my judgements on myself were harsh, it was a rude awakening for me. I then wanted to educate myself on things that I argued about, but was oblivious to. I would search and read up on the school curriculum; I'd read up on dogs, and black history. I would simply just read so I could have a conversation beyond the weather or my boring ass weekend. Like Douglass, reading gave me the will to know knowledge. Reading showed me topics to both talk and write about. Similar to Douglass, reading and writing had freed me, maybe not in all the ways alike, but in some similar way. Reading had not just opened up my knowledge and interest, but it had also broadened my horizon, opening me up to new topics, ideas, and new found understanding. Reading and writing had opened me up to knowledge that could be used as solid support in my writing or arguments. I was free to know that if I truly didn't know, a book would help me to know. You know? Douglass and I wanted to understand our surroundings and didn't want to feel or be oppressed due to our ignorance. Books, reading, letters, and writing did that for us- it freed us.

I read and I write. I read and I write because those two components have gotten me to where I am today. I am proud of myself. I've gone through high school, technical college, my first semester of university, and just everyday life. Reading and writing did that for me, I did that for me. It's amazing, really. I opened myself up to knowledge and from there I couldn't stop. Now that I know what education, reading and writing can do I want to show that to my sisters. I want them to see what can happen when you invest in yourself. Every word you read aloud is an investment; no one can take that away from you. Knowledge it truly power. I want to be a role model to my sisters like Gloria Naylor's mother and mine was to me. I want to show them the beauty in words just as my mom and Naylor's mom did. I want Kami, Shayla, Cheyenne, and Leona to know that if you are willing, reading can bring you to new heights no matter the situation just like Frederick Douglass. I want them to be free in their own right just as Douglass was. And I want their voices to be found and used like Naylor's. So, I read and write to get myself to new found heights, to show them that if I can then they can. I read and write for many reasons and as I've grown the reasons have changed, but one that will never change is that I read and write for my sisters.

Works Cited

Douglass, Frederick. "How I Learned to Read and Write." Introduction to College Writing, McGraw Hill Companies, Inc., 2008, pp. 270–276.

Naylor, Gloria. "The Love of Books." Introduction to College Writing, McGraw Hill Companies, Inc., 2008, pp. 225–231.

He and I

by Chayata Faye Thammarat

Reading and writing have been in human society for a long period of time. People needed to write in order to record their histories so their descendants would not repeat the same mistakes. To understand those records, people needed to know how to read. As time passed, reading and writing turned into daily behaviors. However, people no longer see the importance of literacy and literature. Some even got bored or disliked reading and writing, without knowing how these simple behaviors of reading and writing could benefit and improve their lives. Frederick Douglass wrote "*How I Learned to Read and Write*" to show the importance of literacy to his life. As Douglass was a black man removed from his homeland to be one of the slaves for white men, having knowledge and knowing how to read and write would help him escape from this slavery. For people, nowadays, reading and writing seem to be less important compared to Douglass's life but if we look carefully we recognize easily how reading and writing allows us to be in school, college or university, graduate, know about our environment and other places in the world, get jobs, gain money and support our lives' expenses. Without knowing how to read and write, our lives would end up on the side of the road; not knowing what or how to deal with our lives, working under other people's control and being overworked or underpaid. When I read this story, I recalled how my life has shifted to a better position because of my knowledge in English. I escaped from a place that taught me how to memorize but not learn; and if I did not learn, I knew I would have to work under other people's control for the rest of my life.

For second language learners, it is hard to read and write as there are different ways of writing and reading for different languages. Native speakers might be able to say, "Write like how you talk" but for second language learners, their minds get stuck at how they talked in their own languages which is something the English native speakers might not know. It is even harder if the second language learners were to learn by themselves without a teacher's guidance. Douglass and I started off similarly as we both had someone to teach us once, but soon lost our teacher for different reasons. For Douglass, he lost his teacher as his mistress because she was forbidden by her husband or Douglass's master from teaching him. Douglass wrote:

> Very soon after I went to live with Mr. and Mrs. Auld, she very kindly commenced to teach me the A, B,C. After I had learned this, she assisted me in learning how to spell words of three or four letters. Just at this point of my progress, Mr. Auld found out what was going on, and at once forbade Mrs. Auld to instruct me further, telling her, among other things, that it was unlawful, as well as unsafe, to teach a slave to read (Douglass 270).

Because Auld and other white men did not want their slaves to be smarter than them and get out of their control, people at that time wouldn't teach Douglass or black men how to read and write. Auld and others wanted to keep themselves higher and gained all benefits from black men on their own without caring how their slaves would feel. Douglass was young at that time and Auld might have thought that Douglass would not be able to understand his words but Douglass soon figured out why he and others were forbidden to learn how to read and write. If black men knew what was happening in their lives and what rights they could have had were taken away by these white men, they would not be happy and break out of control which would result in white men losing their workers for their own good.

Similar to Douglass, I was prevented from learning by the education system. When I was in nursery school, I had teachers who taught me A to Z and some three letters words. In my primary school years, I had teachers who taught three to four letter words. However, hiring native English speakers cost more than hiring teachers whose English is their second language, so after my first year of primary school, British and American teachers were replaced by second language learners that made mistakes as they taught. For example, they had difficulties pronouncing some words, got different answers than in the textbooks and failed to answer my questions or give explanation sometimes. Even though I still had teachers for English classes, I did not fully trust the lectures given by teachers but I trusted the books because they were made by English native speakers. The same way Douglass learned by reading books himself-I also learned by reading the books ahead of each class.

If a person has a support system, he or she could do better in anything they were working on. What if they were prevented instead of supported? There were and will be times when people didn't want others to be smarter than them. Not everyone wanted others to be as smart as or better than them, and not everyone wanted to be under other people's controls. To escape from the control means one needs to be smarter; to be smarter has to come from learning more than others; to be able to learn more than others requires better in reading and writing skills. Douglass and I were prevented from learning. For Douglass, his master prevented him from learning as he stated his master's words:

> If you give a nigger an inch, he will take an ell. A nigger should know nothing but to obey his master-to do as he is told to do. Learning would spoil the best nigger in the world. Now, if you teach that nigger how to read, here would be no keeping him. It would forever unfit him to be a slave. He would at once become unmanageable, and of no value to his master. As to himself it could do him no good, but a great deal of harm. It would make him discontented and unhappy (Douglass 270).

To his master and white men, losing their slaves because their slaves knew better to be under their control was not a pleasant thing to happen. But for Douglass, it would be a big change to his life and others' as he stated, "That which to him was great evil, to be carefully shunned, was to me a great good, to be diligently sought; and the argument which he so warmly urged, against my learning to read, only served to inspire me with a desire and determination to learn" (Douglass 271). These quotes showed how Douglass had no support system unlike most students today. He didn't have a family member who could teach him; people around him were preventing him from learning and the only thing he had to escape from this slavery was himself.

Similar to Douglass who was prevented to learn about literacy, I was prevented to learn about every subject I had in school. I had teachers for classes such as Thai, English, Science, Math, and History but we were taught to memorize the material rather than understanding it. Memorizing would not shape young people into smart adults but robots with more memory cards. Most teachers I had would scold or mock students who asked questions or were unable to answer the questions. The exams were the same as 'review' sheets students got from each teacher. These are the two main reasons why most Thai students grew up shy and lacked confidence; not just shy and quiet people but people who had no knowledge. Students were taught to remember by remembering answers and questions from the review sheets and were unable to understand because they wouldn't get answers from asking teachers and were shamed by asking questions. Elders knew about this broken education system but no one made any action to change. My life too would not have changed if I didn't experience a different education system in Michigan when I was a sophomore in high school. After I studied in U.S. for a year, I went back to my home country with more confidence and saw nothing wrong with asking questions. One day when I was a senior in an international high school, I accidentally got involved in a conversation about our country's politics. I got a chance to ask a teacher I trust, "Why do we know that our education system taught students to remember and not to learn, yet no one comes out to make any change, not any little?" My teacher sat there silently for few seconds and replied, "Because there were those who did not want others to be smarter than them. If there are people who were smarter than them then they will lose control of many things and lose the benefits they could get from others." I changed my mind from applying to one of the Thai universities to one of the U.S.'s right away for my own sake. Students who were taught to remember mostly would forget what they were taught after the final exam and would be unable to use what they were taught in their real lives. I did not want to be one of them and be under others' control so I used my experiences in Michigan as a credit and applied for one of the universities in Missouri.

What can second language learners do if there is no teacher and they are also prevented from learning? Other than losing hope and giving up, they could use the first thing they always had-themselves- and then come up with ways to improve this learning process by searching for more resources such as books or people around them. After Douglass knew how important it was to know how to read and write, nothing could stop him from learning how to read and write. He wrote, "The first step had been taken. Mistress, in teaching me the alphabet, had given me the inch, and no precaution could prevent me from taking the ell" (Douglass 272). He came up with plans to escape from his miserable life by exchanging pieces of bread with people in his neighborhood as he stated, "I used also to carry bread with me, enough of which always in the house, and to which I was always welcome; for I was much better off in this regard than many of the poor white children in our neighborhood. This bread I used to bestow upon the hungry little urchins, who, in return, would give me more valuable bread of knowledge" (Douglass 272). Douglass's life changed more and more as he gained more knowledge and with his intelligence he was able to trick those around him into being his teachers. Even he knew how this could put his life to an end, still he struggled for his better life.

He taught himself how to read and write the same way I did when I was in middle school which gave me scholarships to study in U.S. for one year as an exchange student. In my primary school, I was able to guess correctly how to read words in the text books by mainly looking at a, e, i, o, u and letters behind those vowels. By watching other students' mistakes and teachers' corrections gave me better ideas of how to read. I was lucky to always be able to read everything correctly when it was my turn to read. Every time when there were words I didn't know, it was always someone else's turn to read. I felt sorry for others as they lost their confidence in reading and learning English but I gained more confidence. I noticed how foreign teachers never complained when we made mistakes and how they always welcomed us to ask them questions even though sometimes they couldn't answer. Soon after picking up words by listening to teachers talking to one another and through reading, I was able to say longer sentences. Foreign teachers misunderstood that I was the best student in the class and started asking me questions such as how to say words in Thai, what event was being held by the school, ways to go to each specific place, where were my classmates and more. Because they slowly approached me, I answered them easily by using "Yes" and "No" at the very beginning of our relationships. Soon, they asked longer questions and luckily I was ready. My classmates started to drag me along to be a translator for them when they needed to talk with foreign teachers. Thai teachers also asked me to translate their works into English and would drag me along when they needed to talk with foreign teachers as well. By helping out foreign teachers, I gained help in return. Especially when the first teacher from the U.S. arrived to our school to teach us science and math in English. He was told by previous foreign teachers that I was one of very few students in my grade who could communicate in English and had helped them out many times so he reached out to me too. Other than gaining experiences and using my second language that gave me a scholarship to America, I also used every single foreign teacher as my tutor. Because I helped them out with their lives in Thailand, they decided to help me out with my other classes' lectures in exchange. During break, I would bring questions I had to foreign teachers instead of Thai teachers. Even it was not for their classes, foreign teachers were answering all my questions and even conversed with me in person sometimes. It was a huge change like how Douglass moved to another family and learned more by himself. In Michigan, I picked up words by listening and imitating people as they talked to one another. I might not know the exact meaning or the expression of every word but I knew when to use them. Now, I am in Missouri, picking up more words from where I left behind in Michigan, approaching the goal in my life¬ the same way Douglass was.

Frederick Douglass's life story from "*How I Learned to Read and Write*" and my own story showed our struggle in learning English. ·We realized how important this mother language is and how it can change our lives. From A, B, C to three to four syllable words, losing our teacher and struggling to learn by ourselves, we used everything possible around ourselves to teach and move us to a better place which shows that for everyone, reading and writing could be more than just to communicate. It would lead to a better position in our lives as well. Therefore, the first and second language learner must not give up along the way or be careless about it. No matter how much struggles or obstacles we have to face. Everyone can overcome by practicing and using those around us as tools for our own benefits. People, especially the native speakers, could give the most benefit at this point. Unlike Douglass or I who learned mostly by ourselves, the native speakers should be proud and care more of their language. Meanwhile, just like Douglass and me, those who are second language learners shouldn't give in to the obstacles in their lives. Parents, siblings, cousins, books on the shelves, Google, mobile phones, teachers and even strangers can teach you something. If you think your hard work hasn't paid off, work harder and more often. Everything changes over time. Be positive and keep walking.

Work Cited

Douglass, Frederick. "How I Learned To Read and Write" *Introduction to College Writing*. McGraw-Hill Companies,
    Inc., 2010, pp. 270–276.

Appendix
Writer's Workshop

A "best practice" for the developmental writing classroom is the implementation of supplemental instruction and the use of student tutors and mentors. Supplemental Instruction or SI, according to Hunter Boylan in his seminal book, *What Works: Research-Based Practices in Developmental Education*, combines collaborative learning with students learning about strategies that will best aid them in studying and acquiring knowledge in a specific content area. In SI, the sessions, labs or workshops can be led on a weekly basis by a qualified and trained student who works closely with the instructor as well as with the students. Students in these sessions, labs or workshops receive continuous feedback from their SI leader in a structured environment. SI is an invaluable experience to both the writing students and the leader. Boylan, with abundant research to support his argument, claims, "Supplemental Instruction or SI is probably the single most well-documented intervention available for improving the academic performance of underprepared students" (75). The Writing Instruction section of this textbook is organized so any instructor and program can set up their own SI, which is called "Writer's Workshop" in this textbook, conducted by a trained leader, student tutor or Writer's Workshop Leader, using some of the tutorials and activities in the textbook.

Orientation to Writer's Workshop

What Is Writer's Workshop?

This course has both a classroom and workshop component. In addition to your classroom time with your Instructor, you are required to attend your scheduled Writer's Workshop 50 minutes per week. In Writer's Workshop, you will meet with 4–6 other students from your class and a trained Writer's Workshop Leader/Student Tutor for small group tutorials. During these sessions, your Writer's Workshop Leader/Student Tutor will guide you through the writing process for your English essay/paper/Task Paper assignments, helping you freewrite, draft and revise. You will have time to conference with your Writer's Workshop Leader/Student Tutor and obtain feedback not only from them but your peers as well. During some sessions, you will participate in critical thinking, reading and writing lessons and activities that will help you write and revise your course essays. You can look at this time in Writer's Workshop as free tutoring sessions. The time spent in Writer's Workshop, and in working on your papers there, is less time you will have to spend on your own working on your papers. This workshop allows you focused one-on-one time with your Writer's Workshop Leader/Student Tutor in an environment that is nonevaluative and provides you with extra practice and exposure to reading and writing. This dual-component course will prepare you for the rigors of college-level writing and introduce you to college expectations.

What Are the Rules for Writer's Workshop?

Writer's Workshop is an extension of the classroom and, in many ways, is just like your class with similar expectations, rules and policies.

Absences: The Writer's Workshops have a very strict attendance policy. **If you are not present, you will be marked absent regardless of the circumstances that prevent you from attending Writer's Workshops. The fourth Writer's Workshop absence—no matter the reason—results in failure of your entire English class (i.e., ENG 100).** While there are limited grounds for appeal from this policy, in most cases appeals are not granted. You should consider carefully whether you can meet this policy this semester. In addition, if you do not bring the required materials to each session (i.e., assignment sheets, drafts, etc.), you may be marked absent. The attendance policy goes into effect on the first day of class for the university and lasts until the final day of the semester.

Participation and Materials: At every Writer's Workshop session, you will need to fully participate and bring the following materials:

- This textbook
- A pen and pencil
- Notebook/writing paper
- Any additional materials specifically required by the instructions in this textbook or by your Instructor and/or Writer's Workshop Leader/Student Tutor
- A copy of each essay/paper/ Task Paper and any drafts in progress
- Assignment sheets and schedules from your Instructor

Penalties for Unacceptable Behavior: It is imperative that students help us to maintain good conditions for teaching and learning. In Writer's Workshop, everyone must participate, share ideas and questions and support each other. That is how we truly learn. The activities you complete in this workshop are connected to your classroom work and will help improve your comprehension and completion of that work. All students will treat their classmates, instructors, and Writer's Workshop Leader/Student Tutor with civility and respect, both inside and outside the classroom. The following is a list of some (but not all) behaviors that will not be tolerated by your Writer's Workshop Leader/ Student Tutor:

- Not participating in the workshop lesson and discussion.
- Sleeping in class (this includes resting your eyes and laying down your head).
- Arriving late and/or leaving early; disrupting workshop in any other way.
- Using your cell phone or any other device.
- Rude and disorderly conduct; disrespecting peers and/or Writer's Workshop Leader.

Please refer to your student handbook for further information on student conduct and behavior.

Students who violate this policy may, among other penalties, be counted absent and asked to leave. A severe violation and/or frequent violations of conduct rules may result in a student being permanently removed from workshop and class and/or receiving a course grade of F.

What Happens in a Typical Writer's Workshop Session?

Writing is both a personal and social process and Writer's Workshop will introduce you to both of these aspects. Often, in Writer's Workshop, you will be given time to work on your essays/papers/

Task Papers and receive feedback from your Writer's Workshop Leader/Student Tutor. You will also respond to prompts, complete individual exercises, collaborate on writing exercises and discuss your writing with other writers. All of these activities are designed to give you more experience with reading, writing and discussion and, as a result, you will improve your fluency, critical thinking, writing processes and use of written conventions.

Who Do I Contact for Additional Assistance with the Class and Writer's Workshop?

Normally, you should contact your classroom Instructor for assistance. Writer's Workshop Leaders/Student Tutors are not paid for contact outside the assigned sessions, and you should not contact them directly outside of the workshop without their permission. For more serious concerns, please contact the Director.

What Should I Do If I Miss Workshop?

If you miss a workshop session, you do have the opportunity to make that session up at the end of the week. This is a special and extra opportunity and, as a result, we need to restrict the use of these makeup sessions by implementing certain rules.

Makeup Session Rules:

- Makeup sessions will be offered only on **Fridays at 3:00 p.m. during the Spring semester. In Fall semester, sessions will be held at both 2:00 and 3:00 p.m.**
- You may only make up a workshop during the same week that you missed it.
- Students must have good reasons for the absences that they seek to make up.
- Students must notify the Director, by phone or email, before attending makeup sessions.
- Students can attend a maximum of three makeup sessions over the course of the semester. Any student who exceeds the allowed number of makeup sessions will be turned away from the makeup session and the absence will stand.
- Failing to attend after receiving permission may prevent any further use of makeup sessions.
- Failing to participate productively prevents any further use of makeup sessions (you must bring your textbook and any other required materials for the lesson).

Appeal Procedure for Class and Writer's Workshop

The attendance policy for this class and workshop is strict because this class is one that will instruct you on how to become not only a better writer but also a better student. In order for this to happen, you must be engaged with your Instructor, Writer's Workshop Leader/Student Tutor and your peers and you can only do this by being in class and workshop and participating in all activities. The instruction and discussion that takes place in class and workshop is crucial to learning and improving your writing. Attending class, participating in discussion and sharing and questioning ideas and experiences is central to academia. Since you are now part of this academic community, you must follow the rules in order to succeed. Learning and improving your critical thinking, reading and writing skills are all personal and social processes, so you must be in the classroom with your peers every day. This policy will also teach you discipline and responsibility, which you will need in all of your other classes. Contrary to what some think, most college classes do have attendance, conduct and other policies.

If a student violates the attendance policy in class or Writer's Workshop and wishes to begin the Appeal Procedure, the student must meet the following conditions:

- **Each and every absence** (or equivalent failure to attend) was caused by serious, unavoidable circumstances beyond the student's control.
- The student has always acted as promptly as possible to recover from these circumstances and keep up with the class, and the student continues to do so throughout the appeal process.
- The student is working hard and effectively in both the class and the Writer's Workshop, earning no lower than a grade of "C."
- The appeal is presented as soon as possible (within one week after final absence) after it is clear that it will be needed.

Any student who wishes to appeal must submit a written, signed letter of appeal to the Director. The letter of appeal must include the student's college ID number, local telephone number, email address and mailing address and must be accompanied by the following materials:

- **Objective, documented evidence of a good cause for each and every absence** or other failure of diligence (i.e., court documents, hospital records)
- Telephone numbers of all persons who can verify these claims
- Notification of any relevant, documented special needs
- Signed statement from the instructor (and usually from the Writer's Workshop Leader/ Student Tutor, too) stating that the student is working effectively and that they approve of granting the appeal

Students may also use any other campus appeal procedures available to them.

Notice of English Class/Writer's Workshop Policies

This notice alerts students to their responsibilities. These terms are binding by operation of official college documents. They have full effect even without the signing of this notice.

I have read this notice and the "Orientation to Writer's Workshop" set out in the textbook *Discovering the Student, Discovering the Self*. I realize that I am required to purchase that book in order to participate in the course. I realize that the class and Writer's Workshops have strict policies for attendance, participation and behavior. I realize that violating these policies can result in failing the entire course.

I realize that in order to pass, I should attend the workshops, prepare for all scheduled activities, bring my textbook, participate fully, behave with civility and show respect for my peers and for the Writer's Workshop Leaders/Student Tutors. If I have complaints about the workshops, I realize that they should be raised with the Director.

I have also reviewed the Appeal Procedure. I realize that this procedure governs appeals from all policies that might affect my grade. I realize that the Appeal Procedure requires me to keep track of all evidence I may need to prove my appeal case. I realize that if I am unable to comply with that policy, my appeal will fail.

Signature _____

Print Name _____

....

Evaluation of Writer's Workshop

Please answer the following questions in regard to Writer's Workshop only, using the following scale:

    1 = strongly disagree

    2 = disagree

    3 = no opinion

    4 = agree

    5 = strongly agree

I saw the connection between my English class and Writer's Workshop	1	2	3	4	5
I am more comfortable with my writing	1	2	3	4	5
I would not have done as well on my papers if I did not have workshop	1	2	3	4	5
Working with my Leader/Tutor helped me	1	2	3	4	5
Writer's Workshop had no effect upon my writing	1	2	3	4	5
My Leader/Tutor had a positive effect on my writing	1	2	3	4	5
I enjoyed going to Writer's Workshop	1	2	3	4	5
The work I completed in Writer's Workshop helped me in English class and with my papers	1	2	3	4	5
I am a more confident writer	1	2	3	4	5
I thought Writer's Workshop was a waste of time	1	2	3	4	5

Overall rating of Writer's Workshop (1=worst/5=best) _____

Overall rating of Leader/Tutor (1=worst/5=best) _____

Answer the following questions, being as specific as possible. Use back of sheet if necessary.

Explain the best/most helpful aspect or lesson of workshop:

Explain the worst/least helpful aspect or lesson of workshop:

If you could change one thing about workshop, what would it be and why?

Evaluation of Writer's Workshop Leader/Student Tutor

Writer's Workshop Leader/Student Tutor Name:_____

Instructor: _____ **Section:**_____

Attendance

_____ Writer's Workshop Leader/Student Tutor never missed a Writer's Workshop.

_____ Writer's Workshop Leader/Student Tutor missed _____ (number) Writer's Workshops.

Was your Writer's Workshop Leader/Student Tutor well prepared and organized for class? Please explain.

Did your Writer's Workshop Leader/Student Tutor present course material in a clear and understandable manner? Please explain.

Describe your Writer's Workshop Leader/Student Tutor strengths:

What suggestions do you have for improving your Writer's Workshop Leader/Student Tutor skills?

Would you recommend that this Writer's Workshop Leader/Student Tutor be hired again to lead other Writer's Workshops? Why or why not?

Evaluation of Student

Student's Name:_____

Instructor:_____ Section:_____

Writer's Workshop Leader/Student Tutor:_____

Attendance

_____ Student never missed a Writer's Workshop.

_____ Student missed (number) Writer's Workshops.

Work Habits: Please check all that apply

_____ Student exerted leadership in the group and showed initiative in completing work.

_____ Student always completed work as assigned.

_____ Student sometimes resisted beginning assigned tasks and failed to complete assigned work

_____ Student was sometimes disruptive, causing other group members not to be able to complete assigned tasks.

Writer's Workshop Leader's/Student Tutor's evaluative comments about the student (please write specific comments and observations but do NOT assign any letter or number grade):

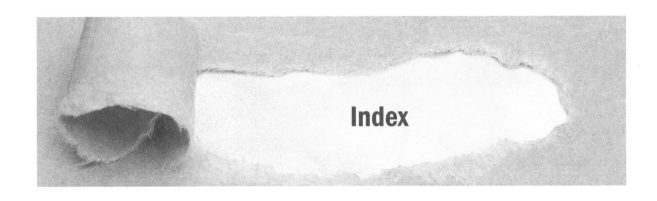

Index